DIVERSITY: GENDER

Labor Force Participation Rates for Women Who Had a Child in the Last Year: Selected Years, June 1976 to June 1998

(In percentages)

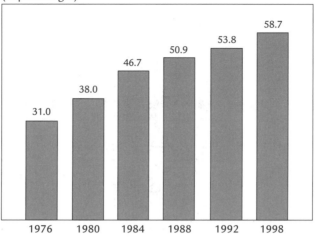

1976	1980	1984	1988	1992	1998
31.0	38.0	46.7	50.9	53.8	58.7

Note: After 1990, the numbers are based on women aged 15 to 44; before 1990, the numbers are based on women aged 18 to 44.
Source: U.S. Bureau of the Census, Current Population Surveys, June 1976 to 1998.

DIVERSITY: CLASS, RACE, AND GENDER

Poverty Rates for Persons and Families with Selected Characteristics, 1999

(In percentages)

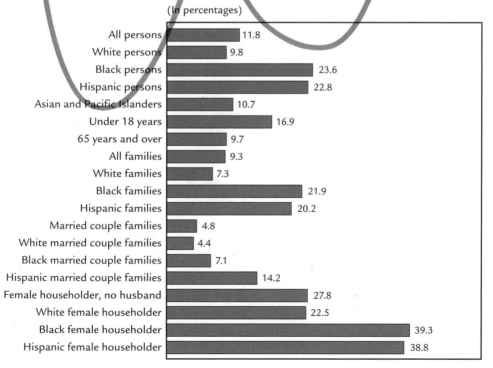

All persons	11.8
White persons	9.8
Black persons	23.6
Hispanic persons	22.8
Asian and Pacific Islanders	10.7
Under 18 years	16.9
65 years and over	9.7
All families	9.3
White families	7.3
Black families	21.9
Hispanic families	20.2
Married couple families	4.8
White married couple families	4.4
Black married couple families	7.1
Hispanic married couple families	14.2
Female householder, no husband	27.8
White female householder	22.5
Black female householder	39.3
Hispanic female householder	38.8

Source: U.S. Bureau of the Census, 2000.

Diversity

IN FAMILIES

SIXTH EDITION

Maxine Baca Zinn
Michigan State University

D. Stanley Eitzen
Colorado State University

ALLYN AND BACON

Boston   London   Toronto   Sydney   Tokyo   Singapore

We dedicate this book to the teachers, students, and scholars who are rethinking family life to meet the challenges of the diverse and changing social world.

Editor in Chief: *Karen Hanson*
Series Editor: *Jeff Lasser*
Editorial Assistant: *Andrea Christie*
Senior Marketing Manager: *Judeth Hall*
Editorial Production Administrator: *Bryan Woodhouse*
Editorial Production Service: *Chestnut Hill Enterprises*
Composition and Prepress Buyer: *Linda Cox*
Manufacturing Buyer: *Suzanne Lareau*
Cover Administrator: *Linda Knowles*
Interior Design, Illustrations, and Electronic Composition: *Glenna Collett*
Photo Editor: *Alan Zinn*

Library of Congress Cataloging-in-Publication Data
Zinn, Maxine Baca,
    Diversity in families / Maxine Baca Zinn, D. Stanley Eitzen.—6th ed.
        p.   cm.
    Includes bibliographical references and index.
    ISBN 0-205-33522-5 (alk. paper)
    1. Family—United States.   2. United States—Social conditions—1980–
    I. Eitzen, D. Stanley.   II. Title.
    HQ536 .Z54 2002
    306.85'0973—dc21   2001046358

Photo and text credits appear on pages 535–538, which are an extension of this copyright page.

Printed in the United States of America
10 9 8 7 6 5 4 3 2   RRD-VA   06 05 04 03 02

Brief Contents

Contents

8   Contemporary Marriages   257

13 Family Policy for the Twenty-First Century   454

Preface

ORGANIZING PRINCIPLES

This book reflects the critical tradition of family sociologists, economists, and historians whose scholarship is structuralist, feminist, and humanist. Several assumptions guide our inquiry. To begin, the understanding of families requires that we demythologize the family, the most myth-laden of all our social institutions. We must separate, for example, the reality of how families are structured from the ideal images of "the family" that are commonly portrayed. The demythologizing of the family also requires that we examine the diversity of contemporary families.

An important aspect of our focus is the critical examination of society. We ask questions such as, "How do families really work?" and "Who benefits under the existing arrangements and who does not?" This critical stance is based on the assumption that the social world is human made and therefore not sacred. Thus a keen sociological analysis demystifies and demythologizes social life by ferreting out existing myths, stereotypes, and dogmas. This means, for example, that families must be examined not only from middle-class, White, male viewpoints, which have dominated the scholarly study of the family, but must be viewed from other vantage points as well. Several bodies of new scholarship are considered throughout this book to show how family organization and experience vary by social class, gender, race, and sexuality.

Conventional research and public policy have long treated families as closed units that can be understood in isolation from outside influences. In sharp contrast, this book assumes that families are not the "building blocks of society," but are, rather, the products of social forces within society. The material conditions of people's lives, for example, shape attitudes, behaviors, and family patterns. The structure of a society's economy affects which family members work outside the home, the lifestyles of family members, how material needs are met, the opportunities for children, and even how the labor and decision making will be divided. Clearly, too, the economic rewards of occupations are key determinants in family diversity.

Contemporary patterns of social inequality influence family formation and family relations. Wealth, race, gender, and sexuality produce diverse family forms and household arrangements. Economic conditions and social inequities in the United States make family life difficult. This does not mean that families cannot be warm and loving places but rather that structural conditions sometimes preclude this ideal. In short, these structural arrangements produce a range of family configurations. Important in our view is that differences are the consequence of structured social inequality rather than the result of family values. This structural perspective does not mean, however, that we ascribe to a rigid structural determinism. There is a dialectic between social structure and human response. Family members do not simply respond to their changing situations. To the contrary, people are agents and actors, coping with, adapting to, and changing social structures to meet their needs. Women, men, and children actively produce their family worlds. This process is called **human agency.** We stress both social structure and human agency in this book.

This examination of families also assumes that they must be understood in historical context. What happens to families today is a continuation of what has been happening to them over time.

THE FRAMEWORK

Several organizing principles guide the analysis of families in this new edition. We call this framework "structural diversity." It differs from functionalism, the dominant paradigm of the 1950s, 1960s, and 1970s. Functionalism posited a monolithic model of the family, in which the nuclear family was viewed as the basis of societal organization and cohesion. The nuclear family was considered essential for the proper socialization of children and for the division of labor that enabled women and men to perform their social roles in an orderly manner. Families that deviated from the standard arrangement were thought to be deficient.

The structural-diversity approach challenges the old paradigm on every dimension. To summarize, the structural-diversity framework incorporates the following themes (these are elaborated more fully in Chapter 1):

1. Family forms are socially constructed and historically changing.
2. Family diversity is produced by the very structures that organize society as a whole.
3. The social locations in which families are embedded are not the product of a single-power system, but are shaped by intersecting hierarchies.
4. Family diversity is constructed through social structure and human agency.
5. Understanding family diversity requires the use of wide-ranging intellectual traditions.

OTHER FEATURES OF THE NEW EDITION

Although the subject of the family has inherent appeal for most students, we have not relied solely on the subject matter to engage students' interest. To draw students into each topic, chapters begin with common myths about families, many of which students may believe, and contrast these myths with reality. The chapters themselves are clearly organized and written, with many examples of contemporary interest to bolster the analysis. Boxed features focus students' attention on family diversity, social science research methods, technology, and global perspectives. Chapter reviews summarize the main points, to help students assimilate the material. And finally, photographs, drawings, and cartoons illustrate many of the ideas and concepts in the text. Relevant websites have been added at the conclusion of each chapter.

Just as families are socially constructed, so, too, is the scholarship on families. As society experiences major "earthquakes," social science thinking about families is undergoing "seismic shifts" as well. These new intellectual developments have required major revisions of the previous edition. Most significant, we have sharpened the focus on the macro and micro and emphasized human agency in the analysis. Each chapter has been reorganized to make the themes of the book more explicit. Each chapter includes material on demythologizing, macro (societal forces) impinging on the micro (families), diversity in families, and human agency.

SUPPLEMENTS

Barbara Wells of Maryville College has prepared a comprehensive *Instructor's Manual/Test Bank* to accompany this text. The *Instructor's Manual* contains chapter overviews, chapter outlines, class activities and projects, and video and film suggestions. The *Test Bank* includes true/false, multiple-choice, and essay/discussion questions. The *Test Bank* is also available in computerized form for Windows and Macintosh. Easy to use and flexible, the test-generating software program allows you to edit existing questions and to add your own items. Tests can be printed in several different formats and can include graphs and tables.

ACKNOWLEDGMENTS

Our thanks to Jeff Lasser, our Allyn and Bacon editor. We thank Alan Zinn, the picture editor, whose skills and creativity bring life and diversity to our approach. Heather Dillaway, Darcel Smith, and Angela Y. H. Pok of Michigan State University were especially helpful as research assistants. Heather Dillaway prepared the information on websites. We also thank the following reviewers whose contributions to the preparation of this edition were extremely helpful: Gary Hampe, University of Wyoming; Augustine N. Isamah, Rutgers University; Phyllis Hutten Raabe; Jack W. Sattel, Minneapolis Community/Technical College; and Anna Zajjicek, University of Arkansas.

Finally, we wish to thank several special colleagues and friends who have influenced our thinking and helped us sometimes so subtly that they and we were unaware of their contributions at the time: Margaret L. Andersen, Bonnie Thornton Dill, Elizabeth Higginbotham, Steven Gold, Pierrette Hondagneu-Sotelo, Michael A. Messner, Kathryn D. Talley, Doug A. Timmer, and Lynn Weber.

Maxine Baca Zinn
D. Stanley Eitzen

Images, Ideals, and Myths

*F*amilies today are very different from what they used to be. They are more diverse and more likely to be formed outside of marriage. They include a complex array of household arrangements, and they are more easily fractured. Family members spend less time together, and parents have less influence over their children. These changes are not unique to the United States. Indeed, they have global dimensions. Throughout the world, every industrialized country is experiencing a movement away from conventional family life. (See Box 1.1.) Women's growing economic independence, widespread divorce, and cohabitation have made marriage optional for many people.

Family change and diversity are now highly charged issues, under fire from many quarters. Many people believe that current developments are symptoms of moral decline and social decay. They think family diversity signals the breakdown of the family and of society as well. Why do so many lament the state of the family? Why has "family" become a rallying cry for politicians and policy analysts? These are disquieting questions that highlight the public anxiety surrounding the state of contemporary families. In the current climate of rapid social change these questions have become politicized, with competing views of the family vying for public attention.

This book presents a sociological analysis of family life in American society. This analysis requires the willingness to call into question existing social arrangements that many people consider sacred. It requires us to expose the mythical ideals that influence our perceptions and replace these myths with an understanding of the historical, social, economic, and cultural forces that create families. Knowing that families are embedded in a larger social context, we can better sort out what is myth and what is reality to make sense of changes in the family.

To begin, we need to be aware that the family is as much a cultural symbol as it is a social form—as much idea as thing (Holstein and Gubrium, 1999:29). Most family images make it difficult to think about family life objectively. As

---

BOX 1.1   **Families in Global Perspective: Family Upheavals around the World**

The rapidity and depth of the most recent period of family transformation which began in the wake of the Second World War rivals any in history. In most Western nations, marriage and family relationships have become more discretionary and variegated while at the same time becoming more precarious than at any time in recorded history. Some of the particular changes that have been most dramatic:

(1) In virtually all Western countries, the link between the onset of sexuality and marriage has been broken. Relatively few young people expect to wait until they wed or are about to wed to initiate sex, and only a small number now expect that their first sexual partner will be their only one. Sexual norms regarding conjugal exclusivity have always been subject to considerable violation. However, for better or for worse, the norms that once confined sex to marital relations have more or less disappeared, leaving individuals to work out their own understandings of when, why, and with whom to have sex.

(2) In most Western nations, cohabitation has now become the initial stage of family formation and in some nations state-sanctioned marriage is postponed until well after childbearing begins or has declined altogether. So children in many countries now enter families where their partners have established a partnership but not a formal contract for their care and upbringing. In some places, northern Europe in particular, childbearing unions are tantamount to marriage but in others such as the United States, they are typically not. And even in northern Europe, the prospects of these unions surviving are far lower than if the couples entered matrimony.

(3) When it does occur, marriage has become less enduring over the past several decades. In virtually all countries, divorce rates have risen sharply despite the fact that those marrying are a more select group whose prospects of divorce should be lower. Couples who wed are older, less likely to be pregnant at the time of marriage, more likely to hold conventional views, and more economically secure than those who do not. Despite these trends that should favor stability, conjugal unions have become less stable over time throughout Europe and North America.

Source: Frank F. Furstenberg, Jr., 1999 "Is the Modern Family a Threat to Children's Health?," *Society, 36* (July/August 1999): 30–37.

much as we seek objectivity, our perceptions are guided by cultural visions of family, by our own family experiences, and, paradoxically, by the very familiarity of family life. Because the family is familiar, we tend to take it for granted, to view it as "natural," without questioning the hows and whys of family life.

When it comes to family, most people think they know it all. Not only have most people personally enjoyed or survived family life, but literature, television, and movies often mask family realities. Many social conditions prevent us from being analytical about families. Families are familiar and they are also mystified. As a result, family behavior can be camouflaged in such a way that individuals may misunderstand family processes in general and may even have some misconceptions about their own families. Family life can be "hidden" by "mystification," which is the deliberate misdefinition of family matters or "complicated stratagems to keep everyone in the dark" (Laing, 1971:77). Objectivity is thus obscured by two different qualities—familiarity and mystification.

Other obstacles that handicap the goal of objectivity are sacredness and secrecy (Skolnick, 1987:58). A discovery of recent family research is that families have myths, secrets, and information-processing rules that determine the kinds of communication that goes on—what can be said and, more important, what cannot be said. Families filter information about the outside world and about their own rules of operation. "Secrets" occurring in the realm of interpersonal relationships can occur in any family, remain hidden for decades, and have unsettling, even destructive implications when they are revealed (Brown-Smith, 1998; Imber-Black, 2000).

The family is not merely a social institution; it evokes deep feelings about morality and proper behavior. At the same time, it is the most private of all society's institutions. The saying that "a family's business is nobody's business but their own" is not merely a statement about the right to family privacy; it is also a statement with strong moral overtones that reflects the sacredness granted to the family. The norm of family privacy gives the family an elusive quality that exists alongside its familiarity. In contemporary Western society, the family is, to use Erving Goffman's (1959) term, a "backstage" area, where people are free to act in ways they would not in public. This accounts for the deceptive quality of family relations. Much of the intimacy of family life remains hidden behind "front stage" performances—behavior characterized by public conformity to role expectations and social norms (Goffman, 1959; Berardo, 1998). Privacy results in "pluralistic ignorance": we have a backstage view of our own families, but we can judge others only in terms of their public presentations. Often we have "inside" interpretations of other families' "outsides." However, the gap between public norms and private behavior can be wide.

The ideals that we hold about "the family" color not only how we experience family life, but also how we speak of our experience. This phenomenon is not unique to our society. Anthropologist Ray Birdwhistell (1980) has found that in all societies a gap may exist between family ideals and family realities—between what people say about their family behavior and the real behavior that takes place in families. This distinction between ideals and behavior, between "talk" and "action," is one of the central problems in the social sciences (Mills, [1940] 1963:467). As we study the family, we cannot ignore the tensions between the

"Family" evokes a warm and caring psychological nurturance.

way families *are* and the way we *would like them to be*. According to historian John Gillis, "we all have two families, one that we live *with* and another we live *by*. We would like the two to be the same, but they are not" (Gillis, 1996:viii).

Many images surrounding the American family obscure our understanding of family life. Images provide an idealized picture of the family by distorting everyday household realities. This chapter narrows the gap between family imagery and family reality. We examine the images, ideals, and myths that shape our perceptions of families and our expectations of what our lives should be inside our own families. Then we provide a sociological framework for looking behind the facades of family life. This framework sets the stage for the chapters that follow.

IMAGES AND IDEALS

"Family" in American society is a symbol, a visual image that speaks to us through the senses, including smells, tastes, textures, motions, and sounds from our own remembered experiences (Tufte and Meyerhoff, 1979:11), as well as through our dreams and longings about what family should be. For roughly the last 150 years, until 1960, most Americans shared a common set of beliefs about family life:

> Family should consist of a husband and wife living together with their children. The father should be the head of the family, earn the family's income, and give his name to his wife and children. The mother's main tasks were to support and facilitate her husband's career, guide her children's development, look after the home, and set a moral tone for the family. Marriage was an enduring obligation for better or worse. The husband and wife jointly coped with stresses. Sexual activity was to be kept within the marriage especially for women. As parents, they had an overriding responsibility for the well-being of their children during the early years until their children entered school; they were almost solely responsible. Even later, it was the parents who had the primary duty of guiding their children's education and discipline (Hamburg, 1993:60).

While these were merely ideals even in 1960, the images they evoke remain with us.

Despite the changes of recent years, the dominant cultural ideal of family life in modern society is the presumably stable, two-biological parent, male-breadwinner, female-homemaker family of the 1950s (Demo, 2000:17). "Family" evokes a mental picture of a warm and happy realm: two heterosexually married adults and their children living together comfortably, and going about their lives in mutually satisfying and harmonious ways. "Family" evokes love, caring, and physical and psychological nurturance in a nuclear family configuration set apart from the troubled world.

The family is quintessentially the private (and some feel the only contemporary private) opportunity for vulnerability, trust, intimacy, and commitment, for lasting pleasant and peaceful relations, for fullness of being in the human realm. The family thus is located as the physical site for a vast (and repressed) range of human expression, the valid arena (and again perhaps the only arena) in which quality of life is a concern. It is in the family that we find the opportunity for psychologically bearable, nonexploitive personal life (Tufte and Meyerhoff, 1979:17–18).

At least three distinct images of the family have emerged: the family as haven; the family as fulfillment; and the family as encumbrance.

Family as Haven

This "family as haven" image of a refuge from an impersonal world characterizes the family as a place of intimacy, love, and trust in which individuals may escape the competition of dehumanizing forces in modern society. Christopher Lasch (1977:8) has named this image a "haven in a heartless world" and described it as a glorification of private life made necessary by the deprivations experienced in the public world. The image has two distinct themes: love and protection. The sentimentalized notion of the family as a refuge from the cruel world reached its fullest expression in the Victorian period (Millman, 1991:136). The family was idealized as a repository of warmth and tenderness (embodied by the mother) standing in opposition to the competitive and aggressive world of commerce (embodied by the father). The family's task was to protect against the outside world. As the nineteenth century passed, the ideal family became "a womblike inside" to be defended against a corrupting outside (Kenniston, 1977:11).

Family as Fulfillment

The protective image of the family has waned in recent years as the ideals of family fulfillment have taken shape. Today the family is more compensatory than protective. It supplies what is vitally needed but missing in other social arrangements. If work does not provide excitement and stimulation, individuals can turn to their family lives. The image of family life today is one of intimacy; that is, spouses, lovers, and even children make us feel alive and invigorated. In short, the family brightens up a social landscape that might otherwise seem gray (Demos, 1979:57). The image is still that of a haven, but now it is a haven of primary fulfillment and meaningful experience. The modern emphasis on "self-actualization" and continuing change and growth in adulthood places more value on being able to choose freely than on commitment. Today, we no longer speak of "true love" as a love we would die for, or die without. Rather, we talk of love that is "meaningful" or "alive" because it involves "honesty" and it stimulates us to discover ourselves and to change (Millman, 1991:140).

Self-fulfillment and enjoyment, the essential qualities of modern family life, may be contrasted with an older morality of duty, responsibility, work, and self-denial. Duty has been replaced with the obligation to enjoy family life. The "fun" morality expressed currently by the advertising industry glorifies the family united in pursuit of common activities that are enjoyed by all.

Family as Encumbrance

Loading the family with compensatory needs has created still another image, this one negative. The anti-image of the family is new. For the first time in American history, we blame the family for inhibiting our full human development. According to this view, domestic relationships look dangerously like an encumbrance, if not a form of bondage inhibiting the quest for a full experience of self. In a culture in which the "restless self" must be kept unfettered, flexible, and ready to change, attachments must be broken when they no longer permit continual development (Millman, 1991:142–143).

Monogamous marriage can become boring and stultifying. After all, variety is the "spice of life." Responsibility for children can compound the problem. The needs and requirements of the young are so constant, so pressing, that they leave little space for adults who must attend to them. "Spice" and "space" are, in fact, the qualities for which we yearn. In this anti-image, the family severely limits our access to either one (Demos, 1979:58).

IMAGES AND REALITY

These three images of family life are different faces of reality. In each image the family is the primary institution through which the goals of personal growth and self-fulfillment are achieved. The differences lie in the effects of family on the individual. In the first and second images the effects are beneficial; in the third they are adverse. What do these images omit, and what kind of distortions do they foster? All three images separate the family from society, creating, in Demos's words, "a sense of inside out in which the family is not experienced in its own right but in relation to other circumstances and other pleasures" (Demos, 1979:58).

Although family imagery has undergone great changes in recent decades, family and society remain polarized. The family still represents a symbolic opposition to work and business. Relations inside the family are idealized as nurturing, whereas those outside the family—especially in business and work—are seen as just the opposite. Families symbolize relationships of affection and love that are based on cooperation rather than competition; that are not contingent, rather than contingent, on performance; and that are governed by feelings and morality instead of law and contract (Collier et al., 1982:34).

Relationships between husbands and wives and between parents and children are especially idealized in the family image. The ideal states that families are formed in the marriage of one man and one woman, who will satisfy each other's emotional and physical needs "till death do them part." When children are added to this exclusive dyad, "parenting" becomes the natural extension of the husband-and-wife relationship. By providing "proper" child care, parents mold and shape happy children who will become successful adults (Birdwhistell, 1980:462–467).

Families have always recognized the difficulty of converting the ideals to reality, yet the images symbolize modern needs for nurturance in an impersonal society. At the same time, they overlook conditions and constraints in family and society that threaten those needs. For example, as women have joined the paid labor force in great numbers, husbands *and* most wives have jobs and families. As they pursue demanding careers or work at jobs with long hours, they may have little time or energy to devote to the family. For women, the difficulties of balancing work and family are widely recognized, and the image of "super-woman" has become a new cultural ideal. The superwoman who appears repeatedly in magazines and on television commercials meshes her multiple roles perfectly. If she has children, she is a supermother, able to work forty hours a week, keep the house clean and neat, entertain, keep physically fit by jogging or taking aerobics classes, and have a meaningful relationship with the superfa-ther, who is both productive and nurturing and who shares fully in the work of running the household. Such superparents have quality time with their children (Galinsky, 1986:20). This upbeat image of the modern superfamily who "has it all" obscures the different and often contradictory requirements imposed by work systems and family systems.

The family ideal no longer describes family experiences, if indeed it ever did. Nevertheless, research on beliefs and behavior indicates that people still hold to the ideal. Even though family images often contrast with the daily realities of most people, we persist in thinking about the family as a peaceful harbor, a shel-ter in the storm. Everything in us resists the idea that this sacred little circle could be disturbed by conflicts of interest, by competition (Millman, 1991:38), or by vast changes in day-to-day living patterns. The traditional family ideology per-sists in spite of societal changes that challenge it. This shows the power of the dominant culture to uphold certain social arrangements whether or not they are attainable for all (Baca Zinn, 1990).

The symbolic families that shape our thinking are misleading when they become standards against which we measure ourselves. They become normative (in the sense of obligatory) and operate as models affecting a great range of action and response, from social legislation to internal evaluations of our own success and failure as family members.

We live in an "information" society filled with images and messages. Much of the vast flood of imagery deals with family life and is aimed at families. The mass media entertains us with endless dramatizations of family normality and deviance. From scenes of domestic perfection exhibited on television by the Cleavers, the Bradys, and the Huxtables, we have been indoctrinated with images of a family life that never existed (Taylor, 1992:64). Certainly, we are past the days of the perfect mom and all-wise dad. Television families are becoming more realistic. Soap opera families and programs like *The Simpsons* and *Malcolm in the Middle* present the nitty-gritty of family life: money problems, divorce, sex, and sibling rivalry. Nevertheless, the families we "live by" continue to shape our expectations. We *expect* families to be happy and harmonious, to soothe away the cares of life outside the home. Disappointments in the home then become an independent source of stress as people criticize themselves because their family life fails to measure up to the imagined harmony of other families (Lerner, 1982:141). Stephanie Coontz, the author of *The Way We Never Were* (1992), a book about family images, myths, and half-truths, finds that guilt is a common reaction to the discord between images and reality:

> Even as children, my students and colleagues tell me, they felt guilty because their families did not act like those on television. Perhaps the second most common reaction is anger, a sense of betrayal or rage when you and your family cannot live as the myths suggest you should be able to (Coontz, 1992:6).

To question the idea of the happy family is not to say that love and joy cannot also be found in family life. Rather, the idealized fantasy overlooks the tensions and ambivalence that are unavoidable in everyday life. Despite the problems resulting from the "family harmony" image, this is the model presented constantly to the public by science, in art, and by the mass media. Even more critical, it is the model used by our legal, social, and psychiatric experts. The result, in Birdwhistell's words, is that the family is an "impossibly overloaded, guilt creating institution" (Birdwhistell, 1980:466).

THE MYTHICAL AMERICAN FAMILY

Family images are a composite of several closely related but distinct myths about the family. **Myths** are beliefs that are held uncritically and without examination or scrutiny (Crosby, 1985). These myths are bound up with nostalgic memory, selective perception, and cultural values concerning what is typical and true about the family. We will address the most prevailing myths that are popularly accepted as true in our society. In subsequent chapters we call into question the prevalent beliefs and folk wisdom that, if left unchallenged and unanswered, will become even more entrenched in the American mind as "the way families are." In this book, we use new knowledge as a "reply to myth" (Crosby, 1985): that is, as a way of challenging the commonly held myths about families in society.

The Myth of a Stable and Harmonious Family of the Past

Most people think that families of the past were better than families of the present. The popular assumption is that families in past times were more stable, better adjusted, and happier. There are two reasons for the assumption. First, we tend to be selective about what we remember. In other words, we romanticize the past. A second basis for thinking that families are worse off today is that so many changes in family life *have* occurred over the past few decades. Recent trends in family life suggest that the twenty-first-century family is in serious trouble. However, fears of family decline are as old as families themselves:

> One thing that never seems to change is the notion that family is not what it used to be. Families past are presented to us not only as more stable but as more authentic than families present. We imagine their times to have been the days when fathers were fathers, mothers true mothers, and children still children. Families past are invariably portrayed as simpler, less problematic. We imagine them not only as large but as better integrated, untroubled by generational divisions, close to kin, respectful of the old, honoring the dead (Gillis, 1996:3).

On closer examination, this glorified family is a historical fiction that never existed (Coontz, 1999a). Such nostalgic images of "traditional" families mask the inevitable dilemmas that accompany family life.

Two important points must be made about the stubborn myth of a vanished family past. First, family historians have found that there has never been a golden age of the family. There have always been desertion by spouses, illegitimate children, and certainly spouse and child abuse. Divorce rates were lower, but this does not mean that love was stronger in the past. Many women died earlier from pregnancy complications, which kept divorce rates lower and which meant that many children were raised by single parents or stepparents, just as now. Divorces were relatively uncommon also because of strong religious prohibitions and community norms against divorce. As a result, many "empty" marriages continued without love and happiness to bind them.

To judge marriage of the past as better than contemporary marriage is to ignore historical changes. We expect more of marriage than did our forebears, but this fact makes modern marriage neither better nor worse, only different. Chapters 2 and 3 examine the new social history of the family, which provides a far different picture of the past.

The Myth of Separate Worlds

The notion that family is a place to escape from the outside world is "the myth of separate worlds" (Kanter, 1984). It makes a distinction between "public" and "private" realms with family as the "haven in a heartless world." Here, social relations are thought to be different from those in the world at large. This myth assumes that families are independent, self-sufficient units relatively free from outside social pressures. Families that are not self-sufficient are judged inadequate.

The idea that family is set apart from the world at large developed during industrialization (Zaretsky, 1976). In response to new economic demands, families certainly changed as communities loosened their grip on family life (see Chapter 2); yet families remained linked to larger institutional structures.

The idea that families and the world exist in opposition to one another is a false dichotomy with contradictory expectations. Although we want the family to protect us *from* society, we also expect families to prepare us *for* society. The myth of separate worlds is ambivalent. On the one hand, the family is considered a private institution providing a haven from the outside world and from the trials of work. On the other hand, families are expected to adapt to the conditions of work, to socialize children to become competent workers, and to provide emotional support to workers to enhance their effectiveness. The myth of separate worlds ignores the many ways in which social structures impinge on family functioning. In many ways families shape themselves in response to the demands of jobs, careers, schools, and other social institutions.

In our family lives we feel family strains from conflicts posed by the relation between family and broader social systems, yet the *popular* conception of the family remains that of an autonomous setting untouched by the external world. This split vision is rooted in certain social realities. Modern society does demarcate public and private spheres, with the family representing the quintessentially private arena. The vision of the family as a private reserve, however, does not prevent society from intruding on every aspect of family life. There are "close and sometimes combustible connections between the internal life of families and the organization of paid work, state-organized welfare, and legal systems, schools, day care centers, and other institutions" (Thorne, 1992:5). This is why we must reject the assumption that the family is a "haven in a heartless world." It cannot function as a haven when outside forces encroach on it (Lasch, 1975).

The myth of separate worlds leads to the belief that the family survives or sinks by its own resources and fitness—a kind of **family Darwinism** that blames families for structural failure (Polakow, 1993:39). This myth ignores the harsh effect of economic conditions (e.g., poverty or near-poverty), unemployment and underemployment, and downward mobility or the threat of downward mobility. It ignores the social inequalities (racism, sexism, ageism, homophobia) that distribute resources differently.

Although the family is under pressure to appear free-standing, all families interact continuously with the workplace, the welfare system, and the schools. Agencies and people outside the family have taken over many functions that were once performed by the family. Children, for example, are raised not only by their parents but also by teachers, doctors, social workers, and television. A study of the family commissioned by the Carnegie Corporation over two decades ago found that parents have less authority than those with whom they share the tasks of raising their children. Most parents deal with persons from outside agencies from a position of inferiority or helplessness. They must compete with "experts," who are armed with special credentials, who are entrenched in their professions, and who have far more power in their institutions than do the parents who are their clients:

> As a result, the parent today is usually a coordinator without voice or authority, a maestro trying to conduct an orchestra of players who have never met and who play from a multitude of different scores, each in notations the conductor cannot read. If parents are frustrated, it is no wonder: for although they have the responsibility for their children's lives, they hardly ever have the voice, the authority, or the power to make others listen to them (Kenniston, 1977:18).

Just as societal changes have weakened parents' authority, so have other large-scale changes revealed flaws in treating family and society in opposition. Structural transformations in the economy and the workplace are among the most important forces shaping family life today (see Chapter 4). Their effect on marital patterns and living arrangements now heighten the interconnections between families and other social structures.

The Myth of the Monolithic Family Form

We all know what the family is *supposed* to look like. It should resemble the 1950s Ozzie and Harriet form. This uniform image has been imprinted on our brains since childhood, through children's books, schools, radio, television, movies, newspapers; through the lectures, if not the examples, of many of our parents; through the speeches, if not the examples, of many of our politicians. Invariably,

The mythical monolithic model.

the image is of a White, middle-class, heterosexual father as breadwinner, mother as homemaker, and children at home living in a one-family house. This model accounts for fewer than 10 percent of families. Today, fewer than one in ten American families fits the model of a go-to-work father and a stay-at-home mother.

The mythical, monolithic model of the typical American family embodies three distinctive features: (1) the family is a nuclear unit; (2) it consists of mother, father, and their children; and (3) it exhibits a gendered division of labor. The first two features are closely related. The nuclear family is separate from society and independent from kin. It consists of a married couple and their children living in a home of their own. The third distinguishing feature of "the family" is its assumed sexual division of labor: "a breadwinner husband, freed for and identified with activities in a separate economic sphere, and a full-time wife and mother whose being is often equated with the family itself" (Thorne, 1992:7).

Although this family type is now a small minority of U.S. families, major social and cultural forces continue to assume a uniform structure. In reality, "the family" today is characterized by its incredible diversity. Contemporary family forms include single-parent households, stepparent families, extended multi-generational households, gay and straight cohabiting couples, trans-national families, and many other kinds of families. The tension between this diverse

Popular TV shows mirror the large variety of family types.

array of family groupings and the idealized 1950s family creates disagreement about what makes up families. In fact, there is no consensus among social agencies or professionals or ordinary people on what currently constitutes a family (Aerts, 1993:7).

One way of moving beyond the distortions in the model of the typical family is to distinguish between families and households. A **family** is a construct of meanings and relationships; a **household** is a residential and economic unit (Osmond and Thorne, 1993:607; Rapp, 1982). To put it another way, a household is a residence group that carries out domestic functions, whereas a family is a kinship group (Holstein and Gubrium, 1999:31). A good example of the importance of distinguishing between family and household is the restructuring of family obligations and household composition after divorce (Ferree, 1991:107). When separation and divorce break the bonds between mother and father, bonds between children and parents remain intact. Consequently, an increasing number of families extend across two or more households linked by the continuing ties between parents and children who live apart but remain family. After all, people may live apart and still feel "family." In fact, household and family are not always the same thing. People may share a household and not consider themselves a family, and people may feel like a family while not living together (Bridenthal, 1981:48).

Although family relations and household arrangements today *are* more diverse than at any time in history, diversity is not new. Throughout history, major social forces have created a wide range of family configurations. Today, the changes most responsible for the proliferation of family types are (1) economic transitions that are creating service-sector jobs and putting women into the workforce (see Chapter 4); (2) new patterns in marriage and divorce; and (3) a decline in the number of children women bear. These developments have added to the emergence of new family types.

Perhaps the most striking change in the national profile of families is the rise in mother-only households, and the poverty that often accompanies them. The vast majority of single-parent households are maintained by mothers. Patterns of sexual inequality in the larger society contribute to "the feminization of poverty," the growing impoverishment of women (and their children) in American society. Many children will not experience the idealized two-parent household during major portions of their childhood years.

A growing trend toward the maintenance of households by persons living alone or with others to whom they are not related has also contributed to the expansion in the variety of living arrangements. Factors contributing to the surge of nonfamily households include the increased tendency of young adults to move away from home at an early age, postponement of marriage, the continued high rate of divorce, and increasing numbers of elderly persons living alone.

Economic and demographic forces are creating other changes as well. At the beginning of the twentieth century, fewer than one in five Americans belonged to a racial or ethnic minority. By 1990 that proportion had grown to one in four. Racial ethnics will account for one-third of the population in the year 2030. As the United States grows ever more diverse in racial and ethnic composition, family diversity will remain evident. Race and class are important structural factors underlying the diversity of family forms. Family differences emerge in the context of race, class, and gender relations in the larger society.

Family diversity has led some social scientists to conclude that the American family does not exist.

> The first thing to remember about the American family is that it doesn't exist. Families exist. All kinds of families in all kinds of economic and marital situations, as all of us can see. . . . The American family? Just which American family did you have in mind? Black or white, large or small, wealthy or poor, or somewhere in between? Did you mean a father-headed, mother-headed, or childless family? First or second time around? Happy or miserable? Your family or mine? (Howe, 1972:11)

The Myth of a Unified Family Experience

Partly because we glorify the family, we assume that family members experience the family in the same way—that family and individuals are merged and that they have common needs, common experiences, and common meanings. The conventional conception of "the family" as a unitary whole is a "glued together family" (Sen, 1983, cited in Ferree, 1991), treated as if it were a single actor with a single set of interests.

New research has cut through romantic assumptions about family and household unity, showing that families produce divergent experiences for women, men, and children. The best way to understand how different realities are produced for family members is to "decompose" the family—that is, to break it down into its essential components (Mitchell, 1966). Two key components of all families are the gender system and the age system. These two systems produce different realities for men and women as well as for children and adults. These systems shape every activity that has to do with daily family living, such as the division of household labor, leisure activities, the giving and receiving of nurturance and emotional support, decisions about consumption, and employment. In addition, age and gender often produce different and conflicting interests among family members. This means that family is not the same for children and adults, nor for women and men. Instead, there are multiple experiences, multiple voices, and different family realities even among members participating in the same family (Wolfe, 1990).

Jessie Bernard's classic work on marriage revealed that every marital union actually contains two marriages—his and hers—and that the two do not always coincide (Bernard, 1971). Researchers who ask husbands and wives identical questions about their marriages often get quite different replies, even to fairly simple, factual questions. The family as a **gendered** institution (Acker, 1992) is one of the most important themes in family research. Gender organizes every aspect of family living—its rules, roles, and relationships. **Patriarchy** is the term used to refer to social relations in which men are dominant over women. Patriarchy in the larger society gives shape to a family system in which men are accorded more prestige and more privileges and in which they wield greater power.

Knowing that family experiences vary by gender, we can better understand the problems associated with the image of the family as a harbor from life's storms. The family is idealized as a personal retreat, yet for most women it is a workplace, a place of domestic labor and child care. For whom, then, is the home a refuge, a nurturant haven? Barrie Thorne has provided the following answer:

> For the vast majority of women, the home is a place of considerable work, even when they are employed full-time out of the home. Researchers have found that women work in and out of the home an average of fifteen hours more than men each week, which adds up to an extra month of twenty-four hour-days a year (Thorne, 1992:18).

Caring for families and caring about them is strongly gendered. Adult women are providers of care but less likely to be recipients of such care. Far more than men, women are the caretakers and the care givers that maintain family bonds (Aldous, 1991:661). A fully differentiated view of family experience is vital if we are to understand family life.

The Myth of Family Consensus

The idealized picture of family life is flawed in still another way. It assumes that families are based on "companionate" or "consensual" relations—in other words, on a harmony of interest among family members. This myth neglects a fundamental family paradox. Family life can be contradictory due to the following conditions: (1) the power relations within the family, (2) the competitive aspects of family relations, and (3) the intense emotional quality of family life.

The family is supposed to be a place of love and solidarity, but people do not always find nurturing and support in their families. Behind the sentimental ideal are the all-too-common rivalries, conflicts, hatreds, and selfishness that are also present in family life (Menaghan, 1989:824). Behind closed doors, the other face of the family may be the opposite of the myth. In marriage, for example, the political reality of husband–wife relationships is evident in household division of labor, in family decision making, and "in extreme form in incidents of wife abuse" (Thorne, 1982:13). Recognizing the political underpinnings of family life does not discount the solidarity and support found within the family realm. Instead, such conditions simply acknowledge families as the site of deep contradictions. Love and conflict can exist alongside each other, often becoming entangled. The tangle of love and domination can create an "arena of struggle" between family members (Hartmann, 1981a).

Though we commonly romanticize the family as a place where all is shared and where nobody measures, new research reveals that money matters often complicate family life. For example, Marcia Millman discovered that there is probably more counting in families than in other settings:

> In many ways, families display the same hard traits of the market. One sees this expressed in the ways we use money, often unconsciously, to control children, punish estranged spouses, measure a parent's true feelings for us, buy freedom from relationships, or stop a partner from leaving. Furthermore, in the family as in the workplace, there is a system of exchange with a perpetual accounting and sanctions for not performing as expected. But because of our image of the family as a place of love and sharing (and our deep wish that it be so) we underestimate the conflicts of interest and rivalries that are common, if not inevitable, and make light of the deadly serious bookkeeping (Millman, 1991:9).

The emotional quality of family life often creates fissures and tensions because emotional relationships inevitably contain negative as well as positive feelings. This combination of love and antagonism sets intimate relationships apart from less intimate ones. Emotional relationships contain negative as well as positive feelings. Therefore, ambiguity is an integral part of family experience.

Because intimate relationships are intense, they can create a cauldron-like setting, one that is "overheated by its seclusiveness, specialization, and uniqueness" (Tufte and Meyerhoff, 1979:17). The family may then become less a refuge and more like a prison from which growing numbers of "refugees" (runaway children, permanently defecting adolescents, wives, and husbands) seek escape. The very closeness, privacy, and intimacy that exist among family members can also create disorder, distance, and conflict.

Families may provide emotional support and nurturance for their members, but they may also inspire violence and brutality. Many family specialists argue that it would be hard to find a group or institution in American society in which violence is more of an everyday occurrence than within the American family. For example, most murder cases involve relatives or people involved in some intimate way. Violence is not found in all families, but there is an emotional dynamic to family life that can generate violence. We must acknowledge this fact if we are to understand the complexity of families in our society.

> Until we admit that families may exhibit the most brutalizing, abusing, dangerous, and inhumane types of interaction patterns as well as loving, caring, protecting, helping, sustaining, and nurturing types of relationships, we will fail to understand the range of human interaction that takes place within families (Eichler, 1981:384).

Family life is fraught with disparities. Families may provide emotional support for some family members but not for others. Or, the support derived from the family may vary by age and gender. Some family members may derive support at great cost to others in the family.

> The modern family has been called a sanctuary, a castle, that succors its beset members from the impersonality of the outside world. And indeed it is a refuge for many. But this kind of family and home has at times been the man's castle, maintained for him by the wife assisted by the children (Tufte and Meyerhoff, 1979:5).

Families are paradoxical. They may provide support for their members, but that support is neither uniform nor is it always present. Lillian Rubin has captured well the duality of family experience: "The family as an institution is both oppressive and protective and, depending on the issue, is experienced sometimes one way, sometimes the other often in some mix of the two by most people who live in families" (Rubin, 1976:6).

The Myth of Family Decline as the Cause of Social Problems

Partly because of the myths about the past, and partly because the family has changed so much in the last few decades, many social analysts conclude that the "breakdown of the family" is responsible for our worst social problems. In the media, on the campaign trail, and in national policy debates, the words "family values" blast out from podiums and headlines. In the early 1990s, former Vice

President Dan Quayle added to the national anxiety by denouncing television character Murphy Brown for having a baby without a husband. Declaring that unwed motherhood was destroying the nation, Quayle blamed the 1992 Los Angeles riots on family decline.

At the end of the twentieth century, rhetoric about family values became broadly accepted as a way of explaining such social ills as poverty, crime, drug abuse, teen pregnancy, and gang violence. According to this logic, the two-parent family is the basis of social organization and cohesion. This family form is extolled as the one in which children are best socialized to become good citizens, and in which women and men perform the roles essential to creating and maintaining social order and continuity from one generation to the next as wives and mothers, husbands and fathers. Any change in family structure is viewed in terms of moral decline. When family moralists say "family values," they really mean family *structure* (Dill et al., 1998). The family-values refrain is nothing more than a way of distinguishing the two-parent family from other family types. Single-parent families produced by divorce and unwed motherhood are denounced as selfish practices that are damaging children, destroying families, and tearing apart the fabric of society. Put very generally, the family-decline position is that "as a result of hedonistic individualism, we are letting our 'family values' slip away and what is needed now is nothing short of a moral rearmament on behalf of parental responsibility" (Mason et al., 1998:3).

What is wrong with the claim that family decline is responsible for social problems? This reasoning is flawed in two fundamental respects. First, it reverses the relationship between family and society by treating the family as the building block of society rather than a product of social conditions. Second, it ignores the structural reasons for family breakdown.

The commonplace belief that changing families threaten society is a form of social reductionism:

> In this simple model of society, the family is the basic unit. . . . Through the magical process called socialization, families cause the attitudes, dispositions, and capabilities of individual children who in turn as adults cause political and economic institutions to work or not to work (Young, 1994:89).

Those who persist in seeing the current shifts in family life as the source of disarray have it backward (Stacey, 1994). Divorce and single parenthood are the *consequences* of social and economic dislocations rather than the cause, as some would have us believe. Disappearing jobs, declining earnings, and low-wage work have far more detrimental effects on families than the demise of family values. Family moralists are blind to the realities of rising inequality, concentrated poverty, and escalating government policies of social abandonment. They reverse cause and effect, thus making single parents a convenient scapegoat. The simple solution that we return to the nuclear family at all costs allows the public and the government to escape social responsibilities, such as intervening in the ghettos, building new houses and schools, and creating millions of jobs that we need. This view shifts the focus from the larger society to individual family members, who must then devise their own solutions for the dilemmas of our times.

Many proponents of strong family values overstate the evidence that divorce produces lasting damage to children and that children are always best off in two-parent families. Not all social scientists agree that family structure is all that matters. As Arlene Skolnick points out, most researchers take a shades-of-gray position on family structure. The evidence does show that children in divorced, remarried, or unmarried families are at greater risk for a number of problems, but there is little support for the frightening picture painted by many (Skolnick, 1997b:16). In fact, the vast majority of children in single-parent families turn out reasonably well. Alan Acock and David Demo, who examined a nationally representative sample of children and adolescents in four family structures, reported few statistically significant differences across family types on measures of socioemotional adjustment and well-being (Acock and Demo, 1994). They found few statistically significant differences in children's well-being in first-married, divorced, remarried, and continuously single-parent families (Demo, 2000:18). Much of the national discussion about the harmful social and cultural effects of family breakdown is a thinly veiled attack on single mothers. Undeniably, many female-headed families are beset with a disproportionate share of family problems. But neither family structure nor lack of family values locks people in a cycle of poverty. Upholding the two-parent family as superior to all other family forms is a way of scapegoating individuals who are adapting to society's changes. Shifts in family life cannot be reduced to moral values.

Healthy families need healthy environments. Many neighborhoods have substandard services such as schools, health care, recreation facilities, sanitation, and police and fire protection. Due to massive economic transformations and various kinds of social disinvestment in the lives of the poor, families across the country are forced to live amidst crime, gangs, pollution, drugs, and inadequate housing. These are the real enemies of strong families. The important question to ask about U.S. families is not how well they conform to an idealized form, but rather, "how well do they function—what kind of loving, care, and nurturance do they provide?" (Mason et al., 1998:2).

A NEW FRAMEWORK FOR UNDERSTANDING FAMILIES

The Sociological Perspective

Commonly held ideas about the family are often "reductionist" in that they focus almost exclusively on individuals as they perform their family roles (Sprey, 2001:4). This book is different. It is firmly grounded in the sociological perspective for a critical understanding of the nation's diverse and changing families. Our central task is to examine how changes in society affect the formation and character of families and how families affect people's experiences in society. To understand family life requires more than family experiences. It requires a perspective that leads to sociological questions and analysis. What is a sociological perspective? How does it apply to family study? Sociology focuses on the structural sources of family life. Since social structures are abstract and often invisible, we must look behind the facades of family life to see how families are organized in socially patterned ways. Two sociological principles are used throughout this book. The first is that there is a close relationship between families and the larger society that shapes them. In studying family life we make a distinction between two levels of analysis. The macro level examines the family in relation to the rest of society. Instead of focusing on family roles and relations in isolation from the rest of social life, families are analyzed in reference to societal trends. The macro level of analysis illustrates how larger social systems shape the smaller family systems. For example, we call on macro structural change to explain why families are far different from what they used to be. A macro level of analysis also looks at how the family as an institution contributes to the organization of the larger society (Kain, 1990:15). For example, the family is a vital part of the economy because it produces both workers and consumers. The family is a primary mechanism for perpetuating inequality through the interlocking systems of race, class, and gender. This enables us to see how "society makes families and families make society" (Glazer, cited in Billingsley, 1992:78).

The societal level is not the only focus of our inquiry. The interior life of families is also emphasized. The micro level of analysis examines the internal dynamics of family life. In this type of analysis, the family is a "small group in which individuals spend much of their lives" (Kain, 1990:15). In micro analysis we examine the varied "experiences of kinship, intimacy, and domestic sharing" (Thorne, 1992:12). This is where the vital interpersonal dramas of love and domination, of companionship and conflict, of happiness and hatred occur. Of course, intimate family relationships reflect the structured inequalities of the larger society. Understanding families requires that we study both the macro level and the micro level and how each affects the other (see Box 1.2 for a look at the methods sociologists use in doing research on families).

Because our emphasis is on social structure, the reader is required to accept another fundamental assumption of the sociological perspective: the adoption of a critical stance toward all social arrangements. We must ask these questions: How does the social system really work? Who has the power? Who benefits under the existing social arrangements and who does not? Questions such as these call into question existing myths and stereotypes about the nation's families.

The Shifting Terrain of Family Studies

Just as families in the nation and the world are changing dramatically, so, too, is the scholarship on families. As society experiences major "earthquakes," social science thinking about families is undergoing "seismic shifts" as well. Today, new ideas about diversity and social context are sweeping the family field and making it more exciting than ever before (Allen and Demo, 1995; Cheal, 1991; Mann et al., 1997; Skolnick, 1993).

These new developments have fundamentally changed our knowledge about the way families operate, producing what is called a paradigm shift. **Paradigm** refers to the basic assumptions that scholars have of the social worlds they study. A family paradigm includes basic conceptual frameworks—in other words, models of families in society, and the field's important problems, questions, concepts, and methods of study.

BOX 1.2 **Researching Families:** How Do Sociologists Conduct Research on Families?

There are many methods for studying families; each has its own purpose and its own underlying logic that justifies using the method. A widely used distinction is that between **quantitative** and **qualitative** methods.

The most frequently used quantitative method is the sample survey (often shortened to "survey"), which focuses on specific behaviors or attitudes and on factors that are hypothesized to influence them. The researcher designs a measure for each behavior or attitude and each potential explanatory factor. As a simple illustrative example, the researcher might expect that how much education a husband has influences how much housework he does. Education is easily measured in years and housework in hours per week, so a survey questionnaire can be designed for interviewing husbands on these matters. The goal is to understand whether such a relationship between education and housework exists for all husbands in the population; since they are too numerous, the researcher must interview an appropriately selected sample. By using suitable statistical procedures, the researcher can find out whether housework is related to education in the sample and whether the results in the sample can be generalized to the population. Measurement, statistical analysis, and generalization of findings from a sample to a population are the distinguishing features of quantitative research.

Qualitative and quantitative methods sometimes have been regarded as incompatible, but several researchers have used them in a complementary fashion. Nevertheless, combining quantitative and qualitative approaches has not been easy because qualitative methods have a different focus and a different starting point than quantitative approaches. Qualitative researchers begin with the premise that human activity is interpretive activity. That is, we cannot do anything without its having some meanings, and qualitative researchers want to discover meanings—how people interpret what they do. Returning to the previous example, the number of hours a week a husband does housework is of some interest, but of more interest is its meaning to him and to his wife. Does he define what he is doing as "helping" his wife in "her" tasks? Or is he a committed believer in gender equality who defines housework as something to be shared equally? Or is there some other, less obvious meaning? And how does she define what he is doing? And how do those meanings shape their interactions and relationships?

The qualitative researcher usually begins research with questions in mind rather than with specific hypotheses, questions about how people do things and what those activities mean. There are two main types of qualitative research procedure. One is called ethnography. The ethnographer observes people and talks with them over a period of weeks, months, or years as they interact in their customary round of life. The researcher compares participants with those being studied and records observations in field notes. The second is known by various names—qualitative interviewing, unstructured or semi-structured interviewing, in-depth interviewing. The researcher designs an interview guide with open-ended questions that invite and allow the interviewee to answer in his or her own words. Qualitative research is a process of discovery of the implicit and explicit categories through which people

(continued)

(continued from previous page)

define and construct their interpersonal activity. The researcher then tries to understand those categories in some larger theoretical framework. He or she creates categories that facilitate understanding the meanings in use by those studied. The distinguishing features of qualitative research are: conversational and participant observation data, discovering meanings in use, interpreting those user meanings, creating interpretive categories and concepts that are general enough to serve in studying other groups.

One of the issues in collecting qualitative interview data is whether family members should be interviewed individually or jointly. Individual interviewing is more common. Important ethical dilemmas are encountered in doing qualitative research on families. By its nature, such research seeks to penetrate family privacy in the interest of increased understanding of how families function. The full consequences of this effort cannot be known in advance either by the researchers or by the participants. Researchers should be sensitive to possible hazards to family members.

Source: Gerald Handel and Gail Whitchurch (eds.), "Introduction to Part II: Research Methods." In *The Psychosocial Interior of the Family,* 4th ed. New York: Walter de Gruyter, 1994, pp. 49–51.

The old family paradigm posited a uniform process of family formation. This model was rooted in concerns that shaped the early social sciences—namely, the shift from traditional to modern society. Modernization was thought to produce a standard family type. In the 1950s and 1960s, the notion of a standard family type was an important feature of the dominant paradigm known as functionalism. Talcott Parsons (1955), the major sociological theorist in the United States and the leading family theorist of the 1950s and 1960s, saw the family as a vital element in the larger social system (Skolnick, 1993:49). According to his theory, the modern nuclear family was the basis of social organization and cohesion in society. This family form was essential for the socialization of children and for the orderly division of labor between women and men. Structural functionalism treated the modern nuclear family as the norm even though there were many varieties of families in different regional, economic, racial, and ethnic groups (Baca Zinn, 2000:44).

Structural functionalism was flawed, however, in that it mistook a historically specific family form as the universal form for families in modern society (Mann et al., 1997:321). This distorted and misrepresented family life because it generalized about families from the experience of the dominant group.

In the past three decades, efforts to challenge the false universalization embedded in structural functionalism have changed our thinking. A flood of new ideas and approaches has produced a shift away from uniformity and changed the field forever. The shift in family sociology has been so pronounced that one scholar calls this stage of development, a "Big Bang"—a dramatic period of diversification in family studies (Cheal, 1991:153).

The Structural Diversity Approach

The perspective used in this book draws on a conceptual framework that we call "structural diversity." This framework goes beyond adding in different group experiences to already established frameworks of thought (Andersen and Collins, 2001). Our coverage of the nation's various family arrangements is not simply for cultural appreciation. We want our readers to understand *why* families are diverse. We provide a coherent analysis as well as a new approach. (Some of the following discussion is based on ideas in Baca Zinn and Eitzen, 1996; Baca Zinn and Dill, 1996; and Baca Zinn and Wells, 2000.) Our approach is based on the premise that families are divided along structural lines that shape their form and dynamics. The new perspective on families incorporates the following themes.

1. *Family forms are socially constructed and historically changing.* Although we think of families as "natural," they cannot be universalized. Social history shows that families vary by economic, political, and cultural conditions. Supporting this view are the social constructionist and social structural theoretical approaches. The social constructionist approach argues that social context creates families. What seems "natural" depends on time, place, and circumstance. How a family is defined depends on the historical period, the society, and even the social stratum within that society (Coltrane, 1998:1–9). "Stages we take for granted like childhood, adolescence, and adulthood are not timeless entities built into human nature but aspects of the human condition that have been reshaped with historical changes" (Skolnick, 1993:45). The point is that the form and meaning of families, gender, motherhood, fatherhood, or childhood are socially and historically varied.

2. *Family diversity is produced by the very structures that organize society as a whole.* Class, race, and gender are axes of social structure that create different contexts for family living through their unequal distribution of social resources and opportunities. Different contexts or "social locations" are the differences that make a difference. Instead of being an intrinsic property of groups that are culturally different, diversity in families is *structural*. The uneven distribution of work, wages, and other family requirements produce multiple family realities (Baca Zinn, 2000:48). At any particular time, a society will contain a range of family types that vary with social class, race, region, and other structural conditions.

One important feature of family variations is that they are "based in social relations between dominant and subordinate groups" (Weber, 2001:81). Not only do power relations produce both opportunity and oppression, "there is a direct relationship between the privileged circumstances of some families and the disadvantaged position of other families" (Garey and Hansen, 1998:xvi). For example, the histories of racial-ethnic families in the United States were not a matter of simple coexistence with dominant race and class groups. Instead, the opportunities of some families rested on the disadvantages of other families (Dill, 1994).

3. *The social locations in which families are embedded are not the product of a single power system, but are shaped by intersecting hierarchies.* Class, race, and gender are social structures that intersect. They work together to place families and their

members in particular social locations. When we examine how families and individuals are positioned within these cross-cutting hierarchies, we have a better grasp of different family arrangements and different family experiences. Not only do race, class, and gender shape families in different ways, they mean that people of the same race may experience family differently depending on their location in the class structure as unemployed, poor, working-class, or professional; their location in the gender structure as male or female; and their location in the sexual orientation system as heterosexual, gay, lesbian, or bisexual (Baca Zinn and Dill, 1996:327).

4. *Family diversity is constructed through social structure and human agency.* The structural diversity model stresses larger social forces in shaping families differently. However, a structural analysis must not lose sight of the family members who shape their families through their own actions and behaviors. Families, after all, are not just molded from the "outside in." What happens on a daily basis in domestic settings also constructs families. Women, men, and children are not passive. They actively shape families by adapting to, and changing, certain aspects of their social environments. Often they must invent new family forms in order to survive. This process is called **human agency**. Behaviors that family members use in adapting to structural constraints and stressful events are called "family adaptive strategies." If used carefully, the concept of human agency can serve as a sensitizing device (Moen and Wethington, 1992), illustrating meaningful interaction between social actors and their social environments (see Box 1.3 for an illustration of family adaptive strategies).

5. *Understanding family diversity requires the use of wide-ranging intellectual traditions.* This differs from past approaches, which were based on studies involving mostly white, middle-class families. Today, the family field takes various standpoints into account. Several bodies of new scholarship by and about marginalized groups are documenting multiple family realities. Feminists representing different schools of thought along with various racial and ethnic groups, members of the working class, and lesbians and gays have pressed for a redefinition of "the family." New scholarship about families as they vary by class, race, gender, and sexuality offer powerful alternatives to the old paradigm. The structural diversity model calls on concepts and approaches in the new fields of women's studies, African American studies, Latino studies, and cultural studies. Their insights can enhance the sociological perspective and offer vital building blocks for understanding the wide variety of family types in the United States.

ADDITIONAL FEATURES OF THIS BOOK

The framework described in this chapter is woven throughout this book. The demythologizing of families is a central theme. Each chapter begins with a list of myths juxtaposed by the facts that are presented in greater detail in that chapter. In addition, the chapters include three distinctive boxes to enhance your understanding of the topics listed on p. 27.

BOX 1.3   **Inside the Worlds of Diverse Families:** Norma's Challenge: Providing for Children without a Husband or a High School Diploma

Women in U.S. society have typically depended on their husbands' earnings to support their children. Increasingly, young women pursue advanced educational credentials that will enable them to provide adequately for their children. Norma's circumstances are different. Norma is a White divorced mother of two who dropped out of high school. She lives in a small community in rural Michigan with her 9-year-old daughter and 8-year-old son. Since her divorce three years ago, Norma's goal has been to be able to support her family financially. She grew up on welfare and also spent time on welfare during her marriage. Now age 33, Norma still remembers that she and her siblings were called "welfare brats" when they were growing up in this community. She is determined that her children will not be called the same.

By implementing a number of adaptive strategies, Norma has been able to achieve the goal of providing for her children without public assistance. Two of the principal strategies she uses to make ends meet are relying on her extended family and commuting to a higher wage labor market. Norma and her children currently live in an extended family household with her mother and stepfather. Norma had her own apartment, but found she was unable to pay the rent. She explains what happened then,

> My mom was having a hard time financially—she was about ready to lose her house. I said, "Well, I can move in and pay you rent." That's helped her out and it has helped me out.

This household arrangement represents an adaptive strategy that serves all involved. Norma pays rent to her mother at a lower than market rate and her mother is now able to cover her house payment.

Wage scales in rural areas are lower than those in urban areas; wage scales for rural women are especially depressed. Norma engages in an economic strategy used by many rural residents: she commutes to a job in or near an urban center. In Norma's case, her previous local jobs paid $4.35 and $5.00 an hour. Now she drives thirty-five miles to a furniture factory where she is paid $8.30 an hour. The wages are higher, but commuting raises a set of difficult issues. Many single mothers are unable to extend their work day by adding commuting time. Others express concern about working at long distance from their children. Norma has resolved these issues by working out a flexible arrangement in which her aunt provides paid childcare. Norma knows that if an emergency arises in her absence—for example, if her daughter or son becomes ill at school—a family member is available and willing to step in for her.

Norma lives on the economic edge; she reports that it is extremely difficult to provide food, clothing, and shelter for her children. In fact, her experience shows that she is unable to live in an independent household on her meager earnings. Nevertheless, Norma is doing as well as is feasibly possible given the constraints of limited education and a low-wage economy. Norma's extended family is the vital resource that enables her to provide the necessities of life for her children.

Norma is motivated by the desire to set a good example for her children. She says, "I want them to know that they have to work for what they get and not just

(continued)

(continued from previous page)

take a free ride through life." But she also acknowledges how hard it is to support her family. "Sometimes," she says, "we don't have nothing."

Source: Barbara Wells, Department of Sociology, Maryville College, 2001. This essay was written expressly for the sixth edition of *Diversity in Families*.

1. *Inside the Worlds of Diverse Families* looks inside micro structural worlds to put a human face on different features of family experience.
2. *Researching Families* presents the main approaches and methods sociologists use in their studies.
3. *Families in Global Perspective* offers an international view of families, with selected illustrations of family life in other societies.
4. *Technology and the Family* explores the effects of new technologies on everyday family life.

We hope that you capture some of our enthusiasm for exploring the intricacies and mysteries of families in society.

CHAPTER REVIEW

1. This book uses a sociological perspective to analyze families. This analysis requires a critical examination of social relations.
2. Families are in upheaval around the world. These changes are confusing to many observers. Although some see this upheaval as a sign of family decline, the real causes of family change lie in larger changes occurring in the nation and the world.
3. Our objectivity as sociologists and students is often obscured by our own experiences and by ideals and myths about the family.
4. Three distinct images of the family can be identified in U.S. society: (a) family as a haven, (b) family as fulfillment, and (c) family as encumbrance. All of these images place family and society in opposition to each other.
5. The disparities between idealized and real patterns of family life become evident when we examine six myths about family.
6. The myth of a stable and harmonious family of the past romanticizes the "traditional" families of our forebears. However, new research has found that problems considered unique in today's families also existed in the past.
7. The myth of separate worlds polarizes family and society. In fact, the family is embedded in social settings that affect the day-to-day realities of family life.
8. The myth of the monolithic family form assumes that all families are nuclear in structure; are composed of a father, mother, and children; and exhibit a sexual division of labor featuring a breadwinner father and a homemaking mother. This model accounts for only 10 percent of families in the United States. Because "family" is an idealized concept, sociologists often find it useful to use the concept of "household," which is a domestic unit.
9. The myth of a unitary family experience is also a product of false universalization. It assumes that all family members have common needs, interests, and experiences.

Gender and age, however, are key components that create different experiences of women and men and adults and children.

10. The myth of family consensus assumes that families operate on principles of harmony and love. Although these ingredients are present in many families, this myth ignores the contradictions that are intrinsic to family life due to power relations, financial concerns, and the intense emotional quality of family life.

11. The myth of family decline blames social problems on deteriorating family values. This myth ignores the changing economic conditions that produce divorce and single-parent families.

12. Sociologists analyze families at two levels. The macro level examines families in relation to the larger society, and the micro level examines the interpersonal features of family life.

13. The sociological perspective stresses structural conditions that shape families differently, but does not lose sight of individuals who create viable family lives.

14. In the past, family sociology marginalized diversity rather than treating it as a central feature of social life. The paradigm known as structural functionalism treated the modern nuclear family as the norm.

15. A new paradigm is emerging in the family field. The structural diversity approach focuses on multiple family and household forms. The key to understanding family diversity is the structural distribution of social opportunities.

RELATED WEB SITES

http://www.contemporaryfamilies.org/

The Council on Contemporary Families (CCF) is a nonprofit organization founded in 1996 by a diverse group of family researchers, mental health and social work practitioners, and activists. CCF's goal is to enhance the national conversation about what contemporary families need and how these needs can best be met. CCF believes that the public is asking for both more accurate information about the condition of America's families and for a more humane and sensitive discussion of the larger social, legal, cultural, and psychological issues that are often simplified under the rubric of "family values." It is their purpose to achieve this goal through the dissemination of educational materials, media coverage, conferences, and seminars.

http://www.familydiscussions.com/

Family Discussions: "Family Discussions" is intended to provide useful resources for anyone interested in the sociology of the family, especially recent sociological discussions of family change.

http://www.gallup.com/poll/reports/family.asp

Family Values Differ Sharply Around the World: The Gallup Organization reported that a poll it conducted in 1997 in sixteen countries on four continents finds people a long way from sharing a global set of family values. In fact, what is considered morally acceptable in some countries is widely deemed immoral in others.

http://www.bccf.bc.ca/

British Columbia Council for Families: Affirming that the family in all its diversity is the foundation of society, the mission of the BC Council for Families is to strengthen, encourage, and support families through information, education, research, and advocacy. The Council was formed in 1977 when representatives from the community, government and churches met to brainstorm about family issues. They believed that the family was the basic unit of society and that supporting and strengthening the family would greatly benefit society as a whole.

Preindustrial Families and the Emergence of a Modern Family Form

Myths and Realities

Myth: Families everywhere are similar in form because the family is a natural unit, based on the timeless functions of love, caring, and childbearing.

Reality: Families are not merely biological arrangements, but are grounded in particular social settings, which produce wide-ranging family differences.

Myth: Traditional American families were stable arrangements of many kinfolk living together in large households. Family members all worked together on Grandma's farm. Life was hard but happy, because family members knew their roles and had strong family values.

Reality: This image is what William J. Goode (1983:43) named "the classical family of Western nostalgia." Few examples of this "traditional" family have been found. Grandma's farm was not entirely self-sufficient. Few families stayed together as large aggregations of kinfolk, and most houses were small, not large. Family discord was as common in the past as in the present.

Myth: Family life among the Puritans in the New England colonies was especially disciplined, harmonious, and stable.

Reality: Although the Puritans valued discipline, family life was neither harmonious nor stable. The family was a breeding ground for tension and conflict, especially during the winter, when its members were forced into close and constant contact with each other in small, cramped houses (Henretta, 1973:36). High mortality rates meant stability was hard to achieve. The average length of marriage was less than a dozen years. One-third to one-half of all children lost at least one parent before the age of twenty-one (Coontz, 1993:36).

Myth: Premarital sex was unheard of in "traditional" America, when young people, especially girls, were likely to be virginal at marriage and faithful afterward.

Reality: Sexual expressiveness outside of marriage is a time-honored practice. Even among the Puritans, fornication and adultery were common in the seventeenth century. Premarital pregnancy is not limited to the twentieth century. In certain communities of eighteenth-century America, 30 to 40 percent of brides were going to the altar pregnant (Demos, 1986:6).

Myth: Industrialization replaced the extended family of early America with the nuclear family form.

Reality: Nuclear families did not emerge as a response to industrialization but were brought here by the nation's earliest White settlers.

Myth: Public anxiety about "the crisis of the family" is a recent development.

Reality: The idea that the family is falling apart is as old as the nation itself. The earliest New England settlers feared that the family was endangered and children were losing respect for authority.

*F*amilies are changing in ways that are troubling to many people. Marriages continue to end in divorce, more than half of all mothers with school-age children are in the workforce, family life is more fluid than ever before, and new family forms are on the rise. These trends suggest to some observers that the American family is in decline. Yet popular notions of what is wrong with the family today are based on misconceptions about how families lived in the past. False images of something called "the traditional family" are used both to idealize the past and to lament the present state of the family. New research, however, has dispelled many myths about earlier family life. Historical studies have begun to paint a new picture of the history of family life (Kain, 1990:4), one that stands in sharp contrast to our images of the past. Knowing about families of the past is important for many reasons; one is to better understand our present. Even though American families are far different from what they used to be, many of these new patterns have roots in the past. Throughout history, families have been in flux. Steven Mintz and Susan Kellogg refer to these ongoing changes as "domestic revolutions."

> Over the past 300 years, American families have undergone a series of far-reaching domestic revolutions that profoundly altered their family life, repeatedly transforming their demographic characteristics, organizational structure, functions, conceptions and emotional dynamics (Mintz and Kellogg, 1988:xiv).

Knowing that families have always been vulnerable to social and economic change is essential for understanding many of the problems faced by today's families.

This chapter examines White families in American society over a sweep of two and a half centuries. The chapter shows how underlying social forces and macro structures encompass families and cause them to bend with time. To illustrate this, we focus on family life among the White colonists, tracing the social forces that, by about 1800, produced a new family form. More important than the precise chronological markings are the ongoing social and economic developments in the larger society that changed the relationship between families and other institutions, especially the workplace. The rise of the **"modern" family** traces the historical development of a race-specific and class-specific form. This development was not universal. Instead, social forces created varied family arrangements within the United States. In every historical period, this society has had several distinct but interconnected family systems. Together, they are

The Lugo family, Bell Gardens, California, 1888.

part of a larger constellation of power relations, unequal access to resources, and struggles over what families "should" be (Coontz, 1999b:ix). Even though family diversity is as old as the nation itself, an emergent "modern" family soon became a mandatory form—a standard against which all other families were and are measured.

We begin with a brief discussion introducing the field of family history. We then examine White families in the premodern period, extending roughly from the early 1600s through 1800. We devote special attention to the unique connections between families and colonial communities. We then turn our attention to the period of transformation, extending roughly from 1800 through 1850. We look at the shift from an agriculturally based economy to an industrial economy and the consequences for family life.

FAMILY AND THE NEW SOCIAL HISTORY

What Is "New" about Family History?

In the past two decades, family history has become an exciting, multidisciplinary field. Research by historians, sociologists, demographers, and anthropologists is profoundly affecting how we view both contemporary and historical developments in U.S. families. Family history is part of "the new social history" that has offered insights about customs and lifestyles of ordinary people during periods of social and economic change. Social history is new in several ways. Instead of highlighting wars, revolutions, and diplomacy, social historians are interested in uncovering many overlooked aspects of everyday living associated with family life (Schvaneveldt et al., 1993:101). Social historians also concentrate on social class and ethnicity. They are interested not only in the elite, who are the most likely to leave behind letters, diaries, and memoirs; the new social historians also concentrate on the hitherto "voiceless": ordinary people, including immigrants, African Americans and other members of minority groups, women, children, and the elderly, which previously had been little studied (Cooper, 1999:26). Family history gained popularity in the 1960s, first in Europe and then in the United States, as scholars began to challenge long-held theories about the family's historical development. Their work has added a new perspective to family studies by providing an intimate perspective of the roles and relationships of spouses, parents, and children within families over time (Schvaneveldt et al., 1993:101). As family history has become more sophisticated and complex over the last decades, it has become clear that no one family form can be understood outside its milieu or context (Coontz, 2000; Cooper, 1999).

Despite these advances, our knowledge about the intimate details of past family life outside the middle class is uneven in the periods we examine in this chapter. The farther back we delve into history, the greater is the difficulty in finding such information, because those outside the middle class "usually did not keep diaries or maintain lengthy correspondence; moreover, even if they did, few were preserved" (Degler, 1980:82).

The Speese family, 1888.

Before we review recent historical findings, a brief discussion of research methods is in order. There is no single historical method, and there is considerable ambiguity as to how historical methodologies are carried out. One useful way of discussing historical methods is to describe historical sources as materials and the various strategies of dealing with sources as the tools of historians (Schvaneveldt et al., 1993:102). **Family reconstitution** is a tool that brings together scattered information about family members in a number of successive generations. Data are collected through a laborious procedure of compiling every available fragment of information about births, marriages, and deaths for all family members (Seward, 1978:42). The aim is to reconstruct the family and household patterns of ordinary people who have passed down little information regarding their way of life. Although data on the upper classes have been more readily available, family reconstitution is one way of retrieving information on people whose everyday lives have been hidden from history (Hutter, 1981:72).

Family reconstitution is generally considered to be very accurate, but it is a time-consuming and expensive procedure that is not suited to all problems in family history. An alternative method is **aggregate data analysis.** This tool involves analyzing records at different points in time in order to develop a picture of trends. Rather than looking at events as they occur in individual families, researchers look at a number of events as they are distributed over time in populations (Gordon, 1983:4). By delving into census records, birth, marriage, and death registers; occupational files, and family letters and diaries, historians have reconstructed the family lives of large numbers of ordinary people in the past. The history of the family has challenged the traditional view of the family in past times and has given us a new picture of family life and social change (see Box 2.1).

Overview of Family History Themes

The most important themes to emerge from historical studies of the family are those of diversity, uneven change, and human agency.

Diversity

Historians have discovered so much diversity that any discussion of "the Western family" must be qualified. Instead of a prevailing type of family at any one time, several types of families were present from the beginning.

> The indigenous peoples who greeted the invaders from across the sea lived under a wide variety of familial arrangements quite alien to the newcomers. The migrants who transplanted themselves to American soil came in many ways and for various reasons as families and as unmarried individuals, in groups of religious refugees, and as single adventurers seeking fortune or at least an initial stake in life. They

The Andrews family at the grave of their son Willie, 1887.

BOX 2.1 Researching Families: The Materials of History

Once an area of interest has been identified, historical researchers are faced with the question of relying on existing sources or uncovering previously unknown materials. Definitive data may not be available or, in fact, may be very difficult to obtain. Also, surviving evidence, often consisting of information found in scattered locations, may not be of great help. Thus, available data may not contain the answers the researcher seeks. This is a particularly salient methodological issue, because the careful selection of data is so crucial to good historiography. Family historians have sought creative ways in which to address this problem, but the matter of missing or misleading data still remains as one of the more difficult barriers to establishing definitive responses to important questions. Nevertheless, even as detectives sometimes proceed with only the scantiest of clues, so must historians carry out their research without all of the pieces of the puzzle. It may be necessary for historians to draw from a wide variety of materials as they seek to clarify a research question.

Documents in Archives, Libraries, and Private Collections

Documents constitute the basic source for both traditional and new historians and are defined as any written or oral accounts of human behavior or social condition. Thus, documents not only consist of written and printed materials: as population censuses, public records, and private papers, but may also include taped interviews.

When family historians conduct research to answer a specific question, and all of the information necessary cannot be obtained from a single document, the use of a number of documents, such as vital statistics, marriage records, tax records, wills, employment ledgers, school rosters, and city registers can yield a composite result. This technique is generally referred to as record linkage, and it is often used with substantial profit, particularly when employing the method known as family reconstitution. Through family reconstitution, profiles of families who lived long ago can be put together to determine structural characteristics and patterns of change.

Letters, being genuine and firsthand, tend to be superior to other material, at least in those respects. Nevertheless, even here there are often problems of content. As people often present themselves differently on paper than they are in real life, the reader is subject to the hidden intent of the writer.

Diaries provide historians with a glimpse into the intimate as well as the public lives of their keepers.

Autobiographies, or memoirs, although very useful to the historian, are problematic for several reasons. When writing for an audience, writers are even less likely than letter writers and diarists to portray themselves candidly. Further, self-knowledge and a good memory are essential for a worthwhile autobiography. Finally, the historian must consider that those who reflect on their own past do so under the influence of the time and situation in which they sat down to relate the details of their lives.

Mission and Church Records

Church records include some of the oldest documents for historical research on families. By and large, historians have diligently searched for data that would indicate the influence of factors such as work and politics on families and societies, yet they

(continued)

(continued from previous page)

have often neglected the impact of religion. Interestingly, religious documents reveal a substantial amount of information about the history of family life in general.

Mass Media Files

Historians traditionally have relied on newspapers as a source of historical data, and often newspapers are the only available source of information on a particular subject. An advantage to using newspapers, and now radio and television materials, is that erroneous assumptions by the public are often corrected by conscientious editors.

Census Data

Census data have long been used by historians to study individual and family trends. Before the nineteenth century, information compiled on public records were often simply lists. It must also be remembered that information contained in such enumerations always reflects the orientation of the person who compiled it. Tax lists could have been drawn up to underestimate or overestimate the number of household members; a military recruiter might have grouped households to facilitate his job; and a household might simply have been described as those who dined together.

Source: Jay D. Schvaneveldt, Robert S. Pickett, and Margaret H. Young, "Historical Methods in Family Research." In P. G. Boss, W. J. Doherty, R. LaRossa, W. R. Schumm, and S. K. Steinmetz (eds.), *Sourcebook of Family Theories and Methods: A Contextual Approach.* New York: Plenum Press, 1993, pp. 102–104.

came under different conditions of wealth and poverty and in different degrees of freedom and bondage, as lords with vast tracts of land; as gentlemen merchants and planters, as yeoman freeholders with just enough land to build and sustain a family, as renters, as indentured servants, selling four or seven years of their labor for fifty or a hundred acres of uncleared land, and as captive chattel slaves. They set up remarkably different societies, ranging from the compact theocratic communities of New England through quasi-feudal Maryland and the scattered farms and plantations of Virginia, to the largely unorganized back country of the Carolinas (Scott and Wishy, 1982:2).

Even White colonial families were diverse, especially in class, gender, and region. Four classes of English men and women made the Atlantic passage: propertyless husbandmen, yeomen farmers, artisans, and common laborers. One in three passengers disembarking in Virginia was a woman, usually in her early twenties; the majority of these women were indentured servants. New England immigrants, in contrast, came more often in family units, two of every three members of which were likely to be women (Ryan, 1983:22).

The principal sources of the population for the original thirteen American colonies were Europe and Africa. European sources were mainly the British Isles and other Western European nations. Of the approximately 2 million White people in the thirteen colonies in 1776, the estimate is that 60 percent were English, 17 to 18 percent were Scotch-Irish, 11 to 12 percent were German, 7 to 8 percent were Dutch, and smaller percentages were French, Scottish, Swedish, Irish, Welsh, Danish, and Finnish (Taft, 1936:71–72).

The other principal group to come to America during the colonial period was from Africa. The earliest recorded Africans to come to America arrived in Virginia in 1619, as indentured servants. As slavery grew in the colonial period, thousands were brought by force from different national and tribal groups in western Africa. The first official U.S. Census in 1790 showed a population of 757,208 Negroes, constituting about 19.3 percent of the total population (Vander Zanden, 1966:25–27). However, slaves' households were not recorded in the Census but were combined with those of their masters.

Not listed on the Census returns for 1790 or any other year were the original settlers, the American "Indians," or Native Americans. They may have numbered half a million and were widely and often thinly spread across the American continent. For more than two centuries, devastating European diseases had reduced their numbers, and the relentless and usually violent encroachment of European settlement had pushed them west or into shrinking enclaves. Living in some 600 societies with a wide variety of residence and marital rules, and speaking almost 200 different languages (Larkin, 1988:4), American Indians created their own forms of diversity.

> Among nomadic foragers, residence rules were flexible and descent was seldom traced far back. Horizontal ties of marriage and friendship were more important in organizing daily life than were vertical ties of descent. More settled groups tended to have more extensive lineage systems, in which lines of descent were traced either through the female or the male line of descent. Most of the Great Plains and prairie Indians were patrilineal; matrilineal descent was common among many East Coast groups; the Creeks, Choctaws, and Seminoles of the South, and the Hopi, Acoma, and Zuni groups of the Southwest (Coontz, 2000:21).

Native American family systems and fertility patterns helped maintain the game and forests that made the land attractive to European settlers. But they also made the Native Americans vulnerable to diseases brought by Europeans and to the Europeans' more aggressive and coordinated methods of warfare and political expansion. Native American family systems were devastated by European colonization. Massive epidemics sometimes killed 60 to 90 percent of a group's members, devastated their kin networks, and disrupted social continuity. Many American Indian groups were either exterminated or driven onto marginal land that did not support their forms of social organization. Yet Native Americans collective traditions were resilient. Euro-Americans spent the entire nineteenth century trying to eradicate them.

Uneven Change

As we place family life within the context of social change, we must also recognize that historical changes never occur uniformly throughout society. Historians have shown that we should not think of family changes as occurring in a linear transition, that is, from one family "type" to another (Coontz, 2001:283). The family type labeled "modern" and linked to the transition from a traditional agrarian society to an industrial society was *not* universal. In fact, "the modern family" is a historically specific form that applies primarily to Whites. Families in different social classes, different races, and immigrant groups all experienced different rates of change, a pattern that can be described as "checkered." This finding belies the existence of any continuous linear pattern encompassing families throughout society moving in the same way to a more "modern" level (Hareven, 1987). In Chapter 3, we examine family diversity by class, race, and gender.

Human Agency

As we link the development of families to time, place, and socioeconomic context, we must remember that people in the past were not passive objects of historical change. They adapted to macro-level social and economic conditions. Historical research has discovered a wealth of information on the varied ways in which family members took charge of their lives and allocated their resources in the struggle to survive and to secure their own and their children's future. In going about their day-to-day lives and adapting to changing social conditions, families and individuals called on whatever resources they had, including their cultural heritage and the economic resources available to them.

Reconstructing the family lives of ordinary people in the past offers us a view of history "from the bottom up." This process represents an effort to reconstruct patterns of people's behavior from their own experience and point of view (Hareven, 1987:37).

FAMILY LIFE IN COLONIAL AMERICA

White families in colonial America had a unique relationship with the larger society. A macro-level analysis is essential for understanding both family form and life within families. Historians have found distinctive patterns in household composition, marriage, and childhood. These patterns also provide a framework for looking at families at the micro level, where the internal workings of colonial families differed profoundly from those in later periods.

Macrostructural Conditions and Family Life

For the original settlers of the American colonies, the family was the most important institution in helping them adapt to New World conditions. The English migrants who ventured to New England sought to avoid the disorder of English family life (see Box 2.2) through a structured and disciplined family. They possessed the idea of a **godly family:** a patriarchal institution ruled by the father, who exercised authority over his wife, children, and servants much as God the Father ruled over his children or a king—the "father" of his country—ruled his subjects. This "Godly Family" (Mintz and Kellogg, 1988:1) was a social, political, and economic unit that performed vital functions for colonial communities.

BOX 2.2   **Families in Global Perspective: English Family Life in the Sixteenth and Seventeenth Centuries**

The disciplined Puritan family of the New World was quite different from the English family of the sixteenth and seventeenth centuries that had been left behind. In fact, it represented an effort to re-create an older ideal of the family that no longer existed in England itself.

English family life in the era of New World colonization was quite unstable. Because of high mortality rates, three-generational households containing grandparents, parents, and children tended to be rare. The duration of marriages tended to be quite brief—half of all marriages were cut short by the death of a spouse after just seventeen to nineteen years. And the number of children per marriage was surprisingly small. Late marriage, a relatively long interval between births, and high rates of infant and child mortality meant that just two, three, or four children survived past adolescence. Despite today's mythical vision of stability and rootedness in the preindustrial world, mobility was rampant. Most Englishmen could expect to move from one village to another during their adult lives, and it was rare for an English family to remain in a single community for as long as fifty years. Indeed, a significant proportion of the English population was denied the opportunity to have a family life. Servants, apprentices, and university lecturers were forbidden from marrying, and most other young men had to wait to marry until they received an inheritance on their father's death.

Source: Steven Mintz and Susan Kellogg, *Domestic Revolutions.* New York: The Free Press, 1988, pp. 7–8.

Although the family was the cornerstone of the new society, colonial communities did not make a sharp distinction between family and society. Family life *was* social life. Boundaries between home and community were almost nonexistent. Families were not private as we know them today, but were domains of work and living connected closely with society. Colonial communities were strong and cohesive, created to deal with questions of land distribution, taxation, and public works. Communities were much like families, and families were much like communities. They ran together at many points, and each was a lively representation of the other. Their structure, their guiding values, their inner purposes were essentially the same (Demos, 1986:28).

Families were not set apart from society, because most social activities or functions took place in family settings. The most important of these activities making up the business of daily living were economic. The household was the basic economic unit of the agrarian-based society. Almost all production was done within the household. The goods created were owned and distributed by family members as part of a broader, interconnected community (Coleman, 1998:79). Historians Louise Tilly and Joan Scott have called this mode of production the **family-based economy.** Each family provided the market with a commodity. Women, men, and children all worked at productive tasks that were defined by age and sex (Tilly and Scott, 1978:44). The family was a unit of production and exchange, of cultivating, processing, and manufacturing all the commodities that ensured survival. Women, men, and children labored in the agrarian family economy that supported the colonial population. The colonial family was not only an economic unit, it also performed many more functions than does its present-day counterpart. It raised the food and made most of the clothing and furniture for the early settlers. It taught children to read, worship their God, and care for each other in sickness and old age (Mintz and Kellogg, 1988:1). John Demos has described the range of activities and functions that have since been taken over by specialized institutions:

> The Old Colony family was, first of all, a business, an absolutely central agency of economic production and exchange. Each household was more or less self-sufficient; and its various members were inextricably united in the work of providing for their fundamental material wants. Work, indeed, was a wholly natural extension of family life and merged imperceptibly with all of its other activities.
>
> The family was also a "school." Parents and masters were charged by law to attend to the education of all the children in their immediate care "at least to be able duly to read the Scriptures." Most people had little chance for any sort of education, though "common schools" were just beginning to appear by the end of the Old Colony period.
>
> The family was a "vocational institute." However deficient it may have been in transmitting the formal knowledge and skills associated with literacy, it clearly served to prepare its young for effective, independent performance in the larger economic system. For the great majority of persons—the majority who became farmers—the process was instinctive and almost unconscious. But it applied with equal force (and greater visibility) to the various trades and crafts of the time. The ordinary setting for an apprenticeship was, of course, a domestic one.
>
> The family was a "church." To say this is not to slight the central importance of churches in the usual sense. Here, indeed, the family's role was partial and subsidiary. Nonetheless, the obligation of "family worship" seems to have been widely assumed. Daily prayers and personal meditation formed an indispensable adjunct to the more formal devotions of a whole community.
>
> The family was a "house of correction." Idle and even criminal persons were "sentenced" by the Court to live in the families of more reputable citizens. The household seemed a natural setting for both imposing discipline and for encouraging some degree of character reformation.
>
> The family was a "welfare institution"; in fact, it provided several different kinds of welfare service. It was occasionally a "hospital"—at least insofar as certain men thought to have special medical knowledge would receive sick persons into their homes for day-to-day care and treatment. It was an "orphanage" in that children whose parents had died were straightaway transferred to another household (often that of a relative). It was an "old people's home" since the aged and infirm, no longer able to care for themselves, were usually incorporated into the households of their grown children. And it was a "poorhouse" too for analogous, and obvious, reasons (Demos, 1970:183–184).

The premodern family, with its permeable boundaries, did not contain or define an individual's social life. Rather, people lived "in the streets" in the community (Cott, 1979:109). Community members often intervened in family matters. A dramatic example of community intervention was the disciplinary technique called the *charivari*, prevalent in Europe and the United States until the early nineteenth century. The *charivari* was a noisy public demonstration intended to subject wayward individuals to ridicule and punishment.

> Sometimes the demonstrations would consist of masked individuals circling somebody's house at night, screaming, beating on pans and blowing cow horns (which the local butchers rented out). On other occasions the offender would be seized and marched through the streets, perhaps seated backwards on a donkey or forced to wear a placard describing his sins. Sometimes the youth would administer the charivari; on other occasions villagers of all ages and sexes would mix together (Shorter, 1975:219).

People in colonial America were not free to do entirely as they pleased, even in their own families. The larger community—the state—was involved in matters of family living. Thus, for example, disobedient children were not only punished with a thrashing at their father's hands; they were also liable to action by the courts. Colonial magistrates might even remove a child from the care of "unseemly" parents and place him or her in some other family. Or again, a local court could order the reunion of a husband and wife who had decided to live apart (Demos, 1977:60).

What went on in families was not "their own business" but was, in fact, a community affair. Even "private" matters took place in the presence of lodgers and neighbors (see Box 2.3). This interpenetration of family and society persisted throughout the eighteenth century.

Family Structure and Household Composition

Common wisdom once held that nuclear families emerged as a response to industrial society. Even sociological theory assumed that families of the past were extended. This theory of "progressive nucleation" (Lasch, 1975) assumed that industrialization and modernization substituted the nuclear family for the extended family of early America. However, this assumption about the relationship between the family and the industrial revolution has been revised. New research shows that the nuclear family was one of several different family systems present in preindustrial Europe (Kertzer, 1991:158).

The study that did most to challenge the myth of the preindustrial extended family was Peter Laslett's *The World We Have Lost* (1971). Laslett showed that a golden age of stable extended families is nothing more than wishful thinking. He used the family reconstitution technique to study family structure and household size in seventeenth-century England. By collecting data from parish registers in scattered villages at scattered intervals in time, he demonstrated the predominance of nuclear families. Couples headed households of small nuclear families. Although many households contained servants, the average household did not contain extended kin and was, in fact, relatively small. As this discovery was applied to the American colonies, scholars found growing evidence that colonial families were typically nuclear in structure. The work of two family historians, John Demos and Phillip Greven, makes this point.

John Demos applied the family reconstitution technique to his study of Plymouth Colony, the seventeenth-century Pilgrim settlement. Entitled *A Little*

Inside the Worlds of Diverse Families: Eighteenth-Century Family and Social Life Revealed in Massachusetts Divorce Records

Nancy F. Cott draws on rich materials contained in divorce records to explore attitudes and practices involved in family relationships. Her findings show that neighbors and lodgers often intervened into couples' affairs.

When men and women of eighteenth-century Massachusetts complained to the court of marital travesties such as desertion, adultery, or neglect, they inadvertently brought these issues to light. Families there experienced none of the isolation or withdrawal from community overseership which presumably characterize the modern family. On the contrary, the divorce records reveal the interconnectedness of family and community, particularly in the form of community members' guardianship over family affairs. Divorce petitioners successfully relied on the proximity and curiosity of neighbors, lodgers, and kin, and on their motives to preserve community norms, in order to obtain material to substantiate their cases. Mary Angel, for example, out walking in Boston with Abigail Galloway one day, saw through an open window her neighbor Adam Air "in the Act of Copulation" with a women named Pamela Brichford. . . .

Whether avid observers were attempting to uphold community standards by surveillance, when it came to adultery—or simply satisfying their own curiosity—may be a fine distinction. When Mary Cole witnessed Hannah Wales invite a strange man to lie down with her in Boston in 1785, Mary left the room, but later admitted that "Curiosity led her to look thro' a hole in the door, when I plainly saw said man Lying upon Mrs. Wales, his breeches were down . . ." and the couple was caught in the act. Mary Knight, living with her husband Russel in Williams Parham's household in Lancaster, was constantly subject to the Parhams' and their neighbors' observation because they doubted her fidelity. One night William and a neighbor, hearing noises in Mary's chamber, rushed up through a cellar trap door to confront her in bed with a strange man. Mary later accused William of sending the man to assault her and "frame" her in the act of adultery. When the justice of the peace asked William whether he had burst into Mary's room "to find out the man and secure him or not"—for he allowed the man to escape—William replied, "I went into the Room to Satisfy myself whether the sd Russel's wife was such a lewd Person as I suspected—and not to apprehend the Man."

Not only did neighbors know each others' business with predictable small town alacrity. The very circumstances of household life facilitated the intervention of neighbors, and even more readily, of lodgers, into a couple's affairs. The construction and population of houses were respectively so thin and so thick that privacy was hard to come by. Mary Angel, who caught Adam Air in the act, also testified that she "live[d] the next door, where only a thin Partition divided us have often heard him beat . . . [his wife] & heard her scream in Consequence of the beating." In Katherine and Elijah Cobb's house in Taunton in 1766, only a single wall separated Ruth Cushman's chamber from the Cobbs' and she "had frequent opportunity of hearing their conversation." The presence and transience of servants, hired laborers, nurses, relatives, and other lodgers in households assured numerous omnipresent eyes and ears.

Source: Nancy F. Cott, "Eighteenth-Century Family and Social Life Revealed in Massachusetts Divorce Records." In Nancy F. Cott and Elizabeth H. Pleck (eds.), *A Heritage of Her Own*. New York: Simon & Schuster, 1979, pp. 109–111.

Commonwealth, the study analyzed wills, inventories, and official colonial records, as well as physical artifacts remaining from seventeenth-century houses—furniture, tools, utensils, and clothing—to reconstruct family patterns. Demos concluded that the colonial family was nuclear rather than extended. A married couple and their children formed the core and most often made up the entire family. While nonkin household members—servants, boarders, and apprentices—were often present, colonial households could be described in terms of simple categories of husband, wife, children, and servants (Demos, 1970:63–67).

Phillip Greven's research on colonial Andover, Massachusetts, during the seventeenth and eighteenth centuries offers further evidence that extended families were the exception rather than the rule. He examined four successive generations in Andover, using the family reconstitution method. Greven found that the basic household was nuclear but that families consisted of kinship networks of separate households. He describes these families as "modified extended," somewhere between a nuclear and extended family. First-generation sons who were to inherit land remained in the parental residence, even after marriage. However, households were nuclear in all other respects (Greven, 1970).

Recent studies have also addressed such matters as the number of children per family and the average size of the family. Historians disagree about the number of children, but they generally agree that family size was smaller than the stereotype assumed. According to Demos, colonial families were larger than families in contemporary society: "What I concluded for Plymouth can be summarized as follows: the average household size throughout the period in question was just under six persons. Typically, this meant a man and his wife and children, and in some cases, a servant or two" (Demos, 1972:56). Where servants were present, households were larger. Looking at summaries of the federal Census for eleven states taken in 1790, Greven found that the presence of slaves could greatly increase the size of a household. Slaves were sometimes listed as members of White families. Since the extent of slavery varied from state to state during the late 1790s, the average family size also varied. Variations ranged from five persons to seven persons per family in 1790. Greven has concluded that the average family in eighteenth-century America was very large in comparison with families in modern America. Still, household size varied.

Thus, both Demos and Greven have concluded that families in eighteenth-century America were smaller than our stereotypes assume, but larger than today's families. As we use family history to correct the myths about extended families of the past, we must be careful not to substitute a new orthodoxy of the nuclear family. While some historians emphasized the long-standing predominance of the nuclear family, others now demonstrate a kernel of truth in earlier generalizations about the decline of extended families (Coontz, 2001; Cooper, 1999). No doubt, some families were extended in form. But because life spans were shorter in the past, comparatively few families had enough members to reside even potentially as a multigenerational household. Even a small number of extended-family households represented a high proportion of all such potential arrangements (Coontz, 2001:81).

The Tilton family, 1837. The early American household was typically a small nuclear family.

The research on the size and composition of colonial families is important, but it tells us little about the quality and texture of family life in past times. Some scholars are critical of research that is limited to the quantifiable part of history. Christopher Lasch, for example, has argued that the study of family structure is not important unless it tells us what these family forms *mean* (Lasch, 1975). However, it is always hard to capture the intent and feeling of historical actors (Cooper, 1999:23). Although studies of family size and composition have some limitations, they also offer valuable insights about the internal dynamics of family life. For example, Laslett's study of preindustrial Europe found populations that were overwhelmingly young. This conspicuous feature of traditional society created a distinctive quality of life:

> We must imagine our ancestors, therefore, in the perpetual presence of their young offspring. A good 70 percent of all households contained children. This figure is remarkably consistent from place to place and date to date and there were between two and a half and three children to every household with them. . . . In the preindustrial world there were children everywhere: playing in the village streets and fields when they were very small; hanging round the farmyards and getting in the way until they had grown enough to be given child-sized jobs to do; thronging churches; forever clinging to the skirts of women in the house and wherever they went; and above all crowding round the cottage fires. The perpetual distraction of childish noise and talk must have affected everyone almost all of the time (Laslett, 1971:109).

Historians now supplement demographic household data. Demos's work is a good example of this. After gathering certain facts about colonial society, such as evidence of large families and small houses and court records reporting contention among neighbors, he contends that family members turned their "natural hostilities" toward neighbors, thereby avoiding domestic conflict (Demos, 1972:569).

Some scholars are now probing the complexities of premodern households though historical records. As Robert Wells explains:

> A simple structural analysis of a seventeenth-century Chesapeake household might provide evidence of a husband and wife and four children living in a household. But with a dynamic perspective, we might learn that this was the second or third marriage for both husband and wife. In addition, the four children, instead of all being born into that particular marriage, might include a child of the father's, a child of the mother's, each from a previous marriage, one child who was the product of this union, and a fourth child who might be an indentured servant of the child of one of the brothers or sisters of the husband or wife who had been taken in either to learn an occupation or because of dislocation in that child's own immediate family (Wells, 1991:48).

Other historians argue that to capture the meanings of families in past times, we must investigate the myths, rituals, and symbols of family life in different times and places. John Gillis (1996) finds that across the ages, symbolic dimensions of family life have produced a sharp contrast between the families people *want* and the families they *have*.

Wives and Husbands

The early colonists organized their families around the unquestionable principle of patriarchy. Patriarchal authority rested ultimately on the father's control of landed property or craft skills. Children were dependent on their father's support in order to marry and set up independent households (Mintz and Kellogg, 1988:9). Marriages were arranged according to the social and economic purposes of larger kin groups. Marriages across social boundaries were not permissible, given the firm colonial hierarchies of rank and order. Among the wellborn, a suitable marriage was one made or arranged as an economic and social alliance, ensuring that the son or daughter remained in the station to which he or she had been bred. Or it was an arrangement that would secure, and perhaps enhance, the status and fortune of the family as a whole. But property was no less important to the making of marriages of more ordinary people. Among the less well off, who and when one married depended on economic circumstances such as the well-being of the family, the number of sons and daughters who had to be settled, or whether their labor was still needed in the family. The size of the dowry or settlement, as well as the timing of the marriage, could vary greatly among siblings. In places where, either by law or by tradition, primogeniture (the transfer of the family estate to the eldest surviving male) held sway, the eldest son stood to receive the greatest portion (Scott and Wishy, 1982:5).

For both women and men, marriage was a central event in life. According to the prevailing doctrine, a wife was to be her husband's helpmate, not his equal

(Mintz and Kellogg, 1988:11). Although marriages were based on social and economic rather than on romantic considerations, romantic love was not wholly absent from colonial society. It was present but was not directly or consistently linked to courtship and mate selection (Adams, 1980:68). Marriage was, for the most part, a relationship in which the husband agreed to provide food, clothing, and shelter for his wife, and she agreed to return frugal management and obedient service. To "act like a man" meant to support one's wife (Cott, 1979:120).

Actual relations between spouses were more complicated than the ideals suggest. According to Mintz and Kellogg, both marital love and marital violence were present in the colonies:

> It was not unusual to find mutual love and tenderness in Puritan marriages. In their letters, Puritan husbands and wives frequently referred to each other in terms suggesting profound love for each other, such as "my good wife . . . my sweet wife" or "my most sweet Husband." Puritan court records further reveal that wife abuse is not a recent development. Between 1630 and 1699, at least 128 men were tried for abusing their wives (Mintz and Kellogg, 1988:11).

Throughout the colonial period, there was a shortage of women, especially in the frontier areas. Since women usually married older men, they tended to outlive their husbands. Widowhood was typically short, as women remarried very quickly. A study of marriage in seventeenth-century Maryland revealed that complex family arrangements and family conflict resulted from such marriages:

> Men found themselves responsible for stepchildren as well as their own offspring, and children acquired half-sisters and half-brothers. Sometimes a woman married a husband who himself had previously been married, and both brought children of former spouses to the new marriage. They then produced children of their own. The possibilities for conflict over the upbringing of children are evident, and crowded living conditions, found even in the households of the very wealthy, must have added to family tensions (Carr and Walsh, 1979:39).

The gender ratio in some ways enhanced the status and position of women in the colonies by allowing them to perform crucial economic duties. Work for women, whether married or single, was not only approved of, it was considered a civic duty. Wives were expected to help their husbands and received approval for doing extra work in or out of the home:

> The vast majority of women worked within their homes, where their labor produced most articles needed for the family. The entire colonial production of cloth and clothing and in part that of shoes was in the hands of women. In addition to these occupations, women were found in many different kinds of employment. They were butchers, silversmiths, gunsmiths, upholsterers. They ran mills, plantations, tan yards, shipyards, and every kind of shop, tavern, and boarding house. They were gate keepers, jail keepers, sextons, journalists, printers, "doctoresses," apothecaries, midwives, nurses, and teachers. Women acquired their skills the same way as did the men, through apprenticeship training, frequently within their own families (Lerner, 1979:183).

Although some women worked at occupations outside the home, they were excluded from roles that yielded the most power and privilege (Huber, 1993).

The great majority, regardless of age or status, worked in the family setting. Each family provided the market with a commodity that other families needed. The members of the household specialized in different parts of the work of the family. Women's work was an integral part of the colonial economy, even though a sharp division of labor existed between husbands and wives. Men worked outdoors and in the fields, while women worked on the home plot, performing tasks associated with housework and child care. Nevertheless, their tasks were diverse and endless:

> Over the long term of a lifetime [their tasks] were probably more arduous and demanding than those performed by men. One traveler in 18th century Carolina reported that "the ordinary women take care of Cows, Hogs, and other small Cattle, make Butter and Cheese, spin cotton, and flax, help to sow and reap corn, wind silk from the worms, gather Fruit and look after the House." Looking after the house was itself a heavy task since that included not only cleaning the physical interior but the washing and mending of the family's clothes, preparing meals under the handicaps of an open fireplace and no running water, preserving various kinds of foods, making all the soap, candles, and most of the medicines used by the family, as well as all the clothes for the family. And then, as the quotation suggests, the women had to be ready at planting or harvest time to help in the fields. On top of this, of course, was the bearing and rearing of children. During the colonial years when families of at least six children were common, this task was close to a full job in itself. It was this almost unending congeries of jobs that probably gave birth to the well-known tag that a woman's work is never done. Unlike the work of the husband-farmer, a woman's work went on after dark and at undiminished pace throughout the year (Degler, 1980:363–364).

Without the labor of women, the economy of the seventeenth century would have been crippled. Although the work was vital, it was done under the heavy dominance of men.

> Woman's vow to obey her spouse was repeatedly underscored by colonial writers and preachers. She owed her mate "reverent subjection" and was obliged to submit to his superior judgement in all things. New England clergymen referred to male authority as a "government" that the female must accept as "law," while Southern husbands, such as William Byrd of Virginia, charged assertive wives with "impertinence." Not only were women obliged to scrupulously abide by the lawful commands of patriarchs, but they were "still subject even to those who are sinful and unkind" (Ryan, 1983:35).

Children

One belief about traditional colonial family life that survives the test of evidence is that families reared large numbers of children in comparison with the norms of our own day (Demos, 1981:6). Women gave birth to an average of eight children, and the number of children living in a household was three times greater than the number in 1950 (Grabill et al., 1973:379). Families of the premodern period reared large numbers of children, yet household size was not very large because of the high child mortality rate.

Children in colonial society were dominated by the "three Rs" of repression, religion, and respect (Adams, 1980:72). The prevailing ideology was that children entered the world with original sin and stubbornness. Even newborn infants were embodiments of sin. Cotton Mather, a famous Puritan preacher of the seventeenth century, gave the advice, "better whipped than damned." This exerted a powerful influence on methods of child rearing (Mintz and Kellogg, 1988:15). Together, parents, schools, and churches kept children in subjugation:

> In some households [children] were made to stand through meals, eating whatever was handed to them. They were taught it was sinful to complain about food, clothing, or their lot in life. Courtesy of a formal sort was insisted upon. Corporal punishment seems to have been liberally employed. Use was made of birchrods, canes, "flappers" [a leather strap with a hole in the middle], and at school dunce stools and caps and placards bearing humiliating names (Queen and Habenstein, 1974:306).

From an early age, religious training was grim and constant. Children were required to learn the Bible by reading it chapter by chapter. This pattern of discipline was consistent with the prevailing view of children as miniature adults. In colonial society, childhood was not a recognizable stage. Children were not considered as a social category separate from adults, requiring special care and treatment. Demos has described the world of the colonial child in the following manner:

> His work, much of his recreation, and his closest personal contacts were encompassed within the world of adults. From the age of six or seven he was set to a regular round of tasks about the house or farm (or, in the case of a craftsman's family,

Flax Scutching Bee, 1885. Rural families included resident servants and kin.

the shop or store). When the family went to church, or when they went visiting, he went along. In short, from his earliest years he was expected to be or try to be a miniature adult (Demos, 1977:64).

Many historians contend that children in the colonies were miniature adults. A classic work by Phillippe Aries, *Centuries of Childhood* (1965), popularized the idea that childhood is a recent social creation and that for most of human history, parents did not perceive young children as different from adults. Although some historians now dispute this view (Juster and Vinovskis, 1987:201), there is no doubt that children in the colonies were not sentimentalized. It was common to send young children or adolescents to live in other people's homes in order to work or learn a trade. This practice of "putting out" children at ten and eleven years of age indicates an attitude far different from the attachment to children that was to develop in later periods. For some children, early development depended a great deal on caretakers other than parents: on siblings, neighbors, or masters. Child abuse was a common feature of poor children's lives in this period (Polakow, 1993:15).

Social class and regional differences made childhood in the colonies highly variable. In the eighteenth century, outside of New England, child rearing was more genteel. Daniel Blake Smith found an affectionate and respectful mode of child rearing in the Chesapeake plantations of Virginia and Maryland:

> The wide open and uncrowded plantation environment, with land abundant and vices scarce, allowed planters to raise their children under more optimistic and permissive assumptions about childhood and parental conduct. Obedience and respect for parental authority remained important for the development of strong character and stable family life, but parents placed considerably more emphasis on developing a child's, and especially a son's, freedom of movement and sense of personal autonomy.
>
> Chesapeake households were often complex units with servants and kin living on the plantation, making constant parental supervision of children unnecessary. Indeed, one senses from the letters and diaries of the period that children were allowed, and perhaps encouraged, to explore their immediate environment with little parental supervision (Smith, 1983a:220).

THE EMERGENCE OF MODERN FAMILY LIFE

Modern family life, with qualities distinctly different from those in colonial society, emerged at the end of the eighteenth century and the beginning of the nineteenth, in the years between the American Revolution and about 1850. These years are not to be taken precisely. Historians use decades, whole centuries, and the expansive categories "premodern" and "modern" in reference to an imaginary boundary line set at roughly the year 1800. We should think in terms of a transitional process in which the end of one stage and the start of the next are fully merged (Demos, 1986:xi, 26). Even then, the shift was slow, varying in a number of aspects, including class, race, gender, and region (Kain, 1990: 34). Table 2.1 summarizes the distinctive characteristics of family life during this period.

TABLE 2.1

Colonial Families and Emerging Modern Families

Dimension	Pre-Revolutionary War Family	Post-Revolutionary War to 1850 Family
ECONOMY, FAMILY, AND SOCIETY		
Economy	Family-based economy	Family-wage economy
Community linkages	Family and community interpenetrated	Development of boundaries around family
Social control	Community involvement in family matters	Family no longer subject to control by outsiders
HOUSEHOLD COMPOSITION		
Structure	Nuclear	Nuclear
Members	Husband, wife, children, servants	Exodus of nonfamily members from household
WIVES AND HUSBANDS		
Marriage	Based on economic considerations	Based on romantic considerations
Division of labor	Women's and men's work converged in the household economy	Separation of men's commercial labor and women's domestic labor
Role of women	Wide-ranging with community obligations	Domestic caretakers
Status of women	Subordinate to patriarchal head of household	Subordinate to patriarchal head of household
CHILDREN		
Dominant ideology	Children require harsh discipline	Children require affection

Unlike the colonial period, the time of transition was not a unique period of American history. Rather, it was part of the transformation from an agricultural to an industrial economy. The rise of the modern family accompanied the shift from production in the home to a market economy. As productive work and family life developed into separate domains, a new family form emerged. Households became smaller and more private. Marriage was based on love and companionship. Families turned inward and became idealized as the domain of women and children.

Macrostructural Changes and Family Life

The War for Independence produced a new nation with a distinctly "modern" family form. Critical family transformations were aspects of macrolevel social, economic, and demographic transformations that were reshaping all aspects of life in the new society (Mintz and Kellogg, 1988:xviii).

Social, economic, demographic, and cultural factors all gave rise to new family patterns. As the country moved from an agricultural to an industrial economy, the nature and location of productive work changed. Households could no longer sustain themselves by making, growing, or bartering goods. Now families acquired what they needed in the commercial economy. Work was done at central locations such as factories and shops. This trend led to the new concept of "going to work" (Jones, 1982:2) and created the **family-wage economy** (Tilly and Scott, 1978:104). In the family-wage economy, goods and services were produced outside the household. Workers earned their living outside the home, and families were supported by their wages.

As goods and labor moved out of the household and into the commercial economy, the family lost many of the functions it had embraced in colonial society. No longer was the family a workshop, church, reformatory, school, and asylum. Now external institutions took over these functions. Families became increasingly private, set apart from society by distinct boundaries. The family took on the particular functions of procreation, consumption, and child rearing (Hareven, 1976a:198). This made the family a "personal" realm; a fortress of protection against the outside world. Aries has described this "emotional revolution:"

> Previously, feelings were diffuse, spread over numerous natural and supernatural objects, including God, saints, parents, children, friends, horses, dogs, orchards, and gardens. Henceforth, they would be focused entirely within the immediate family. The couple and their children became the objects of a passionate and exclusive love that transcended even death. From that time on, a working man's life was polarized between job and family. But those people who did not go out to work (women, children, old men) were concerned exclusively with family life. Nor was the division between job and family either equal or symmetrical. Although there was, no doubt, some room for emotional involvement at work, the family was a more conducive setting; whereas the working world was subject to constant, strict surveillance, the family was a place of refuge, free from outside control (Aries, 1965:229).

In the colonies, when families had been economically productive, work and family were intertwined. But with the separation of family and work activities, the family turned inward and "assumed domesticity, intimacy, and privacy as major characteristics" (Hareven, 1976a:198).

The separation of work and family created a division of public and private spheres of living. The family became the private sphere. As families shifted from being a public to a private domain, people's family activities were observable to fewer and fewer people. As the "audience" of family behavior changed, individuals were less subject to social control by nonfamily members. This fostered individual rights.

Demographic changes were another powerful force for the transformation of family life. (The following is dependent on Mintz and Kellogg, 1988:xix.) Such fundamental characteristics of a population as age distribution and the proportion of the sexes exert strong influences on the size and composition of families, the marriage rate, the death rate, the birth rate, and other features of family life. Two key demographic changes were critical. The first was a gradual reduction of fertility within marriage. Beginning in the last quarter of the eighteenth century, American women began bearing fewer children, spacing children closer together, and ceasing childbearing at earlier ages. Smaller families meant that parents could invest more emotion and financial resources in each child. A second fundamental demographic change was a gradual aging of the population. This meant that a growing proportion of the population began to experience aspects of family life less well known in the past.

Agency, Adaptation, and Change

The emergence of modern family life was tied to broad processes of social and economic change. But we should be careful not to fall back on a totally structural analysis of the shifting family form. Two themes are important in this regard: (1) people were not passive victims of change—they engaged in various active negotiations that gave them control over their lives; and (2) not only did the modern family emerge from macrostructural conditions, family development also shaped the emerging social order. Two historical examples make these points.

Responses to the Dilemma of Declining Land

By the end of the seventeenth century, fathers were losing control of landed property and productive skills. New forms of industrial capital were replacing land as a major source of wealth. This gave many children new opportunities to live away from their parents and permitted greater freedom from parental authority. At the same time, rapid population growth, combined with the practice of dividing family lands among all sons, resulted in plots too small to be farmed viably. This weakened paternal control over heirs. In many older settlements, high birth rates gradually outstripped the amount of cultivable land. Some communities grew by 5 or 6 percent annually, and the number of surviving sons proved to be greater than the resources necessary to establish viable farms. Colonists adapted their family arrangements in devising strategies to meet this dilemma:

> In some instances family homesteads were simply subdivided among all sons. In others fathers encouraged sons to migrate to newer communities where fresh land was available or else converted inheritances into some form other than real estate, such as formal education, an apprenticeship, or a gift of money. In still other cases such as Andover and Dedham, partible inheritance tended to give way to primogeniture; the bequest of land to the eldest son. And in other instances whole families moved to areas with abundant land. . . . In Chebacco, a little village on the Massachusetts north shore, families combined a variety of strategies. First and second sons typically remained in the community, while younger sons migrated to newer areas. To balance the conflicting desires to preserve the family's estate, to allow most children to remain in the village and to provide a legacy for each child, families adopted a complex system of inheritance (Mintz and Kellogg, 1988:18).

How Families Shaped Society

Just as social changes transformed the family, the family also played an important role in adapting different classes to the new social order. Storekeepers, merchants, financiers, and entrepreneurs constituted a wealthier class with material abundance and comfort. But there were also more propertyless workers in the city and countryside. These new inequalities had profound effects on family life. Bernard Farber (1973) studied merchant, artisan, and laboring families of the 1800s. He found that commercialization affected the social classes in different ways. For example, in the merchant class, family alliances fostered entrepreneurship. Relatives were given positions of trust, capital was pooled in family partnerships, and family alliances were created through marriage. These practices fostered a sense of cooperation, and they produced other results as well. First, business decisions sometimes caused merchants to question the motives of relatives (who were also their partners). Second, family coalitions contributed to political factions as well. These factions often became separate worlds, each with

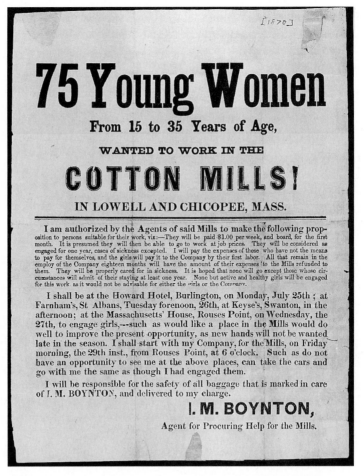

Broadside advertising for women operatives, 1859. With the coming of industrialization, poorer women transferred their traditional home occupations to the factory.

its own set of business arrangements and intermarriages among first cousins and among sets of siblings (Farber, 1973:103).

The artisan class played a different role from that of the merchant class in the development of business enterprise. The artisans' industry was still largely home-based. It provided a place for socializing children well suited to the pursuit of business. Families took on relatives as apprentices. Specialized occupations were then transmitted from one generation to another among relatives who remained in the same general locale and were expected to help one another in time of need. In this way, strong, stable, extended family relationships persisted in the artisan class long after the merchant families had fragmented themselves into many smaller units (Farber, 1973:105–106).

The laboring class, made up of "strangers" to the community, contributed to the day labor of the economy. Laborers' flexible family arrangements provided the economy with a pool of geographically mobile laborers, who were then exploited by the merchant and artisan classes.

Household Size and Composition

Premodern households had included a variety of nonkin: apprentices, servants, orphans or children from broken homes, and dependent members of the community placed there by town authorities. From the late eighteenth century on, apprentices slowly disappeared from American homes, as did servants, except in upper- and middle-class families (Hareven, 1976a:194). The transition to a market economy produced a new class of urban wage workers. As artisans, craftsmen, boarders, lodgers, and others left family settings and moved out into the commercial economy, households became smaller.

Wives and Husbands

The rise of the modern family was accompanied by profound changes in women's and men's roles. Marriage became a companionate relationship rather than an economic union. Mutual affection between spouses replaced duty and obligation.

Romantic love brought couples together, and marriage was transformed into an emotional bond between two individuals. When people in the nineteenth century spoke of the purpose of marriage, they were most likely to refer to "love" or affection as the basis of the attraction between marital partners and the beginning of family formation (Degler, 1980:19). A content analysis of magazines published in the latter part of the eighteenth century revealed that romantic love was thought to be the basis of an ideal marriage (Lantz et al., 1968).

With the transfer of production outside of the family, women's and men's roles became increasingly differentiated. Their activities were split into the male world of work and the female world of the family. Married women lost many traditional "productive" economic roles. Middle-class women, especially, concentrated on keeping house and raising children. According to the new conception of women's roles, their task was to shape the character of children, making the home a haven of peace and order, and exert a moral and uplifting influence on men (Mintz and Kellogg, 1988:xix). Women's household labor took on new social and economic meaning:

> While the good wives of the past produced prosaic and essential goods—homespun clothing, simple foodstuffs, crude soaps, candles and dyes—eighteenth-century women and especially those who resided in commercial centers labored over more refined, if not ornamental creations—chintz curtains, decorated rugs, embroidered coverlets. The diaries and correspondence of urban middle-class women also indicated that they were less involved in both their husbands' business activities and the neighborhood barter system than were their foremothers (Ryan, 1983:80).

Women's definition as homemakers and caretakers rather than as workers was strongest in the middle class. Here, the home acquired a sentimental quality; it was viewed as a retreat where meaning and satisfaction were to be found.

> Women's activities were increasingly confined to the care of children, the nurturing of husband, and the physical maintenance of the home. Moreover, it was not unusual to refer to women as the "angels of the house," for they were said to be the moral guardians of the family. They were responsible for the ethical and spiritual character as well as the comfort and tranquility of the home. In that role they were acknowledged to be the moral superiors of men. Husbands, on the other hand, the ideology proclaimed, were active outside the home, at their work, in politics, and in the world in general. In fact, it was just this involvement of men in the world that made them in need of women's moral guidance and supervision (Degler, 1980:26).

The image of the family as a retreat was also more characteristic of middle-class families than of working-class families. We must keep in mind that changes were gradual and that they varied from class to class. When female occupations such as carding, spinning, and weaving were transferred from home to factory, the poorer women followed their traditional work and became industrial workers. Many families retained their rural economic base while daughters went to work in factories. These women had to meet the demands of the new work system outside their homes and to balance these obligations with traditional domestic and family tasks. Consequently, they retained some continuity between their earlier traditions and their new work experience (Lerner, 1979; Hareven, 1976b).

On the other hand, the middle-class family experience was characterized by a sharp distinction between home and workplace, a role segregation between husband and wife, and limiting of women's activities in the home, along with a glorification of their domestic roles as housekeepers and mothers. The women of the middle and upper classes used their newly gained time for leisure pursuits. They became "ladies" (Hareven, 1976b).

Children

As families became increasingly private and as gender domains became more separate, a new conception of childhood began to emerge. Children were now seen as different from adults. Among other things, they were now considered more innocent. Childhood was perceived much as it is today, as a period of life worth recognizing, cherishing, and even extending (Degler, 1980:66). Now, for the first time in this society, the child stood out as a creature distinctly different from adults: someone with special needs, talents, and character. Around 1800, children started to appear in clothing that was distinctly their own. They were also spending more and more time at play among groups of their peers (Demos, 1977:72).

By the middle of the nineteenth century, a middle-class upbringing differed dramatically from the premodern pattern. Instead of shifting back and forth between their parents' homes and work experiences as members of other households, a growing proportion of children were continuing to live with their parents into their late teens and twenties. Childhood and adolescence began to be viewed as a distinct stage of growth and development in which young people were prepared for eventual emergence into adulthood (Mintz and Kellogg, 1988:58–59). Children were born into families that were White or Black, poor or rich, farmers or wage earners. Their experiences were determined largely by the class and status of the family into which they were born. Few written historical sources have been found on the attitudes of working-class parents toward children in the period of transition. Nevertheless, the limited amount of child labor in the economy at this time suggests that working-class parents saw childhood as a special and different status (Degler, 1980:69).

The most telling evidence of this new view of children, indeed this new social category, was the publication of books about child-rearing methods.

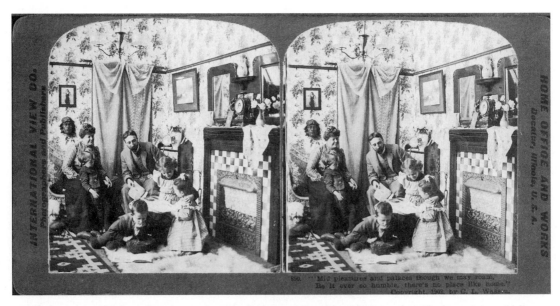

"'Mid pleasures and palaces though we may roam, Be it ever so humble, there's no place like home." As middle-class family life adapted to industrialized society, women and the home acquired a sentimental quality.

For if children were innocent and natural it followed that parents should learn how to care for them, love them, and instruct them properly. And so in the years after 1820 large numbers of advice books on child-rearing came off the presses in Britain and the United States. As one authority on the history of child-rearing remarked, parents thought they "were remiss if they did not obtain and study the expanding body of literature on child rearing." He quoted one mother early in the 19th century as writing "There is scarcely any subject concerning which I feel more anxiety than the proper education of my children. It is a difficult and delicate subject, the more I feel how much is to be learnt by myself." Significantly, he concluded, this interest in child-rearing literature "was a new phenomenon" in the 19th century (Degler, 1980:68).

Other tangible measures of the new status of children were books designed for children themselves and a marked decline in the corporal punishment of children (Degler, 1980:68–72). Not only do historians find a new outlook toward children in this period; some argue that the modern family took hold with the discovery of the child, a social category separate from adults (Aries, 1965). Not all scholars agree on this point. Still, childhood was transformed by the reorganization of work and domestic life.

The new view of childhood went hand in hand with the separation of families from the larger society. In colonial times, children were reared in communities by various community members, including their parents. As families became privatized, however, parents were left to bring up children on their own. Heightened concern with child rearing and with the child's home environment in this historical period gave way to family life that was increasingly child-centered. In fact, the new conception of childhood gave the private family a new reason for being, a justification that remains to the present.

Challenging a Uniform Definition of the Family

Even as the modern family form emerged, it was a race-specific and a class-specific arrangement. Not all groups were not entitled to family life. During the seventeenth century, slaves had few opportunities to establish a stable and independent family life. As their population grew and African slaves were forcibly sold to serve as a labor pool, slave society developed with its distinctive African American kin forms. Among Native Americans, from the Pueblo to the Cheyenne, both matrilineal and patrilineal family structures existed, expressing further diversity and cultural forms. While early American forms varied widely, however, a uniform image of family has dominated historical sensibilities and public memory (Polakow, 1993:25). This monolithic image is traceable to the patriarchal structure of the New England colonies and the emergence of the "modern" family. This stubborn image has long upheld one family form as the norm and the yardstick for judging other family forms. In the next chapter, we examine the varied family arrangements that emerged as U.S. history pressed forward.

CHAPTER REVIEW

1. Common knowledge about families in the past is pure myth. The most persistent myths stem from false images of the "traditional" family nestled within a golden past.
2. Findings from the new field of family history have taken a long time to reach the public. Nevertheless, the work of social historians has confirmed the long-standing diversity of family forms.
3. White middle-class families are idealized and used as a measuring rod for all families, even though social and economic realities gave rise to a range of family arrangements.
4. In the early colonial period, White families were the central units of the larger agriculturally based economic system. This arrangement is called the family-based economy.
5. The family-based economy integrated women's, men's, and children's productive labor. Families were patriarchal. At the same time, women played an important role in the colonial economy.
6. During the colonial period, families and communities were strongly interconnected. Families performed the economic, political, religious, and educational functions for society.

7. After 1800, social, economic, and demographic changes produced gradual changes in family living. The transition to industrial production transformed families from integrated work units into specialized domestic units that were separate from the surrounding communities.
8. Industrialization removed productive labor from the household and transferred family functions to other specialized institutions.
9. As industrialization removed productive labor outside of the family setting, the family-wage economy developed. In the family-wage economy, goods and services were produced outside of the household, where workers earned wages to support their families.
10. The family-wage economy produced a sharp distinction between women's and men's work, especially in the middle class. The family withdrew from the world of work and became a retreat from the outside world. The household became a setting for the care and socialization of children and for the emotional support of adults.
11. Throughout history, ordinary people developed a variety of family strategies for adapting to changing social conditions.

RELATED WEB SITES

http://www.americaslibrary.gov
America's Library: Welcome to America's Story from America's Library! This Web site is brought to you from the Library of Congress in Washington, D.C., the largest library in the world and the nation's library. It represents one of the most comprehensive historical research sites available to students and researchers.

http://www.nwhp.org/index.html
The National Women's History Project: The National Women's History Project is a non-profit organization dedicated to recognizing and celebrating the diverse and historic accom-

plishments of women by providing information and educational material and programs.

http://www.mtsu.edu/~kmiddlet/history/women/wh-manu.html
American Women's History: A Research Guide to Archival Collections: A definitive guide to searching archives: resources, finding aids, and directories of archives.

http://www.datalounge.net/lha/
Lesbian Herstory Archives: A guide to a wide-ranging collection of resources, including many

primary resources—books, manuscripts, magazines and photographs.

http://www.pbs.org/wgbh/aia

Africans in America—PBS Online: The Africans in America Web site is a companion to "Africans in America," a six-hour public television series. The website chronicles the history of racial slavery in the United States—from the start of the Atlantic slave trade in the 16th century to the end of the American Civil War in 1865—and explores the central paradox that is at the heart of the American story: a democracy that declared all men equal but enslaved and oppressed one people to provide independence and prosperity to another. Africans in America examines the economic and intellectual foundations of slavery in America and the global economy that prospered from it. And it reveals how the presence of African people and their struggle for freedom transformed America.

http://www.uvic.ca/hrd/cfp

The Canadian Families Project provides some information about the historical approach to studying families.

http://www.sagepub.co.uk

Journal of Family History: The Journal of Family History is an interdisciplinary journal which publishes scholarly research from an international perspective concerning the family as an historical form, with contributions from the disciplines of history, demography, anthropology, sociology, liberal arts and the humanities.

3

The Historical Making of Family Diversity

Myths and Realities

Myth:	The industrial revolution changed all families by separating them from the world of work.
Reality:	Although middle-class families were separated from the world of work, most families did not experience this separation.
Myth:	Historical development produced a nuclear family form that was independent of kin. Kin networks were inefficient, in contrast with the nuclear family, which was compatible with industrialization.
Reality:	First, the nuclear household predated industrialization. Second, kinship ties in the late nineteenth century and the early twentieth century persisted because they were effective in the modern industrial system.
Myth:	Families that did not conform to the "standard" model (nuclear in form, with a breadwinner father and a homemaker mother) were exceptions to the rule.
Reality:	The breadwinner father/homemaker mother form that developed during industrialization was one of many family forms that emerged in the new society.

Myth: European immigrant families broke down as the old ways clashed with the new in America's industrial cities.

Reality: The immigrant family system made settlement possible in the new society.

Myth: Slavery destroyed African family systems and left a legacy of dysfunctional cultural patterns.

Reality: Although their families were frequently disrupted, slaves rebuilt kinship structures that enabled them to cope with enslavement.

Myth: People of Mexican origin were simply another immigrant group, disadvantaged mainly by their traditional family ways.

Reality: The American takeover of Mexicans on their own land in the mid-1800s and the labor migration that followed disrupted family patterns. Nevertheless, family flexibility sustained Mexican-origin people in the United States.

Conventional wisdom about family history assumes a uniform pattern of development with a "modern" family at the end. But even as the breadwinner father and homemaker-mother form was taking shape among some groups, it was a family type that was particular to certain settings in North America. Other social contexts gave way to widely varying domestic and family configurations.

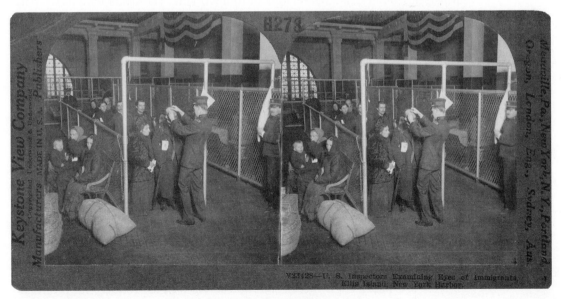

"U.S. Inspectors Examining Eyes of Immigrants. Ellis Island, New York Harbor."

This chapter highlights the social construction of different family forms. We examine some of the broad differences that make up the social history of American families. The threads of diversity, uneven change, and social agency become thicker in this chapter as we trace family development across time and social location.

First, we pick up on developing industrialization to show that "change is seldom unitary in its effects" (Coontz, 2001:83). White women, men, and children in different social classes were affected differently by the changing economy. Here, the theme of uneven change stands out as we contrast the experiences of the White working class with those in the middle class.

We turn then to immigration and racial control in the making of family history. Although the conventional histories of these groups and their families often feature diversity themes, they treat racial and ethnic families as special "cultural" cases that are different from a standard form (Baca Zinn, 1994). Instead, we take a **structural diversity approach**—one arguing that racial and ethnic families are not merely cultural artifacts, but are shaped differently by contextual factors. Both macrostructural forces and different group experience shaped all families in ways that conventional thinking does not consider. First, we consider the impact of immigration on the family patterns of White European immigrant groups who entered the United States voluntarily during the nineteenth century and at the beginning of the twentieth century. Then we examine the impact of racial domination on family life. We draw primarily from the historical experiences of African Americans and Mexican Americans, groups incorporated into our society through force and conquest.

Such diverse contexts led working-class families and racial and ethnic families along different paths from that of White middle-class families. Different labor structures and racial and ethnic domination produced and required different family forms. Structural forces produced varying adaptations on the part of industrial workers, slaves, and agricultural workers. These adaptations were not *exceptions* to the rule; they were, instead, variations created by mainstream forces. As a result, the idealized modern family was not a luxury shared by all. "Even though it was a legally, economically, and culturally privileged family form that conferred advantages to those who lived in it" (Coontz, 2001:83), those advantages were not evenly distributed. Many outside of society's privileged groups share a historical legacy of family devaluation, degradation, and even destruction. At the same time, the theme of human agency is especially powerful here. Family historians have given us richly textured accounts of how people subordinated by class and race used their families to survive and create a history and a place in the United States.

INDUSTRIALIZATION AND FAMILY LIFE

Family life was fundamentally changed during the period of industrialization. The mill towns that grew up along the streams of the Northeast and the steam-powered factories served to dismantle the family-based economy (Ryan, 1983:116). As increasingly more goods and services were produced for profit outside the home, the **family-wage economy** developed.

This period in American history was critical. The nation's economy was transformed from an agricultural system to one based on capitalist industrialization. With industrialization, cities grew rapidly, fueled by rural migrants and, most significantly, by wave after wave of European immigrants. During this period, the frontier was expanded to the West Coast. These developments occurred unevenly and had different effects on families in various segments of society. As Stephanie Coontz expains:

> The changes that helped produce more "modern" family forms, then, started in different classes, meant different things to families who occupied different positions in the industrial order, and did not proceed in a unilinear way. The "modernization" of the family was not the result of some general evolution of "the" family as early sociologists originally posited, but of *diverging* and *contradictory* responses that occurred in different areas and classes at various times, eventually interacting to produce the trends we now associate with industrialization (Coontz, 2000:24–25).

Macrostructural Transformations

The crucial era of transition to capitalist industrialization in the United States occurred in the decade before the American Civil War. The most basic changes produced by the industrial revolution revolved around the reorganization of work and the allocation of different kinds of work to various groups within society. A distinguishing characteristic of capitalist industrialization was the development of sharp distinctions between a middle class whose wealth was based on business and industry and an industrial working class whose labor produced that wealth (Ehrenreich and English, 1978). This differentiated the level of pay, prestige, and power that resulted from various positions within the economy.

Another transformation was the removal of production from the family and the development of the family-wage economy, in which the family was dependent on wages earned outside the home. This shift in economic production, with men becoming wage workers and women staying home to care for the house and children, became sharper in the early decades of the nineteenth century (Glenn, 1992; Osmond, 1996).

Of course, there were varying shapes of industrialization (Coontz, 2000:22). Two concepts help us understand how the new division of labor in the industrial economy took different forms in the middle class and the working class. These concepts are *social production* and *social reproduction*. The term **social production** refers to the varied ways in which people make a living, producing commodities (goods and services) on the job. **Social reproduction** refers to the work of caring for families in the home. This includes the maintenance of life on a daily basis, including food, clothing, shelter, and emotional activities (Amott, 1993:12; Brenner and Laslett, 1986:117). These two forms of work for the family became increasingly divided in the new economy. Before industrialization, both social production and social reproduction occurred within the family setting. Here, family members were engaged simultaneously in maintaining daily life and in the production of foodstuffs, clothing, shoes, candles, soap, and other goods consumed by the household. With industrialization, production of these basic goods gradually was taken over by capitalist industry. Social reproduction, however, remained largely the responsibility of individual households (Glenn, 1992:6). The new economy meant that families were now required to have workers in both arenas.

In the middle class, the family developed boundaries that separated it from the larger society, and it became a distinct sphere for women. While men's activities were increasingly focused on the industrial and competitive sphere of work, women's activities were confined to the care of children, the nurturing of the husband, and the physical maintenance of the home (Degler, 1980:26). This complementary arrangement was possible only where men earned wages high enough to support the whole family. However, vast differences among men's earnings meant that many wives were forced into the public world of work. The new social order had different implications for families in different social classes.

Work and Family in Industrial Society

The Doctrine of Two Spheres

The development of a split between public and private worlds led to an ideology about women's and men's proper places. The doctrine of two spheres called for a gendered division of labor in which married women were to remain in the home, creating a domestic "nest" by looking after their husbands and children, while married men were to venture outside the home, earning a living for the family. This ideology was accompanied by new beliefs about women's moral superiority. Women were thought to be "angels of the house" and spiritual guardians of the family.

The idealization of the women's sphere, called the **cult of true womanhood,** is described in the following manner by historian Barbara Welter:

> The attributes of True Womanhood, by which a woman judged herself and was judged by her husband, her neighbors, and society, could be divided into four cardinal virtues—piety, purity, submissiveness, and domesticity. Put them together and they spelled mother, daughter, sister, wife-woman. Without them, no matter whether there was fame, achievement, or wealth, all was ashes. With them, she was promised happiness and power (Welter, 1973:372).

Women's family roles were simultaneously idealized and restricted to family and church. The cult of true womanhood controlled women, narrowed their options, and lowered their status. Even within the home, women's influence was limited. "A husband's authority was supposed to be absolute in all major family decisions. By contrast, a wife's authority was exerted entirely by way of symbolism. Indeed, her great virtue was submissiveness and obedience to the will of her spouse, and her role was that of a comforter" (Demos, 1977:68).

Scholars have analyzed the development of the specialized, private family in capitalism as oppressive to women (Zaretsky, 1976). As work became increasingly alienating, the new sphere of personal life became more important for individuals. Women were assigned responsibility for maintaining the private refuge, and they were largely restricted by that responsibility. The family life that developed in this "cult of domesticity" was very different for women and men:

Family life emerged with man's separation from the household and his engagement in a distinct, economic sphere. It emerged as women's sphere, as women's work, but a retreat from the world of work, where man could relax and be rejuvenated by the ministrations of his wife. Since the husband centered his life around self-seeking competition in the economy, women as wives became complements to this process of masculine self-seeking, and family life itself became oriented around his struggle in the economy. Husband and wife cooperated in the formation of man's labor-force identity and in his perpetuation through his children. While man could correctly claim that, in the labor force, he was working to support his family, it is also true that the whole of family life, and of women's work, was at the service of man's economic success. Man and woman were dependent as husband and wife, each filling the needs of the other, but in this process man's labor-force activity dominated as the determinant of the activities of his wife and family (Matthaei, 1982:118–119).

The cult of true womanhood was an ideal that not all groups could achieve. Economic necessity frequently forced women to join their husbands (and often their children) in earning money for sheer family survival (Osmond and Thorne, 1993:610). Historian Gerda Lerner (1979) has argued that the cult of true womanhood became a class ideology, a vehicle whereby middle-class women could distinguish themselves from poorer women who were leaving their homes to become factory workers. As class distinctions sharpened, social attitudes toward women became polarized, and the image of "the lady" was elevated to a status symbol. The cult of true womanhood served as a means of preserving class distinctions. Elite and middle-class women had privileges that neither women nor men of other classes possessed. Although "home" was the proper sphere for the expression of true womanhood, much of the household work was done by servants, leaving some leisure for ladies to pursue other interests (Mullings, 1986b:49).

Although domesticity was idealized for all classes of women, many were hardly in a position to be "ladies." For example, women on the Overland Trail to California and Oregon between 1842 and 1867 longed for a return of the separate spheres. On the long journey, they performed both women's and men's work, but they viewed the work as only temporary, and indeed they fought to preserve for themselves a separate women's sphere (Faragher and Stansell, 1979).

Women and Industrial Work

Unlike middle-class women, working-class women in the 1800s were engaged in both social production and social reproduction. Most women lived in households in which the role of full-time homemaker was an unattainable luxury. They bore and raised children during most of their lives. They engaged in both domestic caretaking in the home and wage labor outside the household, mostly in disagreeable and often hazardous jobs in factories and sweatshops (Coleman, 1998:75; Osmond and Thorne, 1993:611).

Women's traditional household tasks were among the first productive activities to be transferred to the factory. Traditionally female production became the first large industries of the capitalist market, including yarn and textile production (spinning, weaving, bleaching, and dying); shoe-binding; palm leaf and straw weaving; food processing; comb and button making; and the production of ready-made clothes (Coleman, 1998:80). When a group of Boston businessmen drew up plans for cotton mills along the New England waterways in places such as Lowell and Waltham, Massachusetts, they designed female boardinghouses as well as spinning, weaving, and warping rooms. This model of early American industry recruited a workforce of young farm girls from throughout New England. The Hamilton Company in Lowell was typical. By 1835, 85 percent of the machine tenders were female, 86 percent were native born, and 80 percent were between the ages of fifteen and thirty. In the large and small textile mills that grew up throughout New England and the Middle Atlantic states, women workers were almost always in the majority. Only shoe manufacturing rivaled textiles in scale of organization and level of productivity. Both industries employed at least as many women as men, and often more women. The development of heavy industries that employed great numbers of males, especially mining and metal workers, would await the post-Civil war period (Ryan, 1983:121).

Wage earning was essentially a domestic obligation; wages earned belonged to families. Research on wage-earning women from 1900 to 1930 points to the intensive family loyalties of working-class girls:

> Although they were generally more successful in school than boys, daughters left school for work or to assist at home about as frequently as their brothers. They worked at dull, ill-paying jobs more steadily than adolescent boys; they usually surrendered their entire wage to their mothers—males often returned only a portion of their pay; and they had more household responsibilities than wage-earning sons. Investigators often reported tension between parents and daughters in working-class families, especially over spending money and social freedom, but most daughters stayed essentially obedient; they remained in the parental home, they surrendered their wages, they compromised with parents on standards of behavior (Tentler, 1979:89).

As industrialization advanced, women continued to inhabit a distinct and separate labor market. Then, as today, low-income family life required cooperation and sharing between the sexes and generations. Family was a primary defense against underclass oppression. Thus, to many working-class women it appeared extremely desirable for the family breadwinner to be the man (Osmond and Thorne, 1993:611).

The Family Wage

In the early nineteenth century, working-class men began agitating for a "family wage," an income advantage that would enable men to keep their wives at home raising the children and maintaining the family. The ideology assumed that all women would sooner or later become wives, making it legitimate to argue for women's exclusion from the labor force (May, 1990:277). Although the family wage was an important victory of the labor struggles of the late nineteenth and early twentieth centuries, it glorified women's domesticity and mandated that men should be the family breadwinners. This legitimated women's exclusion from the labor force. However, the family wage was limited to White men. Others received wages insufficient to support a family alone. The family wage provided a material basis for race and gender domination.

"Boys picking slate in a great coal breaker. Anthrecite mines, Pa." Children from poor families, such as these "breaker boys" working in the coal mines, labored long hours in often dangerous conditions.

Childhood and Adolescence

The new conception of children as separate and different from adults went hand in hand with the doctrine of two spheres. In the nineteenth century, many families became increasingly child-centered. Children were to be reared by women within the domestic setting. Although women had always reared children, in the nineteenth century child rearing was defined as a woman's special task. This concept was reinforced by the industrial changes that were placing women's duties in the home. The separation of family from work also exalted children and raised domesticity within the family to a new and higher level of respectability (Degler, 1980:73).

Childhood was now viewed as a distinct stage in the life cycle. Changes in the economy and the family were giving way to adolescence, a new life stage. The concept of adolescence emerged in the last two decades of the nineteenth century. As families moved away from production and as the population shifted from rural to urban settings, the concept of adolescence gradually took shape. Urban settings provided circumstances that allowed young people to be brought together and to form a distinctive youth culture (Demos and Demos, 1973:209).

Industrial capitalism restructured parent–child relationships. In the family-based economy, children had been little workers who were trained as apprentices. In the new economy, a son's fortune depended on his performance in the labor market, a daughter's fortune on her success in the marriage market and her husband's success. Parenting in middle- and upper-class families became a distinct social and familial activity intended to prepare children for success in economic competition:

> Because successful marketplace competition meant shaping oneself to the needs of capital as they arose and advancing oneself through a series of jobs, preparing a son for economic success could no longer mean instructing him in the skills of a predetermined trade through employment as a little worker. Rather the parenting of a son came to mean teaching him to be a self-seeking competitive individual, instilling in him the drive to succeed and the belief in his ability to do so. . . . The parenting of girls changed with that of boys for it meant, first and foremost, preparing them to be mothers and wife/supporters to these new individuals (Matthaei, 1982:108).

This model of early life was a middle-class phenomenon. It never existed at all for poor children in this country or for poor children in other societies (see Box 3.1 for a discussion of infant abandonment among the poor in nineteenth-century France).

Girls and boys from poor families in the United States were "put out" to labor for wages at unskilled or manual work; they were put to work for the family as much as they had been in the household economy (Cooper, 1999:26; Matthaei, 1982:198). The streets became a vital arena for the social and economic lives of working children (see Box 3.2).

Accordion Households

In Chapter 2 we dealt with myths about "the classical family of Western nostalgia." Industrialization did not create the nuclear family, although it did contribute to household flexibility during certain periods of transformation. Although households after 1830 tended to be nuclear, recent studies have found that they were not always or invariably so. They could expand and contract according to family circumstances. Families could enlarge their households with nonfamily members. At certain points in their development and in response to economic need, families might augment their household composition by taking in boarders or lodgers. When conditions improved, the family would become nuclear again (Modell and Hareven, 1977). Modell and Hareven found that the structure of households of the late nineteenth century varied along the family life cycle. Migration patterns, available housing, and changing economic needs provided contexts for creating "malleable households":

> Boarding in families in industrial America in the late 19th century was the province of young men of age just to have left their parents' homes, and was an arrangement entered into and provided by household heads who were of an age to have just lost a son from the residential family to an independent residence. . . . [Boarding involved] the exchange of a young adult person and a portion of his young adult income from his family of orientation to what might be called his family of reorientation to the city to a job, to a new neighborhood, to independence. It was a transition from a family (often rural, whether domestic or foreign) with excess sons or daughters (or insufficient economic base) to one (usually urban) with excess room (or present or anticipated need). And often both the excess room and the present or

BOX 3.1 **Families in Global Perspective: Discarding Infants in Nineteenth-Century France**

In her illuminating study of abandoned children in nineteenth-century France, Rachel Fuchs (1984) argues that the widespread abandonment of infants and young children was part of the very fabric of the culture and the corresponding lifestyles of the poor and destitute. For mothers it was "a radical solution to the social psychological, and above all economic pressures the woman faced. . . . They abandoned the baby, because to keep the infant meant loss of job, income and even life for them and the child." We read in Hugo's *Les Misérables* how Fantine is forced to abandon her little daughter Cosette in this way.

Abandonment constituted part of the "social question" that preoccupied France as late as the eighteenth and nineteenth centuries; for the rising tide of destitute abandoned children threatened the state as they grew up to form the "dangerous classes." The desperate conditions of poor mothers and their children illuminate not only state policies toward children but also "nineteenth-century French attitudes toward unwed mothers, illegitimate children, working class and middle class families, and the peasantry." Social economists saw all forms of deviance as having their origins in the poor and uneducated population.

The late eighteenth century saw a rise in population and growing rates of illegitimacy, so starvation threatened both the rural and the urban poor and abandonment became a problem of enormous magnitude. Hence France began to develop a state policy for receiving and maintaining destitute and unwanted children. Influenced by the secular reformers, a national, secular, state-supported form of public assistance was initiated. The constitution of 1791 proclaimed that the task of the nation was to raise abandoned children and to make useful citizens by training them for the military, for agriculture, and for populating the colonies. Prostitution and vagabondage were the vices most feared by the authorities. Because abandoned children were believed to "carry the most dangerous instincts in their hearts," France's public policy for children developed two strategies: the first institutionalized abandonment through the notorious "tour," and the second disposed of disposable children through the wet-nurse institution.

The "tour"—a revolving cylindrical box in which mothers placed their babies—was built into the walls of hospices and foundling hospitals, a stark symbol of anonymity. It was stipulated by decree in 1811 that each hospice should have one. The cradle swiveled so that the mother who deposited the baby from the street could not be seen on the inside, and a bell would be sounded to announce that a baby had been dropped. Thus "the tour was deaf, dumb and blind. The total anonymity of the mother and baby was assured, unless the mother or her messenger put some identifying tag or note on the infant." This anonymity was believed necessary to avoid abortion and infanticide, but it was controversial since many authorities believed it encouraged immorality and irresponsibility on the part of destitute women. The tour, in essence, centralized child abandonment. It regulated the process by which the state took control of pauper children and fashioned them into useful capital for the state. When its controversial practice was discontinued, French child policy continued to permit the "displacement" of babies to the countryside.

Source: Valerie Polakow, *Lives on the Edge*. Chicago: University of Chicago Press, 1993, pp. 17–19.

`BOX 3.2` **Inside the Worlds of Diverse Families:** Children's Uses of the Streets: New York City, 1850–1860

Unlike today, the teeming milieu of the New York streets in the mid-nineteenth century was in large part a children's world. . . . Public life with its panoply of choices, its rich and varied textures, its motley society, played as central a role in the upbringing of poor children as did private, domestic life in that of their more affluent peers. While middle-class mothers spent a great deal of time with their children (albeit with the help of servants), women of the laboring classes condoned for their offspring an early independence—within bounds—on the streets. Through peddling, scavenging, and the shadier arts of theft and prostitution, the streets offered children a way to earn their keep, crucial to making ends meet in their households. Street life also provided a home for children without families—the orphaned and abandoned—and an alternative to living at home for the especially independent and those in strained family circumstances. Such uses of the streets were dictated by exigency, but they were also intertwined with patterns of motherhood, parenthood, and childhood. In contrast to their middle- and upper-class contemporaries, the working poor did not think of childhood as a separate stage of life in which girls and boys were free from adult burdens, nor did poor women consider mothering to be a full-time task of supervision. They expected their children to work from an early age, to "earn their keep" or to "get a living"—a view much closer to the early modern conceptions which Phillippe Ariès describes in *Centuries of Childhood* (1965). Children were little adults, unable as yet to take up the duties of their elders, but nonetheless bound to do as much as they could. To put it another way, the lives of children, like those of adults, were circumscribed by economic and familial obligations. In this context, the poor expressed their care for children differently than did the propertied classes. Raising one's children properly did not mean protecting them from the world of work; on the contrary, it involved teaching them to shoulder those heavy burdens of labor which were the common lot of their class, to be hardworking and dutiful to kin and neighbors. By the same token, laboring children gained an early autonomy from their parents, an autonomy alien to the experience of more privileged children. But there were certainly generational tensions embedded in these practices: although children learned independence within the bounds of family obligation, their self-sufficiency also led them in directions that parents could not always control. When parents sent children out to the streets, they could only partially set the terms of what the young ones learned there. Street selling, or huckstering, was one of the most common ways for children to turn the streets to good use. . . . In the downtown business and shopping district, passers-by could buy treats at every corner: hot sweet potatoes, baked-pears, teacakes, fruit, candy, and hot corn. In residential neighborhoods, hucksters sold household supplies door to door: fruits and vegetables in season, matchsticks, scrub brushes, sponges, strings, and pins. Children assisted adult husksters, went peddling on their own, and worked in several low-paying trades which were their special province: crossing-sweeping for girls; errand running, bootblacking, horse holding, and newspaper selling for boys. There were also the odd trades in which children were particularly adept, those unfamiliar and seemingly gratuitous forms of economic activity which abounded in nineteenth-century metropo-

(continued)

(continued from previous page)

lises: one small boy whom a social investigator found in 1859 made his living in warm weather by catching butterflies and peddling them to canary owners.

Younger children, too, could earn part of their keep on the streets. Scavenging, the art of gathering useful and salable trash, was the customary chore for those too small to go out streetselling. Not all scavengers were children; there were also adults who engaged in scavenging full-time, ragpickers who made their entire livelihoods from all the odds and ends of a great city. More generally, however, scavenging was children's work. Six- or seven-year-olds were not too young to set out with friends and siblings to gather fuel for their mothers. Small platoons of these children scoured neighborhood streets, ship and lumber yards, building lots, demolished houses, and the precincts of artisan shops and factories for chips, ashes, wood, and coal to take home or peddle to neighbors.

Source: Christine Stansell, "Women, Children, and the Uses of the Streets: Class, and Gender Conflict in New York City, 1850–1860." In Ellen Carol Du Bois and Vicki L. Ruiz (eds.), *Unequal Sisters: A Multi-Cultural Reader in U.S. Women's History.* New York: Routledge, 1990, pp. 94–95.

anticipated economic need can have come from the departure from the household of a newly independent son (Modell and Hareven, 1977:177).

These accordion households helped families adapt to urban life. They were important in the life cycle of young people as a transitional stage between departing from their parents' family and setting up their own family. The practice of taking in strangers in exchange for pay or services was more widespread during this period than was the practice of sharing household space with extended kin (Hareven, 1977).

Family members were not isolated from kin, although extended kin did not live together in the same household. Distinguishing between households and families is important if we are to correct common misconceptions about family life in past times. Although households as residential units were predominantly nuclear in the past, family units and family activities were not constrained within the boundaries of the household. Family members sustained family ties with relatives outside the household. Kinship ties persisted outside the household even where the residential unit was predominantly nuclear (Hareven and Vinovskis, 1978:15).

IMMIGRATION AND FAMILY LIFE

From 1830 to 1930, the United States witnessed two massive waves of immigration. The first wave (the "old" immigration) began arriving in the 1830s and continued through the 1880s, when more than 10 million immigrants arrived. English, Irish, German, and Scandinavian immigrants predominated in these decades. The opening of large land areas beyond the Mississippi and the building of roads, canals, and railroads, along with increasing industrialization, offered new jobs to immigrant labor and opened up new agricultural areas to settlement.

The "new" immigration took place in the years between 1882 and 1930. This great influx of European people saw the admission of more than 22 million immigrants. This period marked the high point of immigration from northern and western European nations and the beginning of a new influx of peoples from southern and eastern Europe, including Italians, Poles, Greeks, Russians, Austro-Hungarians, and other Slavic groups (Dyer, 1979:103–105).

Immigration, which began as a trickle, gradually gained momentum during the nineteenth century and finally became a flood by the beginning of the twentieth century. This extraordinary population movement—the largest in recorded history—was fundamentally the result of an extraordinary economic expansion—also the largest and most concentrated in American history. Demographers and historians have identified a host of push and pull factors that operated on different groups. In their countries of origin, immigrants were experiencing population explosions and dislocations that provided the major stimulus for emigration. At the same time, industrialization was generating an insatiable demand for labor in the United States. The prospects of economic opportunity on this side of the Atlantic motivated millions of Europeans to uproot themselves. We can hardly overstate the critical role played by immigrant labor in the industrialization of America. In the early stages of industrialization, immigrants performed unskilled labor in mining, construction, and manufacturing. Foreign labor built the industrial edifice:

> By 1910, the foreign-born made up a quarter of the nation's work force, and in many of the industries closest to the industrial center, the foreign-born were a clear majority. In 1910 . . . a survey of twenty principal mining and manufacturing industries found that 58 percent of workers were foreign-born. In coal mines the figure was 48 percent; in iron mines 67 percent; in clothing factories 76 percent; in slaughter and packinghouses 46 percent; in tanneries 53 percent; in steel mills 51 percent; in rubber factories 41 percent; in textile mills 49 percent; in road construction 46 percent (Steinberg, 1981:36).

There was a great deal of variation in immigrant family migration arrangements. Europeans from diverse societies who settled in the industrial cities of the Northeast and Midwest were confronted with numerous problems. They faced discrimination, poverty, and many difficulties in reestablishing families (Hutter, 1991:170). These problems led to the erroneous conclusion that migration destroyed family life.

The Social Breakdown Perspective

Themes of instability and crisis were common in early social science. As a result, turn-of-the-century research on immigrants was steeped in questions about how migration broke down the old ways of life. Immigrants were thought to be uprooted and unstable peasants without family ties in the new society. Such themes appeared in an influential book written by Oscar Handlin. *The Uprooted* (1951) presented immigrants as traditional peasants from small harmonious vil-

"'Imported Americans' shopping from push carts in the lower East Side, N. Y. City." Existing family patterns and values gave an advantage to immigrants who settled into urban enclaves.

lages where family life had been patriarchal and kin-based. In the modern world, these immigrants confronted the overwhelming forces of industrialization and urbanization. As peasants they were torn from their solitary communities and thought to have endured the stresses of urban life alone. Ghetto living, crowding, poor sanitation and nutrition, and above all alienation were characterized as the essence of the immigrant experience. The resulting disorganization contributed to the confusion of roles, the breakdown of patriarchal authority, the isolation of the family from the extended kinship grouping, and general family instability. Eventually, as their "cultural baggage" (values, behavior patterns, and traditional institutions) fell away, the newcomers were assimilated by the dominant society.

This interpretation was in error on almost all counts. To begin with, it does not account for the variety of immigrants that came to the United States. "To speak of the immigrant family is not only to lose sight of diversity but also to miss the important point that ethnic groups sometimes differed dramatically in family patterns" (Degler, 1980:132). More important, immigrants settled in communities with widely differing social and economic structures that produced different family outcomes. Research indicates that the characterization of most immigrants simply as traditional peasants is inaccurate and misleading. Although first-generation immigrants certainly experienced personal and collective cultural traumas, they were neither totally uprooted nor destroyed. Instead, most endured material hardships and emotional stress with remarkable fortitude and dignity (Early, 1983:482).

The greatest misconception about the family life of the immigrants is that their family patterns in the New World were shaped mainly by their Old World cultures. The key ingredients of the old family ways—patriarchal family ideology and kinship orientation—were thought to be obstacles that prevented successful adjustment. Prevailing thought was that the immigrants' "cultural baggage" could be erased through the process of acculturation. Immigrant families were major targets for reform. Settlement workers sought to Americanize the newcomers by ridding them of their old family ways.

This thinking ignores the vital role that families played in migration, recruitment, and settlement. Instead of relinquishing old patterns completely, immigrants "used their cultural baggage to help them control and fashion their own destinies" (Early, 1983:482).

Industrial Work and Immigrant Families

The family was the most important social form in the recruitment of workers to the new industrial society. Family patterns and values often carried over to the urban setting and provided continuity between the Old World and the new industrial setting. Immigrants tended to migrate in groups. They moved into neighborhoods with networks of relatives and friends, where others spoke their language and helped them find work.

> Low-paid industrial immigrant workers were forced by economic pressures to live close to their places of work. The particular choice of residence and occupation was strongly influenced by the presence of friends and relatives in a process that has been called "chain migration." Chain migration refers to the connections made between individuals in countries of origin and destination in the process of international migration and to the process in which choices of residence and occupation were influenced by friends and relatives. . . . Relatives acted as recruitment, migration, and housing resources, helping each other to shift from the often rural European work background to industrial work (Hutter, 1991:177).

Rather than breaking their kinship ties, families used them in the transition to industrial life. A study of southern Italians in Chicago by Rudolph J. Vecoli discovered that solidarity and support rather than alienation and disorganization characterized family life after 1800. The *contadini* emigrated in chainlike fashion. After working a while, men would send for their families. In this way, chains of immigration were established between certain towns of southern Italy and Chicago. By 1920, the Italian population in Chicago had reached approximately 60,000. Within their ethnic communities, families retained their unity and their traditional ways of life:

> Reunited in Chicago, the peasant family functioned much as it had at home; there appears to have been little of that confusion of roles depicted in [Handlin's] *The Uprooted*. The husband's authority was not diminished, while the wife's subordinate position was not questioned . . . nor did the extended family disintegrate upon emigration as is contended . . . [for] the family unit not only includes those related by blood, but those related by ritual bonds as well. . . . The alliance of the families of the town through intermarriage and godparenthood perpetuates a social organization based upon a large kinship group (Vecoli, 1964:409).

The work patterns of southern Italians were influenced by their culture and the city's occupational structure. Few found employment in Chicago's manufacturing industries because of their aversion to factory work and discrimination against them by employers. Instead, they retained their traditional laboring mode by replacing the Irish in excavation and street work, as they did on railroad and construction jobs throughout the west. Engaged in seasonal gang labor, they developed an institution for distributing employment and other kinds of social support. This was the *padrone* system. The *padrone* was an employment agent who mediated between employers and the Italian laborers. He also assisted them in other ways, easing their accommodation to the new society.

Like working-class women in general, immigrant women often entered the industrial labor force in order to make ends meet. Although they shared the domestic ideal of womanhood, many worked simply to provide for their families. The extent to which immigrant wives worked outside the home varied according to ethnic group, but at no time did more than 10 or 15 percent of the wives of any nationality work outside the home (Degler, 1980:140). Hareven (1975) found that French Canadian women continued to work after their marriages despite the expectation prevalent in their culture that married women would remain in the home. On the other hand, historian Virginia Yans-McLaughlin (1973:117) found that southern Italians in Buffalo, New York, opposed women's employment outside the home. Italian women remained in the home, while Buffalo's Irish, Polish, Swedish, and German women were employed as domestics in middle-class homes. Women's preference to remain in the home resulted somewhat from Buffalo's peculiar occupational structure. Unlike many other cities, heavy industry and transportation dominated its economy. The city offered comparatively little in the way of light industrial production for unskilled women.

Recent historical scholarship has shed new light on just how immigrants used their traditional family patterns in accommodating to the new industrial settings. For example, a study of French Canadian families moving to Lowell, Massachusetts, in the 1870s reveals a distinctive family strategy. Frances Early (1983) found that French Canadian families arrived from agricultural settlements in Quebec, where the family was still the main unit of production. All family members had contributed their labor to the family farm. In Lowell, the immigrants patterned their work on the farm economy by using children's labor to contribute to the earning power of families: they sent their children to work. By the age of 13, children worked away from the home: seven in ten children ages 11 through 15 held jobs in 1870 (Early, 1983:485). This was an adaptive mechanism based on the family economy tradition. It enabled the immigrants to survive in a one-industry textile town:

> They created new family economic strategies based on difficult new realities, and thereby exerted a certain control over their lives. However, the vast majority of French Canadians, if they chose to live and work in Lowell, had to accept the socioeconomic configuration of late nineteenth-century industrial-capitalist New England society. In other words, they had to begin their new lives as members of a large, alienated, and often suffering industrial proletariat whose ability to direct and shape the present as well as the future was, indeed, regrettably limited (Early, 1983:494–495).

The Irish in Massachusetts in the late nineteenth century also adapted to poverty by sending children out to work. John Modell (1978) found that poor Irish families removed their children from school in order to place them in the labor force. When economic conditions improved for the family, children were reinstated in school. The family was not simply a passive recipient of social change. It was, however, a vital resource in adapting to the new society. The immigrant family was primarily responsible for "making it" in America (Hutter, 1991:175). Yet the family traditions of these immigrants were not something passed down from generation to generation. Instead, different groups drew selectively from cultural resources, often creating new "traditions" as they adapted to or resisted changing economic or political constraints and opportunities (Coontz, 2001:82).

RACIAL CONTROL AND FAMILY LIFE

New Thinking about Minority Families

The mythical "standard family" has produced far-reaching misconceptions. As the yardstick for judging all family forms, images of what is "normal" have clouded our understanding of minority families. Compared to mainstream families, racial minority families are usually seen as cultural aberrations—products of ethnic lifestyles at odds with modern society. Even some social science treatments of family life are based on racialized images that are part of the American cultural mythology.

The African American family in particular has been equated with family instability and stereotyped as the essence of what families should *not* be. The idea that slavery weakened kin ties and undermined family values gave way to notions of the **matriarchal family,** a form in which power rested in the mother figures, with fathers largely absent from family life. According to this thinking, family disintegration continued into the twentieth century. Black families remained locked in a "tangle of pathology." This was the theme of Daniel Patrick Moynihan's study, *The Negro Family: The Case for National Action* (1965). The Moynihan report identified the family as the main problem facing African Americans:

> At the heart of the deterioration of the fabric of Negro society is the Negro family. It is the fundamental source of weakness in the Negro community at the present time. . . . Unless this damage is repaired, all the effort to end discrimination and poverty and injustice will come to little (Moynihan, 1965:5).

According to this reasoning, the family was a deficient social form that created problems for African American people in American society.

Mexican-origin or Chicano families have been stereotyped as disorganized due to backward Mexican traditionalism. As late as 1966, the Chicano family was seen as the main cause of Chicano subordination:

> The kind of socialization that Mexican-American children receive at home is not conducive to the development of the capacities needed for advancement in a

dynamic industrial society. This type of upbringing creates stumbling blocks for future advancement by stressing values that hinder mobility; family ties, honor, masculinity, and living in the present—and by neglecting values that are conducive to it—achievement, independence, and deferred gratification (Heller, 1966:34–35).

Such explanations rest on ahistoric concepts of family life (Mullings, 1997:73). New research on the family histories of people of color shows how inadequate the old frameworks have been. Rather than trying to explain why family patterns deviate from the so-called normal family, researchers are now investigating the underlying social conditions that lead to different family outcomes. Today, we have a better understanding of why the family lives of people of color have never fit the mainstream model.

In this section we examine the myths and realities of family life among racial minorities from the time these groups entered the United States through 1930. Although we draw primarily from the experiences of African Americans and Chicanos, we also refer to Asian American families. This analysis shows the many ways in which systems of racial control have disrupted family life among people of color.

Macrostructural Connections among Race, Labor, and Family

To understand how race was fundamental in the social construction of families, we must return to a theme that we have followed throughout our historical discussion—namely, the importance of *work* in determining the social placement of people and groups. "In any society the distribution of power and prestige is largely determined by the work people do" (Huber, 1993:43). From the founding of the United States and throughout its history, "race has been a fundamental criterion in determining the kind of work people do, the wages they receive, and the kind of legal, economic, political and social support provided for their families" (Dill, 1994:166). This historical fact can be best examined through an analysis of the placement of people of color in the labor structures of the U.S. economy.

The United States started out as a colonial economy that offered raw resources and land to European and American capitalists. To develop the economy, capitalists needed labor, which was always in short supply. The presence of racially defined groups in the United States is tied to this demand for labor. Most were brought to the United States for the express purpose of providing cheap and malleable labor. Although European immigrants were also welcomed as a source of low-wage labor, they were incorporated into low-wage economies of the North (Glenn, 1992:177).

In his analysis of the different historical experiences of White immigrants and racial minorities in the United States, Robert Blauner (1972) borrows the concept of colonialism from the former colonies of European countries to describe the manner of incorporation and the labor-market status of racial minority people, including African Americans, Asians, and Chicanos. Blauner argues that racial groups were internally "colonized" minorities within the boundaries of the United States, whereas Europeans immigrated to this society (Blauner, 1972).

Racially defined groups were recruited to fill labor needs in economically backward regions: the West, Southwest, and South. In the late nineteenth and

"Japanese Laborers in California." Unlike that of European immigrants, the labor status of people of color severely limited their opportunities.

early twentieth centuries, Chinese men constituted between a quarter and a third of the workforce, reclaiming agricultural lands, building railroads, and working in mines, and 90 percent of the domestic and laundry workers in California. During this same period, native Chicanos and Mexican immigrants (Mexicanos) were employed as miners, railroad hands, and agricultural laborers in the western states. In the years following emancipation, African Americans were concentrated in agriculture, as well as in heavy construction labor and domestic service in the South. All three groups helped build the agricultural and industrial base on which subsequent industrial development rested, but they were excluded from the industrial jobs that resulted (Glenn, 1992:177).

Unlike European immigrants, most people of color were historically incorporated through coercive labor systems. These systems—principally slavery and contract labor—were organized in ways that maximized economic productivity. Maximizing labor productivity meant that few supports were made available for sustaining family life. In some cases family life was legislatively denied (Hondagneu-Sotelo, 1995:183). Bonnie Thornton Dill describes the way in which families were brutally conditioned by the larger political economy:

> In the eighteenth and nineteenth centuries, labor, and not the existence or maintenance of families, was the critical aspect of their role in building the nation. Thus, they were denied the societal supports necessary to make their families a vital element in the social order. . . . In some instances racial-ethnic families were seen as a threat to the efficiency and exploitability of the work force and were actively prohibited. In other cases, they were tolerated when it was felt they might help solidify or expand the work force (Dill, 1994:149–150).

The labor status of people of color prevented them from receiving the kind of legal, economic, political, and social support provided for other families. Lacking these supports, racial-ethnic families devised various solutions for maintaining family life. One vital solution was to extend women's work beyond the private family sphere. This created racial differences in the experience of public-private spheres. Women of color did not share the same separation of the public-private domains that developed in the dominant society. Dill explains why the concept of reproductive labor, when applied to women of color, must be modified.

> Treated primarily as workers rather than as members of family groups, these women labored to maintain, sustain, stabilize, and reproduce their families while working in both the public (productive) and private (reproductive) spheres. . . . Long after industrialization had begun to reshape family roles among middle-class White families, driving White women into a cult of domesticity, women of color were coping with an extended day. This day included subsistence labor outside the family and domestic labor within the family. For slaves, domestics, migrant farm laborers, seasonal factory workers, and prostitutes, the distinctions between labor that reproduced family life and labor that economically sustained it were minimized (Dill, 1994:164–165).

Unlike families of the dominant society, racial minorities had no private domestic arena for mothers and children, supported through the productive

Mexican workers on the urban rail system in Los Angeles, CA, 1903.

work of husbands and fathers. Furthermore, systems of racial control systematically disrupted family life (Amott and Matthaei, 1991:16). We are most familiar with assaults on family ties of African Americans under slavery: sale of individuals, slave-master control over marriage and reproduction, and the brutal conditions of family life. Less well recognized are the assaults on the culture and family lives of Chicanos and Chinese Americans. In both groups, households were broken apart by the demands for male labor (Glenn, 1987:53). Many Mexican American men were employed in mining camps and on railroad gangs, which required them to live apart from wives and children (Barrera, 1979). This was also true for male migrant agricultural workers until the 1880s, when the family-labor system became the preferred mode (Camarillo, 1979). In the case of the Chinese, only prime-age males were recruited as workers, and wives and children had to be left behind. The Chinese Exclusion Act of 1882 not only prohibited further entry of Chinese laborers but also barred resident laborers from bringing in wives and children. This policy was aimed at preventing the Chinese from settling permanently once their labor was no longer needed (Glenn, 1987:53). The high concentration of males in the Chinese community prior to 1920 resulted in a split-household family, in which work life was separated from family life and carried out by a member living far from the rest of the household. The split-household form made possible maximum exploitation of workers, because the cost of family maintenance was borne partially by the unpaid subsistence work of women and old people in the home village (Glenn, 1983:14–15).

Despite the harsh conditions imposed on family life by a racial labor system, families did not break down. Instead, people of color struggled to create livable family environments. Let us turn to the histories of African American and Chicano families, which illustrate how people of color organized their families in ways that allowed them to function.

African American Families in Slavery and Freedom

Until the 1970s, scholars took it for granted that slavery decimated the African American culture and created the foundation for unstable female-headed households. In the past three decades, however, revisionist historians have transformed our conceptions of the slave family. Using an adaptational perspective, they analyzed family life as a positive adaptation to social conditions (Mullings, 1997:78; Taylor, 2000). The television version of *Roots*, which emphasized the strong family bonds among slaves, dramatized the new scholarship. The most significant historical work in the new social history of slave families was Herbert Gutman's landmark book, *The Black Family in Slavery and Freedom* (1976). Inspired by the controversy following the Moynihan report, Gutman examined plantation records and marriage applications during slavery and after emancipation. He provided quantitative evidence to explain how Black Americans developed a culture shaped by adaptation to the harshness of initial enslavement, then dealt with the dislocations associated with the physical transfer of hundreds of thousands of upper-South slaves to the lower South between 1790 and 1860, and later experienced legal freedom in the rural and urban South and in the urban North prior to 1930 (Gutman, 1976:7).

Revisionist history has shown that African American families adapted to adverse conditions and endured with remarkable completeness.

Gutman found that two-parent households prevailed both during slavery and after emancipation (see Box 3.3). The major reason for family breakup during slavery was forced separation through sale. Gutman presents compelling evidence that family formation continued despite the abuses of slavery. The findings challenged the common portrayal of slave families:

> [T]he alleged inadequacy of the slave father and husband, the absence of male "models" for young slave children to emulate, the prevalence of the "sambo" personality, the insistence that slave marriages usually meant little more than successive polygyny, and the belief that the "matrifocal" household . . . prevailed among the mass of illiterate plantation field hands and laborers. These misconceptions accompany another erroneous belief: that when slaves did honor the two-parent household they did so either as a result of the encouragement offered to "favored" slaves by owners or because daily contacts between whites and slave servants and artisans (as contrasted to slaves living in "the quarters") permitted these few slaves to "imitate" marriage "models" common among owners and other whites. Implicit in such arguments, none of which rests on significant evidence, is the assumption that such "models" were infrequent among the slaves themselves, an assumption that has encouraged simplified and misleading descriptions of slave socialization and slave culture (Gutman, 1976:13).

Some historians now challenge Gutman's analysis that two-parent households were the norm among slaves. These "postrevisionist" scholars argue that slave family structure was more fluid and variable than reported in revisionst

Researching Families: Dispelling the Myths About African American Families

Herbert G. Gutman made ingenious use of quantitative data derived from planta-tion birth registers, census data, and marriage licenses to document the predomi-nance of the two-parent household during and after slavery. The following table shows that between 1855 and 1880, as many as 90 percent of Black households contained both a husband and a wife.

Percentage of Male-Present Negro Households, 1855–1880

Place and Date	Number of Households (%)	Male-Present Households (%)	Male-Absent Households (%)
Buffalo, N.Y., 1855	145	90	10
Buffalo, N.Y., 1875	159	85	15
Troy, N.Y., 1880	128	85	15
York County, Va., 1865	994	85	15
Montgomery County, Va., 1866	500	78	22
Princess Anne County, Va., 1865	375	84	16
Natchez, Miss., 1880	769	70	30
Beaufort, S.C., 1880	461	70	30
Richmond, Va., 1880	5670	73	27
Mobile, Ala., 1880	3235	74	26
Rural Adams County, Miss., 1880	3093	81	19
St. Helena's Township, S.C., 1880	491	87	13
St. Helena's Island, S.C., 1880	904	86	14

Source: Herbert G. Gutman, "Persistent Myths about the Afro-American Family." In Michael Gor-don (ed.), *The American Family in Social-Historical Perspective.* New York: St. Martin's, 1983, p. 468.

works (Franklin, 1997; Taylor, 2000). However the debate is eventually resolved, there is compelling historical evidence that African American households and families of varied forms remained relatively intact and survived the experiences of slavery (Taylor, 2000:238). The key to understanding how African Americans forged powerful family ties during slavery and its aftermath lies in the adaptive capacities they constructed from their African and American experiences. Slaves did not simply react to the abuses of the plantation system. Within their work settings and kinship networks, they forged many forms of resistance and main-tained the integrity of family life.

Work and Gender
Slave women and men were laborers on and for the plantation. Sometimes slave labor was gendered. For example, ditching was men's work; sorting cotton was women's work. Exceptions were found in field work when, during the harvest,

both sexes worked in hoeing gangs. Advertisements for women slaves often proclaimed their ability to work like men. Women could be found doing the stereotypically masculine work of plowing (Matthaei, 1982:81; Mullings, 1997:82). Away from the fields, however, work was nearly always based on gender. Craft work or skilled work necessary to produce commodities for the plantations was segregated in the same manner as it was among free women and men:

> An elite of slave men was trained as carpenters, coopers, stonemasons, millers, and shoemakers. Some masters used such promotion as a reward for good field work. Slave women were trained for feminine occupations, such as sewing, spinning and dairy keeping, by their mistress homemaker, by white women bond servants or by the wife of the overseer (Matthaei, 1982:91).

Slave women, in addition to their labor on the plantation or in the "public" slave sphere, were responsible for the domestic care of their own families. A female slave's work also included being "mammy" to her owner's children; she was, therefore, engaged in mothering two sets of children at once. Thus, the "forced participation of the slave mother in labor outside of her home meant that she lived the double day long before it became common among free families" (Matthaei, 1982: 96).

In John Blassingame's collection of two centuries of slave letters, speeches, interviews, and autobiographies, one slave describes the work of his mother, a house servant:

> My mother's labor was very hard. She would go to the house in the morning, take her pail upon her head, and go away to the cow-pen, and milk fourteen cows. She then put on the bread for the family breakfast, and got the cream ready for churning, and set a little child to churn it, she having the care of from ten to fifteen children, whose mothers worked in the field. After clearing away the family breakfast, she got breakfast for the slaves . . . which was taken at twelve o'clock. In the meantime, she had beds to make, rooms to sweep, and etc. Then she cooked the family dinner, which was simply plain meat, vegetables, and bread. Then the slaves' dinner was to be ready at from eight to nine o'clock in the evening. . . . At night she had the cows to milk again. . . . This was her work day by day. Then in the course of the week, she had the washing and ironing to do for her master's family . . . and for her husband, seven children and herself. . . . She would not get through to go to her log cabin until nine or ten o'clock at night. She would then be so tired that she could scarcely stand; but she would find one boy with his knee out, and another with his elbow out, a patch wanting here, and a stitch there, and she would sit down by her lightwood fire, and sew and sleep alternately, often till the light began to streak in the east; and then lying down, she would catch a nap and hasten to the toil of the day (Blassingame, 1977:133).

Slave women's work shaped child-care arrangements. Women organized communal child care in such a way that a few women were responsible for caring for all children too young to work, and women as a group were accountable for one another's children (White, 1990).

Women and men in slavery lived within a gender system that served the needs of plantation owners, yet it was different from the gender system of the dominant society. Women were physical laborers in the public sphere of the plantation. At the same time, they were vulnerable to sexual exploitation.

Women slaves had no legal rights to their bodies, their sexuality, or their children. Nevertheless, slave women found ways to resist. They attempted to work in settings that allowed them to be with their families. Not all slaves could control their working conditions. Some mothers murdered their babies to keep them from being slaves. Others resisted through their fertility, by using various contraception and abortion techniques. All of these actions reflect *human agency*. Anthropologist Leith Mullings calls this transformative work and defines it as the efforts to transform circumstances in order to maintain continuity. "These efforts have spanned the domains of work, household and community" (Mullings, 1997:98).

In contrast to the treatment of women, male slaves were denied manhood in the public sphere of the plantation:

> The slaveholders deprived black men of the role of provider, refused to dignify their marriages or legitimize their issue; compelled them to submit to physical abuse in the presence of their women and children; made them choose between remaining silent while their wives and daughters were seduced and risking death; and threatened them with separation from their family at any moment (Genovese, 1981:241).

New research offers a fresh look at men in slavery. The slave family did rest on much greater equality between women and men than was the case for White families. Furthermore, slavery produced strong women. However, it did not completely undermine male slaves. According to Genovese, men provided for their families to a greater extent than has been appreciated. Many hunted and trapped animals to supplement the meager food supplied by plantation owners. Slave children usually did have an image of a strong Black man before them. Even when a slave boy was growing up without a father in the house, he had as a model a tough, resourceful driver, a skilled mechanic or two, and other field hands. Some of those men devoted themselves to playing surrogate father to all the children. They told them stories, taught them to fish and trap animals, and instructed them in the ways of survival in a White world. The norm called for adults to look after children whether they were blood relatives or not. Every plantation had some men who played this role (Genovese, 1981:243).

Kinship

Strong kinship ties were foremost in the formation of slave families. Kinship patterns connected unrelated slaves into a family. Even when slavery destroyed particular families, kinship networks were recreated. When plantations were initially set up, slaves might be obtained from various sources and would be strangers to one another. Gutman (1976:127–130) found in the records of plantations in Virginia and Alabama that after thirty years slaves on those plantations had established kinship networks such as those found on older plantations.

Slaves devised various practices for maintaining kin ties. For example, "naming" children after blood kin such as aunts, uncles, and grandparents was a family custom. Sons were often named after their fathers. According to Gutman, naming practices defined the place of the child in slave society and preserved symbolic kinship ties. Slave naming patterns reveal a unique conception of family:

> The names of their children suggest that slaves conceived of their families in a broad sense, including extended kin. Owners, in contrast, saw the nuclear family as the primary unit, perhaps because of its reproductive functions, and established rules to maintain this unit when dividing their estate without regard to preserving the larger net of kinship (Cody, 1983:441).

Gutman found that marriages endured, that unions were legitimized by rituals such as "jumping over a broomstick," and that fidelity was expected from male and female slaves after marriage.

Following emancipation, large numbers of slaves, often at considerable cost to themselves, came before authorities to proclaim that they were already married. Under slavery, however, legal marriage did not exist. Gutman used plantation birth records to show that female slaves often had their first child outside of slave marriage, and that this was followed by permanent and settled unions. Important new evidence about the attitudes of freed men and women toward marriage and family life was uncovered in the Freedman's Bureau manuscripts:

> Registers that listed the marriages of former slaves in Washington, D.C., and Rockbridge and Nelson counties, Virginia, between 1865 and 1867 show that models of

The Old Plantation, c. 1800: "Jumping the Broomstick."

stable marriages existed among the slaves themselves, not just among their masters, other whites, or free blacks. Some had lived together as husband and wife for more than forty years in slavery. In all, registers recorded the dates of 1,721 marriages: 46 percent in Nelson county, 43 percent in Rockbridge county, and 36 percent in Washington, D.C., had resided together at least ten years. The Washington register tells even more. It listed 848 marriages, and of them only 34 were between men and women who had lived in the District before emancipation. The rest had moved there, probably as families, mostly from nearby rural counties in Maryland and Virginia. Asked by the registrar who had married them, some did not know or could not remember. Others named a minister, a priest, or, more regularly, a master. Most important, 421, nearly half, responded, "no marriage ceremony," suggesting clearly that slaves could live together as husband and wife in a stable (though hardly secure and ideal) relationship without formal religious or secular rituals (Gutman, 1983:470).

Gutman found that the two-parent household prevailed after slavery. Female-headed households were common but not typical. Between 1855 and 1860, variation was found in different Northern and Southern communities, but everywhere a consistent pattern emerged: "Depending upon the particular setting, not fewer than 70 percent and as many as 90 percent of the households contained a husband and wife or just a father" (Gutman, 1983:468). Other scholars, using manuscript census data, have provided additional evidence of two-parent households. Studying late-nineteenth-century Boston, Elizabeth Pleck (1973) discovered that the most typical African American household included the husband and wife, or husband, wife, and children. "The predominant household form prevailed among all occupational levels and among families of both urban and rural origins" (Pleck, 1973:153). Although there is variation in the proportion of two-parent families among Blacks from place to place and time to time, at no place or time before 1950 does the proportion of two-parent households fall below 65 percent. In fact, most of the studies show no more than 20 to 25 percent of free Black households being headed by a single parent. This is generally true whether the place is the rural or urban South or the urban North (Degler, 1980:128).

Chicano Families in the Southwest

Families of Mexican descent have been incorporated into the United States both by conquest and by migration. In 1848, at the end of the Mexican War, the United States acquired a large section of Mexico, which is now the southwestern United States. With the signing of the Treaty of Guadalupe Hidalgo, as many as 80,000 to 100,000 Mexicans living in that region became residents of U.S. territory. The American takeover disrupted traditional family life through land displacement of the indigenous people, new laws, and new labor systems.

The military conquest was accompanied by the beginnings of industrial development and by the growth of agriculture, ranching, railroads, and mining in the region. Rapid economic growth in that region resulted in a labor shortage. U.S. businesses recruited Mexican workers to migrate north for work at low wages in railroad construction and agriculture (Portes and Rumbaut, 1990).

Prior to the American takeover and the beginnings of industrial development, Mexicanos, whether natives of northern Mexico or immigrants from southern Mexico, were people of Mexican heritage, largely peasants, whose lives had been defined by a feudal economy and daily struggle on the land for economic survival. This pastoral life was disrupted. With the coming of the railroads and the damming of rivers for irrigation, the Southwest became an area of economic growth, but the advantages accrued mainly to Anglos. Mexicans no longer owned the land; now they were the source of cheap labor, an exploited group at the bottom of the social and economic ladder.

Family Life amidst Coercive Labor Systems

Mexican immigration to the United States increased substantially in the early twentieth century, although immigration from Mexico had been growing since the late 1880s. But Mexican workers who migrated north for work in the late nineteenth century and later in the first half of the twentieth century often did not settle down permanently:

> The prevailing "ebb and flow" or "revolving door" pattern of labor migration was calibrated by seasonal labor demands, economic recessions, and mass deportations. Although some employers encouraged the immigration of Mexican women and entire families in order to stabilize and expand the available, exploitable work force, many other employers, assisted at times by government-sponsored "bracero programs," recruited only men for an elastic, temporary labor supply, a reserve army of labor that could be discarded when redundant. Employers did not absolutely command the movement of Mexican workers, but employers' needs constructed a particular structure of opportunities that shaped migration (Hondagneu-Sotelo, 1995:177).

Migratory labor made families highly susceptible to disruption. Historian Richard Griswold del Castillo (1984) provides a powerful historical example of family arrangements among Mexican Americans in southwestern cities during the latter half of the nineteenth century, concluding that a large proportion of households (38 percent) were female headed, even though extended, two-parent families remained the "ideal type." Although migratory labor systems clearly restricted family life, Mexican families were flexible, pluralistic, and adaptive in surviving the rigors of economic marginality and frontier life. Disruptions and reformulations in family structure were commonplace, but family networks were durable (Griswold del Castillo, 1984; Vega, 1995:5).

Cities in the American Southwest served as focal points for reconstituting the Mexican family constellations and the construction of new families north of the border. Extended family networks were crucial in dealing with migration and in reinforcing Mexican customs and values (Sanchez, 1990:252).

Mexican familism (a strong orientation and obligation to the family) took several forms and served many purposes. The family consisted of a network of relatives, including grandparents, aunts, uncles, married sisters and brothers and their children, and also *compadres* (co-parents) and *padrinos* (godparents) with whom Chicanos actively maintained bonds (Ramirez and Arce, 1981:9). The *compadrazgo* system of godparents established connections between families and in this way enlarged family ties. "Godparents were required for the celebration of major religious occasions in a person's life: baptism, confirmation, first communion, and marriage." At these times godparents "entered into special religious, social, and economic relationships with the godchild as well as with the parents of the child." They acted as co-parents, "providing discipline and emotional and financial support when needed." As *compadres* they were expected to become the closest friend of the parents and members of the extended family (Griswold del Castillo, 1984:40–44).

Work and Gender

Chicano family roles in the early nineteenth century were strongly gendered. As economic hardship forced women and children into the paid labor force, the old pattern of women doing domestic work and men doing productive work began to break down. Historian Albert Camarillo has described how traditional patterns of employment and family responsibilities were altered in Santa Barbara, California:

> The most dramatic change was the entrance of the Chicana and her children as important wage earners who contributed to the family's economic survival. As male heads of household faced persistent unemployment, their migrations to secure seasonal work in the other areas of the country or region became more frequent. In these instances the Chicana assumed the triple responsibilities of head of household, mother, and wage earner. No longer able to subsist solely on the income of the husband, the Chicana and her children were forced to enter the unskilled labor market of Anglo Santa Barbara. The work they performed involved domestic services and agriculture-related employment (Camarillo, 1979:91).

Entire families entered the pattern of seasonal and migratory field work. Initially, Chicanas and their children were employed as almond pickers and shellers and as harvesters of olives. During the almond and olive harvests, men were usually engaged in seasonal migratory work. There were seasons, however, especially in the early summer, when the entire family migrated from the city to pick fruit. Chicano family labor had become essential for the profits of growers. Families would often leave their homes in Santa Barbara for several weeks, camping out in the fields where they worked (Camarillo, 1979:93). Women confronted severe hardships in raising their families. In the *barrios,* women's reproductive labor was intensified by the congested and unsanitary conditions. In El Paso, for example,

> Mexican women had to haul water for washing and cooking from the river or public water pipes. To feed their families, they had to spend time marketing, often in Ciudad Juarez across the border, as well as long, hot hours, cooking meals and coping with the burden of desert sand both inside and outside their homes. Besides the problem of raising children, unsanitary living conditions forced Mexican mothers to deal with disease and illness in their families (Garcia, 1980:320–321).

Although women did productive labor, family life was still gendered. As both daughters and wives, Mexican women were instructed to be obedient and submissive to their parents and husbands. Domesticity and motherhood were primary virtues. Whether they labored outside the home or not, they were subject to a sexual division of labor, in which their primary task was to care for their husbands and children. Like other women of color in nineteenth-century America, they were engaged in productive as well as reproductive labor. The wage labor of Mexican-heritage women contributed greatly to family adjustment in a colonized setting (Garcia, 1980). Despite all of these hardships, Chicanos maintained viable families with strong cultural traditions. The Chicano family has acted as a fortress against social displacement by the larger society. Chicanas in particular are described as the "glue that keep the family together." They have been responsible for the maintenance of Mexican traditions (Sanchez, 1990:251), including birthday celebrations, saints' days, baptisms, weddings, and funerals. Through the family, Mexican culture was nurtured.

CHAPTER REVIEW

1. Families are socially constructed in particular political and economic settings.
2. Historical changes did not affect all families in a uniform manner. Industrialization produced and required diverse family forms.
3. Throughout U.S. history, race, class, and gender have been important social divisions that made families different.
4. Social production and social reproduction are two distinctive forms of work for the family. Industrialization separated them and drove middle-class women into a cult of domesticity.
5. For most families, the private/public division was only an ideal. Working-class women and women of color did not experience a private life nor a protected sphere of domesticity, because their work outside the home was an extension of their domestic responsibilities. To maintain even minimal levels of family subsistence, most families sent women and children into the workforce.
6. In the 1800s and through the turn of the century, family systems were indispensable in the settlement and adjustment of the European immigrants. Families played a dual role in the massive social transformations of the period: (1) they provided a sta-

ble home environment with strong traditions; and (2) they played a major role in labor recruitment and the placement of workers in the factories.

7. European immigrants were integrated into the developing industrial society through wage labor, whereas people of color were historically incorporated into the nation through coercive labor systems. Labor defined the place of people of color, but few supports were made available for sustaining family life.
8. Slavery assaulted and broke up African American families, but it did not destroy the strong kinship system. Instead, slaves drew on both their African heritage and their experiences in this society to re-create a complex, kin-based family organization.
9. Families of Mexican descent were incorporated into the United States by both conquest and migration. Family life was greatly altered by economic development in the Southwest. Despite longstanding family fluidity, Mexicans in the United States retained many features of their traditional culture.
10. New research shows that people can create meaningful and workable families even under adverse conditions.

RELATED WEB SITES

http://www.family-tree-research.com/
Discover the easy way to create a family tree. Locate missing links in your family tree. Find

the true and hidden meaning of your surname. Create a family web site and have it hosted free.

http://www.umn.edu/ihrc/profiles.htm

Immigration History and Research Center: The IHRC locates, collects, preserves, and makes available for research the records of 24 ethnic groups that originated in eastern, central and southern Europe and the Near East. In addition, the IHRC's General Collection documents the response to immigration by organizations and individuals who provided services, worked for government policy reform, and educated Americans about immigrant needs and problems.

http://www.ins.usdoj.gov/graphics/aboutins/
history/tools.html

The Immigration and Naturalization Service (INS) provides several historical research tools to help individuals search their family records. In addition, these tools provide a wealth of information for scholarly researchers. INS history is the history of US immigration since the 1890's. Agency records at the National Archives, many of them long ignored and forgotten, constitute a rich resource for social, ethnic, labor, intellectual, and legal historians, as well as all students of US immigration policy.

http://www.usgenweb.com/

The USGenWeb Project consists of a group of volunteers working together to provide Internet websites for genealogical research in every county and every state of the United States. The Project is noncommercial and fully committed to free access for everyone. The USGen-Web Digital Library (Archives) offers actual

transcriptions of public domain records. You will find copies of census records, marriage bonds, wills, and other public documents.

http://www.ins.usdoj.gov/graphics/aboutins/
history/chinese.html

Chinese Immigrant Files: This INS website gives visitors access to information regarding Chinese immigration into the U.S., as well as access to public records. Responsibility for enforcement of US Chinese Exclusion law transferred to the Immigration and Naturalization Service in 1903, and continued until repeal of the Chinese Exclusion Act in 1943. The old Chinese Service transferred into INS along with its records, which INS maintained as a separate set until 1908. Those files on Chinese matters kept separate from general immigration files at Washington, D.C., until 1908 are referred to as Segregated Chinese Files, and are today found at the National Archives in Washington, D.C. INS continued to file records of Chinese in separate file series at major ports of entry and district offices, and those files are today found at Regional Archives across the country.

http://www.siris.si.edu/

Smithsonian Institution Research Information Services: The Smithsonian Institution Research Information System (SIRIS) is the online catalog of resources held by the Institution's libraries, archives, and other specialized research centers.

Economic and Demographic Upheaval in Society and Family Formation

Myths and Realities

Myth: Families are the building blocks of society.

Reality: Families are shaped by specific historical, social, and economic conditions. That is, structural conditions shape families more than families shape societies.

Myth: The dominant family form—intact nuclear household with male breadwinner, full-time homemaker wife, and their dependent children—has persisted over the past fifty years or so.

Reality: "The [institution of] the family has changed more in the last 10 years than any other social institution" (Bianchi and Spain, 1996:5). "Today, many family forms are common: single-parent families (resulting either from unmarried parenthood or divorce), remarried couples, unmarried couples, stepfamilies, foster families, extended or multigenerational families, and the doubling up of two families within the same home. Women are just as likely to be full- or part-time workers as full-time homemakers" (Ahlburg and De Vita, 1992:2).

Myth: Deindustrialization has affected families uniformly across the social classes.

Reality: Deindustrialization has most profoundly reshaped working-class and middle-class families. The poor have always had to adjust to and cope with economic hardship.

Myth: Latino immigrants are a homogeneous group, as are Asian immigrants.

Reality: Within each category there is a wide variation by country of origin in economic resources, educational attainment, poverty rate, and modal type of family.

Myth: The study of culturally diverse families is the study of "others" (i.e., people in families that are different from the mainstream).

Reality: There is no dominant family form against which families are measured and judged. Alternative family forms do not reflect deviance, deficiency, or disorganization. They reflect, rather, adaptations to specific structural conditions.

Myth: The cultural norms emphasizing patriarchal men and submissive women are found uniformly in Latino and Asian American families.

Reality: The degree to which patrarchy is found in Latino and Asian American families depends on structural factors. It is affected by family arrangements induced by the migration process and/or the economic resources of women.

Myth: With a relatively low fertility rate, the proportion of old people in the U.S. population remains relatively stable.

Reality: A low fertility rate translates into a smaller proportion of children in the population. With the elderly living longer and relatively fewer children, the proportion of the elderly population will increase.

*F*amilies are not isolated units free from outside constraints. On the contrary, individuals bring to their family relationships perspectives, needs, and problems, gained from their nonfamily roles and experiences. Their activities in organizations and social networks outside the family—at work, at school, at church, in voluntary associations, and at play—have profound influences on what occurs in families. More fundamentally, families are embedded in a society in which governmental laws and policies, economic forces, population dynamics, institutional racism and sexism, and prevailing ideologies have both direct and indirect effects.

The previous two chapters demonstrated the ways in which social factors have transformed family life historically in the United States. This chapter focuses on the way the structure of contemporary society shapes families and the individuals within them. We examine three societal "earthquakes" and their effects on families: the structural transformation of the economy, the new immigration, and the aging of society. The present generation is in the midst of social changes that are more far-reaching and are occurring faster than at any other time in human history. The purpose of this chapter is to understand these three macro social forces and how they affect social life, especially families. We will examine these three societal upheavals and how each of them has extraordinary consequences for individuals, families, communities, and for the institutions of society.

THE STRUCTURAL TRANSFORMATION OF THE ECONOMY AND FAMILIES

The Industrial Revolution, which began in Great Britain in the 1780s, was a major turning point in human history. With the application of steam power and, later, oil and electricity as energy sources for industry, mining, manufacturing, and transportation, came fundamental changes to the economy, the relationship of people and work, family organization, and the like. In effect, societies are transformed with each surge in invention and technological growth. Peter F. Drucker describes the historical import of such transformations:

The transformation from manufacturing to service occupations in the U.S. changed the nature of work. These women are working as telephone operators.

Every few hundred years in Western history there occurs a sharp transformation. We cross . . . a "divide." Within a few short decades, society rearranges itself—its worldview; its basic values; its social and political structure; its arts; its key institutions. Fifty years later, there is a new world. And the people born then cannot even imagine the world in which their grandparents lived and into which their own parents were born. We are currently living through just such a transformation (Drucker, 1993:1).

For example, the shift from private capitalism to industrial capitalism had profound effects on families (Zaretsky, 1976). In the early stage of capitalism, nuclear families were the unit of production. Each family was a self-contained economic enterprise, with parents, children, and employees working together to produce a product. Although the family was organized hierarchically and strictly disciplined, marriage was understood to be an economic partnership based on common love and labor. With the rise of industrial capitalism, however, the production of goods was removed from the home and shops to factories. The work of men and women was separated, with men working away from home in a highly coordinated, strictly disciplined, bureaucratic, and impersonal environment. "Industrial capitalism required a rationalized, coordinated and synchronized labor process undisturbed by community sentiment, family responsibilities, personal relations or feelings" (Zaretsky, 1976:47–48). Working in such settings, men looked to their families as havens—as places of shelter, caring, and emotional attachment. Women, freed from working in the family enterprise, were expected to devote their full attention to the nurturing of family members. Zaretsky's thesis is that the changing conditions of capitalism affected families dramatically. In effect, the particular form of the family found in society is socially determined, because it arises out of definite social conditions.

The United States is now in the midst of a new transformation, one fueled by new technologies and applications (e.g., superfast computers; the Internet as a distributor of information, goods, and services; fiber optics; biotechnology; the decoding of the human genome; and cell telephony). These amazing scientific breakthroughs have had and will continue to have immense implications for commerce, international trade, global politics, and at the individual level employment opportunities, pay and benefits, and family formation. In Drucker's words:

> The next two or three decades are likely to see even greater technological change than has occurred in the decades since the emergence of the computer, and also even greater change in industry structures, in the economic landscape, and probably in the social landscape as well (Drucker, 1999:54).

The Interrelated Forces Transforming the United States

Several powerful forces converging in the United States are transforming its economy, redesigning and redistributing jobs, exacerbating inequality, reorganizing cities and regions, and profoundly affecting families and individuals. These forces are (1) technological breakthroughs in microelectronics, (2) the globalization of the economy, (3) capital flight, and (4) the shift from an economy based on the manufacture of goods to one based on information and services.

New Technologies Based on Microelectronics

The computer chip is the technology that is transforming the United States into a service/information economy. Microbased systems of information allow for the storage, manipulation, and retrieval of data with speed and accuracy unknown just a few years ago. Information can be sent in microseconds via communications satellites throughout the world. Parallel processing with supercomputers gives machines the ability to reason and make judgments.

Globalization of the Economy

Because of the size of the domestic market, the relative insulating effects of the Pacific and Atlantic Oceans, and superior technological expertise, the U.S. economy throughout most of the twentieth century was relatively free from competitive pressures from abroad. This changed dramatically around 1970. The United States, once the world's industrial giant, now employs fewer workers in manufacturing than at any time since 1850 (Coy, 2000). Many of the goods now used in the United States are produced in low-wage societies.

The shift to a global economy has been accelerated by the tearing down of tariff barriers. The North American Free Trade Agreement (NAFTA) and the General Agreement on Tariffs and Trade (GATT), both passed in 1994, are two examples of agreements that increased the flow of goods across national boundaries.

Capital Flight

Private businesses in their search for profit make crucial investment decisions. The term **capital flight** refers to the investment choices that involve the movement of corporate monies from one investment to another. This movement takes several forms: (1) investment overseas, (2) plant relocation within the United States, and (3) mergers. Although these investment decisions may be positive for the recipients of the move, they also take investment away (disinvestment) from others (workers and their families, communities, and suppliers).

Overseas Investment by U.S. Firms Multinational corporations based in the United States have invested heavily in foreign countries. Corporate capital is invested overseas because manufacturing there is profitable, mainly because of cheap and nonunionized labor, and the relative lack of the kind of regulations (e.g. controlling pollution and promoting worker safety) found in the United States.

Relocation of Businesses Corporate administrators may decide to move their business to another locality. Such decisions involve what is called plant migration or, more pejoratively, "runaway shops." The decision may be to move the plant to Mexico, to the Caribbean, to Central America, or to the Far East, where many U.S. plants involved in textiles, electronics assembly, and other labor-intensive industries are located.

U.S. corporations are also moving some of their operations to other English-speaking countries (such as Ireland, Barbados, Jamaica, India, the Philippines, and Singapore), where cheap labor performs such tasks as data entry for accounting, medical transcription, making airline and hotel reservations, and telemarketing. For example, in 2000, Caltrex Petroleum Corporation moved its headquarters from Dallas to Singapore, shifted its website development to South Africa, and set up its accounting division in Manila (Clifford and Kripalani, 2000).

Capital is also moved within the United States as corporations shut down operations in one locality and start up elsewhere. Profit is the motivation for investment in a new place and disinvestment in another. Corporations move their plants into communities and regions where wages are lower, unions are weaker or nonexistent, and the business climate is more receptive (i.e., it has lower taxes, fewer environmental restrictions, and gives greater government subsidies to the business community).

Regardless of whether plants are moved within the United States or to foreign countries, there are consequences for individuals and communities. Plant closures are devastating. Workers in the affected plants are suddenly unemployed, and so, too, may be many others in the affected communities whose jobs were tied directly or indirectly to that plant (such as transportation, supplies, and services). Real estate, banking, schools, and other areas are also adversely affected. The local governments can no longer provide the same level of services because the tax base has shrunk. The recipient "boom" communities in the United States benefit from the increase in jobs, greater tax revenues, and the image of growth and progress. However, they often cannot meet the greater demand for new roads, sewage treatment, schools, hospitals, recreation facilities, and housing that the new plants create.

Mergers and Takeovers Another type of capital flight occurs when corporations use their capital and increase their debt to purchase companies in related or unrelated enterprises rather than to expand and modernize their plants. In 1999 mergers amounted to $3.48 trillion (Valdmanis, 2000).

This trend toward mergers has at least three negative consequences: (1) it increases the centralization of capital, which reduces competition and raises prices for consumers; (2) as corporations become fewer and larger, they have increased power over workers, unions, and governments; and (3) mergers reduce the number of jobs. As an example of the last point, after Qwest merged with U S West in 2000, the new entity cut 11,000 jobs and 1,800 contractor positions. Along with the downsizing of jobs, Qwest announced that former U S West employees would now contribute to their medical, vision, and dental health plans rather than receive those benefits free as they had previously.

From Manufacturing to Knowledge-Based Corporations

In a special issue devoted to the twenty-first-century corporation, *Business Week* noted the profound transformation of corporations occurring now:

> For nearly all of its life, the modern corporation has made money by making things. It has done so by amassing fixed assets, organizing large workforces, and managing hierarchically. The 21st century corporation will do little of that. It will make money by producing knowledge created by talented people working with partners all over the world. So fundamental will the changes be that the corporation as we know it will likely exist only on the margins of the economy. . . . We are just in the beginning of the beginning. The 21st century is going to be hard on corporations, governments, and all the rest of us. But the changes the century will bring will be nothing short of astonishing (*Business Week*, 2000b:278).

We now have an economy based on ideas rather than physical capital. By 2006 the government estimates that manufacturing jobs will account for just 12 percent of the labor force (McGinn and McCormick, 1999). Thus, the demand for workers is shifting from physical labor to cognitive abilities. The best educated and trained will benefit with good jobs, benefits, and opportunities. The less educated will not benefit in such a climate. When workers had strong union industrialized jobs, their wages and benefits were enough for a middle-class lifestyle. Now, typically, their work provides the services that are poorly paid, and some have few if any benefits, working as clerks, cashiers, custodians, nurses' aides, security guards, waiters, retail salespersons, and telemarketers. As a result, "high school grads' median weekly earnings are 43% less than those of college grads, far worse than the 28% gap in 1979" (Coy, 2000:79).

The New Economy: What Does It Mean for Families?

The transformation of the economy brought about by new technologies, the globalization of the economy, capital flight, and deindustrialization has profoundly affected individuals, families, and communities and will continue to do so for the foreseeable future.

Families are affected when their resources are reduced, when they face economic and social marginalization, and when family members are threatened by unemployment or are actually laid off. This subsection explores these and related consequences of the economic transformation for families and family members. It focuses on the changing nature of jobs and job insecurity, income inequality, the shrinking middle class, the working poor, and the new poor. Two topics—the economic marginalization by race and women workers—fit logically here, but they are discussed at length in Chapters 5 and 6, respectively.

The Changing Nature of Jobs

Joseph Schumpeter (1950) described a process inherent to capitalism that he called "creative destruction." By this he meant that as the economic structure of capitalism mutates, some sectors will lose out while others gain. The shift away from manufacturing to services and information/knowledge, for example, means that some sectors of the economy will fade in importance or even die out completely. These sectors (e.g., steel, tires, shoes, and the various defense industries) are known as **sunset industries.** Over 1500 plants in these industries have closed permanently since 1975. The jobs lost in these industries tended to be unionized, with good pay and benefits.

Many blue-collar jobs have also been lost because of automation. Robots have replaced humans doing routine work such as picking fruit, shearing sheep, as well as welding, painting, and scanning products for defects. Similarly, many white-collar jobs are being lost because of new technologies. The Internet, for example, allows people to make their own travel arrangements (reducing or eliminating the need for travel agents) or to buy and sell stocks (making stock brokers unnecessary). Also, software helps people do their tax returns without the assistance of a tax specialist. Within firms computer programs take care of payrolls, control inventory, and delivery schedules, reducing the need for accountants. Primarily because of voice mail, laser printers, and word processors, hundreds of thousands of secretarial and clerical jobs have been eliminated. To emphasize the force of "creative destruction" on jobs, Tom Peters, the esteemed expert on work, has estimated that 90 percent of white-collar jobs in the United States will be either destroyed or altered significantly in the next ten to fifteen years (Peters, 2000).

However, whereas some jobs have shrunk by the millions, many millions more have been created. Many of these new jobs are in the **sunrise industries,** which are characterized by increased output and employment. Such jobs are involved in the production of high-tech products (computers, software, communications equipment, medical instruments, fiber optics, bioengineering, and robotics). Also, lower-end service jobs such as sales clerks, janitorial, and security guards are plentiful.

Job Insecurity

Despite a booming economy in the 1990s and the lowest unemployment rate in the past thirty years, about one-third of the nation's 140 million workforce fear losing their jobs (Leonhardt, 2000). African American workers are more economically insecure than White workers. On average, they make about three-fourths what White workers make, and their rate of joblessness is twice that of Whites. Not only do women make less money than men (72 cents for every dollar a man made in 1999), women in the labor force clearly are less economically secure than men. Women are easy targets when downsizing occurs, because they tend to have less seniority. And almost six out of ten minimum-wage workers are women, employed where benefits are virtually nonexistent.

Another category of the economically insecure are contingent workers. About 30 million American workers work in temporary, contracted, self-employed, leased, part-time, and other "nonstandard" arrangements (Economic Policy Institute data, reported in Cook, 2000). These workers lack an explicit contract for ongoing employment and thus receive sporadic wages. They earn about 16 percent less than their counterparts who do the same work, and only 5 percent have employer-provided health coverage (Jorgensen and Riemer, 2000).

Income Inequality

The gap between the wealthiest and the poorest families is at its widest point since the Census Bureau began collecting these data several decades ago. It is also the widest of any advanced industrial society. In effect, the top 10 percent of the population have been the big winners over the last twenty-five years while the bottom 10 percent have been the losers. Those in the middle have also fallen in their share of the total wealth and earnings in the United States (Collins et al., 1999). A few illustrations show the magnitude of the inequality gap:

- The top 1 percent of families (the richest 2.7 million Americans) have as many after-tax dollars to spend as the bottom 100 million put together (Reich, 2000a).
- In 1998, 34 million people were below the poverty line ($16,600 for a family of four). The average income deficit for poor families (the average dollar amount needed to raise a poor family out of poverty) was $6620 (U.S. Bureau of the Census, 1999b:v).
- 26.8 percent of workers earned poverty-level wages in 1999 (Lee, 2000).
- Chief executive officers in 1998 made 419 times the pay of average workers, up from 42 times the pay of average workers in 1980 (Sklar, 1999).

The Shrinking Middle Class

The "American dream," in effect a middle-class dream, is that one's family will own a home, own at least one late-model car, and be able to provide college education for the children. Through the 1950s and 1960s, this dream was realized by increasingly more Americans as average real wages (i.e., wages adjusted for inflation) and family incomes expanded and the economy created new jobs and opportunities. The result was that many Americans after World War II were able to move up into a growing and vibrant middle class. This trend peaked in 1973, and since then families have tended either to stagnate or decline in their level of affluence. Comparing 1977 with 1997, for instance, the highest fifth of households increased their share of aggregate income, while the lower 80 percent declined (U.S. Bureau of the Census data, reported in Hurst, 2001:26).

The Increasing Cost of a New Car   For the past twenty years the price of new cars in the United States has risen faster than inflation. As a result, while the average family spent a third of its income to buy an average-priced car two decades ago, it now must spend more than half of its annual income for a new car.

The Increasing Cost of Housing Living standards have also been reduced by the rising cost of home ownership, making this pillar of the "American dream" less and less attainable. In Denver, Colorado, for example, the average price of a previously owned home in August 2000 was $250,787, up from $150,000 just five years earlier. In Denver, while the Consumer Price Index (an indicator of the inflation rate) for the Denver metropolitan area increased 3.8 percent from 1999 to 2000, the cost of housing increased 19.3 percent, resulting in an affordability index of 0.89 (that is, an 11 percent income-to-housing gap—a score of 1.0 means median-income households can afford a median-priced house) (Rebchook, 2000). Those hit hardest are the working poor, young families, and households with just a single income. To achieve the increasingly costly goal of home ownership, many husbands and wives choose to work in the labor force. Thus, the high cost of housing, combined with other factors (see Chapters 8 and 9), result in couples having less time together, delaying children, having fewer children, and children spending more time in day care.

These national data mask two factors that make home ownership especially difficult for some people. First, the cost of housing varies by locality. Cities with desirable climates (e.g., San Francisco and San Diego) have very high housing costs. Cities pumped up with the influx of high-tech companies and high-wage employees (e.g., San Jose, California, and Austin, Texas) have home prices rising at more than twice the inflation rate (Lardner, 2000). In 1999, for example, a family earning a median income could afford only 15 percent of the houses sold in San Francisco and 31 percent of the houses in San Jose, California (El Nasser, 2000).

The national average for the cost of home ownership also hides the difficulty that racial minorities have in obtaining this part of the American dream. While slightly less than half of White families can afford a median-priced house with a conventional, thirty-year, fixed-rate mortgage, about three-fourths of African American and Latino families cannot (Belluck, 1997).

As home ownership has become more problematic, so, too, has the cost of renting, which has outpaced the inflation rate. This inflation in rental housing has been especially difficult for the poor.

> [Jose and Lily Valles have two children. They live in Los Angeles, and each works at a minimum wage job.] "I make $5.75 an hour. That's about $240 a week. One hundred ninety dollars after taxes. You can't really live on that. Lily works in a fast-food place, too. She makes the same as me. Two weeks of my pay and two weeks of her pay every month goes for rent. Then you have to pay the fare to go back and forth to work. You gotta pay for your food. You have bills. We're still paying on the sofa" (quoted in Herbert, 2000b).

According to a U.S. Department of Housing and Urban Development study, no minimum-wage worker can afford the rent for a modest two-bedroom apartment in any county in the United States (reported in McCaffrey, 2000).

The Increased Cost of a College Education The cost of higher education has also made this middle-class goal less and less attainable. Throughout the 1980s and early 1990s, the cost of college rose at a rate more than twice the inflation rate. The result is that the children of the affluent continue to have access to this important societal "gatekeeper," but the access for more and more youth is blocked, especially youth from the racial and social-class margins.

This trend has another implication. Middle-class children, who a generation ago could afford a private education, another form of privilege, now must attend public colleges and universities and community colleges (in 1999–2000, on average, the total expenses to attend a private school as a resident were $23,651, compared to $10,909 for a public school) (Reisberg, 1999). The cost of room, board, fees, and tuition at the nation's most exclusive schools is about $35,000 for a single school year.

> In what is increasingly a winner-take-all society, attendance at a prestigious college is widely viewed as a key springboard to success, so families of kids who are admitted to Yale or Stanford or a similar school feel enormous pressure to come up with the cash. To do otherwise would be to deprive the child of the opportunity of a lifetime, or so it seems. (Crenshaw, 2000:35).

Meanwhile, the children from relatively low-income families are finding financial aid less and less available. Thus, a college education—the major mechanism for achieving upward mobility, or at least for maintaining middle-class stability—has come to be increasingly out of reach for children of the middle and lower classes.

To summarize, shrinking incomes and higher costs have caused many families to slide downward from the middle class. Other families, through both spouses working outside the home, multiple jobs, increased overtime, or increased debts, have retained a middle-class lifestyle.

Coping Strategies

The lowering of living standards for many Americans is actually more severe than the facts appear to indicate. The reduced income, plus higher housing costs and the higher costs of college, result in several coping strategies: dual incomes, working more hours, home-based work, and increased debt.

Dual-Earner Families Making a living has become a family enterprise, since most families now require two incomes to get by, when two decades or so ago one income was usually sufficient to maintain a middle-class lifestyle. For example, in 1998, six out of ten women age sixteen and over were in the labor force, while more than two-thirds of single women with children under six and 64 percent of married women with children that age were working outside the home (see Table 4.1).

This shift toward dual-income families is important in at least four ways. First, there is the perceived *necessity* of two incomes to maintain an adequate lifestyle, which limits the choice for those women or men who would rather stay at home to raise their children (see Box 4.1). Second, women's work tends to be

TABLE 4.1

Women Age 16 and over in the Labor Force,
1970–1998 (percent)

	1970	1980	1990	1998
Total	**43.3**	**51.5**	**57.5**	**59.8**
Race				
White	42.6	51.2	57.4	59.4
African American	49.5	53.1	58.3	62.8
Latino	—	47.4	53.1	55.6
Age				
16 to 19	44.0	52.9	51.6	52.3
20–24	57.5	68.9	71.3	73.0
25–34	45.0	65.5	73.5	76.3
35–44	51.1	65.5	76.4	77.1
45–54	54.4	59.9	71.2	76.2
55–64	43.0	41.3	45.2	51.2
65 and over	9.7	8.1	8.6	8.6
Marital status				
Single	56.8	64.4	66.7	68.5
Married	40.5	45.8	58.4	61.2
Marital status with children under 6				
Single	—	44.1	48.7	67.3
Married	30.3	45.1	58.9	63.7
Marital status with children 6 to 17 only				
Single	—	67.6	69.7	81.2
Married	49.2	61.7	73.6	76.8

Source: U.S. Bureau of the Census, *Statistical Abstract of the United States: 1999,* 119th ed. Washington, DC: U.S. Government Printing Office, Tables 650, 652, 658, 659.

poorly paid (making about 74 cents for every dollar a man makes). When long-time women workers are downsized, they are less likely than men to be reemployed, and if reemployed, they are more likely to work at part-time jobs than men. Women workers are, for the most part, second-class citizens in the occupational world, and this form of patriarchy has implications for marriage dynamics, as we shall see in Chapter 8. Third, although dual-earner families bring in more family income, the amount left after expenses is lowered considerably by the additional costs for such items as transportation, clothing, and child care. Fourth, two-worker families have less time for each other and with their children.

Increased Workload Americans work more hours per week than in any other country in the advanced industrial world. Some 8 million people held down more than one job in 1997, more than double the number of multiple-job holders

BOX 4.1   Families in Global Perspective: Changes in Capitalism Render One-Earner Families Extinct

The traditional family is disappearing almost everywhere.

Worldwide from 1960 to 1992, births among unmarried mothers doubled for those 20 to 24 years of age and quadrupled for those 15 to 19 years of age. The United States is far from being the world's leader in this category, ranking sixth. Divorce rates are rising in the developed and underdeveloped world, doubling in Beijing in just four years. Female-headed households or households where females provide 50% or more of total income are becoming the norm.

The reasons are straightforward. The current economic system is no longer congruent with traditional nuclear family values, just as the Industrial Revolution two centuries earlier was not congruent with the then-traditional extended family values.

In America, 32% of all men 25 years to 34 years of age earn less than the amount necessary to keep a family of four above the poverty line. While male wages are falling at the bottom, the costs of supporting a family are rising. Children need ever more expensive educations for ever longer periods of time if they are to make it in today's global economy. Economically many men, perhaps a majority, are being told that they should not plan to have a family since there is no probability that they will be able to support a family.

Women are under enormous pressures because the economy gives them one message (go to work and make the money the family needs to survive) and old cultural mores give them another message (stay at home and take care of the children). They feel stressed because they are stressed.

Today, family members support the family less because it is now much less necessary to their own successful economic survival. Men end up having strong economic incentive to bail out of family relations and responsibilities because they raise their own standards of living when they do so. Whether it is by fathering a family without being willing to be a father, by divorcing and being unwilling to pay alimony or child support, or by being a guest worker from the Third World and after a short time failing to send payments to the family back home, men are opting out. Among families with dependent children, 25% don't have a male present.

Women get welfare only if no man is present in the home. Children's economic standards of living are often higher as wards of the state in foster care than they would be if they stayed in their disintegrating families.

Values follow economic realities. Individual fulfilment now ranks higher than family in public opinion polls. "Competitive individualism" grows at the expense of "family solidarity." The ideal is "choice," not "bonds." In the language of capitalism, children have ceased to be "profit centers" and have become "cost centers."

The response quite naturally is to form fewer families and to have smaller numbers of children. When children do exist, parents spend less time with them—40% less than they did 30 years ago. With mothers at work, more than 2 million children under the age of 13 are left completely without adult supervision, both before and after school. Effectively, no one ends up taking care of the children, but they have to be left alone because paying for day care would use up most of mother's wages and negate the whole purpose of going to work in the first place.

(continued)

(continued from previous page)

Historically, the single parent has been the norm in no society, but patriarchal linear life is economically now over. Family values are under attack, not by government programs that discourage family formation (although there are some) and not by media presentations that disparage families (although there are some), but by the economic system itself. It simply won't allow families to exist in the old-fashioned way, with a father who generates most of the earnings and a mother who does most of the nurturing. The one-earner, middle-class family is extinct.

Social arrangements are not determined just by economics—there are many possibilities at any point in time—but whatever the arrangements, they nave to be consistent with economic realities. Changes within capitalism are making the traditional family less and less compatible with the market.

As a consequence, the family is an institution both in flux and under pressure. Basic questions about how the family should be organized have been put in play by economic reality.

Source: Lester C. Thurow, "Changes in Capitalism Render One-Earner Families Extinct," *USA Today,* January 27, 1997, p. 17A.

in 1965 (Barten, 1999). Between 1977 and 1997 the average work week increased from 43 to 47 hours, with 37 percent of workers putting in 50 or more hours a week (Zuckerman, 2000). *The State of Working America,* a study sponsored by the Economic Policy Institute (Mishel et al., 2000), reports that from 1989 to 1998 the average number of work hours by all middle-income family members increased by 246 hours, to 3885 (about six extra full-time weeks a year). Middle-income Latino families worked 4050 hours, and African American middle-income families worked 4278 hours per year, almost 500 hours per year more than White families. In effect, then, an average middle-income African American family needed over 12 more weeks of work than the average White family in order to reach the middle-income ranks.

The result of this increased workload, of course, is decreased leisure and decreased family time. The toll is especially hard on parents with young children.

> Families with children have had to work harder and harder over the past few decades to maintain a decent standard of living, and that phenomenon continues. The number of earners per family has increased, as have the average number of weeks worked per year, and the number of hours worked per week. That doesn't leave a lot of quality time for families to enjoy the benefits of their added income. As a woman in New Jersey recently said: "We're a working family all right. That's all we do is work" (Herbert, 2000:1–2).

Home-Based Work The structural transformation of the economy has changed the patterns of work in profound ways. The redistribution of jobs has displaced many workers and has placed many millions, as we have seen, in low-wage service jobs, often without traditional benefits. Included in this last category is the new emphasis on contingent work arrangements, such as part-time work, temporary work, and home-based work, all of which are jobs held disproportionately by women (about three-fourths). We focus here on women.

Home-based work includes word processing, typing, editing, accounting, telemarketing, sewing, laundry, and child care. Women often opt for home-based work because the flexibility permits them to combine work and family obligations. Others choose it because of the autonomy—working on their own, at their own pace, and on their own schedule. Others have no option; they need the money, and some form of home-based work is all that is available. Employers contract women to do home-based work because money is saved—the employers pay only for work delivered, they avoid unions, and they do not pay benefits such as health insurance, paid leaves, and pensions.

The consequences of home-based work are mixed. On the positive side, home-based work allows flexibility and independence not found in most jobs. This type of work allows women to supplement their incomes and maintain skill levels without working full-time. It permits women to stay in the workforce at times when they cannot or will not work full-time outside the home. For some, especially single parents on the economic margin, home-based work is the only way they can earn an income and provide for child care. The dark side of this is that the pay is typically low, and benefits such as health care are minimal or nonexistent. Most important, the strains engendered from combining the work and parent roles may be excessive and overwhelming. Home-based workers are often frustrated because they cannot work for long uninterrupted periods. An office environment is designed to maximize work, but a home is not. Children, spouses, neighbors, the telephone, household tasks, and other home distractions hinder productivity—and pay. "Working at home eliminates the boundary between work and family, so that women often find they never can leave their work" (Christensen, 1988:5). Thus, the combination of work and family in the home setting engenders a form of claustrophobia for some. This is exacerbated further by the common problem of isolation. Home-based workers usually work alone, separated from social networks. Aside from not realizing the social benefits of personal interaction with colleagues, isolation means being cut off from pooled information and the collective power that might result in higher pay, fringe benefits, and supportive legislation and legal decisions. Working alone and doing work for powerful others means that home-based workers will continue to be denied fair pay and appropriate fringe benefits that many other workers receive.

Increased Debt Either because of a wish to consume beyond their means (Schor, 1998) or because of a financial squeeze from the high cost of housing, putting children through college, losing a job, being downsized, or wages not keeping up with inflation, many households borrow money. Cumulatively, U.S. households are on a credit binge, with borrowing increasing by almost 60 percent from 1995 to 1999 to $6.5 trillion, which is a record 101 percent of household income (Zuckerman, 2000a).

The use of credit cards such as Visa and MasterCard is especially tempting to those facing economic difficulties. These cards allow their holders an initial grace period of twenty-five days before the bills are due plus the option of making a minimum payment each month. The trap is that the interest on the amount carried over is excessive (as much as 18 percent). Total credit card debt has more than quadrupled in twelve years to $569 billion in 1999 (Federal Reserve data, reported in Crenshaw, 1999). The average credit card debt per household was $7564 (the average U.S. household has 13 credit or charge cards) by the end of 1999 (Terwilliger, 2000).

Two additional facts show the extent to which Americans are in debt and the consequences. First, the average personal debt load in the United States, excluding mortgages, is about $26,000 (Judson, 1997). Second, in 1999, in the midst of the longest peacetime economic expansion in this century, 1.5 million people filed for personal bankruptcy, up from 400,000 ten years earlier (Terwilliger, 2000). Put another way, in 1999 about six out of every 1000 adults declared personal bankruptcy, almost twice the rate as ten years earlier (Mishel et al., 2000).

What Does It Mean to Move Down from the Middle Class?

The economic transformation has had dire consequences for many in the middle class. Corporate downsizing and other forms of layoffs has meant, for example, that one in five California workers was fired from a job in the past three years, affecting production workers as well as white-collar workers and managers (*Business Week*, 2000). Katherine Newman describes the experience of the downwardly mobile middle class (see Box 4.2 for the methods employed by Newman).

> They once "had it made" in American society, filling slots from affluent blue-collar jobs to professional and managerial occupations. They have job skills, education, and decades of steady work experience. Many are, or were, homeowners. Their marriages were (at least initially) intact. As a group they savored the American dream. They found a place higher up the ladder in this society and then, inexplicably, found their grip loosening and their status sliding.
>
> Some downwardly mobile middle-class families end up in poverty, but many do not. Usually they come to rest at a standard of living above the poverty level but far below the affluence they enjoyed in the past. They must therefore contend not only with financial hardship but with the psychological, social, and practical consequences of "falling from grace," of losing their "proper place" in the world (Newman, 1988:8).

Thus, individual self-esteem and family honor are bruised. Moreover, this ordeal impairs the chances of the children, as children and later as adults, to enjoy economic security and a comfortable lifestyle.

In terms of agency, many downwardly mobile families find successful coping strategies to deal with their adverse situation. Some families develop a tighter bond to meet their common problems. Others find support from families in similar situations or from their personal kin networks. But for many families downward mobility adds tensions that make family life especially difficult. Failure in the work world typically affects relations between breadwinner and spouse, sometimes stretching emotional bonds beyond the breaking point. The loss of one's home and the process of relocation terminate attachments to a neighborhood and a way of life, often causing alienation and anger, which are sometimes directed at family members. Children, so dependent on peer

<hr />

BOX 4.2   **Researching Families:** Ethnographic Field Research

Katherine Newman, a cultural anthropologist, studies the consequences of America's economic decline from the ground up. She says that

> there are many vantage points from which to approach the question of America's economic decline. Most of them, quite properly, involve the structural trends—demographic, industrial, and monetary—that constitute the intellectual terrain of economists, [sociologists], and historians. But if we are to understand what the declining position of the United States means to ordinary people in the late twentieth century—workers, consumers, suburban folk, and urban dwellers—we have to consider how the macro-trends of job markets and housing markets, unemployment and underemployment have impacted upon individual lives. For at the end of the day, it is the dashed hopes . . . that accompany this post-industrial transformation that define the daily experience of economic decline (Newman, 1994:330).

Newman seeks to understand the experience of ordinary Americans on the receiving end of impersonal economic forces. To do so she has examined two forms of downward mobility: **intragenerational downward mobility** (individuals who, in the course of their adult working lives, decline in socioeconomic status) and **intergenerational downward mobility** (individuals who, when compared to the socioeconomic status experience of their parents, do not measure up). To examine intragenerational mobility, Newman did extensive fieldwork (intensive observation, structured and unstructured interviews, and extended conversations) with both managerial/executive workers and blue-collar families affected by the high unemployment of the early 1980s (see Newman, 1988). For the study of intergenerational mobility, Newman did similar fieldwork in a suburban New Jersey community, focussing on two generations in 60 families (Newman, 1993). Collectively the data from these two studies represent a portrait of the personal, local experience of economic decline—unemployment, foreclosure, a crashing of self-doubt, and the growth of the calamitous assumption that America is no longer the country it once was (Newman, 1994:331).

approval, often find intolerable the increasing gap in material differences between themselves and their peers.

Many families who experience a slide in their standard of living attempt to camouflage their deteriorating situation with lies and cover-ups. These tactics sometimes place heavy demands on family members, and relations among them tend to grow more strained. The result is that many members of families facing downward mobility experience stress, marital tension, depression, anxiety, hypertension, high cholesterol, and high levels of alcohol consumption. Newman has suggested that these pathologies are somewhat normal, given the persistent tensions generated by downward mobility. Many families experience some degree of these pathologies and yet they somehow endure. But some families disintegrate completely under the pressure, with serious problems of physical brutality, incapacitating alcoholism, desertion, and even suicide (Newman, 1988:134–140).

The Working Poor

Two of the persistent myths about poverty are that people who work are not poor and that most poor people are poor because they do not or will not work. The facts belie the faulty assumption that poor people are lazy. Census data on the employment status of the poor show that most of them either are working or fall into those categories of people that society does not expect to work—mothers of young children, retired people, the disabled, the sick, or full-time students.

In 1999, slightly more than one in four U.S. workers earned less than $8.19 per hour, the wage required to lift out of poverty a family of four with a full-time, full-year worker. One in three women earned poverty-level wages in 1999, compared to one in five men. Poverty-level work is especially common for racial minorities. Mishel, Bernstein, and Schmitt (2000) found that in 1999, one in three African American men, two in five African American women and Latino men, and slightly more than half of Latino women were in jobs that paid poverty wages. Compounding the economic woes of the poor is that only three in ten workers whose wages place them in the bottom fifth have employer-provided health insurance (Mishel et al., 2000).

Actually, the greatest increase in the number of poor since 1979 has been among the working poor. This increase is the result of declining wages, the rise in the number of working women who head households (who must bear the cost of child care but who earn low wages), and a minimum wage that does not provide a full-time worker with two dependents with the wages to keep above the poverty line. The result is that nearly one worker in five is in the low-pay (i.e., below the poverty line) category. When race is considered, the poverty rate for White workers is the least, followed in order by African American workers and Latino workers. Almost one-fourth (23.8 percent) of Latino men, for example, are minimum-wage workers.

The New Poor

Millions of blue-collar workers have lost their jobs as obsolete plants have closed and as companies have moved overseas or to other domestic sites in search of cheaper labor, or when they were replaced by robots or other forms of automation. Many of these displaced workers find other work, but usually at lower-paying jobs. They are poorer but not poor. Many others, though, especially those who are over forty years old, find employment difficult because their skills are obsolete and they are considered too old to retrain.

These **new poor** are quite different from the **old poor.** The old poor—that is, the poor of past generations—had hopes of breaking out of poverty; if they did not break out themselves, at least they believed their children would. This hope was based on the presence of a rapidly expanding economy. There were jobs for immigrants, farmers, and grade-school dropouts because of the needs of mass production. The new poor, however, are much more trapped in poverty. A generation ago, those who were unskilled and uneducated could usually find work and could even do quite well financially if the workplace was unionized. But now these people are displaced or misplaced. Hard physical labor is rarely needed in a high-tech society. This phenomenon undercuts the efforts of the working class, especially African Americans, Latinos, and other minorities, who face the additional burden of institutional racism (Harrington, 1984:10).

Government data reveal the contours of the new poor. Tens of millions of Americans have lost their jobs in the past two decades because of plant closings and downsizing. Almost half of these newly unemployed were long-time workers (workers who had held their previous jobs at least three years), and seven out of ten of them found new jobs. Of those reemployed full-time, 65 percent end up in jobs that pay less than did their previous jobs (Uchitelle and Kleinfield, 1996:6). These workers were downwardly mobile but likely not poor. About 15 percent, however, did not find employment, and they constitute the new poor.

Family changes result when a breadwinner loses a job. Younger families may delay having children during such a crisis. Families in economic distress may move in with other family members—adult children with parents or parents with adult children. A common coping strategy when the breadwinner is unemployed or reemployed at a low-income job is for the spouse to enter the workforce. Although it helps solve the economic problem, this strategy has some possible negative outcomes for families. For one, it increases the burden on women who work for wages and who continue to do most of the housework. Many tradition-minded husbands find the loss of their breadwinner status intolerable, especially when that role is taken over by their wives. These men lose self-esteem. They may react by withdrawing from social relationships, by drinking, and by physically and mentally abusing their spouses and children.

Families of unemployed workers also suffer from the physical and mental problems associated with the trauma of unemployment. There is evidence that when workers are involuntarily unemployed, they tend, when compared to the employed, to have more hypertension, high cholesterol, ulcers, respiratory diseases, and hyperallergic reactions. Similarly, they are more prone to headaches, upset stomachs, depression, anxiety, and aggression. For example, research on workers in California who were laid off found that regardless of their race, gender, or educational background, they were twice as likely to experience a subsequent decline in health or the onset of a disability as those with continuous employment (reported in *Business Week,* 2000a).

The loss of income from unemployment makes the unemployed vulnerable to unanticipated financial crises such as health problems, a fire, or an automobile accident. These events may result in the loss of a home, bankruptcy, or inadequate health care for the unemployed and family members. In sum, the families of displaced workers experience considerable strain and are thus disproportionately characterized by illness, divorce, separation, physical abuse, and turmoil.

Shifting Family Forms

The theme of this chapter is that family composition and family dynamics are intertwined with social forces. Thus, given the magnitude of the economic transformation, we should not be surprised that family forms are changing.

Case Study: The Shift from the Modern Family to the Postmodern Family
Judith Stacey's important research on working-class families has documented the difficulties these families face and the changes in families as a result. Her description reveals much about changing families. (The following is taken from Stacey, 1990, 1991, 1996.)

The prevailing family form in U.S. society in the 1950s was an intact nuclear household composed of a male breadwinner, his full-time homemaker wife, and their dependent children. In 1950 some 60 percent of U.S. households fit this pattern, whether children were present or not. Although this family form was clearly dominant in society, its prevalence varied by social class. The pattern clearly prevailed in working-class households, for example, but was much less likely among the poor, where women have always had to work outside the home to supplement family income.

This model for the family, which Stacey calls the **modern family**, was disrupted by deindustrialization and the challenges of women to traditional ways. Stacey found that working-class families, especially the women in them, created innovative ways to cope with economic uncertainty and domestic upheavals. In effect, these women were and are the pioneers of emergent family forms. Stacey calls these new family forms **postmodern** because they do not fit the criteria of a "modern" family. Now there are divorce-extended families that include ex-spouses and their lovers, children, and friends. Households now expand and contract as adult children leave and then return home only to leave again. The vast majority of these postmodern families have dual earners. Many families now involve husbands in greater child-care and domestic work than in earlier times. Kin networks have expanded to meet economic pressures. Parents now deal with their children's cohabitation, single and unwed parenthood, and divorce. The result is that only 7 percent of households now conform to the "modern" family form. According to Stacey,

> No longer is there a single culturally dominant family pattern, like the modern one, to which the majority of Americans conform and most of the rest aspire. Instead, Americans today have crafted a multiplicity of family and household arrangements that we inhabit uneasily and reconstitute frequently in response to changing personal and occupational circumstances (Stacey, 1991:19).

Significant in this shift is that working-class families are not clinging to the old "modern" family form. Indeed, they are leading the way toward new forms. Again, according to Stacey,

> [My research findings] shatter the image of the white working class as the last repository of old-fashioned "modern" American family life. The postmodern family arrangements I found among blue-collar people in Silicon Valley are at least as diverse and innovative as those found within the middle class (Stacey, 1991:27).

It is important to note that these postmodern family forms are new to working-class and middle-class families as they adjust to deindustrialization, *but that they are not new to the poor*. The economic deprivation faced by the poor has always forced them to adapt in similar ways: single-parent families, relying on kin networks, sharing housing costs, and multiple wage earners among family members.

The title of this chapter is "Economic and Demographic Upheavals in Society and Family Formation." The changing economy is such an upheaval and results in the formation of new family forms. Michael Elliott, writing about the dawn of a new millennium, captures the magnitude of this change:

The bedrock has shifted. It's now plain that what we misguidedly call the "traditional" family is under threat of collapse. For about a hundred years, the Western world was built on an implicit social unit: a man worked outside the house, a wife worked within it, they had a few children who all survived childhood, and the spouses stayed together till death did them part. . . . American families are now in uncharted territory—economic and cultural pressures have seen to that. Divorce, single parenthood and the rise of working women—and there's good and bad mixed up in that list—have changed the ways in which we can respond to the world outside (Elliott, 1994/1995:131–132).

THE NEW IMMIGRATION AND THE CHANGING RACIAL LANDSCAPE

Another societal "earthquake" that is shaking up society and families is massive immigration. This change is occurring both in numbers and in diversity. *Newsweek*'s special issue anticipating the new millennium describes it this way:

Immigration's vital to understanding the United States today. Americans now aged around 50 built their suburban dreams in places like the San Fernando Valley, the heartland of support for California's Proposition 187 [the successful 1994 vote initiative that opposed education, welfare, and health services for illegal immigrants]. The world of their youth was one in which immigration was rare. . . . Now the Valley's 40 percent Latino and Asian. . . . And it isn't just southern California that's been changed. . . . Just like their predecessors a century ago, today's immigrants will struggle with the twin urges to assimilate and to remember their roots. Just like their forebears, they will be accused of Balkanizing the country and stealing jobs from "real" Americans (Elliott, 1994/1995:131).

This demographic force—the new immigration—is challenging the cultural hegemony of the White European tradition; creating incredible diversity in race, ethnicity, language, and culture; rapidly changing the racial landscape; and leading, often, to division and hostility.

Historically, immigration has been a major source of population growth and ethnic diversity in the United States. Immigration waves from northern and southern Europe, especially from 1850 to 1920, brought many millions of people, mostly Europeans, to America. In the 1920s, the United States placed limits on the number of immigrants it would accept, the operating principle being that the new immigrants should resemble the old ones. The national origins rules were designed to limit severely the immigration of eastern Europeans and to deny the entry of Asians.

The Immigration Act amendments of 1965 abandoned the quota system that had preserved the European character of the United States for nearly half a century. The new law encouraged a new wave of immigrants, only this time the migrants arrived not from northern Europe but from the Third World, especially Asia and Latin America. Put another way, 100 years ago Europeans were 90 percent of immigrants to the United States; now 90 percent of immigrants are from non-European countries, mostly from Latin America and Asia. The result, obviously, is a dramatic alteration of the ethnic and racial composition of the U.S. population (Figure 4.1). The size of the contemporary immigrant wave has

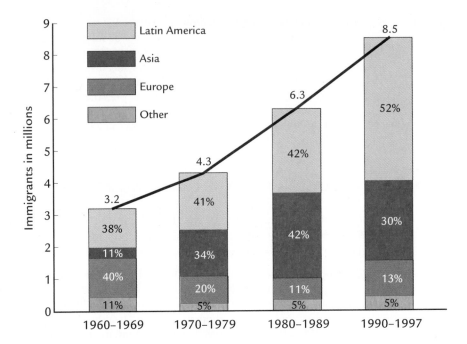

Note: The total for 1990 to 1997 includes 2.2 million immigrants who were legalized in 1987 and 1988 and granted immigrant status in the early 1990s. The sum of the percentages may exceed 100 because of rounding.

Figure 4.1

U.S. immigrants by region of birth, 1960s to 1990s

Source: Philip Martin and Elizabeth Midgley, "Immigration to the United States," *Population Bulletin* 54 (June 1999):5.

resulted in a highly visible and significant number of U.S. residents who are foreign-born (10.4 percent in 2000).

About 1 million immigrants enter the United States legally each year (the following data are from Martin and Midgley, 1999; and Population Reference Bureau, 1999). Another estimated 300,000 unauthorized aliens enter and stay (an estimated 1.5 million to 2.5 million people enter the United States illegally each year, but most return to their native countries either voluntarily or by force if caught by the Immigration and Naturalization Service) for a net gain of U.S. immigrants of about 1.2 million annually. Although the number who enter clandestinely is impossible to determine, the best estimate is that somewhere between 6 million and 11 million illegal aliens reside in the United States. Roughly 60 percent of these undocumented immigrants are Latino (and two-thirds of them are Mexicans).

The settlement pattern of the new immigration differs from previous flows into the United States. Whereas previous immigrants settled primarily in the industrial states of the Northeast and Middle Atlantic region or in the farming areas of the Midwest, recent migrants have tended to locate on the two coasts and in the Southwest. Asians have tended to settle on the West Coast; Mexicans are most likely found in the Southwest; and other Latinos are scattered (for example, Cubans in Florida and Puerto Ricans in New York).

California is a harbinger of the demographic future for the United States. As recently as 1970, California was 80 percent White, but since then it has become uniquely affected by immigration. The result is that Whites now constitute a numerical minority (47 percent in 2000, with 32 percent being Latino, 11 percent Asian, and 7 percent African American), and by 2025 only one-third of California's population will be White (Chideya, 1999). Less than 38 percent of California's public school students are White (Verdin, 2000). Los Angeles has the largest population of Koreans outside Korea, the largest concentration of Iranians in the Western world, and a huge Mexican population. The diverse population of southern California speaks eighty-eight languages and dialects. Greater Los Angeles has more than fifty foreign-language newspapers, and television shows that broadcast in Spanish, Mandarin, Armenian, Japanese, Korean, and Vietnamese (Fletcher, 1998). For all this diversity, though, California, especially southern California, is becoming more and more Latino. California holds nearly half of the U.S. Latino population and well over half of the Mexican-origin population. Latinos are expected to surpass Whites in total California population by 2025 and become an absolute majority by 2040 (Purdum, 2000).

Latinos are also concentrated and growing rapidly in Arizona and Texas. Historian David Kennedy argues that there is no precedent in U.S. history for one immigrant group to have the size and concentration that the Mexican immigrant group has in the Southwest today.

> If we seek historical guidance, the closest example we have in hand is in the diagonally opposite corner of the North American continent, in Quebec. The possibility looms that in the next generation or so we will see a kind of Chicano Quebec take shape in the American Southwest, as a group emerges with strong cultural cohesiveness and sufficient economic and political strength to insist on changes in the overall society's ways of organizing itself and conducting its affairs (Kennedy, 1996:68).

Demographic Trends and Increasing Diversity

The United States is shifting from an Anglo-white society rooted in Western culture to a society with three large racial-ethnic minorities, each of them growing in size while the proportion of whites declines. Five facts show the contours and magnitude of this demographic transformation:

1. *More than one-fourth of the people in the United States are African American, Latino, Asian, or Native American.* The nonWhite population is numerically significant, comprising 28 percent of the population in 1999 (up from 15 percent in 1960), and more than one-third of all children in the United States are non-White. Three states have non-White majorities (California, New Mexico, and Hawaii). Minorities make up the majority in six of the eight U.S. cities with more than a million people—New York, Los Angeles, Chicago, Houston, Detroit, and Dallas.

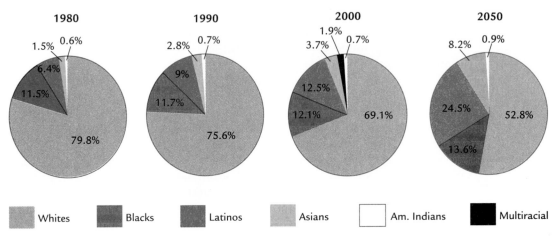

Figure 4.2

U.S. population by race, 1980, 1990, 2000, and 2050

Source: U.S. Census, accessed online at www.census.gov/population/www/cen2000; and U.S. Census, *Current Population Reports*, P25-1130 (1996).

2. *Racial minorities are increasing faster than the majority population.* Whereas more than one-fourth of Americans are non-Whites, by 2030 a majority of children (under eighteen) will be from a minority background (Chideya, 1999:37), and between 2050 and 2060 minorities will surpass the white population in size (Riche, 2000). See Figure 4.2.

3. *African Americans are losing their position as the most numerous racial minority.* In 1990, for the first time, African Americans were less than half of all minorities. By 2000, in a historic shift, Latinos outnumbered African Americans 35.3 million to 34.6 million. By 2050 Latinos will be 24 percent of the U.S. population and African Americans will be 14 percent (*Newsweek,* 1998). This demographic transformation will make two common assumptions about race obsolete: that "race" is a "Black-and-White" issue, and that the United States is a "White" society (Chideya, 1999).

4. *Immigration now accounts for a large share of the nation's population growth.* Today about one in ten current U.S. residents is foreign-born. Since 1970 the number of foreign-borns has almost tripled, from 9.6 million to 28.3 million today. This growth rate far outpaces the growth of the native-born population. Immigration accounts for over a third of the current population growth directly and adds more indirectly, as first- and second-generation Americans have more children on average than the rest of the population (Chideya, 1999).

5. *New patterns of immigration are changing the racial composition of society.* Among the expanded population of first-generation immigrants, the Asian-born now outnumber the European-born, and those from Latin America, especially Mexicans, outnumber both. This contrasts sharply with what occurred as

recently as the 1950s, when two-thirds of legal immigrants were from Europe and Canada.

These trends signal a transformation from a White majority to a multiracial/multicultural society:

> Around the year 2050, whites will become a 'minority." This is uncharted territory in this country, and this demographic change will affect everything. Alliances between the races are bound to shift. Political and social power will be re-apportioned. Our neighborhoods, our schools and workplaces, even racial categories themselves will be altered (Chideya, 1999:35).

The pace of these changes is quickening. From 1990 to 1999, while the White population increased by 2 percent, the Asian and Pacific Islander population grew by 58 percent, the Latino population increased by 53 percent, the African American population by 12 percent, and the Native American numbers grew by 15 percent. Let us examine, briefly, the two categories whose numbers dominate the recent migrants—Latinos and Asians.

Latinos

In 1970, about one in twenty Americans was Latino. In 1999 this proportion had risen to slightly less than one in six, and by 2050 the Latino population is expected to grow to approximately one out of four Americans. Geographically, Latinos are highly concentrated. About four-fifths live in seven states—California, Texas, New York, Florida, Illinois, Arizona, and New Jersey. More than six in ten Latinos live in just twenty-five metropolitan areas, with over 4.1 million living in Los Angeles County, followed by Miami-Dade County, Florida (with about 1.2 million) and Cook County, Illinois (with over 930,000).

Mexicans, Puerto Ricans, Cubans, and other Latino groups differ from each other by history and the timing and conditions of their arrival in the United States (the following is taken primarily from Baca Zinn and Wells, 2000). They differ in size, with Mexicans outnumbering the other Latino groups (see Figure 4.3). They vary in social class. Puerto Ricans and Mexicans are the most economically disadvantaged Latino groups, whereas Cubans are much more likely to be economically advantaged and educated. Some are recent immigrants, either legal or undocumented. Others are descendants of families who have lived in the southwestern United States for over 300 years. Fertility (birth) rates, too, vary by country of origin, with Puerto Rican and Mexicans having the highest rates and Cubans the lowest. These rates also differ by recency of immigration, with first-generation migrants having the highest rates, followed in order by second and third generation migrants.

Latinos are more likely to separate or divorce than are Anglos, but they do so at a lower rate than African Americans. This relatively high rate of family dissolution appears to be related to social class, with the conditions necessary for the maintenance of long-term stable marriages present in the middle class but absent in poor families (Fernandez-Kelly, 1990:185). Cubans, the most affluent Latino category in the United States, have over three-fourths of their families intact, compared to only about half of Puerto Rican families (the poorest and most likely to be unemployed Latino category).

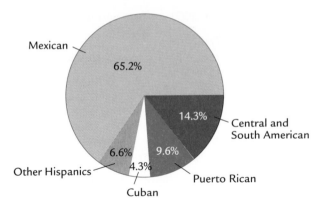

Figure 4.3

Hispanics in the USA, by national origin
Source: USA Today, May 23, 2000, p. 10A.

Diversity is also found within each Latino category, demonstrating a major theme of this book: "families are understood to be constructed by powerful social forces and as settings in which different family members adapt in a variety of ways to changing social conditions (Baca Zinn and Wells, 2000:253). Some examples demythologize common stereotypes of Latinos.

- Strong kin networks are believed to be a defining feature of the Latino population. Studies have found, however, that kinship networks are not monolithic, depending on distinctive social conditions, such as immigrant versus nonimmigrant status, and generational status. First generation immigrants, for example, have smaller social networks than do second-generation Mexican Americans. Contrary to a common assumption that familism fades in succeeding generations, Velez-Ibanez (1996) found that second- and third-generation Mexican Americans have highly elaborated family networks actively maintained through frequent visits, ritual celebrations, and the exchange of goods and services.
- Latino families are typically viewed as settings of traditional patriarchy because of *machismo,* the cult of masculinity. Research has found, to the contrary, that there is considerable variation in family decision making and the allocation of household labor, ranging from patriarchal role-segregated patterns to egalitarian patterns. In general, the more resources and autonomy that Latinas have outside the home through employment, the less patriarchal are the home arrangements. This relationship is impeded, however, for families imbedded in dense familial social networks, which tend to promote traditional gender segregation (Hurtado, 1995; Coltrane and Valdez, 1993).
- Not only is there variation among Latinos, there are differences within a given Latino family—parents and children, women and men—as they experience family life differently. For new immigrants, family adaptation

A Dominican family-owned video store.

to new conditions is not a unitary phenomenon. School-age immigrant children generally become competent in English more quickly than their parents, resulting, sometimes, in the children assuming adult roles as they help their parents negotiate the bureaucratic structures of their new social environment (Dorrington, 1995). Immigration may also create formal legal distinctions among family members. For example, undocumented Central American couples are, by definition, "illegal aliens," yet their children born in the United States are U.S. citizens. This results in a **binational family** (see Chapter 12 for an extended discussion of transnational families).

Asian Americans

In 1970, Asian Americans numbered 1.4 million (1.5 percent of the total U.S. population). They now represent more than one-third of all legal immigrants and are growing rapidly, reaching 9.6 million (4 percent of the population). "Assuming medium levels of fertility, mortality, and net immigration, the Asian American population is likely to exceed 32 million by 2050 and make up about 8 percent of the population" (Lee, 1998:16).

Asian Americans are often characterized as one group because of their seemingly common ethnic origins in Asia and their similar physical appearance. However, to classify them as a single group masks great differences among them. The term "Asian American" applies to members of at least twenty-eight subgroups. Asian Americans are diverse in religion, language, income, education, occupational skills, and in immigration experience (Ishii-Kuntz, 2000). The largest Asian American groups are Chinese (24 percent of all Asian Americans in 1997), Filipino (21 percent), Japanese (10 percent), Vietnamese (11 percent), Korean (10 percent), and Asian Indian (13 percent). Among the rest are such ethnic groups as Laotians, Kampucheans, Thais, Pakistanis, Sri Lankans, Indonesians, and Hmong.

There are some interesting findings concerning Asian American families. First, the number of divorces in this group is lower than the U.S. average, especially among first-generation immigrants. Among the various Asian American groups, Japanese Americans have the highest divorce rate. For the number of households headed by a woman, Asian Indians have the lowest rate, while the Chinese, Filipino, and Korean rates are higher than found for the United States in general. The fertility rate for Asians is the lowest of all racial categories in the United States. The most economically disadvantaged groups (the Vietnamese, Cambodians, Laotians, and Hmong) on average have much higher fertility rates than other Asian immigrants. Japanese Americans and Chinese Americans, however, have much lower fertility rates than found in the general U.S. population. Foreign-born Asian women rarely have children out of wedlock but the rate doubles for U.S.-born Asian American women (Lee, 1998;19). Finally, interracial marriage (that is, marriage outside one's racial group) is more likely among Asian Americans than among African Americans and is as likely as found for Latinos (Lee, 1998). Of the various ethnic categories, the Japanese are the most likely to marry outside their group. Women in all Asian categories consistently outmarry at a higher rate than Asian men, by about two to one. With regard to intermarriage, Asian Indians are the exception to the other Asian groups, having much lower intermarriage rates, and for those relatively few interracial marriages involving Asian Indians, men are much more likely than women to be exogenous (**exogamy** is marrying outside one's group).

The diversity among Asian American families reinforces a major theme of this book, that family forms are shaped by social forces and social location. To reiterate, "Asian American family experiences are diverse because they have been influenced by such factors as socio-economic status, immigration history, generational status, age, gender, and nativity, to name a few" (Ishii-Kuntz, 2000:276). With these structural variables is in mind, let us demythologize two common stereotypes of Asian Americans.

1.   Many Americans believe that Asian Americans are the model racial minority, scoring high in relative income, educational attainment, and on other measures of success. This assumption, however, does not reflect the diversity found among Asian Americans. Whereas most of the pre–World War II Asian immigrants were peasants, the recent migrants vary considerably by education and social class. On the one hand, many arrived as educated middle-class professionals with highly valued skills and some knowledge of English. For exam-

ple, in 1995, when 23 percent of the total U.S. male population had at least a college degree, 49 percent of Asian Indian men, 42 percent of Filipino men, and 35 percent of Chinese men in the United States were college graduates. In sharp contrast, among others, such as the Southeast Asian groups (Cambodians, Laotians, and Hmong), only 3 percent of men had a college degree or higher (Waters and Eschbach, 1995:433). These immigrants arrived as uneducated, impoverished refugees. These initial disparities among Asian groups upon entry into the United States is reflected in the differences in income and poverty level by ethnic category. Asian Americans taken together have a poverty rate about double the rate for Whites, although Japanese and Asian Indians having very low poverty rates and are above the national average in income and educational achievement. The Southeast Asian groups are the most economically disadvantaged, with high poverty rates.

2. It is widely assumed that Asian American families are patriarchal, emphasizing men's superiority and women's obedience to their husbands. Research has found, however, similar to the experience of Latinos, that traditional gender inequality is related to husbands' and wives' differential earning power and gaps in educational attainment. When Asian American women have educations equal to their husbands and contribute significantly to the family income, the relations between wives and husbands is more egalitarian (Ishii-Kuntz, 2000). Also, recent immigrants are more traditional in their gender roles

Members of a Cambodian family behind the counter of their grocery store.

than are those in succeeding generations, reflecting the effects of greater exposure to the mainstream culture.

To summarize, the shape of Asian American families, like that of all families, is the consequence of

> the members' daily interaction with each other and with people in the outside world. Just because one is born into an Asian American family does not mean that one's values, beliefs, and family experiences will be identical to those of other Asian Americans. Rather, these experiences are constructed by social and historical situations that surround the families because these situations provide the concrete resources and constraints that shape family interactions (Ishii-Kuntz, 2000:277).

The Effects of Immigration on Immigrant Families

There are a number of possible consequences of migration for immigrant families. We concentrate on three: (1) the loss of ethnic identity in the new society, (2) family acts of agency, and (3) the effects on family dynamics.

Ethnic Identity: The United States as a Cultural Melting Pot?

Martin and Midgley sum up the universal dilemma for immigrants:

> There is always a tension between the newcomers' desires to keep alive the culture and language of the community they left behind, and their need and wish to adapt to new surroundings and a different society (Martin and Midgley, 1999:35–36).

If the past is a guide, the new immigrants will assimilate. "Our society exerts tremendous pressure to conform, and cultural separatism rarely survives more than a generation" (Cole, 1994:412). For earlier immigrants to the United States, the shift to English usage took three generations—from almost exclusive use by newcomers of their traditional language, to their children being bilingual, and their children's children (third-generation immigrants) being monolingual English speakers (Martin and Midgley, 1999).

An argument countering the assumption that the new immigrants will assimilate as did previous generations of immigrants is that the new immigrants are racial/ethnics, not Whites. As such, they face individual and institutional racism that excludes them from full participation, just as it has excluded African Americans and Native Americans (O'Hare, 1993:2). The current political mood is to eliminate affirmative action (as did California with Proposition 209, which took effect in 1997), a policy aimed at leveling the playing field so that minorities would have a fair chance to succeed. Should these efforts succeed in the courts and legislatures, then the new immigrants will have a more difficult time assimilating than did their predecessors, should they wish to do so.

Another factor facing this generation of migrants is that they enter the United States during a critical economic transformation, in which the middle class is shrinking and the working class and the working poor face difficult economic hurdles. A possible result is that the new immigrants, different in physical characteristics, language, and culture, will become scapegoats for the difficulties that so many face. Moreover, their opportunities for advancement will be limited by the new economic realities. Sociologist Herbert Gans (1990) argues, for example, that the second generation of post-1965 immigrants likely will experience downward mobility compared to their parents because of the changing opportunity structure of the U.S. economy.

The issue of immigrant adaption to the host society is complex, depending on a number of variables. Zhou (1997) describes a number of these critical variables, including the immigrant generation (i.e., first, or second), the immigrants' level in the ethnic hierarchy at the point of arrival, what stratum of U.S. society absorbs them, the degree to which they are part of a family network, and the like.

Immigrants who move to the United States permanently have four options regarding assimilation. Many try to blend into the United States as quickly as possible. Others resist the new ways, either by developing an adversarial stance toward the dominant society or by resisting acculturation by focusing more intensely on the social capital created through ethnic ties (Portes and Zhou, 1993). The fourth alternative is to move toward a bicultural pattern (Buriel and De Ment, 1997). That is, immigrants adopt some patterns similar to those found in the host society and retain some from their heritage. Although this concept of bicultural pattern appears to focus on culture, the retention or abandonment of the ethnic ways depends on structural variables (Kibria, 1997:207). These variables include the socioeconomic resources of the ethnic community, the extent of continued immigration from the sending society, the linkages between the ethnic community and the sending society, and the obstacles to obtaining equal opportunity in the new society.

Immigration and Agency

Immigration can be forced (e.g., the slave trade) or freely chosen. Immigration in this latter sense is clearly an act of human agency. Most people in developing countries do not move. Others move, breaking with their extended family, leaving neighborhood and community ties, mostly to improve their economic situations or to flee repression.

Typically, new immigrants face hostility from their hosts, who, as we have seen, fear them as competitors or hate them because they are "different." Moreover, they face language barriers as they seek jobs. Often, most especially for undocumented immigrants, their initial jobs are demeaning, poorly paid, and without benefits. How do they adapt to these often difficult circumstances? Commonly, migrants move to a destination area where there is already a network of friends and relatives. These networks connect new migrants with housing (often doubling up in very crowded but inexpensive conditions), jobs, and an informal welfare system (health care, pooling resources in difficult times). These mutual aid efforts by immigrant communities have been used by immigrant networks throughout U.S. history, whether by Swedish settlers in Minnesota, Mennonite settlers in Kansas, Irish settlers in Boston, or the Mexican settlers or Vietnamese settlers now (Martin and Midgley, 1994:14–17).

To overcome low wages, all able family members may work in the family enterprise or at different jobs by combining family resources. To overcome various manifestations of hostility by others, the immigrant community may become closer, having as little interaction with outsiders as possible. Some may become involved in gangs for protection. Still others may move to assimilate as quickly as possible.

The Effects of Immigration on Family Dynamics

Under the provisions of the Immigration Act of 1990, gaining immigrant status generally requires a sponsor, who may be a U.S. citizen, a legal resident, a U.S. employer, or, in the case of refugees, the U.S. government. Of these options, the most common route to immigration involves a close family member. Thus, immigration to the United States is largely a family affair.

The immigration laws, which favor migrants with family connections, have a snowball effect, enhancing the potential for further migration (called "chain" migration), both legal and extralegal. Such chaining processes often lead to dense ethnic concentrations in cities, where extended families are closely networked.

> Such spatial concentrations of kin and kith serve to provide newcomers with manifold sources of moral, social, cultural, and economic support that are unavailable to immigrants who are more dispersed and help to explain the gravitational pull exerted by places where family and friends of immigrants are concentrated (Rumbaut, 1997:7).

Family connections not only make immigration possible, they help migrants cope with life in a new social setting.

An exception to the family-oriented immigration often occurs among undocumented migrants. These are typically young manual laborers, who leave their families behind for months at a time while they work in the United States. These **transnational families** find their family ties stretched across national boundaries, which often causes extraordinary emotional, financial, and physical stress for the family members (Chavez, 1992). (See Chapter 12.)

Undocumented immigrants may have families in the United States. This occurs by having their spouse join them or marrying U.S. citizens or legal residents. The children of these unions, if born in the United States, are U.S. citizens. This leads to the unusual situation of families that consist of a mix of legal statuses. Chavez (1992) calls these families **binational,** since they consist of both undocumented immigrants and U.S. citizens or legal residents.

No family action has greater consequences than a family leaving its home society for a new one. The family's economic situation changes; if family members are non-English-speaking, their language is useless outside the immigrant community; their culture is demeaned; their children in time will likely question tradition; and the family members will likely be the objects of discrimination. In addition to these profound consequences, immigration has consequences for family dynamics. To illustrate this, we describe what research has found for Mexican immigrant families and Vietnamese immigrant families.

Case Study: The Reconstruction of Gender Relations among Mexican Immigrant Men and Women

Immigrants from Mexico often arrive in the United States in stages (called family stage migration). The typical pattern is for husbands to leave alone for the United

States, where they work and save in anticipation of their wives and children arriving later, sometimes years later, for permanent settlement (the following discussion is based on Hondagneu-Sotelo, 1992, 1994). In this arrangement, husbands make the decision to migrate. Wives remain behind to run the household.

This migration pattern confronts traditional patriarchy in two ways. First, the longer the spouses are separated, the more independent the women become. While remaining in Mexico, usually with diminished resources, the women devise income-earning activities, take on multiple roles, and become more competent at traditional male activities such as public negotiation. In short, "the long separation fostered by the men's solo sojourns diminished the hegemony of the husbands' authority and increased women's autonomy and influence in the family" (Hondagneu-Sotelo, 1992:404).

Second, access to social networks of women enables women to subvert patriarchal authority by migrating without their husbands' cooperation. Hondagneu-Sotelo compared the experience of families in which the husbands migrated before 1965 with those who migrated after 1965. This date is significant because U.S. legislation granted legal status to many undocumented pre-1965 migrant men by the 1970s. For wives to join their husbands (and also receive legal status), they needed the help of their husbands. This dependence, of course, reduced the independence of wives. Their autonomy was also diminished because there were relatively few Mexican immigrant women in the United States to assist them if their husbands did not.

The wives of men migrating after 1965 were *not* dependent on obtaining legal status through their husbands, because legal status was no longer a viable option for males and females. Many wives did migrate without the assistance of their husbands, but rather with the assistance of a network of immigrant women already in the United States. This network of mothers, sisters, and friends generated independence of wives from their husbands.

Hondagneu-Sotelo's research makes the important point that the strong cultural norms that emphasize patriarchal men and submissive women (*machismo*) are changed not by learning the values of a new society but by "arrangements induced by the migration process itself" (Hondagneu-Sotelo, 1992:394).

Case Study: Migration and Vietnamese American Women: Remaking Gender Relations

Traditional Vietnamese family and gender relations were based on Confucian principles, which placed women in subordination to men in every aspect of life (the following is based on Kibria, 1990, 1993, 1994). Women married at a young age, entering the household of their husband's father, and where they were dominated by their mother-in-law. In this arrangement men controlled economic resources and men controlled women through the isolation of women from their families of origin.

Following the Vietnam War, many Vietnamese migrated to the United States. Several conditions within Vietnamese American communities worked to undermine the bases of male authority found in Vietnam. One of these conditions was downward mobility. Unlike Mexican immigrants to the United States, who rose in economic resources with migration, most Vietnamese who migrated before

1975 shifted from their middle-class occupations in Vietnam to largely unskilled, low-status, and low-paying jobs in the United States. Their difficulties with English and facing continuous discrimination tended to keep them low in status.

One consequence of this downward mobility was that Vietnamese men and women became more equal. Women were low status in Vietnam; now, with migration, men and women shared low status in the United States. Husbands in Vietnam earned the income for the family. In the United States the husband's income was often insufficient, so he was dependent on the income of his wife and children.

Another disruption from the traditional patterns was a change in kinship networks. Family ties in Vietnam were based on the husband's family. In the United States, given the scarcity of relatives, Vietnamese migrants adapted by creating flexible kinship networks that involved the husband's kin, the wife's kin, and **fictive kin** (close friends incorporated into family groups). This reconstruction of kinship had some special advantages for women.

One consequence of the more varied and inclusive nature of the kinship network was that women were rarely surrounded exclusively by the husband's relatives and/or friends. As a result, they were often able to turn to close fictive kin and perhaps members of their families of origin for support during conflicts with men in the family. Another condition that enhanced the power of married women in the family was that few had to deal with the competing authority of their mother-in-law in the household, because elderly women have not been among those likely to leave Vietnam (Kibria, 1994:254–255).

The situation for Vietnamese women, however, is not full equality with men. Kibria notes that while migration enhanced women's power, the women remained attached to the old male-dominant family system because it offered them economic protection and gave them officially sanctioned authority over the younger generation. Kibria summarizes this contradictory situation:

> Migration to the United States has thus had a complex, somewhat contradictory, impact on the status of Vietnamese immigrant women. On the one hand, migration has weakened men's control over economic and social resources and allowed women to exert greater informal family power. At the same time, the precarious economic environment has heightened the salience of the family system and constrained the possibilities for radical change in gender relations (Kibria, 1990:21).

THE AGING OF SOCIETY

During the twentieth century the population of the United States has experienced a pronounced change—it has become older and is on the verge of becoming much older. In 1900 about one in twenty-five residents of the U.S. was 65 years or older. By 1950 it was about one in twelve. In 2000, one in eight was 65 or older, and by 2030 the ratio will likely be around one in five, with more people over 65 than under age 18. In effect, by 2030, when most of today's college students will be around 50, there will be more grandparents than grandchildren. "The Senior Boom is coming, and it will transform our homes, our schools, our politics, our lives and our deaths. And not just for older people. For everybody" (Peyser, 1999:50).

The Demographics of an Aging Society

In 1950 there were about 12.2 million Americans aged 65 and older. In 2000 there were approximately 35 million. Two forces, a falling birth rate and advances in medicine have joined to make the 65-and-older category constitute the fastest-growing segment of the U.S. population, increasing twice as fast as the population as a whole. Also noteworthy is the rapid increase in the "old-old," that is, those aged 85 and older. In 1950 there were 600,000 in this category, compared to 4,300,000 in 2000, a sevenfold increase. In 2030 there will be 8,500,000 aged 85 and over (see Figure 4.4). In 2000 some 72,000 Americans were at least 100 years old. Because of continued advances in medicine and nutrition, it is expected that the number of centenarians will increase to about 1 million by the middle of the twenty-first century.

Because racial minorities have a lower life expectancy than do Whites (African Americans, for example, live about six fewer years), they form a smaller proportion of the elderly category than of other age groups. In 1997, 15 percent of the White population was 65 years of age or over, compared with 8 percent of African Americans, 7 percent of Asian Americans, 7 percent of Native Americans, and 6 percent of Latinos (U.S. Department of Health and Human Services,

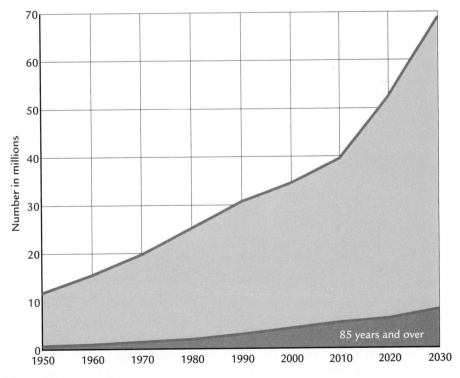

Figure 4.4

Population 65 years of age and over: United States, 1950–2030

Source: U.S. Department of Health and Human Services, *Health, United States, 1999.* Hyattsville, MD: National Center for Health Statistics, 1999, p. 23.

1999:22). It is expected that nonWhites will be one-third of the elderly population by 2050 (with Latinos being the largest elderly minority after 2020).

The elderly population is disproportionately composed of women. Older women outnumber older men by a ratio of 3 to 2. As age increases, the disparity becomes greater—for those aged 85 and older, there are about five women to every two men. Because of pensions through work and the traditional bias of Social Security toward women who had not worked outside the home, elderly women are much more likely than elderly men to be poor (a 13 percent poverty rate compared with 7 percent for men). African American and Latino elderly women had even a higher probability than their male counterparts of being poor—a rate 1.3 times as likely (U.S. Department of Health and Human Services, 1999:28).

Geographically, some states and communities have disproportionately more older residents. Six states have more than 15 percent elderly, with Florida having the highest concentration (18.5 percent, and expected to rise to 25 percent by 2010). Many states with a high concentration of elderly are rural states, where there has been a large outmigration of young people. Most elderly remain in their communities after retirement ("aging in place"), but those who move tend to migrate to the favorable climate found in the Sun Belt states (Florida, California, Arizona, Nevada, and Texas) (Frey, 1999). Those who migrate are not representative of the elderly: they tend to be younger and more affluent than those who stay in their home communities.

The Consequences of an Aging Society on Families and the Elderly

Legally, the elderly are those persons 65 years of age and over. This arbitrary chronological age was set by Congress in 1935 as the age when Social Security benefits went into effect. At that time 65 was old, because the average life expectancy then was 62. Now, however, the average life expectancy at birth is 77 (74 years for males, compared to 79 years for females). Under current mortality conditions women who reach 65 will, on average, live 19.2 more years and men will live 15.9 years more, to 84 and 81, respectively. The implications of living well past 65 are profound for the elderly and their families.

Economic Resources

In general, recent retirees have personal resources—education, income, and assets—unknown to previous cohorts. Many are comfortable, with time for leisure, opportunities for rewarding and productive activity, and a decent standard of living (Treas, 1995). Many have benefited from sharp rises in the stock and real estate markets resulting in extraordinary wealth, which ultimately they will pass on to their fortunate heirs. Yet many elderly have missed out on the economic boom. In 1999 the median net worth for older White families was $181,000, while it was less than $13,000 for older African American families (Federal Interagency Forum on Aging-Related Statistics, reported in Newman, 2000).

The elderly who are members of a racial or ethnic minority are disproportionately poor. In 1997, for example, African American elderly were 2.9 times as likely and Latino elderly were 2.7 times as likely to live in poverty as White elderly persons (U.S. Department of Health and Human Services, 1999:28). This relative lack of resources for racial minorities translates into a reduced likelihood, compared to Whites, of their receiving adequate health care and, if needed, living in nursing homes with full-time skilled nursing care under a physician's supervision.

Social Security is the only source of income for about half of retired people and a major source of income for 80 percent of the elderly in the United States. Since the introduction of Social Security in the 1930s, this program has been a significant aid to the elderly. Social Security has reduced poverty significantly among the elderly—from 35.2 percent in 1959 to 9.7 percent in 1999. "Without Social Security income, 54 percent of America's elderly would live in poverty" (Wellstone, 1998:5).

Despite its considerable strengths, the Social Security program has several serious problems that place a disproportionate burden on certain categories of the elderly and on some portions of the workers paying into the program. An immediate problem is that not all workers are covered. Some groups of workers are unable to participate because they work for states with alternative retirement programs. Also, legislation has specifically exempted certain occupations such as agricultural workers from Social Security.

For workers who are eligible for Social Security, there are wide disparities in the benefits received. The amount of benefits depends on the length of time workers have paid into the Social Security program and the amount of wages on which they paid a Social Security tax. In other words, low-paid workers receive low benefits during retirement. Thus, 30 percent of the elderly who depend almost exclusively on Social Security benefits live *below* the poverty line. These elderly typically are people who have been relatively poor during their working years or are widows.

Living Arrangements among the Elderly

The living arrangements of the elderly vary considerably by age, sex, race, and marital status (see Figure 4.5). Slightly more than seven out of ten elderly men live with their spouses compared to about four in ten elderly women. This is the result of the greater longevity of women and the social norm for men to marry younger women. Thus, to the extent that isolation is a problem of the aged, it is overwhelmingly a problem for elderly women.

Elderly Japanese and Chinese Americans are more likely than Whites to live in their children's homes (Kamo and Zhou, 1994). African American and Latino women are more likely to live with other relatives compared to White women. Compared to White and Latino men, older African American men are more likely to live alone and less likely to live with a spouse (U.S. Department of Health and Human Services, 1999:24).

Two demographic trends—increased life expectancy and few children per family—increase the likelihood of elderly parents living with their adult children. These trends result in a **beanpole family structure**—a vertical, four-generation family structure.

In the decades to come, individuals will grow older having more vertical than horizontal linkages in the family. For example, vertically, a four-generation family struc-

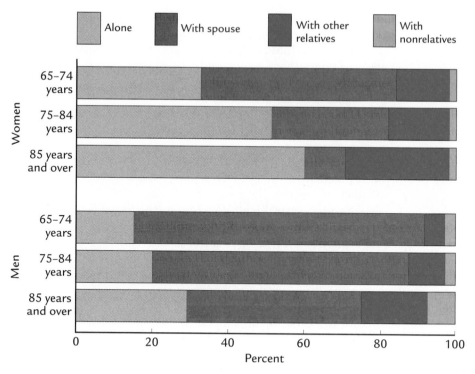

Figure 4.5

Living arrangements of persons 65 years of age and over by age and sex: United States, 1997

Source: U.S. Department of Health and Human Services, *Health, United States, 1999.* Hyattsville, MD: National Center for Health Statistics, 1999, p. 25.

ture has three tiers of parent-child relationships, two sets of grandparent-grand-child ties, and one great-grandparent-great-grandchild linkage. Within generations of this same family, horizontally, aging individuals will have fewer brothers and sisters. In addition, at the level of extended kin, family members will have fewer cousins, aunts, uncles, nieces, and nephews (Bengtson et al., 1990:264)

The decision for the elderly to live with their children is made for one of several reasons. It may be that the elderly persons cannot function alone or are too poor to handle the economic demands of living alone. The decision may be driven by the wish of both parties to be together with shared responsibilities (e.g., the elderly may take care of baby-sitting, cooking, cleaning, and other chores, while the children take care of the added finances). The arrangement can be satisfactory or it may be difficult, as either the elderly or their children or both may resent the lack of privacy and the erosion of independence or there may be disagreements over disparate lifestyles.

About 43 percent of today's seniors will use a nursing home during their lifetime (Greenwald, 1999). At any one time about 4 percent of the elderly live in long-term care institutions, usually nursing homes. The residents of nursing

An elderly parent living with a familiy can have both
positive and negative consequences.

homes are typically over 75, female, White, and currently unmarried, typically
widowed. The economically advantaged are not as likely as their less wealthy
age cohorts to be institutionalized, and if institutionalized, they are apt to be in
private nursing homes and to receive better care.

Paying for Health Care

Of all age groups, the elderly are the most affected by ill health. These problems
escalate especially from age 75 onward, as the degenerative processes of aging
accelerate. Consider the following facts:

- Although the elderly comprise only about 13 percent of the population
  presently, they consume more than one-third of all health care in the
  United States.
- The elderly are four times as likely as the nonold to be hospitalized. When
  hospitalized, they stay an average of about three days longer than the
  nonold.
- The medical expenses of the old are three times greater than those of mid-
  dle-aged adults, yet their incomes are typically much less. The average

person spends $386.09 a year on prescription drugs, while the average elderly individual spends $600 a year on prescription drugs, with one in ten spending more than $2000 a year (Tyson, 1999).

- An estimated 4 million Americans suffer from Alzheimer's disease, the leading cause of dementia in old age. The disease rises sharply with advancing age—from less than 3 percent of those age 65 and doubling every five years of age between 65 and 85 so that for those 85 and older, the rate is almost half (47 percent) (Neergaard, 2000).
- The cost of long-term care is prohibitive, with the average yearly cost in 1999 for nursing home care at $46,000. Because Medicare does not pay for most long-term care, long-term care insurance is expensive, and Medicaid will help only after the patient's resources are exhausted, the result is that many elderly will end their lives impoverished (*USA Today*, 1999).

Medicare, begun in 1965, is the health insurance program for those 65 and over. Everyone is automatically entitled to hospital insurance, home health care, and hospice care through this program. For an additional modest fee Medicare offers a supplemental medical insurance that helps pay for doctors' bills, outpatient services, diagnostic tests, physical therapy, and medical supplies. Overall, Medicare is financed by payroll taxes, premiums paid by recipients, and a government subsidy.

There are two major problems with Medicare. First, it is insufficiently financed by the federal government. From the perspective of the elderly, only about half of their health care bills are paid through the program, leaving them with substantial costs. The affluent elderly are not hurt because they can afford supplemental health insurance. The poor are not hurt because they are also covered by Medicaid, a separate program financed by federal and state taxes that pays for the health care of indigent people. The near-poor, however, do not qualify for Medicaid and they cannot afford additional health insurance.

A second problem with Medicare is that physicians feel that the program pays them too little for their services. As a result, many physicians limit the number of Medicare patients they will serve, some even refusing to serve any Medicare patients. Thus, some elderly have difficulty finding a physician willing to serve them.

Role Transitions

The elderly in society encounter a number of major role transitions—from work to leisure; from marriage to widowhood, from independence to dependence, and from living to impending death.

Retirement

Most of us work all of our adult lives and then, at age 60 or 65 or 70, we exit the work role for a life without work. While the idea of retirement is appealing and many have no problems adjusting to it, for many this is a difficult transition. It involves a loss of identity (i.e., one's work was the center of who he or she is and who others think they are), and a loss of meaning (i.e., being productive). Also, it says to others "I am old," which in U.S. society means "I am no longer important," or, as a movie reviewer in *Time* magazine put it: "To be old in America is almost as uncool as being poor" (Corliss, 2000:70).

Retirement can have beneficial or detrimental effects on marital quality (Myers and Booth, 1996). Positively, retirement means more time together for the spouses. If they can afford it and are in good health, they can engage in travel and other activities of mutual interest. However, after forty years or so of being away from each other while one or both work outside the home, the dramatically increased time together might be seen as an intrusion into each other's space and a source of irritation. Since husbands are typically older than their wives, they will retire earlier than their spouses. This leads to difficulties with the household division of labor, since many husbands resist doing their fair share of the housework, even though they have the time.

Widowhood

Although becoming a widow or widower is theoretically possible at any time, the probability, of course, increases with age, and the likelihood is that women will experience this role transition more than men. In 1998 some 23.7 percent of men 75 and older were widowed, compared to 60.4 percent of women (U.S. Bureau of the Census, 1999:58). The loss of a spouse leads to loneliness and isolation, especially for elderly women, since they are much less likely than elderly men to remarry. They are also more likely than men to have inadequate financial resources.

From Independence to Dependence

A major transition for the elderly, especially for the old-old, is a shift from independence to dependence. Adulthood is a time of financial and social independence from others. Toward the end of life, however, many elderly persons, because of physical or mental health reasons, must be cared for by family members or nurses or placed in an institution. This is a huge shift, one that is often difficult for the elderly as well as their caregivers. For the caregivers, a study sponsored by the Kaiser Family Foundation found that more than one-third of those caring for aging parents were concerned with juggling caregiving with their other responsibilities. More than one-fourth worried about having enough time for their spouse or partner; and 25 percent worried that caregiving interfered with their time with their children. Thirty percent also had missed work as a result of elder care (reported in *USA Today*, 2000).

Impending Death

In 1900 the average life expectancy was fifty years with infectious diseases the most common cause of death. The median age of death now is 77 and the leading causes of death are heart disease, cancer, and stroke (this section depends largely on Meier and Morrison, 1999). Advances in the treatment of atherosclerotic vascular disease and cancer have turned these previously rapidly fatal diseases into chronic illness with which people often live for several years before death. This means that the elderly with terminal diseases become progressively dependent on others, most often by family members, typically, by women (spouses, adult daughters, and daughters-in-law). Thus, the majority of an older person's last months and years is spent at home in the care of family members, with hospitalization or placement in a nursing home occurring only near the very end of life.

The elderly and their kin are well aware that death draws nearer with advancing age. How do the elderly individual, the spouse, and their children prepare for this event? Do they avoid thinking and talking about it? Or do they actively prepare for the inevitable by preparing a will that settles the estate and disburses personal effects, preparing a **living will** (declaring, legally, that unusual efforts to keep the dying person alive, shall not be taken), and making funeral and burial arrangements? As the patient nears death, family members and health care providers "often have to negotiate difficult, often wrenching decisions about the use or discontinuation of such life-prolonging technologies as feeding tubes, ventilators, and intravenous fluids" (Meier and Morrison, 1999:6).

Responses by the Elderly: Human Agency

Being old is a difficult stage in life for many. People who were once attractive, active, and powerful may no longer be so. They must live on restricted incomes that become more constricted by inflation. They must face chronic health problems, pain, and impending death. Many are isolated because they have lost a spouse and their children live at a distance. Some elderly, especially the poor and those in many nursing homes, live lives of desperation and hopelessness.

After studying the aged for fifteen years, Bernice Neugarten and her associates delineated four major personality types among people age 70 and over (Neugarten, 1980). The majority of the elderly retain *integrated* personalities. They function well, are intellectually able, and have competent egos. Another category, the *defended*, are achievement-oriented people who continue to work hard. They fight the aging process by not giving in to it and by remaining very active. *Passive-dependent* people, in contrast, have essentially given in to the inevitability of aging. They become inactive and depend on others. Finally, a relatively small proportion are the *disinterested* (disorganized) elderly. These people have experienced a deterioration of their thought processes. They may be confused, disoriented, forgetful, childish, and paranoid.

These personality types reflect responses to being old, a devalued status in the United States. Being considered old by society and by oneself is a catalyst that provokes the individual to respond in characteristic ways. However—and this is the crucial sociological point—the elderly are reacting to socially structured inequalities and socially constructed definitions, not to age as such. In a different cultural setting in which status increased with age, observers would likely find different personality types and responses.

Some researchers have argued that senior citizens respond to the aging process by retreating from relationships, organizations, and society (called **disengagement**). This behavior is considered normal and even satisfying for the individual, because withdrawal brings a release from societal pressures to compete and conform. Other researchers have quarreled with disengagement theory, arguing that many elderly people are involved in a wide range of activities.

The majority of the elderly do remain active until health problems curtail their mobility and mental acuity. A striking number of them are politically active, in an attempt to change some of the social conditions especially damaging to them. Faced with common problems, many are joined in collective efforts both locally and nationally. Several national organizations are dedicated to political action to benefit the elderly. Most significant is the American Association for Retired Persons (AARP), with close more than 33 million members. Representative other groups are the National Committee to Preserve Social Security and Medicare, the National Council of Senior Citizens, the National Council on Aging, the National Caucus of Black Aged, and the Gerontological Society. Thee organizations work through lobbyists, mailing campaigns, advertising, and other processes to improve the lot of the elderly in the United States.

As the elderly increase in numbers, their sphere of influence will increase as well. Thus, there will be strong and coordinated efforts by the elderly for more generous Social Security and Medicare systems. Seniors, if history is a guide, will likely oppose higher taxes and school bond expenditures. Future politics, then, will be characterized by generational tensions, with the younger generations fighting against higher taxes to fund the elderly and fighting for school taxes for the children's education and seniors resisting them on both fronts. The tensions will be not only generational but also racial (Peyser, 1999). This is because the younger generation, which is asked to pay the bills for the elderly, are increasingly multiracial and multiethnic, whereas the 65-plus population is overwhelmingly White (85 percent).

THE THREE STRUCTURAL TRANSFORMATIONS OF SOCIETY

This chapter focuses on three major transformations occurring in society—one economic and two demographic. These macro forces have huge consequences for society, for communities, for families, and for individuals. These contemporary economic forces have brought about a fundamental transformation in the nature of work. Fewer and fewer workers are engaged in mass assembly-line production, jobs that paid well and had good benefits. Many assumed that new jobs in the service sector and along the information superhighway and cyberspace would absorb those downsized from changing industries. This occurred but to only a limited extent, because the skills required are very different from those of the industrial age, and these high-tech corporations also downsize their workers as they automate and use low-cost labor worldwide. As a result, only 35 percent of displaced workers have found work that equaled or surpassed their previous wage/benefits. In effect, the economic transformation has caused millions of workers to transfer from good wage jobs to lower-wage jobs or to temporary or contingent work, or to no work at all. Also, the unskilled and semi-skilled workers have been either left out or work at low wages without benefits. Thus, many in society must deal with insecurity and downward mobility. Many wives join their husbands in the labor force to supplement family income. This has consequences for childbearing (whether or not to have children, the timing and spacing of children), child care, and the division of labor within families.

Society is also undergoing a racial transformation, fueled especially by massive immigration from Latin America and Asia. Most of these immigrants arrive without the work and language skills to fit into a knowledge society. Past immigrants have succeeded economically, but the realities of the economic transformation increase the likelihood that they will be left on the margins. Moreover, the political climate fosters the elimination of affirmative action and other compensatory programs to aid minorities, as well as the downsizing of public supports to the poor, and the neglect of urban blight and inner city schools. All of these occur as racial minorities move toward becoming the numerical majority by mid-twenty-first century.

In addition to the external demographic force—immigration—there is an internal population shift—the growing proportion of the elderly—that is and will continue to affect society. This increase in the dependent population places pressure on workers and families to provide for them. Their growing political power will affect public policies, the politics of elections, and the political dynamics of certain states and regions.

The consequences of these three powerful macro social forces are many. The most significant for our consideration is that these structural conditions shape families.

CHAPTER REVIEW

1. The economy of the United States is in the midst of a major structural transformation. This fundamental shift is the consequence of several powerful converging forces: (a) technological change; (b) the globalization of the economy; (c) capital flight; and (d) the shift from an industrial economy to a service/information/knowledge economy.

2. These forces combine to create considerable discontinuity and disequilibrium in society. In particular, they have reduced the number of jobs providing a middle-class standard of living and have expanded the number of lower-standard-of-living jobs. This results in greater income inequality, increased job insecurity, a shrinking middle class, downward social mobility for many, and the creation and perpetuation of the new poor.

3. The new economy has generated several difficulties for most workers and their families. While wages have been stagnant or declining, the cost of purchasing a new car has increased, as has the cost of owning or renting housing and the cost of a college education.

4. Families have adjusted to economic difficulties by placing both spouses in the labor force, working more hours to stay even, engaging in home-based work, and taking on increased debt.

5. Downward mobility from the middle class causes personal difficulties, such as loss of self-esteem and self-blame. Economic insecurity is related to stress, marital tension, depression, and high levels of alcohol consumption.

6. The economic transformation has fostered growth among the working poor. This growth is a result of unemployment, underemployment, and a minimum wage that does not lift a family above the poverty line.

7. The new poor are those blue-collar workers who lost manufacturing jobs with good pay and benefits because their companies closed or moved elsewhere or because the workers were replaced by automation.

These new poor are much more trapped in poverty than were the old poor of other generations.

8. Blue-collar workers in this century have experienced a rapid rise and fall in their fortunes. As this happened, they moved from the modern family (an intact nuclear household of male breadwinner, his full-time homemaker wife, and their children) to the postmodern family (emergent family forms that vary considerably). Working-class women, in particular, are the pioneers of these emergent family forms.

9. The second societal upheaval that is shaking up society and families is massive immigration. This wave of immigration (adding about 1.2 million immigrants annually) differs from previous waves because the immigrants come primarily from Latin America and Asia rather than Europe.

10. Racial and ethnic diversity (the browning of America) is increasing, with the influx of about 1.2 million immigrants and differential fertility. The non-White population will be equal in size to the White population in about 2050.

11. The two fastest-growing minorities—Latinos and Asian Americans—are each heterogeneous groups with wide differences by ethnicity in poverty rates, fertility rates, income, and education.

12. The lot of the new immigrants, for the most part, is difficult (hostility from others, language barriers, and demeaning and underpaid jobs without benefits). In response, migrants tend to adapt by moving to a location where there is a network of friends and relatives (moving in with relatives, pooling resources, and helping others in need). To overcome low wages, all able family members work. To overcome hostility from others, the immigrant community closes ranks.

13. Research on Mexican and Vietnamese immigrants shows that the immigration process itself reduces traditional patriarchal relations in families.

14. The third societal upheaval that has profound consequences for families is the extraordinary growth in the proportion of the U.S. population age 65 and over. In this age category, women outnumber men and minorities are underrepresented. Although the elderly are not disproportionately poor, the elderly who are women, minorities, or who live alone are disproportionately poor.

15. The Social Security program is the only source of income for about one-half of retired people and a major source of income for 80 percent of the elderly. Medicare is the universal health insurance program for the elderly.

16. The likelihood of the elderly living with their adult children will increase because of greater longevity. The common result for families will be a beanpole family structure—that is, a vertical, four-generation family structure.

17. The elderly face four major role transitions—from work to leisure, from marriage to widowhood, from independence to dependence, and from living to impending death.

18. For most elderly people, dying is a relatively long process because of advances in the treatment of disease, and the medical ways to prolong life artificially. This relatively slow process often results in many months of dependence on family caregivers, usually women.

19. The elderly respond to this stage in the life cycle in several characteristic ways. They may withdraw from social relationships (disengagement); they may continue to act as they have throughout their adult lives; or they may become politically active to change the laws, customs, and social structures that disadvantage them.

20. The major consequence of the convergence of these three powerful forces—the structural transformation of the economy, the changing racial composition of society because of immigration, and the aging of society—is their effects on family forms, such as dual-worker families, transnational families, beanpole structure families, and elders living with their adult children who care for them.

Related Web Sites

http://opr.princeton.edu/

The Office of Population Research at Princeton University is the oldest population research center in the country.

http://factfinder.census.gov

American Factfinder: In 1996, the U.S. Census Bureau undertook a comprehensive multi-year development effort to build a data dissemination system. In order to expand public access to demographic and economic information, the Bureau wanted to provide access to its data through the Internet. American Factfinder was created in 1999 to help disseminate Census Bureau data to the larger public.

http://ameristat.org/

Ameristat.org is a website developed by the Population Reference bureau in partnership with the Social Science Data Analysis Network. It provides the latest statistics on marriage, family, children, fertility, foreign-born populations, income and poverty, and the elderly.

http://www.aarp.org/indexes/legislative.html

American Association of Retired Persons (AARP): This organization is specifically for individuals over 50 years old, but this website is available to all. This site includes articles and discussion groups on current events as well as issues pertinent to older individuals; it offers a unique perspectives on mainstream issues.

http://www.nih.gov/nia/

National Institute on Aging: The National Institute on Aging (NIA), one of the 25 institutes and centers of the National Institutes of Health, leads a broad scientific effort to understand the nature of aging and to extend the healthy, active years of life. In 1974, Congress granted authority to form the National Institute on Aging to provide leadership in aging research, training, health information dissemination, and other programs relevant to aging and older people. The NIA's mission is to improve the health and well-being of older Americans through research.

http://www.caregiver.org

Family Caregiver Alliance: Founded in 1977, Family Caregiver Alliance was the first community-based nonprofit organization in the country to address the needs of families and friends providing long-term care at home.

http://www.urban.org/periodcl/update25.htm

Keys to Successful Immigration: The New Jersey Experience: This 1997 report by the Urban Institute discusses why immigrants have been successful in some areas of New Jersey.

http://www.NAFTAWORKS.org

The Mexico–U.S. Relationship: This site provides a profile of the relationship between Mexico and the U.S. since the enactment of NAFTA. In addition, this site discusses the importance of the border between these two countries. Due to both its geographical location, as the first point of binational interaction, and to the intensity of exchange registered, the border has strategic importance for both countries.

http://www.immigration.about.com/

About Immigration provides a long list of features, some practical, some scholarly, from a variety of sources.

http://www.cis.org/

Center for Immigration Studies (Washington, DC) is a nonprofit organization founded in 1985 devoted to research and policy concerning the impact of immigration on the United States. It is the Center's mission to expand the base of public knowledge and understanding of the need for an immigration policy that gives first concern to the broad national interest.

http://www.prospect.org/archives/20/20blue.html

Barry Bluestone's "The Inequality Express": A report found in the American Prospect Online Magazine on economic restructuring and its impact on workers and their families.

Class, Race, and Gender

Myths and Realities

Myth: Since the United States is a classless society, there should be commonalities in family structure and family relations. Whatever differences exist in family patterns are due to distinct family values and lifestyles.

Reality: The class structure produces great inequalities in the resources people need for family living, and this creates class variation in families.

Myth: Cultural preferences and deviant family values create problems for minority families.

Reality: Family patterns among racial-ethnics are often adaptations to the lack of opportunities in the larger society.

Myth: Families are women's worlds, in which female control of domestic activities gives women power they lack in the public sphere.

Reality: Families are part of a wider system of male power, giving men privileges largely at women's expense.

*T*oday, families in our society share some common features. All families must acquire provisions for daily living and do the work of feeding and caring for family members. All families must make decisions, use leisure time, and engage in countless other activities that fall within the realm of family life. Beneath the surface of similarities, there are far-reaching differences in *how* these family relations are organized and experienced. Variations in families reflect conditions in the surrounding society, especially the social organization of class, race, and gender.

This chapter examines the different family arrangements produced by social inequalities. First, we introduce class, race, and gender as forms of inequality that make different opportunities available to families. We then turn our attention to class, race, and gender as structural categories. Looking at each system, we discuss conventional explanations about their effects on family life. We critique conventional thought on the grounds that it fails to explain how families are socially constructed. We then use our structural diversity framework to show how class, race, and gender produce diverse family arrangements. We pay particular attention to differences as they emerge out of people's everyday lives in different social locations.

The theme of this chapter is that families are differently embedded in these intersecting systems, and that this is key to understanding family life.

CLASS, RACE, AND GENDER AS STRUCTURED INEQUALITIES

Class, race, and gender are macro structural categories that profoundly affect micro structural family worlds. Of course, the social patterning of inequality occurs along many other dimensions, including age, family characteristics, and place of residence (see Table 5.1). Although many characteristics are associated with varying degrees of inequality, class, race, and gender organize society as a whole and create varied environments for family living through their unequal distribution of social opportunities.

To understand the effects of class, race, and gender on family relations, we must understand four points about these systems: (1) they are forms of stratification that foster group-based inequalities; (2) they distribute social rewards and opportunities differently; (3) they are relational systems of power and subordination; and (4) they are interconnected systems of inequality. Let us look at these points.

The phrase **social stratification** refers, in essence, to structured inequality. The term *structured* refers to stratification as being socially patterned. This means that inequalities are not caused by biological, cultural, or lifestyle differences. Of course, class, race, and gender can also refer to individual characteristics, but they are built into society's institutions in ways that produce advantages and disadvantages for entire groups of people. A crucial feature of social stratification is that groups are socially defined and then treated unequally. Social stratification rests on *group-based* inequalities (Collins, 1997). When groups are differentiated as inferior or superior, we have stratification.

TABLE 5.1

Persons and Families in Poverty by Selected Characteristics: 1998

Characteristics	Below Poverty Percent	Characteristics	Below Poverty Percent
PEOPLE		FAMILIES	
Total	12.7	Total	10.0
Family Status		**Type of Family**	
In families	11.2	Married couple	5.3
Householder	10.0	White	5.0
Related children under 18	18.3	White, non-Hispanic	3.8
Related children under 6	20.6	Black	7.3
In unrelated subfamilies	19.9	Hispanic origin	15.7
Children under 18	50.5	Female householder, no	
Unrelated individuals	19.9	husband present	29.9
Male	17.0	White	24.9
Female	22.6	White, non-Hispanic	20.7
Race		Black	40.8
White	10.5	**Race**	
White, non-Hispanic	8.2	White	8.0
Black	26.1	White, non-Hispanic	6.1
Asian and Pacific Islander	12.5	Black	23.4
Hispanic origin	25.6	Asian and Pacific Islander	11.0
Age		Hispanic origin	15.7
Under 18 years	18.9		
18 to 24 years	16.6		
25 to 34 years	11.9		
35 to 44 years	9.1		
45 to 54 years	6.9		
55 to 59 years	9.2		
60 to 64 years	10.1		
65 years and over	10.5		
Nativity			
Native	12.1		
Foreign born	18.0		
Naturalized citizen	11.0		
Not a citizen	22.2		
Region			
Northeast	12.3		
Midwest	10.3		
South	13.7		
West	14.0		
Residence			
Inside metropolitan areas	12.3		
Inside central cities	18.5		
Outside central cities	8.7		
Outside metropolitan areas	14.4		

Source: U.S. Bureau of the Census. "Poverty in the United States: 1998." *Current Population Reports,* Series P60-207. Washington, DC: U.S. Government Printing Office, 2000. Table A, pp. vi, vii.

"Actually, Tommy, we're just about full-blooded management, except for your grandfather on your mom's side, who was one-quarter labor."

The hierarchies of stratification—class, race, and gender—place socially constructed groups, and the individuals and families assigned to those groups, in different social locations. The crucial consequence of this placement is that the rewards and resources of society—wealth, power, and privilege—are unequally distributed. Crucially, differential access to these societal rewards produces different life experiences and different life chances. The term **life chances** refers to the chances one has throughout a life cycle to live and to experience the good things in life. Life chances are the most critical because they are those things that

> (1) better off people can purchase (good medical care, comfortable homes, fine vacations, expert services of all kinds, safe and satisfying occupations) and which poor people would also purchase if they had the money; (2) . . . make life easier, longer, healthier, and more enjoyable (Tumin, 1973:104).

The converse, of course, is that people at the low end of the stratification hierarchies will have inadequate health care, shelter, and diets. Their lives will be more miserable, and they will die sooner (Eitzen and Baca Zinn, 2001:236).

Not only do class, race, and gender arrange groups and individuals in patterned ways and allocate society's resources unequally, they are also systems of power and domination. Class, race, and gender are made up of structured social relationships in which the affluent dominate the poor, men dominate women, and Whites dominate people of color (Feagin, 1986:21). These hierarchies of domination and subordination are not just rankings of socially valued resources—who has more income or prestige—they are power relationships (Weber, 1998:305). They structure the experiences of *all families,* albeit in different ways (Baca Zinn, 1994:305). Class, race, and gender simultaneously generate advantages for some and disadvantages for others. In other words, social locations of opportunity and oppression are *relational.* This means that men and women from dominant race, class, and gender groups play a part in and benefit from the oppression of subordinates.

The hierarchies of race, class, and gender do not stand alone. They are interconnected systems of inequality. Economic resources, the bases of class, are not randomly distributed but vary systematically by race and gender. For example, people of color and women have fewer occupational choices than do White males. People of color and women often experience separate and unequal education and receive less income for the work they do, resulting in different life chances. These systems of inequality form a **matrix of domination** (Collins, 2000) that affects all families and individuals. The configuration of class, race, and gender relations has several important implications (Baca Zinn and Dill, 1996). First, people experience race, class, gender, and sexuality differently depending on their social location in these structures of inequality. For example, people of the same race will experience race differently depending on their location in the class structure as poor, working class, professional/managerial class, or unemployed, and their location in the gender structure as male or female and in the sexuality system as heterosexual, gay, or lesbian. These systems of inequality create an imbalance of power *within* families as well as *between* families.

Class, race, and gender all play a part in creating varied environments for families. Viewing differences as a consequence of how families are embedded within the larger society challenges many common ideas about family life. Most people (and even some family experts) believe that family differences are rooted in group-specific characteristics; in other words, that distinctive class and race experiences in family living come from unique values, morals, and cultural preferences. Our perspective agrees that families in different race, class, and gender categories often have distinctive values, but we examine family life as it occurs in social contexts that include power relations between dominant and subordinate racial and class groups as well as power relations between women and men.

CLASS

Social class is a complex concept that centers on the distribution of economic resources. That is, when a number of individuals occupy the same relative economic rank in the stratification system, they form a **social class.** (The following discussion is based on Eitzen and Baca Zinn, (2001:265–268). There are no clear-cut boundaries, except perhaps those delineating the highest and lowest classes. A social class is not a homogeneous group, given the diversity within it, yet there is some degree of identification with other people in similar economic situations. Also, people have a sense of who is superior, inferior, or equal to them.

Sociologists agree that there are social classes. However, they disagree on the meaning of class for people and on how to define class. Although this oversimplifies the debate, there are two different ways to think about class. Each approach gives us a distinctive view of family.

The Cultural Approach

Some sociologists use the terms "income," "occupation," and "education" as fundamental indicators of social class, with "occupation" as central. Occupational placement determines income, interaction patterns, opportunity, and lifestyle. Lifestyle is the key feature of social class. Each class is viewed as having its distinct culture. There are believed to be class-specific values, attitudes, and motives that distinguish a class's members from other classes. These orientations stem from income and especially from occupational experience (Collins, 1988:29), which then give rise to class-differentiated family patterns.

Lower-class people are thought to be unmotivated, incapable of deferring gratification, and as a result unable to improve their condition (Miller and Riessman, 1964). Poor families are described in even more negative terms: as apathetic and fatalistic, responding to their economic situation by becoming fatalistic; they feel they are down and out and there is no point in trying to improve, for the odds are all against them (Kahl, 1957:211, 213).

The middle class, on the other hand, have occupations orienting them to success and self-direction. They raise their children differently, stressing

> self-control, curiosity, and consideration . . . cultivating capacities for self-direction and empathetic understanding in their children, while working class parents who focus on obedience, neatness, and good manners, are instilling behavioral conformity (Gilbert and Kahl, 1982:126).

Upper-middle-class "careers" require initiative and self-direction, whereas working-class jobs require workers to follow orders. Although these lifestyles stem from specific occupational experiences, comparisons between the classes usually turn out to be *deficit* accounts of lower-status families. Not only are these characteristics insulting, but they are also conspicuously lopsided, implying that lower-class people fail because something is missing in their families. There is not enough ambition, or stimulation, or loving-kindness, or patience (Connell et al., 1982:27).

One of the most influential concepts in deficit explanations of family life among the poor is the **culture of poverty**. The culture of poverty contends that the poor are qualitatively different in values and lifestyles from the rest of society and that these cultural differences explain continued poverty. In other words, the poor, in adapting to their deprived condition, are more permissive in raising their children, less verbal, more fatalistic, less apt to defer gratification, and less likely to be interested in formal education than the well-to-do. Most important is the contention that this deviant culture pattern is transmitted from generation to generation.

The culture of poverty thesis arose from anthropological case studies of Oscar Lewis (1959, 1966). Based on ethnographies of lower-class family life in Mexico, Puerto Rico, and New York, Lewis argued that the difference between the poor and the nonpoor is cultural, resting in values and attitudes. Poverty is more the result of defective lifestyles than of physical environment. If poverty itself were to be eliminated, the former poor would probably continue to prefer instant gratification, be immoral by middle-class standards, and so on.

Social scientists of previous generations were not the only ones to use culture-of-poverty reasoning. Today we find it in some uses of the term **underclass** by social scientists and media analysts in discussions of urban poverty. The underclass is said to be locked into poverty by a maladaptive culture—a way of life utterly different from that in the American mainstream (Lemann, 1986:32). Like the culture-of-poverty and lower-class-culture concepts, the underclass concept implies that people are poor due to their own behaviors.

Shortcomings of the Cultural Approach

Common values and lifestyles among families with similar occupations, education, and income are real, but emphasizing culture distorts key points. Treating diversity as the result of cultural differences amounts to little more than a statement of the tautology, "Families in different social classes are different because their cultures are different." This may be true, but it is not meaningful. Although subcultural differences are important, they become fully meaningful only when they are related to social and economic context.

Cultural explanations of family life in different parts of the class system ignore the social and material realities of class. Instead of recognizing how the economic system produces different levels of support for family life, the conventional explanations make each class responsible for its fate.

Over the years, social scientists have disputed the typical interpretation of poverty. Today, extensive research offers a different explanation. Here, we review evidence from two studies arguing that family life among the poor is not caused by deviant values. The first study was conducted almost four decades ago by Hyman Rodman (1964). He argued that many so-called lower-class family traits were *solutions* to the problems lower-class people face in life. Consensual unions and female or mother-centered households, "promiscuous" sexual relationships, "illegitimate" children, "deserting" husbands and fathers, and "unmarried" mothers—all are solutions employed by the lower class to problems they face in life. In his study of the lower class in Coconut Village, Trinidad, Rodman found that marital or quasi-marital relationships were related to persistent economic uncertainties. "Marital shifting" and fluid marital bonds were then acceptable alternatives among lower-class families in American society as well.

> Within the United States, the higher rates of divorce and desertion within the lower class, as well as of "common law" unions and illegitimacy, are indicative of such fluidity. If, as I am suggesting, these lower-class patterns are responses to the deprivations of lower-class life, and if they are functional for lower-class individuals, then we can see the sense in which many of the lower-class family patterns that are often regarded as problems are actually solutions to other, more pressing problems (Rodman, 1964:68).

More recent evidence against the culture of poverty comes from a large-scale study conducted by social scientists at the University of Michigan. For over thirty years, the Panel Study of Income Dynamics (PSID) has been gathering data on the economic fortunes of families and individuals over many generations. This study explored a question that most work on the culture of poverty has failed to test—namely, whether the poor constitute a permanent underclass doomed to continuous poverty. By following families since 1968, the PSID has found that poverty is not a permanent condition for most people. For the most part, poor families experience short-term poverty spells as they slip in and out of poverty.

> Over half of the poverty spells experienced by people in the study between 1968 and 1987 lasted one year or less. . . . Over a 20 year period, 12 percent of the poverty spells extended 5 or more years, and only 5 percent of the poverty spells lasted 7 or more years. Among African American families, who tend to have longer spells of poverty than whites, less than 10 percent of poverty spells lasted 7 or more years (Gottschalk, McLanahan, and Sandefur, 1994 cited in O'Hare, 1996:30).

Contrary to the myth that the poor are poor because they lack motivation, the PSID shows that people often fall into poverty because of a dramatic change such as divorce, sudden unemployment, or the birth of a child. Once adjustments are made to those changes, people are often able to climb back out of poverty (O'Hare, 1996; Rank, 2000). (See Box 5.1.)

The experience of long-term poverty varies among population groups. Female-headed families, African Americans, Latinos, and the elderly have longer than average poverty spells once they become poor, because they have fewer routes out of poverty. These facts show how race and gender are interconnected to class in producing poverty. The PSID has found little evidence that poverty is a consequence of the way poor people think or that economic success is a function of "good" values and failure the result of "bad" ones.

The Structural Approach

A very different view of class differences in U.S. families emerges when we examine the institutional features of the class system. The structural perspective is critical of explanations that rest on people's own efforts and abilities. Such explanations neglect the ways in which social class distributes group access to material and social resources. Socially structured opportunities rather than lifestyles determine where people fall in the class system. Occupations are part of the larger opportunity structure of society. Those that are highly valued and carry high income rewards are distributed unevenly. Income has a profound affect on family life. The job or occupation that is the source of the paycheck connects families with the opportunity structure in different ways.

Are occupations, then, the main criterion for social class? The answer to this question depends on which model of social class is used. The first model places families and individuals in social classes according to occupation. Each social class is composed of social equals who share a similar lifestyle. Each class-specific culture is assumed to shape family life differently. Treating classes as groups

BOX 5.1 **Researching Families: The Panel Study of Income Dynamics: Following Parents and Children for Three Decades**

The Panel Study of Income Dynamics (PSID), begun in 1968, is a longitudinal study of a representative sample of U.S. individuals (men, women, and children, and the family units in which they reside). It emphasizes the dynamic aspects of economic and demographic behavior, but its content is broad, including sociological and psychological measures. As of 2000, the PSID had collected information about more than 40,000 individuals spanning as much as thirty years of their lives. The study is conducted at the Survey Research Center, Institute of Social Research, University of Michigan.

Starting with national sample of 5000 U.S. households in 1968, the PSID has reinterviewed individuals from those households every year since that time, whether or not they are living in the same dwelling or with the same people. Adults have been followed as they have grown older, and children have been observed as they advance through childhood and into adolescence, forming family units of their own. Information about the original 1968 sample individuals and their current co-residents (spouses, cohabitors, children, and anyone else living with them) is collected each year. In 1990, a representative national sample of 2000 Latino households, differentially sampled to provide adequate numbers of Puerto Ricans, Mexican Americans, and Cuban Americans, was added to the PSID database.

In the early years, the purpose was to find out more about the policy makers then called the "culture of poverty." Culture-of-poverty theorists believed that lack of motivation and other psychological factors were deeply rooted in the poor and kept many of them isolated from society's mainstream. The panel study measures individual attitudes about achievement, personal effectiveness, and the future with a series of psychological tests. Findings did not support theories that low motivation contributes to poverty. Highly motivated people were not more successful at escaping poverty than those with lower scores on these tests.

If the panel study did not support common ideas about what causes poverty, what did it show? A new and emerging definition of poverty has resulted from the PSID, as the data helped transform research on poverty from a static view of poor and rich to a dynamic view in which families experience *episodes of poverty*. Changes in family living arrangements are important to understand many of the shifts in and out of poverty. Researchers have found that family structure changes such as divorces are as important to well-being as unemployment.

The PSID has been used to design more effective welfare policies nationwide. Citation studies show that it is one of the most widely used social science data sets in the world. In the last five years alone, more than 1000 articles, papers, and other publications were based on the data.

In the next few years, the PSID will pursue a number of bold new directions. These include studies of intergenerational transfers and mobility; research on savings; information technology for home, work, and school; a life course approach to health and aging; studies linking family, school, and community to child development; and research on immigrant adaptation and immigrant children.

Sources: Anne Rueter, "Myths of Poverty." *The Research News,* Ann Arbor, MI: Institute for Social Research, The University of Michigan (July–September, 1984):18–19; PSID Home Page, "An Overview of the Panel Study of Income Dynamics" (April 1997), http://www.umich.edu/psid; PSID Newsletter (April 2000), http://www.isr.umich.edu/src/psid/newsletter/news042000.html.

of occupations has been a useful way of creating a picture of the class structure in which occupations and their resources and rewards are stratified, (that is, divided like a layer cake, with each class or "layer" sharing certain attributes, such as level of income and type of occupation). However, this picture of classes as occupational strata implies that "class" is a static place that individuals and families inhabit, rather than a real-life grouping (Connell et al., 1982:25).

A second model of social class focuses not on occupations but on relationships of power between class groups. A social class in this view is not a cluster of similar occupations, but rather a number of individuals who occupy a similar position within the social relations of economic production (Wright et al., 1982). In other words, what is important in this model is that class relationships are not merely economic relationships, they are *power* relationships, involving domination and subordination. Some groups have more power than others through their structural control of society's scarce resources. The key, then, is not the occupation itself but the control one has over one's own work, the work of others, decision making, and investments. People who own, manage, oppress, and control must be distinguished from those who are managed, oppressed, and controlled.

Both models of social class are important in understanding how class shapes family life. In this section, we refer to families in five categories in order to illustrate two points: (1) that different connections with society's opportunity structure produce and require unique family adaptations; and (2) that structured power relationships produce advantages for some families and disadvantages for others. Class privileges shape family relationships. **Privilege** refers to the distribution of goods and services, situations, and experiences that are highly valued and beneficial (Jeffries and Ransford, 1980:68). **Class privileges** are those advantages, prerogatives, and options that are available to those in the middle and upper classes. They confer dominance, power, and entitlement (McIntosh, 1992:98). They involve help from "the system": banks, credit unions, medical facilities, and voluntary associations. These supportive forces in the larger society create many differences in family patterns.

The family is often thought to be a key unit in the stratification system because it passes on wealth and resources from generation to generation. We will see that although the family is basic in maintaining stratification, life chances are affected by race and gender inequalities as well as by social class. In most families, men have greater socioeconomic resources and more power and privileges than do women, even though all family members are viewed as members of the same social class. Although a family's placement in the class hierarchy does determine rewards and resources, hierarchies based on sex create different conditions for women and men even within the same family (Acker, 1973). Gender cuts across class and racial divisions to distribute resources differently to men and women. Therefore, both family units and individuals are important in our understanding of different family experiences. In the following description of family life and social class, we examine how families in different parts of the class hierarchy are connected to society. The following points are important: (1) class composition and class formation are always in flux; (2) the classes as they are described here contain many contradictions; and (3) the classes are always being entered and exited by individuals in either direction. Nevertheless, the class structure does organize families differently. Poverty, stable wage earning, affluent salaries, and inherited wealth create different material advantages, differences in the amount of control over others, and class differences in how families are shaped and how they operate.

The distinction we have been making between family and household helps us understand why family formation patterns differ by social class. Households are economic sites. They support themselves in different ways: through inheritance, salaries, wages, welfare, or various involvements with the hidden economy, the irregular economy, or the illegal economy. These different ways of acquiring the necessities of life produce variations in family life. Being poor involves more than simply having a low income. It has critical impact on every aspect of family life. The following descriptions situate class-based family differences in factors outside the family.

The Lower Class

The lack of opportunities at the lower levels of the class hierarchy make the nuclear family a difficult arrangement to sustain. Those in poverty are more likely than the nonpoor to use a large network of kin to exchange resources and services (Rank, 2000:308). This extended network provides resources and services such as babysitting, sharing meals, or lending money. It represents a coping mechanism for dealing with poverty.

Poverty reduces the likelihood of marriage. The reason for a great proportion of female-headed households among the poor is that individuals who contemplate marriage generally seek or desire to be economically secure partners. Because poverty undermines the availability of such partners, individuals in these situations are likely to delay or forego marriage (Rank, 2000:309).

These themes are reflected in many studies of the past three decades that show how poverty affects family life. A labor market that fails to provide stable jobs prevents families from lifting themselves out of poverty. The solutions that poor families devise would surprise most nonpoor people. An important addition to the growing body of research on how low-income families *really* get by is Kathryn Edin and Laura Lein's *Making Ends Meet* (1997). They show what poor single mothers who are welfare recipients and those who work in low-paid, unskilled job sectors of the U.S. economy must do to survive. Welfare mothers are not an underclass of women with deviant values. Many mother struggle in low-wage jobs even though they may have been better off on welfare. Over a twelve-month period, Edin and Lein found that both welfare mothers and low-wage working mothers experienced devastating hardships. Both groups faced the same fundamental dilemma each month, and they relied on similar kinds of survival strategies to generate the additional money they needed to bridge the gap between their income and their expenditures.

> These survival strategies were dynamic rather than static. They resembled a continuously unraveling patchwork quilt, constructed from a variety of welfare- and work-based income; cash and in-kind assistance from family, friends, absent fathers, and boyfriends; and cash and in-kind assistance from agencies. Though welfare- and wage reliant mother drew from the same repertoire of strategies, wage-reliant mothers were less likely to rely on supplemental work because they

had so little extra time. For the same reason, they relied much more heavily on their personal networks to meet household expenses. Although maintaining this web of social relations took time, the "work" fit more flexibly into working mothers' schedules (Edin and Lein, 1997:224–225).

This study highlights both the hardships and creativity of poor single mothers. With the high rate of unemployment and limited social opportunities, poor families must do whatever it takes to survive. This often means expanding their family boundaries in order to stretch and sustain the few resources they have. (See Box 5.2.)

The Working Class

Working-class families are the largest single group of families in the country. As Rubin described the working class in the 1990s,

> These are the men and women, by far the largest part of the American work force, who work at the lower levels of manufacturing and service sectors of the economy; workers whose education is limited, whose mobility options are severely restricted, and who usually work for an hourly rather than a weekly wage. They don't tap public resources; they reap no benefit from either the pitiful handouts to the poor or from huge subsidies to the rich. Instead, they go to work every day to provide for their families, often at jobs they hate (Rubin, 1994:30–31).

In Chapter 4 we examined the macroeconomic shifts displacing manufacturing workers and creating new vulnerabilities for family life. These economic pressures are altering the working class and moving them even farther from the idealized nuclear family model. As Stacey (1991:252) argues, working-class families, both Black and White, are the real pioneers of contemporary family patterns. They struggle creatively, often heroically, drawing on whatever resources they can to sustain the family. Support from kin turns out to be one of the most important solutions to social and economic pressures.

Working-class reliance on extended kin, however, is hardly new. Practically every study of working-class families shows that they interact more with kin than do middle-class families. For example, Mirra Komorovsky's study, reported in *Blue Collar Marriage* (1962), which was conducted in the late 1950s, revealed not only that family life was built around kin, but that in many cases kin relations were the sole experience of group membership. Kin relations were governed by principles of reciprocal aid:

> Thus a widowed father shares his home with a married son who pays no rent but is responsible for household expenses; a widowed mother resident with her daughter works as a waitress, paying rent and her share of the grocery bill; a widow and her bachelor brother inherited the parental home and rented rooms to a married daughter who is the homemaker for the whole group and expenses are shared (Komorovsky, 1962:237).

Herbert Gans's study of "urban villagers," Italian American workers in Boston, also painted a kin-based picture of working-class families. Research conducted in the late 1950s revealed "a way of life based on social relationships amidst relatives" (Gans, 1962:245). And Lillian Rubin's classic study, *Worlds of Pain* (1976), described the extended family as the heart of social life. Rubin

BOX 5.2   **Inside the Worlds of Diverse Families:** Survival Strategies

The unskilled and semiskilled mothers we interviewed chose between welfare and work. Their choices were partly shaped by another set of decisions: each mother also had to choose among a range of survival strategies to scratch together enough supplementary income. These survival "choices" were not entirely up to the mother, since other factors, including her personal characteristics and the characteristics of the neighborhood and city she lived in, often limited the range of options available to her. Despite these constraints, however, most mothers said they still had a range of strategies to try.

Some mothers relied on the father of their children or a boyfriend for help. Others relied mainly on their own mother or other family members. In cases where neither a child's father, a boyfriend, nor a relative could help, mothers often relied on an off-the-books job. Some sold sex, drugs, and stolen goods. Still others moved between informal and illegal jobs. When these strategies failed, many went to churches or private charities to get help to pay the light bill or the rent.

Mothers who did not have supportive friends and relatives generally had to find some kind of side-work. But some mothers told us they could not do side-work because they had no one to watch their young children. Others could not get a side-job because they were disabled; still others did not have the know-how to get an off-the-books job without getting caught by their welfare caseworker; and others lived in small, tight-knit communities where a side-job would be hard to hide from authorities.

Mothers who could get neither network support nor side-work were the most dependent on churches and private charities. Not surprisingly, these mothers invested a lot of time learning about the range of public and private sources of help available in their communities. Some mothers had a relatively easy time finding out about agencies because members of their social networks offered them guidance or because such services were well publicized. Other mothers lived in neighborhoods or cities with poor service environments, making agency help more difficult to obtain.

Most women expressed clear preferences for some strategies over others. These preferences had two dimensions. First, most mothers thought some strategies compromised their self-respect more than others. Second, mothers felt that some strategies involved more blatant violations of the welfare rules—and could be more easily tracked by caseworkers—than others.

Self-reliance through work remained most mothers' long-term goal. The vast majority said that they wanted to pay all their bills with what they earned. Full financial independence, allowing them to forgo any outside help, was the only strategy that, in these mothers' eyes, involved no loss of self-respect; yet, not one mother earned enough to make this possible. Instead, they turned to their second-, third-, and fourth-best alternatives to make ends meet. In general, both welfare- and wage-reliant mothers felt that their second-best alternative was to rely on cash help from members of the personal networks. Mothers thought this strategy was the most acceptable for a number of reasons . . . not the least of which was that network help was seen as the best bet for moving from welfare to work. But the quality and extent of mothers' networks varied a lot, and some had no one to whom they were able (or willing) to turn.

Source: Kathryn Edin and Laura Lein, *Making Ends Meet: How Single Mothers Survive Welfare and Low Wage Work.* New York: Russell Sage Foundation, 1997, pp. 143–144.

exclaimed that "even in mobile California, the importance of extended kin among working class families is striking" (Rubin, 1976:197). Of course, living close to relatives can have both costs and benefits. On the one hand, kin can provide support when times are hard. On the other hand, they also require assistance and they can be the source of family conflict.

Those in the working class are more vulnerable to economic slumps. Because they work for wages rather than a salary, their livelihood can fluctuate with the state of the economy. Many working-class families at one time or another live on a combination of wages, unemployment insurance, and Social Security benefits (Bridenthal, 1981). Like those in the lower class, they may depend on welfare, food stamps, and various sectors of the irregular economy. For minorities and women in the working class, economic pressures are compounded by racial discrimination and sex discrimination. Minority groups and women heading households are disproportionately found in this category.

Many blue-collar families keep themselves above the official poverty line through wives' employment. However, not all wives married to blue-collar workers are themselves in working-class occupations. This complicates the class position of families, as David Halle (1984) discovered in his study of blue-collar workers. He found various kinds of "class overlap" that eroded the distinctions between blue-collar families and lower-level white-collar families:

> Better-paid blue-collar workers earn as much as or more than many white-collar workers. This enables workers . . . to move from older neighborhoods to areas that contain a greater occupational mix . . . and their income enables better-paid blue-collar workers to buy the same houses and consumer goods and services as many white-collar employees and to engage in many of the same leisure activities (Halle, 1984:74–75).

The Middle Class

The middle-class family form is idealized in our society. This form, composed of mother, father, and children in a self-supporting, free-standing unit, has long been most characteristic of middle-class and upper-middle-class families. Middle-class families of the new century are quite different from the television stereotyped family of the 1950s, with a breadwinner husband and homemaker mother. Today, many families sustain their middle-class status only through the economic contributions of employed wives. Although middle-class families are less kin-oriented than those in the working class, their "autonomy" is shaped by supportive forces in the larger society. When exceptional resources are called for, nonfamilial institutions usually are available in the form of better medical coverage, expense accounts, credit at banks, and so on (Rapp, 1982:181). These links with nonfamily institutions are precisely the ones that distinguish the family economy of middle-class families.

Class distinctions are often complicated by race:

> Two main things tend to distinguish black middle-class people from middle-class whites. One is the likelihood that many more of their relatives will come to them first for help. The other is that they tend to lack the resources of people who started in the middle class (Billingsley, 1992:284).

Middle-class households are characterized by stable, secure resources provided by both partners.

The salaries of middle-class families provide them with a stable resource base. Even more important, the middle class exerts power and control in relation to the working class. Those in the middle class can control their working conditions in a way that the working class cannot (Vanneman and Cannon, 1987). According to Randall Collins (1988b), this power position distinguishes the middle class from the working class. In his distinction, the middle class are "order-givers" while the working class are "order-takers." This is a useful way of thinking about class as a social relationship. However, gender complicates matters, because paid work gives women and men different connections with society's opportunity structures. Some women's jobs seem to be in middle-class sectors, but Collins argues that, in fact, most women's jobs are "white-collar working-class" because they take rather than give orders:

> Secretaries, clerks, and retail sales positions are order-takers, not order-givers. Many of them are also manual workers, operators of machines (telephones, photocopiers, typewriters, word processors) within an office setting. Nurses, who are conventionally classified as professionals, nevertheless tend to be clerical workers within a medical setting and assistants who perform manual work for physicians (although they may sometimes have some order-giver power vis-à-vis patients). Of the most common female occupations, only schoolteachers (5.3 percent of the female labor force) would be considered genuinely middle class by the criterion of order-giving and order-taking (Collins, 1988b:30).

Gender can create class inconsistencies in middle-class marriages because many middle-class males have married downward to white-collar working-class women.

The Professional Class

Families in the professional class are likely to merge the spheres of work and family. Leisure activities often revolve around occupational concerns and occupational associates. Studies of corporation executives and their families reveal a strong corporate influence. For example, Rosabeth Kanter found that both executives and their wives were closely tied to the corporation. Here is her description of "corporate" wives:

> At a certain point in their husbands' climb to the top [these wives] . . . realized that friendships were no longer a personal matter but had business implications. Social professionalism set in. The political implications of what had formerly been personal or sentimental choices became clear. Old friendships might have to be put aside because the organizational situation makes them inappropriate, as in the case of one officer husband who let his wife know it would no longer be seemly to maintain a social relationship with a couple to whom they had previously been close because the first husband now far outranked the second. The public consequences of relationships made it difficult for some wives to have anything but a superficial friendship with anyone in the corporate social network. Yet since so much of their time was consumed by company related entertainment, they had little chance for friendships and reported considerable loneliness (Kanter, 1984:116).

In many professional homes, family life is subordinate to the demands of the husband-father's occupation. Family can be a respite, "dad's place of leisure" (Larson and Richards, 1994). Or family can take a back seat to the male involvement in work, success, and striving, and its effect on families:

> This is the pressure that often molds the family. Accommodation to it is frequently the measure of being a "good wife," moving when the male's "future" requires it, regulating activities so that the male is free to concentrate on business (Miller, 1972:106).

Typical contacts outside the home support the business orientation of upper-middle-class families.

> Business people live in neighborhoods filled with others like themselves, who share the values of sociability. Their homes are not overcrowded and they can entertain without strain. They become activists in club work and are likely to run into the same townspeople at the parent-teachers association, the Rotary club, or the country club. . . . Even their children form a single extensive web of contacts (Gilbert and Kahl, 1982:151).

What a difference this overarching structure of social class contacts makes in family life! Think back to our review of the working-class family prototype. Komorovsky's study of blue-collar families found no such links with society as may be provided by membership in women's clubs or the Rotary Club. For the great majority, life was narrowly circumscribed by the family, the relatives, a few friends, the union, and the boss. The work sphere and the family sphere of the average male factory worker are totally separate: "He never entertains the foreman, and the foreman certainly gives no thought to a worker's wife before promoting him" (Komorovsky, 1962:154).

Professional families with husbands (and perhaps wives) in careers have both economic resources and built-in ties with supportive institutions. These ties are structural. They are intrinsic to some occupations, and to middle-class neighborhoods. Such class-based connections strengthen the autonomy of these families, allowing them to emphasize the nuclear unit.

The Elite

Vast economic holdings give elite families control over social resources as well as opportunities and choices not available to other families in society. Through their enormous assets, the elite either own or control the major units of the economy. This is class control. Their network of influence in the global economy and their ability to generate additional resources is what most distinguishes the elite from the rest of society. "It is not simply bank interest that generates more money, but income-producing property: buildings, factories, natural resources; those assets Karl Marx referred to as the means of production" (Mantsios, 1996:101). Decisions about what is most profitable for them affect what happens to other families in the nation and the world.

Some examples of upper-class families are the Du Ponts (who control General Motors, U.S. Rubber, and various chemical companies); the Rockefellers (who control Standard Oil and Chase Manhattan Bank); and the Mellons (who control Alcoa, Gulf Oil, the Mellon Bank, and numerous appliance companies) (*Forbes*, 1999). Day-to-day family life among the elite is "privileged" in every sense:

> Wealthy families can afford an elaborate support structure to take care of the details of everyday life. Persons can be hired to cook and prepare meals and do laundry and to care for the children (Stein et al., 1977:9).

Elite family lifestyles are made possible by their control of labor of others—the subordinate classes whose own families must often suffer as they do the work required to support elite privileges. The point is not only that domination and subordination coexist, but that the lifestyles of the wealthy cannot exist without denying the rights and privileges of those who serve them.

The elite have a distinctive family structure. Family boundaries of the elite are more open than those of the middle class, yet *class boundaries* are rigidly drawn. Among the elite, "family constitutes not only a nuclear family but the extended family as well." The elite often have multiple households (Rapp, 1982:182)—that is, numerous townhouses and country places. For years, the Kennedy "compound" at Hyannis, Massachusetts, was an obvious case in point, as were the Rockefeller estates (managed by employees). The compound is usually only one of several residences that serve as community centers for extended kin. Multiple residences are not nuclear households in form, nor are they independent entities (Leibowitz, 1978:165). The concerns and much of day-to-day life exist within the larger context of a kinship network. The kin-based family form of the elite serves to preserve inherited wealth. It is interconnected with other national institutions that control the wealth of society.

Elite families are nationally connected by a web of institutions they control. Families throughout the country are linked by private schools, exclusive colleges, exclusive clubs, and fashionable vacation resorts. In this way the elite remains intact, and the marriage market is restricted to a small (but national) market (Blumberg and Paul, 1975:69). A survey of 500 members of the top 1 percent of the population was conducted by Roper Starch Worldwide. The top 1 percent are people with at least $250,000 in income or $2.5 million in assets. Here are some findings:

Marriage among the elite is more than a legal-emotional commitment. It is a means of concentrating capital and maintaining the in-group solidarity of the class (Langman, 1987:224). Even the division of labor between women and men sustains class solidarity. Research by Susan Ostrander (1984) and Arlene Kaplan Daniels (1987) finds that upper-class women's philanthropic work is vital in preserving the institutions that benefit family and class.

We have reviewed studies showing extensive class variation in household and family formation. Kinship ties, obligations, and interests are more extended in classes at the two extremes than they are in the middle (McKinley, 1964:22). In the upper extreme and toward the lower end of the class structure, kinship networks serve decidedly different functions, but at both extremes they are institutions of resource management.

*R*ACE

Like the class and gender hierarchies, racial stratification is deeply embedded in U.S. society. It operates as a structure of opportunity and oppression through its unequal distribution of privilege. In this section of the chapter, we will show how race shapes family arrangements.

Race is a social category that serves as a basis of power relations and group position. The racial hierarchy, with White groups of European origin at the top and people of color at the bottom, serves important functions for society and for certain categories of people. It ensures that some people are available to do society's dirty work at low wages. The racial hierarchy has positive consequences for the status quo: it enables the powerful to retain their control and advantages. Racial stratification also offers better occupational opportunities, income, and education to White people. These advantages constitute racial privilege. In Chapter 3 we examined the historical developments that produced different family arrangements for Whites and people of color.

Racial distinctions are a way of classifying people with certain characteristics. Although racial categories operate as if they were real, there is no such thing as biological **race**. Instead, the characteristics that distinguish racial categories are *socially defined*. Racial classification in the United States is based on a Black/White dichotomy—that is, the construction of two opposing categories into which all people fit. However, the social definitions of race change over time and vary in different regions of the country. In the Southwest the divide has been between Anglos and Latinos; in parts of the West Coast it is between Asians and Whites (Rosenblum and Travis, 1996:15). In Chapter 4 we saw that new patterns

Racial-ethnic groups are strongly influenced by social, political, and economic forces in the larger society.

of immigration are changing our social definitions of race. Sociologists Michael Omi and Howard Winant (1994:55) call this **racial formation,** meaning that society is continually creating and transforming racial categories. Groups that were previously defined in terms of specific ethnic backgrounds (such as Mexican Americans and Japanese Americans) have become racialized as Hispanics and Asian Americans. Even the U.S. Census Bureau, which measure races on the basis of self-identification, revised its racial categories for the 2000 Census.

Although racial classification has been confounded by a Black/White dichotomy, common thought overlooks whiteness as a racial category. Most Whites do not think of themselves in racial terms because they are not people of color (McIntosh, 1992). Race is treated as something possessed by people of color—racial others—whereas Whites are depicted "(usually implicitly) as having no race and as people whose lives are not affected by race" (Lucal, 1996:245–246). In this view whiteness is the normal or natural condition. It is racially unmarked (Frankenberg, 1993) and, therefore, something immune to investigation. This is a false picture of race. In reality, the racial order shapes the lives of all people, even Whites who are advantaged by the system. Just as we must understand how different social classes exist in relation to each other, we must also use a relational model to see that definitions of all races are possible only in relation to other races. "Black" is meaningful only insofar as it is set apart from, and in contradistinction to, "White." "This point is particularly obvious when people are referred to as "non-White" (a word that ignores the differences in experiences among people of color) (Lucal, 1996:246). Race should not be seen simply as a matter of two opposite categories of people but as a range of power relations among differently situated people.

Whereas race is used for socially marking groups based on physical differences, **ethnicity** allows for a broader range of affiliation. Ethnic groups are distinctive on the basis of national origin, language, religion, and culture. The contemporary world is replete with examples of newly constructed ethnicities. In the United States, people began to affiliate along ethnic lines such as Italian American or German American much more frequently after the civil rights movement.

In the United States, race and ethnicity both serve to mark groups as different. Groups labeled as *races* by the wider society are bound together by their common social and economic conditions. As a result, they develop distinctive cultural or ethnic characteristics. Today, we use the concept racial-ethnic groups (or racially defined ethnic groups). The term **racial-ethnic** refers to groups that are socially subordinated and remain culturally distinct within U.S. society. It is meant to include (1) the systematic discrimination of socially constructed racial groups, and (2) their distinctive cultural arrangements. We saw in Chapter 3 that, historically, the categories of African American, Mexican American, Asian American, and Native American were constructed as both racially and culturally distinct. Each group has a distinctive culture, shares a common heritage, and has developed a common identity within a larger society that subordinates it.

As we saw in Chapter 4, the growing presence of racial-ethnic groups is changing U.S. society. Figure 5.1 shows how the racial composition of the United States is expected to change through the year 2050. Terms of reference are also changing, and the changes are contested within racially defined groups as well as between them. For example, Blacks continue to debate the merits of the term "African American," while Latinos disagree on the label "Hispanic." In this book, we use such terms interchangeably because they are currently used in popular and scholarly discourse.

Racial-Ethnic Families

Although racial stratification affects families throughout society, we focus here on racialized patterns of family formation among African Americans and Lati-

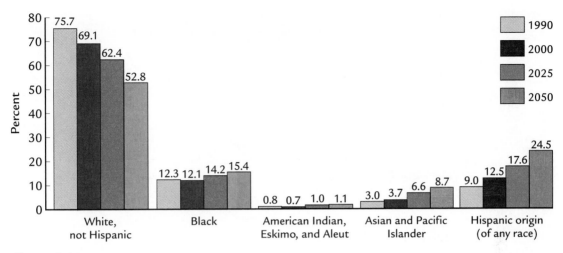

Figure 5.1

Percent of the population, by race and Hispanic origin: 1990, 2000, 2025, and 2050 (middle-series projection)

Source: U.S. Bureau of the Census, Current Population Reports, Series P23-194, *Population Profile of the United States: 1997.* Washington, DC: U.S. Government Printing Office, p. 9; U.S. Bureau of the Census, accessed online at www.census. gov/population/www/cen2000.

nos. Our intent is not to limit our understanding of racial stratification to people of color, but to examine some of the ways in which racially subordinated groups are denied social opportunities that benefit family life.

The Cultural Approach

There is a strong tendency for the public and some social scientists to think of racial-ethnic families as cultural artifacts. When an idealized model of White families is used as the norm, racial-ethnic families are seen as the product of deficient cultural preferences. Group-specific family patterns handed down from generation to generation are said to hinder the development of family characteristics needed in modern society. This type of thinking maintains that African American and Latino families are historic relics. Latinos, among whom extended family networks play a strong part in integrating family and community, are criticized for being too "familistic"—their lack of social progress is blamed on family values that keep them tied to family rather than economic advancement. African American families are criticized as "matriarchal" because of the strong role women play in extended family networks (Dill et al., 1993:16). In both cases, the flawed family structure is said to be responsible for that minority group's status in society. Walter Allen (1978:125) has called this the "cultural deviant" approach. This approach was used in Daniel P. Moynihan's (1965) well-known study of Black families (see Chapter 3). The Moynihan report was widely criticized because it viewed family arrangements among Blacks as deviant and the product of Black culture. The main objection to the Moynihan report is that it is

Murals in Chicano communities reflect their distinct identity within the larger culture.

a classic case of blaming the victim, locating the problems in the so-called matriarchal structure of the Black family, not in the racially organized society.

The deficit model of Chicano families also sparked criticism. Several works on Mexican American families that were published about the same time that the Moynihan report appeared (Heller, 1966; Madsen, 1964; Rubel, 1966) found the problems of Mexican American people to be the result of the patriarchal family structure.

During the 1960s and 1970s, scholars became sharply critical of cultural deficiency approaches. Instead of a cultural deviance perspective, much family research has discovered that racial-ethnic families are resilient and adaptive in responding to racial inequality.

Shortcomings of the Cultural Approach

The cultural argument is deeply flawed. First, and most important, it views the family as the "primary" institution of society (Skolnick and Skolnick, 1983:164), rather than one largely shaped by social forces. Second, and closely related, it blames the victim and ignores the impact of racism and economic structure on family formation. Third, it treats all African American families and all Latino families as monolithic entities rather than acknowledging a wide diversity of family forms among people of color.

Macro Structural Inequalities and Racial-Ethnic Families

Social conditions associated with racial inequalities produce aggregate differences between minority and White families. Different racial groups make their homes in neighborhoods that are typically segregated, thus living in "separate societies." An entire arsenal of social institutions creates paths in which families assigned to one group receive better jobs, housing, health care, schooling, and recreational facilities, while those relegated to other groups do worse, or do without (Collins, 1997:397). For minorities, segregation, employment problems, and poverty are barriers to family well-being and to family formation. As a result, the family arrangements of racial-ethnics, and their definitions of what families *are*, often depart from the idealized family organized around a heterosexual couple living in a single-family dwelling and needing little support from relatives or neighbors.

Extended kinship systems and informal support networks spread across multiple households have long been common among people of color. Extended families and "fictive kin"—people treated like family even though they are not related by blood or marriage—are found in all racial-ethnic groups. These patterns are not merely the result of cultural preferences. Rather, they are often produced by social and economic conditions that fail to meet family needs. Family extension is a way of sharing resources denied by the larger society. In saying that family structure is the result of distinctive social conditions, we should recognize the *varied* social and economic contexts within which different racial-ethnics experience their family lives. There are no "typical" racial-ethnic families. Like families throughout the nation and the world, U.S. people of color live in diverse social and economic settings that produce multiple family outcomes. Furthermore, many characteristics of racial-ethnic families *are* culturally unique. Ways of relating, of spending leisure time, and of worshiping, as well as forms of entertainment, language, and food customs, are different from those of families in the dominant society.

Nevertheless, racism produces many common characteristics associated with limited economic resources. In the past decade, the research emphasis was on how these conditions affect family structure, especially the shift to family types more vulnerable to poverty (McLoyd et al., 2001). Compared with Whites, people of color have higher rates of female-headed households, out-of-wedlock births, divorce, and other factors associated with a general lack of support for family life. In Chapter 3 we saw that minority families have long experienced the juggling of work and family roles for women, single parenthood, extended family relationships, and poverty—conditions that are now affecting more and more families throughout society (Stack and Burton, 1994:42).

Economic hardship among people of color has tended to reinforce the stereotype of poor minority families. However, we must realize that not all people of color are poor. The tendency to view racial-ethnic families as a collection of the problems they face can be misleading. Class differences exist among African Americans and Latinos. For example, several million African Americans are in the middle class, with incomes, education, and lifestyles similar to those of their White counterparts. They are successful professionals, managers, elected officials, and entrepreneurs. In the past quarter-century, many well-educated African Americans have made considerable advances. At the end of the twentieth century, a third of African Americans were middle class (*The Economist*, 1993:17). However, as successful African Americans have improved their life chances, unsuccessful ones have been marginalized.

The Cosby Show notwithstanding, few families of color enjoy an upper-middle-class standard of living. Although the number of affluent blacks has skyrocketed over the past decade, the net worth of Black households is only 12 percent of what White households are worth, while the net worth of Latino households is only 8 percent that of Whites (Collins et al., 1999:55). Minorities are twice as likely to have low relative incomes but three times less likely to be in the high-income tier. Roughly 40 percent of African Americans and Hispanics fall on the bottom rung of the relative income ladder, whereas only about 5 percent have made it to the top (Ahlburg and DeVita, 1992:38). Although the racial income gap is wide, the racial wealth gap is even wider. White families generally have greater net worth than Black or Latino families (Collins et al., 1999), In their book, *White Wealth/Black Wealth*, Melvin Oliver and Thomas Shapiro (1995) define wealth as the command over financial resources that a family has accumulated over its lifetime, along with those resources that have been inherited across generations. White families generally have greater resources for their children, and bequeath them as assets at death. Oliver and Shapiro call this "the cost

TABLE 5.2

Median Income by Race and Family: 1998

All Races

Married-couple families	$54,180
Wife in labor force	63,751
Male householder, no wife present	35,681
Females household, no husband present	22,163

White

Married-couple families	$54,736
Wife in labor force	64,480
Male householder, no wife present	37.798
Females household, no husband present	25,175

Black

Married-couple families	$47,383
Wife in labor force	55,579
Male householder, no wife present	27,087
Females household, no husband present	16,770

Hispanic

Married-couple families	$34,816
Wife in labor force	45,188
Male householder, no wife present	29,227
Females household, no husband present	16,532

Source: U.S. Bureau of the Census, "Money Income in the United States: 1998." *Current Population Reports*, U.S. Department of Commerce, Economics and Statistics; Bureau of the Census Series P60-206. Washington, DC: U.S. Government Printing Office, 2000, Table 4, pp. 13–16.

of being Black." One important indicator of a family's wealth is home owner-ship. Paying off a home mortgage is the way most Americans build net worth over their lifetimes. More minorities are buying homes, but because of discrimi-nation in employment, housing, and insurance, they are still less likely than Whites to own the homes in which they live. In 1995, the home ownership rate was 47 percent for African Americans and 44 percent for Latinos, about two-thirds the rate for White households (Collins et al., 1999). African American and Latino households are likely to be located in segregated neighborhoods, where median home values are lower.

African American and Latino families are three times as likely as White fam-ilies to be poor. In 1999, 23 percent of African Americans and 22 percent of His-panics were living below the poverty level, compared with 7 percent for Whites (U.S. Bureau of the Census, 2000). Whether or not they are living in poverty, most African American and Hispanic families must get by on far less income than White families. Table 5.2 shows clearly that the average income for White fami-lies is greater than the average income for Black and Hispanic families. In addi-tion, per-person income for Black and Hispanic families is lower than for White families because Black and Hispanic families have more children (DeVita, 1996:30; Pollard and O'Hare, 1999.) (Figure 5.2). This difference in household composition reflects the older age structure of White adults, delayed childbear-ing, and lower fertility among White couples (O'Hare, 1992:19).

These inequalities illustrate that race inequality is in part a class issue, because class is linked to low income. However, many economic inequalities

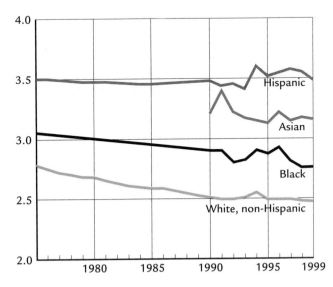

Figure 5.2

Persons per household, by race/ethnicity, 1975–1999

Source: AmeriStat: Population Reference Bureau and Social Science Data Analysis Network. http://www.ameristat.org/marfam/hsehold.htm. Retrieved on January 15, 2001.

have more serious consequences for people of color than for Whites. This illustrates that economic inequality is racialized. Race and low-class position combined reduce the life chances far more than does low-class position alone.

Let us examine some contemporary realities of African American and Latino families. Rather than using a middle-class White family model as the norm, we will examine distinctive family characteristics as they relate to structural conditions.

African American Families at Century's End

Marriage

Although two-parent families were strong during and after slavery, sometime after 1925 the proportion of African American families headed by two parents began to decline, and this decline became more pronounced in the 1960s, 1970s, and 1980s. During this period, divorce rates more than doubled, marriage rates declined, fertility rates fell to record levels, the proportion of families in which children lived with both biological parents declined, and the proportion of children reared in single-parent households rose dramatically (Taylor, 2000). Although the vast majority of African American households are family households (i.e., the household members are related by birth, marriage, or adoption), less than half of the families (47 percent) were headed by a married couple in 1990, down from 68 percent in 1970 and 56 percent in 1980. A much higher percentage (81 percent) of White families are headed by married couples, although this percentage also has slipped over the past two decades (U.S. Bureau of the Census, 1999a).

African Americans tend to marry later and have higher rates of marital disruption than Whites. In 1980, 51 percent of persons 18 years and over were married. In 1998, only 41 percent were married. In 1990, only 39 percent of African American women were married and living with their husbands. Over the same period, the percentage of divorced Black persons 18 years and over grew from 8 to 11 percent, and the percentage who had never married grew from 30 to 38 percent (U.S. Bureau of the Census, 1999a, Table 62). While a similar movement away from marriage occurred among White women, the change was much more dramatic among Blacks (Table 5.3). Furthermore, the marriage gap between Whites and Blacks was just as strong among women without children as it was among women with children. Regardless of parental status, African American women are less likely than those in the general population to be married.

What has caused the movement away from marriage among African Americans? A growing body of research has pointed to demographic and economic factors (Taylor, 2000; McLoyd et al., 2001). Many social scientists focus on the relationship between marriage rates and the relative numbers of women and men. African American women outnumber men in the age range (20 to 49) when most people marry and start families. Following this reasoning, fewer Black women are getting married because there are too few suitable Black male partners (that is, those with a good education and a job (Spain and Bianchi, 1996:42). Various social forces undermine marriage among African Americans. Changes in local labor markets together with racial discrimination in hiring and firing have

TABLE 5.3

Marital Status by Race, 1980 and 1998

Year	Married	Divorced	Widowed	Never Married
		WHITE		
1980	67.2	6.0	7.8	18.9
1998	62.1	9.8	6.9	21.2
		BLACK		
1980	51.4	8.4	9.8	30.5
1998	41.8	11.7	7.6	38.9
		HISPANIC		
1980	65.6	5.8	4.4	24.1
1998	58.9	7.7	3.8	29.7

Source: U.S. Bureau of the Census, *Statistical Abstracts of the United States: 1999*
(119th ed.). Washington, DC: U.S. Government Printing Office, 2000, Table 62.

pushed many African American men to the margins, or completely out of the labor force. African American men with low wages and little job security have difficulty fulfilling the traditional role as the major breadwinner for a family. The rise in female-headed families, whether formed through divorce, separation, or out-of-wedlock childbearing, has exacerbated Black/White differences in economic well-being. Today, the fastest-growing African American families are mother-only families, a relatively disadvantaged group (McLanahan and Casper, 1995:3).

Many studies find a link between economic stressors and marital patterns among African Americans. For example, sociologist Robin Jarrett shows that economic factors play a prominent role in women's decisions to forgo marriage, to bear children outside of marriage, and in some cases to head households. Her interviews with never-married mothers uncovered a range of economic pressures that work against marriage. The prospective mates of Jarrett's informants were generally unemployed, underemployed, or relegated to insecure jobs, including car wash attendants; drug dealers, fast food clerks, grocery store stock and bag clerks, hustlers, informal car repairmen, lawn workers, street peddlers, and street salvage workers. Although most women remained unmarried, this did not preclude strong and stable male/female partnerships existing outside of legal marriage (Jarrett, 1994:40–41).

Marital patterns among African Americans are related to social class. It is not that African American people per se have different values regarding marriage and family. Research indicates that differences in marital patterns are determined largely by economic differentials between the races. Billingsley's detailed analysis of the variation in Black family structures and social class experience indicates that the higher up in the social class structure families are, the more likely they are to be husband–wife families. They are also more likely to have employed wives to help sustain this status. Social class and family status are directly related (Billingsley, 1992:57).

Based on prevailing economic conditions, social scientists have proposed that marriage is less important than kinship ties for Blacks (Cherlin, 1992; 1996).

> The Black family is not primarily based on a conjugal relationship or on a single household as in the case of the idealized American family. Rather, it consists of a wide-ranging group of relatives involved in relationships of exchange and co-parenting (Aschenbrenner and Carr, 1980:463).

This arrangement can be viewed as a protective strategy against the uncertainties of marriage. Marriage involves economic as well as affective relationships. Greater economic support can be provided by a kinship exchange network than by a conjugal bond alone. If we see female-headed households within the context of the larger kinship system, we can appreciate how children and other dependents are cared for when other factors undercut marital unions. Marriage is as much the result as the cause of economic security and well-being. Therefore, marriage is a form of class and race privilege.

Because widespread economic marginality threatens long-lasting marriages, African Americans are more tolerant of out-of-wedlock births and informal adoptions. Some scholars have argued that this is one way in which African Americans have managed a relatively high rate of illegitimacy without widespread use of abortions or access to formal adoption agencies sensitive to their needs (Hill, 1977). Marriage is approached with ambivalence by many young African Americans. Given the high unemployment rates among young Black males, many African American families encourage pregnant girls not to marry the father, who would simply be an additional financial burden. The families absorb the child into the family-kin system (Cazenave, 1980:432).

Social Support Networks

Extended family structure and social support networks among minorities have been consistent themes in social science literature for decades. Although some new research finds a decline in network participation by African Americans and other minorities (Rochelle, 1997), research has consistently documented the fact that Blacks are more likely than Whites to reside in extended-family households (Taylor, 2000). Extended-family arrangements consist of both kin and nonkin spread over several households; networks of unrelated kin (fictive kin as well as persons in separate households) a mother, an aunt, a brother, an in-law, and so forth. They share and exchange goods, services, and emotional support (Hill, 1993).

In a pathbreaking study of ghetto families conducted over three decades ago, Carol Stack revealed that extended-family arrangements are a way of coping with poverty and racism. She found that Black families pooled their limited resources in order to survive and that the urgency of their needs created alliances between individuals. According to Stack, "Kin and friends exchange and give and obligate one another. They trade food stamps, rent money, a TV, hats, dice, a car, a nickel here, a cigarette there, food, milk, grits, and children" (Stack, 1974:32)

While kin networks help compensate for resources withheld by the wider society, they also remain strong among middle-class African Americans. Harriette McAdoo (1978) found that socially mobile Blacks continue to draw on their families for more than financial aid; they depend on their families for strong emotional and cultural support as well. The extended-family pattern is both a racial and a cultural phenomenon; among the lower classes of all races and ethnic groups it is a structural coping tactic. Among middle-class African Americans (and Latinos) it has developed into a strong and valuable cultural pattern because, even for more secure African Americans, finding wider community support is always problematic.

Recent research stresses the role of women in the struggle to maintain family life. For example, caring for other people's children, whether kin or not, is an old tradition. "othermothers" are women who assist blood mothers by sharing mothering responsibilities (Collins, 1990). According to Collins, othermothers are key in supporting children and in helping blood mothers. Men are not absent from these families, but women are central in these resilient networks of grandmothers, sisters, aunts, and cousins that share responsibility for child care.

Similar arrangements are found among other racial-ethnics. For example, an Indian "grandmother" may actually be a child's aunt or grandaunt in the Anglo-Saxon use of the term, and extended families may form around complex kinship networks based on conditions other than birth, marriage, or adoption (Snipp, 1989:129). Asian Americans also have a high proportion of extended families. Therefore, a focus on parents and children alone misses the social and cultural resources that other relatives bring to Asian American families (McLoyd, 2001).

The Underclass Debate

Changing household and family patterns have prompted many observers to proclaim a "crisis" in the African American family. Not only is the family said to be disintegrating, but also the decline in married couple families is viewed as the main cause of the urban underclass. This has revived the old cultural explanation and created a national debate over the relationship between family structure and poverty among African Americans.

Two distinct models of the underclass now prevail—one cultural, one structural. Both focus on issues of family structure and poverty (see Baca Zinn [1989], Marks [1991], and Jarrett [1994] for elaborations of cultural and structural models of the Black underclass). Cultural models assign the cause of the growing underclass to ghetto-specific behaviors and a lifestyle of out-of-wedlock childbearing. These theories argue that family breakdown and welfare dependence lock inner-city people in a cycle of poverty. Like the older cultural models, this explanation is wrong on many counts. It relies too heavily on cultural preferences and behavioral traits to explain poverty. It falls back on blaming the victim to explain patterns that are rooted in social structure. It reverses cause and consequence: single-parent families are not the cause of poverty but the consequence of economic deprivation. The macro structural economic transformations we examined in Chapter 4 have removed jobs and other opportunities from inner-city residents and altered their families. This is a better explanation of persistent and concentrated poverty among African Americans. This explanation is detailed in William J. Wilson's compelling books, *The Truly Disadvantaged* (1987) and *When Work Disappears* (1996). According to Wilson, the social problems of the ghetto are caused by economic marginalization. Wilson draws a connection between African American men's declining employment and nonmarital child-bearing among African American women.

Black men's declining employment has other consequences. Together with high levels of poverty and underemployment, joblessness contributes to the disproportionate number of Black males killed in wars and criminal homicide. This shortage of Black men with the ability to support a family causes many Black women to leave marriage or to forgo marriage altogether. Wilson shows that marriage is itself an opportunity structure that does not presently exist for large numbers of Black people.

The economic foundations of African American families are undermined by changes in the urban economy and the class structure of ghetto neighborhoods. The movement of middle-class African American professionals from the inner city has left behind a concentration of the most disadvantaged segments of the Black urban population. Ghetto residents are socially isolated from both mainstream behaviors and opportunity structures. These forces have led to more unemployment, fewer marriages, more female-headed households, and higher poverty rates among African Americans.

Many scholars agree with Wilson on the causes of family disruption among African Americans, but they argue that this captures only a portion of the problem. Inner-city women are also affected by the new economic realities. They, too, need training, employment, wage equity, and day care. The underclass is not a group of people lacking family values, but a group of people who are outside the mainstream of the U.S. occupational structure (Kornblum, 1991:203). This analysis explains how changing political economies alter family and household patterns. Macro structural transformations in class, race, and gender leave African American women disproportionately separated, divorced, and solely responsible for their children.

When critics lament the state of African American families, they often call for policies that would restore the two-parent family. However, the two-parent family is not a guarantee against poverty for minorities (see Figure 5.3). Although living in a married-couple family generally improves the chances of having high relative income, many young children in married-couple homes are in the lowest income tier: three in ten Black children, four in ten Hispanic children, and two in ten White children (Ahlburg and DeVita, 1992:38). Increasing the proportion of Black children growing up in two-parent families would not by itself eliminate much of the racial gap in the economic well-being of children. Raising the life chances of Black children will require changes in the economic status of their parents.

The recent escalation of African American single parenthood is a social and economic problem that warrants close attention. However, we should not use single mothers and their children as the "typical" African American family. This distorts the complex reality of African American families. Sociologist Andrew Billingsley has examined family myths and stereotypes in his book, *Climbing Jacob's Ladder* (1992). He argues that no one pattern describes African American families. There are both weak families and strong families. Furthermore, contrary to the popular wisdom, Black families are not vanishing. Instead, they are doing what they always do:

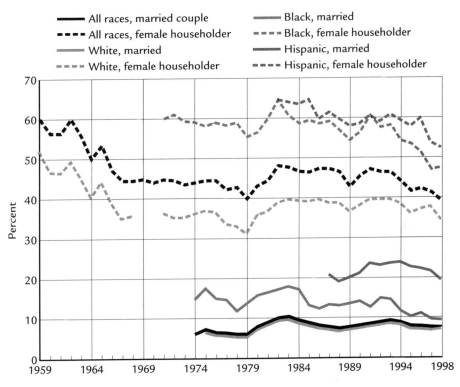

Figure 5.3

Poverty status of families, 1959–1999

Source: U.S. Bureau of the Census, "Poverty in the United States: 1998." *Current Population Reports,* Series P60-207. Washington, DC: U.S. Government Printing Office, Table B-3, pp. B-10 to B-17.

They are adapting as best they can to the pressures exerted upon them from their society in their gallant struggle to meet the physical, emotional, moral, and intellectual needs of their members. It is a struggle for existence, viability, and a sense of worth (Billingsley, 1992:44).

Latino Families at Century's End

In Chapter 4 we examined the diversity among Latinos. In spite of important differences among the groups, Latino families show similarities that stem from racial domination and ethnic patterning, including religion and other cultural forms. Latino families in all regions of the United States are experiencing many of the transitions facing all U.S. families, yet important differences exist. The continuing influx of immigrants combines with systems of class and racial inequalities to produce hardships not faced by mainstream families.

A Hispanic Underclass?
As the Hispanic presence in the United States has increased in the last decade, poverty rates among Hispanics have risen alarmingly. Hispanic children are

more likely than white children to be living below the poverty level. In 1996, 39 percent of Hispanic children under eighteen were living in poverty, compared to sixteen percent of White children (Jones, 1996).

Among Hispanic groups, Puerto Ricans have the highest poverty rates (33 percent compared with 29 percent for Mexicans and 13 percent for Cubans). Over the past three decades the economic status of Puerto Ricans has dropped precipitously. A growing proportion of Puerto Ricans are concentrated in poor urban neighborhoods located in declining industrial centers in the Northeast and Midwest, which have experienced massive economic restructuring and diminished employment opportunities. The rising Puerto Rican poverty rate has also been linked to a dramatic increase in female-headed households (Moore and Pinderhughes, 1993:xix). In 1995, 41 percent of Puerto Rican households were headed by women, compared to 19 percent for Mexicans and 21 percent for Cubans (U.S. Bureau of the Census, 1999b).

Do high poverty rates and changing household patterns among Latinos mean that they have joined inner-city African Americans to form part of the underclass? In other words, do changes in the economy and jobs have the same effects on Blacks and Latinos? Certainly, the broad changes wrought by economic transformations have affected Latinos. Puerto Ricans have been especially hard hit by economic restructuring over the past three decades. For families of Mexican origin, the conditions that place them in poverty are different. A large proportion of Mexican-heritage families have members in the workforce. The problem is that they are in low-wage jobs and do not earn enough to bring them above the poverty line (Aponte, 1991).

Different economic contexts shape Latino families in different ways. The causes of poverty across Latino communities differ. In addition, different patterns of social organization at the community and family levels produce varied responses to poverty. Therefore, the underclass model does not apply evenly to the many diverse Latino barrios across the nation. Poverty dynamics even in the poorest of Latino barrios differ in fundamental ways from the conventional underclass portrait (Moore and Pinderhughes, 1993). For example, research finds that Puerto Ricans have exceptionally high cohabitation rates (Sullivan, 1993), while poverty-stricken Chicanos cope by using their kinship networks to share scarce resources across households (Velez-Ibanez, 1993). Although economic restructuring has strained Latino barrios, family patterns are different from those in the inner city. In the next section, we focus on Chicanos (Mexican-origin Latinos).

Extended Kinship Systems

For decades, **familism**—an obligation and orientation to the family—has been considered a defining feature of the Mexican-heritage population. Presumably, family is one of the strongest areas of life, more important for Mexicans than for Anglos. This attitude pertains not only to the nuclear family but also to a wider circle of relatives—the extended family—which includes aunts, uncles, grandparents, cousins, in-laws, and even *compadres* or co-parents (Alvirez and Bean, 1976:277).

Familism contains four key components. The first component, *demographic familism,* involves characteristics of Chicano families, such as family size. The second component, *structural familism,* measures the incidence of multigenerational households (or extended households). *Normative familism,* the third component, taps the value Mexican-heritage people place on family unity and solidarity. Fourth, *behavioral familism* has to do with the level of interaction between family and kin networks (Ramirez and Arce, 1981).

Compadrazgo is another feature of familism among Chicanos and Mexicans. It encompasses two sets of relationships with "fictive kin": (1) *padrinos y ahijados* (godparents and children); and (2) parents and godparents who become *compadres,* or co-parents. The compadrazgo system of godparents enlarges family ties by creating connections between families (see the discussion of *compadrazgo* in Chapter 3).

Popular thinking and social science as well have assumed that familism among Chicanos produces a kinship structure that is qualitatively different from that of all other groups. However, studies of familism and its varied forms are not conclusive. (The following discussion is based on Baca Zinn and Wells, 2000.) Economic changes and the resulting dislocations of Latinos have raised questions about extended family relationships in today's world. Analyzing a national sample of minority families, Rochelle (1997) argues that extended kinship networks are declining among Chicanos (as well as among Puerto Ricans and Blacks). On the other hand, a large body of past and present research documents longstanding participation in kinship networks. Studies spanning the last three decades have found that kinship networks are an important survival strategy in poor Mexican-origin families (Alvirez and Bean, 1976; Hoppe and Heller, 1975; Velez-Ibanez, 1996), and that they operate as a system of cultural, emotional, and mental support (Keefe, 1984; Mindel, 1980; Ramirez, 1980), as well as a system for coping with socioeconomic marginality (Angel and Tienda, 1982; Lamphere et al., 1993; Glick, 1999; Uttal, 1999). Familism among Mexican-heritage adults has been associated with high levels of education and income (Griffith and Villavicienco, 1985) and among adolescents has been viewed as a form of social capital linked with academic success (Valenzuela and Dornbusch, 1994).

Kinship networks have long been used in the migration of Mexicans to the United States (Chavez, 1992; Hondagneu-Sotelo, 1994; Portes and Beck, 1985; Wells, 1976). As we saw in Chapter 4, Mexican immigrants create a process of chain migration as a buffer against the stress related to immigration and upheaval. This is profoundly important. In contrast to the prevailing view that extended families are mainly an artifact of culture, this research helps us understand that among immigrants, family extension is an adaptation. Transnational families and their networks of kin are extended in space, time, and across national borders. This family form is a means of dealing with the challenges of immigration.

Kinship networks among Mexican-origin people are far from uniform. Differences have been found between immigrants and nonimmigrants and among different generations. Even though immigrants use kin for assistance, they have smaller social networks available than second-generation immigrants, who have broader social networks available consisting of multigenerational kin (Vega, 1990). Regardless of class, studies have shown that Mexican extended families in the United States become more extensive and strong with generational advancement and socioeconomic mobility (Velez-Ibanez, 1996:144). Although a cultural perspective would predict that familism fades in succeeding generations, Velez-Ibanez's study (discussed earlier as a refutation of the underclass) finds highly elaborated second- and third-generation extended-family networks actively maintained through frequent visiting, ritual celebrations, and the exchange of goods and services (Velez-Ibanez, 1996).

Human Agency and Family Formation

People of color use their families in adapting to their circumstances. Family arrangements have been vital in ensuring survival, and they have also served as a means of resisting social domination (Caulfield, 1974). The concept of **family strategies** (or household strategies) helps us think about some of the ways in which people use their families to cope with the problems in their lives. Instead of responding passively to the outside world, family members can take actions and engage in certain behaviors, including labor force participation, migration, co-residence, marriage, childbearing, food allocation, and education, in order to adapt to external structural change (Wolfe, 1992:12–13). Strategies often differ for women and men. Strategies also change as people use their social locations to shape their family lives.

Strategies are always contingent on structural conditions in the immediate environment. Different locations determine the actions people can take in their own interests. Although racial-ethnic families have adaptive capabilities, the constraints of racial oppression mean that strategies do not completely solve the problems at hand. Some adaptations can exact a price in family well-being. If individuals and families are able to survive because of nonconventional family structures, they also pay enormous costs. For example, **household augmentation** among minorities is a common economic family strategy. But when African Americans, Hispanics, or Asian Americans are forced to double-up in households, there may be fewer resources to go around, even though the intent is to add earnings. Ronald Angel and Marta Tienda have studied Black, Hispanic, and White households in which multiple earners had been added. They wanted to know whether additional workers helped buffer the effects of labor-market discrimination, and they discovered that although extension did not lift minority families out of poverty, it did alleviate some of the harsher aspects of poverty. This means that the extent of income inequality between minority and nonminority groups would be even greater without alternative strategies to compensate for the inadequate earnings of household members (Angel and Tienda, 1982:1377). Many of the family adaptations associated with immigration, including binational families and their networks of kin, represent quintessential household "strategies for mustering social resources" (Chavez, 1992:135).

In addition to adapting their household structures, racial-ethnic women and men often use their families politically, as major sources of support in struggling with poverty and the degrading realities of being subordinated by race and class

(Osmond and Thorne, 1993:617). For example, African American women, Latinas, Native American women, and Asian American women have a long tradition of extending their mothering roles to the realm of politics. Nancy Naples (1992) found African Americans and Latinas engaged in different kinds of *activist mothering* for the benefit of the entire community. And in the Chicano movement of the 1960s, the Chicano/Mexicano family was the basis of group solidarity. In *political familism,* the emphasis on family ties was not only symbolic, but also an organizational means of involving entire families in activist work (Baca Zinn, 1975).

GENDER

Gender, like race and class, is a way of organizing the social world. Gender organizes society in such a way that women and men are treated differently. From the macro level of the societal economy, through the institutions of society, to interpersonal relations, gender is the basis for dividing labor, assigning roles, and allocating social rewards. This has become a "core idea in sociology" (Risman and Ferree, 1995:775). **Gender** is the patterning of difference and domination through distinctions between women and men (Acker, 1992:565). Almost everything social is gendered. **Gendered** refers to distinguishing and differentially evaluating males and females. Until recently, gender differentiation seemed "natural." New research shows that gender differentiation is not natural at all but is *socially* constructed. In fact, the point of gender differentiation is "to justify the exploitation of an identifiable group—women" (Lorber, 1994:5).

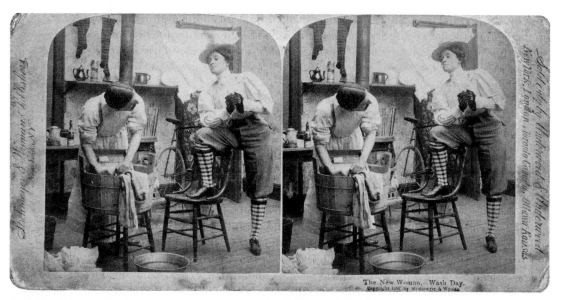

"The New Woman, Wash Day." Stereo image spoofing gender roles.

Gender is not only about women, however. Men often think of themselves as genderless, as if gender did not matter in the daily experiences of their lives. However, their experiences in families and other social settings are deeply gendered (Kimmel and Messner, 1995).

In the big picture, gender divisions make women unequal to men. Still, we cannot understand gender relations in society or in families by looking at gender alone. Gender intersects with other characteristics such as class, race, and sexual preference. As a result, different groups of men exhibit different degrees of power, while different groups of women exhibit varying levels of inequality. Nevertheless, the gender system ranks women and men differently, and it denies both women *and* men the full range of human and social possibilities. The social inequalities created by gender influence family life in profound ways. In fact, "gender relations and family are so intertwined, it is impossible to pay attention to one, without paying attention to the other" (Coltrane, 1998:1).

Like class and race, there are two main ways to think about gender and family. The first, a **sex roles** approach, treats gender differences as roles learned by individuals for family stability. The second approach, a structural or **gendered institutions** approach (Acker, 1992), emphasizes features of social organization that produce sex inequality. The difference between the two approaches lies in whether the individual or society is the primary unit of analysis.

The Traditional Sex Roles Approach

Until very recently, most family scholars operated under the assumption that the modern nuclear family was the basis of social order in a modern society. Industrialization made the various components of society more specialized, and it also produced a division of labor between men and women. Men assumed the breadwinning roles, while women were charged with the physical and emotional care of husbands and children. This division of society into public and private components, with a corresponding division of women's and men's roles, was viewed as a complementary arrangement, well suited to modern society. The family was a haven of protection in an increasingly competitive public world. It socialized the next generation to take their places in society.

This model of the family was developed by Talcott Parsons and called "structural functionalism." It became the dominant family framework in the 1950s and 1960s. Even today, many of Parsons's assumptions about family life are found in popular thought and in many strands of family social science (Mann et al., 1997; Smith, 1993). The strategy of structural functionalism was to posit one family type (by no means the only family form even then) and define it as "the family." This model glorified a historically specific and class-specific family form of the 1950s as the benchmark for all families. It made the modern nuclear family a falsely universal construct. It ignored difference even though race and class differences were at the very foundation of family life.

Shortcomings of the Sex Roles Approach

Throughout the 1970s and 1980s, sex role theory came into question. Real-world changes in gender and family challenged the old framework. Many scholars argued that this model ignored class and race differences in families even though they were at the very foundation of family life. The sex roles approach made it seem that role division between the sexes was necessary if families were to operate efficiently. This view wrongly assumes that expressive and instrumental activities are mutually exclusive (Thorne, 1982:8). It ignores the social conditions that make it impossible for many women to remain in the home because their husbands are deprived of a "family wage."

The sex roles perspective ignores what is most important about roles—that they are unequal in power, resources, and prestige. When terms such as "sex roles," the "female role," and the "male role" are used in an uncritical manner, male dominance can be easily overlooked (Thorne, 1982:8). Furthermore, the older ideas about role division in the nuclear family ignore the conflicts these inequalities produce. Roles are seen as the building blocks of harmonious families.

The sex roles approach assumes that the family is defined by its emotional quality. Families are portrayed as havens of intimacy and love. Husband-wife relations are thought to be simply matters of love and agreement. But whether husbands and wives love one another or not, their relations develop within the larger system of male dominance. Husband–wife relationships are political. What is thought to be a private relationship of love is also a social relationship of power. Recent research has given us a more complex picture of husband-wife relations. Families are not always havens and may often be settings of conflict. Love between the sexes is complicated by an unequal balance of power.

The Family as a Gendered Institution

Sociologists have advanced from studying gender as individuals' learned behavior. Today, the focus is on how gender is built into social institutions. The term 'gendered institutions' means that gender is the basis for distributing resources and opportunities in the various sectors of social life. The institutional structure of the United States and other societies is organized along lines of gender (Acker, 1992:567).

Families throughout society are closely bound up with a broad system of gender inequality. In addition, the family is an important foundation of the gender system. Together with other social institutions, the family does the work of creating two dichotomous genders from biological sex. Understanding the institutional basis of gender does not mean that we should ignore interpersonal relationships. How women and men interact, and what they *do* every day in families is essential in reproducing gender. When we look carefully at everyday family activities, we see how deeply gendered family worlds can be. Few areas of family life are untouched by gender—the allocation of tasks, the experiences of work and leisure, the giving of nurturance, conflicts and episodes of violence, and decisions about employment, and moving are gendered. Even mundane decisions such as what to watch on television are gendered. Women, men, and children experience the family in gender-specific ways that vary by class and race.

Patriarchy is the term used for forms of social organization in which men are dominant over women. Patriarchy is both interpersonal and structural, private and public; therefore, we distinguish between private patriarchy and public patriarchy. The concept of **private patriarchy** refers to male dominance in the interpersonal relations between women and men; that of **public patriarchy** encompasses dominance in the institutions of the larger society.

Patriarchy is interrelated with other structural forces. For example, its development in the United States is closely tied to capitalism. The United States can be defined as a **capitalist patriarchy.** Capitalism and patriarchy are interrelated in complex ways. They should be analyzed together if we are to understand the position of women (Acker, 1980). Women and men do different work, both in the labor force and in the family, and they have different resources in both of these settings. Men have greater control in both public and private arenas. Their economic obligations in the public sphere ensure that they have control of highly valued resources and give rise to male privileges. Male privilege refers to those advantages, prerogatives, and benefits that systematically uplift men and are denied to women.

Structured gender inequality interacts with other inequalities such as race, class, and sexuality to sort women and men differently. These inequalities also work togther to produce differences *among women* and differences *among men.* Some women derive benefits from both their race and their class while they are simultaneously restricted by gender. Such women are restricted by patriarchy, yet race and class intersect to create for them privileged opportunities and ways of living for them (Baca Zinn et al., 2000). Men are encouraged to behave in "masculine" fashion to prove they are not gay (Connell, 1992). In defining masculinity as the negation of homosexuality, *compulsory heterosexuality* is an important component of the gender system. Compulsory heterosexuality imposes negative sanctions on those who are homosexual or bisexual. This system of sexuality shapes the gender order by discouraging attachment with members of the same sex. This enforces the dichtotomy of "opposite" sexes. Sexuality is also a form of inequality in its own right because it systematically grants privileges to those in heterosexual relationships. Like race, class, and gender, sexual identities are socially constructed categories. Sexuality is a way of organizing the social world based on sexual identity and a key linking process in the matrix of domination structured along the lines of race, class, and gender (Messner, 1996:223).

Although there is considerable variation in how different groups of women and different groups of men are placed in society, men in general gain privileges at the expense of women. This is readily apparent from the kind of work women do in the home. As wives and mothers, women earn no money for their household chores of cleaning, ironing, cooking, sewing, and caring for the needs of household members. Although the work is necessary, it is low in prestige. Apportioning household labor and child rearing (reproductive labor) to women upholds male privilege by freeing men from such responsibilities. Individual males—adults, adolescents, and children—gain leisure time, and the opportunity to pursue their own careers or boyhood interests. If wives, mothers, and sisters tend to existence-related needs such as cooking, cleaning, and taking care of clothing, men gain time at women's expense.

> He reads the evening paper and his wife fixes dinner. He watches the news or an informative television show and she washes the dishes. He retires to his study (or his office or his shop or a soft chair) and she manages the children. Men gain

leisure time at the expense of the oppression of women. This is a fundamental priv-ilege which accrues to the division of labor (or lack of division) in the home (New-ton, 1973:121).

The domestic division of labor, in turn, can limit women's occupational activities. Women burdened with domestic duties have less time and energy left over to devote to careers. The gendered division of family labor reinforces the division of labor in the workforce and upholds men's superiority. The interlock-ing systems of capitalism and patriarchy create a cycle of domination and sub-ordination.

Thinking about family activities in terms of power and domination chal-lenges the very concept of "the family" as a unit. Many scholars argue that the image of the unified family is erroneous. As Heidi Hartmann says, the family is a "locus of struggle":

> In my view, the family cannot be understood solely or even primarily as a unit shaped by affect or kinship, but must be seen as a location where production and redistribution take place. As such, it is a location where people with different activi-ties and interests in these processes often come into conflict with one another (Hart-mann, 1981a:368).

Hartmann does not deny that families also encompass strong emotional ties, but she concentrates on the ways in which unequal division of labor inside and out-side the family generates tension, conflict, and change.

Studies of housework and child care (see Chapter 6) have shown that, on the average, men whose wives are employed full-time do little more domestic labor than do husbands of full-time homemakers. We should not take women's dou-ble burden for granted, as if it is in the nature of things that a wife must do most of the housework and child care even when she is employed full-time (Boss and Thorne, 1989:84).

The gender perspective has uncovered many invisible forms of labor that are disproportionately the work of women. Throughout their lives, women do most of the caretaking and caregiving that is required to maintain family bonds (Aldous, 1991:661). Women's invisible work sustains family life. Recent research has found that much of women's exertion in caring for the family remains hid-den. For example, Marjorie DeVault's *Feeding the Family: The Social Organization of Caring as Gendered Work* (1991) brings into view the invisible activities that go into preparing family meals. Not only is feeding the family deeply gendered, but there are also important class differences: "In families with more resources, food becomes an arena for self-expression, providing a chance to experience family as a reward for achievement; in poor families, feeding and eating are themselves the achievement" (DeVault, 1991:201). In Chapter 6, we give further attention to household labor.

Agency within Constraint

Although women are subordinate, they are not passive victims of patriarchy. Like other oppressed groups, they engage in various activities that subvert power and give them some control over their lives. (See Box 5.3.) Women's resistance takes different forms. It can be subtle or passive. It can also be active defiance

BOX 5.3   **Families in Global Perspective: Progress for Women's Rights Worldwide? Beijing Plus Five**

Beijing, China, 1995: Delegates from 189 countries gathered in a conference center downtown. Approximately 40,000 women from around the world travelled to the city to sing, protest, and share life histories under acres of white tents. Despite bad weather and negative reactions from the Chinese government, these women came together to support women's rights and the fight for gender equality worldwide. Four days later, the United Nations' Fourth Conference on Women produced the Beijing Platform for Action—the "most comprehensive set of commitments toward women's equality ever made" by a government body (Luchsinger, 2000:32). The Platform listed recommendations for action in the areas of economics, health, education, violence, political participation, human rights, the environment, and even the portrayal of women in the media. Although Beijing was not the first time women's rights have gotten global affirmation, it was the first time that women participated in policy discussions on a large scale and then lobbied their governments to take action (Luchsinger, 2000).

However, since 1995, many governments have devised empty programs that take advantage of the platform's major weaknesses: it spells out very few specific benchmarks for measuring governments' "progress" towards women's rights (Bunch, 1999). Scholars and activists have discussed how it is "extremely difficult to hold governments accountable" when there are no targeted goals. "We need to ensure implementation because that's what will make the difference." (Luchsinger, 2000:32). Hence the organization of "Beijing Plus Five."

New York, New York, 2000: In early June 2000, at a special session of the U.N. General Assembly in New York, delegates and activists reviewed the progress made towards women's rights globally. This special session, dubbed "Beijing Plus Five," assessed how well the Platform has been implemented. Some have even said that the "key word" at Beijing Plus Five was "implementation" (Luchsinger, 2000:32). At the core of this assessment was also "accountability"—"that it is not just a good idea but a duty of governments and a right of women to seek to implement these commitments" (Bunch, 1999:1). While Beijing Five priorities varied somewhat by region, certain issues seemed to concern everyone. The following is a sampling of important issues discussed at Beijing Plus Five:

· *Women's human rights.* Throughout the Beijing Platform, women's human rights are affirmed. Activists say that governments are now morally bound to take specific actions to implement them.
· *Women's legal status.* Honor killings are still legal in some countries, and other countries exonerate rapists who marry their victims. These are some of the long list of blatant discriminations against women that still exist today, things that the Beijing Platform prohibits.
· *Women and the environment.* The Beijing Platform documents many connections between women and the environment, but this issue has received the least amount of attention. Beijing Plus Five will make the case that "women's issues are anything that affects women's lives" (Luchsinger, 2000:33).

(continued)

(continued from previous page)

· *Women and the economy.* Women's labor, paid and unpaid, in the home, the community, and the workplace, is central to the functioning of society and the economy. Around the world, women's labor has been used to maximize economic competitiveness and profitability. Thus, the availability, quality, level of pay and safety of their jobs is a central issue for Beijing Plus Five. For instance, governments need to ensure that women's wages are above the poverty line. Governments also need to monitor off-shore proportions of women workers (Center for Women's Global Leadership, 2000:4).

· *Women and education.* Education is a human right and an essential tool for achieving the goals of equality, development and peace ("Women Watch," 2000:1). Strategic objectives developed for Beijing Plus Five include ensuring equal access to education for women and men, eventually eradicating illiteracy of women, improving women's access to vacational training, and developing non-discriminatory education and training for women.

While the goal of Beijing Plus Five was to get from "words to deeds," (Luchsinger, 2000), reports from this special session show disappointment among feminists worldwide, and confirmed what activists and government officials had suspected for several years: for the most part, the Beijing Platform for Action has never been put into action. Non-governmental organizations (NGOs) lamented the lack of "more concrete benchmarks, numerical goals, timebound targets, indicators, and resources" aimed at implementing the Beijing Platform (Feminist Majority Foundation, 2000:1).

Significant gains made at Beijing Plus Five, however, included the approval of the Political Declaration that reaffirms and extends governments' responsibility to implement the Platform. Delegates from over 180 countries again agreed on a statement to "eradicate harmful customary or traditional practices against women, including marital rape and forced marriages." They also called for the prevention of sexual exploitation, including the trafficking of women and girls, and condemned the honor killing mentioned earlier. A final two-day negotiation session resulted in the inclusion of the statement that "women have the right to decide feely and responsibly on matters related to their sexuality . . . without coercion, discrimination, and violence" (Feminist Majority Foundation, 2000:1). Other gains came in the areas of women's health, the gendered aspects of infectious deseases, and the realization of the negative impacts of globalization and economic restructuring on women.

Little progress was made of the session's most contentious issues: abortion and sexual orientation. Conservative delegates also blocked language regarding access to birth control (Feminist Majority Foundation, 2000). Despite blocks to progress on reproductive rights and sexual orientation, the final outcome of Beijing Plus Five was fairly positive and the sessions' final reports contained concrete gains for women. Hopefully, the implementation of the original Beijing Platform for Action will now be easier, as governments are held more accountable in securing women's rights. In another five years, perhaps Beijing Plus Ten can report something even more positive for women worldwide.

(continued)

(continued from previous page)

References

Bunch, Charlotte (December 10, 1999). "Women's Human Rights and Beijing + 5." Statement delivered by Charlotte Bunch, Executive Director, Center for Women's Global Leadership, Rutgers University. Website: www.cwgl.rutgers.edu/b5/12.10.99.htm. Downloaded on 7/24/2000.

Center for Women's Global Leadership (February 2000). "Recommendations for Action: Violence Against Women & Women and the Economy." Working Paper on a Human Rights Based Approach to Implementation of the Beijing Platform for Action. Website: www.cwgl.rutgers.edu/b5/approach/htm. Downloaded on 7.24.2000.

Feminist Majority Foundation (June 10, 2000). "Reports from Beijing + 5: Feminists Disappointed with Lack of Progress at UN Conference." Website: www.feminist.org/other/beijing.html. Downloaded on 7/26/2000.

Luchsinger, Gretchen (2000). "From Words to Deeds." *Ms.* April/ May. pp.32-33.

"Women Watch." The United Nations Organization (February 2000). "FWCW Platform for Action: Education and the Training of Women." Website: www.un.org/womenwatch/daw/beijing/platform/educa.htm. Downloaded on 7/24/2000.

Source: Heather Dillaway, Department of Sociology, Michigan State University, 2001. This essay was expressly written for the sixth edition of *Diversity in Families*.

of patriarchal constraints. Within patriarchal settings like the family, women negotiate, strategize, and bargain to get what they can in return for domestic services and subordination. Deniz Kandiyoti (1988) calls these exchanges "patriarchal bargains." Although such bargains do not eradicate women's inequality, they often pave the way for various forms of resistance and control in family matters. In the chapters that follow, we take a closer look at the gendered family and how it varies by class and race.

CHAPTER REVIEW

1. Class, race, and gender interact in complex ways to place individuals and families in the larger society.
2. Class, race, and gender are group-based inequalities that create varied environments for family life.
3. Although macro structural forces press in on families, people are not merely victims of inequalities but are active participants producing family life.
4. Households are material sites with different ways of acquiring the necessities of life. This creates variation in family structure.
5. Two models of social class have different implications for understanding families:

(a) conventional explanations of class differences place families into social classes according to occupation and shared lifestyles; (b) structural explanations of class differences focus on society's opportunity structures, which produce advantages for some families and disadvantages for others.

6. Culture-of-poverty thought treats poor families as a complex of self-defeating behaviors passed down from generation to generation.
7. Contrasting explanations of racial inequality have different implications for understanding families: (a) cultural approaches blame racial-ethnic families for group-

based inequalities; (b) structural approaches focus on the socioeconomic system which creates different contexts for family living.

8. No matter what their structure, White families fare better economically than their minority counterparts.

9. Family structure is a crucial determinant of well-being, because the potential for having two earners in the household increases the likelihood of achieving higher income levels.

10. In the underclass model, inner-city male joblessness has encouraged nonmarital childbearing and undermined the economic foundation of the African American family. This explanation applies more to family changes among African Americans than among Latinos, who require a different model to understand poverty and family issues in each group.

11. Racial-ethnic families in the United States have some important commonalties,

including (a) extended kinship networks and multiple households spread across several generations and (b) high rates of female-headed households, out-of-wedlock births, and other factors associated with family disruption.

12. Two views of gender influence our understanding of families: (a) In the first view, gender inequality is a consequence of behavior learned by individual women and men. (b) In the second view, gender is an institutional force closely intertwined with other forms of inequality. In this view, patriarchy shapes families along with other social institutions.

13. Women of all classes and races are subject to patriarchal control, but they experience that control differently.

14. Families are not cohesive units but settings of power and control in which gendered family roles and responsibilities generate conflict.

ᖇELATED WEB SITES

http://www.isr.umich.edu/src/psid/

The Panel Study of Income Dynamics is a longitudinal survey of a representative sample of U.S. individuals and the families in which they reside. It has been ongoing since 1968. The data are collected annually, and the data files contain the full span of information collected over the course of the study. PSID data can be used for cross-sectional, longitudinal, and intergenerational analysis and for studying both individuals and families.

http://www.ssc.wisc.edu/irp/

Institute for Research on Poverty at the University of Wisconsin: The IRP is a national, university-based center for research into the causes and consequences of poverty and social inequality in the United States. It is one of the two centers designated as a National Poverty Research Center by the U.S. Department of Health and Human Services.

http://www.iwpr.org

Institute for Women's Policy Research: "The Institute for Women's Policy Research (IWPR)

is an independent, non-profit, scientific research organization incorporated in the District of Columbia, established in 1987 to rectify the limited availability of policy relevant research on women's lives and to inform and stimulate debate on issues of critical importance for women. The Institute also works in affiliation with the graduate programs in public policy and women's studies at The George Washington University."

http://www.jcpr.org/

Joint Center for Poverty Research: Sponsored by Northwestern University and the University of Chicago, the Joint Center for Poverty Research is a national and interdisciplinary academic research center that seeks to advance our understanding of what it means to be poor in America.

http://www.nowldef.org/

NOW Legal Defense and Education Fund: In its 29th year, the NOW Legal Defense and Education Fund (NOW LDEF) continues to be at the center of every major social and economic justice concern on the women's rights agenda, defining the issues and bringing them to public attention. NOW LDEF pursues equality for women and girls in the workplace, the schools, the family and the courts, through litigation, education, and public information programs.

http://www.aclu.org/

The American Civil Liberties Union is the nation's foremost advocate of individual rights—litigating, legislating, and educating the public on a broad array of issues affecting individual freedom in the United States.

http://www.geocities.com/CapitolHill/1064/

This "Welfare Moms" Homepage makes its mission the "mauling" of myths and stereotypes of poor women with children. This website argues that stereotypes attributed to welfare recipients are incorrect and offers a variety of resources to support its position.

http://cpmcnet.columbia.edu/dept/nccp/

The National Center for Children in Poverty identifies and promotes strategies that reduce the number of young children living in poverty in the United States, and that improve the life chances of the millions of children under six who are growing up poor.

http://www.naacp.org/

NAACP List of Recommended Links: The NAACP, National Association for the Advancement of Colored People, is the oldest, largest and strongest civil rights organization in the United States. The principal objective of the NAACP is to ensure the political, educational, social and economic equality of minority group citizens of the United States. This website represents a list of links to other Internet resources, supported by NAACP. Most links concern specific racial or ethnic groups, women, and other groups that have historically been disadvantaged.

http://www.census.gov/pubinfo/www/hotlinks.html

U.S. Census Bureau—Minority Links: The U.S. Census Bureau provides some quick and easy links to the latest data on racial and ethnic populations in the United States.

http://www.latinoweb.com

Latino Web: a homepage for Latinos on the Internet.

http://www.hsph.harvard.edu/grhf/WoC/

Women of Color Web explores the intersection of gender and race. It provides material on blacks as well as Chicanas. This website includes research, other Internet resources, and articles.

http://www.coombs.anu.edu.au/WWWVL-AsianStudies.html

Asian Studies WWW Virtual Library: This website represents a conglomerate of research publications and archives on Asian peoples in every country/region in the world. This research tool is produced by the Internet Publications Bureau, Research School of Pacific and Asian Studies at The Australian National University (ANU), Canberra, and is regularly updated.

http://www.webcom.com/~intvoice

Interracial Voice: IV is an independent, information-oriented, networking newsjournal, serving the mixed-race/interracial community in cyberspace. This electronic publication advocates universal recognition of mixed-race individuals as constituting a separate "racial" entity and wholeheartedly supported the initiative to establish a multiracial category on the 2000 Census.

http://www.census.gov/apsd/www/wepeople.html

This is a link to a series of U.S. Census groups on various groups in the U.S. This series is called "We the Americans" and profiles racial and ethnic groups, women, the elderly and immigrants, to name a few.

http://inequality.org/

Inequality.Org provides data and essays on various aspects of inequality in the United States.

Meshing the Worlds of Work and Family

Myths and Realities

Myth: In the past three decades, women have poured into the labor force due to their desire for liberation.

Reality: Economic necessity is the primary reason most women have gone to work. Changing values are important, yet most women have jobs in order to support their families.

Myth: Many women have grown so tired of juggling jobs and families that they are returning to domesticity and starting a new homemaking trend.

Reality: Although newspapers and magazines periodically feature stories about the rush back to homemaking, there is no decline in women's labor force participation.

Myth: The division of household labor in U.S. families is nearly equal now, especially in families where husbands and wives have paid jobs.

Reality: While fathers are spending more time taking care of children, working couples still feature a gender gap. Women spend more than twice as much time on household work as their husbands.

Myth: Children suffer when their mothers work outside the home.

Reality: Evidence does not show that mothers' employment harms their children's development.

Myth: Now that more mothers are in the workforce, children are taking on a greater share of housework for the collective well-being of the family.

Reality: Children are withdrawing from domestic responsibilities, increasing rather than lightening the burdens on their parents.

Myth: The turn-of-the-century workplace is finally supporting workers' family responsibilities. Soon most workers will be able to take advantage of a wide array of family-supportive programs.

Reality: The family-friendly workplace is more talk than action, with only 2 percent of the workforce currently using flexible work programs.

Macro-level social changes are producing major upheavals in family life. In Chapters 4 and 5 we saw how systems of inequality and other social transformations produce a wide range of family structures: one-parent families, cohabiting couples (both gay and straight) with children, co-provider families, and many varieties of extended families, including divorce-extended families and multinational families. A great deal of family diversification is related to changes in the workplace. The struggle to balance work and family is creating deep changes in the day-to-day operation of families.

Juggling work and family is a central concern for most adults. Although there is no typical family form, wives are now more likely than not to be employed. Less than 10 percent of U.S. families are breadwinner-and-homemaker families. A growing portion of families have women as heads of households and sole wage earners. The dramatic rise in women's employment has both positive and negative consequences. Most families are faced with conflicting demands of work and home.

In previous chapters we reviewed the myth of separate worlds, or the belief that work and family are detached. This myth ignores the profound effect that the type of job and the level of workers' earnings have on each family member and on the family as a unit.

New research on work and family has sharpened our understanding of how these "greedy institutions" overlap. In the 1990s, work/family linkages became stronger and more important to study than ever before. The study of work and family has become a major subfield within sociology (Hood, 1994:x). New economic patterns recast the family field in terms of the explicit interdependence of work and family (Dubeck, 1998:4, Haas, 1999). We have discovered that these two spheres were never as separate from each other as was believed. Furthermore, the concept of work no longer refers only to paid employment outside the home, but encompasses the variety of reproductive or caring labor that family members do for which they receive no reimbursement—housework, child care, kin care, the nurturing of interpersonal relationships, and activities in the larger

New employment trends show how larger social and economic conditions are revolutionizing family worlds.

community (Baber and Allen, 1992:176). Today, family researchers pay close attention to how women and men manage both paid labor and unpaid labor.

This chapter is divided into several sections. We begin with the macrostructural context to examine the social, economic, and demographic transformations that are changing the work patterns of women, men, and children in different classes and races. We turn, then, to macro and micro connections between the workplace and families by looking at different kinds of linkages and interactions and how they shape family dynamics. Next we review various forms of family labor that have, until recently, been invisible. Finally, we turn to coping efforts and strategies that family members and some companies have adopted to manage work and family.

THE CHANGING WORK PATTERNS OF WOMEN, MEN, AND CHILDREN

We cannot understand today's families in isolation from changes in the U.S. economy. New employment trends show how larger social and economic conditions are revolutionizing family worlds.

Women's Employment

The increased participation of U.S. women in market work is a story that has been unfolding since the early nineteenth century. In the past five decades, the increase accelerated. In 1940, less than 20 percent of the female population age sixteen and older were in the labor force. By 1999, the figure had risen to 60 percent, compared to 75 percent of men (*Occupational Outlook Quarterly*, 1999–2000). This means that women make up half of the workforce (48 percent of the workforce is female). Although women of all age groups are likely to be employed, women of childbearing age have especially high rates of labor force participation. (See Table 6.1.) In 1980, for the first time in the twentieth century, married women's place was no longer typically in the home. In that year, the number of married women working for pay outside the home exceeded the number of married women who were full-time homemakers.

Women's labor force participation has been growing at a faster pace than men's in recent years. Between 1970 and the early 1990s, women's numbers in the labor force increased twice as fast as those of men. But today, as in the past, the proportions of employed women and men vary by race. African American women have a long history of high workforce participation rates, and those rates increased only modestly after World War II. Much greater rates of increase have occurred among White and Latina women. In 1999, 63 percent of African American women, 59 percent of White women, and 55 percent of Latina women were in the labor force (U.S. Department of Labor, 2000a). (See Table 6.2.)

As women add more workers to the workforce, their share approaches that of men. By 2008, women are projected to comprise 48 percent of the labor force,

TABLE 6.1

Labor Force Participation Rates for Women, by Age Groups, 1999

Age Group	Participation Rate (percentage)
All women	60.0
16–19 years	51.0
20–24 years	73.2
25–54 years	76.8
25–32 years	76.4
35–44 years	77.2
45–54 years	76.7
55–64 years	51.5
65 and over	8.9

Source: Facts on Working Women. "20 Facts on Women Workers" U.S. Department of Labor, Women's Bureau. http://www.dol.gov/dol./wb/public/wb/pbs/20fact00htm p.1

TABLE 6.2			
Labor Force Participation Rates for Women, by Race, Selected Years			
Year	Black	White	Hispanic
1975	48.8	45.9	n.a.
1980	53.1	51.2	47.4
1985	56.5	54.1	49.4
1990	57.8	57.5	53.0
1995	59.5	59.0	52.5
1999	63.5	59.6	55.9

Source: Facts on Working Women. "20 Facts on Women Workers" U.S. Department of Labor, Women's Bureau. http://www.dol.gov/dol./wb/ public/wb/pbs/20fact00htm p.2 Retrieved on 9/3/00.

compared with 52 percent of men (*Occupational Outlook Quarterly*, 1999–2000:37). (See Figure 6.1.) Businesses will be utterly dependent on the labor of millions of women.

Dual-earner families now outnumber breadwinner/homemaker families two to one. And although the workplace still operates as if households had only one full-time worker and the support of a full-time homemaker, no change has had as much impact on family life.

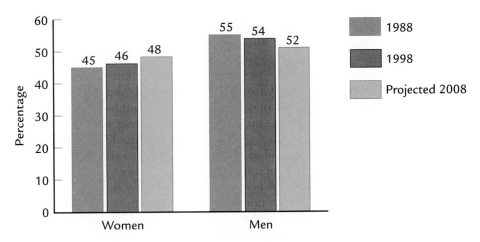

Figure 6.1

Labor force share by sex, 1988, 1998, and projected 2008 (percentage)

Source: Occupational Outlook Quarterly, Winter 1999–2000. Washington, DC: U.S. Department of Labor, Bureau of Labor Statistics, p. 37.

Although women are now firmly attached to the labor force, their employment patterns remain different from those of men: Somewhat more of women's work is part time, part year, or both, and it is more often interrupted to care for ill, aged, or young family members. Women and men are also differentiated by what they do in the labor market and the sectors of the economy in which they perform their work for pay. These differences are important because they limit women's earning abilities (Bianchi, 1995:122; Haas, 1999).

The most remarkable trend in women's employment has been the rapid rise in the percentage of married women with children in the paid labor force. Families in which both parents are working have become the majority among married couples with children (Lewin, 2000). All racial groups have experienced an increase in mothers' labor force participation. Despite family obligations, a majority of women now work outside the home during the years they are raising children. In the late 1970s and early 1980s, less than half of all mothers with infants were labor force participants. By the mid-1990s, almost three-quarters of married women with dependent children were employed. Increasingly, it is normal for adult women, regardless of parental status, to be employed outside the home (Spain and Bianchi, 1996:79; Haas, 1999).

Causes of Increased Labor Force Participation

What explains the dramatic changes in women's labor force participation? Three major push and pull factors account for women's new work patterns. First, large-scale changes in the U.S. economy have pulled women into the labor force; second, families have become dependent on women's income, thereby pushing women into the labor force; and third, women themselves find fulfillment in working.

Changes in the Economy The most important reason for the surge in the number of employed wives has been the transition from a manufacturing to a service economy, which creates a labor market with more of the jobs that traditionally hire women. The demand for workers in service-producing industries such as government, education, real estate, health care, and clerical work has been met by women. Since 1980, women have taken 80 percent of the new jobs created in the economy. Most women found traditionally female jobs in secondary-sector service and administrative support occupations. Since 1992, the largest job growth occurred in jobs with people working evenings, nights, and weekends— in other words, jobs filled disproportionately by women (*Population Today,* 1997b). The influx of women into the labor force is a direct consequence of structural changes in the economy.

Decline in Real Earnings Economic needs of families themselves have pushed many women into paid work. As we saw in Chapter 4, economic problems, such as inflation, deflation, high interest rates, unemployment, shrinking wages, and the eroded buying power of the male wage, have made two incomes crucial for maintaining a standard of living. The "male family wage" is no longer a reality. Even though males' earnings are higher than women's, most men do not earn a wage sufficient to support a wife and children (Catanzarite and Ortiz, 1996:124).

Women's work maintains the standard of living. Without it, many couples could not achieve what their parents had at the same age. Unless both partners have jobs, many would be unable to survive economically (i.e., pay the mortgage or the rent).

By 1990, working wives were contributing about 30 percent of their families' incomes—40 percent in those families in which the wife worked full-time, year-round. In 1999, one in four working wives earned more than their husbands (Riche, 2000:29).

To a greater extent than ever before, the income level for families with young children is being determined by the extent to which mothers are employed, especially in single-mother families (Bronfenbrenner et al., 1996:109). Sixty-eight percent of women in mother-only families work outside the home to secure adequate support for their children (Herz and Wootten, 1996:51). In 1998, the median annual income of married-couple families in which the wife was in the paid labor force was about $63,751, compared with $37,161 for those without the wife in the paid labor force. Women who maintain families had the lowest median family income ($22,163) (U.S. Department of Labor, Women's Bureau, 2000).

Personal Fulfillment   The economy is not the only force driving women into paid work. In the late 1960s and early 1970s, many women began questioning their traditional roles in family and society. The steady rise in the number of women working outside their homes had started to break down the social and ideological barriers to women working. Many women want to do paid work. They want to be rewarded for their work. Work outside the home gives them pride, worth, and identity, and it allows for some economic independence from men (Albelda, 1992:7).

Problems of Women Workers

Despite the massive entry of women into the paid labor force, the economy still restricts women's employment in several ways. Women who live in labor market areas with high unemployment rates or with low demand for labor in "female jobs" are less likely to be employed. Problems in finding child care can be another constraint. Many women are limited by the lack of child care; more women would be working and more would work more hours if child care were available. Single-parent families are especially affected. Lack of affordable child-care often prevents single mothers from holding jobs. The child care dilemma, in which parents must find "private" solutions to their child care needs, is especially acute in the United States. Our government lags behind those of other developed nations in providing child care for the children of working parents.

Men's Employment

Recent changes in the labor force itself have altered men's employment patterns as well as those of women. The revolution in paid employment for women coincides with declining employment for men. Since 1960, labor-force participation rates among men have edged down gradually from 83 percent to 75 percent in

1999. Declines were steeper for African American men than for White men, with Hispanic men more likely to be in the labor force than White or Black men. Among White men, the declines were importantly due to lower age of retirement, whereas among minorities, the "discouraged worker effect" (the unemployed dropping out of the labor force after an unsuccessful period of job search) on prime working-age males played a greater role. Diminished opportunities for urban minority men (discussed in Chapter 5) have seriously affected their work patterns.

Causes of Decreased Labor Force Participation

Men's work experience is especially affected by three macro-level trends: (1) structural unemployment, (2) the redistribution of jobs, and (3) the low-income-generating capacity of jobs.

Changes in the Economy Technology and the shift from manufacturing to services and information have had serious consequences in industrial work. Although women have been affected by downsizing, men have been more likely to be employed in hard-hit manufacturing jobs. Men, especially those working in heavy industries, are finding their skills unneeded. Economic survival in these instances depends on unemployment insurance and union benefits (which are short-lived) and their wives' employment. These wives have better luck in finding and keeping jobs because of the growth in the service sector, where the majority of workers are female.

As manufacturing jobs become scarce, young men have increasingly turned to the lower-paying but rapidly expanding service sectors. Since 1973, one of the fastest-growing occupations for men has been sales. Men's employment in other service occupations (for example, security guards, orderlies, waiters, day-care workers, and janitors) has also increased. Service work generally pays low wages, offers few benefits, and produces limited opportunities for career advancement.

The declining share of men who earn enough to support a family is affecting family patterns in several ways. The number of divorces and single-parent families increases. If men are employed, unmarried mothers have less of an incentive to marry the father of their children. Married women are not forced to stay married (Riche, 1991:44-45).

Decline in Real Wages Men's shrinking wages have also dealt a serious blow to the "good provider" role. According to Jessie Bernard, the "good provider" role became the standard against which masculinity was measured:

> The good provider was a "family man." He provided a decent home, paid the mortgage, bought the shoes, and kept his children warmly clothed. He might, with the help of the children's part time jobs, have been able to finance their educations through high school and, sometimes, even college. There might even have been a little left over for an occasional celebration in most families. The good provider made a decent contribution to the church. His work might have been demanding, but he expected it to be (Bernard, 1984:47).

"All This family needs is one more worker
and we'll be middle class."

Macro-level economic conditions have eroded men's ability to be the sole breadwinner in the family. Yet most men continue to provide the largest source of income—on average, about two-thirds of total family income (Ahlberg and De Vita, 1992:27). However, men's share of family income is steadily declining. As men's economic power declines, the old models of men's family roles are falling away. Thanks to wives' rising incomes, men are being freed from the demands of the good provider role. On the one hand, they have greater opportunities to participate more fully in the family. At the other extreme, they are freed from family responsibilities (Jacobsen and Edmondson, 1993:22. Gerson, 2000), a change that makes marriage more fragile.

Children's Employment

Child labor is on the increase, especially in the teen years. The rise of a service economy has produced a new demand for adolescent workers. Teens form the core of our low-wage retail and restaurant workforce (Hine, 1999). This trend has only recently begun to capture the attention of family researchers. One feature of a service economy is the proliferation of part-time jobs, many of which require little skill, necessitate work at "off" hours (evenings and weekends), and offer low wages. These jobs, "bad" for adults, are in some ways well suited to teenagers, who have not developed a high level of job skills, whose regular work hours are committed to schoolgoing, and whose wage requirements are lower than those of self-supporting adults. Almost all U.S. adolescents now work at some time during high school (Mortimer and Finch, 1996). National studies show that nearly three-fourths of students work for pay during their last year of high school (Crispell, 1995). American students are far more likely to have part-time jobs than their counterparts in underdeveloped countries, and to work longer hours. The difference is that their families do not depend on their wages for their livelihood. Teen earnings are often used for luxury items such as cars, stereos, "extra" clothing, concert tickets, and drugs. Researchers are finding that only a small percentage of high school seniors save all or most of their earnings for long-term purposes. (See Figure 6.2.) This has created, for many, a "premature" affluence, an unrealistic level of discretionary income that they find impos-

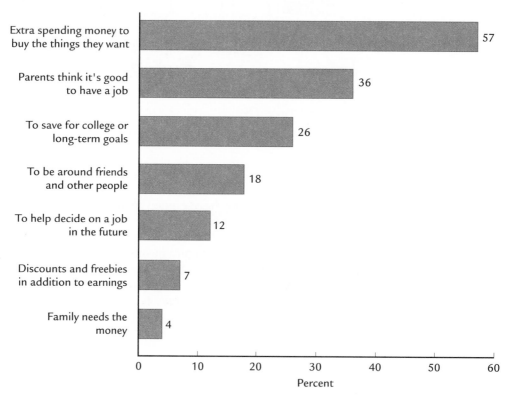

Figure 6.2

Why high school students are working

Most students who work during the school year say they learn things that will be helpful in the future. But 36% said they would do better in school if they didn't have a job and 35% said their jobs kept them from participating in sports and other school activities. Here's why students work, according to the Families and Work Institute survey "Ask the Children 2000: Youth and Employment."

Source: Occupational Outlook Quarterly, Winter 1999–2000. Washington, DC: U.S. Department of Labor, Bureau of Labor Statistics, p. 37.

sible to maintain at college unless they have extravagant parents (Woodward, 1990:57; Hine,1999:75).

How does adolescent employment affect family life? Researchers have only recently begun to address this question. Conventional ideas about the benefits of paid labor suggest that jobs improve teen autonomy and self-reliance. However, there are some indications that teenage employment has more negative than positive consequences. Among other things, part-time employment (1) erodes parental authority, because working adolescents are less economically dependent on the parents; (2) interferes with school work; (3) is associated with higher rates of alcohol and drug use, because adolescents have more money to spend; and (4) may foster the development of negative attitudes toward work itself, given the high-stress, low-paying jobs that most teenagers have (Gecas and Seff, 1991; Greenberger and Steinberg, 1986). Recent research finds that seniors who work 30 hours or more a week display higher levels of aggression, are more likely to use drugs and alcohol, and are less satisfied with their lives in general. Different types of jobs, however, make a difference. When jobs are relevant to educational and career goals, teens are less likely to experience the problems associated with heavy work hours (Crispell, 1995). The primary outcome of adolescent employment is a higher standard of living for teens themselves. This differs from children's work in the past, which contributed to the economic well-being of the family.

WORK AND FAMILY OVERLAP

Many connections and interchanges make it impossible for work and family to be separate worlds. Work shapes family life, and family overlaps with work. The economy provides goods and services for consumption by families. Families use their earned income to buy these goods and services. The economy provides jobs to family members, while the family supplies skilled workers to the economy. Work/family relationships generate difficulties for workers. The term **work–family interference** refers to the ways in which the connections between jobs and family life may be a source of tension for workers and family members (Hughes et al., 1992:32). One of the ways that work-family problems are expressed is through **spillover**—that is, the carrying over of the concerns, responsibilities, and demands of one part of life to another. Spillover can go in two directions: home-to-job spillover or job-to-home spillover. It can also be positive or negative (Galinsky and Bond, 1996:97).

Just how work and family interact depends on the structural features of each. Job characteristics profoundly affect day-to-day family relations. For example, the demands of professional and managerial occupations, in contrast to those of lower-paid white-collar and blue-collar jobs, pose very different problems for the family. Family characteristics are also important. Is there only one working member, or are there two? Is there only one or are there two parents? These work and family characteristics are important because they set up different work opportunities and demands, as well as different family needs and resources, of both an economic and an interpersonal nature.

Work–family relations also vary because they are linked within a larger society that is stratified by class, race, and gender. Family structure and employment are major components of family well-being. Regardless of race, dual-earner families are associated with high standards of living. Married-couple families in which the wife is employed have the lowest poverty rates of all family types, whereas families headed by nonemployed single mothers have the highest poverty rates (McLanahan and Casper, 1995:20). Can we conclude, then, that poverty would disappear if people lived in co-provider families? This conclusion would be misleading because work and family connections are different across the racial hierarchy. Neither marriage nor employment offer the same rewards to women of color as to White women. Certainly marriage and employment matter a great deal, but they matter *differently* for Black and Latina women than they do for White women: they matter less. "Minority women are more likely to be poor than are comparable Whites of the same marital status and at every level of work effort" (Catanzarite and Ortiz, 1996:133). Employment by itself does not eradicate poverty for minorities. For example, the low earnings of Latinos mean that even when they "play by the rules"—that is, live in married-couple families where parents work—they are more likely to be poor than White families (Lichter and Landale, 1995:346). Structures of inequality produce different rewards for workers and their families.

Work and family connections are complex. They change in both expected and unexpected ways over the life course. Here we focus on how the linkages vary according to the gender of the workers, the requirements of work roles, and the composition of families.

Gender Inequality

Although work and family roles are changing, the gender order shapes everyday relations in the family and the workplace. Both settings impose uneven demands on women and men, and women's demands are higher overall (Milkie and Peltola, 1999). Even the metaphor of "balance" is gendered, with women doing most of the balancing (Moen and Yu, 2000). Not only are women more likely to work part-time, earn less, and receive fewer benefits than men, they assume more family responsibility than men and they report greater stress in both work and family roles.

The demands of the family intrude more on women's work roles than on those of men. If an emergency or irregularity arises, requiring a choice between the two, the family usually takes priority. For example, when there is a crisis for a child in school, it is the child's working mother, rather than the working father, who will be called on to take responsibility. For husbands, the relationship is reversed. The work role takes priority over the family role. Many husbands take work home with them or use their time at home to recuperate from the stresses they face in the work role. Husbands are expected to manage their families so that family responsibilities do not interfere with their work efficiency and so that families will make any adjustments necessary to the work role. Joseph Pleck (1977) has termed women's and men's uneven relationship to work and family the **work–family role system.** This system reinforces the traditional division of

The working mother is more likely than the father
to care for a sick child.

labor in both work and family. This system also ensures that wives' employment
does not affect their core responsibilities for housework and childcare. Employed
wives generally have two jobs, while employed husbands have only one.

Despite these different orientations to work and family, pressures of balancing work and family are increasingly an issue for men as well as women. Fathers'
involvement in family life is taking place across race and class. Research on
men's family lives offers a contemporary and hopeful perspective on gender
equality in family and society. Although true "role-sharing" couples remain a
minority, men are taking on more of the family workload, a necessary step in the
transformation of both the male role and the patriarchal family (Coltrane, 1996).

Although work and family roles remain strongly gendered, women and men
are making adjustments in the workplace and in the home. Most studies of
changing commitments to families and jobs have focused on women, because
they are the ones who make more adjustments. Yet men, too, are adapting in
diverse ways. Kathleen Gerson's (1993) research led her to divide contemporary
men into three groups: (1) breadwinners or career men, who contribute little to
domestic work and child rearing; (2) autonomous men, who skip or flee family
commitment by remaining single or getting divorced and ignoring their obligations; and (3) involved men, who are willing to sacrifice career advancement to
share family responsibilities with their wives. Gerson found that men could
move across the typology over their lifetimes and that shifts now taking place in
men's lives are redefining the meaning of manhood in America.

Work Characteristics

A variety of job characteristics affect families. Two major aspects of work affect family life directly: (1) the level of economic rewards associated with work, and (2) the conditions associated with performing a job. These are structural job characteristics that organize the worker's time, determine when and where one works, and include work hours, travel demands, weekend work, and flexibility in job scheduling (Hughes et al., 1992:32).

Increased Work Time

Time is a scarce commodity in U.S. families. As the economy moves steadily to a 24-hour, 7-days-a-week economy, Americans are left with too little time for their families. Long work hours have become a standard part of life. Both women and men now work longer hours than they did 20 years ago. The average U.S. workers now works 1966 hours per year, 83 hours more than in 1980. In other nations, hours on the job have gone *down,* yet workers here spend 40 percent more time on the job than Norwegians and 26 percent more time than Germans (Longworth, 1999). (See Figure 6.3.) No wonder Juliet Schor's book, *The Overworked American* (1991), became a best-seller in the 1990s. According to Schor, a Harvard economist, the rise in work is not confined to a few selective groups, but has affected the great majority of Americans. Hours have risen for men as well as women; for those in the working class as well as professionals; for all marital status and income groups; and across a wide range of industries. What Schor calls a "profound structural crisis of time" is taking a serious toll on family well-

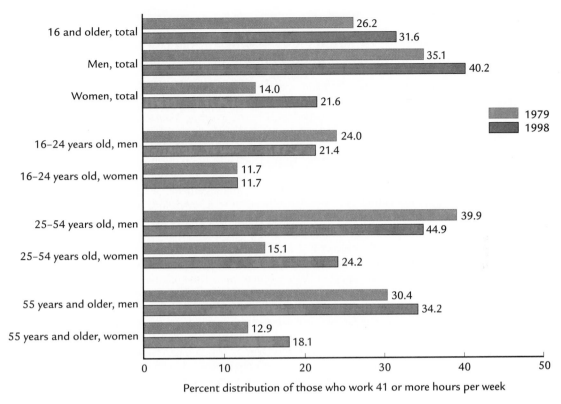

Figure 6.3

More workers have a long work week.

Source: The Career Quandary. Reports on America, Vo. 2, No. 1. Washington, DC: Population Reference Bureau (February 2001).

being. Although many families are better off economically, they are "time poor." The time crunch reduces time that parents might spend with their children and places tremendous burdens on marriage, as couples have less time to talk with each other (Schor, 1991:5; Berry, 1999; Morin, 1998).

Should we assume, however, that spouses *want* more time with their families? In a new study of the work-family squeeze, Arlie Hochschild finds that, instead of trying to arrange shorter or more flexible work hours, many women and men are choosing to work longer hours. This research challenges the taken-for-granted idea that home is a respite from work. Hochschild observed and interviewed workers at all levels of a *Fortune* 500 company she calls "Americo" (see Box 6.1). She discovered a growing tendency for workers to escape family pressures by taking refuge in the efficiency, predictability, and camaraderie of the workplace. For them, work was more like family and family was more like work. What has caused such a reversal? According to Hochschild, the social world of work has become more important and the social world at home less important:

Researching Families: How Sociologist Arlie Hochschild Studied the Work-Family Squeeze in Corporate American Families

I was asked to give a talk at Amerco, a company about which I knew little except that it had been identified as one of the ten most "family-friendly" companies in America by the Families and Work Institute, by *Working Mother* magazine, and by the authors of *Companies That Care*. At a dinner given after my talk, a company spokesman seated next to me asked if I had ever thought of studying family-friendly policies in the workplace itself. To tell the truth, I could not believe my luck. If there was ever a chance for families to balance home and work, I thought to myself, it would be at a place like this. Amerco's management clearly hoped my findings would help them answer a few questions of their own. In the late 1980s, the company had been distressed to discover a startling fact: they were losing professional women far faster than they were losing professional men. Each time such a worker was lost, it cost the company a great deal of money to recruit and train a replacement. The company had tried to eliminate this waste of money and talent by addressing one probable reason women were leaving: the absence of what was called "work-family balance." Amerco now offered a range of remedial programs including options for part-time work, job sharing, and flextime. Did these policies really help Amerco? Given current trends, it seemed crucial to top management to know the answer. Six months later I found myself lodged at a cozy bed-and-breakfast on a tree-lined street in Spotted Deer, ready to begin finding out.

The receptionist at company headquarters issued me a magnetized badge, a bit like one of those magic rings that children once found in cereal boxes, which opened company doors everywhere day and night. Over the course of three summers between 1990 and 1993, I "badged in" and "badged out" behind employees I was following around.

I interviewed top and middle managers, clerks and factory workers—a hundred and thirty people in all. Most were part of two-job couples, some were single parents, and a few were single without children. Sometimes we met in their offices or in a plant break room, sometimes in their homes, often in both places. Early mornings and evenings, weekends and holidays, I sat on the lawn by the edge of a series of parking lots that circled company headquarters, watching people walk to and from their vans, cars, or pick-up trucks to see when they came to work and when they left.

I talked with psychologists in and outside the company, child-care workers hired by Amerco, homemakers married to Amerco employees, and company consultants. Along with the Spotted Deer Childcare Center, I visited local YWCA after-school programs as well as a Parent Resource Center funded by the company. I attended company sessions of the Women's Quality Improvement Team and the Work Family Progress Committee, a Valuing Diversity workshop, and two High Performance Team meetings. A team in Amerco's Sales Division allowed me to sit in on its meetings. To their surprise—and mine—I also became the fifth wheel on a golfing expedition designed to build team spirit. During several night shifts at an Amerco factory, tired workers patiently talked with me over coffee in the break room. One even took me to a local bar to meet her friends and relatives.

The company gave me access to a series of its internal "climate surveys" of employee attitudes, and I combed through research reports on other companies,

(continued)

(continued from previous page)

national opinion polls, and a burgeoning literature on work and family life. I also attended work-family conferences held in New York, San Francisco, Los Angeles, and Boston by The Conference Board, a respected organization that gathers and disseminates information of interest to the benefit of the business management community.

Six families—four two-parent families and two single-mother families—allowed me to follow them on typical workdays from dawn until dusk and beyond. I found myself watching a small child creep into her mother's bed at dawn for an extra cuddle and snooze. One day I sat for over an hour on a green plastic turtle watching two giggly girls slither down a small water slide into a pool. Many times children approached me to locate a missing button on a shirt or—more hopelessly for me—to play Super Mario Brothers on the Nintendo set, while a busy parent cooked dinner.

Source: Arlie Russell Hochschild, *The Time Bind*. New York: Metropolitan Books, Henry Holt and Company, 1997, pp. 7–9.

In this new model of family and work life, a tired parent flees a world of unresolved quarrels and unwashed laundry for the reliable orderliness, harmony, and managed cheer of work. The emotional magnets beneath home and workplace are in the process of being reversed. In truth, there are many versions of this reversal going on, some more far-reaching than others. Some people find in work a respite from the emotional tangles at home. Others virtually marry their work, investing it with an emotional significance once reserved for family, while hesitating to trust loved ones at home (Hochschild, 1997:44–45).

The extent to which this reversal affects U.S. workers across occupational settings is controversial. Nevertheless, Hochschild's provocative conclusions raise important questions about the changing worlds of work and family.

Stress is produced by two kinds of interference: structural interference and psychosocial interference. **Structural interference** is the extent to which the organization and demands of one work role (work or family) promote practical difficulty in managing the demands of the other. **Psychosocial interference** is the transfer of moods from one setting to another (Hughes et al., 1992:32). Most of the research on both forms of interference has investigated job-to-family interference. Although workers' family responsibilities also shape their work, we know less about how employees manage children or other family concerns from the workplace. This issue is important to both employers and employees.

Workers often have to deal with emergencies, large and small, while at work: they have to arrange a different car pool ride for a child, make a doctor's appointment for an elderly parent, or deal with a family conflict, such as a teenager who is suspected of drinking or using drugs. For those employees who have children who care for themselves after school, there can be a period of tension until the child telephones to say he or she is safe at home. (This applies to employees who have access to a telephone; many don't.) Employers know this as the "3:15 syndrome," sometimes noting that productivity slumps at this time (Galinsky, 1986:17).

Timing and Scheduling of Work

Timing affects the rhythm and quality of daily life directly by determining when, where, and how much a worker can be with his or her family. Some jobs are rigid, requiring employees to punch a time clock, while others are more flexible. With flexible jobs, workers are better able to handle personal emergencies at home, visit with their children's teachers, and the like. Some jobs demand that one be away from home for days or even weeks at a time. This separation requires that one spouse take on a greater share of responsibility for the day-to-day decisions about home and children. Other forms of work-related travel take people away from their families. Some live at a distance from work, losing several hours a day to commuting. Most working hours occur from Monday through Friday during the daylight hours. This arrangement permits workers to have greater interaction with spouse and children in the evenings and weekends because their schedules coincide. Other jobs, however, have odd schedules (e.g., working at night, four 10-hour days a week, and swing shifts, in which the work hours rotate from week to week). Many workers are expected to put in overtime hours, either at the workplace or by bringing work home, and many workers take on additional jobs to make ends meet.

The timing of work is a strong determinant of family life. Workers who put in long hours often have higher levels of work–family conflict and strain; that is, work and family life interfere with each other. Women and men who work similar hours experience less strain (Moen, 1999). Gender differences emerge in studies of how work schedules impose on families (Galinsky and Bond, 1996; Stains and Pleck, 1983). For men, long work hours often prevent them from fulfilling their family responsibilities, whereas women workers tend to experience more stress arising from scheduling work and family responsibilities. When employees can exercise some control over their job schedules, they and their families suffer fewer ill effects. Theodore Cohen's (1993) research on men's parenting roles found that timing of work was the most important shaper of their fathering activities. The men in his study had to fit children around their jobs. On the other hand, men's paid work schedules sometimes offered them unique opportunities to engage in more extensive activity with their children:

> Two fathers who worked nights, a third who as a teacher returned home early from work, and a fourth whose job included two weekdays off all associated their work schedules with higher than expected levels of involvement in child care. . . . Thus, whereas some fathers felt that their jobs restricted their parenting activities, others owed their high levels of involvement to their work schedules. In both directions, work became a dominant influence over the nature of men's relationship with their children (Cohen, 1993:16).

Work schedules vary considerably in the 24–7 economy. There is no such thing as an average workday when husbands and wives work different hours. Shift work is on the rise for women and men alike. As of the early 1990s, about one-fourth of dual-earner couples worked split shifts (*Population Today*, 1997b). A recent poll of working women commissioned by the AFL-CIO found that nearly half of working women work a different shift than their husband (Love, 2000; Swoboda and Joyce, 2000). A reason for this new pattern lies in the growth of

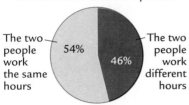

Almost two-thirds of working women
are married or live with a partner.

The two people work the same hours — 54%

The two people work different hours — 46%

IRREGULAR WORK

Percent of working women who
work some evenings and/or
weekends:

All working women	28%
With children under 18	26%
Single women	40%
Under age 30	35%
Earn less than $25,000	42%

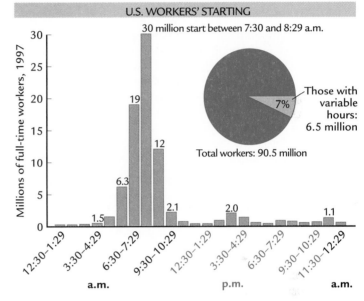

U.S. WORKERS' STARTING

30 million start between 7:30 and 8:29 a.m.

Those with variable hours: 6.5 million — 7%

Total workers: 90.5 million

Figure 6.4

Working women's hours

Source: Alice Ann Love, Associated Press. "Survey Shows 46% of Couple Work Different Shifts," *Albuquerque Journal,*
March 10, 2000, pp. A1, A2.

America's service industries, which require shift and weekend work (McEnroe, 1991:50). Shift work can be a strategy for managing childcare needs (Garey, 1999; Lamphere et al., 1993). Nevertheless, shift work often precludes the sharing of routine family activities. As full-time workers and full-time caregivers, parents have little time for leisure, to rest, be together, or even sleep (Funk and Hughes, 1996:407). (See Box 6.2.)

Geographic Mobility

High mobility underlies business and work institutions and, increasingly, the family. Two types of geographic mobility are common in this society: work-related travel and job-related moves and transfers. The large majority of Americans work and live in different places. Commuting extends the workday and requires reliable access to transportation.

Inside the Worlds of Diverse Families: Constructing Motherhood on the Night Shift

Cultural definitions of a *good mother* conflict with cultural definitions of a *good worker*. Sociologist Anita Garey interviewed hospital nurses to find out how they resolved the conflicting demands of work and family. She found that night shift nurses construct themselves as "stay-at-home" moms. This strategy offered several advantages, including being at home when their children returned from school. Doing things with and for their children enabled them to retain the symbolic definition of "good mothering." The following excerpted interviews reveal how they reconciled some incompatibilities of being working mothers.

Janice Ho, Doris Chavez, and Julia Ginzburg each have one child in elementary school and a child under five years old in some form of day care. Differences in ethnicity, age, and seniority at the hospital notwithstanding, their stated reasons for working the night shift are remarkably similar. Janice, a 30 year old Filipina registered nurse, told me:

> I was always working nights. Cause it's easier to work nights with my young children. I like to be home with them, even [if] I'm sleeping, I like to be, you know, around.

Doris, a 34-year-old Mexican American registered nurse, immediately mentioned being home during the day in response to my request that she "tell me about working and having children." Doris replied:

> It's hard, real hard. I want my kids to go to college; we bought a house. I want them to have a house. And that's one of the reasons I work night shift. I feel more comfortable being at home in the daytime while they're—well, they go to day care. So my husband takes them to day care and then I get home in the morning and sleep. And I know that I'm home by the phone in case something happens to them.

For Doris, being available to her children means being by the telephone, at home, close to her children's school, in case the school needs to reach her. Julia Ginzburg, a 43 year old Jewish registered nurse, gave a similar response to my question about her reasons for working the night shift.

> For me, it allows—I mean—I'm available. There's always a parent at home. If there's anything that comes up; if the kid is sick, it's no big deal, I'm here. Like now, during the summer, when my son is finished with his program at noon he comes home. I'm here. He can handle himself around the house. My small one (one year old) I have in child care, but the big one (nine years old) comes home and can go and play with friends, he can go to the library himself, but—I'm here. Whereas, if I were working in the daytime, I wouldn't be comfortable with him coming home to an empty house. I don't want him to be—I don't feel like he's a latchkey kid. I'm here. I'm asleep! But I'm here. If something comes up, I'm available.

"I'm here," "I'm home," "I'm around," "I'm available" are striking refrains in two ways. First, they are coupled with the statement "I'm asleep." Second, for a large part of the time these women are home, their children are not. Notice that both Doris and Julia use the word "comfortable" to describe their reasons for wanting to be home during the daytime. Being at home during the day, even if they are asleep and even if their children are at school or in child care, "fits" with their construction of motherhood. It not only enables them to respond instrumentally to daytime child-related needs and emergencies and to be home when children return from school, but it places them in the symbolically appropriate place for mothers: in the home. A look at how they each organize their daily schedule illustrates this.

Janice Ho gets home from the hospital at about 8:30 in the morning. Her husband has already gotten their older child off to school, taken the baby to the neighbor who does child care for them, and left for work. Janice returns to an empty house and immediately goes to sleep. At 1:30 p.m., she wakes up, picks the baby up from the neighbor's house and meets her son at the bus stop. She spends the next few hours feeding the children, playing with the baby, and helping her son with his homework. When her husband returns from work in the evening, Janice goes back to bed and gets a few more hours sleep until it is time to wake up to get ready to leave the house at 10:00 p.m. for another night shift. The routine that Janice reports is in some ways an exception to the reported routines of the other night-shift nurses in that she goes back to bed after her husband returns from work. Her intended routine gives her more sleep than the other nurses I interviewed and her husband does more of the care when she is home than do the husbands of the other night-shift nurses. However, my interview with Janice indicated that things were rarely routine in her household and that she averages far less sleep than claimed in her report of a "typical" day.

Except for her two days off each week, Janice reports spending about three hours a day with her children. The rest of the time they are either at school or child care, or she is sleeping. For Janice, working nights is not a way of spending more time with her children, since day shift workers would have about as many child contact hours as Janice does. But, as Janice says, working nights allows her to "be around" during the day.

Doris Chavez lives over an hour from the hospital and usually doesn't get home until 9:00 in the morning. Her husband, who has a two hour commute to work, gets the children up at 5:00 a.m., leaves the house by 5:30 a.m. to drop them at the child care center and then continues on his way to work. Doris's oldest child will then be bussed from the child care center to his elementary school. Unlike Janice, Doris doesn't immediately go to sleep when she gets home; she does housework, starts dinner preparations, unwinds a bit. She averages four hours of sleep on the days she works. She wakes about 3:00 p.m. to welcome her son home from school and goes to pick up her youngest child from the child care center. Doris spends the rest of the afternoon preparing dinner, helping her son with his homework, and caring for the children. When her husband comes home from work, they all have dinner together. She leaves the house at 9:30 p.m. to drive back to the hospital for another night shift.

Doris reports spending about twice as much contact time with her children as Janice but, for both of them, what is most salient is *which hours* they are home. As Doris said, "I know that I'm home by the phone in case something happens to them," and she adds:

> But I'm usually home by 9 a.m., and I have been called [by the school] before . . . I get that straight with the teacher right off the bat. You know "I work nights, I'm home."

Doris lets her children's teachers know, and she emphasizes the importance that they know, that she is a mother at home during the day.

Source: Anita Ilta Garey, "Constructing Motherhood on The Night Shift: 'Working Mothers' as 'Stay-at-Home Moms,'" *Qualitative Sociology* 18(4): 424–426 (1995).

Employment-related considerations comprise slightly more than a quarter of all reasons for moving. In 1990, a move for a new job, transfer, or the desire to be close to work or school accounted for about 20 percent of all moves among home owners and 30 percent among renters (Gober, 1993:29). Some job-related moves occur because individuals must move to find work; others are made to improve an individual's economic and occupational status. Individuals move to find work, for example, in beginning a career after completing school or losing a job because of plant or office closings or cutbacks (Voydanoff, 1987:66). Moving depends largely on the type of job people hold. Doctors, lawyers, and others who rely on local bases of operation have low rates of mobility, while business executives are highly mobile (McFalls, 1998:19).

Success and promotions within a work organization may involve the move to a new geographic location. Married-couple families usually move in response to husbands' job opportunities (Spitze, 1991:390). Migration is a common practice in large corporations, the rationale being that "rising stars" should have varied management experiences and should be familiar with the company's operations in the field. Typically the case involves a male company executive who is promoted and must relocate. His transfer to a new location often requires his wife and children to pay a heavy price. While husbands often fit into a ready-made work structure complete with colleagues (though not always successfully), wives must find their way around a new community without the status and achievements from their previous community (McCollum, 1990).

Corporate marriages demand that the male (typically) be dedicated to his job and move as the corporation dictates. His wife, in turn, must be willing to sacrifice for his career. A person who moves or stays because of a spouse's opportunity contrary to his or her own optimal economic choice is said to be "tied." Given current market opportunities, a "tied mover" is likely to be a wife and a "tied stayer" a husband (Spitze, 1991:390).

High levels of geographic relocation can result in family stress (Ammons et al., 1982; Gaylord, 1979; McCollum, 1990). Nevertheless, spouses and children appear to manage. With difficulty, they survive quite well the traumas of moving. These families of geographically mobile executives may even benefit as they pull together because of the disruption.

Type of Work
Different kinds of work have different consequences for families. Jobs vary in wage levels and other benefits, such as health insurance, Social Security, private pensions, disability, and unemployment insurance. Thus, employment is the major source of economic and social well-being.

White Collar and Professional   Different kinds of carryover have been found in both middle-class and working-class families. This research has focused on the father's occupation. In general, occupational prestige and income increase marital stability and marital satisfaction, yet occupational success may offset the rewards. Although a family benefits monetarily from such success, it may also suffer because of the successful worker's absence or neglect. Years ago, Arlie Hochschild (1975) observed that "the clockwork of male careers" imposed unrelenting demands. Family obligations must be canceled, interrupted, or post-poned if need be. This time-devouring form of work, deeply embedded in the male career model, is increasingly the model adopted by career women.

All occupations can extend into family life, but specific occupations are sin-gled out for their high rates of negative carryover. For example, problems asso-ciated with family disorganization and personal stress—divorce, family vio-lence, and alcoholism—are particularly common in the families of urban police officers (Hoffman, 1987:366).

Blue Collar Many classic family studies have found blue-collar working condi-tions spilling over into the family. Inadequate resources, monotonous and unchallenging work, unsafe working conditions, dead-end jobs, the unrelenting threat of unemployment, and low self-esteem affect family life. Richard Sennett and Jonathan Cobb (1972), in their analysis of the working class, found that these workers find their search for respect thwarted and blame themselves for the fail-ure because of their lack of ability and for not working hard enough. These feel-ings of inadequacy and self-blame have profound effects on relationships within the family. These husbands may refuse to allow their wives to work because work is their own single source of self-worth; they may rule the home in an authoritarian manner; they may abuse their wives and children; or they may withdraw from social relationships, even within the family. Lillian Rubin's path-breaking study of working-class families found that most men are in a constant struggle to make some order and continuity out of the fragments of their lives. Thus, they come home after work and plunge into projects that offer the possi-bility for feeling useful, competent, and whole again—fixing the car or truck, remodeling the kitchen, building something for the kids. Others—those who seem already to have given up life and hope—collapse into a kind of numbed exhaustion from which they stir only to eat, drink, and watch television. Either way, the implications for family life are clear. Husbands and fathers are removed from active involvement, some because they are in a desperate struggle to retain some sense of their humanity, others because they have given it all up (Rubin, 1976:161).

Professional Satisfaction from Work Work may or may not be a source of per-sonal satisfaction. In the past, most research focused on fathers' jobs. Today, researchers are asking questions about women's work lives and learning about job conditions that foster greater control. These include having more flexible time and leave options, greater autonomy, and greater control over work sched-ules (Galinsky and Bond, 1996:102). Chances are that the higher the prestige, the more autonomy; the greater the income received from the job, the greater the importance of work to the individual's well-being. Occupations offering less desirable working conditions offer fewer intrinsic benefits and exacerbate other negative characteristics (Menaghan, 1996:411).

Although it is generally assumed that blue-collar work produces greater negative carryover than white-collar work, we should caution against this sim-ple generalization. It is difficult to untangle the effects of type of work and social class. Psychologically demanding jobs such as those with high pressure and low support have negative effects and prevent workers from meeting family demands (Hughes et al., 1992:40). We need to know more about the effects on family life of the working conditions in different occupations. For example, the computer revolution may diminish the time workers spend in family activities. New requirements that employees check voice and e-mail after hours and on vacation erodes the boundaries between work and home (Gerson, 2000; West, 2000). They introduce new time constraints for today's overworked families.

Work demands have a profound impact on how people behave in their families. It is unrealistic to expect that these dynamics can be overcome through individual or family efforts alone—they require, instead, a restructuring of the workplace.

Family Characteristics

Women, men, and children live in a wide range of family forms that must be taken into account when considering work–family linkages. Two-parent families, two-earner families, single-parent families, and other variations have different connections with the workplace. Especially important are the ages of workers; stage in the family life cycle; employment status of workers; number, age, and sex of children; and the presence of aging parents. For example, the ages of the workers' children make a big difference. Employed workers with young children are more likely to find it difficult to manage both their work and family

"I'm off now to reproduce—but I'll be back!"

responsibilities, as do workers who care for aging parents. Children's adolescence can be a stressful time for employed parents, particularly executive fathers (summarized in Galinsky, 1986:3; Haas, 1999:573–574).

Dual-Worker Families: The Dominant Pattern

Dual-worker families are now the dominant family model among workers in the labor force (Ahlburg and De Vita, 1992:25; Waite, 2000). Whatever their social class, all dual-earner couples confront the challenges of negotiating roles and a division of labor, setting priorities for work and family, and, if children are present, arranging for their care.

Costs and Benefits of Having Both Spouses in the Labor Force   Although research finds that dual-earner families experience tremendous stress, employed wives also have high levels of self-esteem and well-being (Spitze, 1991:384).

The chief disadvantages of combining roles for women stem from greater marital stress. Many husbands are reluctant to share household responsibilities. Women have absorbed the male work ethic much more readily than men have absorbed their share of domestic and care taking roles (Hochschild, 1997:11). Occupationally, women sacrifice more and compromise career ambitions in making the dual-earner pattern work.

What happens when women add employment to their other roles? How does the combination of marriage, motherhood, and employment affect them? We have seen that across the races, marriage and employment are associated with a higher standard of living for women (McLanahan and Casper, 1995). In addition, women in co-provider marriages are consistently found to be healthier, less depressed, and less frustrated than wives who are homemakers (Coontz, 1997:67). Because roles provide a sense of social integration, multiple roles enhance well-being (Miller et al., 1991:566). Women's power within the family is greater when they produce income. Some wives who feel trapped by the homemaker role are liberated when they go to work. This is ironic, given the tedious and dead-end jobs they typically fill and the relatively low pay they receive. However, these faults are offset by a new sense of independence, of feeling competent, of having pride in doing a good job and in contributing monetarily to the family. Women can "escape" (at least temporarily) the routines of housework when they go to work.

Employment is an important predictor of physical health and lack of psychological anxiety among women. Why would multiple roles, despite the time crunch and conflicting obligations, often lead to more happiness? Several studies suggest that multiple roles provide many types of gratification including a sense of accomplishment, improved interpersonal relationships, opportunities to develop talents and abilities, clear goals and priorities, and a greater variety of experiences (summarized in Haas, 1999).

Studies comparing overall levels of life satisfaction among employed and nonemployed women show that physical and mental health favor the employed (see Spitze [1991] for a decade review of women's employment and family relations). The key factor seems to be employment preferences. Wives are least depressed when their employment status is consistent with their own and their husbands' preferences and most depressed when they are not employed but would prefer to be.

Mothers' Employment and Children Does mothers' employment damage children? Decades of research have shown that employed mothers pose no harm to their children. In fact, some children are actively helped by maternal employment (Coontz, 1997; Gerson, 2000). Not even national longitudinal child–mother surveys find harmful effects of women's employment on young children. However, certain conditions, such as both parents' working overtime, create negative effects. Other conditions intrinsic to dual-earner families increase tensions. The major problems are the coordination of family roles, caring for children, and a decline in family time. The increased time parents have spent at work in recent years has reduced the time they spend at home. This has left them less time to spend with their children.

Work and Family Priorities among Different Categories of Women The impact of women's employment on family life has not been uniform. When we assess changes that occur in the family once women enter paid employment, we must be careful not to accept as "universal" the changes that are unique to women in elite professions. Class and race bring different linkages to work and family. Married women in working-class jobs may appear to be far more "traditional" than professional wives—that is, more willing to accept patriarchal authority, less "committed" to their work, and prepared to sacrifice themselves endlessly to family demands. We should be critical of this stereotype because it presents women in elite professions as exemplary, as if their norms, values, and behaviors in "balancing" work and family are superior. The "lesser work commitment" of working-class wives must be seen in the context of the work they do; after all, a job is not a career. On the other hand, their jobs do make it possible to provide for their families, albeit in settings where advancement, achievement, and financial success are structurally limited (Ferree, 1987).

The Wife as Sole Provider

While multiple earners have become more necessary, changes in family composition have left growing proportions of families with a single adult earner. Deteriorating economic conditions have thrust many wives into the provider role. They have had no choice but to enter the labor force. Job loss among working-class and minority men affects family life. Unemployment generally hits hardest where there is less tolerance of employed wives. Men getting laid off and becoming dependent on their wives for economic support creates tensions in the marital relationship.

Often wives continue working after husbands retire. This occurs with ever greater frequency because increasingly more middle-age women are in the labor force and because so many men reach retirement age years before their wives do.

In some other cases, though few, wives choose to be the providers and the husbands the homemakers. The arrangements are often experimental, with each spouse taking a turn alternating a career with home and childcare. The number is small in this category for several related reasons. First, whether acquaintances, friends, or relatives, others tend to be very unsupportive of this nontraditional arrangement. The cultural ideal remains strong that says that men should always be involved in full-time employment while women should combine work and family responsibilities, and those who defy this norm experience ridicule and scorn. Second, men resist because they have been taught that their primary contribution to the family is as financial provider.

Single-Parent Families

Today, almost a third of family households with children are maintained by a single parent, nine out of ten of whom are women (Berry, 1999). While such parents do not have to negotiate with an unemployed spouse about schedules or housework, neither do they have the income assistance or the emotional support that a spouse can provide. One-parent families with one earner are relatively more disadvantaged than two-parent families with two breadwinners. The economic circumstances of never-married mothers are worse than those of divorced mothers (Spain and Bianchi, 1996:141–166).

Both single fathers and single mothers must do housework, yet women and men define the responsibility differently. Interviewing single mothers and fathers, Polly Fasinger (1993:211) found that although men reported doing housework as single fathers, they defined it differently than single women and used different rationales for requesting help from their children. "Whereas mothers ask for help because they 'need it,' fathers tell their children that 'housework is not my job.'" According to Fasinger, men may do more housework as single fathers, but they do not necessarily feel responsible for these activities. The demands of employment add to the difficulties of single parenting.

INVISIBLE AND UNPAID FAMILY WORK

When most people hear about the massive entry of women into the workplace, their minds turn to one type of work: participation in the paid labor force. Women have always worked in the household, but such labor has not been included in the definition of work. After industrialization divided work and family, men's work evolved into paid labor outside of the home while women's work (whether they labored outside the home or not) became associated with unpaid work in the household. This division obscured all of those activities that are done inside the household to keep the family going. Feminists have long argued, however, that "outside" employment is not the only activity that qualifies as "work" (Garey, 1999:41). If we think about work in a more inclusive way, to include as any individual effort or activity that produces goods or services of value to others, it becomes clear that a vast amount of unpaid work is done in the family, much of it by women.

Gendered Labor in the Household

Housework is the quintessential example of work that is done inside the family without extrinsic rewards. "We are discussing a set of work activities engaged in

daily by many millions of people. Most of them are women, a class of workers who, although socially invisible, collectively devote billions of hours to their work" (Berk, 1988:288).

Household work done each day provides cooked meals, clean clothes, scrubbed floors, and a host of other "commodities." It also reproduces the important rituals that constitute family living. For example, preparing and providing food are important activities in the construction of family life. Not only is meal preparation part of the work of caring, it is a central ritual that organizes people and activities (DeVault, 1991:263).

Domestic labor maintains families and it sustains the economy. Without shopping, cooking, housework, and other forms of "caring work," the economy would be at a standstill, because society requires workers that are "serviced." Yet much of this service work remains unpaid.

Since increasingly more wives share the provider role, it is reasonable to ask if husbands share the family labor. The answer to this question can be summed up in the familiar tag, "Man may work from sun to sun, but women's work is never done." Household tasks continue to differ by gender, even among women who work full-time. Over the past three decades, married mothers have experienced a decline in their hours of housework (from about 30 to about 20 hours or less per week) (Ehrenreich, 2000). However, "married fathers picked up only part of the slack, increasing their household work from about five hours a week to about ten hours" (Spain and Bianchi, 1996:169). No matter how housework is defined and measured, wives still do two-thirds of the housework. This finding is repeated in study after study (see Shelton, 1992, and reviews in Ferree [1991] and Thompson and Walker [1991]; and Milkie and Peltola [1999]). These studies yield the following conclusions:

1. Family tasks are strongly gendered whether the wife is employed or not. Men work on cars and do yardwork, home repairs, and household errands, while women almost exclusively do the cooking, cleaning, laundry, mending, and child care.
2. Husbands of working wives spend about one-third as much time on housework as do their wives (about an hour and a half per day, compared to four and a half hours for their wives).
3. Husbands do not share equally in the housework even if the wife works full-time, even if the husband is unemployed, and even if the husband professes that spouses should share equally in domestic work.
4. Husbands tend to do relatively more housework if there is a child under the age of two, if they are better educated, and if they are younger.
5. The domestic contribution of husbands does not change much, whether their wives work or not.
6. The general pattern of gendered household labor does not vary greatly by social class or race.

Housework carries different meanings for women and men. It is *gendered* labor, a set of specific tasks that convey social meanings about masculinity and femininity (Ferree, 1991:111; Arrighi and Maume 2000; Risman, 1998). This is a fundamental privilege that benefits individual men and boys within families. Women tend to men's "existence needs," such as cleaning, cooking, and taking care of clothing, while men gain time at women's expense.

Women's responsibilities for housework, child care, and home management have produced what Arlie Hochschild (1989) calls **the second shift** for employed wives. Hochschild interviewed fifty couples of different classes and races to find out how families attend to the tasks that must be accomplished before and after paid work. She discovered that most women work one shift in their workplace and a second shift at home (see Box 6.2). Hochschild found that wives devoted more time to housework than did husbands and more time to all forms of family work than did husbands; that coping by performing the second shift left wives much more deeply torn than were their husbands about the burdens of paid work and family work. The additional hours that working women spent on the so-called second shift of housework, Hochschild calculated, add up to an extra month of work each year! Even though social class is important in determining how the household labor gets done (more affluent families can afford to purchase more labor-saving services), Hochschild found that social class, race/ethnicity, and personality gave limited clues about who does and does not share the second shift.

Although gender is paramount in the allocation of household labor, men are doing more housework than they used to (Shelton, 1992). For example, Joseph Pleck (1993) argues that men are making more accommodations to family demands and experiencing greater stress than Hochschild and others suggest. Other research also finds that "variation among couples is increasing, with some men now making much larger contributions to some forms of family work" (Coltrane, 1996:53). Conditions associated with domestic sharing include high levels of education (for both wives and husbands) and having a young child (Shelton, 1992; Spain and Bianchi, 1996), and wives working full-time (Figert and Mutari, 1998).

What about children's contributions to household labor? In two-parent working families, children don't relieve their parents of much day-to-day housework. Apparently, children are withdrawing from domestic responsibilities. What little household labor they contribute is strongly gendered, with girls having more responsibility than boys. Daughters of mothers who work full-time spend 10.2 hours per week on housework, in contrast to sons' 2.7 hours. Even in more egalitarian couples, the picture is one in which both parents are picking up after and waiting on their children (Waite and Goldscheider, 1992).

Few families escape the demands of household labor, but some have the resources to hire others to do their domestic work and child care. Some professional lifestyles have long been dependent on the labor provided by domestic workers in private homes (Dill, 1983; Glenn, 1992; Rollins, 1985; Romero, 1992). Today, hiring household help is becoming more common. In 1999, between 14 and 18 percent of households employed an outsider to do their cleaning (Ehrenreich, 2000). Private household workers are still disproportionately women of color. In 1998, the Bureau of Labor Statistics reports that 36 percent were Hispanic, 15 percent were African American, and 2 percent were "other." (Ehrenreich, 2000:63). African American, Asian American, and Latina women have a long history of performing intimate household services for affluent families. Career women increasingly hire help from a new Latino servant class—women whose own families must accommodate to their work in other people's homes (Hondagneu-Sotelo and Avila, 1997).

How is domestic labor allocated in immigrant families? Research finds that whereas patriarchal norms organize daily household chores, immigration and settlement in the United States can push immigrant men to take on some household responsibilities, especially when their wives enter the workplace (Hondagneu-Sotelo and Messner, 1994).

Nevertheless, women's employment by itself does not produce role-sharing couples among racial-ethnics. This is one of the main lessons of Patricia Zavella's (1987) study of Chicana cannery workers in California's Santa Clara Valley. Women's paid work and their family work are both bound up with broader systems of class and racial inequality. Chicana working mothers faced occupational segregation by race and gender on the job and the double day at home. Seasonal jobs in the canneries created temporary shifts in day-to-day family life, but they did not alter traditional marital roles. Although financial incentives kept wives employed, they were workers in a declining industry and were still economically dependent on husbands. These structural conditions supported and reinforced the gendered division of household labor, yet these are not group-specific or cultural conditions.

Although race/ethnicity does not by itself determine how families organize household labor, minority men spend more time on household tasks than White men. Recent studies (Coltrane and Valdez, 1993; Shelton and John, 1993b) uncover two conditions that are more important than ethnicity in determining the amount of time husbands devote to household labor. Being employed or unemployed together with the relative earning power of husbands and wives shapes the household division of labor. These studies reveal that whereas minority men may have different ideals about men's family work, Black and Hispanic men actually do more housework than White men because they earn less.

This gender-based imbalance in household work has the potential to create divisiveness within marital relationships. Much depends on how women perceive the unequal burden they carry. Husbands are more satisfied with their marriages and less critical of their wives if their wives do more than their "fair share" of housework. Among wives, however, there is a clear and positive connection between fair division of family work and marital and personal well-being. Studies show that wives whose husbands do their share of family work are more satisfied with their marriages, whereas wives who feel overworked as mothers tend to evaluate their husbands more critically (Thompson and Walker, 1991:89).

The question, then, is this: Why can't women and men share housework? When both spouses work outside the home, the work can be assigned randomly or otherwise fairly distributed. Or if one spouse chooses to be a full-time homemaker, must it always be the woman? Why can't the roles be reversed periodically?

There are indications of change on the horizon. The catalyst for change is the ever-increasing number of dual-earner families. Employed wives, especially those who work full-time, have less time, less energy, and fewer inclinations to follow the old ways governing housework (Risman, 1998).

Other Forms of Family Work

We have redefined work as a social activity that produces "value" even when it is invisible because it is unpaid and done inside the home. This definition includes work other than household labor that is done both within and outside the home. A wide variety of activities that go into creating and sustaining family life have previously gone unrecognized not only as work, but as effort of any sort. For example, Pamela Fishman (1978) calls attention to the **interaction work** that women do to sustain communication with their mates. Arlie Hochschild (1983b) shows how women engage in **emotion work,** the work of trying to find the right feeling, to make and keep everything fine.

Other forms of invisible labor have been identified. For example, **consumption work,** which involves selecting goods and making purchases, links the needs of families with products in the market (Weinbaum and Bridges, 1979). Women's invisible and unpaid work often does more than contribute to family well-being; it elevates the family's place in the class hierarchy. Martha Fowlkes (1987) reveals the varied supports, services, and career enhancements that professional men receive from their wives. The volunteer work that upper-class women do in communities is labor that legitimizes the family class position. At the other end of the spectrum, women's invisible work in "family-owned" but husband-controlled enterprises provides access to the middle class. As Ferree notes (1991:110), Cuban, Korean, and Vietnamese family enterprises provide contemporary examples. Among racial-ethnics, mothers labor in domestic service and sweatshops to keep their children in school and to make upward mobility possible (Dill, 1983; Glenn, 1985).

Women are involved in still another type of work that sustains family—the work of kinship. **Kin work,** according to Micaela di Leonardo (1987:110), is the upkeep and ritual celebration of cross-household kin ties, including visits, letters, telephone calls, presents, and cards to kin; the organization of holiday gatherings; the creation and maintenance of quasi-kin relations and decisions to neglect or intensify particular ties. Kin work is like housework and child care: Men in the aggregate do not do it. Yet it is kinship contact across households, as much as women's work within them, that fulfills our cultural expectations of satisfying family life (di Leonardo, 1987:442).

COPING WITH WORK AND FAMILY

Family Coping Strategies

Coping as Human Agency
Balancing work and family produces considerable stress and strain. When both spouses are employed, they must manage the competing demands of their work and family roles, which are often contradictory. If they are to construct workable family relationships, they must cope with interference and overload. Although the burdens of work and family responsibilities can strain individuals and families to the breaking point, people are devising adaptive strategies to cope with the stresses of jobs and family responsibilities. This illustrates human agency in operation. At the same time, family strategies always depend on available options (Moen and Yu, 2000). Even though dual-earner families are on the rise, structural patterns are modeled on a breadwinner/homemaker family. Without wider social changes in workplaces, individual family members must devise their own solutions for meeting structurally induced dilemmas.

How Parents Are Coping
Coping is "an active process in which individuals manipulate their role expectations and behaviors to deal with stressful situations" (Voydanoff, 1987:189). Research shows that coping (like the other features of family life that we have examined in this chapter) is strongly gendered, with women taking on greater responsibility and men resisting change. A national study of the changing work-

force found that women feel more able to cope when they are married and when they have more help at home with chores and child care, mainly from their husbands. "They are also more satisfied with their overall ability to handle problems when they have higher household incomes, which is largely a function of being married; however, women who contribute a higher proportion of family income—that is, single mothers and those whose husbands contribute less—feel that they are coping less effectively" (Galinsky and Bond, 1996:102).

For most working families, housework and child care create the most difficult problems. Parents use a variety of coping strategies for solving these problems. Strategies differ, depending on the resources of couples, on their work schedules, on the demands of their jobs and careers, and on the ages of their children. Common strategies for dealing with work overload and the resultant strain are as follows:

> 1) reducing the standards of domestic work; 2) purchasing domestic and childcare services; 3) having other family members (e.g., husbands, children, parents) perform more domestic work; 4) refusing to comply with the demands or requests of greedy employers (with a cost to one's career success, probably most often the woman's); and 5) choosing an occupation (e.g., school teaching) which allows more time for the family (with a cost to one's income, usually the woman's) (Chafetz 1997:120).

Most families rely on several strategies (Haas, 1999). Coping falls unevenly on women's shoulders. Hochschild discovered that couples created **gender strategies** that fit conventional gender beliefs and needs with the realities of women's and men's daily lives. In her study, wives ended up doing most of the coping, yet the couples developed family myths—versions of reality that emphasize "sharing" in order to preserve harmony and camouflage conflict (Hochschild, 1989:17–31).

Although Hochschild found that employed wives devoted more time to housework while their husbands did "more of what they'd rather do," other research has uncovered strategies in which working families are changing the gendered patterns of family labor rather than accommodating to it. For example, shift work is a common solution for solving child-care problems. A study of household and employment patterns among working-class Hispanics and Anglo dual-earner families living in the Sunbelt illustrates how spouses can help one another out:

> If a couple decided to use a "split-shift" day care arrangement, in which each parent took care of the children while the other worked, men tended to do more child-care tasks and, in some cases, more housework. Yet if husbands worked evening or night shifts and their wives worked on day shifts, women could end up doing most of the housework when they were home in the evenings. Child-care arrangements were closely related to the shifts a couple worked. Often there was a tradeoff between housework and child care: if a husband took care of his children, the wife would overlook his lack of responsibility for doing housework (Lamphere et al., 1993:190–191).

More dual-earner families are now using split-shift parenting to ease the strains of combining employment with child care. This strategy avoids the cost of daycare and maximizes the amount of time that children are cared for by at least one parent. According to a report from the U.S. Bureau of the Census, fathers are increasingly important as child-care providers, particularly in families where mothers work part time and on non-day shifts. By 1991, 20 percent of primary child care for preschool children was provided by fathers in the home while mothers were at work (O'Connell, 1993:3; Helburn, 1999).

For women, a common way of dealing with work/family overload has been to juggle competing demands by adjusting the timing of events over the life course. This adjustment process is known as **sequencing.** It involves alternating paid work and child raising rather than trying to combine them (Coontz, 1997; Granrose, 1996). After establishing themselves in their career or earning an advanced degree, the women step off the career ladder for a few years to focus on children and home. When their children reach school age, they return to full-time jobs. However, women can pay a high price for having children. (See Figure 6.5.) When they return to work, many women find that their employers place them on the so-called **mommy track,** which leads to fewer promotions and opportunities for advancement. Although the mommy track has been widely criticized for the way in which it makes women suffer vocationally for bearing the brunt of family responsibilities, there is some evidence that a "daddy track" exists as well. Fathers suffer in promotions and other salary increases when they curtail their work involvement in order to care for children (Waite et al., 1986).

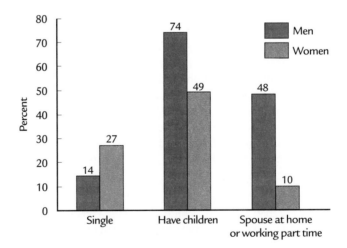

Figure 6.5

What price success?

Do women with high-powered jobs have less of a chance of having a family? Yes, says a recent Catalyst study of MBAs—men and women at an average age of 40—who have risen to top jobs in their corporations.

Source: Michele Conlin, "The New Debate over Working Moms," *Business Week,* September 18, 2000, pp. 102–104.

Family-Supportive Employer Responses

Unlike some other countries, the United States has only recently become aware of the complex struggle that most workers face in trying to combine paid work and family work (see Box 6.3). Only in the past decade or so have political, business, and professional leaders had very much to say about work and family.

BOX 6.3 **Families in Global Perspective: Time Off with Pay**

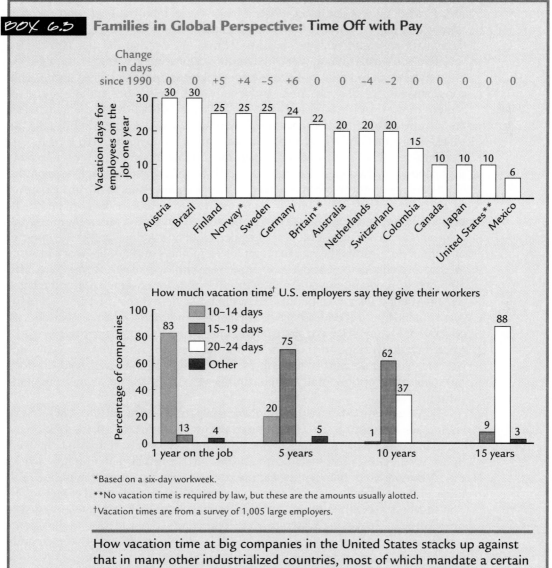

*Based on a six-day workweek.

**No vacation time is required by law, but these are the amounts usually alotted.

†Vacation times are from a survey of 1,005 large employers.

How vacation time at big companies in the United States stacks up against that in many other industrialized countries, most of which mandate a certain amount of vacation for workers in the private sector.

Source: Leah Beth Ward, "Working Harder to Earn the Same Old Vacation," *The New York Times,* May 11, 1997, p. 12F.

Presidents tended to pass the responsibility to the states and the private sector. State leaders often passed responsibility to the federal government or to the cities (Hamburg, 1993:63). Workplaces were slow to respond to workers' needs. The traditional organization of work—an inflexible 8-hour workday—was an obstacle for parents trying to balance family and work demands.

A U.S. Department of Labor survey published in the mid-1990s asked a quarter of a million women what it means to be a working woman in the United States today. The report, called *Working Women Count*, paints a complex portrait of U.S. working women in the 1990s. Most women reported pride and satisfaction at being breadwinners for their families. Seventy-nine percent of respondents said they either "love" or "like" their jobs overall. Yet the report also reveals a consensus among working women about what is wrong with their jobs and what needs to be fixed—namely, workplace support of family needs. This consensus crosses all occupations and incomes, all generations and races, and all regions of the country. The study reported that "the difficulty of balancing work and family obligations is the number one issue women wanted to bring to the president's attention" (U.S. Department of Labor, Women's Bureau, 1994).

Only recently has the federal government made modest efforts to help families cope with child care through tax credits, special funds for subsidizing the child-care costs of low-income parents, and the **Family and Medical Leave Act of 1993** (Haas, 1999:575). The law requires employers of fifty or more people to provide 12 weeks of unpaid leave to any worker who has a medical emergency or needs to care for an adopted or newborn child or a seriously ill child, spouse, or parent. But despite the fact that employed mothers and fathers work in similar-size organizations (almost half work for employers with fewer than fifty employees), fewer mothers than fathers are eligible for coverage under the Family and Medical Leave Act because of mothers' higher rates of part-time employment (Galinsky and Bond, 1996:80). The Family and Medical Leave Act does not cover 41 million workers in the United States—nearly half of the private workforce. People working for businesses with fewer than fifty employees are not covered. Neither are part-time workers. The Family and Medical Leave Act does not cover many critical family responsibilities that require time away from work (Morin, 1998).

Corporate work–family programs have expanded since the late 1980s. Many companies are touting new family-friendly policies. But for all the talk about accommodating work and family needs, for most workers, life has not changed much at all. Studies conducted through the 1990s suggest that "the new workplace" is more myth than reality. Family support programs are often public relations gimmicks, costly to implement in an era of heightened global competition. The Business Work-Life Study by the Families and Work Institute revealed a mixed picture. Surveying 1000 major U.S. companies, the study found that many family-friendly policies—job sharing, flexible hours, and the like—are expanding. At least, many companies are flexible: 72 percent offer flextime; 64 percent permit part-time employment; 36 percent provide job sharing; and 20 percent allow employees to work from home (Jackson, 1998).

Flexible Work Schedules

As we discussed earlier in this chapter, shift work is on the rise for women and men. Flextime typically allows an employee to choose his or her own work schedule within specified limits. "Flexible" is a term that covers a variety of arrangements—unconventional hours, part-time work, job sharing, leaves of absence, and working at home. In the past decade, companies have been systematically trying to promote flexibility throughout their organizations.

However, the publicity may overstate the changes. Even though most employers say they offer programs such as flexible scheduling, they actively allow it informally, have no written policy, or limit it to a few workers. Having a program available to workers does not translate into a family-friendly environment. Managers and top executives must be supportive and employers must know about the programs to make use of them. Recent studies have found that less than half of all companies hold supervisors accountable for sensitivity to their employees' family needs (Jackson, 1998).

Employer-Assisted Dependent Care

A second option available to employers involves the provision of care for children and elders. According to recent studies, little progress has been made in offering dependent-care assistance. The Business Work-Life Study found that only 9 percent of companies offered child care at or near the workplace and 23 percent offered elder care and referral services (Jackson, 1998).

Leaves of Absence

Another set of policies that affect child-care issues directly are those governing the use of employee leave. At present, most medium and large firms with at least 100 to 250 employees provide some form of maternity leave, although few provide paternity leave. Thirty-three percent of companies offer maternity leaves more than 13 weeks long (Jackson, 1998). However, there is wide variation in whether maternity leave is paid or unpaid, whether other fringe benefits continue while employees are away from work, and whether employees have the right to their old jobs when they return to work.

Another important issue involves the use of paid sick leave to stay home and care for ill children. Mothers (or, less often, fathers) forfeit salary or annual leave if they cannot use their earned sick leave to care for their ill children. A small number of firms permit employees to use their paid sick leave in this way (O'Connell and Bloom, 1987).

These and other changing corporate policies can reduce or remove some of the stresses for workers who earn a living and raise children. However, work and family benefits will never reach a broad spectrum of workers as long as they are bargained workplace by workplace and company by company. "We need a national work and family policy that will guarantee the kinds of benefits that families need. Such a policy would include paid family and parental leave, flexible work schedule, and affordable, quality child care" (Grundy and Firestein, 1997:19).

CHAPTER REVIEW

1. Contemporary families across the economic spectrum are being reshaped by changes in the workforce.

2. The number of women in the workforce has increased from under 20 percent in 1940 to over 60 percent today. There is virtual parity among Black and White women, while Latina women have somewhat lower rates of labor force participation.

3. The most important factors influencing the rising number of women in the workforce are changes in the economy, families' economic needs, and women's fulfillment in their work.

4. Recent social and economic changes have fostered the demise of men's "good provider" role. Three structural changes have been most responsible for men's changing work patterns: structural unemployment, redistribution of jobs, and shrinking wages. Men of color and young men have been the most negatively affected.

5. The service economy has produced a new demand for teen workers, especially in part-time jobs. Almost all U.S. teens now work at some time during high school. Long work hours may negatively affect family life and school work.

6. The worlds of work and family overlap and interact. Work and family linkages vary based on the structural characteristics of each. Variance is also created through class, race, and gender inequalities.

7. Work and family roles are strongly gendered. Men's paid employment is taken for granted, but women's paid employment is often seen as problematic.

8. The gender-structured workplace and the gender-structured family take a toll on the well-being of women workers, even though men in all class and racial groups are taking on more of the family workload.

9. Family life is directly affected by two aspects of work: (a) earnings, and (b) conditions associated with performing a job.

10. Structural interference, or the job-related constraints imposed on families, comes from the following: timing and scheduling of work, geographic mobility, and different types of work.

11. Family characteristics, such as employment status of workers and number, age, and sex of children, shape the work–family interface.

12. Women's labor in the home has been excluded from traditional definitions of work, yet unpaid work contributes to the economy and to the maintenance of daily family life.

13. Housework in most families is strongly gendered. Women do it whether they work for pay or not. Most women in dual-earner families work one shift on their jobs and a second shift at home.

14. In addition to tasks commonly associated with housework, there are many kinds of domestic labor, including interaction work, consumption work, and kin work.

15. Juggling work and family is a complicated process that requires creative solutions. Workers must devise their own solutions for coping with the demands of child care and housework. Sequencing the timing of life events is a strategy women use to manage conflicting demands of work and family. Shift work and shared parenting are also commonly used strategies.

16. The traditional workplace is not conducive to meeting the conflicting needs of family members. Although recent changes have heightened public awareness, family-supportive employer responses, such as flexible work schedules, employer-sponsored child care, and flexible benefits, are limited and motivated by business needs rather than concern for family well-being.

RELATED WEB SITES

http://www.bc.edu/bc_org/avp/csom/cwf/aboutdatabase.html

This is the home page for the Work-Family Researchers Electronic Network. The Sloan Electronic Researchers Work-Family Literature Database is a collection of nearly 2,500 entries providing bibliographic information with selected annotations for journal articles, books, chapters in books, reports, papers, and dissertations that present information about work and family research.

http://www.la.psu.edu/lsir/workfam/

The Work-Family Newsgroup: A newsgroup on the changing worlds of work and family.

http://www.jobsmart.org/hidden/bestcos.htm

Best Companies: You may discover a potential employer on these lists of "best" companies. You'll also learn more about what makes a company "best" so you can compare other employers. This site has links to many well-known listmakers like Fortune Magazine and Forbes Magazine, as well as sources for ranking companies for women and different racial and ethnic groups.

http://www.shrm.org/diversity/

Workplace Diversity Initiative: The Society for Human Resource Management (SHRM) is the leading voice of the human resource profession. SHRM provides education and information services, conferences and seminars, government and media representation, online services and publications to more than 150,000 professional and student members throughout the world. This Diversity Initiative is one new effort SHRM is trying to provide, which includes defining "diversity" and starting discussions about it.

http://www.lpa.org/

Labor Policy Association Online: LPA is a public policy advocacy organization representing corporate executives interested in human resource policy from more than 200 leading corporations doing business in the United States. LPA's purpose is to provide in-depth information, analysis, and opinion of current situations and emerging trends in labor and employment policy.

http://violet.berkeley.edu/~iir/workfam/home.html

The Labor Project for Working Families: The Labor Project for Working Families is a national advocacy and policy center providing technical assistance, resources and education to unions and union members addressing family issues in the workplace including child care, elder care, flexible work schedules, family leave and quality of life issues.

http://www.familiesandwork.org/

Families and Work Institute: Families and Work Institute is a non-profit organization that addresses the changing nature of work and family life. We are committed to finding research-based strategies that foster mutually supportive connections among workplaces, families, and communities.

http://www.workoptions.com/

Work Options, Inc.—"The Working Mother's Resource for Negotiating Flexible Work": This is the Web's only place for working mothers and others to get this exclusive combination of content and resources which, together, will help you develop a solid negotiating position for your request and get your alternative work schedule request approved. Working mothers and others who want more time outside of their job find that a flexible work arrangement paves the way to lifestyle balance and enjoyment. If you want to restructure your current job into a telecommuting, part-time, job sharing or compressed work week arrangement, WorkOptions.com helps you go from 'I want one' to getting the boss's approval—fast.

http://www.wfbenefits.com/

Work & Family Benefits, Inc. was founded in 1992 by William H. Mulcahy, President, and is dedicated to the transformation of employee benefits to meet the needs of today's workforce. Our cornerstone is the Work & Family Benefits, Inc. Values Package(r). WFB's Values Package delivers child and elder care consultation and referral as a low-cost, high-return employee benefit. Employers of ANY size can invest in productivity and give employees convenient access to real solutions.

CHAPTER **7**

The Social Construction of Intimacy

Myths and Realities

Myth: Sex is a "natural" drive, rooted in biological urges and innate differences between males and females.

Reality: Sexual attitudes and behaviors are shaped by social conditions and cultural meanings that often vary by class, race, gender, and sexual orientation.

Myth: Variations in sexual habits are produced by individual variables such as hormone levels, psychological makeup, and sex role socialization.

Reality: Sexual practices are shaped primarily through social experiences in the social groups to which people belong.

Myth: This society offers us infinite possibilities for falling in love with whomever we wish.

Reality: Our romantic partners and those we marry are people very much like ourselves in class, race, and level of education.

Myth: Current teen pregnancy rates are skyrocketing in the United States, leading to a sudden epidemic of children having children.

Reality: Teenage pregnancy has decreased by 15 percent in the past twenty years.

*I*ntimacy, like other social relations, is shaped by society. Patterns of intimacy among women and men, in heterosexual, lesbian, and gay relationships, reflect the organization of society. In this chapter we examine intimacy through a sociological lens. We begin by examining the changing historical and social context giving rise to intimacy as it is defined today. We then look at patterns of courtship and mate selection by connecting them to historical developments. Turning to sexuality, we describe the macro structural conditions that shape our most private behaviors. We look at sexual trends in the contemporary United States. We also consider connections between sexual practices and public health and policy issues. Finally, we turn our attention to the ways in which love and sex are structured along the lines of class, race, and gender inequality.

Applying our sociological perspective to intimacy requires that we accept the following assumptions: (1) intimacy is experienced at the micro level, yet it is shaped and given meaning by macro level forces; (2) human sexuality is not simply a biological drive but is socially constructed within particular sociohistorical conditions and sanctioned by social institutions; (3) although social forces influence sexuality and love, people can take deliberate actions to create rewarding relationships.

We live in a society consumed with intimacy. At the same time, there are few prescribed forms of conduct for establishing intimate relationships. Things were not always like this. In the past, intimate relationships followed socially defined steps:

> . . . marriage used to be the endpoint of a series of distinct stages, each involving a greater degree of commitment—dating, keeping company, going steady, a private agreement to be married, a public announcement of the engagement, and finally marriage, presumably for life. A different level of sexual intimacy was permitted at each stage of the relationship (Skolnick, 1983:260).

In the last two decades, a new emphasis on relationships and sexuality has emerged to create an "intimacy revolution" (Whyte, 1990). Young people develop intimate relationships earlier, and people move in and out of marriage, friendship, romance, and cohabitation throughout the life course (Surra, 1991:70). Turn-of-the-century technology, including electronic communication, travel, and improved contraception, offers the opportunity for instant intimacy. (See Box 7.1.)

In preindustrial America, work relationships and personal relationships were not sharply divided. In Chapter 2 we traced the separation of public and private spheres. When work moved out of the home, two types of relationships developed. One was personal and private, the other was impersonal and public (Gladin, 1977:33). Since then, social and cultural changes have increased the intensity of intimate relationships. These forces have moved us away from a society in which an individual's social identity was provided by family and community. With the loosening of ties to place and kin, individuals in the modern world are often "atomized" individuals. Families move frequently; they live in cities where they are essentially anonymous much of the time. Family members work away from home in impersonal, bureaucratic settings.

In our global society, identities are fragmented and disconnected. Our private selves are separated from the public roles we assume. This separation has crucial consequences. The discrepancy between our inner selves and the roles we

BOX 7.1   **Technology:** Cyber Love: What Is Real and What Is Virtual

The conventional bar scene of the 70s and 80s is no longer the accepted place to meet prospective dates. Lately, more and more singles are turning to the Internet for better dating opportunities. Talk show hype over cyberspace love encounters and the recent movie *You've Got Mail* have popularized the romantic potential of the Internet. The process of an online relationship, however, is very different from real time dating processes. The online environment is, by it very nature, restrictive. For new Internet users, the online culture shock can be daunting.

Learning to communicate on the Internet is the first obstacle for newbies. *Emoticons* such as :-), LOL, and <G> are used liberally to express emotion, and can be like learning a foreign language. The rules are different online as well. There are protocols to follow in chat rooms; for example, to avoid accidentally offending others, sarcasm must be spelled out. Devoid of body language and intonation, the typed word is the only way to get the message across. Most novice Internet chat users first begin as "lurkers," content to quietly watch others interact. This way, the Internet culture is safely and quietly experienced before a user feels comfortable interacting within it.

Another noticeable inconvenience, especially for women, is the seemingly endless number of chatters who want casual "cyber sex." This affront discourages many new chat users from returning, and also perpetuates the image of the Internet being "dirty." These cyber sex offenders are attracted to the anonymity of the Internet. Where else can they act so rudely without getting caught?

However, all novice chat users are mesmerized to some degree by the extreme anonymity and fantasy potential the Internet provides. Often, the user eventually realizes the sensitivity needed to interact with others—a transition is made from relating to the computer to relating to other people online. Often, this transition is coupled with an event that brings about this reality—such as "falling in love" with a fantasy and dealing with the reality that follows, meeting a chat partner face to face, or realizing that careless actions have hurt another person. Once this transition occurs, the chat user suffers a period of disillusionment, and then chooses to continue chat use—now wiser and kinder, or abandons Internet chat altogether.

MIT sociology professor Sherry Turkle has extensively studied people's relationships to computers. In her book, *Life on the Screen,* Turkle defines the aspects of the self as they relate to the new Internet culture.

According to Turkle, "people are able to build a self by cycling through many selves" on the Internet (Turkle: 1995, p. 178). This is a new phenomenon, and counters the psychoanalytic definition of identity as being forged early in life. By trying on various personas, Internet users are able to experiment with their own identity.

This identity experimentation, however, is not without risks and complications. While experimentation can be a healthy exploration, it can also be damaging to self-esteem. Turkle describes cases where the Internet users feel more confident as "altered selves," losing confidence in their real identity (Turkle, 1995). Often, it is the state of the self-esteem at the beginning of the experimentation that determines whether the experience is positive or negative. For example, someone who suffers from depression, will likely realize a negative impact by experimenting with his or her identity online.

Identity experimentation also complicates the Internet dating area. Not all identity experimentation is intentional. Some Internet users involved in online romances

(continued)

(continued from previous page)

describe their relationship in these terms: "I'm a different person when I'm with him [online]" or "I'm happy and confident when we are talking online. I'm not like that any other time." These feelings might be incorrectly attributed to the relationship's success, when the reality is that behavior has been altered through subconscious self-exploration. Once these relationships move off line, they often wane, since the magic (and the altering of identity) cannot be maintained without the online illusion.

Turkle describes two phases of Internet relationships.

> In a first phase, [Internet] players feel the excitement of a rapidly deepening relationship and the sense that time itself is speeding up. . . . In a second phase, players commonly try to take things from the virtual to the real and are usually disappointed (Turkle, 1995, 206).

Another complication of Internet dating is the use of the Internet as an escape. The Internet can become a fantastic and unreal world. Online, we are who we say we are, if only for a few hours. This escape from reality, however, makes online dating more difficult.

Here are some other suggestions for successful online dating:

- *Be safety and security conscious.* Do not readily make available your name, address, phone and social security number online.
- *Beware of "players."* Not everyone on the Internet is honest and decent. Be cautious with your safety as well as your heart. To some people, an online romance is a game. Look for inconsistencies in what they say, or pressure for you to do something that you are uncomfortable with.
- *Dishonest is the same as anonymous.* It is appropriate to remain anonymous online until you establish mutual trust. However, it is not right to be dishonest, especially regarding your marital status.
- *Practice courtesy.* Don't think that the anonymity of the Internet allows you to be invasive. Demanding to know someone's weight, age, or sexual secrets is as rude online as it is off line.
- *Realize that what you see online isn't the whole picture.* There are many characteristics that make up a person. Online typing does not afford the experience of a person's temperament, work ethic, parenting skills, or bad breath. Keep everything in perspective and don't fall in love too quickly with the person you've envisioned.
- *Avoid intimate online conversations until later.* The sense of anonymity frees individuals to speak more frankly than they would in person. However, a relationship should progress at a comfortable pace. If you confess all your inner secrets to your new online lover, you might later regret it during your first face-to-face encounter.
- *Don't make hasty commitments.* "Love at first type" is romantic, but not always realistic. Take your time and do it right.
- *Consider free online dating web sites.* Most of these are divided into major cities or geographical areas, increasing the chance of finding the right person locally. Also, because there is more of an expectation to meet in real time, there are fewer lurkers. However, as with dating services, you must contend with candidates with less-than-noble motives. Always be aware.

(continued from previous page)

· *Make friends.* You will certainly meet many people that aren't right for you, but they are still interesting. The Internet is a great place to make friends.
· *Meet early.* Once you like someone online and they like you, progress to a real time meeting. Until you hit it off on all levels, keep your options open.
· *When you meet in real time (RT), play it safe.* Remember that you are meeting a stranger. Opt for public places, such as a restaurant. Or consider bringing along a friend.

Source: Cindy Grant, *Cyber Love: What Is Real & What Is Virtual?* http://www.creativehat.com/cyber_love.htm. Retrieved July 31, 2000.

are playing in work and public life creates the need for intimate relationships—"a private world where we can express our real and whole selves" (Skolnick, 1983:122). Using the theater as a metaphor, Erving Goffman (1959) has also made this point. Life in large, impersonal bureaucracies, whether at work, school, church, or in the community, requires "frontstage behavior"—the formal playing of roles by participants. Intimate relationships permit people to behave as if they were "backstage"—to be themselves, rather than acting a role, in a relaxed and informal manner. Until recently "courting" was a process in which young women and men moved from casual dating to formal commitment and finally marriage. In other words, the participants gradually moved from frontstage to backstage behavior.

In the modern world, the intense need for intimate relationships creates a contradiction—the very intensity of emotional and physical intimacy makes the bond increasingly fragile. Individuals burden their relationships with too many expectations. They demand too much of intimacy. A romantic partner must provide all things that family and community once provided. A romantic partner must be all things—"lover, friend, companion, playmate, and parent" (Piorkowski, 2000:37).

Some couples are indeed successful, but many people fall short of sustaining the intimacy required by their partner. This often results in a search for a new partner or partners who will provide the intimacy so intently craved. This is a major source of marital strain and helps account for the high divorce rate in contemporary America.

Heterosexual Courtship and Mate Selection

Macro-level changes have reshaped courtship, moving mate selection from an orientation toward family influence to one that emphasizes the autonomy of the partners. The decline of parental influence over children's courting behavior reflects the many changes occurring in the larger society. In the past, when people remained in their community of birth after marrying, the bond of strong kin networks was crucial. With a changing economy, the decline of rural America, changing work patterns, the lure of cities, new opportunities far from home, the importance of education, and the relative emancipation of women, young people began to seek more independence from their parents. One major result of this change was the rise of romantic love as the basis of marriage. This freedom of young people to choose their partners is, as we will see, partly illusory, because relationships are still "arranged" by parents, peers, and other social forces, but it is surely more pronounced than in most societies, and much more so than in earlier times in this society.

A major break with the past was the emergence of dating. Couples in 1900 got to know each other on the front porch of their parents' home. Young men went a-calling and a-wooing at the homes of young women. By the 1920s courting couples began to go out on "dates" without adult supervision. By mid-century, "going steady" was a regular feature of high school and college life (Coontz, 1992; Kass, 2000). Rules governing dating were defined by peers rather than by adults. Courting, once a way to select a mate, gave way to dating, which was done for enjoyment. During its initial decades, dating had several goals—namely, pleasure, romance, and learning to relate to the so-called opposite sex. Although dating has changed greatly, our culture is still based on the premise that dating provides valuable experience that will help individuals select mates and achieve happy marriages. Yet dating today is far removed from mate selection. Evidence suggests that dating is going out of style, replaced by informal pairing off in larger groups, often without the prearrangement of "asking someone out" (Whyte, 1992:73-76).

An emerging trend among adolescents and on college campuses is semiplatonic "group dating," an activity also known as "hanging out" (Annin, 1996). Table 7.1 shows a comparison of various aspects of students' behaviors in the years 1947, 1967, and 1977. In 1947, dates were traditional. In 1967, couples might pair off at a party and there might be some traditional dating. By 1997, however, dating was characterized by the single word "rare." As sociologists Mary Riege Laner and Nicole Ventrone (1998) put it, "hanging out" implies a much more informal kind of interaction than dating. Today, we must use the term "mate selection" cautiously, for choosing a spouse is only one of the many forms that close heterosexual relationships take. The term is no longer useful for describing the variety of premarital relationship experiences (Surra, 1991:54).

Variations in "Dating" Practices

Gender

Gender differences are exceedingly important in today's romantic relationships. In their study of college dating, Laner and Ventrone originally decided that the words "hanging out" denoted a "nondate." They first surveyed college students about their gendered experience with dating (as if a date were a romantic encounter between two strangers), and then later about their experience with friends who turned into dating partners (to get at the notion of "hanging out"). Interestingly, they found the same results each time: that heterosexual "dating"

TABLE 7.1

Hanging Out at the University of New Mexico

	Today	30 Years Ago	50 Years Ago
Hair:	Women—short Men—long coming back, but mostly short	Women—ratted, bouf-fante, fante, smooth, sometimes with a flip Men—Beatles' cuts, over the eyebrow	Women—medium to long, wavy Men—short
Dress:	Backpacks, worn t-shirts, cut-offs, Tevas, sandals Women—dresses, no purses	Women—knee-length skirts, shifts, stretch pants tennis shoes w/o socks Men—(Greek) Madras shirts and bermudas, tight straight pants, narrow ties, loafers, (non-Greek) Mexican wedding shirts, denim work shirts, Levis, sandals	Women—skirts, blouses, sweaters Men—uniforms or Levis and shirts
Hang-out:	Frontier, SUB, downtown bars (e.g., Dingo, University Draft House), coffee-houses	SUB (Friday night dances), Drink Inc., Okie Joe's, Jack's, Ned's, coffee-houses	Oklahoma Joe's, La Grande, Casa Mañana, Barbers Super Market, Student Union
Music:	Alternative, jazz	Beatles, Janis Joplin, Country Joe and the Fish, Mo-Town, jazz	Orchestras, big band
Dating:	Rare	Groups, couples might pair off at a party. Some traditional dating.	Traditional
Curfews:	None	Yes, for women	Yes. Navy men in by 10
Greeks:	Dwindling	More prevalent but with an anti-Greek, pre-hippie group	Strong, although military groups lived in the Greek houses
Smoking:	Not so much . . . cigars are in	Lots	Women were starting to
Drinking:	Mostly beer (dark, heavy)	Draft beer, mixed drinks, Mateus wine	Some
Drugs:	Marijuana is around	Some marijuana and hard drugs	None, but aware of marijuana
Communicating:	E-mail	Phone	Letters

Source: "Hanging Out," *Mirage: The University of New Mexico Alumni Association* Vol. 4, No. 5 (Spring 1997). Albuquerque: The University of New Mexico, p. 17.

behavior is very gendered. College students believed that it was still men's responsibility to decide where to go, prepare the car, get money, pick up the date, open the door, pay the bill, and so on. Women-exclusive behavior (regardless of the formality of the "date"/"hang out" session) still included talking with friends about the date, taking extra preparation time, waiting for the date to arrive, and being the recipient (not the initiator) of any affectionate or sexual moves, such as being kissed or having the man put his arm around her (Laner and Ventrone, 1998:473).

Of course, the sexual double standard has weakened. Today, many women initiate relationships with men to whom they are attracted. This change has two profound implications. On one side, it creates havoc in many relationships. Some individuals are torn between the traditional standards and new expectations. They are in a quandary as to what are appropriate behaviors: When should a woman take the initiative? Should men never act chivalrous? As relationships form, the parties must now define and redefine the rules.

Class

Dating and courtship behaviors vary with social class. Several generalizations apply. First, the higher the class, the more control parents have over the dating activities of their children. Middle- and upper-class families have more control over desirable resources that they can use (Whyte, 1990:70). The upper class lives in a privileged social world with exclusive neighborhoods, private schools, and country clubs. This social homogeneity continues even during vacations, which tend to be spent in exclusive resorts (Domhoff, 1970). Supervised dances and parties are provided for young people at exclusive schools and country clubs, where social mingling most assuredly occurs among social equals. At eighteen years of age, many young women in this class are formally "presented" at expensive galas.

Middle-class youths have more freedom of choice than those from the upper class, but they too are controlled more by their parents than are lower-class youths. Middle-class youths are more likely to attend school, church, and civic-sponsored social events than lower-class students. Middle-class parents are also more likely to move to a different neighborhood or to change their child's school in order to narrow the social choices in the desired direction.

Lower-class youths are less likely to use structured activities for their cross-sex encounters and more likely to gather in streets, bowling alleys, or taverns to meet others.

Stratification in the larger society promotes courtship patterns that are based on social class. In a typical high school or college, for example, men are rated according to such criteria as their resources, family background, group member-ships, potential occupation, accomplishments, behavior, and appearance. Women are also ranked in terms of their desirability in regard to these charac-teristics, but with special emphasis on physical beauty and popularity. Decades ago, sociologist Willard Waller (1937) theorized that social stratification shaped intimate relationships. Ranking systems punish those with low status by nega-tively affecting their self-esteem and increasing their isolation (as seen in shy-ness, inept social behavior, and refusing to date for fear of rejection). Individuals in each level tend to date within their "dating desirability level." When this behavior occurs, dating partners have relatively equal bargaining power, reduc-ing the potential for exploitation.

Whenever people date outside their stratum, however, the possibility of exploitation increases. According to Waller's "principle of least interest," the

"It's a courtship thing, Megan —
The dude brings the babe flowers."

person with the least interest in continuing the relationship has the power to control it. Since the high-status person has less to lose by discontinuing the relationship, she or he can make excessive demands on the lower-status partner. The high-status male, for example, can demand more sexual favors from his low-status partner than would be the case if her status were equal or reversed. Similarly, the high-status female can make excessive demands on her lower-status partner for gifts and costly dating activities than she would if the status situation were otherwise. The class hierarchy influences courtship as "people from higher social classes are likely to be viewed as more attractive dating partners than those from lower social classes" (Whyte, 1990:70).

Race

Because people of color are vastly overrepresented among the poor, their dating and courtship patterns are most likely to resemble those found in the lower classes. There are exceptions to this, of course, as the children of African Americans and Latinos who are economically and professionally successful obtain the benefits of class privilege. In many urban areas, for example, there are "coming out" parties for the daughters of the Black elite. These children often attend private schools, and they, like other children of the middle and upper classes, tend to marry late.

Being a person of color often means being situated in social networks and activities that differ from those of Whites. For example, many Mexican American families hold quinceanera rites for young women on their fifteenth birthday. The quinceanera ritual is the parents' way of introducing their daughter to the ethnic community as a young girl who has become eligible for marriage (Williams, 1990:39).

From high school through college to work settings, dating and mating take place within race- and class-based networks. This may be changing as teens across the country are crossing racial barriers when dating. According to a 1997 *USA Today*/Gallup Poll of teenagers across the country, 57 percent who go out on dates say they have been out with someone of another race or ethnic group—whether White, Black, Latino, or Asian. Another 30 percent say they would have no objection to doing so (Peterson, 1997:1A). See Figure 7.1. Findings from this poll as well as other studies suggest that younger individuals are making interracial dating more acceptable (Jet Magazine, 1997). New patterns of interracial dating could signal important shifts in marital patterns and race relations.

Interracial dating trends could influence attitudes about race.

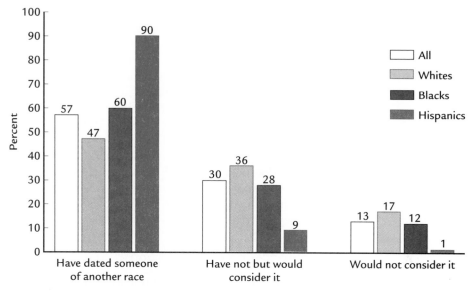

Figure 7.1

Who dates interracially?

Source: Gallup/*USA Today* Poll of 602 teenagers aged 13 to 19. Karen S. Peterson, "Interracial Dating," *USA Today*, November 3, 1997, p. 1A.

Factors in Mate Selection

In some societies the choice of a marriage partner is the exclusive responsibility of the kinship group. This choice is made on practical grounds, with these considerations paramount: Do the two families to be joined have similar social and economic standing? Do the two principals share the same religious values and other important traditions? Does the union make economic sense to the two kinship units?

In contemporary U.S. society, young people rather than the kin group make the choice of marriage partner, and this choice is governed by such nonpractical considerations as the personality traits, behavior patterns, and attractiveness of the potential partner. Even in our society, however, the choices are not entirely free. There are laws governing the permissible age for marriage. Some states do not permit marriage by those defined as mentally incompetent. Until the U.S. Supreme Court declared them unconstitutional in 1967, some seventeen states had laws forbidding interracial marriages. And all states prohibit marriage between close relatives (although the definition of "close" varies from state to state). Beyond the legal requirements there are social expectations by peers, family, neighbors, and others in the community that narrow the choices of potential spouses. Commonly, one is expected to marry someone from the same racial category. This norm remains strong even though intermarriage rates are rising. At the end of the century, 8 percent of marriages involving an African American were interracial, while approximately a quarter of Asian Americans and Latinos were married to someone outside their own race (U.S. bureau of the Census, 1999). The rate of interracial marriages among African Americans is six times the rate in 1960. Some say the increase in interracial marriages is due to the disappearance of strict residential segregation and to the 1967 elimination of antimiscegenation laws in the U.S. Other cite individual choices as the reasons for more interracial dating and marriage (Norment, 1999).

In the study of mate selection, the question "who marries whom?" is called **assortive mating** (Whyte, 1990:99). Even in recent years, mate choice in the United States is far from random. Individuals marry within their class, race, ethnicity, religion, and educational level. This is called **homogamy.** Although ethnicity and religion are playing a less important role in influencing who marries whom, homogamy remains "one of the robust social facts of romantic life" (Schwartz and Rutter, 1998:18).

Structural Influences on Mate Selection

Patterns of mate selection reveal how influences other than personal ones affect mate choice. The structural composition of the population shapes demographic trends in two ways. First, the availability of marriageable partners (those with qualities that make them desirable spouses, such as the appropriate age or economic circumstances) is limited. Research on sex ratios has found that imbalances in the number of women and men in a given population affect mate choice. The undersupply of men among African Americans contributes to mate selection differences between Blacks and Whites. African American females have a much more restricted field of eligibles than White females.

A second structural influence on mate selection lies in individuals' varied affiliations with different groups. Diverse affiliations provide opportunities to meet and stay in contact with dissimilar others. Summarizing the research, Surra concludes that people marry outside their social group, not because they have a preference for doing so, but because of their multiple and interwoven group affiliations. Indeed, there is some evidence that, although personal preferences affect social choice, heterogeneity influences social contacts above and beyond preferences (Surra, 1991:57).

Although young people in American society choose their own dating partners and eventual marriage partners, parents are not passive witnesses to the process. They can be very much involved:

> Parents threaten, cajole, wheedle, bribe, and persuade their children to "go with the right people," during both the early love and later courtship phases. Primarily, they seek to control love relationships by influencing the informal social contacts of their children: moving to appropriate neighborhoods and schools, giving parties and helping to make out invitation lists, by making their children aware that certain individuals have ineligibility traits (race, religion, manners, tastes, clothing, and so on) (Goode, 1959:45).

Although parental involvement occurs to some degree in most families, we must emphasize again that the higher the social class, the more involved the parents are in who their children marry. This tendency has neither increased nor decreased in recent times (Whyte, 1990:110). People within the same social class are most comfortable with each other because they tend to have the same work and leisure interests, hold similar values, behave alike, and have comparable levels of achievements.

The schools play a prominent role in narrowing the choice of eligible partners in terms of social class. Neighborhood schools tend to be homogeneous in social class. In high school, students tend to stratify themselves according to the socioeconomic status of their parents. The tracking system in the schools is highly correlated with social class. This finding is significant because the tracking system formally segregates students, promoting interaction among those preparing for college on the one hand and among those taking technical and commercial courses on the other.

College further restricts the pool of eligibles along social class lines. College attendance is strongly determined by the socioeconomic status of one's parents. Colleges self-select by social class because of the high cost of tuition. Moreover, the colleges and universities are themselves stratified by prestige, cost, and eventual benefit of attendance. Children from the upper classes cluster in the most costly and prestigious private schools. Middle-class young people are most likely to attend state colleges and universities, and those with the fewest resources are most likely to enroll in community colleges.

Within a given college, fraternities and sororities play a role in mate selection by social class. These organizations carefully scrutinize prospective members for the right social characteristics (social class, race, and ethnicity). Although technically open, sororities and fraternities tend to restrict their membership to Whites, Christians, and individuals from the upper-middle and upper classes. Sororities control dating by scheduling dances, parties, and other get-togethers with fraternities and by applying peer pressure on a "sister" who dates someone who does not fit in (Scott, 1965). It is important for women from the most prestigious sororities to date men from the highest-ranking fraternities, thus promoting homogamy by social class and other social characteristics (Krain et al., 1977).

The intraclass pattern of courtship and marriage so prevalent in U.S. society is occasionally broken. When this happens, the pattern is generally for a woman to marry a man of higher status (**hypergamy**) rather than a man of lesser status (**hypogamy**). This tendency for women to marry upward occurs because of the patriarchal tradition in American society, according to which women are evaluated in terms of their husbands' social status rather than their own accomplishments. Thus, women can improve their social standing by marrying upward. Men, on the other hand, do not lose status by marrying women from a lower social class. Some theorists suggest that equity is achieved in such relationships when men marry someone of lower social rank who brings the highly valued qualities of youth and physical attractiveness (Elder, 1969). This tendency toward hypergamy when dating or marrying has an interesting consequence: it results in reducing the dating and marriage prospects for upper-status women and lower-status men.

At the personal level, some cultural proclivities affect the chemistry between potential spouses. Cultural standards of beauty make certain people more physically attractive and sexually exciting than others. A cultural mandate dictates that the man be older than the woman. Similarly, another cultural demand requires men to be taller, heavier, wiser, and that they make more money than their mates. As Judith Stiehm (1976) has shown,

- If pairing were random, the woman would be taller than the man in one out of six couples, but such couples are much rarer.
- Similarly, more couples than expected would have a weight gap between the male and female exceeding the average if the pairing were random.
- Men marry younger women. Among first marriages, the gap is more than 2 years (for divorced men it is 4.5 years). Widowers choose women 8.3 years younger than themselves.
- Women tend to marry men who are better educated. With few exceptions, men make more money than their wives.

These cultural prescriptions determine what males and females find attractive in each other. What may seem like natural attraction patterns, then, are really dictated by subtle but still potent social-cultural demands.

CHANGING SEXUAL BEHAVIOR

Society and Sexuality

We think of sexuality as private, yet dictated by the body's "natural" urges. In fact, human sexuality is far from being purely natural. In treating sexuality sociologically, we must keep in mind two points: (1) human sexuality varies across time, space, and the life of any individual; and (2) sexuality is a power system, closely connected with society's institutions and with the systems of class, race, and gender.

Sexual behavior refers to the sexual acts that people engage in. Sexual desire, on the other hand, is the motivation to engage in sexual acts—in other words, what turns people on. A person's sexuality consists of both behavior and desire (Schwartz and Rutter, 1998:2). Sex is grounded in the body, but biology alone does not define human sexuality. If sex were purely natural, we would expect to find uniformity across the world's cultures, yet sexual behavior and sexual desire are incredibly diverse. Activities condemned in one society are encouraged in another; and ideas about what is attractive or erotic or sexually satisfying, or even sexually possible, vary a great deal. Even deeply felt personal identities (for example, masculinity/femininity or heterosexuality/homosexuality/bisexuality) are not privately or solely the product of biology but are created by social, economic, and political forces that change over time. Furthermore, sexuality is situational and changeable, modified by day-to-day circumstances throughout the life course.

Although human beings are capable of a variety of sexual expressions, social institutions try to channel and direct sexual behavior in socially legitimate directions. Heterosexuality, which is considered "normal" and natural, is but one imaginable arrangement of the sexes and their pleasures (Katz, 1990; Messner, 1996). Larger forces of social control go to great lengths to define heterosexuality as natural. **Compulsory heterosexuality** refers to the practices that enforce heterosexual behavior as normal and natural while stigmatizing other forms of sexual expression.

When we demystify sexuality, we can begin to see how socially dominant groups use sexuality to their own ends. For example, images about sexuality among African Americans are central to maintaining institutional racism. Similarly, beliefs about women's sexuality operate to maintain gender control. Heterosexuality is the privileged form of sexual behavior. It is protected and rewarded by the state and subsidized through social and economic incentives such as the right to marry. On the other hand, homosexuality and bisexuality are controlled through the denial of marriage. Gays and lesbians are not allowed to marry. This denies them spousal health-care benefits and the option of filing joint tax returns (Schwartz and Rutter, 1998:89). (See Chapter 8.) Of course, dominant sexual meanings are being challenged by many social groups, including feminists (both lesbian and straight), gay men, and bisexuals. Through daily practices and political activism, many are working to change the societal structures unfair to them.

Enlarging the Sexuality Frame

Understanding sexual marginality is important in its own right and is vital for a larger understanding of social and cultural organization (Epstein, 1994). The study of gay and lesbian experience has generated new questions about how sexualities should be defined. The sociological view tends to see homosexuality as a social construction, both at the macro level—where society defines what same-sex relationships means within its cultural boundaries, and at the micro level— where the individual, in interaction with others, acquires his or her own personal sense of a sexual identity (Heyl, 1996:120). The terms **sexual identity** and **sexual orientation** refer to how people classify themselves—as gay, lesbian, bisexual, or straight. Sexual identity and sexual behavior may differ, if people identify themselves as heterosexual and desire people of the same sex (Schwartz and Rutter, 1998:26).

One of the most important debates in the social science literature centers around the question of whether homosexuality has genetic or social origins—on whether it is inborn or shaped by social experience. The debate is between *essentialists* (those who identify biological, or essential determinants of sexuality) and *social constructionists* (those who emphasize the social conditions leading to the choice of sexual partners). Unfortunately, the debate has polarized nature and nurture rather than seeing them operating in combination. There is a growing literature that provides evidence of a biological basis for homosexuality (for summaries, see Burr, 1993; Gelman, 1992; Gorman 1991a; Angier, 1991). Despite the biological facts, sexualities are always social as well. Lesbian and gay *identities* are a twentieth-century phenomenon, whereas homosexual behaviors are universal and have always been practiced (D'Emilio and Freedman, 1988).

Even though scholars have documented a wide range of sexual experiences, sexual orientation is commonly placed into two mutually exclusive categories— gay and straight. But because sexuality is comprised of many different elements,

*"The love ballad I'm about to sing will pose
a lot of uncomfortable questions about gender identity and
class-based issues. I hope you can handle it."*

including physical, social, and emotional attraction as well as actual sexual behavior, the gay/straight dichotomy masks great variability. Being gay, straight, or bisexual is a social role as well as a sexual preference. Desire is one thing; behaviors and lifestyles are quite another. Homosexual, heterosexual, and bisexual lifestyles are not merely a matter of genital activity. They are social creations with identifiable norms and values about sexuality.

The Sexual Revolution

Over the last three and a half centuries, the meaning and place of sexuality in American life have undergone great changes. Sexuality moved from a family-centered reproductive system in the colonial era to a romantic, intimate, yet conflicted form in nineteenth-century marriage, to a commercialized sexuality in the modern period, in which sexual relations were expected to provide personal identity and individual happiness apart from reproduction (D'Emilio and Freedman, 1988). By the 1920s, sexuality had entered the public sphere, becoming a major source of identity and self-discovery. Sexual liberalization continued through the next three decades. By the 1960s, sexuality had been transformed. According to historian Stephanie Coontz (1992:197), this sexual revolution had three components:

- The first stage of this sexual revolution was the growth of a "singles" culture, predating the rise of political and cultural protest, that accepted sexuality activity between unmarried men and women.
- A second stage was reached when women began to demand that this singles culture be readjusted to meet their needs.
- A third stage came in the 1970s, as the gay movement questioned the exclusive definition of sexual freedom in terms of heterosexuality.

These transformations did not occur overnight. Instead, as Coontz (1992:197) details, their roots can be traced to social, demographic, and economic changes occurring in the United States:

- The rising age of marriage
- Educational convergence of women and men
- Women's growing autonomy
- The invention of birth control methods that are independent of coitus (first the oral contraceptive pill, introduced in 1960, then the IUD)
- The sheer rise in the absolute number of singles as the baby-boom generation reached sexual maturity
- The revulsion of a politically active generation against what they saw as the hypocrisy of their elders

Along with the aforementioned factors, advertising has been an important force contributing to sexual permissiveness. As manufacturers use sex to sell products, it has become a central and omnipresent feature of U.S. mass culture (D'Emilio and Freedman, 1988:327). Many television programs are characterized by their critics as guilty of "sexploitation." Cable television is less restricted than the networks and therefore is free to show nudity. Movies are free to display whatever sexual activities they choose, within the guidelines set for each rating category by the movie industry. Advertisers blatantly use sex, even "sexy" poses by preteens, to sell their wares. Popular music, whether country, pop, or rock, is commonly sexual in its message. The media's fixation on sex has served to involve children and youth earlier and earlier in thinking about sex and acting sexually.

Hard-core pornography is pervasive and readily available everywhere in every medium. The global reach of the Internet make all types of pornography accessible from any computer that is connected to a phone line.

Scientific Research on Sex

Much of what we know about sex in this society is based on a few surveys in which a sample of people are selected from the population to answer questions about sexual thoughts, feelings, and behaviors. Since Alfred Kinsey's pioneering research (1948, 1953), social scientists have asked people about their sex lives. In the years since Kinsey, national magazines such as *Redbook* and *Cosmopolitan* and men's magazines such as *Playboy* have done surveys asking people what they do in the bedroom. Sex surveys have shown substantial changes in women's sexual behavior, and smaller but significant changes in men's sexual behavior. In the 1980s, Philip Blumstein and Pepper Schwartz (1983) conducted an important study that included married, cohabiting, gay, and heterosexual respondents. Their sample was drawn from volunteers, and data were gathered in New York, Seattle, and San Francisco.

Although there are many sex surveys in the research literature, many are flawed because they sample a narrowly defined group of people. Kinsey's research was based on 18,000 interviews. Although his research did a great deal to break down stereotypes, his landmark study was not based on a representative sample of the U.S. population. Kinsey's respondents were volunteers, a self-selected group, "leading to the suspicion that the more libidinous members of the population were over represented and that the incidence of homosexuality in particular was exaggerated" (Robinson, 1994:3).

More than 44 years after Kinsey, a team of University of Chicago researchers led by Edward O. Laumann completed the nation's most comprehensive representative survey of sexual behavior in the general population. The 1992 National Health and Social Life Survey (NHSLS) was designed to learn about the sex lives of the U.S. public. The NHSLS is based on interviews with nearly 3500 adults. The study explores the extent to which sexual behaviors are influenced by gender, age, marital status, and other demographic characteristics. Among the topics considered by the NHSLS are early sexual experiences, masturbation, contraception and fertility, sexual abuse and sexual coercion, sexual health, satisfaction, sexual dysfunction, and homosexuality. Survey findings are detailed in two books: *The Social Organization of Sexuality* (Laumann et al., 1994) and *Sex in America* (Michael et al., 1994). The new study differs in several ways from its predecessors. Respondents were randomly selected from a cross section of U.S. households. Even though the sample is far smaller than Kinsey's, the sophisticated sampling techniques make its findings generalizable to the population at large. (See Box 7.2.)

The most valuable contribution of the survey is that it looks at sexuality in its *social* context. The finding the authors stress more than any other is that people's sexual choices are shaped by the social networks in which they operate. Using what they call networks analysis, the authors show how most people meet their sexual partners through family members, friends, and acquaintances—in other words, through their social networks. This finding flies in the face of an old image—that of meeting an alluring and mysterious stranger across a crowded room. This is how the authors of the survey explain how we find our partners:

> People's choices of sexual and marriage partners are severely constrained but also greatly facilitated by their social networks. It's not that you never see a stranger across a crowded room and fall instantly in love. It's more that the stranger you notice will look just like you. This stranger will be of your race, educational status, social class, and probably religion too. The single biggest reason why, of course, is that most of the people in that crowded room are preselected to be alike. The social world is organized so that you will meet people like yourself (Michael et al., 1994:69).

Among the major findings of the NHSLS are as follows:

- Adultery is the exception rather than the rule. Both men and women are remarkably faithful to their partners. Nearly 75 percent of married men

BOX 7.2   Researching Families: The Sex Survey

Our study, called the National Health and Social Life Survey, or NHSLS, . . . in contrast to the "reports" that preceded it, was a truly scientific endeavor, using advanced and sophisticated methods of social science research. Although these methods had been developed and used in the past for investigations of such things as political opinions, labor force participation and hours of work, expenditure patterns, or migration behavior, they work equally well in studying sexual behavior. Like studies of less emotionally charged subjects, studies of sex can succeed if respondents are convinced that there is a legitimate reason for doing the research, that their answers will be treated nonjudgmentally, and that their confidentiality will be protected. . . .

The most important part of our study was the way we selected the people to be interviewed. Of course, the most obvious way might be to randomly select individuals from households across the country. But finding and interviewing people across the United States can be very expensive, so social scientists have found a cheaper, but equally valid, way of identifying a representative sample. Essentially, we choose at random geographic areas of the country, using the statistical equivalent of a coin toss to select them. Within these geographic regions, we randomly select cities, towns, and rural areas. Within those cities and towns we randomly select neighborhoods. Within those neighborhoods, we randomly select households.

We selected the individual in a household to interview by a random process. In effect, if there were two people living in a household who were in our age range, we flipped a coin to select which one to interview. If there were three people in the household, we did the equivalent of flipping a three-sided coin to select one of them to interview. . . .

A much trickier problem arose when we wrote our questionnaire. We had to decide how, and with what language, to ask people about their sex lives. We did not want to confuse people by using technical language. Even words like *vaginal* and *heterosexual* were not well understood by many people, we found. Yet we did not want subtly to make the interview itself sexy or provocative or offensive by using slang terms. We wanted to create a neutral, nonjudgmental atmosphere in which people would feel comfortable telling us about one of the most private aspects of their lives.

We also needed to make the questions flow naturally from one topic to another and without prejudicing people's replies because of the order of the questions. We began by asking people about their backgrounds, their race, education, and religion, for example, and moved on to marriages and fertility. Then we gradually moved on to ask about sex. We asked for many details about recent sexual events and we asked for fewer specifics about events further in the past, reasoning that inability to recall details from long ago could result in erroneous, if well-intentioned, answers.

We decided to administer the questions during face-to-face interviews, which lasted an average of an hour and a half. By asking people directly, we could be sure that the respondents understood the questions and that the person who was supposed to be answering really did answer. . . .

The survey was an expensive proposition, far different from mailing out questionnaires and tallying those that came back, as others have done. But we could be assured that the designated person answered our questions and not someone else.

(continued)

(continued from previous page)

Each interview cost, in the end, an average of about $450, including the interviewer training, the several trips to the residence when necessary to do the interview, and entering the data into a computer for analysis.

Our study, of course, has limitations that are inherent to all survey research. It is a snapshot of the American population, with all of its diversity and all of its similarities. It is not precise, like the calculations of space scientists who guided the shuttle, nor is it as precise as a chemical experiment.

The end result of our work is a huge and complex data set that can shed light on some of the most pressing social questions in America today.

Source: Robert T. Michael, John H. Gagnon, Edward O. Laumann, and Gina Kotata, *Sex in America: A Definitive Survey.* New York: Little, Brown, 1994.

and 85 percent of married women say they have never been unfaithful. Over a lifetime, a typical man has six partners, a typical woman two.

- People in this country are divided into three categories according to how often they have sex. One-third have sex twice a week or more, one-third a few times a month, and one-third a few times a year or not at all.
- Married couples have the most sex, they enjoy it most, and they are the most likely to have orgasms when they do. Nearly 40 percent of married people have sex twice a week, compared to 25 percent for singles.
- The incidence of homosexuality is lower than the 10 percent reported by Kinsey and widely reported since then. Just 2.8 percent of men and 1.4 percent of women identify themselves as homosexual or bisexual. Still, 9 percent of men and 4 percent of women report that they have had a sexual experience with someone of the same sex since puberty. While these numbers are surprisingly low, the research team admits that stigmatization probably makes people reluctant to discuss homosexual behavior.

Laumann recently reanalyzed the data to learn more about variations in sexuality by education and life circumstance. He found that being more highly educated is associated with greater sexual satisfaction and that declining fortunes contribute to sexual dysfunction (Herbert, 1999).

The NHSLS makes important contributions to research on the social construction of sexuality. Of course, questions remain about whether people reveal the truth about their sexual behaviors. Other shortcomings make the survey too limited to reveal much about subgroups of the population (such as gay Hispanics) and people over age 59 (who were omitted from the survey). Nevertheless, the survey goes a long way toward demythologizing sexual behavior in the United States. More research is needed to shed light on how sexual practices are linked to public health and policy issues such as AIDS and teenage pregnancy, problems that may have worsened because of the public reluctance to confront basic questions about sex.

AIDS

Common knowledge has it that the fear of AIDS (acquired immune deficiency syndrome) is causing many in the United States to moderate their sexual behaviors. Indeed, the number of AIDS cases reported has declined every year since 1993, when there was a sharp increase in reported new cases due to the implementation of more careful reporting techniques. This decline is a reflection of the aggressive approach taken toward expanding safe-sex education over the last decade. This education changed sexual practices, especially among middle-class homosexual men. Another sign of changed sexual practices is that the age-adjusted death rate from HIV infection in the United States declined an estimated 21 percent to a rate of 4.6 deaths per 100,000 in 1998, the lowest rate since 1987, after a 48 percent decline from 1996 to 1997. HIV mortality has declined more than 70 percent since 1995. The disease was the eighth leading cause of death in 1996, dropping out of the top leading causes of death last year, and no longer ranks among the top fifteen leading causes of death today (National Center for Health Statistics, 1999). However, despite the declines in HIV/AIDS cases overall, an estimated 412,471 individuals were currently living with HIV or AIDS in the United States in 1999 (CDC, NCHS: HIV/AIDS Surveillance Report, 2000).

The numbers and proportions of HIV/AIDS cases among certain populations have increased over the last few years, while overall rates have declined. The greatest increases have been for women, youth, and people of color. The trends of AIDS death rates are particularly uneven across racial groups. HIV remains the leading cause of death among African men ages 25-44, and the third leading cause of death among African American women in that age group. The 1998 rate of reported AIDS cases among African Americans was more than two times greater than the rate among Hispanics and eight times greater than the rate for Whites. African Americans make up only an estimated 12 percent of the U.S. population, but almost 37 percent of all AIDS cases reported in this country. Hispanics are also disproportionately affected by HIV/AIDS. In 1998, they accounted for 13 percent of the total population, but for 20 percent of new AIDS cases reported in that year (CDC, NCHS: HIV/AIDS Surveillance Report, 2000).

Women have also felt the brunt of increased AIDS infection. Among U.S. women, the disease has increased significantly, especially in communities of color. In 1992, women accounted for 13 percent of persons living with AIDS. By 1997, the proportion had grown to 19 percent. Finally, it is estimated that at least half of all new HIV infections in the United States are among people under 25, and the majority of young people are infected sexually. Furthermore, even though AIDS incidence is declining, there has not been a comparable decline in the number of newly diagnosed HIV cases among youth (CDC, NCHS: HIV/AIDS Surveillance Report, 2000).

Teen Sexuality

Over the course of the last century, young people became sexually active earlier than their parents' generation (Darling et al., 1989). Due in part to their freedom from community and parental control, today's young people have more sexual freedom than ever before. They are bombarded by sexual stimuli from the media and have an intense desire to be treated as adults, with the opportunities to behave as they please sexually. They feel pressure from their peers to be sexually active, yet they often experience conflicting pressures from tradition, religion, and parents.

Data on sexual activity are inexact, but most experts in the field agree that approximately 66 percent of U.S. teenagers have had sexual intercourse by the time they finish high school (Planned Parenthood Federation of America, 2000). In 1998, 48 percent of high school girls and 49 percent of high school boys were sexually active (Mackay, 2000). According to the latest data, the median age for first intercourse is 16.6 years for boys and 17.4 for girls (Alan Guttmacher Institute, cited in Ingrassia, 1994:61). New research has found that while the average age of first intercourse hovers at about 16, there is some variation by race and gender in the percentages of teens that have intercourse during their high school years. For example, a recent study of first sexual intercourse among 13,000 high school students found higher percentages of African Americans having sex before graduation, followed by Hispanics, Whites, and Asian Americans. In all racial groups, however, more males than females had sex in their teen years (Frisco et al., 2000). Because boys and men have always had more sexual leeway than girls and women, changes in adolescent sexuality are especially profound for girls (Rubin, 1990; Brumberg, 1997).

Many teens who have never had sexual intercourse are having oral sex. Apparently they are unaware that sexually transmitted diseases can be contracted through oral sex, which they do not count as "having sex" (Peterson, 2000). Even very young teens report "hooking up," which means having oral sex and other intimate contacts at parties, with people they hardly know (Gilbert, 2000).

Research finds that educational programs addressing teen sex make a difference. For example, condom programs in schools increase condom use; they do not increase sexual activity. A recent study compared the rates of condom use and sexual activity by thousands of high school students in New York City schools, which offer condoms, and by students in Chicago, where HIV/AIDS education is promoted but condoms are not made available in schools. The study concluded that condom access in schools is a low-cost, harmless addition to AIDS prevention efforts (Richardson, 1997:3A). Studies also show that teenagers whose parents talk with them openly are less likely than others to engage in risky behaviors such as casual sex or neglecting to use birth control (Gilbert, 2000).

Teenage Childbearing

In some cultures over time, teenage pregnancy and childbirth have been a normal reproductive pattern. Over the past several decades, however, this pattern has been viewed as a social problem. Particularly in the United States, which has the highest rates of adolescent pregnancy among Western industrialized nations, the issue has prompted growing concern (Lawson and Rhode, 1993:1).

What is the best way to think sociologically about teenage childbearing? Is it a matter of morality, fertility, or poverty? Is it an epidemic? Is it a social problem? For whom? Under what circumstances? Answering these questions requires that we become skeptical about some basic assumptions about teen pregnancy. In her book, *Dubious Conceptions* (1996), sociologist Kristin Luker argues that parenthood among teens is not the problem we think it is. Her point is not that there is no problem at all, but rather that the "facts about pregnancy among teenagers are based on a fundamental misunderstanding of the problem" (Luker, 1996:13). Three trends are important: (1) the United States is not experiencing a sudden epidemic of "children having children"; (2) although teen birth rates rose in the early 1990s, current levels of teenage childbirth are not out of control. Better use of contraception among teens has meant that teen birth rates have *declined* 18 percent since 1991, according to the National Center for Health Statistics (Ventura et al., 1999); and (3) teen pregnancy is not uniquely a U.S. phenomenon.

In the quarter-century between 1960 and 1985, adolescents' sexual activity and their rates of pregnancy rose, but their rates of childbearing declined, largely as a result of greater access to abortion. Although the U.S. teenage fertility rate began to rise slightly after 1985, it still remains substantially lower than that of preceding decades (Lawson and Rhode, 1993:3). This means that even as concern about teenage childbearing has grown during the past three decades, the probability that a teenage woman from virtually any racial, ethnic, or economic category will become a mother has actually diminished. Why is there a discrepancy between levels of concern and actual demographic trends? First, the teenagers of the 1960s were members of a baby-boom generation. This group was so enormous in size that, even with a smaller percentage becoming mothers, the absolute number of babies born to teenagers went up. This made teenage childbearing more visible than it had been before. At the same time, birth rates among older women were declining, and doing so more quickly than the birth rates among teenagers. As a result, births to teenagers began to comprise a larger percentage of total babies born than in the past (Astone, 1993:9).

The real source of alarm about teenage birth rates in the United States is closely tied to changes involving race, gender, age, and poverty (Luker, 1996:13). Even though teen childbearing occurs in other societies, the United States has high rates compared to other countries. (See Box 7.3.) Because teenage childbearing is increasingly concentrated among the inner-city poor, it is viewed by many as a racial problem—associated in the public mind with stereotypes of poor, young, Black women. Research does reveal racial differences in the rates of teen pregnancy, but important changes occurred in the last half of the 1980s as rates remained highest among African Americans but rose most rapidly among Latinas (Usdansky, 1993:1).

Today, at every age, young Blacks and Hispanics are more likely to give birth than are young White women (Sidel, 1996). African American and Hispanic teenagers are less likely than Whites either to use contraception consistently or to have abortions. As a consequence, the rate of adolescent childbearing among African Americans is almost two-and-a-half times higher than among Whites, and among Hispanic teenagers it is about twice as high as among Whites. In 1997, 12 percent of all births were to teens, regardless of race. Eleven percent of

BOX 7.3   Families in Global Perspective: Teen Birth Rates around the World

The birth rate refers to the number of live births per 1000 women in a particular year. Demographers compute the birth rates for women of various ages, racial-ethnic groups, and nationalities.

The 1998 teen birth rate was 51.1. Is this number high or low? One way of answering that questions is to look at birth rates over time. The U.S. teen birth rate for 1970 was 68.3, and it was 53.0 in 1980. In 1990 it was 59.9. The rate has gone down by 18 percent since 1990. Whether a particular rate is seen as high or low depends on the comparison year.

Another way of approaching the U.S. teen birth rate is to reference it to the rates for other countries. The following table illustrates that teen birth rates vary widely across the globe. Comparatively speaking, teen mothering is more a part of U.S. society than of most other societies worldwide.

Teen Birth Rates around the World (from last available year):

Bahrain (1995)	21.7	Iceland (1995)	23.0
Israel (1994)	18.9	Ireland (1995)	15.4
Japan (1995)	3.9	Netherlands (1995)	5.8
Malaysia (1990)	18.5	Norway (1992)	16.0
Thailand (1994)	41.3	Poland (1994)	25.5
Austria (1995)	17.5	Romania (1995)	42.5
Bulgaria (1994)	61.3	Switzerland (1995)	5.5
Martinique (1992)	28.0	United Kingdom (1995)	28.3
Chile (1995)	65.1	Australia (1995)	20.5
France (1993)	7.9	New Zealand (1992)	33.8

Source: United Nations, *Demographic Yearbook.* New York: United Nations, pp. 353–364.

White births were to teen mothers, 22 percent of African American births were to teen mothers, and 17 percent of Hispanic births were to teen mothers (Ventura et al., 2000).

Conventional thinking presumes that early motherhood dooms young mothers and their children to a life of poverty, but many sociologists challenge this assumption. They argue that although teenage pregnancy correlates with poverty, it does not cause poverty because most teen mothers were poor before becoming pregnant.

Early motherhood makes young women vulnerable. Having a baby poses barriers to completing high school and good job possibilities. Yet avoiding early parenthood does not affect all teenage girls in the same way. Research by economist Elaine McCrate has found that, in strictly economic terms, African American teenagers have less to gain from delaying motherhood than do White teenagers. Her study found that women who postponed their first birth until after age seventeen tended to earn higher hourly wages, to experience lower levels of unemployment, and to be more likely to improve their status in the job market. However, in each case, the economic payoff was markedly smaller for Black women than for White women. The differences are explained by Black women's disproportionate confinement to poor schools and labor markets with low pay, little opportunity for advancement, and low job security. This finding provides a basis for rejecting the popular caricature of teen mothers as irresponsible and irrational (cited in Lee, 1989:10). Instead, early childbearing among some women can be explained as a rational response to a social context of race- and class-based deprivation (Geronimus, 1992).

DIFFERENTIATED FORMS OF INTIMACY

Throughout this chapter, we have examined intimacy in the context of structural forces. Gender, class, race, and sexual orientation shape intimate behaviors and experiences. In this section we look more closely at some of the ways in which intimacy reflects social inequalities. Far from being personal and private, our intimate experiences are shaped by power relations in the larger society.

Gendered Love and Sex

The most significant dimension of sexuality is gender. It relates to the biological and social contexts of sexual behavior and desire (Schwartz and Rutter, 1998:2). Women and men often want different things from their intimate heterosexual relationships. They have different expectations and experiences (Baber and Allen, 1992:62) that are the products of social processes and beliefs about gender.

His and Her Sex

Despite the wide range of sexualities among women and among men, gendered experiences have a great deal of influences on sexual behavior and sexual desire:

> As a boy enters adolescence, he hears jokes about boys' uncontainable desire. Girls are told the same thing and told that their job is to resist. These gender messages have power, not only over attitudes and behaviors. . . but over physical and biological experience (Schwartz and Rutter, 1998:4).

The familiar double standard that men are more sexual than women while women are more driven by love captures both the historical reality and the current imbalance in sexual conduct.

Images and statistics show that women and men have distinct patterns of sexual expression (see Figure 7.2). One difference is that men tend to be more casual about sex. They can more easily compartmentalize their feelings about sex and love, while women view sex as more of a bonding experience. In Lillian Rubin's words, women depend on the emotional attachment to call up the sexual, while men rely on the sexual to spark the emotional (Rubin, 1983:102).

The distinction between women's stress on the emotional relationship and men's stress on performance is illustrated in a qualitative study of sexual experiences. Researchers asked their informants

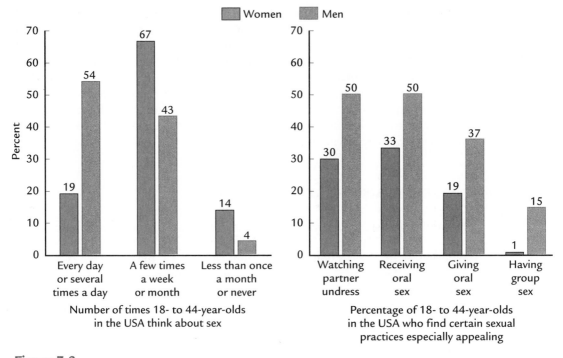

Figure 7.2

Sex and gender

Source: Judith Mackay, *The Penguin Atlas of Human Sexual Behavior.* New York: Penguin Putnam, 2000, p. 21.

to fill in the blank in a sentence that read, "A penis is to a man what a _____ is to a woman." Men had no trouble with the task, almost all referring either to a clitoris or a vagina. Women, by contrast, resisted giving any simple answer, objecting that it was not a matter of one tiny organ but far more diffuse—that is, for them sex was only one outlet to express and experience a better, deeper feeling of intimacy. No man in the study spoke in terms of intimacy: sex for them was a matter of drive, vigor, and technique (cited in Rossi, 1994:27).

How can we explain the imbalance of love and sex in intimate relationships? Part of the split stems from sexual meanings learned in the separate and unequal socialization experiences of girls and boys. In these two separate worlds, boys learn about genital sexuality and masturbation, while girls learn about love and the importance of boys (Gagnon, 1983:164).

Compared to boys, young girls do not engage in an upsurge of experimental, impersonal, and autoerotic sexual activity during adolescence. More than girls, boys arrive at a non-relationship-based experience of sexual feelings and encounters. Females live primarily in homosocial worlds in which adult women reinforce the girl's future status as wife and mother. Women tend not to seek sex for its own sake, and far more than men, they establish their sexuality through a relationship (Fowlkes, 1994:167).

The double standard creates problems for men because it demands that they be skilled, experienced, and competent in sexual matters. For adult men, this has three main negative effects: (1) it perpetuates sexual ignorance, (2) it prevents them from discussing sex with their partners, and (3) it prevents seeking help when a sexual problem does occur. Adolescent boys are under pressure as well. Today, "it's harder than ever for a young man to admit he's never had sex" (Manning, 1997:4D). Joseph LoPiccolo attributes the greatest blame for the model of male sexuality to a mythic masculinity and its embodiment in advertising, television, and the mass media.

> If we look at the type of male who is used as a status model to sell everything from cars to beer, he is clearly an achieving, strong, unemotional, expert, and highly competent man. Many of the male role models we see in novels and television similarly do not include men who cry, who are vulnerable, need help, and have egalitarian, communicative relationships with women, especially in regard to sex. Instead, we see the image of masculinity as extremely "macho," dominant, aggressive, or, in short, suffering from what might be called *testosterone poisoning* (LoPiccolo, 1983:48).

Women may be attracted to men's independent, self-contained ways because such ways reassure women of men's strength. As relationships develop, however, women often resent men for being distant and invulnerable. Many relationships are devoid of emotional intimacy. Male inexpressiveness can so hinder communication between men and women in intimate relationships that it has been labeled a "tragedy of American society" (Balswick and Peek, 1971). However, Jack Sattel (1976) argues that men's tendency to withhold such aspects of emotional intimacy as tenderness and affection is not simply a matter of their socialization, but a way of controlling the intensity of the connection and gaining the upper hand in relationships with women. Keeping cool in private is a way of maintaining the dominance and power that men hold in public.

Some feminist scholars argue that sexuality is the arena in which male dominance and female subordination are produced and reproduced (Dworkin, 1981; MacKinnon, 1989). While men's control of women's sexuality has been an important issue for many feminists, others caution against characterizing women simply as victims. Some claim that the emphasis on violence can eclipse attention to women's experiences of sexual pleasure (Rubin, 1984; Vance, 1984). This debate dramatizes the complexity of sexuality, which many women experience as a contradictory mix of pleasure and danger. The debate also entails questions about "structure and agency" (Osmond and Thorne, 1993). To what degree are women's sexualities shaped by external forces (including male dominance), and to what degree are women "agents," taking actions to resist control and to develop satisfying sexual relationships?

His and Her Love

Most individuals experience at least one love relationship in the course of their lives. To be in love is to be in a special world that centers on a relationship of two people. Romantic love is essentially, but not exclusively, sexual. It is a complex social and psychological state involving thoughts and feelings that provide humans with a powerful sense of intimacy and self-worth. Poets, novelists, and social scientists have disagreed on the nature of love, on whether it is trivial and selfish or ennobling and enriching. Undoubtedly, it can be any of these and can encompass different emotions with different meanings and consequences.

Do women and men differ in what they expect from love as well as in their styles of being in love? According to folklore, it is women who are most concerned with love. The common assumption that men work and women love has a basis in truth (Hatfield, 1983:109). Social historians have helped us identify how these differences are socially created. As economic production became separated from the home and from personal relationships, women's and men's roles became polarized (see Chapters 2 and 3). Love became "feminized" with the rise of capitalism and women became responsible for the emotional management of marriage and family relationships (Baber and Allen, 1992; Cancian, 1987). Men were assigned the duties of the larger world and were defined by their responsibilities in the public setting. Therefore, love could be secondary, a less important part of men's life.

Even today, many studies show that women's and men's styles of love are different. Women work harder at love and at staying attractive and interesting to their partners (Rubin, 1983). Women, more than men, closely attend to, scan, and scrutinize their experiences of love. They do what sociologist Arlie Hochschild (1983a:255) has called "emotion work" or "feeling work"; that is, they work on their emotions and feelings to coincide with what "should" be felt. They do this in order to control and direct love relationships in a "useful" direction. In contrast, men tend to fall in love more quickly and less deliberately than women:

> Men, having a more romantic notion of love, cast a different map over their experience than do women. This sets up different expectations about "what might happen" and affects how men attend to experience. The romantic rendering of love suggests a less managerial, more passive stance toward love. Romantic love is by its nature something that cannot be controlled; it occurs automatically, "at first sight," and is predestined. Love feelings are in a particular way ascribed, not achieved. Indeed, the data suggest that men manage and work on love less. On the other hand, women understand love more as something which can, in its nature, be managed and indeed they seem to perform more feeling work upon it. By deromanticizing love, women appear to professionalize it more. Why? (Hochschild, 1983a:255).

The answer Hochschild provides is that young men hold hegemony over the courtship process, while at the same time women, for economic reasons, need marriage more.

Gendered love styles bolster men's power over women. Because our society defines love in a feminine way, women's emotional expressiveness and their connections with and dependence on others are readily acknowledged. But men's acceptance of love, which emphasizes instrumental activities, conceals their dependency on close relationships. This gives men greater power in intimate relationships (Cancian, 1987).

Public schools are challenged to teach teens responsible family behavior.

Same-Sex Orientation and Intimacy

We cannot generalize about intimacy from the experiences of heterosexuals alone. The social context in which intimacy between lesbians and gay men occurs is markedly different from that of heterosexuals. A crucial difference is that the support network available for both the individuals and for the relationship is missing for the gay couples (Meyer, 1990). Although intimacy among gays is not sanctioned by social institutions, women and men who identify as lesbian or gay draw strength from their shared identities, from their own support networks, and from gay and lesbian rights organizations. From this strength, they challenge prevailing cultural attitudes, customs, and laws.

The experiences of gay, lesbian, and bisexual individuals are unique, but some commonalities have been established by social science research. Sociological research challenges common stereotypes by showing that same-sex couples are not completely dissimilar from other kinds of intimate dyads:

> Gay men and lesbians are as oriented to steady relationships as are heterosexual men and women; they use their relationships as a main source of affection and companionship; they have as high or higher satisfaction as other couples, show similar "adjustment" scores, and report similar relationship quality on a variety of measures. Furthermore, gays and lesbians have certain advantages, such as role flexibility and greater equality (Risman and Schwartz, 1988:134).

Gender exerts a great influence on the intimate relationships of lesbians and gays, often a greater influence than sexual orientation. In this respect, "lesbians resemble heterosexual women just as gay men are similar to heterosexual men" (Risman and Schwartz, 1988:135). Lesbians establish ongoing love relationships earlier than gay men and are more likely to commit to a homosexual identity within the context of an intense emotional relationship, whereas gay men do so within the context of their sexual experience. In general, emotional attachment is the most significant aspect of relationships for lesbians, but sexual activity is most important for gay men. Although this pattern may have changed as a result of the AIDS epidemic, gay men have historically been involved with many more one-time-only sexual partners than have lesbians (Levine and Evans, 1996: 130–131).

Social Class and Intimacy

The conditions under which sexuality and love are experienced also vary with social class. Since Kinsey, other research studies on the premarital sexual activities of Americans have found consistently that certain categories of young people tend to be overrepresented among the sexually active: those from broken homes, those from poverty, those with low levels of educational achievement, and those from minority groups. Kinsey found, for example, an inverse relationship between socioeconomic status and premarital sexual permissiveness—the higher the socioeconomic status, the lower the rate of sexual permissiveness. Using educational level as the indicator of status, Kinsey found that males and females with only an eighth-grade education began their coital behavior five or six years earlier than high school and college graduates (Kinsey et al., 1948:550).

Differences in sexual behavior by social class are becoming less clear. Nevertheless, many studies have found differences in the way sexuality is defined and experienced. Is one class's normal behavior another class's deviance? To test this idea, Raymond Eve and Donald Renslow conducted an exploratory study based on a sample of seventy-two college students who filled out questionnaires about sexual behavior. The study did find that the actual occurrence of different varieties of sexual behavior (and fantasies about these behaviors) is often related to social class. The higher the respondents' socioeconomic status, the greater was the likelihood that they were willing to accept a wider variety of sexual expression as normal (Eve and Renslow, 1980:97).

The NHSLS discovered that sex is very much class-coded. Put broadly, the poorer segments within society incline toward an unadorned, no-nonsense, silent approach to sex, while the more affluent practice a more self-conscious, elaborate, even mannered sexuality, especially when it comes to masturbation, oral sex, and foreplay (Robinson, 1994:22). The most striking finding is that oral sex is most popular among better-educated Whites and less popular among less educated Blacks (Michael et al., 1994:139).

Love and Social Class

Little information exists on love relationships in various parts of the class structure. Although the American ideology of love is held by most people regardless of their social location, there are class differences in the resources required to sustain the ideal. Not only do the social networks that surround couples differ; the impact of economic resources also creates differences in "loving" experiences. Intimacy in marital relationships is also affected by economic conditions. In the 1970s Lillian Rubin asked working-class wives and middle-class wives what each group most valued in their husbands. She found that middle-class women valued intimacy, sharing, and communication.

> Does this mean, then, that working-class women are unconcerned about the emotional side of the marriage relationship? Emphatically, it does not. It says first that when the material aspects of life are problematic, they become dominant as issues requiring solutions; and second, that even when men are earning a reasonably good living it is never "taken for granted" when financial insecurity and marginality are woven into the fabric of life (Rubin, 1976:94).

Economic differences, then, can create vast differences in private relationships.

Race and Intimacy

Inequalities of race and social class have long been sexualized. Throughout our history, the powerful have used images of sexual depravity to justify control of the powerless. The link between sexuality, power, and exploitation is an important aspect of U.S. history, as John D'Emilio and Estelle Freedman explain:

> European settlers justified their superiority over native people in terms of a need to civilize savages, and whites imposed on blacks an image of a beastlike sexuality to justify both the rape of black women and the lynching of black men (1988:xvi).

Social historians do not agree on the origin and meaning of racial differences in sexual practices, but they agree that premarital sexual patterns differ between African Americans and Whites. Racial differences in sexual norms have been suggested by some of the earliest social surveys (Furstenberg et al., 1987:511). Variant patterns of sexuality among people of color should not be considered deviant. Here, we examine racial differences not to contrast them with a mythical norm, but to show some of the ways in which institutional structures of racism create differences in sexual behaviors and sexual meanings.

Contemporary Differences in Sexual Behavior

All studies agree that African Americans become sexually active earlier than Whites (Udry and Campbell, 1994). How can we explain this? Joyce Ladner (1971), a social scientist who has investigated poor Black women, has argued that there is a strong Black culture that is different from that of the dominant White middle class. The Black community has a unique culture because of some African customs that have survived and because of adaptive responses to discrimination. We assert, along with Ladner, that the social context shapes the sexual behaviors of poor minorities. The behaviors of those who are poor and people of color are shaped in unique ways that are conditioned by poverty, discrimination, and institutional subordination.

Over three decades ago, Lee Rainwater (1966) argued that the peer group system of Black lower-class adolescents has encouraged both boys and girls to experience an early initiation into sexual activities. Boys tend to use sex exploitively and competitively for status among their peers, whereas girls participate as a symbol of their maturity.

Elijah Anderson's study (1990) of life in an inner-city neighborhood shows how poverty creates its own sex code. Young men and young women scramble to take what they can from each other. Sexual conquests result in pregnancies, and girls often have little to lose by having a child out of wedlock. Anderson argues that the situation must be viewed in its social and political context:

> It is nothing less than the . . . manifestation of persistent urban poverty. It is a mean adaptation to blocked opportunities and profound lack, a grotesque form of coping by young people constantly undermined by a social system that historically has limited their social options. . . . Like all adolescents, inner-city youths are subject to intense, hard-to-control urges. Sexual relations, exploitative and otherwise, are common among middle-class teenagers as well, but most middle-class youths take a stronger interest in their future and know what a pregnancy can do to derail it (Anderson, 1990:113).

Finally, sexual activity among the poor may be encouraged because it serves as a substitute for other forms of gratification that cannot be fulfilled. Ladner (1971:212) has argued that this takes two forms. On the one hand, sex can provide one with a sense of identity and worth. "Some girls engage in premarital sex because it provides them with a sense of belonging, of feeling needed by their boyfriends." Sex can also be viewed as a system of exchange. "Often in the absence of material resources (such as money to purchase gifts for a boyfriend's birthday, etc.) sex becomes the resource that is exchanged."

The gender ratio among African Americans gives men great power over sex. As Robert Staples has put it,

> the system inherently favors men. With an effective sex ratio of three black women to every male, the females have little, if any, bargaining power where men have such a large number of women from which to choose. In a sense, black women often find themselves in the position of sexually auditioning for a meaningful relationship. After a number of tryouts, they may find a black male who is willing to make a commitment to them (Staples, 1978a:19).

Black men are hardly alone in their exploitation of women for sex. Many men, in all racial and class categories, are similar in the selfish, peer-oriented nature of their sexual behavior. Thus, Staples contends that Black men and White men are much more united in terms of the meaning of sex than are Black men and Black women. According to Cornel West, Black men's sexuality is different from that of Black women because of their different locations in the matrix of inequalities:

> For most young black men, power is acquired by stylizing their bodies over space and time in such a way that their bodies reflect their uniqueness and provoke fear in others. . . . In this way, the black male search for power often reinforces the myth of black male sexual prowess, a myth that tends to subordinate black and white women as objects of sexual pleasure. . . . The case of black women is quite different partly because the dynamics of white and black patriarchy affect them differently [whereby] . . . black women are subject to more multilayered bombardments of racist assaults than black men in addition to the sexist assaults they receive from black men (West, 1996:228–229).

We know far less about intimacy among other racial-ethnics. Latinos are stereotyped as "naturally" sexual: women are "hot tamales" or sexual firebrands

"Be discreet with the girls, Son."

(Ortiz, 2000), while men are "machos," an image that conjures up the rough, swaggering men who are abusive and oppressive toward women. However, Olivia Espin (1984:156) notes that sexual machismo is "nothing but the Hispanic version of the myth of male superiority supported by most cultures."

Two facts account for the lack of social science information about love in the lives of people of color: (1) stereotypes that portray racial-ethnic women and men as more sexual and therefore less capable than Whites of controlling animal instincts (Jagger and Rothenberg, 1984:385); and (2) the prevailing ideology of love as a White, middle-class emotion. The study of love should not be restricted to privileged categories but should be linked to social and cultural factors throughout class and racial hierarchies.

Claiming Control of Intimacy

Because intimacy is socially constructed, it offers the possibility for agency, change, and growth. One of the most important developments leading to greater agency in sexual behavior is the ability to separate sexuality from reproduction (Baber and Allen, 1992:81). This has given many women a wide range of options and enabled them to seek intimate relationships based on mutuality rather than male dominance (Giddens, 1992). A just society would guarantee "basic individual human rights including the rights to chose their own sexual, romantic, and marital partner, as well as to chose one's own sexual practices (as long as they are consensual and do not harm others)" (Schwartz, 2000:215). People throughout society are struggling to transform intimate relationships and to enhance pleasure and love. The sexual revolution is occurring on many fronts. People in all walks of life, both young and old—homosexual and heterosexual—are questioning the old definitions of sex and love. Just as lesbian and gay rights movements challenge the exclusive definition of sexuality in terms of heterosexuality, women and men redefining intimate relationships to create sexual justice.

CHAPTER REVIEW

1. The sociological study of intimacy is not limited to interpersonal relations, but includes the macro structural context.

2. The transition from traditional to modern social conditions created greater needs for intimacy.

3. Courtship patterns have been affected by the changing economy, urbanization, and job and educational opportunities away from home. For most of U.S. history, parents controlled the courtship patterns of their offspring. In this century, personal choice has emerged as the primary determinant.

4. Dating and courtship patterns vary by social class and by race. The higher the social class, the more parental control is involved in the process. Class-based and race-based courtship patterns are due largely to the stratified social worlds in which young people live.

5. Mate selection does not occur entirely through free choice, even in contemporary U.S. society. Homogamy governs mate selection. Factors such as social class, race, and religion limit choice. Schools play a large part in narrowing the range of marital partners.

6. Sexual orientation is a power system operating much like the race, class, and gender hierarchies. Although human beings are capable of various modes of sexual expres-

sion, social institutions enforce compulsory heterosexuality.

7. As lesbians and gays have emerged into the mainstream of society, new understandings of sexuality have been developed.

8. Human sexualities vary from one culture to another, within any one culture over time, over the life course of women and men, and between and among different groups of women and men depending on class, race, ethnicity, region, and sexual orientation.

9. Sexual behavior in the United States has changed from a family-centered reproductive system in colonial days to a romantic sexuality in the nineteenth century to a modern sexuality with sexual relations as a source of happiness and personal identity by the 1920s. Over the next several decades, social changes further liberalized sex.

10. The 1992 National Health and Social Survey is the most comprehensive representative survey ever done of sexual behavior in the U.S. population. This survey looked at sexuality in its social context and found that sexual behaviors are shaped by the

social networks in which individuals operate.

11. Changing sexual practices, especially among gay men, have leveled off the spread of AIDS in this country. In the 1990s, the incidence of AIDS increased among women and people of color.

12. Teenage pregnancy rates have diminished in the past three decades. Still, the United States has the highest rates of teenage pregnancy of any industrialized country, a condition closely related to poor economic opportunities.

13. Gender differences in love and sex are produced by power relations in the larger society.

14. Although intimacy among lesbians and gay men is not sanctioned by the larger society, lesbians and gays can draw support from their own social networks.

15. Love and sexual experiences vary by social class. Research documents that certain categories of young people are overrepresented among the sexually active.

16. Racial differences in sexual norms are evident. Some factors influencing Black and White differences include poverty, discrimination, and institutional subordination.

RELATED WEB SITES

http://www.agi-usa.org/

The mission of The Alan Guttmacher Institute (AGI) is to protect the reproductive choices of all women and men—in the United States and throughout the world. To fulfill this mission, AGI seeks to inform individual decision-making, encourage scientific inquiry and enlightened public debate, and promote the formation of sound public- and private-sector programs and policies. The aims of AGI's domestic and international projects and activities are to 1) foster sexual and reproductive health and rights; 2) promote the prevention of unintended pregnancies; 3) guarantee the freedom of women to terminate unwanted pregnancies; 4) achieve healthy pregnancies and births; 5) secure societal support for parenthood and parenting; and 6) promote gender equality within sexual, familial and social relationships.

http://www.indiana.edu/~kinsey/SSRC/sexreas.html

Sexuality Research: This website was created by the Social Science Research Council, and represents a summary of a report done on why sexuality should be researched in the U. S. This summary comes from a more comprehensive report, done by the Social Science Research Council: Sexuality Research in the United States: An Assessment of the Social and Behavioral Sciences.

http://www.siecus.org/

SIECUS Home Page (Sexuality Information and Education Council of the United States): The Sexuality Information and Education Council of the U.S. (SIECUS) is a national, nonprofit organization which affirms that sexuality is a natural and healthy part of living. Incorporated in 1964, SIECUS develops, collects, and disseminates information, promotes comprehensive education about sexuality, and advocates the right of individuals to make responsible sexual choices.

http://www.lovemore.com/

Loving More is an organization that publishes a magazine, holds annual conferences, and provides information and inspiration for people of all orientations who are interested in exploring healthy relationship options including group marriage, open couples, intimate networks, expanded families, and intentional community.

http://www.sexuality.org/

The Society for Human Sexuality is an all-volunteer social and educational organization devoted to the appreciation of the myriad consensual forms of human relationships and sexual expression. Their site is packed with great resources and information.

http://www.biresource.org/

Bisexual Resource Center: A resource of information about bisexuality from the creators of the Bisexual Resource Guide. Contains pamphlets on bisexuality available for download, sells bi books, music, and products, and lists online resources.

http://www.ifge.org/

The International Foundation for Gender Education (IFGE), founded in 1987, is a leading advocate and educational organization for promoting the self-definition and free expression of individual gender identity. IFGE is not a support group, it is an information provider and clearinghouse for referrals about all things which are transgressive of established social gender norms. IFGE maintains the most complete bookstore on the subject of transgenderism available anywhere. It also publishes the leading magazine providing reasoned discussion of issues of gender expression and identity, including crossdressing, transsexualism, female-to-male and male-to-female issues spanning health, family, medical, legal, workplace issues and more.

Contemporary Marriages

Myths and Realities

Myth: The typical marriage arrangement in the United States is a couple in a life-long marriage with the husband employed and the wife at home as a homemaker and caregiver to her husband and children.

Reality: There are many variations from the presumed marriage norm, with no one arrangement dominant: divorce and remarriage are commonplace; dual-earner marriages are typical; in one out of six marriages, the wife is the economic dominant; and some marriages remain childless by choice.

Myth: Each partner in a heterosexual marriage experiences that relationship in more or less the same way.

Reality: Heterosexual marital relationships are gendered, with wives and husbands acting and perceiving differently from each other. Although marriage is generally beneficial to both husbands and wives, husbands benefit more.

Myth: Married couples have more economic resources, which explains why they provide more benefits to the partners than those experienced by the unmarried.

Reality:	Marriage actually decreases the economic benefits for many of the poor, especially minority poor. The lack of resources of poor couples adds stress as they have difficulty meeting basic family needs.
Myth:	Because of more positive views on gender equality in this generation, husbands and wives in dual-worker families share more or less equally in housework.
Reality:	In the average dual-worker family, the husband contributes only about one-half the hours to housework that the wife does.
Myth:	Happy marriages are alike. That is, there is a cluster of behaviors that identifies successful marriages.
Reality:	There is an enormous variation among stable marriages.
Myth:	Children improve the quality of a marriage.
Reality:	Numerous studies find that marital happiness is lowest when children are in the home and highest in homes without children.
Myth:	As indicated by the trends of increased cohabitation, marrying later, and high divorce rates, Americans are becoming disillusioned with marriage.
Reality:	Marriage is as alive as ever: 90 percent of adults eventually marry; and 80 percent of divorced people remarry.

This chapter examines the institution of marriage in U.S. society. Marriages in this society are interesting phenomena to analyze. Marriages, contrary to public opinion, are varied in form. These forms change as social forces affect them differently at different times and places. However, although marriages must be understood in their social context, we must not forget that these arrangements are intensely personal. This chapter is divided into several parts to capture this duality. The first provides an overview by showing the duality of marriage—the private and the public aspects of this complex social relationship. The second part reviews the facts and trends regarding marriage, revealing its changing nature. The third part examines the benefits of marriage. The fourth part focuses on the micro aspects of marriage—that is, the correlates of marital success, patterns of sexual intimacy, and how decisions are made by married couples. Then we examine strategies for reconstructing gender roles to foster egalitarian marriage. Finally, we address the question of whether marriage is a dying institution.

MARRIAGE: PRIVATE AND PUBLIC SPHERES

A fundamental contradiction characterizes marriages in U.S. society. A marriage is a multifaceted bond based on commitment, love, and intimacy. Yet while this relationship is an intensely private affair, it is also shaped by macro forces, such as the law, economics, religion, and gender expectations. Let's look at the private side first.

Each couple creates its unique social organization within the marriage.

The Private Nature of Marriage

It is easy to treat marriage as a concrete entity with features as readily observable as any three-dimensional object—with volume, density, and a visible surface. However, a marriage is actually a relationship between two people, not a concrete object. It is a dynamic system that emerges from the actions and interactions of two people, who are in many ways strangers to each other, as noted by anthropologist Mary Catherine Bateson:

> We live with strangers. Those we love most, with whom we share a shelter, a table, a bed, remain mysterious. Wherever lives overlap and flow together, there are depths of unknowing. . . . Strangers marry strangers, whether they have been playmates for years or never meet before the wedding day. They continue to surprise each other through the evolutions of love and the growth of affection. Lovers, gay and straight, begin in strangeness (Bateson, 2000:3–4).

The marriage of two "strangers" creates a unique relationship in profound and complex ways. Two individuals with different histories, from different social networks, and (usually) of opposite genders create a novel household. Sociologist Elise Boulding has described this complex process:

> The profound, multidimensional bonding experienced by the founding members of a new household is the primal stuff of the familial reality. All past training in role

To live a successful marriage, each couple must define what works for them in their shared world.

behaviors, all past experience in interpreting reality and coping with its highs and lows, all expectations of the future, must be reforged for each member in the ambiance of a new bond that defines them as new persons. The reality-construction process is breathtaking in its complexity. The process of individuation for each person accelerates in response to the shock of having to assimilate the "alien culture" of the other in the intimacy of the familial partnership. The social space of the household is filled with gossamer social webs that impinge everywhere on the intimacy of pair interaction and make that interaction in fact a miniparliament representing many interests (Boulding, 1983:261).

Within the intimate environment of the marriage and the constraints of society, each couple creates its own unique social organization. As Peter Berger and Hansfried Kellner have said,

Marriage in our society is a dramatic act in which two strangers come together and redefine themselves. . . . The marriage partners [embark] on the often difficult task of constructing for themselves the little world in which they will live. To be sure, the larger society provides them with certain standard instructions as to how they should go about this task, but this does not change the fact that considerable effort of their own is required for its realization (Berger and Kellner, 1975:221, 223).

The couple must work out mutually satisfactory solutions to such crucial areas of potential conflict as the division of labor, making decisions, the spending of money, the use of leisure time, sexual behavior, whether or not to have children (and, if so, how many and when and how they will be raised), the resolution of conflicts, and the like. Needless to say, couples vary in their ability to achieve satisfactory arrangements in these critical areas of married life.

Macro Influences on Marriage

Marriages do not occur in a vacuum. Both members of the marriage union have expectations of the relationship based on broad cultural prescriptions and proscriptions, their religious beliefs, the norms of their community, and their family background. Thus, while each couple forges a unique relationship, there are patterns across marriages that vary by social class, race, gender, and locality. These patterns involve gendered behaviors, how decisions are made, appropriate sexual behaviors, and the division of housework. Moreover, these relationships are patterned by structural arrangements such as the law, differential job opportunities for men and women, and institutional sexism and racism. This section examines three macro forces that affect the human actors in marriages—the law, religion, and gender.

The Law

Marriage is a legal contract. Each state determines the criteria for a legal marriage within its boundaries. Although there are minor differences from state to state on the legal specifics regarding marriage, there are general principles that are more or less universal in the United States.

Each state stipulates the legal age of marriage, the allowed distance between relatives, health requirements, the length of the waiting period required before marriage, rules concerning inheritance, Social Security, and the division of property in the case of divorce. Although it has been ruled unconstitutional now, states at one time had laws against interracial marriages.

Laws Banning Homosexual Marriages   One rule found in every state is that for a marriage to be legal the couple must be heterosexual (for international exceptions to this rule, see Box 8.1). This rule has significant negative consequences for gays and lesbians. Most obvious, when state law formally rejects a marital relationship among homosexual couples in committed relationships, it condemns their living arrangements. Thus, state law, in effect, affirms homophobia. Consider, for example, this letter directed to the well-known newspaper advisor, Ann Landers:

> Dear Ann Landers: Last year, I married the woman of my dreams. She is funny, intelligent, loving, caring, exciting, and gentle. Ours is a full and rewarding life together. We have traveled to several states for both business and pleasure. We go to church, get together with friends and relatives, and share the household chores. We have known good times and bad, and our commitment to one another is stronger now than ever.

So why am I writing to you? Because I hope you will help educate a few million people today. Our marriage, blessed by a minister and approved by many friends and family members, is not legal in the United States. And if Congress has anything to say about it, we may never have a chance to make it legal. You see, Ann, I am also a woman.

My wife and I are hard-working professionals who pay our taxes and vote regularly. We pay our bills on time and are law-abiding citizens. However, we are not accorded all the civil rights that most Americans assume to be their privilege.

BOX 8.1   **Families in Global Perspective: Legalized Marriages for Homosexuals in Other Societies**

Typically, the marriage code of a nation or state specifies that marriage is entered into between a women and a man. Denmark in 1989 became the first nation in the world to allow homosexual marriages. Norway became the second nation to permit these marriages. Norway's law permits homosexual marriages by not mentioning sexuality in the official procedures for a marriage:

> A marriage is contracted when the parties to the marriage come together before a solemnizer [clergyperson or authorized government official] of marriage. While both parties are present, they shall declare that they wish to contract a marriage with each other. The solemnizer shall thereafter declare them to be married (Norwegian Parliament, 1991:13).

In 1994 the Swedish parliament voted to accept the Registered Partnership Law. This law gives gay and lesbian couples the same inheritance, tax, and other benefits and obligations as married heterosexuals. The presider at the first homosexual wedding in Sweden said, "This is a victory for justice and equality. Just 51 years ago, homosexuality was a crime in Sweden" (cited in Associated Press, 1995). In 2000, lawmakers in the Netherlands approved a law that converted the country's registered same-sex partnerships into full-fledged marriages, complete with divorce guidelines and adoption rights for gays. Thus, the Netherlands joined Sweden, Denmark and Norway as the only nations to allow homosexuals to marry.

In 1999, Canada's Supreme Court declared by a vote of 8 to 1 that for the purposes of family law, same-sex partners must be considered spouses. In effect, the decision conferred common-law marital status on cohabiting same-sex couples. The Court ruled

> definitively that same-sex partners must be included under the term "spouse"—so for better or worse, Canadian lesbian and gay couples now have to worry about such things as alimony, child support, shared taxes and separation oversight, while gaining the rights to shared pensions, wrongful-death benefits, immigration, hospital visitation and much more (Graff, 1999:23).

In 2000 the European Union's parliament adopted a resolution urging the 15 European Union nations to grant same-sex couples rights equal to those of heterosexual couples. The nonbinding resolution said EU nations should "guarantee one-parent families, unmarried couples and same-sex couples rights equal to those enjoyed by traditional couples and families, particularly as regards tax law, pecuniary rights and social rights" (Associated Press, 2000).

> Because we are not legally married, we have none of the legal rights married couples enjoy, such as gaining immediate access to a loved one in case of an emergency, sharing insurance policies at reduced rates, holding property together, filing joint returns and so on.
>
> We are not seeking "special rights." We simply want the same rights every other American couple has: the right to be free from discrimination in housing and employment, the right to legal protection from harassment and, most importantly, the right to marry whomever we choose and to enjoy the benefits of marriage (Landers, 1996:12D).

(Landers, by the way, although she supports of the gay rights movement and the rights of same-sex couples, does not support same-sex marriage because, for her, marriage is a union between a man and a woman.)

As noted in this letter to Ann Landers, since same-sex partners are not recognized by the state as legally married couples, they do not receive the legal benefits of marriage. Thus, a surviving partner in a gay or lesbian committed relationship is not eligible to receive Social Security benefits or other pensions. For similar reasons, a partner in a homosexual relationship cannot receive health benefits from his or her partner's company health plan, unless the company provides for same-sex domestic partner benefits (as do such corporations as Microsoft, IBM, Walt Disney, Honeywell, and Boeing).

There are some exceptions to the states' exclusionary policies regarding homosexuals in committed relationships. A few cities, most notably San Francisco, New York City, Madison, Wisconsin, and Boulder, Colorado, allow gay or lesbian couples to register as "domestic partners." This permits partners to receive limited spousal benefits. In New York City, for example, a gay or lesbian may inherit an apartment lease if a partner dies. These domestic arrangements, however, continue to carry minimal legal weight because same-sex marriages are not recognized by any of the states. In 1997 Hawaii became the first state to allow its government employees who were in same-sex relationships to qualify for health and other benefits reserved for married couples. Hawaii's Supreme Court ruled in 1999, however, that gay marriages were illegal. In 2000 Vermont became the first state to grant same-sex couples the legal status of a "civil union" (technically not marriage), qualifying them for more than 300 rights and benefits that flow from marriage under Vermont law, including inheritance, property transfers, medical decisions, insurance, and filing joint state income tax returns. The action by Vermont has led some thirty-one states to ban gay marriages and for Congress to pass the Defense of Marriage Act, which denies federal recognition of homosexual marriage and allows states to ignore same-sex unions licensed elsewhere.

This legal practice of banning same-sex marriages raises the question, What is a marriage relationship? Is the key element in a marriage the sexuality of the partners or their commitment to each other? U.S. society has chosen to define marriage narrowly, as a heterosexual union. Thus, the state supports loving relationships—but only for heterosexuals (Delgado and Yun, 1997).

Religion

By definition, religions constrain their members to behave in particular ways. Thus, as Tim Heaton has said, "religious involvement creates a context, not only for indoctrination into a particular theology, but also for socialization regarding normative expectations" (Heaton, 1986:249). This normative aspect of religion has profound consequences for behaviors within marriage. Almost universally, religions prohibit sexual relationships outside of marriage. Many fundamentalist groups oppose homosexual sex and homosexual marriages. Those religions within the Judeo-Christian tradition limit marriage to one spouse at a time. Some religions do not permit remarriage after a divorce. Some oppose the use of contraceptives. Many formally oppose abortion. Some encourage large families—most notably, the Roman Catholic Church and the Mormon Church. Some religious groups use Scripture to justify patriarchy within a marriage. In 1997, for example, the First Baptist Church of Berryville, Arkansas, closed its day-care center, arguing that working mothers neglect their children, damage their marriages, and set a bad example. The board of directors of the day-care center said that it could not continue to run the center because it encouraged mothers to work outside the home. They cited the Bible for justification: "In Titus 2:5, women are instructed to be 'discreet, chaste, keepers at home, good and obedient to their own husbands'" (cited in Dodds, 1997:36A).

Obviously, the more intense one's belief in a religious ideology, the more control that ideology will have on one's behavior. When a couple shares that ideology, their marital behaviors will be shaped by the moral authority of their religion.

Societal Gender Expectations

Couples have always faced adjustments, but the problems inherent in marriages are now compounded by a critical difference—the changing societal definitions of roles for men and women. In the past, women and men entered into the marriage relationship with an unquestioned set of roles and responsibilities that each would fulfill. The husband would work outside the home and provide for the family's material needs, while the wife would take care of the home, raise the children, and provide for the emotional needs of the family members. He would achieve and she would support. Power would be asymmetrical, with the husband in charge. "She'd subordinate her life to his, and wouldn't even notice it; her needs for achievement and mastery would be met vicariously through his accomplishments or those of the children" (Rubin, 1983:1).

Contemporary U.S. society, however, is undergoing a profound shift in role expectations for men and women. Economic conditions in society that require greater numbers of women to work outside the home are creating new roles. Wives with outside jobs have less time and energy to spend on household tasks. They also have new income and skills that increase their decision-making status within the family. This is crucial, because the marriage relationship is affected vitally by who makes the money, how much discretionary income is available, the demands of the workplace on one or both marital partners, and other work-related issues.

Whereas before each partner knew with certainty what behaviors were expected, now there is ambiguity. Couples must now decide who will do what household tasks, who has the power and in what domains, and whether one or both partners will work outside the home. Most couples now enter marriage without a blueprint or any sure answers to these questions. As Lillian Rubin has said, "We know that the old ways are not for us, but have no clear picture yet of what the new ones will be. We know there's a new vision of masculinity and femininity, but can't figure out how it fits each of us" (Rubin, 1983:8).

Another difference with the past is that marriage and childrearing now define less of a person's social identity than at any time in U.S. history. According to Stephanie Coontz,

> A white woman can now expect, on the average, to spend only 43 percent of her life in marriage, while an African American woman can expect marriage to occupy only 22 percent of her life. Marriage has ceased to be the main impetus into or out of other statuses, and it increasingly coexists for women, as it has long done for men, with several other roles. The orderly progression from student to single job-holder to wife to mother to married older worker that prevailed from the 1920s to the 1960s, for example, is now gone. Modern women take on these functions in different orders or occupy all of them at once (Coontz, 1992:186).

RECENT TRENDS

For most of U.S. history, Americans have shared with virtual unanimity the following cultural beliefs (Cuber et al., 1975):

- Adults should be married.
- Marriage is a life-long commitment.
- Married couples should have children.
- A wife's place is at home as nurturer, mother, and caretaker.
- A husband's role is provider and decision maker.

Although many still hold fervently to these traditional beliefs, the behaviors of contemporary couples often contradict them. This raises the question: To what degree do U.S. marriages now conform to these traditional ideals of what family life should be? The statistics on contemporary marriages in the United States show a gap between the traditions of marriage and reality. Actually, only 7 percent of U.S. households fit the model of the father as sole breadwinner, and the mother staying home to raise their children. Families in which both parents work make up 17 percent of the population, 13 percent of working couples are childless, and 12 percent of all households are headed by women with children (*Population Today*, 1999b). This section surveys the statistical evidence on contemporary family patterns (see Figure 8.1 for a summary of how the composition of households changed from 1960 to 1998).

Nonmarried Adults

People living alone make up one-fourth of all households. There are three categories of nonmarried adults: never-married singles, lesbian and gay couples, and nonmarried heterosexual couples (for more details on these categories, see Chapter 12). The single-adult category ("one-person households") is on the rise. The proportion of never-married women and men between the ages of thirty and

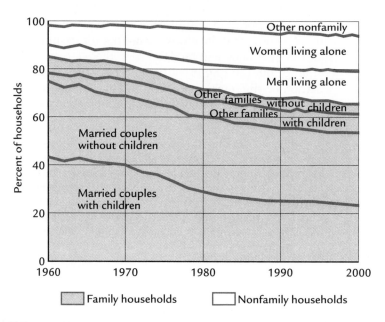

Figure 8.1

Trends in U.S. households, 1960–2000

Source: Suzanne M. Bianchi and Lynne M. Casper, "American Families," *Population Bulletin* 55 (December 2000):8.

thirty-four is more than triple the percentage of never-married single people in 1970. Of special note, demographers estimate that 25 percent of African American women will never marry, nearly three times the rate for White women. This gap reflects social developments, such as the shrinking pool of African American men that African American women would consider good partners, which is the result of disproportionately high unemployment, incarceration, and homicide rates for African American men.

Because state laws do not permit marriage between homosexuals, a long-term relationship between homosexuals is defined by the U.S. Census Bureau as a cohabitation arrangement. Because known homosexuals face discrimination, many keep their same-sex committed relationships secret. Thus, it is impossible to know the precise numbers. We do know that in 1998 there were 5.9 million households with two unrelated adults. Of these, 1.7 million were headed by adults of the same sex. We do not know how many of these were same-sex, sexual arrangements.

We do have a better estimate of heterosexual cohabitation. In 1998 there were 4.2 million households headed by unmarried couples (36 percent of all unmarried-couple households included a child under eighteen), up considerably from 1.6 million couples in 1980 and 523,000 in 1960 (Peterson, 2000a). More than half of opposite-sex first marriages are now preceded by cohabitation (most cohabiting couples either marry or split up within eighteen months). About half of cohabitating couples do marry each other. Ironically, cohabitating couples who marry have a somewhat higher divorce rate than those who marry without having lived together (Brown and Booth, 1996).

Another fact of interest is that 40 percent of all children will spend some time living with their mother and her cohabiting partner before they are age sixteen. Some will begin their lives in such a family. Others will be born to single mothers who later enter a cohabiting relationship. Still others will see their mothers enter such a relationship after a divorce. These data reflect profound changes in family forms.

> At the end of the twentieth century, the rapid increases in cohabitation and unmarried childbearing have dramatically altered family life in the United States (and, indeed, in most Western societies). Family boundaries have become more fluid and ambiguous, and the significance of marriage as a life-course marker in society appears to be declining. (Bumpass and Lu, 2000b:5).

Unmarried people live together for a number of reasons. Some are in same-sex relationships. Some want to share expenses. Some choose this option as a prelude to marriage. Others are older and do not want to lose financial benefits by marrying (Block, 1999). In this instance, many elderly couples choose cohabitation over matrimony because pensions are based on the status of being a widow or widower. Some estate plans are set up on the condition that the surviving spouse remain unmarried. And Social Security benefits can differ depending on the amount of assets someone holds singularly or jointly in a marriage. For example, Social Security regulations require seniors to remain below certain fixed income and asset levels to qualify for governmental benefits such as Supplemental Security Income and Medicaid. The combined incomes and assets of a married couple often exceed these limits. Moreover, recipients of Social Security, by staying single, receive $25,000 each in deductions toward paying taxes on their benefits. If married, and filing jointly, their maximum deduction would be $32,000. By not marrying, the cohabitating couple receive $18,000 in additional deductions (Chevan, 1996:660). Thus it is advantageous not to marry although continuing to live together as a couple.

Age at First Marriage

Marriage is still very much the norm, with about 90 percent of the population eventually marrying. However, the number of marriages is declining. From 1982 to 1999, the number of marriages per 1000 people declined from 10.5 to 8.4, the lowest since 1977. This relatively low rate is partly because people are marrying later. In 1960, the median age at first marriage for men was 22.8 years and for women 20.3 years. This contrasts with the 1998 statistics of 26.7 years for men and 25.0 years for women. Examined another way, the percentage of American women between the ages of 20 and 24 who had not yet married more than doubled, from 28 percent in 1960 to 66 percent in 1994. Figure 8.2 shows the historical trend for age at first marriage for more than 100 years. Most significant, these data show that the age of first marriage is higher for women now than at any time since data were first collected on this subject in 1889.

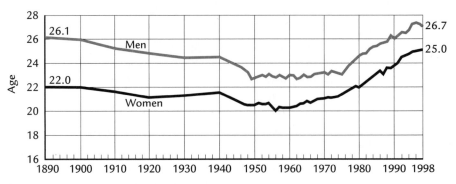

Figure 8.2

Median age at first marriage by sex: 1890–1998

Source: "Marital Status and Living Arrangements: March 1998," *Current Population Reports,* Series P-20, no. 514. Washington, DC: U.S. Bureau of the Census, 1998.

Philip Blumstein and Pepper Schwartz have summarized the major consequences of this trend:

> Delaying marriage gives a woman more opportunity for advanced education and training, reduces the number of children she will have, and ultimately gives her more independence and flexibility in making life choices. Its secondary effect is to give exactly the same advantages to her husband (Blumstein and Schwartz, 1983:31).

Family Size

Earlier we noted that marriages are expected to result in children. Several facts suggest that this expectation has undergone some changes. Some couples have chosen to remain childless, an almost unheard of alternative just a generation ago. Although it is impossible to predict with any accuracy because people do change their minds, it appears that about one in six women will never have children. Moreover, couples who choose to have children are having fewer of them than at any time in U.S. history (see Chapter 9). About 12 percent of households are headed by women. The result of these trends is that the average household is now 2.6 persons per household, compared to 3.1 some 30 years ago. Household size varies by race/ethnicity, with the size of White households in 1998 being 2.5, African American households at 2.8, Latinos at 3.0, and Asian Americans at 3.2 (*Population Today,* 1999a).

Racial or Ethnic Mixed Marriages

Interracial marriage was illegal in a number of states until 1967, when the U.S. Supreme Court overturned **miscegenation laws** in sixteen states, most of them southern. Those laws reflected the social norms of the time, that marrying someone outside one's race or ethnicity or even religion was wrong. But these age-old barriers are breaking down as the demographic landscape is changing from White to more and more non-White (much of the following is from Suro, 1999). The data show that there were 2.9 million interracial marriages in 1998, up from 1.5 million in 1980. Expressed as a percentage of all marriages, interracial marriages increased from 3 percent of the total in 1980 to 5 percent in 1998 (*Population Today*, 1999a). But while some are calling this trend "the beginning of the blend," the overwhelming tendency remains to marry within one's race (**homogamy**), with 95 percent of all marriages between partners of the same race.

Interracial and interethnic marriages vary by race and sex. African Americans are the least likely of all racial groups in the United States to marry outside their race. African American women, compared to African American men, are about one-third as likely to marry someone of another race. The dominant pattern for African American/White marriages is for African American men to marry White women, occurring almost twice as often as African American women marrying White men (Williams, 1999). This pattern is reversed for Asian Americans: a fifth of all married Asian American women have chosen a spouse of a different race or ethnicity, nearly twice the rate among Asian American men. Slightly more than half of all intergroup married couples in the United States have Latino and White spouses. Among Latinos, women are somewhat more likely to marry Whites than are men. Among the Latino subgroups, there is an overwhelming tendency to marry within one's group (i.e., 85 percent of Mexican Americans marry other Mexican Americans; Puerto Ricans and Cubans marry within their subgroups about 75 percent of the time) (Farley, 1996:262). To summarize,

> African Americans have the strongest endogamy, followed by Asian Americans, by Hispanics, and then by Whites. Marriage across racial barriers is much less common than marriage within each racial group. Marriages between Whites and a racial minority are the most typical type of interracial marriage [because of the disproportionate number of Whites in the marriage pool]. Interracial marriages are highest between Whites and Asian Americans, followed by those between Whites and Hispanics. Though on the rise, interracial marriage between Whites and African Americans is the lowest (Qian, 1997:271).

The extent of interracial marriage depends on a number of factors, not the least of which is availability. When social contact is restricted by race, interracial marriage is rare. Social contacts among racial groups depend on the race relations in a community and the extent of residential and school segregation. Intermarriage between Whites and Latinos or Asian Americans is more likely than between Whites and African Americans because the former are much more likely than the latter to live in predominantly White neighborhoods and attend integrated schools. Similarly, the higher the educational attainment, the greater is the likelihood of interracial marriage. Men and women with higher educational attainments are more likely to live in racially integrated neighorhoods and to have more interracial contacts in the workplace. "Therefore, they may be less prejudiced against people of other racial groups, mix relatively freely with people of a similar bent in other racial groups, and consequently, be more likely to intermarry based on 'romantic love'" (Qian, 1997:273).

Couples have the potential to live together for fifty years or more.

Life Span and Marriage

A critical difference between this and earlier generations is that people now live much longer. Between 1920 and 2000, for example, the life expectancy for women increased by 24 years—from 55 to 79 years. And men's life expectancy increased by 19 years—from 54 to 73 years. This dramatic increase in longevity means that now couples have the potential to live approximately 50 years together, the last 25 of which are free of child-rearing responsibilities. This shift has contradictory effects on marital relationships. On the one hand, there is more time to build an enduring bond that provides for mutual sharing and happiness as the needs of each are met in a growing commitment to the relationship. More realistically, though, people often change through the life cycle, with alterations in personality, identity, and needs. With longer life spans, there is the greater possibility of people growing apart. The type of partner one required at the age of 25 may be quite different from the type desired at 50 or 70. This new longevity is one explanation for the relatively high divorce rate. Clearly, the understanding of contemporary marriages requires examination of the different and changing forces that act on the relationship throughout the life cycle.

Divorce

The divorce rate accelerated in the 1970s and peaked in 1981 at 5.2 couples divorcing per 1000 people in the population (for an elaboration on divorce, see Chapter 11). Since then it has declined a bit and appears to have stabilized at 4.2 couples divorcing per 1000 people (1998). At current rates, about half of all marriages will end in divorce. The divorce rate varies by race and ethnicity. African American couples are more likely than White or Latino couples to divorce. At current rates, as many as two-thirds of all recent African American marriages will end in divorce. By the age of sixteen, only about one out of every three White children, compared with two out of every three African American children, will experience the dissolution of their parents' marriage.

Remarriage

More than four out of ten marriages in the United States involve a second or higher-order marriage for one or both of the marriage partners (Miller, 1993). Remarriage has been common throughout U.S. history, but until the last fifty years or so, the typical remarriage followed widowhood (see Chapter 11). Now more than 90 percent of remarriages involve either a bride or a groom who was divorced.

The majority of divorced persons remarry: five out of six men and about three out of four women eventually do so.

Several variables affect the probability of remarriage. The age of women is crucial, with older women much less likely to remarry than younger women. The remarriage prospect of younger women with children is less than it is for younger women without children. Race is also significant. African Americans, for example, are much less likely than Whites to remarry. Whereas two-thirds of White women remarry, only about one-third of African American women do so. This, of course, is another reason why African American women are more likely than White women to head households that have children under the age of eighteen with no husband present. If we do not take race into account, the evidence is that those who remarry tend to do so soon after the divorce, with about one-half of all remarriages occurring within three years. One result of this trend is that about one-fifth of all existing marriages include at least one previously divorced spouse. This strong propensity for divorced persons to remarry suggests that people are not disillusioned with marriage as such but with a specific spouse.

ARE THERE BENEFITS TO MARRIAGE?

Sociologist Linda J. Waite has argued that married people, when compared to the never married, the divorced, and the widowed, are happier, healthier, and better off financially. Waite's research and argument are efforts to promote marriage in the face of a number of societal trends that diminish the importance of marriage, such as increased rates of cohabitation, later age of first marriage, fewer children per family, and a high divorce rate. Moreover, her argument represents one side in a debate between those who wish to promote traditional marriage (organizations such as the Institute for American Values) and those who argue that family forms are shaped by social and economic forces (organizations such as the Council on Contemporary Families).

The Benefits of Marriage

Individuals marry for a variety of reasons. These include the obvious ones, such as companionship, intimacy, economic security, and stability. This section focuses on other benefits that derive from being married (the following is primarily from Waite, 1995; 1999; 2000; and Waite and Gallagher, 2000).

To begin, the marriage relationship promotes healthy behaviors. Research shows that the unmarried are far more likely than the married to die from all causes, including heart disease, stroke, pneumonia, many kinds of cancer, cirrhosis of the liver, automobile accidents, murder, and suicide. There are many reasons why marriage promotes better health. When the married are compared with the nonmarried of the same age and the divorced, the married, especially husbands, are less likely to engage in risky behaviors such as excessive drinking, drinking and driving, substance abuse, and multiple sexual partners (smoking, however, is unaffected by marital status, except that pregnant women are likely to quit cigarettes). Divorce is associated with a return to bad habits, whereas remarriages drive down drug and alcohol use once again (Schwartz, 1997). Waite and Gallagher (2000) posit that marriage affects health by providing individuals, especially men, with someone who monitors their health and who encourages self-regulation. Moreover, the support by a spouse, usually the wife, helps individuals deal with stressful situations and to recover more rapidly from surgery and other health problems. Marriage also provides individuals with a sense of meaning in their lives and a sense of obligation and responsibility to others.

The married have better mental health than the nonmarried. Summarizing the research, Waite and Gallagher say, "Married men and women report less depression, less anxiety, and lower levels of other types of psychological distress than do those who are single, divorced, or widowed" (2000:67). Their interpretation of the research findings is that

> New marriage partners together create a shared sense of social reality and meaning—their own little separate world, populated by only the two of them. This shared sense of meaning can be an important foundation for emotional health. Ordinary, good-enough marriages provide the partners with a sense that what they do matters, that someone cares for, esteems, needs, loves, and values them as a person. No matter what else happens in life, this knowledge makes problems easier to bear (Waite and Gallagher, 2000:75).

Marriage also enhances the sex lives of the partners. Waite and Gallagher, after surveying the research, conclude that "Married people have both more and better sex than singles do. They not only have sex more often, but they enjoy it more, both physically and emotionally, than do their unmarried counterparts. . . . Marriage, it turns out, is not only good for you, it is good for your libido too" (Waite and Gallagher, 2000:79).

B. Smaller

"Do you realize we've been together through three versions of Windows?"

The married have more economic resources (income, pension and Social Security benefits, financial assets, and the value of their primary residence) than the nonmarried. This economic advantage stems from the increase in productivity by husbands (compared to nonmarried men) and because both spouses in so many marriages are now in the labor force. The greater economic advantages of married couples explain many of the benefits that Waite and others associate with the marriage bond itself. With greater affluence comes better nutrition, better access to private dentists, physicians, psychiatrists, and hospitals, a greater likelihood of living in a safe neighborhood, more travel and quality leisure, and the opportunity to experience the good things in life. So, it may not be the marriage bond itself that generates better emotional and physical healthy for the partners, but the greater resources generated.

This raises the question as to whether marriage produces these results or the effects of marriage are due to selectivity (that is, those with more orderly and healthy lives, and who are responsible and hard-working, are more likely to marry than those with opposite traits). Selectivity may explain some of the differences, but the experts conclude that marriage *causes* some of the better outcomes we find for the married. Waite (1995:498) argues that there are four factors surrounding marriage that make it cause the aforementioned outcomes: (1) the institution of marriage assumes a long-term contract, which provides the couple with social support by imposing social and economic costs on those who dissolve the union; (2) marriage assumes the sharing of economic and social resources, which is a form of co-insurance, protecting the partners from unexpected events; (3) married couples benefit from economies of scale (that is, two can live almost as cheaply as one in terms of transportation, electricity, telephone, appliances, residence); and (4) marriage connects people to others, to social groups, and to other social institutions. These connections provide individuals with a sense of obligation to others, which gives life meaning beyond oneself.

The Benefits of Marriage Reconsidered

Marriage matters. Married people have more resources, are better networked, and are healthier, leaving little doubt that marriage is beneficial. But we must evaluate this generalization cautiously. Obviously, not all marriages are advantageous to the partners. Some marriages are abusive. Some partners are abandoned by their spouses. Some marriages are empty of love and caring. Clearly, the emotional needs of the partners are not being met in these marriages The relatively high divorce rate is ample evidence that marriages are not blissful for millions of couples. But let's go beyond these obvious negatives. Consider, first, the generalization that married couples have more resources than the unmarried. Marriage actually decreases the economic benefits for some. The marriage of two poor people, especially among the poor from racial minorities, results in being poor *within* marriages (Catanzarite and Ortiz, 1996). The economies of scale that benefit most marriages are reversed when both spouses are unemployed or underemployed. Many of these couples "play by the rules"—that is, they are married and they work—but they are still poor, poorer than White couples (Lichter and Landale, 1995). Put another way, "The issues facing impoverished Black families [and Latino and Native American families] are different from those facing poor Whites: Low-income African Americans are much more likely than low-income Whites to have an income only *half or less* of the poverty-level figure, and to be trapped in areas where at least 40 percent of the population is also poor" (Coontz, 1997:24). The lack of resources of poor couples adds stress as they have difficulty meeting basic family needs for shelter, clothing, health care, and safety. "In communities where men have historically had limited ability to be breadwinners, the decline in employment has brought an increase in domestic violence, alcoholism, and other problems associated with joblessness" (Dill, 1998:B8). Lower wages or underemployment, more common to racial minorities than to Whites, requires working longer hours, which means less companionship and more pressure on the marital bond. Thus, generalizations about the benefits of marriage are neutralized or even reversed when the social locations of class and race and included (Wells and Baca Zinn, 2000).

Most crucial is the inclusion of gender into the equation. Each marriage is the creation of a new social unit. The two members of this unit—in which the interaction is intense and the feelings intimate—do not, strange as it may seem, always share the same interpretations and reap the same rewards from their shared life. The fundamental reason for this is that the two members in a marriage differ by gender. Society, through the socialization process and through various institutions, imprints girls and boys, women and men with the customary expectations and behaviors deemed appropriate for each gender within a marriage.

By dissecting the family, we see that the sex-gender system structures women's and men's family lives differently. One of the most useful ways of understanding this is Jessie Bernard's concept of "his" and "her" marriages. Bernard's classic work (1972) on marriage revealed that every marital union actually contains two marriages, which do not always coincide.

The Husband's Marriage

Men receive greater health benefits than women from marriage. Waite and Gallagher conclude: "Marriage does not affect men and women in exactly the same ways. Both men and women live longer, healthier, and wealthier lives when married, but husbands typically get greater health benefits from marriage than do wives" (Waite and Gallagher, 2000:163). One advantage is that husbands, in general, receive more social support in commitment and caring from their spouses than they return. They do, in general, work more hours outside the home than their wives, but the work load is rarely equal when housework, child care, and emotional work are tallied.

The Wife's Marriage

Waite's research shows that wives, generally, benefit from marriage, but less so than husbands. Wives are relatively disadvantaged in marriages; typically, they have to deal with patriarchy (the dominance of the husband), their secondary status at home, at work, and in society, and their "triple" day's work. A full-time homemaker does the family's "dirty work"—cooking, cleaning, and other household chores that she may interpret as drudgery and even demeaning. Her wishes are secondary to those of her breadwinning husband. Two-career families generate stressors for wives as they, typically, work full-time and still do the majority of the housework. When children are added, mothers devote much more time and emotional energy to their children than fathers do. "The failure of men to share housework and child care with their partners. . . is a primary source of overload for working mothers and a major cause of marital conflict. . . . Marital dissatisfaction and divorce frequently originate when modern parents backslide into traditional roles after the birth of a child" (Coontz, 1997:109-110). The problem is especially acute for employed housewives who work "three shifts": a day job; family and household chores at night; and relationship maintenance (Peterson, 1993b).

To summarize, the generalization that marriage is beneficial to the spouses is too facile. We can only answer the question, "Who benefits from marriage?" by examining the social location of the partners in a marriage. This means including the social class and race/ethnicity of the spouses. And we must include the lesson of Jessie Bernard that every marriage union is actually two marriages. In effect, then, marriage matters, but the degree to which it matters is affected by social class, race, and gender.

MICRO ASPECTS OF MARRIAGE

In addition to the dynamics of gender, the partners in a marriage must deal with three issues on an ongoing basis: communication and other correlates of marital success, sexual intimacy, and decision making.

Marital Success

Studies of marriage have uncovered some of the diversity in the quality of modern marriages. A well-known study by John Cuber and Peggy Haroff (1965) revealed that enduring marriages differ in important ways from one another, and they differ as well from the ideals of happy marriages. The intent of these researchers was to study "normal" couples rather than those in crisis. Their sample represented the upper end of the occupational distribution, and they interviewed 437 American women and men between the ages of thirty-five and fifty. One of the most widely quoted findings of the study is its description of five types of enduring marriage. Cuber and Haroff (1965:43–65) discovered enormous variation within a group of stable marriages among people of similar class positions, thus destroying the myth that happy families are all alike (Skolnick, 1983:276).

- *Conflict-habituated marriages* centered on tensions, arguments and fights. Conflict in these marriages was not always readily observable to outsiders, but it was always present in various forms including nagging, quarrelling, sarcasm, put-downs, and even physical combat (although it may not include that). A conflict-habituated way of interaction could last a lifetime.
- *Devitalized marriages* involved couples who were once in love but had drifted apart over the years. They remained together in a relationship bound by duty.
- *Passive congenial marriages* were those in which love was not expected, but the marriage provided stability for the couple to direct their energies elsewhere.
- *Vital marriages* differed greatly from the foregoing types in that spouses shared true intimacy in all important life matters. Husbands and wives found their central satisfaction in the life they lived with and through each other.
- *Total marriages,* the fifth type, were like the vital relationship with the important addition of being more multifaceted. Such marriages involved couples who were completely absorbed in one another's life activities, often including their work.

Cuber and Haroff's successful American marriages were by no means all happy, but they remained intact. Are they successful if they remain intact, or is there more to marital success?

There are two measures of marital success. The first is marital stability (the subject of Chapter 11). This variable is easily measured because it refers to the simple and objective reality of whether the marriage is intact. The problem, as illustrated by some of the marital types delineated by Cuber and Haroff, is that this is not necessarily an indicator of marital quality because one or both of the partners in an intact marriage may not find the relationship satisfying at all, yet they do not separate.

Marital quality, the focus of our discussion here, is the other measure of marital success. This refers to the ways in which the husband and wife describe and evaluate the character of their relationship. This subjective and therefore elusive evaluation of marriages goes to the heart of the matter. The questions directed by researchers to spouses involve such matters as the degree of conflict, success at conflict resolution, extent of shared activities, feelings of happiness, communication patterns, sexual behaviors, and financial planning.

The Correlates of Marital Quality

Literally hundreds of studies have examined marital quality, and their findings are summarized here.

Shared Social Characteristics Research has shown consistently that spouses who are alike in the social characteristics of socioeconomic status, religion, race, age, and intelligence (i.e., they are homogamous) tend to have marriages that are higher in quality than those who differ on these dimensions. The underlying explanation for the relative success of **homogamous marriages** is that persons who share similar characteristics adjust more easily to each other and are more likely to agree on values, politics, and religion, thus increasing the chances for harmony.

Economic and Personal Resources The higher the income, education, and occupational status of the couple, the more they are likely to evaluate their marriage as good. Actually, such a positive evaluation may not reflect happiness per se but rather a convenience that both affluent spouses find important to their well-being. Randall Collins (1988b) has suggested that success itself can hold a marriage together, given the economic incentives to do so. Couples lower in the class system have more reason to separate, which, in fact, they do.

Dual-Earner Couples Both spouses in the labor force has contradictory effects on marital happiness. Positively, working wives have better mental health (e.g., better self-concept, less depression). Dual-career couples are more able to live a middle-class lifestyle. Also, having more discretionary income than single-career marriages eliminates or at least alleviates one major source of marital stress.

On the negative side, many wives in the labor force work at menial jobs for minimum wages. More than 70 percent of wives in the labor force work at such jobs as clerks and cashiers, nurses' aides, secretaries, and maids, compared to the less than 30 percent of wives who hold executive or professional jobs (Kilborn, 1994). This means that most working wives have demanding but low-status jobs at which they take orders. They may bring their job-induced resentments home with them. Husbands, too, may resent the extra demands on them as their wives work outside the home. Wives may also be burdened with the guilt of leaving their children with caretakers. Two solutions to the day-care dilemma may also have negative effects on marriages. The first is to be employed but work at home doing such work as word processing or phone solicitation. While doing this contingency work the mother is with her children, but she has now stacked her outside work demands on top of child-care demands. A second solution is for the spouses to work different shifts so that one spouse is always home with the children. The obvious downside to this is that the spouses spend little quality time with each other. Sociologist Lynn White, in a study of 1700 night-shift employees, found that they were one and a half times more likely to divorce than those who work normal hours (cited in Ingrassia, 1993).

Noteworthy is that when both spouses are in the labor force, the strategy these couples adopt to cope with family needs (reduced work time, contingency work, or dual work shifts) "may 'work' in terms of allocating time to home and family, but only serves to perpetuate gendered relations and inequalities at home and at work" (Moen and Yu, 2000:316).

The Division of Household Labor   The division of labor at home is another factor in marital quality (see Chapter 6). Research shows that among dual-earner families, wives spend on average about twice as much time on household tasks (34 hours per week) as their husbands (18 hours per week) (Presser, 1993). In general, the greater the educational attainment of men, the more they share in traditionally female housework. Also, husbands whose wives have similar or more prestigious occupations than their own do more housework than other husbands. Race/ethnicity is also an important variable, as Asian American and Latino men of all ages are more likely than Anglo men to do *less* housework. This is even stronger when the "Latino and Asian men live in ethnic neighborhoods—settings where they are embedded in an intergenerational community and where the language and culture of the home country is kept alive by a steady stream of new immigrants" (Rubin, 1994:91).

Even when the housework assignments are shared, wives often feel more responsibility than their husbands to take charge. Consider the following situation, described and explained by Terri Apter:

> "I'll be trying to work upstairs and he's supposed to be in charge," explained Ann Nuccio, who was preparing for an exam to obtain a real estate license. "But I hear the children fighting and Gail is crying and Sam is screaming, and he's just sitting there in front of the TV. So I march down and say 'What's all this about?' and he says it's okay, they'll be all right. When are they going to be all right? When Sam's nose gets smashed. I say 'The boy's crying, it's not all right.' Does he think this house is a boxing ring? What's this 'all right' business? It's all right for him because he doesn't hear. Just doesn't hear it the way I do." (Apter, 1993:159)

Agreements to share child care often founder on this impasse, as the "off-duty" mother is quicker to see the children as needing a parent's input than is the "on-duty" father. Hence the mother either steps in herself, and in taking charge shows the father that he is not doing what they both agreed would be his job, or confronts the father directly, positioning herself as overseer of the job her husband should be doing, and thereby increasing her tasks. Either way, she is no longer free for her "off-duty" work (Apter, 1993:159).

The division of the housework is a source of marital tension in at least two additional ways. Obviously, wives who work outside the home tend to resent their husbands who work only half as much as they do on household maintenance. In the words of Lillian Rubin,

> Now, women feel obliged to hold up their share of the family economy—a partnership men welcome. In return, women believe they're entitled to their husbands' full participation in domestic labor. And here is the rub. For while men enjoy the fruits of their wives' paid work outside the home, they have been slow to accept the reciprocal responsibilities—that is, to become real partners in the work inside the home (Rubin, 1994:87).

Husbands often resent the escalating demands of their wives to engage in housework because they are (in five out of six marriages) making the larger income. This makes them feel more powerful but also more vulnerable to economic uncertainties as companies downsize or move their operations to low-wage locales (Rubin, 1994:87). Husbands, at least the more traditional ones, even when they do only half as much household work as their wives, may also resent it because what they are doing is much more than their fathers did. This leads to the next source of marital difficulties—**role fit.**

Role Fit The term *role fit* refers to the degree of consensus between the spouses on decision making, the division of household labor, spending money, and issues involving children, such as how many to have, when to have them, and how to discipline them.

Social Class Research has shown that couples vary by social class in what their expectations are for husbands and wives in a marriage (see Box 8.2). The consistent finding is that working-class couples are more likely than middle-class couples to accept the traditional gender roles in marriage.

Children There is a consistent curvilinear relationship between family stage and marital quality. Mary Benin and Linda Robinson (1997), for example, found in a study of 6785 couples that, on average, marital quality is higher in the preparental and postparental states (see Figure 8.3). Children doubtless enrich couples in many ways, but marital quality tends to suffer nonetheless. A major reason for this is that time once devoted to the marital relationship now is directed toward the child or children. Children are costly, and the resulting economic stress may also lead to marital stress. The problems of children, especially older children (e.g., school performance, social relationships, sexual behavior, and adolescent rebellion), are crucial concerns and may produce tension between spouses.

Research also shows that marital quality tends to suffer when a child has special needs (e.g., is hyperactive) or is handicapped in some way. Especially difficult is a situation where the parents must take care of their child throughout the couple's life. Factors affecting marital quality are the strength of the marital relationship before the birth of their handicapped child, the severity of the child's handicap, the availability of a support network including health and education services, and the economic resources of the family.

Researching Families: The Effects of Gender and Social Class on the Division of Labor and Perceptions of Equality in Dual-Earner Marriages

Maureen Perry-Jenkins and Karen Polk (1994) investigated the possible effects of gender and social class on the division of labor in dual-earner marriages. Using data from a national sample, the researchers isolated 656 dual-earner couples where both spouses were employed full time. Social class was defined individually for each spouse in a marriage, taking into account the nature of his or her work (skill level, giving or taking orders). Thus, each spouse was designated as either working class or middle class. This resulted in four categories of families: (1) both spouses middle class; (2) both spouses working class; (3) husband working class/wife middle class; and (4) husband middle class/wife working class.

Findings

1. Wives in all categories performed the majority of the typically "feminine" tasks within the household.
2. Working-class wives, regardless of whether they were married to working-class or middle-class husbands, did a significantly higher proportion of traditionally feminine household chores than families in which the wife was in a middle-class occupation. Thus, "it is actually wives' class level, not husbands,' that is related to the division of feminine tasks" (p. 177).
3. Wives in the both-working-class group reported significantly higher amounts of marital conflicts than wives in the both-middle-class group.
4. Perceptions of what is a fair domestic workload in a marriage relationship differ by gender and social class.
5. The perception of equity in household work was positively related to marital satisfaction for wives in all categories, whereas for husbands no relationships emerged between household work and marital satisfaction.

Source: Maureen Perry-Jenkins and Karen Polk, "Class, Couples, and Conflict: Effects of the Division of Labor on Assessments of Marriage in Dual-Earner Families," *Journal of Marriage and the Family* 56 (February 1994):165–180.

Life Cycle Marital quality appears to change through the life cycle. The level of satisfaction, typically, is highest in the early years of marriage and is lowest when children are teenagers. This may be the result of the strain added to the relationship by children, or it may just be a function of time. Norval Glenn (1989) found that marital success, as indicated by the percentage of married persons who say that their marriages are "very happy," goes steadily and appreciably downward in a marriage cohort for at least the first ten years. Although the evidence is conflicting, there appears to be some increase in satisfaction when the children leave home and the couple is more financially secure. In general, however, there tends to be a loss of intimacy in marriages over time. For many couples marriages become devitalized. The frequency of sexual intercourse and

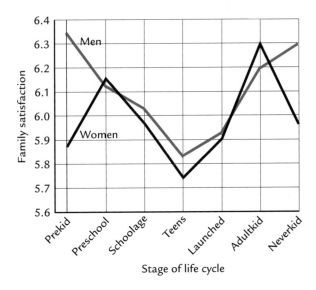

Figure 8.3

Family satisfaction by sex of respondent (scale of 1 "very unhappy" to 7 "very happy")

Source: Mary Holland Benin and Linda B. Robinson, "Marital Happiness across the Family Life Cycle: A Longitudinal Analysis," a paper presented at the American Sociological Association annual meeting, August 1997.

other forms of physical intimacy diminishes, the number of shared activities declines, and the frequency and quality of communication drop.

Communication in Marriage

Mary Anne Fitzpatrick, a keen analyst of communication in marriage, argues that communication is the crucial determinant of marital success:

> For many years, scholars tried to find predictors of marital success or failure by looking at social/demographic factors such as income, education, age at marriage, and the age difference between husband and wife. But social scientists now believe that these factors are far less important than the communication between partners. For example, it is not the lack of money that causes marital problems, but rather how the couples communicate and negotiate with each other about their economic difficulties (Fitzpatrick, 1988:31).

Marriage is the most intimate of relationships. The partners in marriage must continually define their relationship through communication. They must work out their own miniculture, with rules that will guide their living together. They must determine such things as how the money will be managed, how work will be divided, how clean their house will be, and how they will spend their leisure time. Moreover, they must work out their rules for communication with each other. How critical will they be of each other in dealing with the other's mistakes, failures, irritating mannerisms, emotional hang-ups, and lifestyle? Which topics are appropriate for discussion, and which are taboo (e.g., sexual matters are a common communications problem)? In short, how open shall the communication be? As Kenneth Kammeyer has put it, "Knowing when to and when not to say something to one's spouse requires both skill and sensitivity. Many married people know intuitively there are limits to openness and honesty in marriage" (Kammeyer, 1987:240).

Communication in intimate relationships is a complex and powerful phenomenon. Words can be emotionally charged, but the interpretations of these words vary from individual to individual and can evoke different responses in the same individuals depending on their mood or the setting. Moreover, nonverbal behaviors such as facial expressions and body language produce strong positive or negative messages. These nonverbal cues also run the risk of being misinterpreted. The refusal to speak—"clamming up"—communicates a strong message to the other and may drive a wedge between the spouses. At the other extreme, one partner talking incessantly likely will not enhance intimacy among the spouses. Likewise, nagging, complaining, ordering, and scolding communicate, but they do not strengthen the marriage bond. On the other hand, positive communication, such as words of endearment, support, care, praise, and respect, is likely to draw the spouses together.

The degree of intimacy in marriages can be revealed in the different styles spouses use to communicate with one another. Their interaction may be aggressive or passive. They may be verbal or nonverbal. Affection may be expressed with "I love you" or through touching, listening, gifts, time, favors, food, or sexuality (Galvin and Brommel, 1999:111–114).

Role segregation makes communication problematic for many couples. As they go about their separate activities, they may find that they have less and less to talk about. This is especially true in blue-collar families, where roles are traditionally segregated. Lack of economic resources makes it difficult for wives and husbands to go out by themselves, and so they spend time with relatives in sex-segregated activities (e.g., the men watching a ball game on television while the women prepare meals and watch over children). Leisure time spent in the home includes little real interaction. The following excerpt from Lillian Rubin's study of working-class families illustrates the separateness of wives and husbands:

> Frank comes home from work; now it's about five, because he's been working overtime every night. We eat right away, right after he comes home. Then, I don't know. The kids play a while before bed, watch t.v., you know, stuff like that. Then, I don't know . . . maybe watch more t.v. or something like that. I don't know what else— nothing, I guess. We just sit, that's all. The husband: I come home at five and we eat supper right away. Then, I sit down with coffee and a beer and watch t.v. After that, if I'm working on a project I do that for a while. If not, I just watch t.v. (Rubin, 1976:93).

Gender differences make communication in intimate relations sometimes difficult. Men and women are different in their linguistic habits. Men talk more, interrupt more, and dominate more in conversations. Women listen more, ask more questions, and are less assertive (Basow, 1992). Deborah Tannen, a sociolinguist, argues that men in conversations seek to dominate, while women seek to connect. Consider Tannen's analysis of a situation with her husband:

> My husband was simply engaging the world in a way that many men do: as an individual in a hierarchical social order in which he was either one-up or one-down. In this world conversations are negotiations in which people try to achieve and maintain the upper hand if they can, and protect themselves from others' attempts to put them down and push them around. Life, then, is a contest, a struggle to preserve independence and avoid failure.
>
> I, on the other hand, was approaching the world as many women do: as an individual in a network of connections. In this world, conversations are negotiations for closeness in which people try to seek and give confirmation and support, and to reach consensus. They try to protect themselves from others' attempts to push them away. Life, then, is a community, a struggle to preserve intimacy and avoid isolation. Though there are hierarchies in this world too, they are hierarchies more of friendship than of power and accomplishment.
>
> Women are also concerned with achieving status and avoiding failure, but these are not the goals they are focused on all the time, and they tend to pursue them in the guise of connection. And men are also concerned with achieving involvement and avoiding isolation, but they are not focused on these goals, and they tend to pursue them in the guise of opposition (Tannen, 1990:24–25).

Gay and lesbian couples, like their heterosexual counterparts, have to negotiate their roles, the division of labor, disputes, and develop problem-solving strategies (Galvin and Brommel, 1999). They are at a disadvantage, however, given their marginal status in society. Blumstein and Schwartz (1983) note that young homosexuals are denied role models of positive images of long-term same-sex relationships. Society denies them legitimacy. Often they lack a full support network, not even their own families. Without these social supports, the lesbian or gay couple negotiates each situation without relying on societal expectations or previous gender role models for their answers. This increases the potential for increased tensions within each relationship.

The Sexual Relationship in Marriage

The marriage relationship assumes sexual relations. The patterns of sexual behavior that develop between spouses depend on the particular combination of the spouses—their histories, needs, religious beliefs, sexual interests—as well as such factors as work schedules, the demands of parenting, how much privacy they have at home, physical and emotional health, and stress. Each couple must work out their unique sexual life, gradually determining such issues as the best time for sex, the appropriate frequency of sex, the desires of their partner, and the most satisfying form of foreplay and afterplay for both. Obviously, these will vary from couple to couple. But while the patterns of sexual intimacy in marriage are in some ways unique to each couple, there are some general patterns.

Gendered Sexual Intimacy

Women and men differ in their sexuality (the following information is taken from Thompson and Walker, 1991). Women, more so than men, get pleasure from the entire sexual experience—kissing, holding, touching, and intercourse—while men tend to focus more on intercourse. Men are more likely than women to be less inhibited about oral sex and to receive more pleasure from it. Men find the physical attractiveness of their partners more important to their sexual interest than do women. Men are more likely to initiate sexual behavior than women. When married couples disagree on sex, the man's wishes are more likely to prevail. Summarizing the differences between wives and husbands on sexual behaviors, Thompson and Walker state that "in general, then, men are more likely than women to orchestrate sexual intimacy in marriage, and wives often alter their own sexual desires and actions to please and protect their husbands" (Thompson and Walker, 1991:78).

The Sexual Stages of Marriage

In general, marriages in the United States are founded on romantic love. This type of love involves an obsessive focus on one person, a person to whom one is drawn personally, emotionally, and sexually. This total absorption in one's lover continues, typically, through the first months or years in a marriage. During this period, compared with later stages, sexual contact occurs most often. For example, Blumstein and Schwartz (1983) studied 12,000 couples and found that 45 percent of couples married less than two years had sex three or more times a week, while 27 percent of those married from two to ten years and 18 percent of those married more than ten years had sex that often.

Frequency of intercourse, of course, is not necessarily a measure of marital satisfaction. The decline in coital frequency over time does indicate a fading of romantic love. It does not necessarily indicate a lessening of love and affection.

"How am I this morning? Frankly, Mister Never-Around,
I'm as horny as the middle-school band."

At the risk of oversimplifying a complex phenomenon, marriages appear to move through three sexual stages (Frank and Anderson, 1989). The first is the romantic stage, during which the partners are greatly involved with each other and there is considerable erotic activity. The second stage, which occurs in the middle years, is one in which sexual behaviors become less important to the relationship. Wives and husbands in this stage widen their focus beyond each other to children, career advancement, and economic uncertainties. The later years of marriage are characterized by less frequent intercourse and more sexual dysfunction (older men have more difficulty in achieving and maintaining erections, while older women are more likely to be less excited about sex and more resigned to the sexual relationship than when they were younger).

Sex as Power

Sexual behavior can be more than an expression of physical desire. It can involve a power struggle between wives and husbands. Kenneth Kammeyer has summarized the ways in which couples, even "happy" couples, can use sex as an instrument of power:

> This is often done through the necessary acts of initiating sex and refusing it. Someone has to take the first step, and when either the husband or wife does so, the other person has to respond. That response can be positive or negative. Both of these actions have implications about power. How individuals use these actions can tell us about how much power each partner has and how sex can be used to control the other person. . . . When husbands and wives are equally committed to a relationship there is a greater freedom to share equally in initiating sex and being able to refuse without seriously hurting the other. Some indirect evidence for this interpretation is found in the observation that the partner who is more committed to the relationship (more in love) is more likely to be refused after taking the initiative. When husbands are more in love than their wives, their requests for sex are refused much more often than when the wife is more in love. This suggests that refusing sex (or not refusing it) is not simply a reflection of sexual desire, but is used as an instrument of power (Kammeyer, 1987:284).

Power and Decision Making in Marriage

Power is defined as the ability of an individual to produce intended results from the behavior of others (Szinovacz, 1987:652). Power in a marriage involves the ability of a wife and husband to influence each other. The questions regarding which spouse in a marriage has power, and over what, are complex ones involving a number of dimensions.

Sources of Power in Marriage

The sources of marital power are several, involving social stratification, societal norms, social class, race/ethnicity, and individual factors.

Social Stratification U.S. society is stratified by gender, race, and social class, which, of course, affects all families embedded within it. Women because of their secondary status in society are limited, typically, to lower-status occupations, with fewer benefits, and relatively low wages—all of which reduce their power within families. The limited opportunities for racial minorities translates into economic disadvantages for them, which affects the distribution of power within their families.

Social Class Husbands in all social classes generally have greater power than wives, although we find important differences in the operation of marital power. "Patriarchal" and "traditional" are terms frequently applied to working-class families, while "democratic" and "egalitarian" are terms applied to middle-class families. Many studies have shown that not all working-class or middle-class families conform to these descriptions. In fact, it can be argued that the power advantage of middle-class husbands is greater than that of working-class husbands simply because they possess the resources and the status that can be translated into power. The stereotype of the egalitarian middle-class marriage persists partly because the middle class has a more egalitarian ideology than the working class. However, the ideology and the actual distribution of power are at odds. As William Goode has observed, "Lower class men concede fewer rights ideologically than their women in fact obtain, and the more educated men are more likely to concede more rights ideologically than they in fact grant" (Goode, 1963:21).

Rubin's (1976) comparison of working-class and middle-class marriages revealed differences in the expression of male power. Even in the middle class, however, the ideology of equality conflicts with the superior power held by husbands. White middle-class wives who do not work outside the home have less power in the marital relationship than any other group. The better educated and more successful the husband, the less power the wife is likely to have. Middle-class husbands actually have several sources of power that working-class husbands do not have. Male dominance is legitimized by the patriarchy in the larger society. Furthermore, material and professional resources justify control of family decisions and activities. This means that middle-class men can "accept the doctrine of equality without having to live it" (Gillespie, 1972:134). Working-class and lower-class men have culturally legitimized power resting in their masculinity, but few material sources of power. William J. Goode has pointed to the

> frequent assertion from families of professional men that they should not make demands which would interfere with his work: He takes preference as a professional, not as a family head or as a male; nevertheless, the precedence is his. By contrast, lower class men demand deference as men, as heads of families (Goode, 1963:21).

The "traditionalism" of working-class men must be seen in the larger context of societal patriarchy that upholds male control but distributes unequally the resources needed to exercise control. In the absence of resources and status, masculinity itself takes on a distinctive significance. And in the absence of a valued "place" in institutions of the larger society, the family remains a setting in which male control can be imposed. It is not that working-class men are more authoritarian, but that they have fewer arenas in which power can be exercised.

> The professional middle-class man is more secure, has more status and prestige than the working-class man—factors which enable him to assume a less overtly

authoritarian role within the family. There are, after all, other places, other situations where his authority and power are tested and accorded legitimacy. . . . In contrast, for the working-class man, there are few such rewards in the world outside the home; the family usually is the only place where he can exercise power, demand obedience to his authority (Rubin, 1976:99).

Race and Ethnicity Power in racial-ethnic families has often been reported to be different from that in White families. African American families have been described as less male-dominated, and Latino families as more male-dominated, than White families. These portrayals are oversimplified accounts of power and authority in minority families. Although racial-ethnic variations do exist, new research contradicts the assumption that culture alone shapes the marital power structure. Husbands and wives in both African American and Latino families may hold some cultural ideals about power, yet they often depart from them in day-to-day behavior. In studying racial-ethnic families, it is especially important to distinguish between family ideals and family behavior due to the past emphasis on culture as the sole determinant of family life.

Joyce O. Beckett (1976) found that African American and White families differ in the ideologies they hold about power. African American families have more traditional ideas about family interaction; that is, they tend to hold the belief that the husband's interests are more important than those of the wife. In their behavior, however, African American wives and mothers are more egalitarian—that is, they are more likely than White women to believe that their own interests are as important as those of their husbands and children. Whites, in contrast, are more egalitarian than African Americans in ideology and more traditional in their behavior.

Husbands' and wives' involvement in social networks outside of the family have a great impact on family organization. African American wives have always had high rates of employment. This is reflected in the internal structure of family power. Sandra DeJarnett and Bertram Raven (1981) found a more equal distribution of power that was similar in middle- and lower-class couples. This finding is probably due to the resources African American women derive from working outside the home. African American middle-class wives are more likely to work than White middle-class wives. As Harriette McAdoo (1978) has noted, their income is necessary to keep the African American family in the middle class.

Male dominance, or **machismo,** is a popular stereotype associated with Latino families. However, research has challenged the widely accepted notions of rigid *machismo.* Studies show that changes in the family lives of Latinos are closely associated with wives' employment. For example, Maxine Baca Zinn (1980) and Lea Ybarra (1977) found that Chicano families are more equal when wives work outside of the home. Still, it is important to keep in mind that not all types of employment offer resources that wives can use to change the traditional balance of power in marriage. This is the conclusion that emerges from Patricia Zavella's study (1987) of Mexican women (Chicana) cannery workers in the Santa Clara Valley of California. Cannery jobs did give wives some leverage in the home, yet, as seasonal, part-time work, their jobs were defined as an extension of their household responsibilities and did not fundamentally transform family roles.

Gender There is a long history in Western civilization of **patriarchy**—that is, the idea that ultimate authority (legitimate power) resides in the husband and father. This belief is supported by the Old and New Testaments and remains a cornerstone of some contemporary religious groups (e.g., the Promise Keepers, fundamentalist Christian denominations, and the Mormon Church). In this view, the wife is to be obedient, reverent, and submissive to her husband. For example, the Southern Baptist Convention at its annual meeting in 1998 amended its essential statement of belief to include the statement that a woman should submit herself graciously to her husband's leadership and that a husband should provide for, protect, and lead his family.

In addition to religion, male dominance in organizations and relationships is sustained and promoted by language, the schools, the media, the law, and politics.

Resources An important source of marital power is the amount of resources each spouse brings to the relationship. Research shows that, within families, power tends to accrue to the partner with the highest occupational level, the highest income, the highest educational level, and the one most involved in outside organizations. Husbands are more likely than their wives to rate higher on each of these achieved statuses.

The most important resources are economic, involving not only income but also status and prestige based on success in the occupational world. Husbands, typically, are the main providers in families, with only about 20 percent of two-spouse families having wives as the primary source of income. This is because husbands have always been more likely than wives to work in the labor force and because women in the labor force tend to be denied equality in pay, promotions, and access. Thus, husbands, because of their relative economic clout, have greater power than wives in marriage. It is important to note, however, that employed wives, even when they make less money than their husbands, have increased say in decision making, less traditional gender role ideologies, and more egalitarian family roles than do nonemployed wives. This relationship between income and power in marriage is buttressed by the study of over 7000 couples by Philip Blumstein and Pepper Schwartz (1983), who found that in three-fourths of the couples the amount of money one partner earns relative to the other establishes relative power in the relationship.

Blumstein and Schwartz (1983) found one exception to this pattern of partner income determining domestic power. Among lesbian couples, if one partner makes more income than the other it makes no difference in the decision making and the division of labor in their relationship. This is not true, however, among gay couples, where differences in income between the partners, as in heterosexual couples, translates into power.

Noneconomic resources more typically favor wives. These include companionship, emotional support, sex, and home management (meals, purchases, cleaning, maintenance). Wives may use the giving or withholding of these behaviors for power. Ultimately, either spouse may use the threat of divorce to shape the behaviors of the other.

Husbands also have noneconomic resources that generally favor them. Compared to their wives, husbands tend to have the same amount of education or more, and thus have the advantage of greater skills in communication, decision making, and manipulating others. Husbands also are more likely than their wives to be successful in the occupational world and to have community acclaim for their accomplishments, which gives them power over their spouses.

Individual Factors Several ascribed characteristics tend to favor husbands over wives. Husbands usually are older than their wives (in excess of two years for first marriages and more for remarriages), and age is related to authority. Also, husbands are almost always taller than their wives, and tallness in U.S. society tends to denote power. Finally, men are physically stronger than women, and this strength gives men the potential for coercive power.

Another ascribed characteristic works to the disadvantage of women. Only they can have children, and research shows that power declines with the birth of the first child and declines further with each succeeding child (Szinovacz, 1987).

In sum, husbands tend to have more marital power than wives. First, husbands tend to be the main providers and, by virtue of their gender, age, education, skills, and physical stature, are advantaged in the marital relationship. Although women tend to have less power, certain changes are reducing the impact of men's authority in contemporary marriages. More and more wives are in the labor force; they are thus less dependent economically on their husbands and are developing communication and other assertive skills. Second, although such women are still clearly in a minority, more and more wives are outperforming their husbands in the occupational world in income and prestige, which gives them power. Third, the gender norms are changing in society. Many couples have developed relationships based on egalitarian principles and shared decision making.

RECONSTRUCTING GENDER ROLES: BUILDING AN EGALITARIAN MARRIAGE

The discussion in this section focuses on successful marriages. But successful marriages are not all alike. The research of Mary Anne Fitzpatrick (1988) demythologizes the strongly held notion that there is a universal path toward marital success. She found that some happily married couples are extremely close, while others nurture distance in their relationship. Some couples are comfortable with conventional male and female roles, whereas marital success for others depends on their relationship being egalitarian. What is "good" communication in one marriage may not work in another. This is a problem when a couple seeks help for their ailing relationship. According to Fitzpatrick,

> The [social science] literature needs a more pluralistic view of what constitutes "good" communication in marriage and close relationships. The potentially oppressive result for couples seeking help is that "good communication" may require

conformity to someone else's idea of what constitutes a satisfying relationship. Within prescriptive communication programs, couples are urged to confront conflicts, self-disclose, and speak in terms that are descriptive, consistent, and direct (Fitzpatrick, 1988:202).

This is not to say that there are general guidelines for success in intimate long-term relationships, but that couples must define what works for them in their shared world.

Although there is no universal path to marital success, a key problem for contemporary marriages is a mutual understanding of responsibilities by gender. In times past this was not a problem because there were clear norms regarding the responsibilities of husbands and wives. They lived in separate spheres and led parallel lives. The economic dominance of husbands gave them power in the home. Their domestic chores were gender-specific and less demanding than those of their wives. Wives were responsible for the caring of children and the emotional and expressive needs of their husbands. Traditional couples today continue this legacy. If husbands and wives agree on these norms, their marriages can work. However, it is likely that more and more couples will have one spouse, usually the wife, who rejects these traditional arrangements. These wives resent working at a job and then a second shift at home, while their husbands do half as much work at home. They resent being subservient to their husbands. Sociologist Pepper Schwartz says that "the power structure of traditional relationships is a wellspring of resentment that ultimately undermines love" (Schwartz, 1994:54).

Schwartz has identified an emerging type of relationship in which couples successfully reconstruct gender roles on a genuinely equitable basis. She calls this new type of marriage **peer marriage.**

> Peer couples trade a frustrated, angry relationship with a spouse for one of deep friendship. . . . Theirs is collaboration of love and labor that produces profound intimacy and mutual respect. . . . Above all, peer couples live the same life. In doing so, they have found a new way to make love last. . . . These couples . . . base their marriage on a mix of equity—each person gives in proportion to what he or she receives—and equality—each has equal status and is equally responsible for emotional, economic, and household duties. But these couples have more than their dedication to fairness. They achieve a true companionship and a deep collaborative marriage. The idea of "peer" is important because it incorporates the notion of friendship. Peer marriages embody a profound psychological connection (Schwartz, 1994:54, 56).

Schwartz studied peer marriages among same-sex and heterosexual couples and found that their partnerships were based on equality, equity, and intimacy and shared four characteristics:

- The partners do not have more than a 60/40 traditional split of household duties and child raising.
- Both partners believe the other has equal influence over important decisions.
- Both partners feel they have equal control of the family economy and reasonable access to discretionary funds.

- Each person's work is given equal weight in the couple's life plans. Whether or not both partners work, they do not systematically sacrifice one person's work for the other's.

These peer marriages are, in Schwartz's words, "made, not born" (1994:58). The partners must agree on values, such as the primacy of the relationship over work, and the particulars, such as who does what. The husband must overcome the traditional male role and accept his partner as an equal. He must make their relationship primary, which means that his career becomes secondary. He must accept equal responsibility for the expressive aspects of their relationships (communication, warmth, displays of physical and verbal affection, romance). The wife in a peer marriage must shed traditional female role expectations. She must not accept anything less than equal status. Women are more likely than men to have a vision of a peer relationship. Thus, according to Schwartz, "it is often the woman's responsibility to get across to her partner the relationship style she wants" (1994:58).

Schwartz envisions peer marriages as the direction marriages are moving toward:

> I do not see all of us in the same kind of relationship. We're all too different from one another for that. I wouldn't sentence everyone to the same kind of roles in marriages. But peer marriage will become a predominant cultural theme and perhaps the predominant type of marriage in the very near future (Schwartz, 1994:86).

THE FUTURE OF MARRIAGE: CHANGING OR DYING?

The statistics of marriage show that behaviors are changing—the young delay it, older people often get out of it, and some skip it altogether (the following information is from Furstenberg, 1996). These trends have led some social observers to predict that marriage is a dying institution (see, for example, Popenoe, 1993). But 90 percent of adults will marry, and if they divorce, they tend to remarry. The pessimists are concerned about marriage because it no longer fits the idealized 1950s version, in which people married rather than cohabited, the husband was the breadwinner and the wife the homemaker and nurturer of her husband and children. Although this is the standard by which many measure contemporary families, we must remember that the 1950s version of marriage was a historical anomaly. "The middle-class nuclear family that became the norm at mid-century was a stripped-down version of the extended families of previous decades" (Furstenberg, 1996:36). A new family form emerged in a time of economic prosperity and societal stability for the middle and working classes (not, we must remember, for the poor and racial minorities). A single wage earner could provide enough for a family. A full-time worker earning only the minimum wage earned 118 percent of the poverty rate for a family of three. In 1995, in contrast, that minimum-wage worker could earn only 72 percent of the poverty level (Coontz, 1997:41). The government invested in families (e.g., the GI Bill paid for the education of veterans, the building of the interstate highway system opened up relatively cheap land for housing, and the government encouraged low down payments and interest on housing purchases).

Marriages are different now because of several key changes in social conditions. First, in the past twenty years or so there has been a transition from a gender-based division of labor, in which men were in the workforce and women did the domestic work, to one in which household tasks are more contested and the majority of women are now formally employed.

> The traditional bargain struck between men and women—financial support in exchange for domestic services—is no longer valid. Men now expect women to help bring home the bacon. And women expect men to help cook the bacon, feed the kids, and clean up afterward. In addition, the old status order that granted men a privileged position in the family is crumbling. . . . [These] moves toward gender equality have come with a price. Both men and women enter marriage with higher expectations for interpersonal communication, intimacy, and sexual gratification. If these expectations are not met, they feel freer than they once did to dissolve the relationship and seek a new partner (Furstenberg, 1996:37).

Another stress point affecting contemporary marriages is economic. The transformation of the economy (Chapter 4), with downward pressure on wages, corporate downsizing, and a growing gap between the haves and the have-nots, has had an unsettling effect on "marriage in the short term by making marriage a risky proposition, and in the long term by generating larger numbers of people who are the products of unstable family situations" (Furstenberg, 1996:40). The pressure on marriage is exacerbated by the lack of government supports. "So politicians are practicing quite a double standard when they tell us to return to the family forms of the 1950s while they do nothing to restore the job programs and family subsidies of that era" (Coontz, 1997:43).

To conclude, as this and the other chapters point out, marriage (and the family) is not a dying institution but one that is changing as society changes. To paraphrase family historian Stephanie Coontz, marriage is not a dying institution, but it certainly is a *transformed* institution (Coontz, 1997:31).

*C*HAPTER REVIEW

1. Within the intimate environment of a marriage and the constraints of society, each couple creates its own unique social organization.

2. Marriages do not occur in a vacuum. Although each couple forges a unique relationship, these relationships are patterned by structural arrangements. Among the macro forces affecting the partners in marriages are (a) the law, (b) religion, and (c) societal gender expectations.

3. There are three categories of nonmarried adults: singles, cohabiting heterosexuals, and cohabitating homosexuals.

4. The number of marriages is declining, partly because people are marrying later.

5. With minor variations, the fertility rate has declined steadily throughout U.S. history. This rate varies, however, by race and ethnicity, with Latinos highest, followed in order by African Americans, Whites, and Asian Americans.

6. Interracial marriages are becoming more common, with about 5 percent of marriages involving partners of different races.

7. With the increase in life expectancy, marriages now have the potential to last approximately fifty years, an increase of

twenty years or so from 1920. This new longevity is one explanation for the relatively high divorce rate.

8. The divorce rate accelerated in the 1970s, peaked in 1981, with a slight decline since. At current rates, about half of all marriages will end in divorce. African American couples are more likely than White or Latino couples to divorce.

9. The vast majority of divorced persons remarry (five out of six men and about three out of four women).

10. Women and men often have different expectations of marriage, and their experiences in marriage differ. Although, generally, both men and women benefit from marriage, men gain more.

11. Although marriage matters for most couples, the benefits are decreased, even reversed, for some poor couples, especially minority poor, who face greater threats of unemployment, underemployment, and lower wages than Whites. There are differences, too, by gender. So marriage matters, but the degree and the way that it matters is affected by social class, race, and gender.

12. Among the correlates of marital quality are (a) shared social characteristics (homogamy); (b) economic success; (c) role fit (i.e., the degree of consensus between the partners on decision making); and (d) the absence of children. Both spouses in the labor force has contradictory effects on marital quality.

13. A crucial determinant of marital quality is communication. There is a tendency, especially in blue-collar marriages, for communication to lessen over time as the partners go about their separate activities. Gender differences also make satisfactory communication in intimate relations difficult.

14. Another important factor in marital quality is sexual intimacy. Each couple must work out their unique sexual life, which is complicated by differences in their religious backgrounds, parental role models, and gender.

15. The sources of marital power are (a) societal norms, (b) resources (the spouse with the most economic resources typically makes the most important decisions), and (c) individual factors (which also tend to favor husbands). Husbands in all social classes generally have greater power than wives.

16. Some couples resist the traditional gender expectations for marriage by consciously building egalitarian marriages. Pepper Schwartz calls this new type of marriage "peer marriage." In such a marriage (whether same-sex or heterosexual), the partners split the household duties and child raising, share equally in the decision making, have equal access to discretionary funds, and give each person's work equal weight in the couple's life plans.

17. Contemporary marriages are affected by contemporary social conditions. The institution of marriage is not dying, as some observers claim; rather, it is adapting. As a result, marriage is not declining but is being transformed.

RELATED WEB SITES

http://www.hawaiilawyer.com/same_sex/samesex.htm

While the December 1999 Hawaii Supreme Court rejected same sex marriages, Hawaii remains one of the forerunner states in legal decisions regarding domestic partnerships and same sex marriages. Few issues in Hawaii legal history have been as controversial as the "Same Sex Marriage Issue." As a service to readers, a group of Hawaii lawyers present this website as a resource for information on same sex marriage.

http://www.religioustolerance.org/mar_bene.htm

Legal and Economic Benefits of Marriage: Information on this website was provided by the Lambda Legal Defense and Education Fund. The lists of benefits to marriage originally were compiled for couples living in the

United States. However, similar provisions exist in many other countries. Long lists of economic and legal benefits are listed.

http://www.joi.org/

The Jewish Outreach Institute—Interfaith Marriage: Since 1988, the Jewish Outreach Institute has been a leader in the development of Jewish community-based outreach programming. Our objective is to expand the boundaries of Jewish inclusiveness. This institute works to secure the future of Jewish intermarried and interfaith families.

http://www.ncfr.org/

National Council of Family Relations: The National Council on Family Relations (NCFR) provides a forum for family researchers, educators, and practitioners to share in the development and dissemination of knowledge about families and family relationships, establishes professional standards, and works to promote family well-being. The Council provides several sources and articles on topics related to marriage.

http://www.couples-place.com/

Marriage Support—"Resources for Marriage and Other Committed-Couple Relationships": Your online learning community for solving marriage problems, improving relationship skills, celebrating marriage, and achieving happiness with your partner.

http://www.ngltf.org/

NGLTF is the national progressive organization working for the civil rights of gay, lesbian, bisexual and transgendered people. NGLTF's vision and commitment to social change is building a powerful political movement in the fifty states and the District of Columbia. NGLTF serves tens of thousands of gay, lesbian, bisexual and transgendered people who are in need of resources, training and technical assistance to pass pro-GLBT legislation. NGLTF helps those fighting for their families, employment, health care, hate crimes and more.

http://www.abanet.org/family/home.html

The Family Law Section of the American Bar Association: The Family Law Section was organized in 1958 to improve the administration of justice in the field of family law. Today, family law is a fast-growing, complex area with an interstate and at times international character. Well known but rapidly changing areas such as divorce, custody, adoption, alimony and support are within the scope of the Section, as are emerging issues such as third-party parental rights, marital torts, federal and interstate legislation, mediation, and the complicated questions of paternity, perinatal drug addiction, bankruptcy to deprive divorcing spouses of property, and genetic engineering.

Parents and Children

Myths and Realities

Myth: The parental division of labor is the result of biological imperatives.

Reality: Aside from conception, childbirth, and nursing, parental roles by gender are a social
    construction, the result of historical, economic, and social forces.

Myth: Children increase marital happiness.

Reality: Research shows that children increase marital happiness in only about one-fifth of
    marriages.

Myth: Modern fathers share the parenting duties with their working wives.

Reality: Although there are exceptions, the overall pattern is for husbands to leave the child-raising chores to wives. Even among couples who deliberately share parenting equally, mothers do much more of the emotion work than do fathers.

Myth: The socialization process is one-way—the child is a passive receptor of parental influences.

Reality: Socialization works both ways—children learn from parents and parents learn from children.

Myth: Children raised in nontraditional gender role families are adversely affected.

Reality: Research findings indicate that children raised in families with mothers in the labor force and in which there is a more egalitarian division of labor are not negatively affected.

Myth: Children raised by gay or lesbian parents are harmed in their psychosocial development.

Reality: When the children of gay and lesbian parents are compared with the children of heterosexual parents, there is no difference in their psychosocial development.

*I*n most societies there is a pervasive cultural pressure toward parenthood. There are strong expectations that married couples should not only have children but should also want to have them. Indeed, approximately 85 percent of married couples in the United States have children, and about two-thirds of childless couples want children but are infertile. This chapter examines parenthood, the contours of which have changed dramatically in the past two generations. More children now are being raised in families in which both parents are in the labor force. More children now are being raised by a single parent. More children now are being raised by same-sex parents. More children now are being raised by grandparents. And more children are now in households with a step-parent and step-siblings. What are the causes and consequences of these new and pervasive parenting arrangements? In particular, what are the effects of these diverse family forms on the well-being of children? These questions guide our inquiry in this chapter. We begin with a discussion of the social construction of parenting. Second, we describe various demographic trends regarding parenting in U.S. society. Third, the effect of children on the marital relationship are considered. Fourth, we describe the impact of parents on children. Finally, we examine two significant types of situations in which contemporary children are raised: dual-earner families and single-parent families.

THE SOCIAL CONSTRUCTION OF PARENTING

Typically, we think of families as biological units based on the timeless functions of love, motherhood, and childbearing. Moreover, parenting activities are viewed as "natural" behaviors found universally. This idealized version of the family assumes a gendered division of labor, a husband/father in the workforce, and a wife/mother at home nurturing her husband and children. This image of the family does not fit historical fact nor contemporary reality—only 7 percent of households currently fit this description (AmeriStat, 2000e)—yet it continues to be the ideal. The idealized image is inaccurate because "family forms are socially and historically constructed, not monolithic universals that exist for all times and all peoples, and . . . the arrangements governing family life are not the inevitable result of unambiguous differences between women and men" (Baca Zinn et al., 1997:255). Or, put another way, by Terry Arendell: "human parenting is not only or even predominantly the outcome of biological imperatives or genetic imprinting. Parenting activities are not 'natural' behaviors derived from the capacity to reproduce. How children are cared for, reared, and socialized into group life are social processes—dynamic, open-ended, and mutable" (Arendell, 1997:3).

Supporting this view are the social constructionist and social structural theoretical approaches (the following information is from Coltrane, 1998:1-9). The social constructionist approach argues that what seems "natural" or "real" depends on time, place, and social location. What is sexy, feminine or masculine, or even a family depends on the historical period, the society, and the social stratum within that society. Consider the example provided by Coltrane: "Among noblemen in 17th-century France, it was manly to wear perfume, curly wigs, high-heeled shoes, and blouses with frilly lace cuffs. Today, the same attire would be considered unmanly or effeminate" (1998:7). The point is that the meaning of gender (or family, or motherhood, or fatherhood) changes in response to differing cultural and historical contexts. Hence, it is socially constructed. These social constructions are the result of economic and other social forces. In short, people's lives and behaviors are shaped by social forces. As Coltrane says, "Only by looking at the structural constraints people face—such as access to education or jobs—can we understand how cultural definitions and practices governing gender and families have developed" (Coltrane, 1998:3). Summing up this important and sociological way of looking at families, Coltrane states, "In our nostalgia for a mythical past, we tend to envision an ideal family that transcends time and place. In reality, families are very specific forms of human organization that continually evolve and change as they respond to various pushes and pulls" (Coltrane, 1996:22).

To examine the social construction of parenting further, let's consider some related questions: Why is child care and housework obligatory for women and mothers, yet still optional for men and fathers (Coltrane, 1996:7)? Why is being a housewife acceptable and choosing to be a househusband much less so? Why are women who voluntarily release custody of their children to their former husbands defined much more negatively than men who give up the custody of their children to their former wives? Similarly, why do we feel much less incensed when a father abandons his family than when a mother deserts her family? Why does the verb "to mother" include in its core meaning the caring of children, whereas the verb "to father" does not (Shehan and Kammeyer, 1997:219)? In short, why are a father's family obligations less important than a mother's?

Biological differences (e.g., genetic programming, hormones, size, strength, and traits such as nurturance and aggressiveness) do not explain these inconsistencies by gender. Beyond conception, giving birth, and nursing the infant, there are no biological imperatives concerning parenting. Mothering and styles of mothering are tied to social rather than biological sources (much of the following is from Glenn, 1994). This assertion questions the presumed universals of motherhood as the most important source of a woman's fulfillment, mothers as nurturers, and even maternal instinct. There are variations on each of these themes, thus belying their universality. A few examples make this point.

We typically assume that the White, middle-class experience is the norm (Collins, 1990). To do so promotes mythology. Bonnie Thornton Dill (1988) shows how mothering has differed historically along racial and class dimensions. Privileged women (usually White), historically, have been able to escape the more difficult parts of mothering by having other women (White working-class women and women of color) do the tedious child-rearing tasks for them. This frees the privileged mothers for leisure or career pursuits while retaining the status of "mother," and forces much less privileged surrogate mothers to spend less time with their own children. In effect, institutional racism and economic necessities required lower-class women to give precedence to the care of the children of others over their own. Thus, the responsibility for their own children often had to be shared with other family members of other women from the minority community. This "shared mothering" or "othermothering" has been and continues to be characteristic in African American communities.

This chain of "othermothering" extends to other societies as well. Sociologist Arlie Hochschild (2000) illustrates the globalization of child care as mothers from poor countries hire poor women to take care of their children while they migrate to the United States to work to care for someone else's children for better wages.

> A typical global care chain might work something like this: An older daughter from a poor family in a third world country cares for her siblings (the first link in the chain) while her mother works as a nanny caring for the children of a nanny migrating to a first world country (the second link) who, in turn, cares for the child of a family in a rich country (the final link). Each kind of chain expresses an invisible human ecology of care, one care worker depending on another and so on (Hochschild, 2000:33).

Another false universal of motherhood is maternal instinct (that is, the assumption that there is a biological imperative of mother love that compels mothers to protect their children from harm against any odds). This is a myth because historians, anthropologists, and sociologists find that mothers do not protect their children universally in all stages of history and across all cultures. Some cultures accept infanticide, usually the killing of girl babies because they are considered a financial burden to the family. Other societies permit the killing of one or all multiple-birth babies because of the belief that animals have multiple births, not humans. There is also the widespread practice in some societies of poor parents selling their offspring as slaves or prostitutes.

Anthropologist Nancy Scheper-Hughes presents an interesting case of accepted infanticide in northeast Brazil. She found that when infants and toddlers from poor families were quite sick from diarrhea and dehydration, mothers could not be convinced to use medicines to save their children. These mothers would not even accept back into their homes those children who recovered on their own. They believed that these children were sickly and fragile and would always be a burden. Thus it was better to let them die, so the family's few economic resources would be more generously divided among the healthy. When this occurred, parents accepted their sickly child's death with stoicism and equanimity. Scheper-Hughes concludes that mother love is not absent (because it is lavished on other children), but that maternal thinking and practices are shaped by overwhelming economic and cultural constraints: "Mother love is anything other than natural and instead represents a matrix of images, meanings, sentiments, and practices that are everywhere socially and culturally produced" (Scheper-Hughes, 1992:340).

As a final illustration of the social construction of parenting, let's look at the changing views of motherhood and fatherhood in the United States during different historical periods. The expectations of mothers and fathers have changed throughout U.S. history, paralleling economic conditions (see Chapters 2 and 3). When the economy was based on agriculture, parenting (and the farm work) was a joint venture for all family members. Child rearing in this historical setting was not the defining characteristic of wives. Mothers and fathers cared for children because both worked at home. So did other relatives because households often included grandparents, older sons and daughters, and perhaps hired help. Fathers were responsible for the educational, moral, and spiritual development of their children. During this era fathers were patriarchs, with complete authority in the home. Child rearing involved instilling submission to authority. Two interesting differences from the present are that, in divorces involving children, their custody was usually given to the father. Second, the literature on child development during colonial times was directed at fathers, not mothers.

During the late eighteenth and early nineteenth centuries, a philosophical movement called the Enlightenment changed child-rearing practices. Fathers were still expected to rule the family sternly, but with more sensitivity than in earlier times. As LaRossa describes it, "Patriarchal fatherhood was not eliminated, by any means, but it did lose some of its edge" (1997:27).

With the industrial revolution fathers became removed from their children as they commuted to jobs, leaving their wives alone to care for children. In this arrangement fathers became the "sole economic providers" (except for single mothers, poor women, working-class women, and women of color), and mothers became responsible for the educational and moral development of their children. Fathers, on the other hand, became more disengaged from their children and their direct authority over family members declined. Now the great majority of custody suits ruled *against* fathers, and the child-rearing literature now placed mothers at the center of families and fathers on the periphery.

Since the 1960s, family life has changed in response to global and domestic economic restructuring. As noted in Chapter 4, wages for working people stagnated or declined while the costs of housing, health care, transportation, education, and consumer goods increased, sometimes dramatically. This was also a time characterized by corporate downsizing, contingent work, and declining work benefits. Thus, in the last generation, mothers in most families have become essential to supplement the economic resources by working in the paid labor market. Moreover, the ideological terrain shifted as various oppressed groups sought equality, including women. Included in this new way of thinking was that women can be fulfilled in a number of ways, not just through mothering. As a result of the economic and ideological changes, there has been a rapid shift in women's employment since 1960, when only one out of four mothers was employed outside the home. By the 1990s some 75 percent of mothers with school-age children were in the paid workforce (thus, a shift in thirty years from 75 percent stay-at-home mothers to 25 percent). Now it is acceptable for women to have babies and return to work soon thereafter, because their incomes are so necessary for family survival. Now, commonly, child care during the day is shifted from parents to other caregivers, sometimes kin and otherwise to day-care providers, preschool, and school. Sometimes mothers and fathers work different shifts so that one is at home with the children. More fathers are "helping" with domestic chores and child care, but the bulk of these duties is still left to mothers. Thus, in response to changes in the responsibilities of mothers, there is a shift, still slight but real nonetheless, for fathers to become more equal partners in parenting.

Other consequences of so many women working in the paid labor force are that (Coltrane, 1998:105) (1) the isolated homemaker is no longer dominant; (2) compulsory motherhood is weakening as more women choose not to marry, postpone marriage, and elect to remain childless; and (3) the relationship between marriage and childbearing is weakening, as increasing numbers of women are becoming parents without husbands.

DEMOGRAPHIC PATTERNS

Examining a number of demographic factors allows us to describe the changing nature of parenting in the present-day United States. This section considers birth rates over time, differential birth rates by race and socioeconomic status, the facts about those who choose to remain childless, the trend toward delayed childbearing, and the changing composition of households, including adoption, mixed-race children, children of gay or lesbian parents, the dramatic rise of single-parent households, and multigeneration households.

Fertility

The long-term **fertility** (total childbearing rate) rate has declined steadily since 1800, when the average woman gave birth to seven children, compared to a current average of two children per woman. This general downward trend obscures four important swings in the birth rate during the past fifty years. The years of the Great Depression (1930–1939) showed a drastic drop, as wives and husbands limited the number of children they had because of the economic hardships and uncertain future during that period. The baby boom that followed World War II (1947–1964) was just that—a boom in the fertility rate (a rate of 3.8 births per woman in 1957, compared to 2.1 during the Depression). This was followed by a precipitous decline in the birth rate to an all-time low of 1.7 in 1975. Most recently, however, there has been a slight increase in the fertility rate, to 2.07 (see Figure 9.1). This translates to about 4 million new births a year.

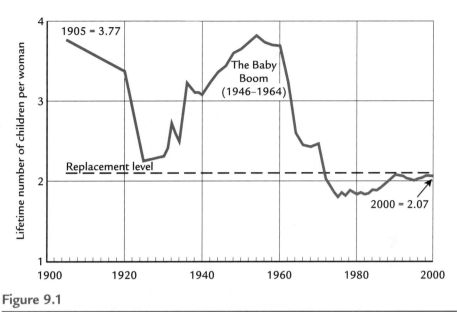

Figure 9.1

Total fertility rate (lifetime number of children per woman)

Source: Theodore Caplow, Louis Hicks, and Ben J. Wattenberg, *The First Measured Century: An Illustrated Guide to Trends in America*. Washington, DC: AEI Press, 2000, p. 85.

The reasons for the relatively low fertility rate today are several. First, marriage tends to occur now at a later age, reducing the number of potential childbearing years for women. Second, the relatively high divorce rate also reduces the number of childbearing years for many women. Third, the majority of women work in the labor force, which adds to family income and the social status of women. The greater the number of children, the more the career development of women is stifled. Fourth, the economic situation of many families demands two incomes to cover mortgages, car payments, and the other elements of a desired lifestyle. Finally, the rise in the number of abortions since the Supreme Court legalized the practice in 1973 (*Roe v. Wade*) has reduced fertility. About one-fourth of pregnancies not ending in miscarriages or stillbirths are aborted. Most women getting abortions are under the age of twenty-five, White, and single.

The Consequences of Low Fertility

That most family units are relatively small has several important consequences for the family members. The fewer the children, the more family wealth is available to be spent on their health and educational benefits—improving their life chances and the well-being of family members.

Research has shown that small family size is related to positive physical and intellectual endowments for the children. Shirley Hartley (1973:195; see also Blake, 1989) has summarized these findings: (1) in terms of health, height, weight, vital capacity, and strength, all decline as the number of children goes up; and (2) children from small families consistently score higher on intelligence tests than children from large families. Although both large families and lower scores on intelligence tests are related to social class, the explanation for family size and intelligence is not. When family income, or the occupation of the father, is held constant, there is still a substantial decline in IQ with an increasing number of children in the family. This relationship is most likely the result of less parent-child interaction, because, as family size increases, the amount of verbal interactions between parents and their children (such as talking, singing, reading, and playing) is reduced.

Increased marital satisfaction is another benefit of small families. This most likely results from fewer economic problems and because wives and husbands have more time to devote to their relationship. Also, spouses (especially wives) who have few or no children are freer to pursue educational and career opportunities.

Differential Fertility

Fertility rates in the United States vary in a consistent pattern by social factors **(differential fertility),** most notably social class and race. The patterned behaviors are that: (1) the higher the income, the lower the fertility; (2) the greater the level of educational attainment, the lower the fertility; and (3) Whites have the lowest fertility rates, followed in order by Asians and Pacific Islanders, Native Americans, African Americans, with Latinos considerably higher than the rest. See Table 9.1. Not shown in this table but significant nonetheless are two additional facts concerning differential fertility. First, the fertility rate for foreign-born adult women is about 50 percent higher than the rate for native-born adult women. Second, the fertility rate for any racial/ethnic category masks the diversity found therein. For example, the average number of children a woman will have during her lifetime varies among Latinos, from a high of 3.2 for women of

---

TABLE 9.1

Fertility Rates by Race and Hispanic Origin (births per 1000 females aged 15 to 44) for Selected Years

Racial/Ethnic Category	1980	1990	1997
All races	68.4	70.9	65.0
White	65.6	68.3	63.9
Black	84.7	86.8	70.0
Hispanic	95.4	107.7	102.8
Asian/Pacific Islander	73.2	69.6	66.3
American Indian	82.7	76.2	69.1

Source: U.S. Department of Health and Human Services, *Trends in the Well-Being of America's Children & Youth: 1999.* Washington, DC: U.S. Government Printing Office, 1000, pp. 32–33.

Mexican ethnic origin to a low of 1.56 for Latino women of Cuban heritage (*Population Today*, 2000b:7).

Generally, the pattern shows that those least able to afford children have more than those who are better able to afford larger families. Several factors combine to explain this seemingly illogical behavior. First, those with the least amount of education are most likely to hold traditional beliefs, including the acceptance of traditional gender roles and **pronatalism** (the high value given to childbearing). Viewed the other way, the more education a woman has, the more likely she will be to hold feminist ideals, pursue a career, and limit her childbearing.

In traditional settings, being a mother or father brings social approval from family, friends, and one's religious community. Parenthood facilitates integration into one's kin network and the community. Children may also be considered a benefit to a poor family by supplementing the family income even during their elementary school years. And the poor may desire a large family as a source of retirement security—so that the grown children can support their elderly parents.

Social Class From the perspective of those with more income and education, the costs of children tend to be perceived as exceeding the benefits. The presence of children negatively affects the chances to complete an education, to pursue a career, to engage in certain leisure activities, and to earn a good income.

In short, as the alternatives grow in number and attractiveness, especially for women, the costs of having children go up. With high educational attainment, career and income potential increase markedly for women. These rewards, then, may outweigh or even replace the rewards of motherhood. This leads to the corollary conclusion that the more prestigious and well-paid the career for a woman, the more deliberately will she restrict family size and maximize time in the labor force.

Another reason for the inverse relationship between social class and fertility is that the more economic resources and educational attainment one has, the later one marries. And there is a strong relationship between the age of the mother at marriage and the pace of subsequent fertility. Lower-class women are more likely to marry soon after high school, whereas middle- and upper-class women are much more likely to complete college first and perhaps even begin a career before marrying. Achieving higher levels of education increases the opportunities to pursue careers, both of which are likely to delay childbearing and, in the long run, to reduce the number of children born to these women (Rindfuss et al., 1996).

Race/Ethnicity The relationship between race/ethnicity and fertility is also strong. The data over a number of decades show consistently that Whites and Asian Americans have lower fertility rates than African Americans, and that Latinos have the highest rate. In time this difference in fertility by race (coupled with immigration) will result in non-Whites surpassing Whites in population size. At mid-twenty-first century, for example, the proportions of Whites and nonWhites will be about equal. According to a U.S. Census Bureau projection, at that time, 40 percent of all births will be White, compared to almost two-thirds in 1995 (U.S. Bureau of the Census, 1996b:2).

An interesting pattern seen over time is that fertility rates by race rise or fall in tandem—for example, the fertility rate for each category was the highest in 1955 and lowest in 1976. This demonstrates that fertility rates fluctuate according to economic and other social factors, regardless of race/ethnicity.

Why is there such a strong relationship between race/ethnicity and fertility? Foremost are the socioeconomic factors—income, education, and occupation—that press the disadvantaged toward pronatalist beliefs and practices. People of color are disproportionately poor, uneducated, unemployed, or, if employed, in the low-paying, low-prestige segment of the economy. Thus, they experience the same pressures and rationales as do other disadvantaged persons to have large families. For example, the total lifetime fertility for Latino women with only a grade school education is 4.1 children and for African American women is 4.5 children. However, with some college or a college degree the African American and Latino rate ranges from 1.6 to 2.0 children, quite similar to the fertility rate of Whites (Children for the Future, 2000).

A second argument is that people make different sacrifices to get ahead. Because people of color are so severely limited by structural barriers to the normal avenues to success, a common strategy among them has been to have large families. Large families mean more workers. They also make it more likely that the parents, when elderly, will receive help from their children. Also, there is a type of "lottery logic"—that is, as the number of children increases, so does the probability of having a child with unusual abilities (in music or sports, two of the few relatively open areas for people of color) that might lift the entire family out of its marginal economic situation. Thus, large families are a form of adaptation to economic deprivation and a hope to overcome it.

Religion Two generalizations hold for the relationship between religion and fertility. First, people who actively practice a religion tend to have higher fertility than nonreligious people (McFalls, 1998). And second, certain religions encourage high fertility. Traditionally, Catholics have had more children than Protestants, but since the 1980s that pattern has all but disappeared. Mormons, on the other hand, have larger families than non-Mormons. Utah, which is 70 percent Mormon, has the highest fertility rate of the states, at 2.64 children per adult woman. Assuming the non-Mormon population in Utah has a fertility rate at the national average, that would place the Mormon rate at 2.91 (Children for the Future, 2000).

Voluntary Childlessness

Despite the strongly held beliefs of most Americans that children are the inevitable and desirable consequences of marriage, some couples choose to remain childless. For most of this century the proportion of childless marriages ranged from 5 to 10 percent. The percentage of women still childless at ages 40 to 44 (most of whom will remain childless) has increased from 10 percent in 1980 to 19 percent in 1998 (AmeriStat, 2000a). These data include the voluntarily and the involuntarily childless (about 8 percent of women who wish to have children are unable to bear them [Coltrane, 1998:95]).

Because of the **pronatalistic** proclivities of Americans, those who reject this prescription often face the stigma associated with being deviant. They are considered by some as less-than-whole persons, emotionally immature, selfish, and lonely. Childless women are more likely than childless men to be negatively stereotyped. This is because motherhood

> is much more salient to the female role than fatherhood is to the male. Whereas masculinity can be affirmed by occupational success or sexual prowess, femininity has traditionally been closely linked with bearing and caring for children, with other roles remaining relatively peripheral. Although the paternal role is also important, it does not have the same centrality that makes motherhood almost a woman's *raison d'être* (Veevers, 1980:7).

Given the strong pronatalist ideology and the negative labels that accompany voluntary childlessness, why do some couples choose this "unnatural" option? There appear to be two common paths to this decision. One pattern, found about one-third of the time, is for two persons to make a commitment before marriage that they will not have children. The other and more common route is for a couple to make a series of decisions to postpone childbearing until a time when it no longer is considered a desirable choice (Veevers, 1980:17). The former path explicitly rejects childbearing, whereas the latter accepts it in the abstract but never finds it convenient, resulting, finally, in a permanent postponement.

A rising number of childless adults are voicing their concerns over the benefits that many companies give to their employees who are parents but not to nonparents (the following is from Belkin, 2000; Briggs, 2000; and Erbe, 2000). Among the list of complaints is that "family-friendly" companies allow parents time off to take care of their children's needs, attend a teacher conference, or to be exempt from working on holidays, nights, and weekends. To the extent that this occurs, workers without children must take up the slack. There is also considerable grumbling by childless workers about company benefits to parents such as subsidized day care, costly but free health benefits to an unlimited number of dependents. Elinor Burkett (2000) says that subsidized day care amounts to about $5000 per child plus health insurance packages for an average family, at a total value worth twice as much as the coverage plans given to childless employees. "The irony is that all this is happening at a time when we're supposed to be increasingly sensitive to the fact that families come in many forms. We say we want diversity, then we define benefits and tax breaks in terms of the most traditional families. . . . If compensation packages given to parents are worth $10,000 more than those given to nonparents, then we're compensating parents for their fertility and not their work" (Burkett, quoted in Briggs, 2000:3F).

Delayed Childbearing

There is a clear trend for contemporary couples to delay childbearing. Two statistics show this. First, the number of women having their first babies in their

"You'd think we'd have a grandchild with all the romantic vacations the kids take."

thirties has increased dramatically since the 1970s. Second, of all age groups, only women in their thirties show significant increases in fertility since 1976.

This shift toward more mature parenthood has several interesting consequences. First, the age gap between parents and their children is significantly greater than it was a generation ago. This may affect the quality of the parent-child relationship. It may be a positive development, as older parents have certain advantages over younger parents, such as more money and more maturity for dealing with the children. On the other hand, older parents, compared to younger parents, may have less patience and a diminished awareness of the needs of the young, especially when children reach adolescence. Second, while older parents will likely be more financially secure, having children later in life places the financial burden of a college education nearer the time of parental retirement, when it may deplete retirement savings. Third, children may push egalitarian couples back toward a more traditional division of labor—husband as provider and wife as homemaker. Aside from the traditional cultural prescriptions, which insist that the father work and the mother stay at home, there are the structural constraints that inhibit a role reversal. In most cases it makes more sense for the father to work because he can make more money than the mother. Many mothers, however, will continue their careers. Even those who might prefer to stay at home continue to work because their lifestyle depends on two incomes. The result is that more than half of all children under the age of eighteen live in homes with fathers and mothers in the workforce. The majority of children, then, spend time away from their parents in child-care centers, in preschools, and with peers—all of which lessen the parental influence on their socialization.

Family Composition

Size

Voluntary childlessness and delayed childbearing combine to shrink the size of families. The proportion of couples with no children has risen in the past twenty years, as has the number of one-child families. The result is a gradual shrinking of family size.

Form

The demographic trends noted in this chapter and elsewhere in this book have combined to alter the traditional family pattern. The typical family just a generation ago was composed of a working father, a homemaker mother, and their children. Now only a small minority of families—7 percent—meet that description.

As shown in Table 9.2, about two-thirds of children live with two parents. About three-fourths of White children live with two parents, almost two-thirds

TABLE 9.2

Percentage Distribution of Living Arrangements of Children under Age 18 by Race and Hispanic Origin: Selected Years

	1970	1980	1990	1998
Total				
Two parents	85	77	73	68
Mother only	11	18	22	23
Father only	1	2	3	4
No parent	3	4	3	4
White				
Two parents	90	83	79	74
Mother only	8	14	16	18
Father only	1	2	3	5
No parent	2	2	2	3
Black				
Two parents	58	42	38	36
Mother only	30	44	51	51
Father only	2	2	4	4
No parent	10	12	8	9
Hispanic				
Two parents	78	75	67	64
Mother only	—	20	27	27
Father only	—	2	3	4
No parent	—	3	3	5

Source: U.S. Department of Health and Human Services, *Trends in the Well-Being of America's Children & Youth: 1999.* Washington, DC: U.S. Government Printing Office, p. 39.

of Latino children live with two parents, but only slightly more than one-third of African American children do. In each instance the proportion of children living with two parents has declined significantly since 1970. These data, while informing about the rise of single-parent households, mask various other family forms—the children raised in stepfamilies, the children with same-sex parents, the children living in grandparent-maintained households, and the percentage of children living with several generations in the same dwelling.

Unmarried Parenting In sharp contrast to the traditional family pattern is the family now headed by a single adult (almost always a woman) and the dependent children By 2000, two-fifths of single mothers had never married. The rate of nonmarital births (the number of births per 1000 unmarried women) increased from 7.1 in 1940 to 43.9 in 1999. As a result, by 2000, single-mother families accounted for 22 percent of all families with children, up from 6 percent in 1950 (Bianchi and Casper, 2000:21).

In 1998, nonmarital fertility rates were highest among Latino women (90.1 births per 1000 women) and African American women (73.3 births per 1000 women), with White women at 27.4 births per 1000 women (AmeriStat, 2000b).

Annually, about 800,000 U.S. teenagers become pregnant, and 500,000 babies are born to them. The nation's highest teen birth rate was in 1957, with 96.3 births per 1000 teenage girls. Since then the rate has dropped to 49.6 in 1999 (AmeriStat, 2000c). These declines occurred in all racial and ethnic groups, but the greatest percentage drops have occurred among Puerto Rican and African American teenagers (Stolberg, 1999). Despite the significant decline in the teenage birth rate, the United States still has the highest adolescent pregnancy rate among developed countries.

Adoption Adoption creates a family form that differs from the traditional biologically related nuclear family. It "creates a family that is *connected* to another family, the birth family, and often to different cultures and to different racial, ethnic, and national groups as well" (Bartholet, 1993:186). Because the blood bond serves as the basis for kinship systems, adoptive family ties have been viewed traditionally as "second best" and adoptive children as "second choice" (March and Miall, 2000; Wegar, 2000). Research has revealed that both adoptive parents and adult adoptees have felt stigmatized by others who question the strength of their adoptive ties.

Adoption is relatively rare. Only about 3 percent of White teenage girls and 1 percent of African American teenage girls and an even smaller percent of adult women choose to give their babies up for adoption (Pollitt, 1996). Although many White families are eager to adopt an African American child, there are difficult hurdles to overcome (Smolowe, 1995). So, too, are the barriers, economic and bureaucratic, for adopting children from other societies. As a result, in an average year in the United States some 60,000 children are adopted. More than one-fourth of these adoptions involve children with "special needs," such as older children or children with mental, physical, or emotional handicaps (Fishman, 1992). Although many adopted children have typical childhoods, on average they are more likely to have problems than nonadopted children. As noted expert David Brodzinsky has suggested, "The experience of adoption exposes parents and children to a unique set of psychosocial tasks that interact with and complicate the more universal developmental tasks of family life" (quoted in Fishman, 1992:46).

Despite this obstacle, most adoptions do work. As Katha Pollitt has observed, "Of course adoption can be a wonderful thing; of course the ties between adoptive parents and children are as profound as those between biological ones" (Pollitt, 1996:9).

Solo Childhood In 1998, of women who were age fifty or more and therefore finished with childbearing, some 17.5 percent had given birth to only one child. That rate was up from 10 percent in 1980. All indications are that more and more families are choosing to limit their families to just one child (Swingle, 2000). This trend reflects other societal trends such as adults marrying later in life and the relatively high divorce rate. Also, some parents choose to have one child for career, financial, or other reasons, clearly different rationalizations than from generations ago.

Multigenerational Families Recent trends indicate the increase of multigenerational households. There are several types. One is the household in which children live in grandparent-maintained households. In 1997 approximately 3.9 million (5.5 percent of all children under age eighteen) children lived in such an arrangement (the following is primarily from Bryson and Casper, 1999). Some of these families have one or both parents present, but the fastest-growing situation is one in which grandchildren live with grandparents with no parent present ("skipped generation" households). The reasons for this growth of grandparents as surrogate parents are teen pregnancy, divorce, drug use by parents, economic marginality, the incarceration of parents, child abuse and neglect, mental and physical illness, and changes in welfare which are added to the pressures of

Recent trends indicate an increase in the number of multigenerational households.

single parents. Of all the grandparent-maintained households, 48 percent are White, 31 percent are African American, and 16 percent are Latino. When both grandparents are raising grandchildren without parents, the families are over-whelmingly White (57 percent), but when the children move in with a single grandmother, the families are predominantly African American (54 percent). The children living with only their grandmother are disproportionately poor and tend to be without any health insurance. Grandparents assuming the parental role are usually stretching meager resources, reducing freedom, and adding responsibility. At a time when they should be slowing down, they have the added burdens of providing emotional and economic support, transportation, guidance, and discipline for their grandchildren. The result, typically, is a high level of stress. Although the negatives are real, some positives are: (1) providing a sense of usefulness and productivity for the grandparent; (2) making the grandparents feel good that they are able to help both their child and grand-child; and (3) providing a more stable situation for the grandchild (Giarrusso et al., 2000).

In another type of multigenerational household, adults are taking care of their aging parents and their children simultaneously (known as the **sandwich generation**). Only a relatively few are caught in this bind, because it generally means the combination of two factors: having children late in life, and parents who suffer from premature disability.

A final type of multigenerational household, one that is on the rise, is one in which adult children, usually sons, who had lived on their own move back home to live with their parents. Some of this **"boomerang generation"** fit the stereo-type: unfocused, lazy, and immature. The majority, however, are students, the rest are unemployed, recently divorced or separated, or working at low-wage jobs. About 15 to 20 percent of adult children aged twenty to thirty and nearly 10 per-cent aged thirty and older live with their parents (Ward and Spitze, 1996). These rates are more than double those found in 1970. These rates, the highest on record, appear to be the result of economic hardship, the high cost of education (the aver-age total debt of students who have graduated from college was $18,800 in 1997, compared to $8200 in 1991; Associated Press, 1997a), unmarried parenthood, the tendency to marry later, and the ambivalence some young adults feel about play-ing adult roles (Goldscheider and Goldscheider, 1994; Mogelonsky, 1996).

Mixed-Race Children About 1.35 million of the 55.3 million married couples in the United States in 1998 were matches between people of different races (a rise of over 300 percent since 1970). The result, of course, is biracial children, who have increased about 400 percent in the past twenty-five years, while the num-ber of all births increased by just over 18 percent. This difference in growth rate will increase with the continued influx of immigration from Asia and Latin America, the trend toward numerical parity between Whites and non-Whites by 2050, and the increasing acceptance of racial intermarriage.

Same-Sex Parents Although it is impossible to know exactly, because some par-ents have not acknowledged to anyone else that they are gay or lesbian, a study using 1990 Census data indicated that a number of gay and lesbian families include children: 22 percent of lesbian families and 5 percent of gay families (Black et al., 2000). This adds up to more than 1 million children living in gay and lesbian families (Stacey, 1998). The existence of same-sex cohabitation, combined with the wish by many lesbian and gay couples for children, has resulted in a variety of family forms despite an array of social, legal, and practical challenges. The legality of homosexual parenthood varies from state to state, and the interpretation of the law often varies from judge to judge. Consider adoption: By the end of 1997 some twenty-two states allowed lesbians and gay men to adopt children, but no state permits a homosexual couple to adopt a child jointly. To circumvent this there is the practice of double-adopting, where the child is adopted by one person and then adopted again later by the other. This requires separate petitions, extensive delays, and twice the legal costs.

There are only a few hundred documented cases of adoption by openly homosexual couples. Of course, many adoptions take place in which a single person seeks the adoption while concealing her or his sexual orientation. Concealing one's homosexuality is common because gays and lesbians fear harassment and job discrimination, and, in the case of children, they wish to shield children from taunts and turmoil.

Another situation is custody of children by a homosexual parent following a heterosexual marriage. In such a situation judges are likely to give custody routinely to the heterosexual parent, assuming that this is better for the child.

It is important to note that many lesbian mothers had children before "coming out" and were awarded custody *as women,* not as lesbians. The point is that lesbian mothers can, and do, lose custody of their children *because of their sexual orientation.*

A third method to achieve parenthood is the practice by lesbians of artificial insemination (see Box 9.1). The partner of the mother in this arrangement often has difficulty in adopting the child. Presently only eight states permit a lesbian to adopt her lover's child and become a second parent.

The majority of same-sex parents are women because the courts are more likely to award custody to mothers and because of the lesbian baby boom through artificial insemination.

A final issue: Do children raised by gay or lesbian parents differ from those raised by heterosexual parents? A growing body of research indicates that the children of gay and lesbian parents develop normally, including their sexual identity. Charlotte Patterson, a psychologist, reviewed thirty studies of gay and lesbian parents and concluded that

> . . . despite longstanding legal presumptions against gay and lesbian parents in many states, despite dire predictions about their children based on well-known theories of psychosocial development, and despite the accumulation of a substantial body of research investigating these issues, *not a single study has found children of gay or lesbian parents to be disadvantaged in any significant respect relative to children of heterosexual parents.* Indeed, the evidence to date suggests that home environments provided by gay and lesbian parents are as likely as those provided by heterosexual parents to support and enable children's psychosocial growth (Patterson, 1992:1036; see also Patterson and Redding, 1996; Allen and Burrell, 1996; and Patterson, 2001) (emphasis added).

BOX 9.1   New Technologies and Family Life: The Consequences of Assisted Reproductive Technologies for Families

In July 1978 Louise Brown was born in England, the world's first child created as a result of in-vitro fertilization. Since then more than 300,000 "test-tube babies" have been born, and many more medical interventions have become available to infertile couples or same-sex couples who cannot become pregnant through regular biological means (much of this essay is taken from Stephen, 1999). These procedures, when successful, are modern miracles that fulfill the wishes of the parent(s). Moreover, they can be used to make sure that genetic diseases such as Tay-Sachs are not passed to the next generation. There are consequences and issues, however, that represent a down side for families as well.

One problem is that some procedures are very costly (e.g., $10,000 for one cycle of in-vitro fertilization; donor eggs cost $3000), and insurance coverage for infertility services tends to be limited or not available at all. The result is a class bias, as poor infertile couples and poor same-sex couples are denied the possibility of having children because of their economic situation.

Another issue involves obtaining "designer genes" through the careful selection of egg and sperm donors for all manner of desirable traits. An advertisement in a college newspaper, for example, said that "a couple was willing to pay $50,000 to an egg donor with SAT scores over 1400 who was at least 5'10" tall" (cited in Stephen, 1999). *USA Today* reported that models were requesting as much as $150,000 for their ovarian eggs, and that male models were asking $10,000 to $50,000 for sperm, which, presumably, will result in beautiful babies (Horovitz, 1999). This practice is legal, but is it ethical? Robert Stillman, medical director of a fertility center, says that this practice "is deplorable, unethical and speaks [to] only the basest of human desires. This speaks of human genetic engineering like the Nazis" (quoted in Horovitz, 1999:2B).

The next step in creating "designer genes" is the manipulation of the human genome (the 70,000 genes carried by every human) by inserting certain desirable genes into human eggs. Although not presently available to humans, it has been used successfully with rhesus monkeys (Begley, 2001). When the experiments lead to use in humans, the potential for genetic enhancement will increase exponentially. Although this breakthrough has the potential to conquer various diseases, there are potential dangers. Bioethicist Margaret Somerville asks: "[The human genome is] the patrimony of the entire species, held in trust for us by our ancestors and in trust by us for our descendants. It has taken millions of years to evolve; should we really be changing it in a generation or two?" (quoted in Begley, 2001:52). Another bioethicist, Arthur Schafer, worries about affluent parents-to-be having superior babies. He warns of new social divisions: in addition to the haves and have-nots, we will have the gene-rich and the gene-poor (paraphrased by Begley, 2001:52).

A common procedure for women with impaired fecundity is to take fertility drugs. One consequence of this is multiple births. In 1971 the rate for triplets or above was 29.1 per 100,000 live births. In 1996 the rate had risen dramatically to 152.6 (about one-third of this increase is due to delayed childbearing to the late reproductive years, which increases the likelihood of multiple births). Multiple births increases the risks to infants of problems such as preterm birth, low birth weight,

(continued)

(continued from previous page)

developmental brain damage, and cerebral palsy. Having twins, triplets, or quadruplets, of course, also increases the economic burden as well as overwhelming the parents with double, triple, or quadruple demands on their time and emotions.

An especially thorny problem involves the legal issues "in establishing parenthood when there may be as many as five people involved: a sperm donor, an egg donor, a gestational mother, and the contracting mother and father" (Stephen, 1999:2). Consider, for example, a lesbian strategy where

> . . . an ovum from one woman is fertilized with donor sperm and then extracted and implanted in her lover's uterus. The practical and legal consequences of this still "nascent" practice have not yet been tested, but the irony of deploying technology to assert a biological, and thereby a legal, social, and emotional claim to maternal and family status throws the contemporary instability of all relevant categories—biology, technology, nature, culture, maternity, family—into bold relief (Stacey,1998:121).

What if, in such an instance, the relationship is broken and both parties seek custody of the child in the courts? Who is the biological parent? Is it the woman whose egg was fertilized, or is it the woman whose uterus was used to bring the fetus to birth? What about the sperm donor, who could actually be a relative (a common occurrence, with often the brother of one of the lesbian partners donating his sperm): does he have a claim? Similar questions occur with heterosexual couples who have used reproductive technology to produce a child. There can be later claims by surrogate mothers (whose uterus brought the fetus to term), egg and sperm donors. The result is a legal quagmire.

These conclusions are challenged by sociologists Judith Stacey and Timothy Biblarz (2001). They re-evaluated 21 psychological studies conducted between 1981 and 1998, which found that children raised by same-sex parents were no different from those reared by heterosexual parents. Their analysis of those studies revealed that: (1) the emotional health of youngsters with heterosexual or gay parents is essentially the same; (2) the offspring of lesbians and gays, however, are more likely to depart from traditional gender roles than the children of heterosexual couples; and (3) children with same-sex parents seem to grow up to be more open to homoerotic relations. Stacey and Biblarz conclude that nothing in their work justifies discrimination against gay families or alters their conviction that gays and lesbians can be excellent parents raising well-adjusted children.

Earlier in this chapter we considered parenting as a socially constructed phenomenon. The existence of lesbian and gay parents demonstrate this.

> Lesbian and gay parents challenge the primacy enjoyed by "traditional" heterosexual marriage and parenthood. They reveal, by their innovation in creating and maintaining families that thrive even in a hostile social environment, that parenting is not an essentialistic or inherently natural experience. Lesbian and gay parents exemplify that families are constructed by a variety of biological, adoptive, and chosen kin ties (Allen, 1997:198).

THE IMPACT OF CHILDREN ON MARRIAGE

Probably no single event has more impact on a marriage and on the marriage partners than the addition of a child. This momentous event impacts the career patterns of the parents, the pattern of housework, the distribution of power, marital satisfaction, and the economic well-being of the unit. Significantly, when spouses become parents, they shift to responding to each other in terms of role obligations rather than as intimates. Interaction patterns shift, as do the patterns of domestic work, communication, and the distribution of power, and the shift is usually toward more traditional gender roles. In effect, then, the addition of a child changes the social organization of the family. To discuss these consequences, this section is divided into four parts—the transition to parenthood, the benefits of parenthood, the costs of parenthood, and gendered parenting.

The Transition to Parenthood

The birth of the first child to a couple brings enormous changes to the parents and their relationship. The structure of their daily lives is altered. The workload of the parents grows with the time devoted to child care. Their living space is more constricted. The freedom the couple had previously is now curtailed severely. The attention that was once lavished on each other is now interrupted by the new arrival. Their lovemaking may become less frequent and more inhibited. There are heightened financial problems. The new mother and new father

> . . . find themselves riding the same roller coaster of elation, despair, and bafflement. . . . [They approached] parenthood full of high hopes and soaring dreams . . . [yet] six months or a year after the child's birth they . . . find themselves wondering "What's happening to us?" (Belsky and Kelly, 1994:4).

Jay Belsky and John Kelly's research on new parents found, among other things, that parenthood presents a fundamental source of tension between the parents. Most couples approach parenthood assuming that the new baby will bring them closer together. In time this often happens, but initially a child has the opposite effect. Couples, even those who consider themselves

> . . . as like-minded often find their priorities and needs diverging dramatically when they become parents. Differences in family background and personality also contribute to transition-time marital gaps. No matter how much they love each other, no two people share the same values or feelings or have the same perspective on life, and few things highlight these personal differences as pointedly as the birth of a child (Belsky and Kelly, 1994:12).

Differences emerge over new concerns, such as whether to minister to every demand of the infant or not, or feelings intensify over old disagreements about the division of labor, which, with the arrival of a baby, is so relentless.

There is considerable evidence that children have a negative effect on marital happiness. Representative of these findings is the research from a national survey of families (Heaton et al., 1996). The researchers found that the child's influence on marital relationships varies with the age of the child. When parents

have very young children, the parents tend to perceive positive parent-child relationships, but these couples spend less time together and have more marital disagreements. Marital stability, however, is greatest in the first five years following
the birth of a child. During the early adolescent years, on the other hand, there
is a declining closeness in the parent-child relationship and high marital disagreement about children. The researchers also found that the greater the behavior problems of the child, the greater the marital disagreement, the less time
together, and the lower marital happiness. They conclude that couples tend to be
happiest before the arrival of the first child. This happiness declines with the
arrival of a child and reaches a low point as children reach adolescence. Marital
happiness increases after the children leave home.

These and other concerns alter marriages. The research of Belsky and Kelly
found that the entry of a child into a marriage relationship changes marriage in
one of four ways (Belsky and Kelly, 1994:14–15):

1. About 13 percent of new parents are what Belsky and Kelly term "severe
   decliners." These new parents become so split by their differences that
   they lose faith in each other and in their marriage. Their communication
   diminishes, as does their love.
2. Another 38 percent are "moderate decliners." These couples avoid a dramatic falling out, but their love and communication is less than before the
   birth of their child.
3. About 30 percent of the couples experienced "no change." Their marriage
   neither declined nor was enhanced by their child.
4. Nineteen percent of the couples in Belsky and Kelly's study were
   "improvers." These couples found that their new child brought them
   closer together, increased communication, and enhanced their mutual love.

The Benefits of Parenthood

Throughout U.S. history the role of parenthood has been exalted, especially for
wives. The assumption has been that a woman's destiny and her ultimate fulfillment were wrapped up in motherhood. This pronatalist belief was fostered by
the encouragement of young girls to play at motherhood (e.g., playing with
dolls, "playing house"), by children's literature that presented women mainly in
nurturing roles, by the Madonna theme in art, and by kinship expectations to
marry and have children. The consequence of this usually unquestioned sanctity
of childbearing is that today 85 percent of marriages produce children. Although
most marriages include children, becoming parents is not a trivial event. The
partners in a marriage now add the roles of mother and father to their already
complex relationship, and this has profound implications.

The benefits of parenthood are several. First, children can positively affect
the marriage bond. The partners share in the miracle of birth, their creation of a
common product, their new and enhanced status in two kinship networks, and
pride in their offspring's accomplishments. They can experience mutual satisfaction in nurturing the emotional and physical growth of the child. The pres-

ence of children may also encourage communication between spouses as they share experiences and work through problems.

A second benefit of having a child is that it symbolizes a kind of immortality, a link with the past and the future. Related to this is that parents often find it exhilarating to see themselves in their children, as the personality traits of parents, their mannerisms, and their values are passed on and acted out by their child. Third, having a child may give the lives of parents a sense of meaning and purpose. This may be especially true for those with low social status. The pride they do not find in their work may be found in their child.

A fourth benefit, and related to the third, is the enhanced status one has as a parent. Parenthood is tangible evidence of one's adulthood to almost everyone—kin, colleagues, friends, neighbors, employers, and community agencies. Fifth, with children there is the ultimate giving and receiving of unconditional love. Sixth, parents can benefit by symbolically recapturing their youth through their child's activities and accomplishments as well as by vicariously having experiences they were denied as children themselves.

A final benefit is that parents are more likely to be integrated in their communities than childless adults (Ambert, 1992). As parents meeting their children's needs, they interact with physicians, teachers, coaches, sitters, daycare providers, and other parents. They become connected to organizations such as schools, churches, sports leagues, children's clinics, daycare and preschool centers. Children may act as social facilitators as they introduce their parents to the parents of their friends and classmates. Similarly, the children of immigrants who do not know the language of the host country may be the catalysts in connecting their parents with the larger community.

The Costs of Parenthood

While children bring joy to parents, the realistic examination of parenthood requires that we examine the negatives as well as the positive. Almost all of the benefits just listed have a negative side: children can adversely affect marital happiness, children can have negative personality traits, they can get into trouble, and they may not return their parents' love. Added to these are other emotional costs to parents. They worry about the child's safety, physical and emotional development, progress in school, potential negative influences of the child's peers, and the like. When the child fails in school or at work, becomes a social misfit, gets arrested for driving under the influence of drugs or alcohol, or becomes a criminal, the parents tend to blame themselves. Adolescence, in particular, is an emotionally difficult time for parents and adolescents as there is the inevitable clash of wills.

Financially, children are a significant burden. According to the U.S. Department of Agriculture, the average middle-income, two-parent family will spend an average of $160,140 to feed, clothe, house, and educate a child born in 1999 to age 18 (reported in *USA Today*, 2000:9D).

In addition to the direct costs of raising children, there are also indirect costs, including the lost wages of the parent (typically the mother) who leaves the workforce to take care of the child. This means a significant loss in lifetime earnings and retirement income.

Gendered Parenting

There has been a shift in men's involvement in pregnancy. Just a generation ago, most fathers-to-be were not involved in preparation for the impending birth. Most were not witnesses in the birth. Now, many prospective fathers join their pregnant wives in prenatal classes. These husbands are present at the birth, helping their wives with breathing and other relaxation techniques. They may hold the newborn and present it to the new mother in a significant symbolic gesture. They may even take time off from work for a week or two to help care for and bond with the infant.

This relatively new involvement of men with pregnancy and birth, however, has *not* resulted in equal responsibility for child care: "The mother still does most of the work not because she is more nurturing or competent but because the culture ideologically and practically structures women's and men's parenting behavior and the time spent in paid work" (Lorber, 1994:162).

Michael Lamb (1987) divides child care into three components: *accessibility,* or being on call near the child but not directly engaged in care; *direct interaction or one-on-one care,* such as feeding, bathing, playing, reading, helping with homework; and *responsibility,* thinking about the child's emotional, social, and physical development, and making arrangements for such activities as babysitting, doctor visits, and school visits.

> Lamb found that in two-parent families in the United States in which mothers did not work outside the home, fathers spent about 20 to 25 percent of the time that mothers spent in direct interaction with children, and about a third of the time in

"It's O.K. by me — Ask your Mom."

being accessible. They assumed no responsibility for children's care or rearing. In two-parent families where both mothers and fathers were employed thirty or more hours a week, fathers interacted with children 33 percent of the time that mothers did and were accessible 65 percent of the time mothers were, but they assumed no more responsibility for children's welfare than when mothers were full-time home-makers. *In fact, the higher proportional level of their day-to-day child care was due to employed mothers' spending less time with the children; it did not reflect more actual time spent with children by the father* (Lamb, 1987; summarized by Lorber, 1994:163; emphasis added).

The parenting pattern, then, is clear—mothers are the primary caregivers, while fathers are passive; mothers spend more time actually doing things to and for their children as well as doing the emotional work or caring and worrying about them. Just as with housework, women are the givers and men the takers.

There are exceptions to this overriding tendency. First, "the overall pattern for all regions, ethnic groups, and religions in the United States was that fathers spend more time with sons than with daughters and were more likely to play with them than do things for them" (Lorber, 1994:163).

A second exception occurs when fathers become the primary parent because of widowhood or divorce. In these instances, single fathers develop relationships with their children that are intimate and nurturing.

A final deviation from the typical male parenting pattern is when couples deliberately share parenting. Here children have two primary caretakers. Parents divide chores and spend time with the children equitably, as noted in the title of a book on shared parenting *Halving It All* (Deutsch, 1999). This sharing, however, is not as easy as it may appear on the surface. Research has shown, for example, that couples find it easy to divide the work (e.g., changing diapers, giving baths, taking them to lessons) but that mothers tended to do more of the emotion work: "Women feel on call for their children all the time; men do not. Men can more easily distance themselves from their children, letting them cry, not paying attention to their every move, and not thinking about them at work" (Lorber, 1994:166). Thus, parenting often remains gendered even among those who work at overcoming the inequitable arrangements between more traditional couples.

There is a major debate over the consequences of gender egalitarianism of the parents for their children. Conservative scholars claim that contemporary egalitarian lifestyles are undermining families and placing children at risk (Glenn, 1997; Popenoe, 1993). Progressive scholars, in contrast, argue that families are changing but not declining. They see egalitarian marriages as an improvement over traditional families because they provide increased opportunities for adult self-fulfillment, especially equitable arrangements for women (Coontz, 1997; Stacey, 1996).

Family sociologists Alan Booth and Paul Amato (1994), using a twelve-year longitudinal study, examined whether nontraditional gender roles among parents are associated with later life outcomes of children. They defined nontraditional families as those in which mothers are employed, fathers contribute to household and child care, and parents hold egalitarian attitudes toward gender roles. Booth and Amato found very little evidence that being raised in nontraditional families had adverse or positive effects on offspring well-being. Adult children from nontraditional families are less likely to live with their parents, they have slightly poorer relationships with their fathers, and they are more likely to have nontraditional gender attitudes. Many aspects of the parent–children relationship are unaffected. The children of nontraditional families are just as likely as those from traditional families to get married and have children, to be happily married, to have positive self-esteem, to experience psychological distress, and to achieve similar levels of education. The authors conclude that

> . . . our evidence does not support the notion that nontraditional families are creating serious problems for their offspring. This is not surprising in that, through history and across cultures, there have been a variety of ways of organizing the family division of labor. Long-term offspring outcomes probably have more to do with economic well-being, parental warmth and competence, social support, and other resources than with family organization. In contrast to the claims of those on the religious and political right, our research suggests that the current trend toward a less traditional, more egalitarian division of labor in the family poses relatively few problems for the youth of today (Booth and Amato, 1994:874).

Houseknecht and Sastry (1996) compared the well-being of children in four societies, from the least traditional (Sweden), followed in order by the United States, the former West Germany, and the most traditional, Italy. They found that the decline of the traditional family is not associated with the kind of deleterious consequences for child well-being asserted by conservatives.

THE IMPACT OF PARENTS ON CHILDREN AND OF CHILDREN ON PARENTS

Parents, more than anyone else, interact with their children on a continuing basis and, therefore, have a crucial impact on their children's physical, social, and emotional development. Ideally, parents provide children with communication skills, the interpretation of events and behaviors, identity, a haven in time of distress, a source of emotional attachment, a sense of what is right and wrong, and skills for competence in the social world.

> When [the child] enters the human group, he is quite at the mercy of parents and siblings. They determine both what and when he shall eat and wear, when he shall sleep and wake, what he shall think and feel, how he shall express his thoughts and feelings (what language he shall speak and how he shall do it), what his political and religious commitments shall be, what sort of vocation he shall aspire to. Not that parents are ogres. They give what they have to give: their own limited knowledge, their prejudices and passions. There is no alternative to this giving of themselves; nor for the receiver is there any option. Neither can withhold the messages conveyed to the other (Wilson, 1966:92).

Although parents are clearly important socializing agents, this observation must be balanced by the reality that the child is not an empty vessel that the parents fill but, to the contrary, the child is an active social being who often shapes the parents.

Historically, theories of childhood have focused on children's internalization of and adaptation to their parents and societal constraints. In this deterministic

Influence flows both from parents to children and from children to parents.

view children were believed to be shaped and molded by adults who reinforced proper behavior and punished inappropriate behavior. More recently, less deterministic, more constructionist theories of childhood have been advanced. "In this perspective, *children are seen as negotiators and co-creators of their own worlds*" (Shehan, 1999:6). In other words, the child is not assumed to be a passive receptor of parental influences but rather influence flows both from parents to the child and from the child to parents. The joke that "insanity is hereditary—parents get it from their children" illustrates this point. Parents respond to the smiles, sighs, irritability, and crying of infants. The infant with colic acts in ways that exert control over the parents. The gender of the infant affects parents as they, typically, treat boys differently than girls, have different expectations according to gender, and structure the play and room environments of children according to gender stereotypes. The child may resist the demands of parents, such as toilet training. Younger and older children can manipulate their parents through their behaviors (e.g., showing affection or being difficult). Clearly, the power and authority of parents to form their child is not total: the child is not a blank slate to be filled in by parental instruction but is rather an active agent in its own construction of knowledge about the world (Kuczynski et al., 1999). This construction will not necessarily be the same as that held by the parents. Thus, the child may have insights, the child may teach, and the child may even lead.

For example, older children may pressure their parents to quit smoking, to eat a healthier diet, and to act more positively toward the environment (Garekik, 1991). In short, the child, while being shaped by the parents, is also active in shaping them. This is known as the **bilateral model of parent child relations** (Kuczynski et al., 1999).

THE STRUCTURE OF THE FAMILY EMBEDDED IN A LARGER NETWORK OF INFLUENCES

Several family structure variables profoundly affect the social and emotional development of the child regardless of overt attempts by parents to socialize their young in particular ways. This section examines first the variables related to family structure and then some extrafamilial factors.

Family Structure

One-Child Families

Only children are commonly believed to be worse off than children with siblings. They are stereotyped as self-centered, lonely, spoiled, and anxious. These are faulty beliefs, however. Research finds that only children are superior to children with siblings on virtually all positive dimensions including intelligence, achievement, maturity, leadership, health, and satisfaction with friends and family.

Family Size

With the addition of each child, the resources that a family has for each is diminished. Douglas Downey (1995) analyzed data from a national sample of 25,000 eighth-graders and found that parental interpersonal resources such as interaction with children and knowing their friends were negatively affected by additional children. Similarly, parental economic resources for their children, such as a personal computer, a place to study, money saved for college, and music or art lessons were all negatively related to additional children (summarized in Eshleman, 2000). Of course, the economic resource problem is minimized when the family is relatively affluent.

The average American has one or two siblings. This is compounded as many sibling relationships have become "a tangle of steps and halves created by multiple marriages" (Crispell, 1996:24). Having siblings as a child and later as an adult has profound effects on family members, as they share genuine emotional ties. The strength of sibling bonds is related to gender, as girls and women have stronger sibling bonds than boys and men.

Birth Order

A significant family structure variable affecting the child is ordinal position. As Jerome Kagan has pointed out:

> Despite the importance of parental behavior, the mere existence of a younger or older sibling in the family is a salient force in the psychological development of the child. The mechanisms that account for these differences do not rest only with the

practices and communications of the parents, and, therefore, they are not solely a function of what is normally meant by "direct family experience." Rather, the catalyst of change is simply the introduction of "another," like the introduction of a crystal into a cloud to precipitate rain. The "other" is the catalyst that creates uncertainty in the child. In response to that uncertainty, the child alters his beliefs, behaviors, and roles (Kagan, 1977:53).

Therefore, when compared with later-born children, firstborns have a strong tendency to adopt the values of their parents and to be less influenced by peers. They tend to be more achievement-oriented, to excel in school, and to have higher verbal scores on aptitude tests. These advantages accrue from the time they had the exclusive attention of parents and because they want to differentiate themselves from their younger brothers or sisters. Thus, "the first-born is propelled to adulthood by the presence of the younger sibling" (Kagan, 1977:51). Later-born children never have the exclusive attention of their parents. They have the additional disadvantage of always appearing less competent than the firstborn. The result is for later-born children, when compared to firstborns, to be less cautious, more impulsive, and more involved in physically dangerous activities. They are more peer-conscious and more willing to challenge authority.

Primary Parents

The question of who does the primary parenting, while seemingly straightforward, is quite complex because there are so many possible variations. These possibilities depend on the number of parents in the household (or even if there are no parents in the "parental" role, such as households headed by grandparents or foster parents); if there is only one parent, the gender of that parent; the presence or not of an extended family; parents' marital status; the sexual orientation of the parents—and each of these may have different effects on children depending on their age (Demo and Cox, 2001). For example, a study of African American children in the Woodlawn community in Chicago distinguished 86 different combinations of adults living in households with first graders (Hunter and Ensminger, 1992). Of crucial importance is the timing and sequencing off changes in children's living arrangements.

The following are some research-based generalizations concerning some of these variations:

- The absence of a same-sex parent for daughters of solo fathers and sons of solo mothers tends to have a negative impact.
- The presence of two adults, even if the second adult is not a legal parent, has been found to diminish adolescent behavior problems.
- Growing up in nontraditional gender role families does not have adverse effects on the children (see Box 9.2).
- Children of lesbian and gay parents have normal relationships with peers and their relationships with adults of both sexes is satisfactory.
- Children do better in stable living arrangements than transitory ones even if the stability involves living with a single parent. For example, children experiencing multiple transitions (e.g., from two parents to single parent to parent and stepparent) and experiencing them later in childhood fare

---

BOX 9.2   **Researching Families:** Parental Gender Role Nontraditionalism and Offspring Outcomes

As we have noted throughout this book, the emerging family of the 1980s and 1990s differs significantly from the traditional nuclear family of the 1950s. Now the majority of mothers are in the labor force. Many contemporary mothers and fathers share child-care and household tasks (albeit still unequally for the most part). And the attitudes of spouses concerning gender roles have changed in many families. What, if any, are the outcomes for children raised in families with nontraditional gender roles?

Sociologists Alan Booth and Paul Amato (1994) investigated this question using data from a longitudinal study of a representative sample of 471 parents and their adult offspring. This procedure allowed the researchers to interview children at least nineteen years of age in 1992, whose parents had been interviewed in 1980, 1983, 1988, and 1992. Thus, they were able to determine the behaviors and attitudes of parents as their children were being raised as well as how the children were affected as adults. They were interested in the effects of maternal employment, paternal involvement in home activities, and parental attitudes regarding gender roles. In their analysis they controlled for the possible confounding effects of parent's gender and race, mother's education and age, and offspring's age and gender. In other words, they compared respondents similar on a variable to assess whether or not another variable was making a difference.

When comparing the children of traditional parents with those of nontraditional parents, Booth and Amato found that the latter (1) were more likely to leave home prior to marriage; (2) were less likely to be close to their fathers (possibly because the fathers were not living at home); (3) were similar to the former in ties to close relatives and friends; (4) were just as likely as those from traditional homes to get married and to parent; (5) were the same as the children from traditional families on measures of psychological well-being; and (6) were comparable to their traditional counterparts in educational attainment.

---

poorly compared to those living their entire childhood in stable single-parent families (Demo and Cox, 2001:105).

- Children in stepfamilies, compared with those in first-married families, are more likely to experience a broad range of adjustment problems.

Extrafamilial Factors

As parents interact with their children, they are not free from outside influences. A number of work-related factors, for example, affect parents and their interactions with children. Some of these are the level of job satisfaction, promotions or demotions, transfer to a new community, level of pay, work schedules, job-related stress, layoffs or threatened layoffs, sexual harassment at work, job discrimination, and the presence of both parents in the workforce.

The influence of parents on their children is diminished by a number of other outside forces as well. When both parents work, preschool children will be

The familiy's resources and educational achievements affect how children perceive themselves.

cared for by someone other than the parents. Once the child is of school age, the school (that is, its teachers, policies, and curriculum) becomes an important socialization agent, sometimes in opposition to the wishes of the parents, causing some to move their children to other school environments or to home schooling.

As children grow they spend less time under the direct supervision of their parents. They are increasingly supervised by others such as teachers, coaches, and youth leaders. Most important, though, is the influence of peers on young people, especially adolescents. Especially disconcerting to parents is that their adolescent children are learning to deal with potentially risky behaviors at the very time peer influence increases (Furstenberg, 2001).

The neighborhoods in which families reside can be mixed in terms of social class and race/ethnicity but more likely they will be relatively homogeneous composed of neighbors of the same social class and race/ethnicity. Thus, living in an area of concentrated poverty such as an urban ghetto or in affluence (gated suburban community), provides peers with the same backgrounds, and privilege or the lack thereof in terms of opportunities, well-financed schools, and community services.

The economic resources of families is a crucial factor affecting the outcomes of children. The amount of family income available to children depends on the type of family in which he or she lives (Bianchi and Casper, 2000:27). Most basically, social class position provides for the child's life chances. The greater the family's economic resources, the better the chance to live beyond infancy, to be in good health, to receive a good education, to have a satisfying job, to avoid being labeled a criminal, to avoid death in war, and to live the "good life." Negatively, this means that millions of America's children are denied these advantages because they were born to parents who were unemployed, underemployed, stuck in the lower tier of the segmented labor market, handicapped, victims of institutional racism or sexism, divorced or separated, or otherwise disadvantaged.

Significantly, the family's resources and educational achievements affect the way in which children perceive themselves. These ascribed characteristics (along with race/ethnicity and gender) place children in the perceptions of others, in turn giving children an understanding of their worth. If the family has favored characteristics, children are very likely to gain nourishment from the social power and esteem that come from high social position. But the children of the poor and minorities find they are devalued by persons outside the immediate family and kin network; this perception can have a profound effect on their psyches and behavior regardless of the efforts of their parents (Kagan, 1977:35, 47).

PARENTS AND CHILDREN IN DUAL-EARNER FAMILIES

Since 1960, the rise of women's participation in the labor force has been dramatic. For example, the percentage of women in two-parent families with children under six years old in the workforce increased from around 19 percent in 1960 to almost two-thirds in 1999; for mothers with school-aged children, the percentage of mothers in the labor force increased from less than 40 percent in 1960 to slightly more than three-fourths in 1999. Most significant, 1987 was the first time that more than one-half of all mothers with babies one year old or younger were working or looking for work, and that percentage continues to increase.

This phenomenal rise is a consequence of several factors. Feminism has encouraged many women to seek fulfillment in a career outside the home. Wives in many husband-wife households work outside the home to supplement family income, since one-wage families have lost purchasing power since 1973. The rapid rise in the numbers of working women is also a consequence of the growth in the divorce rate and in female-headed households, where their participation in the labor force is an economic necessity.

Working mothers in both categories, single and married, share similar problems, such as low pay (74 cents for each dollar earned by men in 2000), juggling the demands of a job, housework, and parenting, as well as finding good child care. One critical difference, however, is that single mothers tend to raise their children with inadequate financial resources, whereas married mothers in the workforce tend to have an adequate financial base.

Social Supports for Working Parents

Dual-earner families and single-parent families (the subject of the next section) share a common problem—the lack of adequate social supports in the community and workplace to ease the strains of their dual roles of workers and parents. In general, U.S. society is unresponsive to the needs of working parents. Single women especially need supplementary help, such as subsidies for food, housing, health care, and child care, but the government in recent times has restricted and even denied rather than enlarged such supplementary aid to the poor and the near poor.

Places of work have been slow to respond to the needs of their employees who are or who soon will be parents. The traditional organization of work—an inflexible eight-hour workday—makes it difficult for parents to cope with family problems or the conflicting schedules of family members. Many European countries have some form of "flextime" arrangement that allows workers to meet their family and work obligations, but in the United States only about one in six employees has such an opportunity. About 80 percent of industrialized countries offer paid maternity leave to women workers (Canada, for example offers 17 weeks). The United States, in contrast, passed the Family and Medical Leave Act in 1993, which permits up to 12 weeks of unpaid leave in companies with more than fifty employees (Heintz and Folbre, 2000:63)

Aside from the issue of availability of good child care, there is the crucial question of the effects of child care on children. The common assumption is that a preschool child deprived of maximum interaction with its parents, especially the mother, will be harmed. Because this belief is widely accepted, many working parents feel guilty for their assumed neglect.

The relationship between child care and child development is complex, involving sources within the child (e.g., temperament, impairment), factors in the child's immediate environment (such as the quality of relationships with parents), and factors in the child's larger social environment (e.g., neighborhood). Although this complexity prevents us from gaining a full understanding of the relationship between child care and child development, the cumulative evidence from empirical studies does permit some conclusions (the following is from a thorough review of the research by a panel on child care of the National Research Council, as reported by Hayes et al. [1990:47–144]; and Belsky [1991]; for findings from other research, see Burchinal [1999]).

1. Young children need to develop enduring relationships with a limited number of specific individuals, relationships characterized by affection, reciprocal interaction, and responsiveness to the individualized cues of young children.
2. There is a normal tendency for children to form multiple, simultaneous attachments to caregivers.
3. Children can benefit from "multiple mothering" if it provides affection, warmth, responsiveness, and stimulation in the context of enduring rela-

tionships with a reasonably small number of caregivers (usually assumed to be five or fewer).

4. For children beginning child care after their first year of life, there is little indication of differences in the mother-child relationship. Children beginning full-time child care within the first year, however, increase the risk of insecurity in their attachments to their mothers than children at home full-time with their mothers.

5. Children reared in child care orient more strongly to peers and somewhat less strongly to adults than their home-reared counterparts.

6. Child care does not negatively affect the cognitive development of middle-class children, and it has positive consequences for the intellectual development of low-income children (if the child-care programs emphasize cognitive enrichment, as Head Start does).

7. The overall quality of child care (group size, caregiver/child ratio, caregiver training, and educational material available) is associated with children's cognitive as well as social development.

8. The children who experience quality care in their families and child-care environments have the strongest development. Children from low-income families are the most likely to be found in lower-quality care settings; thus, they experience double jeopardy from encountering stress at home and stress in their care environments.

The most comprehensive research on the effects of daycare on children was sponsored by the federal government's National Institute of Child Health and Development. Researchers from fourteen universities tracked children from birth to age three, comparing those cared for full-time by their mothers with those spending time in daycare centers for varying amounts of time. Among the findings were that children in daycare develop as normally and as quickly as children who stay home with their mothers; and children cared for by adults other than their parents have normal cognitive, linguistic, social, and emotional development (Scarr, 1997).

Thus, we conclude that daycare under the right conditions can be a positive experience for children. Over three-fourths of preschoolers are cared for on a regular basis by someone other than the parent. The Urban Institute estimated that in 1997 more children under age five were in center-based care (32 percent) than in any other form of care; 24 percent were under the care of parents; 23 percent were cared for by relatives and 16 percent by non-relatives; and 6 percent were cared for by nannies and babysitters (cited in Greenberg and Springen, 2000). Unfortunately, many of these children are in daycare situations that do not meet the standards that lead to positive experiences for children. A key problem is the hiring and retaining of high-quality, well-trained daycare workers. The problem with most daycare centers is that they are underfunded. This results in low wages, which creates a shortage of qualified staff. Whereas the average kindergarten teacher makes $19.16 an hour, the average center-based child-care teacher nationwide earns about $6.70 an hour (Whitebook, 1999). With pay so low and benefits so meager, the annual daycare worker turnover is relatively high and the training expected of workers prior to being hired is minimal. The result, often, is inadequate care. The child-care providers claim that they would pay their employees more if they could, but that would mean charging parents more, which is difficult because daycare is so costly now. According to a 1999 survey of seventy-five cities, a child in a for-profit daycare center eight hours a day each weekday costs annually anywhere from $3120 (Tampa) to $8616 (Boston) (reported in *Parade*, 1999). For the fortunate few there are posh centers such as the Creme de la Creme child-care center in Denver, which charges a tuition of $14,000 a year (Biondo, 2000). In return, the preschoolers study French, use state-of-the-art computers, participate in plays, make use of math labs and dance studios, listen to classical music, and exercise in three playgrounds and a water park—another instance of the benefits of privilege.

What should be done to improve daycare for the children of working parents? This issue was addressed in the previous chapter and will be addressed further in the final chapter, so we will discuss conflicting solutions here. There are two fundamental policy issues involving child care—should the government intervene with subsidies and standards; and if the solution is governmental, then at what level? Conservatives oppose government intervention for several reasons. Some conservatives oppose the government's subsidization of child care because it encourages mothers to leave their homes for the workplace.* The Christian Coalition supports this view and is thus opposed to the funding of child care. Others oppose it because of higher taxes. Still others fear governmental intervention in what they consider issues best left to individual families and the marketplace. Progressives argue that the United States provides the least assistance to working parents and their children of any industrialized nation (Helburn, 1999). As a result, many of our children are neglected. And, as usual, the neglect is correlated with social class, as the affluent can afford the best care for their children and the poor are left to fend for themselves.

The second issue—should the federal or state governments help to fund child care—also divides conservatives and progressives. Conservatives seek governmental help at the local and state levels because they fear federal bureaucracy and the universal standards that may not apply to local conditions. Progressives, on the other hand, argue for federal programs because they will ensure that every child, regardless of location, will receive approximately the same benefits. If left to the states, some legislatures and governors will be generous while others will do little, if anything, to provide benefits to the children of working parents. For example, Georgia is presently the only state to provide free child care for all four-year-olds, while forty-one other states provide some assistance, but eight states do not provide any help, and New Hampshire still doesn't mandate public kindergarten. Thus, if left to the individual states, the benefits to children will be very uneven at best.

---

*There is a major contradiction among conservatives on this point. On the one hand, they favor strongly incentves to encourage middle-class women to forgo employment while their children are young, so that they can care for them at home. At the same time, conservatives approve of government policies such as eliminating welfare to poor mothers (Aid to Families with Dependient Children) and forcing them into the labor force in spite of inadequate provision of early child care (Helburn, 1999:9).

☉INGLE PARENTS AND THEIR CHILDREN

More than one fourth (27 percent) of all U.S. children live with just one parent, up from 12 percent in 1970. Half of all children spend some of their childhoods in single-parent families (Children's Defense Fund, 1997:13). (See Figure 9.2a.) One in five children spends his or her entire childhood in a single-parent household (Demo and Cox, 2001). Over 80 percent of single-parent families are headed by a woman. Single mothers, on average, spend a total of about nine years raising children without a partner present (Bianchi and Casper, 2000:22). In 1999 over half of all African American children (51 percent) lived in mother-only families, compared with 27 percent of Latino children, 16 percent of White children, and 15 percent of Asian American children (AmeriStat 2000d). (See Figure 9.2b.)

The disproportionate number of single-parent families headed by a woman is a consequence, first, of the relatively high divorce rate and the very strong tendency for divorced and separated women to have custody of the children. Second, there is the relatively high rate of never-married mothers (in 1960, 5 percent of U.S. babies were born to unmarried mothers; in 1999, one-third were) To counter the common myths, the facts indicate that two-thirds of unwed mothers

Figure 9.2

(A) Living arrangements of children, 1980 to 1999. (B) Living arrangements of children by race/ethnicity, 1999.

Source: http//ameristat.org/children/image3.html, 11/6/01.

are *not* teenagers. Moreover, while the unwed birth rate for African Americans is higher than for Whites, there are more unwed births among Whites than among African Americans. Figure 9.3 presents the data on unmarried births by race and ethnicity. Note the variation within the Hispanic and Asian American categories.

The important question to answer concerning this trend is: What are the effects on children of living in mother-only families? Research has shown consistently that children from single-parent homes are more likely than children from intact families to have behavioral problems. McLanahan and Booth's (1991) review of the recent research on children from mother-only families, compared to children from two-parent families, shows that:

- They have poorer academic achievement. This relationship is more negative for boys than for girls.
- They are more likely to have higher absentee rates at school.
- They are more likely to drop out of school.

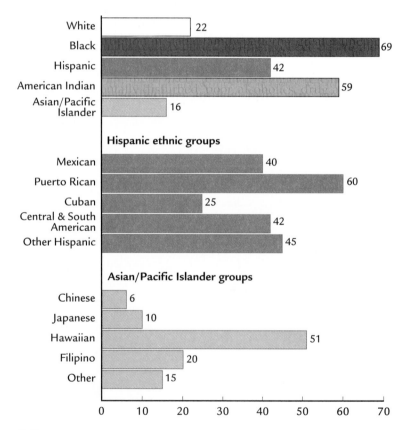

Figure 9.3

Percentage of births to unmarried women, 1998

Source: Suzanne M. Bianchi and Lynne M. Casper, "American Families," *Population Bulletin* 55 (December 2000):22.

- They are more likely to have lower earnings in young adulthood and are more likely to be poor.
- They are more likely to marry early and to have children early, both in and out of marriage.
- If they marry, they are more likely to divorce.
- They are more likely to commit delinquent acts and to engage in drug and alcohol use.

Because over 80 percent of one-parent families are headed by a woman, the common explanation for the disproportionate pathologies found among the children of single parents has been that the absence of a male adult is detrimental to their development. The presence of both mothers and fathers contributes to the healthy development of the child (Marsiglio et al., 2001). Also, the absence of a spouse makes coping with parenting more difficult. Coping is difficult for any single parent—female or male—because of three common sources of strain: (1) responsibility overload, in which single parents make all the decisions and provide for all of their family's needs; (2) task overload, in which the demands of work, housekeeping, and parenting can be overwhelming for one person; and (3) emotional overload, in which single parents must always be on call to provide the necessary emotional support (see Box 9.3). Clearly, when two persons share these parental strains, it is more likely that the needs of the children will be met.

The children of a single parent, whether living with their mother or father, can have emotional difficulties because they have experienced the stress, often traumatic, that accompanied the separation or even death of one of their parents.

Another reason for the disproportionate behavioral problems seen among children living in one-parent families is that their families, for economic reasons, move more often than two-parent families. Moving is a source of emotional strain as old friends are left behind and children experience social isolation in the new setting.

The stress that mothers face also can have negative effects on their children. Changes in residence require that they, too, leave their social networks and sources of support. These moves are sometimes to disadvantaged neighborhoods, with high rates of crime, poverty, unemployment, and poor educational facilities. Often these mothers must enter the labor force for the first time or increase their working hours. Such changes add stress to their lives as well as to the lives of their children.

Although the factors just described help to explain the behavioral differences between children from one-parent and two-parent homes, they sidestep a major reason—a fundamental difference in economic resources. As Andrew Cherlin has argued, "it seems likely that the most detrimental aspect of the absence of fathers from one-parent families headed by women is not the lack of a male presence *but the lack of a male income*" (Cherlin, 1981:81; emphasis added). There is a strong likelihood that women raising children alone will be financially troubled. In 1999, for example, 28 percent of the children living in single-parent families headed by a woman were poor, compared with 5 percent of children in two-parent families. The percentage varies considerably by race/ethnicity, with 19 percent of White children in woman-headed families poor, compared to 23 percent

BOX 9.3 | **Inside the Worlds of Diverse Families:** A Single Mother with Children Struggles to Make Ends Meet

Regina Johnson's children are her alarm clock, and they start ringing too early most mornings.

"Mom, I'm hungry!"

"Mom, look what Mark did!"

Such cries punctuate her mornings starting around 8 a.m.

The single mother of three young children would like to stay in bed a while longer, after working until midnight and getting to sleep about 2 a.m.

Instead, Johnson asks what the children want for breakfast and heads to the kitchen. Then it's time to bathe and dress everyone before cleaning their modest central Denver apartment.

The inevitable rough moments of the day crop up: red Kool-Aid spills on the worn carpet. The kids fight over a toy and cry.

All the while, Johnson worries about making ends meet on her $5-an-hour salary as a printer's assistant for Communications Packaging Inc.

"It's not easy and sometimes I feel like I want to fall apart," said Johnson, 24. "But the kids are here and I know I have to keep them going and keep a roof over their heads."

Michael 3, nestles his head in his mother's lap in the mid-summer heat.

"He's still kind of sick, and when he's sick, he lays around all day," she says.

Johnson worries about how Michael, Mark, 2, and Paula, 1, will turn out. She acknowledges it's hard to find the energy to play with them as much as she would like.

She feels they will drift toward drugs or crime. Or that they'll grow into the type of kids "who just don't care."

She wonders if they'll be more financially secure than she has been. Johnson would like to buy a savings bond for each child. But money is too tight.

Last month, she mailed the rent about a week late. She can't afford a phone. She's bought herself only one new outfit since the kids were born.

"I don't have a checking account," Johnson said, "I live from paycheck to paycheck. I keep enough to get us by through the week."

She was receiving child-support payments from the children's father. But when he quit his job recently, the $114-a-month checks stopped.

Still, Johnson said he helps out when he can and takes the children sometimes on weekends.

Johnson left home and school in eighth grade because she said her father threatened her. She lived for a while with an uncle, and then with the children's father, whom she never married. When they split, she landed on welfare for brief stints.

"It made me feel like a prisoner," she said. "It wasn't for me. I can't sit around all day. I have to go to work and make my own money."

Besides, Johnson didn't want her children teased as "welfare kids."

She went back to school, earned her General Educational Development degree and found her first job paying more than minimum wage.

"I was so excited. I felt like things were turning around. It was neat."

But her next thought was where she would find an affordable baby-sitter. Relatives agreed to watch the children for $5 each per day.

(continued)

(continued from previous page)

Paula, just up from a nap, comes to sit on her mother's lap.

"I want her to grow up and be a model, lead a glamorous life, wear nice clothes and see different parts of the world," says Johnson, stroking her daughter's hair. "I don't want her to have kids until she's 25."

And she wants all her kids to finish high school.

"If something happened to one of my kids, I'd go crazy. I don't think I could handle it. I guess I'm real protective."

When she grows depressed over financial matters or the condition of her house, Johnson says the children are her best tonic.

"I got in a better mood after I started playing with them," she says of one recent bout of depression. "They were making me laugh."

Source: Rebecca Cantwell, "It's Not Easy," *Rocky Mountain News,* August 28, 1989, p. 43.

of Asian American and Pacific Islander children, and 39 percent of African American and 39 percent of Latino children (U.S. Bureau of the Census, 2000). The reasons why there is a disproportionate number of mother-headed families that are poor are obvious. First, many single mothers are young and never married. They may have little education, so if they work, they have poorly paid jobs. Second, many divorced or separated women have not been employed for years and find it difficult to reenter the job market. Third, and more crucial, jobs for women, centered as they are in the bottom tier of the segmented job market, are poorly paid (women, we must underscore again, presently earn about 74 cents for every dollar earned by men). (See Figure 9.4.) Fourth, half of the men who owe child support do not pay all that they owe, and a quarter of them do not pay anything; those women who do receive child support find that the amount covers less than half the actual cost of raising a child.

The economic plight of single-parent families is much worse for families of color. Women of color who head households have the same economic problems as White women who are in the same situation, plus the added burdens of institutional racism. In addition, they are less likely to be getting child support (their husbands, unlike White husbands, are much more likely to be poor and unemployed), and they are more likely to have been high school dropouts, further reducing their potential for earning a decent income.

The financial plight of women heads of households is sometimes alleviated in part by support from a kinship network. Relatives may provide child care, material goods, money, and emotional support. The kin network is an especially important source of emergency help for African Americans, but for many women, kin may not be near or helpful.

In sum, the behavioral social costs attributed to the children of single mothers, noted earlier, are, in large part, the result of living in poverty. Lack of income has negative effects on intellectual development and physical health (Guo and Harris, 2000). Living in poverty translates into huge negatives for single mothers

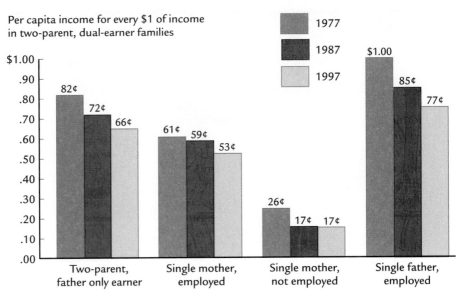

Figure 9.4

Per capita income of selected family types relative to two-parent, dual-earner families, 1977, 1987, and 1997

Source: Suzanne M. Bianchi and Lynne M. Casper, "American Families," *Population Bulletin* 55 (December 1000):27.

and their children—differences in health care (including prenatal and postnatal care), diet, housing, neighborhood safety, and quality of schools, as well as economic disadvantages, leading to a greater probability of experiencing low self-esteem, hopelessness, and despair.

REPRISE: THE DUALITY OF PARENTING

How desirable are children? In the not too distant past children were an asset to their families as they worked in the fields or for merchants, or in the shops of their parents. Not too long ago adult children provided a form of retirement insurance by taking care of their elderly parents. However, as we have shifted from an agrarian society to an industrial society and then to a highly technological information/service economy, children are no longer the assets they once were. Now they are an economic liability. Moreover, children now often hinder the career aspirations of their mothers, and they can reduce marital happiness. The information in this chapter has focused on the reality of modern parenting, with its risks and liabilities. We should not forget, however, that most adults want children; most adults cherish and celebrate their children. They are fulfilled through parenting. Sylvia Hewlett, upon the birth of her daughter, Emma, penned the following poem which enunciates what that child means to her and the value of children even in a contemporary world where they no longer are economic assets:

I glory in her gummy grin which lights up the whole world,
and her infectious giggle.
When she lets loose that bubbling crescendo of pure joy,
I stop whatever I am doing and allow it to wash over me.
Such unstinting, unedited delight cleanses the soul.

    . . . .

I am deeply grateful for this bonus child,
for Emma brings with her special joys and special responsibilities.
In midlife I am much more in touch with that which is miraculous and glorious in a new life.
But I am also more in touch with the awesome risks—hers and mine.
Some are straightforward enough;
Emma can choke on a pea or drown in three inches of bathwater.
Others are more complicated.

I now have another hostage to fortune,
one more life that is more precious than my own. And I now know what that means.

It means a loss of freedom. It means dealing with an undertow of care and anxiety that permeates
    every hour of every day.
For I know full well that if I fail to keep my children safe, I will not find life worth living.

One thing is clear, the loss of freedom is a small price to pay for this,
most sublime of earthly connections.
Being a parent, cherishing a child, brings out the better angels of human nature,
drawing upon our most selfless instincts.
For myself it has brought a measure of wisdom, and a great deal of happiness.
(excerpted from Hewlett and West, 1998:xvi–xvii)

CHAPTER REVIEW

1. Parenting roles by gender, aside from conception, childbirth, and nursing, are not based on biological imperatives. Styles of parenting, expectations of parenting, and behaviors associated with parenting are social constructions, resulting from historical, economic, and social forces.

2. The long-term fertility rate has declined steadily since 1800. The reasons for the low rate now are (a) marrying late; (b) a high divorce rate; (c) a majority of women in the labor force; (d) two incomes required for many couples to maintain a desired lifestyle; (e) delayed childbearing; and (f) legal abortions.

3. Fertility rates vary consistently by social class and race. The higher the social class, the lower the fertility. In terms of race/ethnicity, Whites have the lowest fertility, followed in order by Asian Americans, African Americans, and Latinos.

4. Lesbian and gay parents create and maintain families that thrive even in hostile environments, thus illustrating human agency and that families are socially constructed.

5. The addition of a child affects a marriage dramatically. This event affects the career pattern of parents, the patterns of housework, the distribution of power, marital satisfaction, and the economic well-being of the family.

6. Parenting is gendered, with mothers the primary physical and emotional caregivers. Power tends to become more patriarchal with parenthood.

7. The prevailing view is that parents of young children are all-powerful, shaping them irreversibly. Although parents are powerful socializing agents, they are not omnipotent: (a) the child is an active social being who often shapes the parents; (b) the

structure of the family (i.e., two parents; a solo parent [if so, whether that parent is the same sex as the child]; and ordinal position) affects children and parents in predictable ways; (c) extrafamilial caregivers influence children; (d) peers become increasingly important socializers especially in adolescence; and (e) social class position is the determinant of the child's life chances as well as the child's experiences.

8. Most children live in dual-earner families. The effects of extrafamilial child care are complex and depend on a number of variables: attentiveness and affection of caregivers, the ratio of caregivers to children, the small number of caregivers available, group size, and the availability of stimulating materials. Children from low-income families are the most likely to be found in lower-quality care settings.

9. More than one-fourth of all families with children under age eighteen are headed by a single parent, and these families are almost always headed by a woman. Children living in mother-only families (especially boys) are negatively affected in school performance, delinquent behaviors, early marriage, and divorce. These negative probabilities are the likely result of (a) the single parent being strained by parental responsibilities, tasks, and emotional overload; (b) the children being separated from one of their parents; (c) emotional strains resulting from moving away from friends and neighbors; (d) the strains the mothers feel in the labor force; and most important, (e) economic deprivation.

10. The majority of single mothers have inadequate economic resources. Thus, the social costs attributed to single mothers and their children are largely the costs of poverty.

ℛELATED WEB SITES

http://www.bls.gov/nlsyouth.htm

The National Longitudinal Survey of Youth is a nationally representative sample of 12,686 young men and young women who were 14 to 22 years of age when they were first surveyed in 1979. Data collected during the yearly surveys of the NLSY chronicle important events in the lives of these youth, and provide researchers a unique opportunity to study in detail the life course experiences of a large group of young adults who can be considered representative of all American men and women born in the late 1950s and early 1960s.

http://www.childrensdefense.org/

The Children's Defense Fund exists to provide a strong and effective voice for all the children of America, who cannot vote, lobby, or speak out for themselves

http://www.childrennow.org/

Children Now is a nonpartisan, independent voice for children, working to translate the nation's commitment to children and families into action. Recognized nationally for its policy expertise and up-to-date information on the status of children, Children Now uses communications strategies to reach parents, lawmakers, citizens, business, media and community leaders, creating attention and generating positive change on behalf of children.

http://www.childtrends.org/

Child Trends is a nonprofit, nonpartisan research organization that studies children, youth, and families through research, data collection, and data analysis.

http://www.acf.dhhs.gov/programs/cse/index.html

Home page of the U.S. Department of Health and Human Services Administration for Children & Families Office of Child Support Enforcement.

http://www.pactadopt.org

This is the site for PACT, An Adoption Alliance, which helps African-American, Latino, Asian and multiracial children in the U.S. find permanent adoptive homes. Founders

Beth Hall and Gail Steinberg are strong educators in the area of multicultural adoption and family dynamics.

http://adoption.com

Adoption.Com is a rapidly growing commercial site that offers visitors a comprehensive array of informative sites, articles, chat rooms, and links to every aspect of adoption. A good place to start for both researchers and prospective parents.

http://www.momsonline.com/

Moms Online: Moms Online is a virtual community of mothers working collaboratively to create a friendly site for Moms in cyberspace. By "Mom" we include anyone engaged in nurturing the next generation—from stay-at-home Moms to working Moms, married Moms to single Moms, teen Moms to Grandmoms to Dads.

http://www.surrogacy.com

This is the site for The American Surrogacy Center, Inc., the most complete source of surrogacy and egg donation information on the web, is a growing family-building option and alternative to adoption for couples experiencing infertility. They provide legal, medical, psychological, personal, agency, and surrogacy directories, message boards, classified advertising, e-mail discussion groups, and on-line support groups.

http://www.plannedparenthood.org/

Founded in 1916, Planned Parenthood is the world's largest and oldest voluntary family planning organization. Planned Parenthood is dedicated to the principles that every individual has a fundamental right to decide when or whether to have a child and that every child should be wanted and loved.

http://www.aclu.org/issues/gay/parent.html

Facts about lesbian and gay parenting: The last decade has seen a sharp rise in the number of lesbians and gay men forming their own families through adoption, foster care, artificial insemination, and other means. Researchers estimate that the total number of children nationwide living with at least one gay parent ranges from six to 14 million. Thus, the ACLU put together a fact sheet on lesbian and gay parenting in 1999, to make people aware of issues and realities that these families face, as well as the research that has been done on gay and lesbian families.

http://www.fathermag.com

FatherMag: "The on-line magazine for men with families." This represents one of the only more liberal sites on fathers. FatherMag includes lively discussion on definitions of fathers, divorce, single fatherhood, gender, and many other controversial topics.

http://www.fathersnetwork.org/

The Fathers Network web page: This organization's mission is to celebrate and support fathers and families raising children with special health care needs and developmental disabilities.

http://now2000.com/cbc/

Childless by Choice is an information clearinghouse for people who have decided not to have children, and for those who are deciding whether or not to become parents. CBC materials provide support, humor, and social commentary for and about childless or childfree people.

http://www.childfree.com.au/

Child-Free Zone: An on-line community for people choosing NOT to become parents.

http://aecf.org/

The Annie E. Casey Foundation, through its project "Kids Count," provides national and state-by-state data on child well-being (educational, social, economic, and physical).

Violence in Families

Myths and Realities

Myth:		Battering is about couples who beat each other up.
Reality:		In domestic assaults, one partner is beating, intimidating, and terrorizing the other. It is not "mutual combat" but rather one person dominating and controlling the other.
Myth:		The problem is not really woman abuse. It is spouse abuse. Women are just as violent as men.
Reality:		In over 90 percent of domestic assaults, the man is the perpetrator. In 1994, 28 percent of all female murder victims were slain by husbands or boyfriends. Only 3 percent of male victims were killed by wives or girlfriends. Between 1987 and 1991,

females experienced over ten times as many incidents of violence by an intimate than did males (American Bar Association, 1997).

Myth: Domestic violence is usually a one-time event, an isolated incident.

Reality: Battering is a pattern in a relationship. Once violence begins, it gets worse and more frequent over time.

Myth: Domestic violence, child abuse, and elder abuse occur only in poor, poorly educated, and minority families.

Reality: Domestic violence, child abuse, and elder abuse occur throughout society. Intimate violence is more likely to occur in lower-income and minority households; "violence and abuse, however, *are not* confined to the poor or blacks" (Gelles and Straus, 1988:43). Physical violence happens in rich, White, educated, and "respectable" families as well as in poor, nonWhite, and uneducated families.

Myth: Wife batterers and child abusers are mentally ill.

Reality: A small percentage of abusers are mentally ill. "In fact, only about 10 percent of abusive incidents are caused by mental illness. The remaining 90 percent are not amenable to psychological explanations" (Gelles and Straus, 1988:43).

Myth: Battered women stay in violent relationships. If they wanted to leave, they could just pack up and go somewhere else.

Reality: Battered women are in the most danger when they leave. Perpetrators dramatically escalate their violence when their victims leave (or try to), in an attempt to reassert control and ownership. Assailants deliberately isolate their partners and deprive them of jobs and opportunities for acquiring education and job skills. This, combined with unequal opportunities for women in general and lack of affordable child care, makes it extremely difficult for women to leave. Despite these obstacles and dangers, many battered women leave their abusers permanently.

Myth: Children who are abused grow up to be abusers.

Reality: There is a greater likelihood that abused children will grow up to be abusive, but "there is absolutely no evidence to support the claim that people who are abused are *preprogrammed* to grow up to be abusers" (Gelles and Straus, 1988:49).

Myth: Family violence is a minor problem, overall. The instances are few and isolated.

Reality: The threat of violence in intimate relationships exists for all couples, for children, and for the elderly.

*T*he family has two faces. It can be a haven from an uncaring, impersonal world and a place where serenity, love, and security prevail. The family members can love each other unconditionally, care for each other, and be accepting of each other. The family can provide its members with emotional support; stability; the necessities of food, clothing, and shelter; and the tools to fit into society.

But there is also a dark side of the family. The family is a common context for violence in society. "People are more likely to be killed, physically assaulted, sexually victimized, hit, beat up, slapped, or spanked in their own homes by other family members than anywhere else, or by anyone else, in our society" (Gelles, 1995:450). About 25 percent of women have been raped or assaulted by a current or former partner (Centers for Disease Control and Prevention, reported in Hopper, 2000). In an average week, thirty women across the United States will be killed by a husband or boyfriend; 16,000 will be assaulted by one, with 4000 requiring medical treatment (*USA Today*, 1994b:14A). In 1998 intimate partner homicides accounted for about 11 percent of all murders nationwide (Rennison and Welchans, 2000). In that year, African American women were victims of domestic killings at a rate of 4.5 per 100,000, compared with 1.75 per 100,000 for White women (U.S. Department of Justice, reported in *Society*, 2001). Every year in this country, 1000 to 1200 children die from abuse and neglect by their caretakers, usually their parents. According to the Centers for Disease Control and Prevention, nine out of ten of these victims are under the age of five and more than 40 percent are infants under a year old (cited in Frerking, 1994). Finally, reversing the trend just noted, more than one out of ten murder victims aged sixty or older is killed by a son or daughter (Dawson and Langan, 1994).

Violence in families is difficult to examine because we prefer to picture the family "as an arena for love and gentleness rather than a place for violence" (Steinmetz and Straus, 1974:3), yet the facts of family life in U.S. society cannot be ignored. To disregard them would be to present an inaccurate and unrealistic view of families.

The organizing principle for this chapter is the interaction of the family through the life cycle. The first family relationship is that of the married couple; like other family relationships, this relationship involves intense interaction in a wide range of areas. This interaction often produces strong emotions such as love and sometimes hate. We usually ignore the hate and violence found in marriage, but it is real for many couples. The result for such couples is spouse abuse. The second stage of the life cycle after marriage is parenting, with the intensity of emotions between a parent and child leading some parents to punish their children physically beyond the societal norms. The final stage in the life cycle presented in this chapter is that in which the aged parent lives with an adult child. This, too, is a relationship fraught with the potential for violence.

For each of these types of family violence, we will consider the incidence, causes, and consequences of family violence in an effort to understand the underlying factors and motivations related to this anomaly—the willful inflicting of pain and suffering on family members. We begin with a discussion of how the phenomenon of family violence is related to violence in the larger society. This sets the macro context for understanding violence in micro settings.

FAMILIES IN A VIOLENT SOCIETY

One sociological truism is that each of society's institutions (e.g., the polity, economy, education, religion, sport, and family) is a microcosm of the larger society. Each mirrors society and in its own way contributes to the reinforcement of those practices and beliefs that give society its uniqueness. Thus, in our investigation of violence in the family, we must be aware that families do not exist in a vacuum but are shaped by the history, culture, and distribution of power in society. Our thesis is that U.S. society has always manifested and glorified violence. This is not to say that American society is always violent. We argue, however, that society—like the family—has two faces.

> America: a symbol of freedom and discussion, rational thought, tolerance of new ideas, equality and justice for all. America: a symbol of violent brawls, unrestrained vigilante activity, forcible suppression of political dissidents or "undesirables," racist attitudes (Iglitzen, 1972: 144).

U.S. Violence Rates in Comparative Perspective

Elliott Currie, the esteemed criminologist, says "What most distinguishes America from other developed countries is the extent to which Americans are willing to rob, maim, kill, and rape one another" (1998:116) The murder and rape rates in the United States, for example, are at least four times that of other advanced industrial nations. Currie (1998:120–149) suggests several root causes for the disturbingly high levels of violence in the United States, compared to other developed nations.

- Children and families in the United States are far more likely to be poor, and, if they are poor, are more likely to be *extremely poor*. The links between disadvantage and violence are strongest for the poorest and most neglected of the poor.
- The poor and near-poor receive fewer government benefits to offset their problems such as health care and child care. This represents a crucial difference in the United States, compared to its counterparts—our willingness to tolerate extremes of deprivation and social insecurity rather than a sense of collective responsibility for the well-being of others (see Chapter 13).
- Economic inequality combined with racial or ethnic discrimination leads to higher rates of violent crime in the United States.

Institutionally Sanctioned Violence

Violence is promoted in a number of important areas of society. Historically, violence between family members has been legitimized by the law.

> In 1824, the Mississippi Supreme Court was the first of several states to grant husbands immunity from assault and battery charges for moderately chastising their wives. Such legal support can be traced back to English common law, which gave husbands the right to strike their wives with sticks no wider than their thumbs— hence the classic "rule of thumb." Similarly, historical evidence indicates legal precedents allowing for the mutilation, striking, and even killing of children as part of the legal parental prerogative (Gelles, 1990:106).

Although the legal system no longer legitimizes wife beating and child abuse, the criminal justice system often looks the other way. The police and the courts often err on the side of letting domestic disturbances alone. The commonly held assumption is that the privacy of marriage should be upheld. For example, in the infamous case of O. J. Simpson, police were summoned on at least nine occasions because of Simpson's physical abuse of his wife Nicole. Like many batterers, Simpson felt that what occurred between him and his wife was not the concern of the police. He reportedly said after one call, "What are you doing here? This is a family matter" (quoted in Lewin, 1994:21). Despite Simpson's history of attacking his wife, he never went to jail for those crimes or received any court-supervised counseling.

There are other institutional supports for violence in society as well. Some of these are as follows.

- Congress has rarely limited the right of citizens to own guns, despite evidence that the easy availability of guns, especially handguns, is directly correlated with the murder rate. The result is that approximately 240 million are guns owned by U.S. citizens.
- Corporal punishment—the use of physical force with the intention of causing pain but not injury for the purposes of correction or control—is legal in every U.S. state. Over 90 percent of U.S. parents use corporal punishment on toddlers, and just over half continue this practice into their children's adolescence (Straus and Donnelly, 1994; Straus and Yodanis, 1996).

- In education, the U.S. Supreme Court ruled in 1977 that teachers had the right to use corporal punishment if their state legislatures approve. Use of the paddle in schools is legal in twenty-three states. Paddling in schools is permitted in only three industrialized nations: the United States, Canada, and Australia (Lang, 1998).
- Schools also promote aggressive, violent sports. The sport with the largest budget and most participation is boys' football. In this sport, players are explicitly taught to be "hitters." Moreover, males "do gender" as they participate in school sports. One ethnographic study of male locker rooms found that common conversations and banter there involved sexual boasting, talk about women as sex objects, and aggressive and hostile talk toward women (Curry, 1991).
- Religion, too, supports violence. The Bible states, "He who spares the rod hates his son, but he who loves him is diligent to discipline him" (Proverbs 13.24, Revised Standard Version).

Violence in the Media

Television and Movies

Violence is glorified both in the movies and on television. By the time a child finishes elementary school, she or he on average will have witnessed 8000 murders on television. By the age of eighteen, the average American child will have seen 200,000 violent acts on television, including 40,000 murders (Briggs, 1997). Most significant, women are often the victims.

In many situations portrayed in the media, frustrated people hit, shoot, or bomb other people. These scenarios may be cathartic for viewers, allowing them to get rid of their pent-up aggression in socially acceptable ways. Some are concerned, however, that seeing so many acts of violence by media heroes and heroines provides models for impressionable viewers. Moreover, experiencing so much violence through films, television, and even in popular music desensitizes people to the real violence that is woven into the social fabric of society (Zoglin, 1996).

Pornography

The widespread dissemination of pornography (a $10 billion industry) is believed to encourage male dominance.

> The outlandish scenarios and vivid crotch displays in the men's magazines . . . are designed to make men believe that a woman is under control, submissive, willing to be dominated. Pornography feeds on frustrations; it helps build them too. And, as the social taboos fall away and the portrayals become more and more desperately explicit, violence lunges in (Shapiro, 1977:11).

Music

The lyrics of some popular music (e.g., rap music) degrade women as "bitches" and "ho's," often portraying them as enjoying coercive sex. In addition to this **misogyny** (hatred of women), rap music sometimes glorifies physical aggression in general (Wiehe, 1998:8-9).

Video Games

The U.S. home video game industry is huge (expected to exceed $18 billion in 2003). The theme of many of these games is violence. In the top-selling "Mortal Kombat," for example, a beating heart is pulled from the vanquished competitor's chest. In the sequel, "Mortal Kombat II," players are encouraged to tear off their foes' heads and rip out their hearts, and one of the bad guys rips the skin off his opponents, leaving a bloody pile of muscle. In "Night Trap," when a player loses, four thugs take a power drill to a coed's neck.

Literature and Folklore

Violence has always been a dominant theme in American literature and folklore. Children's stories and even nursery rhymes are often quite violent. Consider the following familiar examples that describe spouse abuse, child abuse, and elder abuse, respectively:

> Peter, Peter, Pumpkin Eater,
> had a wife and couldn't keep her;
> He put her in a pumpkin shell,
> and there he kept her very well.

> There was an old woman who lived in a shoe.
> She had so many children she didn't know what to do.
> She gave them some broth without any bread;
> She whipped them all soundly and put them to bed.

> Lizzie Borden took an ax
> and gave her father 40 whacks.
> When the job was neatly done
> she gave her mother 41.

It is important to note that the empirical research linking violent behavior to the watching of violent movies, playing violent video games, or watching violent pornography is inconclusive. Clearly, most Americans observe media violence and are not violent in their relationships. Looking at adolescents, Mike Males argues:

> If media is any kind of significant cause of youth violence, we should find violence levels among different subgroups of youth, all of whom are exposed to similar amounts of media influence, quite similar. . . . Hundreds of millions of American youth have patronized John Wayne, James Cagney, and Schwartzenegger, tuned in Megadeth, the Beatles, and Ice-T, pored over the Bible, and even become Eagle Scouts—and haven't murdered anyone (Males, 1996:124,126).

Thus real-world violence cannot be blamed on the media, but media violence does contribute to a climate in which violence is often viewed as legitimate. It does desensitize its observers to the consequences of violence. However, and this is the crucial sociological point, the concern over the effects of media violence on its viewers must not obscure the real sources of violence in U.S. society. Referring to street crime, but applicable at least in part to family violence, Todd Gitlin points to the real causes of violence:

> Violence on the screens, however loathsome, does not make a significant contribution to violence on the streets. Images don't spill blood. Rage, equipped with guns,

does. Desperation does. Revenge does. As liberals say, the drug trade does; poverty does; unemployment does. It seems likely that a given increase in decently paying jobs will save thousands of times more lives than the same percent decrease in media bang-bang (Gitlin, 1994:45).

Customs and Beliefs

Many customs and beliefs support violence. For example, males are socialized to be dominant. Parents often encourage their sons to be aggressive. "The overwhelming proportion of American parents consider it part of their role to train sons to be tough. The Violence Commission survey reveals that 70 percent of the respondents believed it is good for boys to have a few fist fights" (Gelles and Straus, 1988:26-27).

Adults in our society consider it normal to discipline children by hitting them. Gelles and Straus, the acknowledged experts on abuse in families, say that

> . . . in general, the large majority of Americans believes that good parenting requires some physical punishment. Over and over again, when we interview parents about hitting their children, we are told that kids "deserve to be hit" or "need to be hit." Among the thousands of people we have interviewed, it was absence of physical punishment that was thought to be deviant, not the hitting of children (Gelles and Straus, 1988:27).

In short, our society accepts physical punishment in the family as "normal violence."

Violence and the Social Organization of the Family

Although the family is based on love among its members, the way it is organized encourages conflict (the following is taken from Gelles and Straus, 1979, 1988; and Rouse, 1997). First, the family, like all other social organizations, is a power system; that is, power is unequally distributed between parents and children and between spouses, with the male typically dominant.

Male dominance has been perpetuated by the legal system and religious teachings. Threats to male dominance are often resisted through violence. Parents have authority over their children. They feel they have the right to punish children in order to shape them in the ways the parents consider important. Also, because marriage is between a woman and a man, this sets the stage for a "battle of the sexes." This may not present a problem in some homes, where there is a basic agreement on gender roles, but for many couples these problems are a constant source of stress. Gelles and Straus summarize the importance of this dimension for understanding family violence:

> The greater the inequality, the more one person makes all the decisions and has all the power, the greater the risk of violence. Power, power confrontations, and perceived threats to domination, in fact, are underlying issues in almost all acts of family violence (Gelles and Straus, 1988:82).

Unlike most organizations, in which activities and interests are relatively narrow, the family encompasses almost everything. Thus, there are more "events" over which a dispute can develop. Closely related to this phenomenon is the vast amount of time in each day that family members spend interacting. This lengthy interaction increases the probability of disagreements, irritations, violations of privacy, and the like, which increase the risk of violence.

Not only is the range of activities greater in the family than in other social organizations, the feelings are also more intense. As Gelles and Straus have put it:

> There is . . . a greater intensity of involvement in family conflict. Love, paradoxically, gives the power to hurt. So, the degree of distress felt in conflicts with other family members is likely to be much greater than if the same issue were to arise in relation to someone outside the family (Gelles and Straus, 1979:35).

Family privacy is another characteristic that enhances the likelihood of violence. The rule in our society that the home is private has two negative consequences. First, it insulates family members from the protection that society can provide if another family member becomes abusive. Second, privacy often prevents the victims of abuse from seeking outside help.

SPOUSE ABUSE

The marriage license, for many, is a license to hit. Violence between husbands and wives in the form of beating, slapping, kicking, and throwing objects is relatively common in U.S. society. That such violence occurs between persons who supposedly joined together because of their mutual love is puzzling indeed.

The discussion of spouse abuse here is limited in two ways. First, we are concerned only with physical violence. Thus, we do not consider verbal abuse and psychological forms of violence, although these are also cruel and coercive. Second, the discussion of spouse abuse focuses exclusively on the most common type—male abuse of wives. Violence directed by wives at husbands is much less likely to occur and is often the result of self-defense because of an abusive husband. Estimates from the federal government's National Crime Victimization Survey for 1998 reveal how much more likely women than men are the victims of violence by intimate partners (Rennison and Welchans, 2000):

- Women were three out of four victims of the 1830 murders attributed to intimate partners.
- About 85 percent of victimizations by intimate partners (876,340) were against women.
- Women were more likely to be victimized by a nonstranger, which includes a friend, family member, or intimate partner, whereas men were more likely to be victimized by a stranger.
- Domestic violence causes more injuries to women than automobile accidents, muggings, and rapes combined (Koop, 1989).

In focusing on women as the abused, we do not negate the existence of physical violence by wives, because it does occur; but since the frequency and severity are so much less than in husbands' attacks on wives, we describe in detail only physical abuse of wives.

Incidence of Wife Abuse

As with other forms of family violence, the actual data on wife battering are impossible to obtain. First, the events generally take place in private, with no witnesses other than family members. Second, battered women are often attended to by physicians who treat their wounds without asking embarrassing questions; or, if they know the cause, the physicians do not report the abuse to the authorities. Third, the victims, most commonly, lie about the causes of their injuries because of shame or fear. Last, many victims do not go to public agencies for help because they have found these organizations often to be unresponsive. This situation is especially true of the police and the courts, who typically feel that most domestic violence is a private affair and none of their business. Also, the situation often comes down to the wife's word against her husband's word, making prosecution difficult, if not impossible, under existing laws.

The data available on spouse abuse are also unreliable because they come either from self-report surveys or from victims seeking help. Self-report surveys are undependable because victims and abusers are generally reluctant to admit their problem. The second source of data, victims seeking help, may themselves be different from the entire population of victims. For example, are the victims of abuse who seek a divorce or who have sought out a community agency for their problems representative of those women who do not seek a way out of their abusive situations? The result of these difficulties in obtaining reliable data is that we have information revealing only the "tip of the iceberg" and can only speculate about its actual size.

Within the limitations of the data, the following are some estimates of the extent of wife abuse.

- Criminologist Jim Fyfe estimates that 35 to 45 percent of U.S. homicides stem from domestic fights (cited in Davis, 1994).
- The U.S. Justice Department estimates that two-thirds of the 2.5 million women victims of violence are attacked by intimate friends or family (Bachman, 1994).
- Up to 15 million women have been abused at least once by a male partner. Every 12 seconds, a woman in the United States is beaten by her husband or lover (Peterson, 1994).
- In 1992 the U.S. Surgeon General ranked abuse by husbands and partners as the leading cause of injuries to women ages fifteen to forty-four (cited in Ingrassia and Berk, 1994:26–27).
- Johnson and Ferraro (2001), after reviewing the research on domestic violence, suggest that about two million women in the United States are terrorized by husbands or other male partners.

Conditions That Favor Wife Abuse

Although the statistics on wife abuse are somewhat unreliable, we do have a more precise understanding of the conditions under which this phenomenon occurs.

Economic Conditions

Foremost, although battered women are found in all social strata, they tend to be found in families threatened by economic hardships. "Less income usually means more problems and fewer possibilities for solving them" (Chasin, 1997:80).

Unemployment is a very significant variable. Reviewing the research, Stephanie Coontz notes that the risk of family violence is nearly six times greater among people laid off from their jobs than among their employed peers, regardless of whether the perpetrators had a prior history of psychiatric disorder or alcohol abuse (Coontz, 1997:145).

Race and Ethnicity

The 1995–1996 National Violence against Women Survey (Tjaden and Thoennes, 1999) found that 13 percent of Asian and Pacific Islander women reported having been physically assaulted by an intimate partner. For White women, the figure was 21 percent, for African Americans 26 percent, and for Native Americans it was 31 percent. These data apparently show that except for Asian Americans, people of color are more prone to domestic violence than Whites. There is some basis for this generalization because racial minorities experience the difficult stressors related to being a racial minority, such as a relatively high probability of joblessness, being paid low wages for doing society's "dirty work," living in substandard housing, children attending inferior schools, living in high-crime-rate neighborhoods, and police harassment (Smith, 1997). However, we must view this apparent overrepresentation of people of color among the abusers and abused with caution. First, when demographic and socioeconomic factors are controlled, minorities are no more likely than nonminorities to be violent (Hutchinson et al., 1994). In other words, racial differences in domestic abuse have less to do with race than they do with socioeconomic status (Johnson and Ferraro, 2001). Second, although official reports of abuse indicate that poor and minority families are overrepresented, *these data tend to distort the actual incidence for these categories.* This is because "the poor run the greatest risk of being accurately and inaccurately labeled 'abusers' (Gelles and Straus, 1988:43) (see Box 10.1). Also, statistics based on police arrest records may overrepresent minorities and the poor because of differential arrest policies (Barnett et al., 1997:195).

Third, the recency of immigration is crucial. For example, "Mexican Americans born in the U.S. reported rates 2.4 times higher than those born in Mexico" (Sorenson and Telles, 1991:3). "This finding can serve to remind us not only of the importance of differences among specific groups in North America, but also of matters of cultural roots and immigrant status that have global implications" (Johnson and Ferraro, 2001:957).

A final note of caution regarding generalities about racial/ethnic groups. These groups are not monolithic, homogeneous populations. Asian Americans, for example, include tremendous diversity.

> Included under this rubric are Asians who have deep historical roots in this country such as the Chinese and Japanese populations; recently arrived immigrants, such as Filipinos, Koreans, and South Asians from India, Pakistan, and Sri Lanka; and even more recently arrived Pacific Islanders and Indochinese refugees, such as Guamani-

---

BOX 10.1   Researching Families: Is There More Child Abuse among the Poor and Minorities?

Do medical practitioners treat data on patients the same or is there a systematic bias against the lower classes and racial minorities? If there is a bias, the data, of course, are distorted and commonly held myths perpetuated.

Sociologists Patrick Turbett and Richard O'Toole investigated this possibility as it relates to child abuse (Turbett and O'Toole, 1980, reported in Gelles and Straus, 1988:43–44). They conducted an experiment with physicians and nurses to determine whether an injured child from a disadvantaged background is more likely than a middle-class child with the same injuries to be labeled "abused."

> Each group was divided in half. One-half received a medical file that described a child, the child's injuries, and facts about the parents. Unbeknownst to the participants in the experiment, the files were systematically varied. For one-half of the subjects, the child's father was described as being a teacher, while the other half read the father was a janitor. Even though the injury to the child was identical, the son of the janitor was more likely to be described as a victim of abuse than the son of the teacher. Turbett and O'Toole next kept the occupation and injury the same but varied the race of the child. Half of the subjects read that the child was black, while the other half had a file that described the child as white. The black children were more likely to be labeled as "abused."

Gelles and Straus conclude:

> Here again we see evidence that people want to see abuse as occurring in families "other than theirs." Seeing abuse as confined to poor or black families is yet another way people construct the acts of others as deviant and their own behavior as normal (Gelles and Straus, 1988:43–44).

---

ans, Samoans, Cambodians, Laotians, Vietnamese, Thai, and Indonesians. All of these ethnic groups have their own culture, language, and history. Furthermore, there is also considerable variation within, as well as between, these various Asian ethnic groups (Huisman, 1996:261).

Abuse in Latino Domestic Relationships Straus and Smith (1989) find that Latino couples experience intimate violence at a higher rate than do Anglo couples. Although research is lacking to help us understand this high rate for Latinos, there are two possible reasons. The cultural reason is that Latino men are socialized to believe in the ethnically derived beliefs of male domination and authoritarianism **(machismo).** Latino women are socialized to accept these norms **(marianismo).** Thus, these beliefs support coercive power by men and the subordination of women (Torres, 1987). For example, the sense of powerlessness of marginalized Latino males may lead to their violent behavior in families, where they have power (Fernandez Kelly and Garcia, 1990). The structural explanation, called the "family stressor model," considers structural factors such as low employment status, low educational attainment, and low income as sources of stress that lead to family violence.

Abuse in Asian American Domestic Relationships There is general agreement that wife battering occurs about as frequently in the Asian population as in the general population (Eng, 1990). However, the formal data do not necessarily reflect the extent of wife battering among Asian Americans. Thus, the facts are difficult to determine because Asian American women who are battered are less likely than women from other racial and ethnic groups to report the abuse, and those who do typically wait until the battering has reached a crisis level (Huisman, 1996). There are several cultural and structural reasons for this reluctance to seek a shelter or tell the police. First, there are traditional cultural beliefs such as patriarchy, obedience, and self-control. Moreover, there is pressure on women to maintain familial harmony and not to bring shame on the family. Eng (1995) has noted that recent Asian women immigrants because they hold these traditional beliefs, are much less likely to report battering than second- and third-generation Asian Americans. Another obstacle to the reporting of abuse is the extended family system, with the typical Asian pattern of women moving in with their husband's family. This arrangement tends to isolate wives, because the husband's family usually sides with him. The length of residence in the United States is a crucial variable for abused women; the more recent the immigration to this country, the more likely the immigrants are to adhere to the traditional beliefs and customs that support patriarchy and, indirectly, wife battering. Length of time is also related to language, with recent immigrants likely to be monolingual, which isolates them further.

Structurally, immigration laws have historically discriminated against Asians. Thus, many Asians fear deportation if they are labeled by the authorities as troublesome. This fear is compounded for undocumented Asians. Institutional racism and sexism also constrain battered Asian women to stay in abusive relationships because of restricted opportunities.

Interpersonal Marital Interaction Patterns

Those couples who are given to verbal aggression are more prone to engage in physical violence than those couples who are not (Gelles, 1977). Verbal assaults by a spouse, because they can be so devastating, are likely to lead to physical violence. Partners become expert at attacking each others' weaknesses, and because such attacks are damaging to the victim's ego strength, he or she may be driven to an act of physical aggression. One interesting point about this tendency for verbal aggression to lead to physical aggression is that it is contrary to the catharsis hypothesis, which argues that verbal aggression allows couples to get out their pent-up hostilities, thereby reducing the potential for physical violence.

Inadequacy of Husbands

Wife beating can be generated by a number of problems the husband faces in his marriage, his work, or other situations. These may include financial difficulties, sexual dysfunction, and jealousy (see Box 10.2).

Research on husbands known to be wife abusers has also found that these men tend to be underachievers when compared to their wives. They may be less intelligent, less successful in their jobs or school, or lower in certain status characteristics (occupation and education) compared to their wives. The inability to be superior to one's wife in a male-oriented society apparently leads to the desire to prove one's superiority over her in physical ways.

Alcohol Abuse

The most common trait associated with wife abuse is the excessive use of alcohol. The problem with assuming a relationship between alcohol abuse and wife abuse is that the relationship is not causal, but contributory. Put another way, stress may be the antecedent to both drinking and spouse abuse (Barnett et al., 1997:198).

Family History of Abuse

It is commonly believed that spouse abuse is transmitted across generations. That is, children learn to behave both by experiencing how others treat them and by observing how their parents treat each other. The assumption is that "children who grow up in families in which they witness interparental violence or experience child abuse are more likely to imitate or tolerate these behaviors than are children from nonviolent homes" (Stith et al., 2000:640). Research, however, finds only a weak relationship between growing up in an abusive family and becoming involved in a violent marital relationship. Thus, we conclude "that while growing up in a violent family may put one at risk for using violence as an adult, the relationship is far from absolute. The fact remains that most adults who grow up in violent homes do not become violent adults" (Stith et al., 2000:641).

In sum, a number of variables are associated with wifebeating. Gelles and his associates (1994) provide an overall risk profile: (1) male unemployed; (2) male uses illicit drugs at least once a year; (3) male and female have different religious backgrounds; (4) male saw father hit mother; (5) male and female cohabitate and are not married; (6) male has blue-collar occupation, if employed; (7) male has some high school education; (8) male is between eighteen and thirty years of age; (9) male or female uses severe violence toward children in home; and (10) total family income is below the poverty line.

> For households with none of the ten risk markers, the rate of male-to-female severe violence was 14 per 1,000; for households with two risk factors, the rate was . . . 35 per 1,000; for households with seven or more risk factors, the rate was 610 per 1,000, more than 17 times the base rate [34 per 1,000] (Gelles et al., 1994:10).

Patriarchal Terrorism: Power and Control

Examining the correlations among social conditions and spouse abuse is helpful in dissecting this phenomenon, but these quantitative data obscure the harsh reality of spouse abuse and the underlying explanation for why some men batter. The key, as pointed out by feminists, is power and control. Researchers relying on data collected from battered women (rather than surveys of the population that revealed correlations and probabilities), especially those who have come into contact with the courts, hospitals, and shelters, have emphasized the traditions of the patriarchal family that in the extreme lead to a phenomenon called patriarchal terrorism (Johnson, 1995; Pence and Paymar, 1993). **Patriarchal**

terrorism is violence initiated by men as a way of gaining and maintaining absolute control over their female partners. This pattern of violence is rooted in patriarchal ideas of male ownership of their spouses and involves the systematic use of violence, economic subordination, threats, intimidation, isolation, and other control tactics (see Figure 10.1). From this perspective the focus is on the perpetrator (rather than the battered wife) and on the systematic, intentional nature of this form of violence.

Feminist legal scholar Donna Coker describes the link between the act of battering and the institutional patterns that provide the context of domestic male dominance and control.

> Battering may be experienced as a personal violation, but it is an act facilitated and made possible by societal gender inequalities. The batterer does not, indeed could not, act alone. Social supports for battering include widespread denial of its frequence or harm, economic structures that render women vulnerable, and sexist ideology that holds women accountable for male violence and for the emotional lives of families, and that fosters deference to male familial control. Batterers often use the political and economic vulnerability of women to reinforce their power and dominance over particular women. Thus, their dominance, or their attempts at dominance, are frequently bolstered by stigmatization of victims through the use of gender social norms that define the "good woman" (wife/mother). Batterers also take advantage of the vulnerabilities of their victims, such as the victim's economic dependence on the batterer, or on her state as an illegal immigrant, her alcohol or drug dependency, or her responsibility to provide and care for children (Coker, 1999:39).

For this type of violence, some men feel the need to control "their" women and in the process assert their authority. If the partner resists being controlled, the perpetrator escalates the level of violence until she is subdued. This pattern was observed by Dobash and Dobash, who showed that women in this situation cannot behave in ways to avoid being beaten.

> For a woman to live her daily life she is always in a position in which almost anything she does may be deemed a violation of her wifely duties or a challenge to her husband's authority and thus defined as the cause of the violence she continues to experience (Dobash and Dobash, 1979:137).

The research on the women who seek help from the criminal justice system, hospitals, and shelters finds that the beatings occur on the average of more than once a week and escalate in seriousness over time (Johnson, 1995:287).

Why are some men patriarchal terrorists, systematically battering their partners? The correlates related to battering husbands provide some clues. For example, low economic status plus traditional gender role expectations by males also explains wife abuse: "Men whose masculinity is tied to norms of dominance but who do not have the economic status to back up a dominant stance are likely to be abusive to the women they love, either psychologically or physically, and often both" (Lorber, 1994:71). Or, as Gelles and Straus argue, "Perhaps the most telling of all attributes of the battering man is that he feels inadequate and sees violence as a culturally acceptable way to be both dominant and powerful" (1988:89).

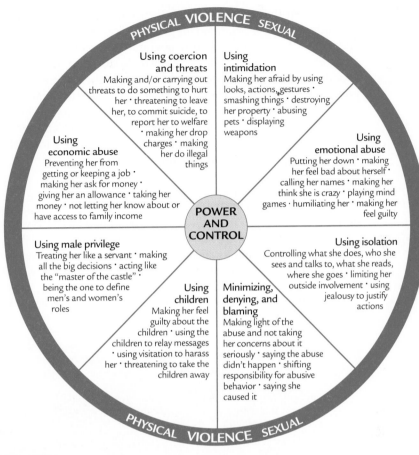

Figure 10.1

Power and control wheel

Source: Reprinted from Elaine Pence and Michael Paymar, *Education Groups for Men Who Batter: The Duluth Model.* New York: Springer, 1993.

Why Does She Stay?

Before we examine the intriguing question of why battered women stay with their batterers, there are four caveats. First, although this is a common question, it misplaces the responsibility on the victim rather than on the perpetrator (thus, blaming the victim). The more appropriate question is: Why doesn't he let her leave (Jones, 1994)? The previous subsection, on patriarchal terrorism, answers this question. Second, we must not interpret wives remaining in this situation as victims bringing violence on themselves by not leaving (Andersen, 1993:170). The blame rests with the perpetrator. Third, the majority of wives do leave their homes for some period of time when their situations become intolerable. And, fourth, many women show great resourcefulness in resisting the pattern of violence in which they are trapped (human agency). Campbell and her colleagues

(1998) found that for the women they studied, after $2\frac{1}{2}$ years, three-fourths of the battered women were no longer in a violent relationship (43 percent had left, and 32 percent had successfully negotiated an end to the violence).

Some wives do not leave an abusive situation, however. As irrational as it sounds, many victims choose to stay with their violent husbands when they know they are in peril. However, they do not stay because they are masochists—experiencing some perverse pleasure in being beaten—as has often been alleged. They have difficulty leaving for a variety of social and psychological reasons. Let's begin with one theory that has been proposed to explain this seemingly irrational response of **"learned helplessness."**

Learned Helplessness

When we perceive that the negative things happening to us are arising through no fault of our own, we tend to become resigned and to give up trying to change the situation (Walker, 1979:34–37). Experiments on cats, fish, rodents, birds, and primates confirm this tendency. One experiment with dogs, for example, gave them random shocks at varied intervals while they were caged. At first the dogs tried to escape, but nothing they did stopped the shocks. In time, they no longer tried to get out of the cages and became compliant, passive, and submissive.

Battered women may remain with an abusive husband for a number of complex reasons.

Wini Breines and Linda Gordon (1983) have criticized the "learned helpless-ness" theory because the research on which it is based has not been done on humans and because it is oversimplified. They do believe, though, that learned helplessness, if understood metaphorically, does illuminate some aspects of women's victimization. Most battered women have, in fact, tried to avoid beat-ings and have "learned" that they cannot do so; they are in fact in "cages" con-structed of the law, poverty, dependent children, lack of child care, and so on. Furthermore, many battered women also suffer from a deformation of self-esteem, another kind of learned helplessness (Breines and Gordon, 1983:518).

The helplessness of women in an abusive situation is enhanced further by traditional gender roles. Women are expected to be passive. They have been taught since childhood that men and women are unequal. Add to this the often superior physical strength that men possess, and women feel hopeless to change the intolerable situation.

Although there is some evidence to support this theory of learned helpless-ness, the key is that "a substantial number of women do not fall into the depths of learned helplessness. They search for avenues of reconciliation, therapy, and escape" (Gelles and Straus, 1988:143).

Self-Blame

A number of other reasons help explain why women remain in abusive relation-ships. The women may blame themselves. In a curious twist of logic, the struc-ture of society not only forces battered women to endure such abuse, it also cre-ates a situation in which the victims see themselves, as do others, as the source of the problem. Michelle Fine has argued that a patriarchal society offers few options to the victims of domestic violence. Social, economic, and legal services are inadequate to provide realistic alternatives to the violent home. Most women are financially dependent on men. Society does not provide protection, shelter, and economic help to the victims of domestic violence. The law tends to support male supremacy, ignoring women's complaints of injustice on the basis of the argument that the privacy of the home should be honored. For example, some states do not allow one partner in a marriage to sue the other for damages. Thus, women cannot easily leave an abusive situation and live on their own. For Michelle Fine, "a social structure which deprives women of alternatives is a social structure likely to keep the violence closeted and privatized (in the 'pri-vacy' of the family), encourage self-blame by the women (and victim-blame by others in society) and perpetuate social abuse" (Fine, 1981:48–49). In this context, a psychology of the victim emerges that conforms to, rather than challenges, the optionless reality. Dissonance reduction and relative deprivation theories both suggest that if individuals invest pain and effort into an unfair system and are ignorant of a "better life," they are likely to justify the experience.

Victims may ultimately convince themselves that their lives aren't "that bad," or that they "deserve the treatment," or that it "really doesn't happen too often" so as not to have to face the dreadful reality that both their spouses/lovers and society are unjust in their treatment of victims of domestic abuse. In an effort to assume psychological control over her life, the victim of abuse may convince herself that she causes it, that she can control it, that it is worth the pain. These

BOX 10.2 **Inside the Worlds of Diverse Families:** Leaving an Abusive Situation

My answer to the question, "why don't you just leave?" was "where would I go?" When you're literally locked into a domestic violence situation, the very notion of leaving is terrifying. People assume that there are choices. I had a choice: I could leave and he would steal my children, or I could leave and he would find me and hurt or even kill me. Everyone has advice, but it seemed as though no one really understood the consequences of my departure with three children. Why don't you leave? It seems like an innocent question, but to a victim of violence it may very well be a death sentence. If I were to leave with my children, who would take us in? Would it be okay to place others in that kind of danger? I was told about a shelter in the neighboring town, and that was where my children and I fled. However, what was going to happen after our maximum thirty day time period in the shelter ran out? Who would help us then?

For eight years, I had always felt as though something was wrong with my marriage. Although, my husband was not physically abusive, he was extremely emotionally, psychologically, and sexually abusive. Because no one could see my bruises, others doubted my claims. My life was one filled with isolation and fear. The abuse was patterned, a cycle of every three days he would be angry, and that I would be his target. The isolation became so immense that I was not allowed to talk to or visit my family, and when I talked to my neighbors he wanted me to record the conversations. When I approached him about my feelings, he simply told me I was crazy and a detriment to our children. This label of insanity left me the only option I thought I had, I attempted suicide. Two months later I fled for my life and for my children's. It is really powerful to think that this abusive person constructed my reality.

I left, ten years ago; with three children, two suitcases, a box of pictures, birth certificates, and eighty dollars. I fled to a woman's safe house in a neighboring town. This was the most terrifying day of my life. However, I was relieved to be alive the morning I left. I stayed in the safe house for 38 days, and left ten days before Christmas, to live in another shelter. For two and a half years I lived in this shelter with my children.

To others I was considered suicidal, a battered woman, a welfare mom, homeless, and a single parent. All of these labels depicted me as a non-productive member of society. These labels had an incredible effect on my life. Soon I would alter my attire to go grocery shopping, including not wearing any jewelry, not dressing up, and being careful about what I put into my grocery cart. People insulted me, saying, for example, "I wish I could buy food like that for free" or "maybe you should have not had three kids if you couldn't support them." The cashiers would not speak to you if you paid with food stamps. And the glares began to make me believe that perhaps they were right, I was no good. Even in the banks, when cashing a welfare check, the teller would not look at my face or even wish me a "good day." When I went to the community college, I had to have all of my instructors sign this paper that said, "welfare recipient" across the top. This is, of course, only a sample of the discrimination that labeling did. It, at many times, made me second-guess my decision to leave.

(continued)

(continued from previous page)

What were my options? I had to go on welfare, because working would not even pay for daycare. Then one afternoon at the safe house, my counselor told me I should go to college. I laughed, and proceeded to tell her how stupid I really was, in case she could not see for herself. This incredible woman took me by the hand, and sat with me through all of the terrifying paper work and testing. Soon I was enrolled in the community college, and finished my Associates degree in two years. I then transferred to the university and received my Bachelor's degree and then a Master's degree. Today I am working on my Ph.D. I am one of the few lucky ones. I continue to do battle with the effects of the abuse, and the effects of the labeling on my self-identity, even after ten years out. I try to remember that I deserve to be loved. Today I love life, go figure.

Source: Eileen Breen, Department of Sociology, Colorado State University. This essay was written expressly for the sixth edition of *Diversity in Families*

internalized messages are produced by a set of capitalist/patriarchal relationships, with economic, legal, social, and psychological consequences, colluding to deny her options, blame the victim, and justify the victimization (Fine, 1981:50).

Fear

The most obvious deterrent for the abused is that leaving *increases* the danger to her and her children. According to a U.S. Department of Justice study, the victimization rate of women separated from their husbands is three times higher than that of divorced women and about twenty-five times higher than that of married women (Bachman and Saltzman, 1996). If caught by the husband, the physical abuse escalates, with murder becoming more likely. For the abusive husband, control of his wife is paramount. Obviously, when she leaves, he loses control over her.

Hope

Abused wives may stay because they are convinced that their husbands will somehow reform. They may believe the myth that it is always best for the children if the parents stay together. This avenue is often encouraged by psychologists, clergy, and friends, who counsel abused wives to keep the family together no matter what the price because they believe that it will work out favorably in the long run.

Economic Dependency

Economic concerns are especially important deterrents to leaving the abusive situation. The lack of marketable skills and jobs with decent pay and benefits often trap women in abusive relationships. Women who leave must find a way to pay for housing and provide care for dependent children, usually on low earnings. If her job does not provide for health care, that will be another burden.

"Even obtaining insurance can be difficult as a number of companies refuse to provide life, medical, or mortgage insurance to women they think have been physically abused. In short, there are few social supports for an abused woman wanting to make a new life" (Chasin, 1997:81).

Women may also fear that their husbands will default on child support payments. If wives have little education and few job skills, they will most likely feel there is no alternative but to stay in their troubled relationship. There is also the difficulty of working and taking care of the children. For middle- and upper-class women, divorce or separation usually means losing the lifestyle and status to which they have become accustomed. For many women who are insecure and have negative self-concepts, it is better to cope with the known than to face the unknown. "Many flee one problem—battering—only to become part of another: 'the feminization of poverty'" (Jones, 1994:200–201).

To summarize, wife abuse is a complex phenomenon. Although many factors contribute, the most significant factor is a social climate that supports violence, that keeps women in a secondary status, and that accepts the use of physical violence to control women. Murray Straus, a leading expert on family violence, is convinced that the causes of wife beating are found in society itself:

> The causes of wife-beating are to be found in the very structure of American society and its family system. Demonstrating this, even in principle, is a vast undertaking. All that can be done here is to identify seven of the main factors and to give the general flavor of the argument. . . . They are:
>
> - The family is a type of social group characterized by a high level of conflict;
> - The United States is a nation which is fundamentally committed to the use of violence to maintain the status quo or to achieve desirable changes;
> - The child rearing patterns typically employed by American parents train children to be violent.
>
> This in turn:
>
> - Legitimizes violence within the family and builds violence into the most fundamental levels of personality and establishes the link between love and violence;
> - Reinforces the male dominant nature of the family system, with a corresponding tendency to use physical force to maintain that dominance when it is threatened.
>
> The sexual inequalities inherent in our family system, economic system, social services, and criminal justice system effectively leave many women locked into a brutal marriage. They literally have no means of redress, or even of leaving such a marriage. It is the combination of these factors which makes the family the most violent of all civilian institutions, and which accounts for that aspect of family violence which we call wife-beating (Straus, 1977–1978:445, 447).

The key determinant, then, is the dominance of males throughout society—in politics, the media, the economic system, the schools, and all other institutions—that makes women "inferior." The secondary status of women makes them subjects of those with power. One response for men, when faced with threats to their dominance, is to use physical force. Thus, the reduction and eventual elimination of sexism throughout society will be a major step in solving the problem of wife beating.

Domestic Violence in Same-Sex Relationships

Only recently have researchers begun to study the dynamics of same-sex relationships, including violence (Island and Letellier, 1991; Renzetti, 1992; 1997). When comparing physical violence in same-sex domestic relationships with that in heterosexual unions, the rate is approximately the same (Elliott, 1996; Barnett et al., 1997). As in abusive heterosexual relationships, the explanation seems to center on power/control over a partner. "A desire for power and control drive the abuser to beat, insult, or threaten the victim into submission to her or his wishes" (Elliott, 1996:4). Because the partners are of the same sex, however, the dynamics of gender/patriarchy are missing.

There are some crucial differences between the patterns of violence in heterosexual and homosexual relationships. Both partners in same-sex relationships have the opportunity to batter instead of the overwhelming preponderance of male perpetrators in heterosexual relations. Second, abusers in same-sex relationships have a unique form of control over their victims—the threat of "outing" (i.e., others revealing one's homosexuality publicly against their wishes) to family, landlords, employers, or others. As difficult as it is for the abused in heterosexual relationships to seek help, it is more so for the abused in homosexual relationships. This occurs because seeking help as a gay or lesbian victim is tantamount to "coming out of the closet" but more than that, to say that you are gay and a victim of domestic assault makes you twice cursed (Simpson, 2000). Gays and lesbians also face unique challenges when they seek a criminal justice response to domestic violence. The police, because of homophobia (this varies by locality, with rural areas more homophobic than urban areas; some cities, such as San Francisco and Seattle, are less homophobic than others), cultural stereotypes, or inappropriate training, respond ineffectively to domestic violence among gay couples (Miller and Knudsen, 1999). The courts also find it difficult to deal with same-sex violence by partners. State statutes concerning domestic violence refer to "spouse" and "battered wife" but have no reference to gay or lesbian victims. In many states, because same-sex unions do not have the legal status of marriage, lesbians and gays cannot get protective orders in Family Court, even though married couples can (Leland, 2000). Gay men and lesbians are more cut off from the usual support systems in society (such as their families, who often reject their homosexuality; the church, which tends to condemn homosexuality as a sin; and the medical and mental health professions, which have a history of diagnosing homosexuality as a mental illness) (Island and Letellier, 1991:100). There are shelters for battered women, but no shelters exist for battered men. In short, same-sex battering victims are even more isolated than battered heterosexuals. The level of isolation is compounded for battered homosexuals of color because of the homophobia and racism prevalent in society (Waldron, 1996). Lesbians of color are thrice cursed by homophobia, racism, and sexism.

CHILD ABUSE AND NEGLECT

Gelles and Straus have concluded that "with the exception of the police and the military, the family is perhaps the most violent social group, and the home the most violent social setting, in our society" (1979:15). "A small child has more chance of being killed or severely injured by its parents than by anyone else. For children, the home is often the most dangerous place to be" (Collins and Coltrane, 1995:476–477). Of the various forms of family violence, violence by parents toward their children is the most prevalent. This problem is reviewed in this section with a focus on the definition, incidence, causes, consequences, prevention, and treatment of child abuse and the characteristics of abusing parents.

What Is Child Abuse?

What constitutes child abuse? The extreme cases of torture, scalding, beatings, and imprisonment are easy to place in this category. However, there are problems in determining whether many other actions are abusive. For example, one definition of child abuse is violence "carried out with the intention of, or perceived as having the intention of, physically hurting the child" (Gelles and Straus, 1979:136). This definition includes everything from spanking to murder. The problem is that spanking is used by nine out of ten parents and is considered legitimate and acceptable behavior. At what point does punishment become excessive? This is an important question for which there is, as yet, no universally accepted answer. It is important for counselors, social workers, health practitioners, and the courts to agree on such a definition because the consequences for children and parents are enormous. To have a definition that is too lax imperils the health and safety of children, and to have one that is too stringent jeopardizes parents who might incorrectly receive the label of "child abuser," have their children taken from them, and even be imprisoned.

Perhaps the most useful definition, focusing on violence, is that child abuse occurs when there is a nonaccidental physical injury requiring medical attention. However, this definition ignores the area of child neglect. This type of abuse involves a range of behaviors, including the inadequate feeding of a child or lack of provision of sanitary living conditions. These forms of neglect may be just as damaging to children, physically and mentally, as physical aggression. This type of problem is complicated, too, because the neglect may or may not be willful on the part of parents.

Given these problems with defining **child abuse,** we have chosen an all-inclusive definition: "The distinctive acts of violence and nonviolence and acts of omission and commission that place children at risk" (Gelles, 1976:136). We should not be misled, in using this broad definition, into thinking that all the forms of child abuse and neglect are essentially alike, caused by the same sources, and subject to a uniform treatment mode (Gelles, 1976). We generalize about this problem, but the reader is warned that child abuse is, like all social problems, very complex.

Incidence of Child Abuse

The precise extent of child abuse and neglect is impossible to know, for two reasons. First, studies of the phenomenon have not used uniform definitions; and second, the issue is extremely sensitive to the persons involved. To be the perpetrator or victim of child abuse is generally something for which people are stigmatized. Acts of violence and neglect are hidden from society because they occur in privacy. When asked by a survey researcher if they have ever physically abused their children, abusing parents will most likely deny such an act. Thus, many of the statistics are taken from police, teachers, social workers, and medical personnel, who must assume that the children were victims of abuse. Obviously, such subjective observations are subject to error. As one illustration of the problem of subjectivity, authorities commonly view the parents and children of the middle and upper classes quite differently than those from the lower classes. Trained personnel are more likely to label as a victim of child abuse a poor child who has a black eye than a rich child who has a black eye. Also, of course, authorities never see many cases of abuse and neglect. Official statistics, then, always underreport the actual incidence.

Given the problems with defining and determining the exact incidence of child abuse, probably the best estimate currently available on violence toward children is from a national self-report study by Straus and Gelles (1986). They found for that year that: (1) two-thirds of parents had used some form of violence toward their children; (2) about 2 percent of parents engaged in a violent act with a high probability of injuring the child; and (3) for those children who experienced beatings, it was repeated an average of once every two months.

The best official estimate found that in 1994 social service agencies received 3.14 million reports of child maltreatment (physical and sexual abuse, neglect), which translates into a rate of about 47 in every 1000 children (Weise and Daro, 1995).

Causes of Child Abuse

The reasons for the abuse and neglect of children by parents are complex and varied, involving personal, social, and cultural factors.

Personal Factors

The most commonly assumed cause for abusive behavior toward children is that the perpetrators are mentally ill. This assumption, however, is a myth that hinders the understanding of child abuse (Gelles, 1976:138). In the view of experts, only about 10 percent of maltreating parents have severe personality disorders or psychoses. This is not to say that personal factors are unimportant. Obviously, abusive parents let their aggressive feelings go too far. There are several possible reasons for this. One important reason is that abused children have a higher probability of becoming abusive parents than do nonabused children. In short, violence tends to beget violence. Some caution is advised concerning this relationship, however. The evidence is that about 30 percent of physically abused children grow up to be abusive adults. Although this is much higher than the overall societal rate of between 2 and 3 percent, we must not ignore the fact that seven out of ten abused children *do not* become abusive adults (Gelles, 1993:15).

The failure to learn parenting skills may also be the reason that children who have lost a parent, who have been separated from their mothers, or who come from a disrupted home show some tendency to become abusing parents themselves.

> Abusive parents, for whatever reason, tend to be more demanding than other parents. Abusing parents demand far higher performance from their children than ordinary parents. What they demand is beyond the capacity of their children even to understand, much less perform. Typically they become angry because the child will not stop crying, eats poorly, urinates after being told not to do so, and so on. In fact, they feel righteous about the punishments they have inflicted on their children. They avoid facing the degree of injury they have caused, but they justify their behavior because they feel their children have been "bad" (Goode, 1971:633).

A relatively common trait of abusing parents is chronic alcohol consumption. This activity reduces the normal restraints inhibiting aggression in the individual. Chronic alcoholism is also associated with a number of other factors that produce strain and disruption in stable family patterns: greater unemployment, poor health, low self-esteem, isolation, and preoccupation with self.

Finally, a caution from Gelles and Straus: "When our explanations focus on "kinds of people"—mentally disturbed, poor, alcoholics, drug abusers, etc.—we blind ourselves to the structural properties of the family as a social institution that makes it our most violent institution with the exception of the military in time of war" (Gelles and Straus, 1988:51).

There is a strong propensity among the lay public to explain child abuse (or wife abuse) in individual terms. Although personal factors should not be ignored, social factors are extremely important for an understanding of this complex phenomenon.

Economic Conditions

The data from a number of studies indicate that child abuse is more likely to occur in families of low socioeconomic status. We must be careful in interpreting these data, however, because wealthier families are simply better able to hide abuse (e.g., they go to private physicians, who may be more reluctant to report signs of abuse in their "respectable" clients than the doctors who minister to the poor in general hospitals). Nonetheless, the generalization is appropriate that children of the poor are more likely to be abuse victims (Straus and Smith, 1990:250). However, as Gelles reminds us, "This conclusion . . . does not mean that domestic violence is confined to lower-class households. Investigators reporting the differential distribution of violence are frequently careful to point out that child and spouse abuse can be found in families across the spectrum of socioeconomic status" (Gelles, 1990:115).

Unemployment is another condition associated with child abuse. This may lead to poverty, low self-esteem because of being a "failure" in a success-oriented society, and depression. The unemployed are also homebound, increasing their interaction with children.

Race and Ethnicity

From the foregoing discussion we might assume that African Americans would have a higher rate of child abuse than Whites because African Americans are more likely to be unemployed and poor. However, data from Gelles and Straus show that there is no difference between African Americans and Whites in the rates of abusive violence toward children. The reason for this seeming anomaly is that African Americans are generally less socially isolated than Whites. That is, they have more contact with relatives and receive more help from them in financial support and childcare (Gelles, 1990:115).

Other research shows that African Americans have higher rates of child abuse than Whites or Latinos. Kathryn Lindholm and Richard Willey (1983) analyzed data obtained from the Los Angeles County Sheriff's Department on 4132 victims of child abuse and 3583 suspected perpetrators to find similarities and differences in child abuse patterns by ethnicity. They found, first of all, when comparing the reported child abuse cases by ethnicity with the proportion of each ethnic group in the general population, that Anglos were underrepresented as victims, Latinos were slightly underrepresented, and African Americans were disproportionately abused. Second, Lindholm and Willey found that abusers tended to be males among Anglos (63.7 percent) and Latinos (61.2 percent), but not among African Americans (49.3 percent). This is a direct consequence of the strong likelihood that African American women are single parents. In this sample, 34.6 percent of the Anglo suspects, 42.4 percent of the Latino suspects, and 61 percent of the African American suspects were female heads of households (Lindholm and Willey, 1983:15). This study also found that female children are more likely to be abused than male children, but again with variation by ethnicity. Among abused Anglo children, 55.1 percent were female, and among Latinos, 60.6 percent were female; but the proportion for African American children was almost evenly distributed, with 50.4 percent being female (Lindholm and Willey, 1983:17).

These data on child abuse by ethnicity should be treated with some caution. What may appear to be determined by ethnicity may actually be explained by social class. Moreover, we should not forget that the overrepresentation of an ethnic group in the abuse category may be a function of the well-to-do being better able to hide the problem, or it may be the result of bias by reporting agencies. As examples, Lindholm and Willey (1983:29) found that 15.6 percent of the abuse cases in their sample were reported by county hospitals, but only 1.1 percent were reported by private physicians. And Raymond Buriel and associates (1979) found that schools were twice as likely to report Latinos as child abuse victims as they were to report Whites. Thus, minority children are more likely than White children to be labeled as abused.

Despite these problems with the data, we can see variations by ethnicity in the patterns of child abuse. These variations are the result of differences in family structure, differing placements in the opportunity and reward structures of society, and contrasting parenting styles. The relationship between social class and child abuse and between ethnicity and child abuse suggests that child abuse is a result of structural stress (i.e., stress from social sources). Most incidents of abuse appear to be related to a central factor in child abuse—"inadequate resources available to the parent who is charged with the 24-hour-a-day responsibility to raise and care for the child" (Gelles, 1976:139). In a society in which violence toward children is culturally acceptable (as noted earlier), those parents in unusually difficult social circumstances may go beyond the cultural norm.

Gender

Men are much more likely than women to be the assailants in all forms of family violence except child abuse, in which women are the perpetrators as often as men. Not only are women with children more susceptible, they are much more likely than men to be in stressful economic situations (to head households alone, to be poor, and to do less fulfilling and less economically rewarding work). Because she is the primary parent, a mother also feels more responsibility and guilt than the father for the failures of her children. Given all of these differential pressures on women, it is impressive that women commit only 50 percent of child abuse (Breines and Gordon, 1983:504).

Gertrude Williams (1980:597) has argued that some additional gender-related issues also promote child abuse by women. In her opinion, a primary reason for child abuse is the **pronatalist bias** in society. **Pronatalism,** as discussed in earlier chapters, is the widespread belief that a woman's only fulfilling activity is motherhood. This ideology forces many women into a role that they may not want. They are also forced into the mothering role by the lack of interesting and well-paid work options, and by unwanted pregnancies. Unwanted children born to a woman in a marginal economic situation are prime candidates for abuse and neglect.

With respect to the gender of the victims, boys are at greater risk for major acts of physical abuse, while boys and girls are equally at risk for minor acts of abuse. Adding age to the mix, we find that boys are more likely to be victims of abuse for children under twelve, whereas for ages thirteen and older, girls are more likely to be victims (Barnett et al., 1997:48).

Lack of Social Support

The lack of social supports is also related to child abuse. The research by Gelles and Straus found that the most violent parents lived in the community less than two years; belonged to few, if any, community organizations; and had little contact with friends and relatives.

> This social isolation cuts them off from any possible source of help to deal with the stresses of intimate living or economic adversity. These parents are not only more vulnerable to stress, their lack of social involvement also means that they are less likely to abandon their violent behavior and conform to community values and standards (Gelles and Straus, 1988:87–88).

Consequences of Child Abuse

Many of the consequences of child abuse are obvious. About 1200 children die annually from abuse. Hundreds of thousands endure physical injuries, such as fractures, burns, internal damage, and neurological dysfunctions, which may lead to permanent damage or even death. The physical disabilities and/or mental anguish resulting from abuse may lead to problems with learning, speech, and acceptable behavior patterns for the victims. Psychological problems are another obvious consequence of the trauma of being abused by one's parents.

Parental abuse, including incest, has been found to be responsible for children running away from home. Running away during childhood or adolescence generally has additional negative consequences—a higher incidence of malnutrition; health problems; being victims of assault; and criminal activity, especially prostitution, both male and female.

Adults who were mistreated as children have a greater tendency to be violent when compared to those who were not mistreated. As noted earlier, they are more prone to be child abusers themselves. "The rate of abuse in families where the parents were themselves abused as children is approximately six times higher than the rate in the general population" (Vandeven and Newberger, 1994:371).

There appears to be a strong relationship between being abused as a child and juvenile delinquency. A study by the Child Welfare League of 75,000 children between the ages of nine and twelve in Sacramento, California found that abused or neglected children in this age category were 67 times more likely to be arrested during those pre-teen years than those who were not (reported in Whitmire, 1997).

INCEST

Incest is a special case of child abuse involving sexual behavior. The legal definition of incest is sexual intercourse between persons so closely related that marriage is prohibited by law (incest is illegal in all fifty states). This definition includes sexual behavior between close relatives, including siblings, first cousins, and the like. We restrict our use of the term here to cases of inappropriate sexual contact between a parent (or a person in the parent role, such as stepparent) and a child. Sexual contact includes petting, fondling, mutual masturbation, oral sex, or intercourse (Geiser, 1979:53–45).

An inappropriate sexual relationship between a parent and child is the most common type of incest, and that is the focus of this section. This relationship is a form of child abuse because the victim usually interprets the experience as coercive and assaultive; the child is powerless to do anything about it. Children are powerless because parents are stronger physically, because children have been socialized to obey their parents, because they may be too young to understand what is happening, and because, if they do understand, there is such a societal stigma attached to incest that they dare not, except in unusual circumstances, inform persons outside the family. This reluctance is changing a bit as celebrities such as Oprah Winfrey, Roseanne, La Toya Jackson, and former Miss America Marilyn Van Derbur have gone public with their stories of childhood sexual abuse.

Incidence of Incest

Because of the stigma and secrecy associated with incest, accurate statistics on incidence are impossible to obtain. Margaret Andersen, after reviewing the literature, feels that the most accurate estimate of incest is that "16 percent of women have been sexually abused by a relative by the time they are eighteen years old" (Andersen, 1997:177).

Although accurate data on incest are unknown, the information from reported cases provides some ideas about the incidence of incest by type. We know from various studies that (1) the victims of incest are usually female (a ratio of 3:1); (2) the offenders are almost always male; (3) the median age of first encounter is under twelve years, with the age ranging from a few months to the late teens; (4) nine out of ten cases involve father and daughter, stepfather and stepdaughter, and grandfather and granddaughter; of the remaining 10 percent, half are sexual relationships between fathers and sons.

Recent research on incest has also found a number of false beliefs about the phenomenon. Incest offenders are not all psychotic. Moreover, the children are *not* seductive connivers who want sex, power, and gifts. Many incest victims try to stop the incestuous encounters, but many are too fearful. Other family members, including the mother, are sometimes aware of what is going on, but, typically, are powerless to stop it.

Mothers may be aware of incestuous abuse, but they are typically powerless to stop it. A mother may become a silent bystander because her emotional and/or economic dependence on her husband prevents her from confronting the situation. Particularly in families in which mothers are unusually powerless as a result of battering, disability, mental illness, or repeated childbearing, there is an especially high risk of sexual abuse, especially among daughters who have taken on the household responsibilities (Andersen, 1997:178).

Incestuous relationships typically last an average of two years. And, most important, incest occurs throughout the social structure, among all races and religions, and in all geographical areas (Finkelhor, 1993). As one researcher has put it:

> The true range of families dealing with incestuous assault has little to do with class, race, economic class or social background. Were it possible to provide a more realistic profile of a typical family in which incestuous abuse occurs, it would more likely be a middle-class family composed of husband, wife and children living together in a nuclear situation. The adults would be Republicans as often as Democrats, involved in their church and active in community affairs, the same people you and I pass on the street each morning (Butler, 1978:11).

Causes of Incest

The explanations for incest are varied. There are psychological reasons, such as low self-esteem, immaturity, and **pedophilia** (sexual interest limited to children) on the part of the perpetrators. Some psychological theories misplace the blame for incest. Some blame wives whose lack of sexual interest toward their husbands turns the men's interest to a daughter. Others place the responsibility on the seductive daughter who is competing with her mother. Some have criticized these theories for blaming the victim. They see the source of the problem, rather, in patriarchy. Some feminists point to the research finding that the greater the paternal dominance and authoritarianism in a family, the more likely it is that incest will occur (James and MacKinnon, 1990). In a patriarchal society, male dominance is normal in sexual relations. Judith Herman and Lisa Hirschman (1981) found that many fathers felt no guilt for their aggressive sexual behavior toward daughters. This may result from being accustomed to forcing sex on weaker and unwilling partners, a common condition in a patriarchal family. Thus, "father-daughter incest will disappear only when male supremacy is ended" (Breines and Gordon, 1983:527).

Consequences of Incest

The experts agree that the children who are victims of incestuous relationships are negatively affected. Clearly, their self-esteem is severely damaged. One researcher asked a victim who was now an adult how the incest experience had affected her:

> Her reply still haunts me: "Think of the lowest thing in the world, and whatever it is, I'm lower." That is the motto of the incest victim.
>
> Incest is almost always a devastating experience for the victim. Its emotional and psychological impact is destructive for several reasons—partly because of our cultural reactions to incest, to a greater degree because the child is thrust into an adult role for which he or she is unprepared, and, most tragically, because of the aggressor's betrayal of the child's trust and dependence. The victims are not always innocent in a sexual context, they are not always virginal, but they are generally too young and naive to understand treachery, and that is the innocence that is so traumatically betrayed in incest. The people they have learned to depend on, trust, and love suddenly turn on them in a bewildering, terrifying, often physically painful fashion.
>
> Incest is powerful. Its devastation is greater than that of non-incestuous child molestation or rape because incest is set within a constellation of family emotions and conflicts. There is no stranger to run from, no home to run to. The child cannot feel safe in his or her own bed. The victim must learn to live with incest; it flavors the child's entire world. The aggressor is always there; incest is often a continuing horror for the victim (Forward and Buck, 1978:19).

The fundamental problem with parent–child incest is the violation by the adult of the child's trust. The father's sexual misuse of his daughter is clearly an abuse of the social role "of father, of power, and of parental authority over a child. To make it worse, this offense occurs in the context of a supposedly caring relationship. It is this caring relationship that precludes any need for force in most cases. The child is not raped but seduced by the father. It is worse than an assault, it is a betrayal. The child grows up distrusting adults and men in particular" (Geiser, 1979:58).

Incest is a devastating experience for most. One estimate is that less than one-fourth of the children involved in incestuous relationships escape with no apparent ill effects (Geiser, 1979:58). For the remainder, there are two common effects. The first involves the suppression of feeling, a coolness in relationships with persons of both sexes, withdrawal, and trouble relating to peers. In later relationships with men, many female incest victims remain aloof; they are turned off by sex, and they may be unable to achieve orgasm. The other typical response is to become self-destructive. Studies have found that a relatively high proportion of prostitutes were sexually abused as children. Abused children are also more likely to run away from home. "Sexually abused female runaways are . . . more likely than nonabused female runaways to engage in delinquent and criminal activities" (Andersen, 1997:178).

*B*ATTERED ELDERS

In the 1960s, child abuse gained attention as a serious family problem. This occurred for spouse abuse in the 1970s. The problem of the battered elderly has, until recently, gone unnoticed. Elder abuse, although certainly not new, has become more of a problem because people are living longer and the numbers of elderly are increasing. This means that as an ever-larger number of adult children must assume a caretaker role, elders are more likely to be physically abused by their children.

What Is Elder Abuse?

We examine the type of abuse in which elderly persons are abused by children with whom they live. The forms that this abuse can take include the following (from Boudreau, 1993:145):

- Physical abuse, such as hitting, slapping, shoving, use of physical restraints, as well as the withholding of personal care, food, medicine, adequate medical attention, and the like
- Psychological abuse, such as verbal assaults, threats, fear, and isolation
- Drug abuse, in which the elderly are encouraged by their doctors and families to take too many drugs, a practice that serves the families by keeping the elderly more manageable
- Financial exploitation, involving the theft or misuse of money and other personal property of the elderly
- Violation of rights, such as forcing a parent into a nursing home or reducing personal freedom/autonomy

Incidence of Elder Abuse

A government study revealed that 11 percent of all murder victims aged sixty or older were killed by a son or daughter (Dawson and Langan, 1994). For the most part, though, accurate information regarding how many elderly persons are subjected to these abusive acts is impossible to obtain. The elderly victims are in a double bind that traps them in an abusive situation in which they feel they cannot notify the authorities.

The abuser is providing financial and other resources necessary for the victim's survival. Thus, the [elderly victim recognizes his or her] dependency on the abusing caretaker. These battered parents, whose attacks cover an even wider range of abuse than that perpetrated upon children, often refuse to report the abuse for fear of retaliation, lack of alternative shelter, and the shame and stigma of having to admit that they reared such a child. Paralleling the battered wife, these abused old people prefer the known, even when it includes physical abuse, to the unknown, if they seek to leave the situation (Steinmetz, 1978:55).

As a result, as many as five out of six cases of elder abuse go unreported (National Center on Elder Abuse, 1998). This is because, in addition to the reasons just mentioned, many mistreated elders are homebound and isolated, and thus are unlikely to be seen at banks, senior centers, hospitals, health programs, and police stations (Wolf, 2000b:8).

Despite these problems with underreporting, Rosalie Wolf (2000) summarizing the findings from five community surveys, found that 4 to 6 percent of older adults report experiencing incidents of domestic elder abuse, neglect, and financial exploitation. With about 35 million Americans age sixty-five and older, a middle estimate of 5 percent yields an estimated 1,750,000 who are victims of some form of abuse. The prevalence studies have identified some important characteristics of abused elders. First, they tend to be in poor health. Second, they tend to be living with someone else. Third, they are isolated and thus have no one to turn to for support (Biggs et al., 1995:41).

Causes of Elder Abuse

The most typical setting for elder abuse is situations in which adult children are overwhelmed by the role of taking care of their parent or parents. The emotional, physical, and financial costs can be enormous. Hospital and other medical care is extremely expensive for the elderly, since they are more prone to illness. There are the obvious additional food and housekeeping costs. The additional financial burden may be especially difficult because it is likely to coincide with higher expenses for the caretakers' own children (e.g., college, a wedding, or assistance with the purchase of a first home).

Parents living with their adult children cause stress and resentment in a number of other ways. The household is more crowded, causing different sleeping arrangements, overcrowded bathrooms, and the like. The caretaking responsibility is most likely assumed by the wife, and she may resent the elders' presence because of the extra work, the intrusion into her privacy, and the excessive demands on her time. As the parents age and their disabilities become more pronounced, the care they need can become overwhelming. The wife may be especially hostile to the parents because, with her own children gone, this could be a time for more freedom—freedom to travel, to go back to school, or to take a job. But with elderly parents to restrain her, she is thrust back into the parental role. Parents living with an adult child can cause special problems when they have not resolved their problems from an earlier time. The parents may continue to treat their adult children like youngsters, taking over or trying to take over the decision-making role. Or the hostile feelings generated when the child was an adolescent may return to haunt both parties.

Clearly, there is tension when the behaviors and values of the adult child do not coincide with those of the elderly parent. They may differ on political issues, religious issues, how the grandchildren should be raised, doing household chores, and what television programs to watch. Adult children may resent the parents living in their home because they feel forced into the situation. The other children may live in other communities, and the parents, no longer able to live alone, moved in with the child who happened to be living in their own community. The hostile feelings increase if the family feels that other relatives are not sharing the burden, at least financially.

This emphasis on the elderly causing stress among caregivers tends to blame the victim. In the words of Karl Pillemer, a major researcher in the field:

> In the same way that some writers held that "spoiled" children were more likely to be abused, or that nagging, demanding wives were more likely to be battered, the elderly themselves have been cited as the cause of abuse. Focusing on caregiver

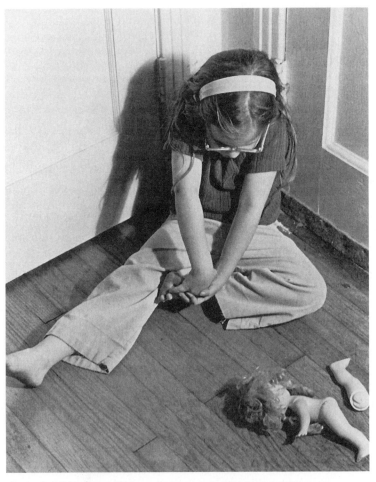

Abused children are likely to become abusive parents.

stress normalizes the problem; it relieves the abuser of much of the blame because, after all, the elderly are demanding, hard to care for, and sometimes even downright unpleasant (Pillemer, 1993:246–247).

Despite this disclaimer, the stress generated between the elderly and their caregivers is a major source of abuse. Stresses and tensions between the generations are inevitable. For some families, such a situation results in actual physical and mental abuse of the elderly. The psychological and social factors related to child and spouse abuse are also pertinent for the abuse of the elderly. One additional catalyst that must be considered is the ageism prevalent in society. This provides an atmosphere in which the elderly are devalued, negatively stereotyped, and subjected to discrimination. To the extent that older people accept these negative definitions of the aged, they may view abusive treatment as deserved or at least as unavoidable. Similarly, if their children accept the tenets of ageism, then they are likely to assume that the elderly deserve their mistreatment.

Macro and Micro Linkages

Violence in the family presents the ultimate paradox—the physical abuse of loved ones in the most intimate of social relationships. The bonds between wife and husband, parent and child, and adult child and parent are based on love, yet for many these bonds represent a trap in which they are victims of unspeakable abuses.

Although it is impossible to know the extent of battering that takes place in families, the problem these forms of violence represent is not trivial. The threat of violence in intimate relationships exists for all couples, and for all parents and children. For many the threat becomes real as the strong abuse the weak. Violence in the family, however, is not only a problem at the micro level of family units. It also represents an indictment of the macro level—society, its institutions, and the cultural norms that support violence.

The forms of intimate violence occur within a social context. This social context of intimate violence includes a patriarchal ideology that condones and maintains the power of men over women. The social context includes a media barrage with the consistent message that violence solves problems. The social context includes an economy in which poverty, unemployment, underemployment, and corporate downsizing jeopardize millions of families. The social context includes institutional sexism, institutional racism, and institutional heterosexuality, which make life more difficult for certain categories of people, especially limiting the possibilities for women, women of color, and gays and lesbians. The social context includes the breaking up of kin networks as household units move for better opportunities, thus increasing social isolation. These social forces cause and perpetuate violence toward spouses, children, and elders. In short, these social forces create the conditions that foster abuse in intimate relationships. Personal suffering at the micro level, then, is a result of macro forces. However, this type of determinism can be resisted, challenged, and changed. These efforts are the topics of the next section.

AGENCY

Although the existence of family violence is strongly affected by social forces, individuals acting singly or with others can and do shape, resist, and challenge the forces affecting their lives.

At the individual level, abused women (the discussion here is confined to spouse abuse) are not always passive and defeated victims. Some fight back against the aggressors, demanding fundamental changes in the relationship. Some seek help from the police and other governmental agencies. Some bring lawsuits against their spouses or perhaps the police for negligence. Still others leave their abusive relationships, often at great personal physical and economic peril. Other women connect in organizations with those in similar circumstances.

Individuals who have experienced abuse can affect the macro level by making their situations known to authorities and through the media. This helps to make the public aware of this usually hidden problem. Most important, abused women aid the reform process by informing the public of inadequate laws, uninformed police procedures regarding the handling of domestic violence situations, and the bureaucratic mishandling of domestic cases by social agencies; and by articulating their rights and their children's rights.

Concerned citizens—abused women, feminists, and others—have worked through organizations to change the societal forces that encourage abuse. They have also worked to change laws and procedures to protect the victims of abuse. And they have worked to provide viable alternatives for abused women.

The Women's Movement

The credo of feminists is that domestic violence cannot be treated in isolation. Legal remedies, mediation, or therapy will not work without considering the issues of women's equality and gender subordination (Schneider, 2000:28). Thus, the agenda of the women's movement, through various organizations, has focused on changing society to bring sexual equity before the law, equal pay for equal work, and the end of oppression of women in all areas of society. The women's movement has been successful, although not completely, and each success has helped to reduce violence in families. Most pertinent, out of the women's movement came a movement to provide shelters for battered women.

The Battered Women's Shelter Movement

Beginning in the early 1970s, women's groups (also church groups and other civic organizations) in various communities formed residential sanctuaries for battered women and their children after they escaped an abusive home (Schneider, 2000:11–28). This movement has swept the country, and shelters are now found universally in cities. These shelters typically provide protection, food, clothing, legal assistance, personal counseling, assistance in obtaining welfare, child care, and job counseling. Obviously, when a community provides these services to abused women, many who otherwise would have no place to turn can leave their abusive situations for a safe haven.

Legal and Criminal Justice Remedies

Several key events have changed the legal situation regarding abused women in the last two decades or so (this information is taken from Gelles and Straus, 1988:160–177). (For the situation in Sweden, see Box 10.3.)

- In the mid-1970s three successful class-action suits set the stage. One, against the New York City Police Department, argued that the police failed to prosecute abusive husbands. Another, against the Cleveland district attorneys, said that they denied battered women equal protection under the law by not following through on the prosecution of abusive husbands. In the third case, the Oakland, California, police department was accused of illegal conduct in its discouragement of arrests in domestic violence cases.
- In 1984 the results of a key study in Minneapolis were published (Sherman and Berk, 1984). Over almost a year and a half, some thirty-five cooperating police officers employed three different tactics to handle domestic violence cases—arrest, advice or mediation, or ordering the violent spouse to leave the house for eight hours. The police were assigned the tactics randomly before they arrived at the home to eliminate police discretion. Each family in the study was followed for six months following the altercation. The study's findings were that *automatic arrest had the greatest deterrent effect*.
- In 1985 a jury in the U.S. District Court for Connecticut awarded Tracy Thurman $2.3 million in compensatory damages against twenty-four police officers. Ms. Thurman, a victim of a vicious physical attack by her husband, had called for help (on this and many previous occasions) but the police took too much time in answering the call and then were lax in restraining her estranged husband. Her civil suit argued that the police treated her numerous requests for help differently because her assailant was her husband. Had he been a stranger, the police would have given her more protection.
- In 1986 the governor of Connecticut signed into law a family violence bill that required police officers to arrest offenders in domestic assault cases, regardless of whether the victim was willing to sign a complaint.
- The Violence Against Women Act, a $1.6 billion inclusion in the Clinton administration's 1994 budget provided funding to support the criminal justice system's response to violence against women.

The result of these (and other) actions was that "public policy in cases of family violence . . . swung from indifference to control" (Gelles and Straus, 1988:167). More states now have mandatory arrest statutes. The police, prosecuting attorneys, and others in the criminal justice system are now much more likely than twenty-five years ago to deal harshly with abusive husbands. These new policies give hope to women in abusive situations.

Families in Global Perspective: Public Policy and Violence against Women: The Swedish Response

Legislation

Violence against women was not generally regarded as a social problem [in Sweden] until the 1970s. Before that, assault against women was "invisible"—a private matter that was supposed to be resolved within the family. Legislation focused on protecting the sanctity of the family and private life. In 1864 a husband's right to beat his wife without punishment was abolished, but not until a century later—in 1965—was rape within the family declared illegal. Since the 1970s, however, there has been extensive legislation in this field. For example, new rules of assault have further emphasized the seriousness of these crimes by making the penalties more severe.

One such rule classifies assault against women as a criminal offense that falls under the jurisdiction of the public prosecutor. This means that an investigation may take place and charges may be filed whether the crime is reported by the victim herself or by someone else, such as medical care personnel.

In 1988 a law on restraining orders went into effect. A restraining order means that a person who threatens or commits violence against a woman may be prohibited from visiting or coming near her. . . .

Shelters and Hot Lines

The first women's shelter in Sweden opened in Göteborg during 1978. In the 1980s, shelters and crisis hot lines were established all over the country. . . . Women's shelters now receive municipal subsidies, which vary in size. The Swedish Organization of Emergency Shelters for Battered Women receives State grants. . . .

Action Program

In 1990 the Swedish government approved an action program on violence against women. Its purpose was to streamline and intensify the work of the judicial system, social services, the health care system and other public agencies.

One important element of this program was to increase the visibility of violence against women and heightened public awareness of the often sex-specified mechanisms that underlie this violence. Some parts of the program were targeted primarily to people in occupational categories that come into contact with women subjected to or threatened with violence. The National Police Board, the National Courts Administration, the National Board of Health and Welfare and the Office of the Prosecutor-General were asked to organize joint training courses on violence against women for the occupational categories within their purview. . . .

Steps have been taken to enable the police to supply technical aids, such as alarms and mobile telephones, to women who have been threatened or harassed. . . .

A number of sexual equality projects aimed at generating greater public awareness of violence against women have received financial aid from the government in recent years. A few of these projects have been targeted especially toward men.

Source: Ranveig Jacobsson and Karin Alfredsson, *Equal Worth: The Status of Men and Women in Sweden*. Stockholm: The Swedish Institute, 1993, excerpts from pp. 85–88.

CHAPTER REVIEW

1. Families reflect the society in which they are embedded. Thus, a violent society, as seen in its history, laws, media, pornography, folklore, and customs, will have violence in its families.

2. The ways that families are organized in American society encourages conflict. This occurs through the unequal distribution of power, patterns of male dominance, the intensity of interaction, and privacy.

3. The data on spouse abuse, child abuse, incest, and elder abuse are unreliable because the events usually take place in private, physicians treating the battered tend to protect the well-to-do, and the victims often lie about the causes of their injuries because of shame or fear.

4. Despite the unreliability of the data, we do know that wife abuse is a fairly common practice and we do know some facts about the conditions under which it occurs. It is more probable when (a) families are threatened by economic hardships; (b) males hold traditional gender role expectations; (c) verbal aggression is a common part of the interaction; (d) husbands feel inadequate; and (e) husbands came from homes in which they were beaten or in which they observed their fathers beat their mothers.

5. The most relevant explanation for why some men batter their wives is patriarchal terrorism—the use of violence and intimidation to maintain absolute control over their partners.

6. There are five reasons why some women remain in abusive situations: (a) learned helplessness; (b) self-blame; (c) fear of increased violence by the assailant; (d) belief that it is best for the children if the family remains together; and (e) lack of economic opportunities.

7. Comparing the pattern of violence in same-sex relationships with heterosexual unions, we find two commonalities: (a) The rate is about the same; and (b) the explanation seems to center on power/control in both. The differences are as follows: (a) When the gender of both partners is the same, patriarchy is missing and both partners have the same opportunity to batter; (b) abusers in same-sex relationships have a unique form of control— the threat of "outing" the other; and (c) the abused in same-sex relationships are even more isolated than the abused in heterosexual relationships. This isolation is even greater for homosexuals of color, and especially for lesbians of color.

8. Child abuse occurs when parents (a) are too demanding; (b) do not have adequate parenting skills; (c) were victims of child abuse; and (d) face economic hardships. Men are most likely to be the assailants in all forms of family violence except child abuse.

9. Incest, the special case of child abuse involving sexual abuse, usually involves a male perpetrator and a female victim. Just as with spouse and child abuse, the offenders are not all psychotic.

10. The problem of elder abuse in family situations occurs when adult children are overwhelmed by the role of taking care of their parent or parents.

11. A number of macro social forces maintain family violence—patriarchal ideology, laws, the media, institutional sexism and racism, and an economy that encourages inequality. These social forces affect families, leading some to be physically violent. Thus, macro forces lead to micro suffering.

12. The abused in families need not be passive and, indeed, most often they are not. Human beings have agency—they can resist, they can cope, they can change social arrangements. Many victims leave abusive situations. Many take their assailants to court. Many join with others to make the problem of family abuse more visible, to change laws and police procedures, and to work for gender equity.

RELATED WEB SITES

http://www.mincava.umn.edu/

The Minnesota Center Against Violence and Abuse (MINCAVA) seeks to provide a quick and easy to use access point to the extensive electronic resources on the topic of violence and abuse available through the Internet.

http://www.dvalianza.com/

This is the home page of the National Latino Alliance for the Elimination of Domestic Violence. Originally, forty Latinos and Latinas— activists, clinicians, researchers, lawyers and survivors—from the United States and Puerto Rico met in Washington, D.C. in November, 1997 for the National Symposium on La Violencia DomÈstica: An Emerging Dialogue Among Latinos. The Symposium steering committee, composed of eight men and women who have exercised leadership in domestic violence work nationally in Latino communities, organized and led this meeting with the support of the U.S. Administration for Children and Families, Family Violence Prevention and Services Program. Now this organization runs this website to disseminate information on domestic violence and a greater understanding of how family violence affects Latino communities nationally.

http://www.cavnet2.org/

The Communities Against Violence Network (CAVNET) is an international network of anti-violence experts and advocates. The website serves as a tool for disseminating new research information about violence and abuse, as well as tips for avoiding it.

http://www.vix.com/pub/men/domestic-index.html

There are many studies demonstrating men's capacity for violence. Many of these are referenced in feminist servers on the net. The intention of this website is to make difficult-to-find and poorly-known material on men and domestic violence available more broadly.

http://bcifv.org/

BC Institute Against Family Violence: The BC Institute Against Family Violence was established in 1989 as a private, non-profit organization. The Institute works to increase public awareness and understanding of family violence through education and dissemination of information. The Institute provides continuing education for professionals, conducts research, and develops and distributes resources to community organizations.

http://www.nncc.org/Abuse/abuse.links.html

National Network for Child Care: Child Abuse Links: National Network for Child Care offers an internet source of over 1000 publications and resources related to child care, an e-mail listserve, support and assistance from experts in child care and child development, and quarterly newsletters for family child care, center-based care, and school-age child care. This particular page offers many links to Internet resources dealing with child abuse.

http://www.igc.org/nonviolence/

Nonviolence International: Nonviolence International (NI) assists individuals, organizations, and governments striving to utilize nonviolent methods to bring about changes reflecting the values of justice and human development on personal, social, economic, and political levels. NI is committed to educating the public about nonviolent action and to reducing the use of violence worldwide.

http://child.cornell.edu/

The Family Life Development Center: The Family Life Development Center was established by New York State in 1974. Its mission is to improve professional and public efforts to understand and deal with risk factors in the lives of children, youth, families and communities that lead to family violence and neglect. It focuses on strategies and programs to help vulnerable children and youth by strengthening families and communities. As an interdisciplinary unit of the College of Human Ecology, the Center accomplishes its mission through research, training, outreach and education.

http://www.unh.edu/frl/

Family Research Laboratory: Since 1975, the Family Research Laboratory (FRL) has devoted itself primarily to understanding family violence and the impact of violence in families. As public and professional interest in family violence has grown, so has the need for more reliable knowledge. The FRL has tried to fill that need in a variety of ways: through comprehensive literature reviews, new theories, and methodologically sound studies. Researchers such as Murray Strauss at the FRL pioneered

many of the techniques that have enabled social scientists to estimate directly the scope of family violence. These efforts have brought international recognition to the FRL.

http://www.elderabusecenter.org/

The National Center on Elder Abuse (NCEA) is funded by the U.S. Administration on Aging. It exists to provide elder abuse information to professionals and the public; offer technical assistance and training to elder abuse agencies and related professionals; conduct short-term elder abuse research; and assist with elder abuse program and policy development. NCEA's website contains many resources and publications to help achieve these goals.

Divorce and Remarriage

Myths and Realities

Myth:	High divorce rates mean that marriage is becoming less popular.
Reality:	Actually, marriage is still popular. Divorced people overwhelmingly tend to remarry.
Myth:	Marriage and divorce rates are more or less stable across racial groups in the United States.
Reality:	There are differences across racial groups because of social class, cultural, and religious differences.
Myth:	Divorces occur throughout the life cycle, with little pattern according to length of marriage.
Reality:	Divorces tend to occur early in marriages—about half by the seventh year of marriage.
Myth:	Ex-husbands and ex-wives suffer about equally from the consequences of divorce.
Reality:	The consequences of divorce are different by gender, with women experiencing many more negatives than men.

Myth: Having learned from their mistakes, remarried couples have more marital success than do couples in first marriages.

Reality: The divorce rate for remarrieds is higher than for first marriages.

*A*lthough many marriages do not end in divorce, about half do. Some marriages become intolerable as they are filled with more and more tension and even violence, as shown in the previous chapter. Some marriages fail because the love the wife and husband once shared diminishes for various reasons. Still other marriages break up because of the relentless strains brought about by poverty. For these and countless other reasons, **divorce**—the formal dissolution of marriage—is a relatively common experience in the United States.

This chapter examines divorce rates (past, present, and future), the correlates and causes of divorce, and the consequences of the divorce experience for the former spouses and their children. Divorce apparently is not a repudiation of marriage, because most divorced persons eventually marry again. We examine this phenomenon of remarriage, looking at the remarriage rates, prospects for marital success, and the role of the stepparent. The final section looks briefly at the politics of divorce.

*D*IVORCE RATES

Recent divorce rates show that, overall, the chances that a first marriage in the United States will end in divorce are about one in two. This section examines the historical patterns in divorce, the variables associated with marital breakdown, the sources of the marital strains that lead to divorce, and the predictions for future divorce rates.

Trends in Divorce

Many politicians, clergy, editorial writers, and others have shown great concern over the current high rates of marital dissolution in the United States. The historical rate reveals three trends. First, the rate has been rising since 1860 (see Figure 11.1). Second, although the current divorce rate is near its historical peak, it has been declining slowly for the past twenty years (see Table 11.1). And third, as revealed in Figure 11.1 the divorce rate is clearly affected by social and economic conditions. Note, for example, that the rate increased after wars: slightly after the Civil War, more noticeably after World War I, and then dramatically after World War II. Note also that there was a downward shift during the economic depression of the early 1930s and an increase in the prosperous 1970s.

From 1990 through 1993, the U.S. divorce rate was 4.7 per thousand population, since reduced to 4.1 in 1999. This rate, although lower than the all-time high of 5.3 in 1981, far surpasses the rate of comparable nations reporting divorce

Figure 11.1

Annual divorce rates, United States, 1860–1998. Divorces per thousand married women aged fifteen and over.

Sources: Andres J. Cherlin, *Marriage, Divorce, Remarriage.* Cambridge, MA: Harvard University Press, 1981, p. 22; U.S. Bureau of the Census, *Statistical Abstract of the United States 1984,* 104th ed. Washington, DC: U.S. Government Printing Office, p. 84; Sar A. Levitan, Richard S. Belous, and Frank Gallo, *What's Happening to the American Family?* Rev ed. Baltimore: John Hopkins University Press, 1988, p. 27; *USA Today,* July 9, 1991, p. 1; and current U.S. Census Bureau documents.

data. Box 11.1 compares the divorce rate for selected Western nations for 1996. Whereas the chances for divorce in the United States are about one in two, "the corresponding ratio in Europe is about one in three to one in four" (Sorrentino, 1990:44). (See Box 11.2 for the methodological issues on computing the divorce rate.)

The next two subsections discuss the correlates of divorce and the explanations for divorce rates, both of which will help us understand the social factors that affect the fluctuating divorce rate and, at the personal level, the degree of happiness in marriages.

Correlates of Divorce

The probability of divorce is associated with a number of variables, the most significant of which are cohort, premarital cohabitation, age at first marriage, circumstances of the first birth, the presence of children, income, race, religion, and intergenerational transmission of divorce.

TABLE 11.1

Incidence of Marriage and Divorce for Selected Years

Year	Number of Marriages	Number of Divorces	Number of Marriages Per Divorce	Divorce Rate per Thousand Population
1960	1,523,000	393,000	3.90	2.2
1965	1,523,000	479,000	3.80	2.5
1970	2,159,000	708,000	3.10	3.5
1975	2,153,000	1,036,000	2.10	4.8
1980	2,390,000	1,189,000	2.00	5.2
1985	2,477,000	1,162,000	2.13	4.9
1990	2,425,000	1,161,000	2.09	4.7
1995	2,355,000	1,184,000	1.99	4.5
1996	2,310,000	1,157,000	1.99	4.4
1998	2,244,000	1,135,000	1.98	4.2
1999	2,318,000	—	—	4.1

Source: U.S. Bureau of the Census, Statistical Abstract of the United States, Washington, DC: U.S. Government Printing Office, various years; and "Population Update," Population Today, various issues.

Cohort

A **cohort** is a category of people who were born during the same time period and thus subject to similar social factors as they move through the life cycle. For example, children born in the economic depression of the 1930s are different as adults than children born after World War II. Among those differences is a much lower probability of divorce among the pre-world War II cohort.

Premarital Cohabitation

Logically, it would seem that cohabitation before marriage would increase the stability of later marriages for those couples who eventually marry, but research consistently finds that the opposite occurs (for a review, see Faust and McKibben, 1999:484). There are several possible reasons for this seeming anomaly. First, research shows that cohabitators differ from noncohabitators in that they are less likely to adapt to traditional marital expectations, and they are more approving of divorce as an answer to marital problems. Also, those who are used to greater freedom in the cohabitation arrangement may find marriage too stifling. Cohabitators, too, are more likely to have divorced parents, which leads to higher risks in marriage (see the next section). Finally, cohabitators who marry are more likely to have stepchildren in their relationships, which leads to higher rates of marital dissolution in cohabitational unions.

Age at First Marriage

The age at which persons marry plays a major role in whether marriages will remain intact. Martin and Bumpass (1989) conclude that age at first marriage is

BOX 11.1   Families in Global Perspective: **Marriage and Divorce: International Comparisons**

· We're number one in marriage.
· We're number one in still believing in marriage.
· We're number one in divorce.
· We're number one in children involved in divorce.

In 1998, approximately 2.24 million Americans married, and in that year 1.135 million split apart in some state of acrimony (*Population Today*, 2000a:7). Marriages in the United States is at best a delicate institution, at worst a vestige of a bygone era. Yet only 9 percent of Americans, the smallest number of any of the nineteen major industrial nations surveyed, say they think marriage is outdated. Are we fooling ourselves?

The United States leads the nineteen major industrial nations in marriage, but weare also number one in divorce. Although the U.S. divorce rate is the highest in the Western world, it is important to note that divorce rates have increased dramatically in all the Western countries.

Divorce Rates for Selected Industrialized Nations, 1996

Country	Divorce Rate per 1000 Population
United States	4.3
Canada	2.6 (1995)
France	1.9
Germany	2.1
Japan	1.6
New Zealand	2.8
Norway	2.3
Spain	0.8
Sweden	2..4
Switzerland	2.3
United Kingdom	2.9 (1995)

Source: United Nations, *Demographic Yearbook 1997.* New York: United Nations, Department of Economic and social Affairs, 1999, Table 25, pp. 520–522.

the strongest predictor of divorce in the first five years of marriage. "Men and women who are under the age of 20 when they first marry are two to three times more likely to divorce than their counterparts who first marry in their 20s" (Price and McKenry, 1988:17).

There are several reasons for this relationship between youth and marital instability. An obvious one is that teenagers may lack the maturity to handle the responsibilities of marriage. Their youth and relative inexperience in relationships also may lead them to make less sensible choices in marital partners (Booth and Edwards, 1985). Couples who marry young have restricted opportunities for

BOX 11.2   Researching Families: Computing the Divorce Rate

The divorce rate is calculated in several ways by official agencies and the media. Each of these methods is based on certain assumptions that can, in some instances, lead to faulty generalizations.

One method is to count the number of divorces per thousand population in a given year. In 1980 there were 5.2 divorces for each 1000 Americans, compared to a 1960 rate of 2.2 divorces per thousand. The problem with this measure of divorce is that it is too sensitive to the nation's age distribution. From 1960 to 1980 there was a very large increase in the age group in which divorces are most likely to occur, so this inflated the rate. In future years the nation's population will be aging, and this fact will deflate the divorce rate if this measure is used.

A second method is to count the number of divorces per thousand marriages in a given year. In 1960 the ratio was 258 per thousand, compared to 490 in 1980. This ratio is inaccurate, however, because it matches the divorced against the married, including those who have been divorced and remarried. Thus, this rate tends to minimize the actual divorce rate.

A third method—the divorce/marriage ratio—is the least satisfactory, yet it is a favorite of the popular press. This ratio compares the number of marriages in a given year with the number of divorces occurring in that year. In 1980, for example, there were 2,413,000 marriages and 1,182,000 divorces, giving a ratio of 490 divorces per thousand marriages. Many would misinterpret this to mean that 49 percent of all marriages end in divorce. Such a reading is inappropriate because the ratio compares two quite different populations. It compares the marriages in a given year with the divorces in that year that came from all existing marriages, not just those from that year.

A realistic measure of divorce reverses the method for the divorce/marriage ratio just mentioned. Instead of comparing the number of marriages in a given year with the number of divorces in that year, this measure divides the number of divorces in a year by the number of existing marriages. The resulting fraction is multiplied by 1000 so that the rate is expressed as a whole number. If we use this measure, the divorce rate was 9.2 per thousand marriages in 1960 and 21 per thousand marriages in 1994 (down slightly from 22.6 in 1980).

A final statistical measure, recently employed by the U.S. Census Bureau, is the divorce ratio, which divides the number of currently divorced persons, regardless of when the divorce occurred, by the number of married persons, excluding those who were separated, and multiplies by 1000. In 1982 the divorce ratio was 114 divorced persons per thousand, compared to 47 per thousand in 1970. The only drawback to this technique is that it is deflated by remarriages.

Sources: Andrew Hacker (ed.), *U/S: A Statistical Portrait of the American People.* New York: Viking Press, 1983, pp. 106–108; George Ritzer, Kenneth C. W. Kammeyer, and Norman R. Yetman, *Sociology: Experiencing a Changing Society,* 2nd ed. Boston: Allyn & Bacon, 1982, pp. 330–332; Constance L. Shehan and Kenneth C. W. Kammeyer, *Marriages and Families: Reflections of a Gendered Society.* Boston: Allyn & Bacon, 1997, p. 311; and Arlene F. Saluter, "Marital Status and Living Arrangements," *Current Population Reports.* Series P-20, No. 380 (May 1983):3.

college education and tend to have financial difficulties, especially if they have children early. Since premarital pregnancy is a common reason for early marriages, many young people enter marriage for the wrong reasons, have reduced chances for education and income, and are likely to feel prematurely limited in their search for potential spouses. Women especially find that early marriages and parenthood restrict their options, and this feeling increases the potential for resentment and strains, leading to eventual marital dissolution.

Circumstances of the First Birth

Premarital pregnancy and births increases the risk of divorce. Women who have never married and who either had a premarital first birth or a premaritally conceived, but postmaritally delivered, first birth have higher divorce rates after their first marriage than do mothers whose first child was postmaritally conceived (Norton and Miller, 1992:7). A quick marriage that often accompanies an unplanned pregnancy works against marital success because the newlyweds may feel that they are trapped with little choice, that the swift arrival of a baby does not give them sufficient time to adapt to married life, and that the timing limits educational and career opportunities, especially for the young women (see Faust and McKibben, 1999:482–483).

The Presence of Children

The presence of children in a family affects marital stability in several ways (from a review of the research literature by Faust and McKibben, 1999:483–484):

- Couples with children are less likely to divorce than childless couples.
- The likelihood of divorce decreases as family size increases, although having more than four children makes couples more likely to divorce than those couples with four or fewer children (Heaton, 1990).
- Divorce rates are lower in families with children under the age of three, while rates are higher in families with children over the age of thirteen.

Do these findings mean that the presence of children makes for happier unions? Actually, as noted in Chapter 9, the opposite is more likely to be the case: couples tend to be happiest before children and after their children leave the nest. If children do not necessarily increase marital happiness, then what is the explanation for the greater durability of marriages that involve children? There are several possible explanations: (1) Couples at risk of dissolving their marriage may decide not to have children unless their difficulties are mended. (2) Couples with children may be as unhappy as those without, but they may tend to stay together "for the good of the children." (3) Couples with large families have, by definition, been married a relatively long time, and longevity in a marriage increases its chances for survival. In this last instance, when families become too large, the economic and time demands on parents may detract from marital stability.

Research suggests that under certain circumstances the presence of children increases the likelihood of divorce (Faust and McKibben, 1999):

- The presence of children born prior to the marriage increases the likelihood of divorce.

- The presence of stepchildren increases the probability of divorce in second marriages (this relationship will be elaborated later in this chapter).
- Families whose children are exclusively daughters have a higher divorce rate than families whose children are limited to sons (Katzev et al., 1994). This appears to be the result of fathers being more actively involved in childcare and family activities when raising sons than daughters.

Income

The research evidence indicates an inverse relationship between divorce and socioeconomic status. In other words, the lower the income, the higher the probability of divorce. In fact, poor two-parent families are twice as likely to break up as are two-parent families not in poverty (Pear, 1993b). The difference is even larger for African Americans, with 21 percent of two-parent families breaking up after two years in poverty, compared to 12 percent of White two-parent families dissolving (Hernandez, 1993). Moreover, the likelihood of marital breakup increases when a husband does not work, and it is even greater when neither spouse works (Pear, 1993b).

The lack of adequate resources places a burden on intimate relationships. Sudden financial difficulties such as unexpected unemployment also increase the possibility of marital breakdown. Low income, for example, is one of the basic reasons for the high probability that teenage marriages will end in divorce. If, however, these youthful unions have sufficient incomes, the negative effects of youth are moderated.

An important exception to this generalization that income is inversely related to divorce is that wives' earnings are positively associated with divorce rates. Apparently, when women have independent sources of income, the likelihood of divorce rises (Carlson, 1990:443).

Race

The divorce patterns in the United States differ by race. The data since 1960 show consistently that that White and Latino marriages are the most stable, with the divorce rate for African Americans more than twice as high.

Marital Instability among African Americans Why is there such a difference between White and African American marriages in terms of their stability? One set of explanations traces the difference back to the long-lasting effects of slavery on African American family life. These are the cultural arguments of E. Franklin Frazier (1939) and Daniel P. Moynihan (1965); they can be summarized as follows:

> The fundamental source of weakness in the black community is an unstable family structure caused by the experience of slavery, the absence of husbands and a high rate of illegitimacy. The model family type, then, is a matriarchy. A matriarchal form of family is detrimental because it is at variance with the standard pattern in American society. It is especially harmful to boys who will be denied adequate sex role models. Thus, the institution of the black family is assumed to be defective. Black culture produces a weak and disorganized form of family, which, because it is self-perpetuating, is the obstacle to full realization of equality (Eitzen, 1974:270).

This explanation, however, does not satisfactorily explain contemporary trends in African American family life (Cherlin, 1992:109–113). First, historian Herbert Gutman (1976) has found evidence that most slaves formed life long stable unions and that long after slavery a high proportion of African American families included both parents. The prominence of single-parent African American families has been a phenomenon of the past fifty years and especially since 1960 and thus cannot be a lingering effect of a slavery system that ended over 130 years ago.

Andrew Cherlin has argued that the differences between African American and White family patterns are not only of relatively recent origin, but that they also reflect the life of African Americans today in cities, where their economic lot continues to deteriorate. Cherlin's findings reveal that those African Americans who differ most from Whites are the least educated, have the most unstable work history, and have the least income. In short, marital instability appears to "represent the response of the poorest, most disadvantaged segment of the black population to the social and economic situation they have faced in our cities over the past few decades" (Cherlin, 1981:108). The economic changes accompanying the transformation of the economy especially have placed African Americans at a disadvantage. Many of the jobs that once provided economic stability for African Americans have left the central city areas for the suburbs and the Rustbelt for the Sunbelt, leaving African Americans with lower-paying jobs or no jobs at all. As a result of these and other social factors, African Americans and Whites differ significantly in occupation and income, with more than one-fourth of African Americans living below the poverty line in 1998 compared to about 8 percent of Whites; also, African Americans are consistently twice as likely as Whites to be unemployed. Clearly, the disparities between these two racial groups show that African Americans are more likely to experience economic hardships and insecurities that lead to marital disruption. Added to these economic differences are the racial inequities that continuously confront people of color.

Marital Instability among Latinos   The rate of marital instability among Latinos is about the same as the rate for Whites. This is curious, because Latinos share more characteristics with African Americans than they do with Whites. The members of both groups suffer discrimination because of skin color; both groups are disproportionately poor, unemployed, employed in the secondary labor sector, negatively impacted by the economic transformation, undereducated, and more likely to marry at a young age. How, then, are we to account for the marital patterns of Latinos, which approximate more closely the patterns of Whites than of African Americans?

First, we must remember that Latinos are not a homogeneous category. The marital disruption rate for Cuban Americans, for example, is relatively low, whereas it is quite high for Puerto Ricans.

The most common explanation for the relative stability of Latino marriages is a cultural one. This explanation focuses on the traditional Latino family, which is typically a strong unit embedded in a very significant kin network. Also, Catholicism, the religion of most traditional Latinos, is absolute in its prohibitions against divorce. Although these cultural explanations appear to make sense, they are too simplistic because they do not take into account the diversity among Latinos.

Peter Uhlenberg (1972), for example, compared two groups of Latinos—first-generation immigrants in rural Texas and third-generation urban Latinos in California—and found some interesting differences. The first-generation immigrants, although very poor, rarely divorced (having a rate actually less than that found for Whites), the reason being that these people were extremely traditional in their attitudes and behaviors. Also, these new immigrants tended to stay together because they were aliens in a strange land, with nowhere else to turn for refuge other than their immediate and extended families. The third-generation Latinos in California, on the other hand, had a high rate of unstable marriages, similar to that for African Americans. They were not constrained by tradition but were affected rather by structural variables. Wives in these families were much less dependent on their husbands than were wives in first-generation immigrant families because these third-generation Latino women had more education and better employment. Thus, for them, traditional gender roles were less tenable. Males were relatively weak compared to females because of their low wages and widespread unemployment. This inability of males to be adequate providers, along with the wives' questioning of gender roles, tends to lead to strain in marriages. "For a male unable to fulfill his role as economic provider, leaving his family reduces the gap between what is socially expected of him and what is possible" (Uhlenberg, 1972:55–56). Uhlenberg's research is important because it demonstrates that Latinos are not a homogeneous group constrained uniformly by the strong traditions brought from Mexico and by the hold of Catholicism. Moreover, we see that the divorce rate for Hispanics is an average that masks the diversity in family experiences among this minority.

Interracial Marriages Interracial marriages have a higher divorce rate than intraracial marriages. Moreover, the type of intermarriage makes a difference. For example, the most common type of Black/White marriage (four times more likely) is for a White woman to marry an African American man, rather than for an African American woman to marry a White man. Among these types, divorce is more likely to occur among those interracial couples who do not follow the typical pattern of a White woman married to a African American man (Collins, 1988a:362).

Religion
A 1999 national survey conducted by the Barna Research Group found that 24 percent of all adults have experienced at least one divorce during their lifetime (reported in Matthews, 1999). Concerning religious affiliation, this study found that Jews had the highest divorce rate (30 percent). Among Christian denominations, Baptists have the highest rate (29 percent), those identified as "born again" have a rate higher than the average (27 percent), while those from the mainline Protestant denominations and Mormons are no different than the national average (25 percent). Atheists and agnostics were below the norm, with the same rate (21 percent) as Lutherans and Catholics.

Matthews suggests that these findings raise "questions regarding the effectiveness of how churches minister to families. The ultimate responsibility for a marriage belongs to the husband and wife, but the high incidence of divorce within the Christian community challenges the idea that churches provide truly practical and life-changing support for marriages" (Matthews, 1999:2). Most important, these findings underscore the importance of social, demographic, and economic influences beyond the relative commitment of two people (Carman, 2000). For example, the relatively low rate for Catholics is due, of course, to the unyielding opposition of the Catholic Church to divorce and the more accepting attitudes of most Protestant denominations. Although the Catholic divorce rate is lower than the Protestant divorce rate, it is important to note that the rates move in tandem. That is, when the divorce rate is going up in society, it moves upward for both religious categories, indicating the importance of other social factors affecting marriages.

Interreligious couples have higher divorce rates than couples with the same religious beliefs. This fact indicates that couples who are alike on social variables **(homogamy)** will have lower divorce rates than those who are different **(heterogamy).** Gender and religion combine for an interesting pattern. The divorce rate is lower when the woman is a Catholic and the man a Protestant than when the man is a Catholic and the woman a Protestant.

Intergenerational Transmission of Divorce

Adult children of divorce are more likely to experience divorce than are adult children from intact families (for a review of the research, see Faust and McKibben, 1999:484–485). There are several possible reasons for this tendency. First, the children of divorced parents usually live with their mother and this often means a decline in standard of living. Children growing up with economic disadvantages are more likely to have lower educational attainment and an increased probability of premarital pregnancy, all of which are characteristics associated with a higher divorce rate (McLanahan and Sandefur, 1994).

Second, children experiencing their parents' divorce may lead to their experiencing feelings of depression, anxiety, and stress, which may have long-term negative effects leading to poor preparation for marriage.

Third, parents who divorce are not good role models for their children. Those children in observing the ongoing conflicts between their parents before the divorce do not learn how to resolve conflicts satisfactorily.

Finally, as a result of accepting their parents' divorce, the children from divorced households, more than the children of intact families, are more accepting of divorce as the only way to deal with a troubled marriage.

This tendency for the children of divorce to end their own marriages disproportionately seems to be lessening. Nicholas Wolfinger's research (1999) finds that the rate of intergenerational transmission of divorce declined by almost 50 percent in a twenty-five-year period ending in 1996. He suggests that because this was a period with a high divorce rate, the stigma associated with divorce diminished, thus reducing the negative psychological effects of divorce on the children affected. Also, prior to no-fault divorce laws, couples had to demonstrate the absolute deterioration of their relationship. "When couples finally ended their marriages, the situation may have deteriorated far more than is typical in divorces today, thereby bringing greater harm to children" (Wolfinger, 1999:415).

PREDICTING THE DIVORCE RATE: UP OR DOWN?

As noted earlier, the divorce rate has steadily risen in the United States since at least 1860, with a dramatic rise from 1960 to 1981, followed by a mild decline from the historic high. But what of the future? Is this recent decline the beginning of a downward trend in the rate or at least a leveling off, or only a pause in the long-term upward trend? The experts are divided on this issue. This section examines the arguments for both sides, looking especially at the societal forces that impinge on the correlates of divorce and on individual couples.

The Prediction of a Declining or Leveling of the Divorce Rate

The predictions about future divorce rates should be viewed with considerable caution since they are based on what has happened to earlier marriages (Kammeyer, 1981; Kammeyer et al., 1990:399). We simply do not know whether this and future generations will follow the patterns of previous generations. With this caveat in mind, let's review first the factors that will have a dampening influence on future divorce rates.

Young adults now are marrying about two years later than in 1960, reducing the number of very young brides and grooms. Moreover, the proportion of first marriages preceded by cohabitation has increased from 8 percent for marriages in the late 1960s to about 50 percent now. If these unmarried cohabiting couples break up, they do not add to the divorce statistics, as they would have done a generation ago, when they most likely would have been married (Bumpass et al., 1991). However, contrary to logic, when cohabiting couples marry, they have a higher probability of divorce than couples who did not live together before marriage (Peterson, 1993a).

A basis for the high divorce rate in the 1970s was the ideological gap between the rise of new feminists and their traditional husbands. Many wives developed a keen awareness of gender inequities *after* they were married. When their challenges to traditional gender patterns were resisted by their traditional husbands, the chances for divorce increased. Although these gender battles are still being fought in contemporary marriages, there is a greater likelihood that both partners are aware from the beginning of marriage of their spouse's beliefs concerning gender roles. Thus, there are fewer surprises, and the demands by wives that their husbands participate in household chores and child care are viewed as less threatening and less challenging. As a result, it is argued, gender battles have diminished as a source of marital disruption.

On the legal side, there is a concerted attempt by conservatives to make divorces more difficult to obtain, which, if successful, will bring the divorce rate down. This is a reaction to no-fault divorce laws, which were passed by every state since the 1970s and which made divorces easier and faster to obtain. These laws made it possible for either spouse to cancel a marriage at any time. Some have argued that the divorce rate, which jumped 30 percent since the passage of no-fault divorce laws, is a consequence of those laws. Research substantiates this. One study found that no-fault laws raised the divorce rate by about 15 percent (Nakonezny et al., 1995), but, as Larry Bumpass has argued, no-fault laws "account for a short-term rise in divorce by speeding those cases that were already coming down the pipeline" (quoted in Johnson, 1996:80). Many states are trying to legislate ways to discourage divorce (that is, bringing back fault-based divorce law). A different legislative strategy with the same presumed outcome is to make marriage more difficult to obtain. Another option with the expressed hope of deterring divorce, passed by the 1997 Louisiana legislature, is a voluntary method called "covenant marriage" (Nock et al., 1999). Arizona enacted similar legislation in 1998 and other states, mostly southern, are considering this attempt to strengthen marriage (Latham, 2000). In Louisiana it works this way: although couples may opt for marriage as before, they now also have the option of a "covenant marriage." Couples choosing this option must receive premarital counseling and promise to marry for life. Divorces are granted only after counseling and only under certain conditions: (1) the couple has been separated for more than two years; (2) either spouse has committed adultery; (3) a spouse is convicted of a felony and sentenced to prison; (4) a spouse physically or sexually abuses his or her spouse or child; and (5) a spouse abandons the house and refuses to return for at least a year.

Clearly, the enactment of laws making marriage and/or divorce more difficult to obtain will bring divorce rates down. Contrary to the assumption of the proponents of such legislation, however, these efforts will not enhance the quality of marriages. Nor will this legislation increase marriages. What will likely occur is that there will be a greater reluctance to marry, increasing the likelihood of cohabitation as a substitute for marriage.

Joshua Goldstein (1999), after analyzing data on divorce rates, predicts that the divorce rate will not decline but rather they will continue at its present level.

The Prediction of a Rising Divorce Rate

The historical pattern for divorce has been for a rise over the past 150 years, with a slight decline from the historical high in the past twenty years. Is this decline a pause in the overall tendency for the divorce rate to increase over time?

A number of plausible reasons lead us to expect the divorce rate either to remain at its present high level or even increase. These reasons are grouped into demographic factors, cultural factors, and structural factors.

Demographic Factors

At least three demographic factors increase the likelihood of the divorce rate remaining at a relatively high level or even increasing in the near future. First, the age structure of the population should increase the number of divorces and the divorce rate. The proportion of young adults will increase over the next decade or so. This will likely increase the divorce rate because of the increased proportion of the population in the divorce-prone years. Second, the bulge in the population of children of divorced parents (i.e., those born after 1970) will increase the present and future divorce rate. As noted earlier by Wolfinger (1999), the children of divorce are somewhat more likely to divorce but not as much as earlier research has indicated. Third, there is the long-term consequence of people living longer. In 1890, the average wife was a widow when her last child left home. In 1970, in contrast, the average intact couple lived together thirty more years after the last child left home. Since then, the number of potential years married people spend together has increased even more, adding to the possibility for separation before the death of one spouse.

Cultural Factors

The high divorce rate of the 1960s and 1970s has a cultural basis that should continue. Social attitudes have changed since the 1950s, to the point where society is now relatively accepting of divorce. As early as one generation ago, divorce was stigmatized in communities and in churches and by acquaintances, friends, and family members. A divorced politician would rarely be elected (Reagan was the first divorced President to be elected). A divorced minister would most likely seek employment in another occupation, because parishioners would not accept such behavior from their spiritual leader. And divorced persons, especially women, faced social ostracism. But these constraints have loosened considerably.

Structural Factors

The major reasons for a predicted high future rate of marital instability are structural. First, with all of the states adopting liberal no-fault divorce laws, divorces have been easy to obtain, low in cost, and moral issues have been removed from the decision. Friends and families now recognize that a divorce may be preferable to an unhappy marriage. Furthermore, being divorced no longer precludes one from finding employment in any field. In effect, then, divorce has become socially acceptable, and the legal and attitudinal supports for divorce will make it an ever-easier option in the future.

Most significant, the forces of technological change, deindustrialization, and globalization are transforming the economy, shifting jobs from one sector to another, eliminating some occupations while creating new ones, thus generating instability and insecurity, reducing further opportunities for the poor, and shrinking the size of the middle class. These changes have had serious consequences for families. If anything, the repercussions will increase over the next generation.

Deindustrialization, for example, has meant the sudden unemployment of many relatively well-paid industrial workers. Many of these newly unemployed find their skills and work experience unwanted. Many, as they seek new jobs or try to be retrained, experience discrimination because they are considered too old. Those who find work most often find it in the service sector, where the pay and benefits tend to be considerably lower than before. The effects on marriages of these consequences of deindustrialization can be devastating. Studies consistently confirm the strong relationship between unemployment, low income, and marital dissolution. Divorce is twice as high among families in which the husband is unemployed as among those families experiencing stable employment.

*"Could you write, 'To Penny, my darling ex-wife, who
nurtured me and supported me all through my struggles as a fledgling
writer, and whom I blew off the minute I had my first big success.'"*

Moreover, the longer the period of joblessness, the greater is the likelihood of
marital dissolution.

Those who believe that divorce rates will decline have argued that the proportion of working women, which was so instrumental in the past increases in
the divorce rate, will level off. They have not taken into account, however, the
realities of the economic transformation taking place now. The economic hardships brought about by male unemployment or underemployment force many
former housewives into the workplace. This trend will have two possible negative outcomes for marital stability. First, many women who were dependent on
their husbands will find that they can make it in the occupational world and thus
will be more likely to leave unhappy marriages in which they feel trapped. Second, traditional men, already devastated by unemployment, may find it all the
more damaging to their wounded self-esteem to be dependent on their wives for
economic security. The resulting tensions (added to by the apportioning of many
household chores) increase the instability of many marriages.

The arguments on both sides of the question of future divorce rates are per-
suasive, although we believe that the arguments supporting the continued high
divorce rates or even rising rates are the most convincing. However, consideration of this debate, while important, should not obscure an important fact: the
divorce rate reflects the composite picture of marital instability. Thus, this single
rate, whether rising or falling, masks the variation in marital disruption by class,
race, and ethnicity.

THE CONSEQUENCES OF DIVORCE FOR ADULTS AND CHILDREN

The previous section on divorce rates examined divorce in a detached manner, considering divorces in the aggregate rather than as the personal dramas of individuals at the micro level severing the most intimate of relationships. Divorce is an intensely personal event, and this intensity makes the breakup a painful experience, even when both parties want the marriage to end. The uncoupling process begins with feelings of estrangement.

> Because virtually all people enter marriage with the expectation (or the hope) that it will be a mutually supportive, rewarding, lifelong relationship, estrangement from one's spouse is typically a painful experience. Estranged spouses might spend considerable time attempting to renegotiate the relationship, seeking advice from others, or simply avoiding (denying) the problem. Consequently, the first negative effects of divorce on adults can occur years prior to final separation and legal dissolution (Amato, 2000:1271–1272).

Both of the partners in a divorce are victims. Each is affected, in the typical case, by feelings of loneliness, anger, remorse, guilt, low self-esteem, low levels of psychological well-being, depression, and failure. Although ex-spouses tend to share these negative feelings, the divorce experience differs for husbands and wives in significant ways because of the structure of society and traditional gender roles. This section scrutinizes the personal side of divorce—the consequences for ex-husbands, ex-wives, and their children (this section is dependent on the review of the literature on divorce by Amato, 2001).

"His" Divorce

Ex-husbands have some major advantages and a few disadvantages over their ex-spouses.

Improved Standard of Living

On the positive side, they are almost always much better off financially. Typically, they were the major income producers for their families, and after the separation, their incomes stay disproportionately with them. Suzanne Bianchi and her associates (1999) found, for example, that custodial mothers experienced a 36 percent decline in standard of living following separation, while noncustodial fathers experienced a 28 percent increase.

Increased Personal Freedom

A second benefit that men have over women after divorce is greater freedom. If children are involved, they usually live with the mother (about 85 percent), so most men are free from the constraints not only of marriage but also of child care. Thus, they are more free than ex-wives to date, travel, go to school, take up a hobby, or work at a second job. Especially significant is sexual freedom, since males tend to have more money and leisure time. Moreover, because older men in American society are considered more attractive to younger women than older women are to younger men, men have a much wider selection of dating partners and potential spouses than do women.

Personal Isolation

The experience of ex-husbands on some counts, however, is more negative than that of ex-wives. Many divorced men, especially those from traditional marriages, experience initial difficulty in maintaining a household routine. They are more likely than divorced women to eat erratically, sleep less, and have difficulty with shopping, cooking, laundry, and cleaning. And because ex-wives usually have legal custody of the children, ex-husbands see their children only relatively rarely and at prescribed times. Thus, they may experience great loneliness, having lost both wife and children.

The image of liberated ex-husbands as swinging bachelors does not fit many men. Some find dating difficult. They find that women in general have changed or that they themselves have changed. Many men withdraw from relationships because of feeling awkward, or because they fear rejection. They may also be wary over concerns about AIDS or other sexually transmitted diseases.

One consequence of the difficulties males experience in their adjustment to divorce is poorer health and even higher death rates. Epidemiological studies indicate, for example, that separated and divorced men have higher death rates than separated and divorced women (Zick and Smith, 1991).

"Her" Divorce

The benefits of divorce for women are few. To be sure, many ex-wives are relieved to have ended an onerous relationship, and some are even freed from a physically abusive one. Some are now liberated from a situation that stifled their educational and career goals. Of course, divorce also frees them to seek new and perhaps more fulfilling relationships.

Personal Isolation

For women, the negatives of divorce clearly outweigh the positives. Especially those women oriented toward traditional gender roles tend to feel helpless and experience a loss of status associated with their husbands' identity and status. Divorced mothers who retain sole custody of their children often feel overwhelmed by the demands of full-time parenting and economic survival. The emotional and schedule overloads that usually accompany solo parenting leave little time for personal pursuits. The result is that divorced women often experience personal and social isolation, especially the feeling of being locked into a child's world. Also, White women cope less well with divorce than do African American women (Price and McKenry, 1988:63). Presumably, this is because African American women have better social supports (extended family networks and friendship and church support networks) than do White women (Taylor et al., 1991:280–281).

Both ex-husbands and ex-wives tend to lose old friends. For the first two months or so after the divorce, married friends are supportive and spend time with each of the former mates. But these contacts soon decline because, as individuals, divorced people no longer fit into couple-oriented activities. This disassociation from marital friends is especially acute for women, because their child-raising responsibilities tend to isolate them from adult interactions.

On the positive side, women tend to have stronger family and friendship networks than men. These networks provide support, explaining, in part, why women fare better emotionally than men after divorce (Faust and McKibben, 1999). Moreover, because most women receive custody of their children after divorce, they are more connected to their children than noncustodial fathers.

Those few women who give up custody of their children face a two-edged sword. On the one hand, they have lost their children, and on the other, they face society's double standard—it is appropriate for divorced men to give up custody of their children, but not for women to let fathers have custody. By giving up their children, these women experience social ostracism and the attitude that they are uncaring and unfit mothers.

Decreased Standard of Living

The biggest problem facing almost all divorced women is a dramatic decline in economic resources. Paul Amato, after examining the relevant research, concludes that "overall, mothers postseparation standard of living [is] only about one half that of fathers" (Amato, 2001:1277). As Lenore Weitzman argues, for most women and children,

> . . . divorce means precipitous downward mobility—both economically and socially. The reduction in income brings residential moves and inferior housing, drastically diminished or nonexistent funds for recreation and leisure, and intense pressures due to inadequate time and money. Financial hardships in turn cause social dislocation and a loss of familiar networks for emotional support and social services, and intensify the psychological stress for women and children alike. On a societal level, divorce increases female and child poverty and creates an ever-widening gap between the economic well-being of divorced men, on the one hand, and their children and former wives on the other (Weitzman, 1985:323).

Research shows, further, that there has been little change in the gender disparity in the economic costs of marital disruption since the 1960s: "The economic costs of marital disruption for young women are as severe today as in the 1960s and 1970s. Both cohorts lose, on average almost half of their income when marital disruption occurs" (Smock, 1993:367).

Sources of Income

Depending on the situation, divorced women have one or more of five meager sources of support.

Alimony One source is alimony ("spousal support"), which is awarded only rarely by the courts (about 15 percent of all cases), usually for a specified brief time. This is generally an option only for the very affluent, who seek to maintain the high standard of living to which they have become accustomed.

Marital Property A second source of wealth for divorced women is their share of marital property. Of course, for a poor couple who separate, there is essentially no property to divide. Even for a couple somewhat better off, there may not be much to apportion beyond cars and furniture, because the house is likely to have a large mortgage, with payments the wife will not be able to afford.

*"My mom has a new boyfriend, my dad has a new
girlfriend, and all I got was a new therapist."*

Presumably, when there is property to divide, the gender-neutral rules that accompanied "no-fault" divorce laws will treat women and men equally. However, as Lenore Weitzman's analysis (1985) has shown, the effect of these laws has been, rather, to deprive divorced women, especially older homemakers and young mothers, of equitable economic settlements. The problem is that the courts assume that, at the time of divorce, husbands and wives are equal. This assumption ignores the economic inequalities created during marriage. The rules do not compensate wives for the years they spent making a home and providing emotional support while husbands moved ahead in their careers. "By far the most important property acquired in the average marriage is its career assets, or human capital, the vast majority of which is likely to be invested in the husband" (Okin, 1989:163). What of the wives' lost educational opportunities, impaired earning capacities, lost job seniority, and lost pension benefits? Judges typically overlook the husband's career assets, which are almost always are superior to those of the wife—his salary, pension, health insurance, and potential earning power. Most husbands and wives, in short, are *not* equal at the time of divorce. Wives are clearly disadvantaged economically in both the short and long term, facts ignored by the supposed fairness of the law.

Child Support A third source of income for divorced women is child support paid by absent fathers. However, this is not universally granted by the courts or, when granted, actually paid by nonresident fathers. About two-thirds of ever-divorced mothers have child support awards requiring nonresident fathers to pay child support. However, in at least 60 percent of the cases, the fathers are either entirely or partially delinquent in the payments (Johnson, 1999). The poorer the family, the less likely they will receive child support. This is related to race, as people of color are the poorest members of U.S. society. Thus, White women are much more likely than women of color to be awarded child support payments. The lack of adequate child support compounds the economic strain on women who have low earning prospects and poor marriage prospects. African American women are especially exposed to these sources of poverty:

> Formerly married black women and their children are especially vulnerable. . . . They have limited earnings capacity, face bleak prospects of remarriage, and receive less help from noncustodial fathers than do previously married white women (Furstenberg, 1990:387).

Welfare Traditionally, welfare assistance has been a possible source of economic support for the economically disadvantaged. Prior to the welfare reform legislation of 1996, about 4 million women (not all divorced, of course) received Aid to Families with Dependent Children (AFDC) for themselves and their 8.5 million children. Although AFDC was meager, it at least provided some assistance. The new welfare legislation eliminated AFDC and cut various welfare programs by $55 billion over six years (see Chapter 13). Federal welfare monies now are distributed to the states to be administered by the rules of each state (and, if the states elect, by counties), thereby providing less assistance to families than before.

Employment The fifth source of support for single women is a job. Most of these women, including those with non-school-age children, are employed, but they are disadvantaged in at least three ways. To begin, the average pay for female workers in the United States is slightly more than 74 percent of the average male pay. This relatively meager pay is reduced even further by the necessity of paying for child-care costs. Finally, women's work is concentrated either in the secondary tier of the labor market—where job security is tenuous, pay is low, fringe benefits are weak or nonexistent, and the chances for advancement are poor—or in the service sector (e.g., nursing, teaching, sales, and secretarial jobs), where "women's work" is clearly underpaid.

The Feminization of Poverty

The economic situation for most divorced women is grim. The **"feminization of poverty"** is a reality that reflects in large part the growing divorce rate of the 1960s and 1970s and the relatively high rate since then. But more than just a mere reflection of a high divorce rate, it is the consequence of a sexist society in which women earn much less than what men earn and almost always end up with the children. The no-fault divorce laws have compounded this problem because their assumption "that men and women are equally capable of self-sufficiency after divorce does not reflect labor-market conditions for most women" (Carlson, 1990:441). Add to this that many women do not receive child support, even if it

"He didn't exactly ask for a divorce—he offered me an early-retirement package."

is awarded by the courts, and the decreases in public welfare programs, then the conclusion is clear that the division of winners and losers in divorce is clearly gendered (Bartfield, 2000).

Divorce as an Opportunity for Change
Before divorce was widely accepted in this society, marriage was literally "until death do us part." Such a life long commitment works for many, but for other couples marriage becomes a trap. Love atrophies, partners change, interests diverge, the interaction becomes abusive—for whatever reason, some marriages are not happy unions. In this sense, divorce allows people to end difficult and sometimes destructive relationships and start anew rather than be condemned to "life imprisonment" (this section is dependent in part on Ahrons, 1994). Severing a marriage relationship, although traumatic as we have seen, allows each partner to go her or his own way—to find a new partner who meets his or her needs in a cohabitating or remarriage relationship; to move to a different locale and begin afresh; to go back to school; or to change jobs.

This renewal through divorce is especially meaningful for many women, because of traditional gender roles, traditional husbands, and being on their own, but others seize the opportunity and develop a new identity, forge ties with others in order to survive, and delight in becoming competent to do things they could not do or were not allowed to do.

Children and Divorce

Approximately 65 percent of the divorcing couples each year have minor children, meaning that about 1 million children are involved in new divorces annually. This means that about two-fifths of children—one in every three White children and two in every three African American children—by age sixteen will experience the permanent disruption of their parents' marriage. Figure 11.2 shows the percentage of children living in various family arrangements. Most of them will remain with their mothers and live in a fatherless home for at least five years. Most significant, many children of divorce effectively *lose* their fathers (Amato and Booth, 1996). "Ten years after a divorce, fathers will be entirely absent from the lives of almost two-thirds of these children" (Weissbourd, 1994:68). Some are twice cursed by the broken relationships of their parents— about one-third of White children and one-half of African American children whose mothers remarry will experience a second divorce before the children reach adulthood. Table 11.2 shows the breakdown in living arrangements of children by race/ethnicity for 1998. These data reveal that children of color, especially African American children, are much more likely than White children to live with one parent (about four of ten children live with two parents, biological or stepparents), whereas more than three of four White children and two of three Latino children live with two parents.

The crucial question is: What are the consequences of divorce for children? There is clearly the possibility of emotional scars from the period of family conflict and uncertainty prior to the breakup. Children will be affected by the permanency of divorce and the enforced separation from one of the parents. Most commonly this is separation from their father.

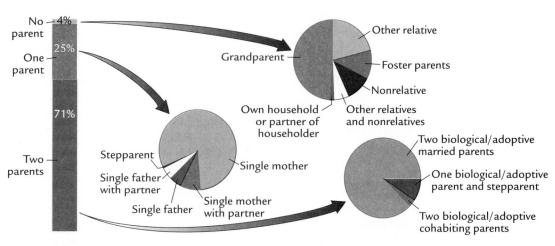

Figure 11.2

Percentage of children under age eighteen living in various family arrangements, 1996.

Source: America's Children: Key National Indicators of Well-Being 2000. Washington, DC: Federal Interagency Forum on Child and Family Statistics, July 2000, p. 7.

TABLE 11.2

Living Arrangements of Children under Eighteen
Years Old Living with One or Both Parents by
Race/ Ethnicity: 1998

Children Living with	White	Black	Latino
Both parents	76.5%	39.8%	67.0%
Mother only	18.8	56.1	28.3
Father only	4.7	4.0	4.7

Source: U.S. Bureau of the Census, *Statistical Abstract of the United States, 1999,* 119th ed., Table 84, p. 68.

There are the possible negative effects of being raised by a single parent who is overburdened by the demands of children, job, economics, and household maintenance. And there are the negative consequences that may result from the sharp decline in resources available to the family when the parents separate. The data are consistent: female-headed single-parent families, compared to two-parent families and to male-headed single-parent families, have much lower incomes. This severe decline in family resources for female-headed single-parent families produces a number of challenges for children's adjustment, often including moving to a different home and school, eliminating or greatly reducing the probability of a college education, and other alterations in lifestyles. As a result of all of these possible outcomes of divorce, children may experience behavioral problems, decline in school performance, and other manifestations of maladjustment.

Summaries of the research on the consequences of divorce on children (Amato and Keith, 1991; Amato and Booth, 1997; Amato, 2001) reveal that children with divorced parents score lower than children with continuously married parents on measures of academic success, conduct, psychological adjustment, self-concept, and social competence. Although the differences between children from divorced and two-parent families were small, they were consistent. Research also finds that children are better off on a variety of outcomes if parents in high-conflict marriages divorced than if they remained married. But because only some divorces are preceded by a high level of conflict, "divorce probably helps fewer children than it hurts" (Amato, 2001:1278).

Before discussing the problems that arise from divorce, we must note that the long-term effects of divorce are difficult to measure. Does divorce actually cause the problems displayed by divorced children? Could it be that these troubled children are being raised by troubled parents who eventually divorce (Cherlin, 1999a). Also, we simply cannot know how the children from a particular family would have fared if their parents had stayed together. Most important, we do not know what the consequences would have been if a couple stayed together in a tension-filled household. Also, we must be aware that children with divorced parents are not doomed to be misfits. As Stephanie Coontz says:

While it is true that children in divorced and remarried families are more likely to drop out of school, exhibit emotional distress, get in trouble with the law, and abuse drugs or alcohol than children who grow up with both biological parents, most kids, from *every* kind of family, avoid these perils. And to understand what the increased risk entails for individual families, we need to be clear about what sociologists mean when they talk about such children having more behavior problems or lower academic achievement. What they really mean to say is *not* that children in divorced families have more problems but that *more* children of divorced parents have problems (Coontz, 1997:99).

Note this well: Reviews of the studies on the effects of divorce on children find that "the 'large majority' of children of divorce . . . do not experience severe or long-term problems: Most do not drop out of school, get arrested, abuse drugs, or suffer long-term emotional distress" (Coontz, 1997:100; see Amato and Keith, 1991; and Acock and Demo, 1994).

With these caveats in mind, let us examine the evidence from research according to the characteristics of the children and their families.

Characteristics of the Child

The age of the child at the time of divorce appears to be related to personal adjustment problems. The younger children are at the time of marital disruption, the more likely they are to have adjustment problems. However, after the initial trauma of divorce, most children are as emotionally well adjusted as those in two-parent families.

The gender of the child appears to be an important variable, with boys being more handicapped by divorce than girls. Boys affected by divorce show more aggression, have a greater need for attention, and are lower achievers in school; when these boys are adolescents, they have more problems than do girls with alcohol and drug use (the studies finding these differences compared boys and girls from divorced homes with boys and girls from intact homes). Boys seem to take about twice as long as girls to adjust to a divorce, and they are more likely to have a relapse during adolescence. Girls, too, are affected, but in different ways. As Furstenberg has put it, "The hazards of divorce may not be greater for boys than for girls—only different. Boys 'act out' in response to divorce, while girls exhibit less socially visible forms of maladjustment" (1990:392).

The seemingly greater resilience of girls to the potential trauma of divorce may, however, be a consequence of the living arrangements made after divorce rather than the divorce itself. Since about 85 percent of children of divorced parents live with their mothers, the negative behaviors of boys may be the result of living with a female rather than a male parent. Boys in families headed by a single mother are less well adjusted than are girls. However, boys living with single fathers are better adjusted than are girls living with single fathers (Seltzer, 1994:241).

Adolescence appears to be a particularly troublesome time for children of divorced parents. They are more likely to begin sexual intercourse at an earlier age, and they are more apt to engage in delinquency, deviancy, and antisocial behavior (McLanahan and Bumpass, 1988). The research indicates that all of these behaviors are more the result of living with one parent than of divorce per se. That is, "antisocial behavior is less likely to occur in families where two adults are present, whether as biological parents, step-parents, or some combination of biological parents and other adults" (Demo and Acock, 1991:179). Thus, antisocial behavior on the part of adolescents is more a function of less parental control than the result of the trauma of parents divorcing.

Characteristics of the Family

The children of divorced parents face difficult adjustments, and many suffer. We should remember that although the finality of the divorce is important, the conditions and situations leading up to the divorce also may have a negative impact on the children.

> Families that eventually divorce may be different in a variety of ways from those that do not long before marital disruption occurs. They may be more likely to exhibit poor parenting practices, high levels of marital conflict, or suffer from persistent economic stress. Many of the same processes that are often thought to be initiated when marriages dissolve actually antedate the separation event. Our analysis suggests that exposure to these conditions may compromise children's economic, social, and psychological well-being in later life whether or not a separation takes place (Furstenberg and Teitler, 1994:187).

The size of the family after divorce has been found to be related to maladjustments among the children. The larger the family, the greater is the amount of stress (scheduling and economic demands) experienced by single parents, and this stress may negatively affect children. Also, the more children in a family, the more restrictive are the child-rearing techniques employed by the parent, resulting in possible hostility.

The socioeconomic status of the family is a significant variable affecting the adjustment patterns of children. As we have seen, divorce results in a lower socioeconomic status for families headed by a single mother, and this reduced income and accompanying shifts downward in lifestyle have a negative effect on children. Parents of higher socioeconomic status are more likely to assume joint legal custody of their children. This is significant because, compared to fathers whose former wives have sole legal custody, nonresident fathers with joint legal custody spend more time with their children (Seltzer, 1994:242).

Race appears to be significant for children from divorced families. People of color are disproportionately at a disadvantage economically in U.S. society. At divorce, the meager resources are reduced substantially, putting these children further at risk. Moreover, African American children are less likely than White children to experience their mothers' remarriage or informal cohabiting union, which keeps them, typically, from enhancing their economic situations.

Finally, maternal employment in the labor force is a family-related variable. A single working mother has a negative impact on her children if she goes to work for the first time after the divorce, giving the child an additional feeling of loss and deprivation.

To conclude, we quote from the presidential address to the Population Association of America by noted family sociologist Andrew Cherlin:

> Whether a child grows up with two biological parents, I conclude, makes a difference in his or her life; it is not merely an epiphenomenon. Not having two parents

at home sometimes leads to short- and long-term problems, but not all the differences we see in outcomes are the results of family structure. Some of the differences would have occurred anyway. Moreover, parental divorce . . . does not automatically lead to problems. Many (perhaps most) children who grown up in single-parent or in stepfamilies will not be harmed seriously in the long term (Cherlin, 1999:427).

REMARRIAGE AFTER DIVORCE

Although there has always been a strong tendency in the United States for the formerly married to remarry, there has been a shift in the pattern in this century. For most of American history, people remarried after the death of a spouse, not after a divorce. Even as late as the 1920s, more remarriages occurred after widowhood than after divorce. Now close to 90 percent of those remarrying were divorced. This increase in remarriage by the divorced is the result of two fundamental demographic facts. The first is that people are living longer, reducing the time of widowhood. Second, this trend is also simply the consequence of the ever-greater proportion of divorced people in the population. Divorce, as we have seen, is common now and is considered a relatively acceptable alternative to an unhappy marriage.

Divorce and remarriage after divorce are now common experiences. The next subsection examines the phenomenon of remarriage, focusing especially on the demographic facts of remarriage after divorce and the unique problems experienced by the partners in remarriage and by their children.

Statistical Facts about Remarriage

About one-third of all Americans will marry, divorce, and remarry. Most divorced people remarry—three-fourths of divorced men and two-thirds of divorced women (Cherlin and Furstenberg, 1994). The rate is even higher for divorced parents—"75 percent of custodial mothers and 80 percent of fathers remarry" (Weissbourd, 1994:70). The remarriage rate has declined since the 1960s, but this is likely the result of the cohabitation rate increasing. "Divorced persons, in other words, have not reduced their propensity to live with someone; rather, they have substituted cohabitation for remarriage (Cherlin and Furstenberg, 1994:362). Yet even as the remarriage trend declines, remarriage is still significant, with more than four in ten marriages in the United States involving a second or higher-order marriage for one or both of the marriage partners. The probability of remarriage is affected by several important variables: age, socioeconomic status, race, and religion.

Age

The older a woman is at the time of her divorce, the lower are her chances of remarrying. The National Center for Health Statistics (cited in Levine, 1990:50) showed, for example, that the marriage rates per 1000 divorced women were 256.7 for those 24 years old or less, 133.1 for those between 30 and 34, and 64.0 for those 40 to 44. Put another way, although almost "90% remarry among

"We're saving his toddler clothes for my Dad's new baby."

women whose marriages terminate while they are under age 25, this proportion declines sharply with age to about 60% for women in their 30s, and to less than a third for women over age 40" (Bumpass et al., 1990:753).

As we have already noted, more men than women remarry, and they are more likely than women to marry soon after the divorce. This is because divorced women who seek remarriage are at a disadvantage compared to men, since the size of the pool of potential spouses for these women is relatively small. One reason for this shortage in available men is the shorter life expectancy for men than for women. The second and more important reason for this imbalance is the propensity for men to remarry younger women. Given the sexism present in the occupational patterns of the United States, men generally gain in property, prestige, and power as they age. Therefore, they tend to retain or even improve their attractiveness to women as they age. These differences in the attraction patterns by sex and age result in a great imbalance in the number of eligible marriage partners, as most men marry younger women, and women must therefore marry older men. Consequently, although the male–female ratio is approximately the same in the 45-to-64 age bracket, there are three times as many single, divorced, and widowed women as there are single, divorced, and widowed men in that age category.

Socioeconomic Status

Socioeconomic status is related to remarriage rates. Income, for example, is significant, but the relationship differs by gender. The more money a divorced man has, the more likely he is to remarry. The reverse is true for women (Coleman and Ganong, 1991:193). Similarly, among women, remarriage is negatively correlated with their educational level. Those with less than a college education remarried quickly, whereas those with more education tended to remarry later or not at all. This is most likely because college-educated women have more career options than less educated women and therefore do not have as much pressure to marry for economic reasons. Also, the lower the socioeconomic status, the earlier that first marriage occurs. If women divorce in the average time of seven years, they will still be in their twenties and thus will have a higher probability of remarrying.

Race

The race of the divorced who remarry is a significant factor, with African Americans and Latinos remarrying at lower rates than Whites. Data from 1990 showed that 65 percent of divorced White women were remarried, compared to 51 percent for African Americans and 52 percent for Latinos (Norton and Miller, 1992:8).

Divorced White women wait an average of 26.5 months to remarry; Latino women 29.9 months; African American women 38.3 months (Dunn, 1991). Put another way, "although three-quarters of separating white women are likely to remarry, less than half of separating black women are likely to do so" (Bumpass et al., 1990:753).

There appears to be a difference in remarriage patterns by race and education. Pamela Smock (1990) found in her research that although the likelihood of remarriage did not differ significantly by schooling level for White women, it did for African American women. For African American women, the relationship between remarriage and education is a positive one; that is, those with the worst socioeconomic prospects are the least likely to marry.

Religion

A final factor affecting remarriage rates is religion. In the past, most Christian religious groups disapproved strongly of divorce, with varying severity in sanctions for those who defied the doctrines of the church on this matter. The ultimate church sanctions were for the divorced who remarried to be considered adulterers. Most denominations have shifted considerably on this issue and show ever greater tolerance, even bestowing the church's blessing on remarriages. The exception has been, and continues to be, the Catholic Church, which officially does not recognize remarriage. Thus, the more devout Catholic is more likely to remain in an unhappy marriage and, if divorced, is likely not to remarry or at least to delay remarriage.

Finally, we must recognize that the remarriage of divorced persons may also end in divorce. Actually, remarriage divorce rates are slightly higher than the divorce rates for first marriages (about 60 percent of the remarried divorce). Also, second divorces occur, on the average, after five years compared to seven years for first divorces. There are two reasons why divorce among remarried people is more prevalent and happens more quickly than in first marriages: (1) The once-divorced are less likely than the never-divorced to stay in a poor marriage out of fear of social pressure; and (2) remarriages, especially those involving stepchildren, have stresses not found in first marriages. We now turn to the description of the advantages and especially the problems of remarried couples that lead to this greater likelihood of redivorce.

The Uniqueness of Remarriage

Marriages following divorces have strengths and weaknesses not found in typical first marriages.

The Advantages of Remarriage

On the positive side, many factors should lead to marital satisfaction and more successful marriages among the remarried. Having chosen badly the first time, people are likely to be more careful in their selection of second partners. When people remarry, they are older and presumably more mature than when they married the first time.

Partners in a remarriage should, when compared to first marrieds, be more tolerant, more willing to compromise, more aware of the need to integrate their different styles of living, and better able to anticipate problems and work them out before they snowball. Moreover, the pooling of economic resources and the greater probability of better-paying jobs (because of being older) should ease or eliminate the economic problems that plague many first marriages. Also, these older partners should be more likely than first marrieds to have worked out their solution to the division of household chores, work outside the home, and other matters concerning gender roles.

Remarriage, just like divorce, offers positive opportunities for growth. Step-family researchers Mavis Hetherington and James Bray summarize the possibilities: "Although divorce and remarriage may confront families with stresses and adaptive challenges, they also offer opportunities for personal growth and more harmonious, fulfilling family and personal relationships" (cited in Rutter, 1994:32).

The Disadvantages of Remarriage

Although there are these advantages to remarriages, these marital unions entail very special problems that make marital success more difficult to attain than in first marriages. The once-divorced individuals in remarriages may be less mature, less responsible, and less supportive than the never divorced. Their first marriages may have been troubled precisely because of their immaturity, and unresolved personal problems may haunt the second marriage relationship as well. The once-divorced may, as a group, be more willing to bail out of a difficult relationship than to try to resolve the problem. The remarried person may, as is also sometimes the case in first marriages, marry for the wrong reasons. A man may be overly enthralled by the attentions of a much younger and more physically attractive mate, only to find later that they have little in common. A woman may remarry too soon after a divorce in her eagerness to find economic security, or a father for her children, or both, and thus end up with an incompatible partner.

Remarried spouses generally report higher levels of tension and disagreement than do spouses in first marriages. These disagreements typically center on issues related to stepchildren, such as discipline, rules for children, and the distribution of resources to children (Coleman et al., 2001). The evidence is, then, that the presence of stepchildren tends to lower marital quality for remarried adults. Consequently, remarriages dissolve at higher rates than first marriages.

Blended Families

The family form created in a remarriage that involves one or more children from the previous marriage of either spouse is called a **reconstituted family** or a **blended family.** This type of family has a special problem with family unity (see Box 11.3) and therefore is at a relatively high risk of divorce. Let's begin with some facts about stepfamilies (Coleman et al., 2001; Mason and Mauldon, 1996; Whitmire, 1994):

- About 40 percent of remarriages involve stepchildren.
- About 40 percent of adult women will likely reside in a remarried or cohabiting stepfamily household as a parent or stepparent at some time.
- About one-third of children will live in a remarried or cohabiting stepfamily household before they reach adulthood.
- One in three Americans is a stepparent, a stepchild, a stepsibling, or some other member of a stepfamily.
- Sixty-five percent of children living with a stepparent live with a stepfather.
- Overall, 60 percent of remarried couples divorce, however, the divorce rate is 50 percent higher in stepfamilies than in those in which no stepchildren are present (Tzeng and Mare, 1995).

Cherlin argues that the difficulties of couples in remarriages after divorce derive from the lack of societal guidelines for solving many of the common problems of remarried life. These reconstituted families have

> . . . problems for which institutionalized solutions do not exist. And without accepted solutions to their problems, families of remarriages must resolve difficult issues by themselves. As a result, solving everyday problems is sometimes impossible without engendering conflict and confusion among family members (Cherlin, 1978:642).

The problem is that remarriage, especially when it involves children from one or both of the previous marriages, greatly increases the complexity of familial relationships. There are additional social roles, such as stepparents, stepchildren, stepsiblings, stepgrandparents, noncustodial parents, and the spouses of noncustodial parents—in short, a new type of extended family of "thin kin," as Furstenberg and Cherlin (1991) have labeled it. Society has not provided a useful way to handle these complex social roles. Even the language fails. What does the child who already has a "mom" call his or her stepmother? There is no term

BOX 11.3   **Inside the Worlds of Diverse Families:** In Stepfamilies, Blending Yours, Mine, and Ours

At first, Christa and Shayne Johnson treated each other with the wariness of two hungry cats who suddenly have to share the same food bowl. Each was 8 years old and used to being the only child of a single parent. When those parents were married eight years ago, Shayne and his father moved in with Christa and her mother.

"They were each used to getting all of the attention," said Christa's mother, Mary Lou Johnson, a nurse in suburban Minneapolis. "They weren't real happy about having to wait their turn. They had some very choice names for each other."

For many children, having a new stepparent means gaining new brothers or sisters as well. Sharing with these other children may be the most difficult challenge of all. Giving up the privacy of one's room or the status of being the oldest or youngest child in a family can be as stressful as coping with a new parent. Having stepsiblings forces children to re-evaluate themselves.

The teasing, tattling and tussles that routinely mark sibling rivalry can become a special problem for blended families. Cries of "Mom always liked you best!" have a sharp and bitter edge. Newly married parents find themselves pulled in different directions by their feelings of love and protectiveness for their spouse and their children.

"It caused trouble between my husband and me," Ms. Johnson said, "We were defensive about our respective children when we argued. We never argued about anything except the children."

Such fights are common among stepparents and stepchildren. They reflect the large number of dramatic and subtle changes children must undergo when they enter a blended family. Child psychologists say most parents underestimate the extent and importance of those changes.

"Children in blended families are asked to share, all of a sudden, their room, their toys, their clothes," said Dr. Emily B. Visher, a psychologist in Palo Alto, Calif., who has written extensively about such families. "It's a very dramatic transition, and it's very unsettling."

Teenagers often have more difficulty than younger children adapting to a blended family. Parents wonder if the apparently rebellious adolescent who stays away from the house and who doesn't participate in planned family activities is trying to sabotage the new family.

Often, the problem is not the child's attitude but a conflict between the stage of development of the child and that of the new stepfamily. Adolescent behaviors that would draw little attention in a traditional family—for example, not wanting to spend time at home—sometimes become a serious problem for a new stepfamily. When misunderstood or dealt with poorly, they can escalate into conflicts that last well into adulthood.

Among the developmental tasks of adolescence are separating from family and developing an individual identity. It is important that teenagers place some distance between themselves and what they perceive as the dependent behavior of their childhood. Spending time with friends away from home and arguing over parental restrictions are ways of safely testing the turbid waters of adulthood.

(continued)

(continued from previous page)

The newly formed stepfamily, however, is at a developmental stage much closer to that of a younger child. Parents strive for their new family to be surrounded by symbols of harmony and closeness. The adolescent perceives those same symbols as signs of the very dependence he is trying to escape. The more the parents promote togetherness, the more the teenagers strive for separation, both from their parents and from their new stepsiblings.

High-school seniors and other teenagers who are about to leave home may have a very different reaction to a parent's remarriage than younger adolescents. While a 15-year-old may rebel against the new family, an 18-year-old will often embrace it.

"A child who has one foot out the door may feel relieved that the parent is going to be taken care of," said Dr. Sheldon M. Frank, a psychiatrist in Westchester County and president of the New York Council on Child and Adolescent Psychiatry.

Private space is a major area of conflict for stepsiblings. Arguments over who gets which bedroom or who has to share a bedroom can make some international political negotiations pale by comparison.

Researchers and family therapists generally agree that, although having one set of children move into the house or apartment lived in by the other set of children may be a financial and human necessity, it is likely to lead to bitter territorial squabbles. The children who are already in the house may feel imposed upon and threatened. The entering children may feel out of place.

"When you move into a place where one family has lived, everyone has their own territory staked out," said Mala S. Burt, a social worker in Baltimore and president of the Stepfamily Association of America. "They have to give up some of it to make room for new people."

Birth order becomes confused in blended families, causing additional friction. Children view themselves, in large part, by their position within the family. After a remarriage, a girl who has been the oldest child for 10 years may suddenly have two older stepsisters. A boy who was the baby of the family suddenly loses the advantages of that position to a younger, and perhaps cuter, stepbrother.

Holidays and birthdays can develop an unpleasant edge. Each set of children, unsure of what the new family means for their future, clutches at the past by insisting that theirs is the "right" way to celebrate. Stepsiblings will sometimes divide a Christmas tree in half for decorating, especially on the first Christmas together. One side of the family puts their ornaments on one side of the tree; the other children decorate their half.

Some parents in blended families say holidays and birthdays pose special rivalry problems because of gifts from the noncustodial parents. Dramatically unequal gifts or the lack of a gift from a parent who no longer lives with the child can spark nasty comments and feelings of superiority or inferiority.

"To this day, its hard for us" said Ms. Johnson, recalling how her children would tease each other about the presents they would get from their noncustodial parents. As they became teenagers, however, the tone changed.

"Now my son feels bad for my daughter because she hardly ever hears from her biological father," Ms. Johnson said.

Source: Lawrence Kutner, "In Stepfamilies, Blending Your, Mine and Ours," *The New York Time,* January 5, 1989, pp. B1, B6.

in the language to describe a child's relationship to the woman his or her father remarried after he divorced the child's mother. What are the rights and duties of the child and this woman to each other? Where is "home" to a child whose remarried parents share her or him in a joint custody arrangement? What people constitute that child's "family"? As Cherlin has noted, the absence of clarity in our language about these roles and relationships in families of remarriage "is both a symptom and a cause of some of the problems of remarried life" (Cherlin, 1978:644). Thus, in contrast to the nuclear family, divorce and remarriage have created what anthropologist Bob Simpson has called "the unclear family" (Simpson, 1998:xi).

The complexity is compounded further by the linkages among several households—among the remarried couple's household and that of the household of each former spouse, and with the households of the child's grandparents. The entanglements arise because the new kin in a remarriage do not replace the kin from the first marriage, as they more typically do in a remarriage after widowhood. Rather, in a remarriage, the effect is cumulative. Research has revealed that the biggest problem in a remarriage is stepparenting. There is the problem of acceptance—by the child of the stepparent and by the new spouse of the stepchild. Love for a spouse does not automatically transfer to that spouse's children, just as love for a parent does not mean love for that parent's new spouse. This problem is compounded for the children because they tend to remain loyal to both of their original parents. Also, since children typically are angry at their parents for divorcing, they may project this anger onto the new stepparent.

The problem of acceptance is difficult because stepparents must work their way into a closed, special group. Paul Bohannan and Rosemary Erickson have addressed this problem specifically for stepfathers.

> Stepfathers take on a functioning in-group. The mother and the children share a common history, the man coming into it has quite a different personal history. . . . The new family has basically two subgroups: the husband and wife are one and the old mother-headed family is the other. Only the wife is a member of both, and for this reason she is pivotal. The mother-cum-children group is one with which the stepfather must deal; the children, in turn, must deal with the husband-wife power bloc. There are four possible outcomes: the stepfather may take control; he may be assimilated into the mother-headed family; both he and the mother-children group can change and reach a new status quo; or he can be driven away. (Bohannan and Erickson, 1978:54).

Several factors determine how stepchildren and stepparents view each other (the following information is from Cherlin and Furstenberg, 1994:367). The younger the age of the child, the more likely he or she will consider the stepparent a "real" parent. A second factor is frequency of interaction between the stepchild and his or her nonresident parent: the less frequent their interaction, the more likely the stepparent will take on the parentlike role. A third factor is the quality of the relationship between the stepparent and the biological parent in the home. The better this relationship, the more the stepchild will accept the stepparent as a "real" parent. A final factor is the number of stepsiblings in the blended family.

Stepmothers have a more difficult time integrating into stepfamilies than do stepfathers because they are expected by their husbands to assume the primary caretaker role (Hetherington and Stanley-Hagan, 2000:187). A crucial problem for stepparents, especially stepmothers, is the issue of disciplining stepchildren. Should the stepparents assume the parent role in disciplining their spouses' children, or should they back off? The child may resent this intrusion, as may the natural parent. On the other hand, the natural parent may wish for the spouse to assume the parental obligations in full. In many households, this becomes a no-win situation for all parties.

Another problem stepparents create is that they often bring different values, different expectations, and different routines to the reconstituted family. This phenomenon encourages ambiguity and has the potential to add stress to the family relationships. The spouses in the remarriage may find that what they had worked out in the abstract does not work in the real world of the reconstituted family, with differences in what should be the division of labor, in parenting roles (especially in the discipline of children), and the like creating stresses in the marital relationship.

In sum, society, in its language, customs, and laws, does not provide guidelines for how a remarried couple and their children should solve their special problems. Without sufficient guidelines, each remarried couple must work out for themselves definitions for the obligations of each role. They must learn how to reconcile competing claims for time and resources from their own children, the children they are raising who have an absent natural parent, and the children being raised by an ex-spouse. The complexity of these problems that each couple must work out through trial and error means that many will fail. Family unity will not be achieved, tensions will mount, feelings will be hurt, and relationships will be strained. The consequence is that remarried divorced couples, especially with children from previous marriages, have an increased probability of redivorce when compared to first marriages.

The Special Case of Remarriage among the Elderly

As the population of seniors grows, so, too, will the number of elderly who remarry after divorce or widowhood. About 500,000 people over the age of sixty-five remarry each year, a number that will likely increase in the next decade as the baby boom generation begins reaching retirement age (Coleman et al., 2001). Although remarriage among the elderly is often rewarding in companionship, mutual caring, and pooled resources, it brings a special set of problems that younger remarrieds do not face (the following is from Barton, 1994). Foremost is the problem of money, not so much the lack of money but who controls the combined assets. Second, and often related to the first problem, are adult children. Daughters are more accepting of the remarriage of their parent than are sons. Sons, it appears, are more concerned than daughters about their inheritance, which is now diluted by the presence of a stepparent. Finally, seniors who remarry often face difficulty because of their differing expectations for the relationship. Men typically remarry because they want someone to cook for them, take care of the home, and take care of them. Women, in contrast, are more interested in the affective parts of the relationship (companionship and romance). Thus, just as in marriage the first time, marriage late in life is typically more difficult for women than for men.

THE POLITICS OF DIVORCE

There is an ongoing, contentious debate among scholars, religious leaders, marriage counselors, and others over divorce and its consequences for individuals and society. The two positions, as summarized by Paul Amato, are:

> [The family] is the setting in which adults achieve a sense of meaning, stability, and security and the setting in which children develop into healthy, competent, and productive citizens. According to this view, the spread of single-parent families contributes to many social problems, including poverty, crime, substance abuse, declining academic standards, and the erosion of neighborhoods and communities. . . . In contrast, [others] argue that adults find fulfillment, and children develop successfully, in a variety of family structures. According to this view, divorce, although temporarily stressful, represents a second chance for happiness for adults and an escape from a dysfunctional home environment for children. Poverty, abuse, neglect, poorly funded schools, and a lack of governmental services represent more serious threats to the well-being of adults and children than does marital instability. (Amato, 2001:1270; for arguments supporting the conservative position, see Wallerstein et al., 2000; Popenoe, 1997; and Glenn, 1996; for the liberal position, see Stacey, 1996; Coontz, 1992.)

Amato's review of the accumulated scholarship on the consequences of divorce leads him to conclude that both of these views are one-sided accentuations of reality.

> The increase in marital instability has not brought society to the brink of chaos, but neither has it led to a golden age of freedom and self-actualization. Divorce benefits some individuals, leads others to experience temporary decrements in well-being that improve over time, and forces others on a downward cycle from which they might never fully recover (Amato, 2001:1282).

As for the effects on children, "the fact of the matter is that most kids from divorced families do manage to overcome their problems and do have good lives" (Amato, quoted in Kirn, 2000:78).

The leading conservative treatise on the negative impacts of divorce on children is by Judith Wallerstein and her associates (2000). They argue that the children of divorce suffer greatly from this trauma, with only a minority managing to construct successful personal lives. Consequently, the authors conclude that parents in unhappy, loveless, but low-conflict marriages should stay together for the sake of their children. Andrew Cherlin, the highly respected family scholar, in his review and critique of this book, questions the research and conclusions of Wallerstein and her colleagues. His conclusion, as did Amato's, takes the middle ground in the political debate over divorce.

> What divorce does to children is to raise the risk of serious long-term problems, such as severe anxiety or depression, having a child as a teenager or failing to grad-

uate from high school. But the risk is still low enough that most children in divorced families don't have these problems. . . . Wallerstein encourages readers to believe that most of their commitment problems stem from their parents' divorces. But parental divorce isn't that powerful, and its effects aren't that pervasive. To be sure, it raises the chances that children will run into problems in adulthood, but most of them don't. (Cherlin, 2000:68)

Is MARRIAGE A FAILED INSTITUTION?

This chapter has considered failed marriages and the attempt by many of those who divorce to create new marriages. The media and politicians, looking at the statistics on divorce, portray an image of marriage in American society as a failed institution. But we must not lose sight of three facts: (1) Overwhelmingly, most people want to get married. As Margaret Talbot has put it: "The right to divorce is deeply ingrained in American culture precisely because so is the ideal of a mutually fulfilling marriage" (2000:2); (2) half of all marriages do not end in divorce; and (3) the overwhelming majority of those who divorce remarry. Thus, we must conclude that the institution of marriage in the United States is not dying but is, rather, quite alive.

CHAPTER REVIEW

1. Looking back over the past 100 years, divorce rates have trended upward. The rate is affected by social and economic conditions (up after wars and during prosperity and down during economic depressions).

2. About one in two contemporary marriages ends in divorce. The probability of divorce is correlated with a number of variables: cohort, premarital cohabitation, age at first marriage, the circumstances of the first birth, the presence of children, income, race, religion, and whether one's parents were divorced.

3. The factors leading to a prediction of a declining divorce rate are (a) high rates of unmarried cohabitating couples; (b) declining birth rate; (c) increased educational attainment of women; and (d) a diminishing gap between wives and husbands on gender expectations.

4. The factors leading to a prediction of a rising divorce rate are (a) the greater proportion of the population in divorce-prone years; (b) the increase in the number of adults, who as children experienced their parents' divorce; (c) greater longevity; (d) greater public acceptance of divorce; (e) economic transformation, which continues to reduce opportunities for the poor and shrinks the size of the middle class; and (f) greater independence by women.

5. Divorce gives ex-husbands two major advantages: (a) an improved standard of living; and (b) increased personal freedom. There is one major disadvantage—personal isolation.

6. Divorce is much harsher for ex-wives than for ex-husbands. Ex-wives face personal isolation but, most important, they face a significant decline in their standard of living.

7. About 1 million children are involved in new divorces annually. About 85 percent will remain with their mothers. How these children adjust to the divorce of their parents is related to the age and gender of the child, family size, the socioeconomic status of the family, race, and the employment of the mother in the labor force.

8. Although divorce is a traumatic event for children, leading to some negative behav-

ioral and emotional problems, the large majority do not suffer long-term distress.

9. Most divorced people remarry—three-fourths of men and two-thirds of women. The probability of remarriage is affected by several variables: age for women, income and education, gender, race, and religion.

10. About 40 percent of remarriages after divorce involve one or more children, thus creating reconstituted or blended families. This greatly increases the complexity of familial relationships, linking several households and creating stepparents.

11. Rather than considering divorce as pathological, we should remember that there is also a healthy element to the breaking up of marital bonds. Some marriages are destructive or just are not working for one or both partners. Rather than being condemned to a life sentence in a dysfunctional relationship, the actors break it off. This event leads, potentially at least, to greater personal growth and the establishment of a new relationship that works.

12. There is a contentious debate among observers concerning the consequences of divorce for individuals and society. The conservative position is that divorce contributes to social problems such as poverty, crime, substance abuse, and declining school performance. The progressive position is that although divorce is temporarily stressful, it represents a second chance for happiness for adults and an escape from a dysfunctional home environment for children. The research on divorce and its consequences shows that the reality lies between these two extreme views.

13. The relatively high divorce rate does not mean that marriage is a failed institution. We conclude that the institution of marriage is not dying because (a) most people want to marry; (b) half of all marriages do not end in divorce; and (c) the vast majority of those who divorce choose to remarry.

RELATED WEB SITES

http://www.divorce-online.com/network/

The American Divorce Information Network, Inc., is a group of professionals who believe in an interdisciplinary approach for dealing with divorce and family law. They are members not only of the legal system, but also therapists, accountants, financial planners, educational planners and other consultants. The American Divorce Information Network publishes an online newsletter called Divorce Online. This organization desires to build and make available a strong (and free) support system for helping families who go through the challenges and frustrations of divorce.

http://www.divorceabc.com/

Divorce ABC's is a website provided as a service by the Children of Separation and Divorce Center (COSD). This is a private nonprofit organization helping people adjust to the continuous process of separation, divorce and remarriage.

http://www.divorceonline.com/

Divorce Online, an electronic resource for people involved in, or facing the prospect of, divorce. Divorce Online provides free articles and information on the financial, legal, psychological, real-estate, and other aspects of divorce. Additionally, you can turn to the Professional Referral section of Divorce Online to locate professional assistance near you.

http://www.stepparenting.about.com/

About Stepparenting contains a mixture of information and practical subjects. This site even has a section on stepgrandparenting. It is a popular rather than educational website.

http://www.stepfam.org/

The Stepfamily Association of America: The Stepfamily Association of America is a national organization dedicated to providing support and guidance to families with children from previous relationships . . . stepfamilies. This association's vision is that stepfamilies in the United States will be accepted, supported, and successful.

http://www.stepfamily.org/

The Stepfamily Foundation: The Stepfamily Foundation provides counseling, on the telephone and in person, and information to create a successful step relationship. Their website also provides articles and helpful discussion on key issues that stepfamilies deal with. Founded in 1975, the Stepfamily Foundation has pioneered this particular method of counseling. We provide the vital training, information and counseling to avoid the pitfalls which often stress these relationships and forcing them to become just another negative statistic.

12

Emergent Families in the Global Era

Myths and Realities

Myth: Alternative lifestyles are destroying the family.

Reality: The retreat from universal marriage and its accompanying family arrangements reflect global changes and greater choices available to women and men, but they are not threatening the nuclear family.

Myth: Being single is a lonely existence, especially for never-married women, who miss out on the best things life has to offer.

Reality: Research belies this stereotype and shows that never-married women can lead meaningful lives, complete with intimate relations and strong family ties.

Myth: Because living together is practicing for marriage, cohabitants who later marry have more successful marriages than those who do not.

Reality:	Some couples live together to test their compatibility before marriage, but others live together without marriage simply as a non marital family form. Couples who live together before marriage are more likely to break up than those who do not.
Myth:	Lesbian and gay partnerships are incompatible with family life.
Reality:	A family-centered discourse is becoming more pervasive in gay communities, as gay men and lesbians establish families of choice, raise children, and create their own kinship networks.
Myth:	When they become separated from families in their country of origin, today's immigrants to the United States sever their ties to families in their homelands and settle amid a chaotic pattern of living arrangements.
Reality:	Rather than severing family ties, contemporary immigrants retain strong family bonds that often cross national boundaries and sustain them in the new society.
Myth:	Commuter marriage is a romantic lifestyle, much like a honeymoon when partners are together.
Reality:	Commuter marriage is a difficult alternative, and most commuters are ambivalent about their way of life.

Throughout this book we have examined the social forces that produce and require diversity in family life. In the past three decades, domestic and household arrangements diversified as our population adapted to evolving technologies, economic changes, and social developments in the external world. All of these forces have fueled a movement away from the idealized family model of the 1950s. This chapter is about the growing fluidity of family life in an era of unprecedented change.

First, we set forth the close connections between emerging family forms and larger social trends. We use the social constructionist perspective to set the stage for thinking about the growing diversity in domestic life. We show how structural changes are freeing women and men from conventional marriage, enabling them to accommodate their family arrangements to the new social realities they face. We move beyond a simple "lifestyles" approach to see that pluralism is a central dynamic in family formation. We turn, then, to the four domestic arrangements that are the central subject of this chapter: singlehood, heterosexual cohabitation, lesbian and gay families, and family arrangements involving separations of space and time.

THE RISE IN NEW FAMILY ARRANGEMENTS

Families in Transition

To understand current trends in living arrangements, we must return to the distinction between households and families (see Chapter 1). (The following is based on Ahlburg and DeVita, 1992:5; and Bianchi and Casper, 2000:8). The U.S. Bureau of the Census defines a *household* as all persons who occupy a housing unit, such as a house, apartment, or other residential unit. A household may consist of one person who lives alone or of several people who share a dwelling. A *family*, on the other hand, is two or more persons related by birth, marriage, or adoption who reside together. All families comprise households, but not all households are families under the Census Bureau's definition. Indeed, the growth of the **nonfamily household** (that is, persons who live alone or with unrelated individuals) is one of the most dramatic changes to occur during the past four decades, as shown in Figure 12.1. In 1960, 85 percent of households were family households; by 2000, just 69 percent were family households. At the same time, nonfamily households, which consist primarily of people who live alone or who share a residence with roommates or with a partner, have been on the rise. The fastest growth has been among persons living alone. The proportion of households with just one person doubled from 13 percent to 26 percent between 1960 and 2000 (Bianchi and Casper, 2000:8).

Nonfamily households are a diverse group. They may consist of elderly individuals who live alone, college-age youths who share an apartment, cohabiting couples, individuals who delay or forgo marriage, or those who are "between marriages" (Ahlburg and DeVita, 1992:5; Rawlings, 1995:22).

Another dramatic shift in household composition between 1970 and 1995 was the decline in the percentage of households with children. (The following is based on Bianchi and Casper, 2000:8). Two-parent households with children

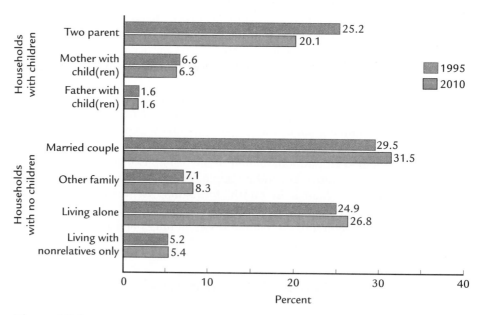

Figure 12.1

Projections of changing household composition: 1995 and 2010.

Source: Jennifer Cheeseman Day, "Projections of the Number of Households and Families in the United States: 1995 to 2010." U.S. Bureau of the Census, *Current Population Reports*, Series P-25-1129. Washington, DC: U.S. Government Printing Office, April 1996, p. 11.

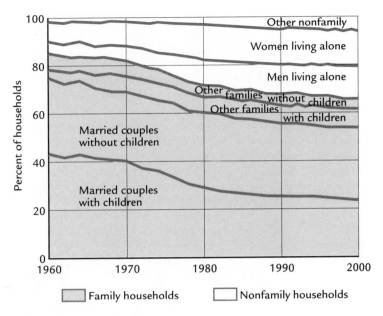

Figure 12.2

Trends in U.S. households, 1960 to 2000.

Source: Suzanne M. Bianchi and Lynne M. Casper, "American Families." *Population Bulletin* 55 (December 2000):8.

dropped from 44 percent to 24 percent of all households between 1960 and 2000 (Figure 12.2). This downward trend reflects the decline in birth rates, the shift toward smaller families, and the extended period of time before young adults marry. During the next fifteen years, the overall composition of households is projected to shift, with a decreasing proportion of family households with children and increasing proportions of family households with no children and people living alone (Day, 1996:11). However, household composition varies considerably among different segments of the population. Minorities are much more likely than Whites to live in households that include children. Over 40 percent of minority households in 1995 had at least one child under age eighteen compared with 32 percent of White households. This difference arises primarily because minority populations tend to have a younger age structure than the White population (that is, a greater share of minorities are in the prime child-bearing ages) and minorities tend to have higher fertility rates than Whites (DeVita, 1996:34).

Global Trends, Individual Options, and the Decline of Marriage

Current household and family patterns are not the result of overnight changes but a continuation of forces set in motion long ago. These changes are not uniquely a U.S. phenomenon; instead, they have global dimensions. Research of the last two decades has revealed five global trends in family formation:

A grandparent raising a child is an example of an alternative family lifestyle based on available resources.

1) women's average age at first marriage and childbirth has risen, delaying the formation of new families; 2) families and households have gotten smaller; 3) the burden on working-age parents of supporting younger and older dependents has increased; 4) the proportion of female-headed households has increased; and 5) women's participation in the formal labor market has increased at the same time that men's has declined, shifting the balance of economic responsibility in families (Bruce et al., 1995:5).

Many family changes reflect new social attitudes toward a variety of living arrangements outside of marriage. Many new types of families do not have marriage at their core. Declining proportions of adults are married. Indeed, nonmarriage has nearly doubled in the past three decades, from 28 percent of the adult population in 1970 to 40 percent in 1996 (Saluter and Lugalia, 1998:1). Many adults now push beyond current definitions of "the family," choosing to live as a single person, to live with another adult of the same or the other sex without marriage, or to live separately from a spouse. Still, the focus on choice should not ignore the socially produced conditions that sustain and even require changes in household formation. Emerging domestic arrangements reflect the complex interaction of social structure and human agency. Individual choice is now an important facet of alternative household and family formation, but structural conditions that lie beyond individual choice help explain the long-term trends.

How to Think about Family Diversification

Rethinking Family Categories

Many people now choose from a wide range of lifestyles and family configurations. For others, family adaptations emerge in response to changes and constraints in the external world. The growing diversity in family forms does not in any way signal the breakdown of the nuclear family, but it does require a rethinking of the categories we use for sorting out the complex array of family relationships we find in society today.

The family field has long made a distinction between "the traditional family" and "nontraditional alternatives." Although so-called nontraditional families make up a diverse array of forms, they all tend to be categorized in *opposition* to the family ideal of the working father, stay-at-home mother, and their children. This dichotomy has become less useful as new family and household forms emerge. Not only does it simplify the incredible array of contemporary family arrangements, it also miscasts the idealized family as the *normal* family—the standard from which "alternatives" depart. But how can *one* family form be the standard when all family forms are adaptations to their social contexts? In fact, the 1950s model was itself made possible by certain historically specific forces. At the same time, other social conditions, such as the growing participation of married women in the paid labor force, rising divorce rates, and the rise of lesbian and gay communities, have led a variety of domestic arrangements. According to Linda Nicholson, new family types are no more alternative to what had preceded them than had been the 1950s (traditional) type to its historical predecessors; and to believe otherwise is to construct a false distinction between "traditional" and "alternative" family forms (Nicholson, 1997:28).

Rather than categorizing varied family arrangements as *alternatives* to an idealized traditional form, we should think of all family forms in their own right. No family structure is better than others. All families are social forms that emerge in response to different conditions. This gives us a better understanding of today's emergent and reconfigured families. As the larger social world in which families are embedded grows more complex, families, too, become more diverse and fluid. Today, different family forms coexist in society. As individuals move through the phases of their lives, their family and household arrangements are increasingly marked by family diversity.

The Question of Lifestyles

Past scholarship often used the term "alternative lifestyles" to refer to new family and household arrangements. However, the concept of "lifestyle," which refers to the "relational patterns around which individuals organize their living arrangements" (Stayton, 1985:17), has become less useful. In fact, the concept of "alternative lifestyles" can be misleading in that it must be alternative *to* something. Alternative lifestyles prompt the question: "alternative to what?" (Fowlkes, 1994:152), presuming a family form shared by most people in society. As the number and significance of families formed outside of marriage has grown in recent decades, scholarship moved away from "lifestyles" to a broader emphasis on nonmarital families. "Although studies of non-marital relationships are not new phenomenon, recent data facilitate a broader conceptualization of families than was possible before this decade" (Seltzer, 2001:466).

Throughout this book, we have argued that social and economic forces in society produce and require diversity in family life. Therefore, family variation is not new. What *is* new is a greater recognition of diversity and ongoing public outcries of groups insisting that "they too are families." These changes have given a new urgency to questions about family diversity. "What makes a legitimate family? Who is entitled to family status and the social support associated with it? Who should or does define appropriate family formation?" (Lempert and DeVault, 2000:6). Family forms differ in the degree to which the large society accepts them. For example, lesbian and gay families are often stigmatized, whereas blended stepparent families or living arrangements created by career choices are more likely to be viewed as legitimate. When variations are associated with subordinate class and racial categories, they are judged against a standard model and found to be deviant. Many alternative lifestyles that appear new to middle-class Americans are actually variant family patterns that have been traditional within African American and other ethnic communities for many generations. Presented as the "new lifestyles of the young mainstream elite, they are in fact the same lifestyles that have in the past been defined as pathological, deviant, or unacceptable when observed in Black families" (Peters and McAdoo, 1983:288). Many of the family patterns among racial-ethnics have been adopted as available and logical life choices in a society that has denied them a full range of resources.

The family and household configurations discussed here represent additional adaptations to those already discussed in previous chapters. Like the variations in family living produced by class, race, and gender inequality, these variations have always existed.

Singlehood, heterosexual cohabitation, lesbian and gay alternatives, and families separated by time and space represent an array of adaptations that cannot be neatly tied to a single cause. They are part of a larger web of economic, demographic, and social trends. Women's economic independence, later age at marriage, and the high divorce rate are some of the trends associated with these forms, but no one explanation covers all of them. Although these arrangements appear to be a heterogeneous mixture of lifestyles, in fact they all embody new definitions of women's and men's public and private roles. Singlehood, heterosexual and homosexual cohabitation, and families separated by time and space expand the traditional boundaries and behaviors associated with gender. Each form, in its unique way, modifies the relational patterns around which women, men, and sometimes children organize their living arrangements. In this way, these domestic arrangements represent adaptations to both particular social arrangements and the times in which we are living.

The question "What is a family?" will grow more contested as household and family patterns fall outside the nuclear mold. The U.S. Census Bureau's definition of "two or more persons related by birth, marriage or adoption who live in the same household" fails to include many arrangements in which people live and relate as families; practical and legal considerations require that we modify the conventional definition of the family.

⌒INGLE LIFE

"Single" used to mean what people were before they settled down to marriage and family. Over the past four decades, a growing proportion of adults spent a larger proportion of their lives in a single status and in one-person households. People who live alone now make up over one-fourth of households; 60 percent are women, 40 percent are men. By the end of the twentieth century, 12 percent of all adults lived alone. Although women accounted for the larger share of people living alone (six in ten), the number of men living alone increased at a faster pace. Between 1970 and 1996, the number of women living alone doubled, from 73 million to 14.6 million, while the number of men living alone tripled, from 3.5 million to 10.2 million (Lugaila, 1998:26). As a result of the rise in single living, there are now as many households of those alone as there are of married couples with children. Reasons for the increased members of those living alone include more people living independently before marriage, more who are divorced, and a boom in the aging population, including many who have lost partners (Peterson, 1996:4d).

Today, a growing share of adults are unmarried. One in three men and more than one in four women were unmarried in 1997, compared with fewer than one in ten in 1900 (Caplow et al., 2001:68). (See Figure 12.3.) Although more women and men now live alone for part of their adult lives, most people do marry, at least once. In 2000, 91 percent of women and 94 percent of men ages forty-five to fifty-four had been married (Bianchi and Casper, 2000:15). For young women and men today, it is plausible to assume that approximately 10 percent will never

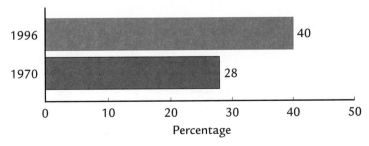

Figure 12.3

Unmarried adults as a percent of all adults: 1970 and 1996.

Source: Arlene M. Saluter and Terry A. Lugaila, "Marital Status and Living Arrangements: March 1996." U.S. Bureau of the Census, *Current Population Reports,* Series P-20-1496. Washington, DC: U.S. Government Printing Office, March 1998, p. 1.

marry in their lifetime. For those who do marry, approximately 50 percent will divorce, and the surviving marriages will eventually end in widowhood.

The Singles Population

The growing disinclination to marry among people of all ages means that there are many different ways of being single and consequently many different ways to depict the experience of singlehood. In the broadest sense, the term "single" refers to all unmarried adults over the age of eighteen. This population represents a wide-ranging demographic diversity with respect to age, race, ethnicity, education, occupation, income, and parental status. Singlehood also has different connections to the institution of formal, legal marriage, including as it does those who have never married, together with the divorced, the separated, and the widowed (Fowlkes, 1994:153).

Peter J. Stein (1981) proposed a useful typology for distinguishing the varieties of single status in the contemporary United States. His typology is based on whether an individual's single status is voluntary or involuntary, stable or temporary. Of particular interest here are those described by Stein as voluntary stable singles, "those who have never married and are satisfied with that choice; those who have been married but do not want to remarry; cohabitors who do not intend to marry; and those whose lifestyles preclude the possibility of marriage (e.g., priests and nuns)" (Stein, 1981:10; cited in Fowlkes, 1994:153).

"This is Larry. If I were Matt Damon, he'd be Ben Affleck."

Formal marriage no longer organizes life decisions and transitions, as it did in the past. In colonial times, almost all unmarried persons lived in a family environment, either with parents or in the homes of their employers. Only with marriage did they become fully independent members of society. This pattern began to change in the nineteenth century, when increasing numbers of single people worked for wages outside the family and lived in boardinghouses. The dramatic shift, however, occurred in recent years, as divorce, cohabitation, remarriage, and single motherhood all contributed to the growth of the single population (Coontz, 1997:79).

Women's economic independence has had a great impact on the rise of singlehood as a viable option. Many women have jobs that pay enough that the women do not require a partnership with a man to have a decent living. They need not marry for economic support or for social identity. Many women with strong career aspirations have opted for singlehood because marriage and domestic demands greatly lessen their chances for career success. Other social and cultural reasons make marriage less desirable. Marriage may be less necessary for happiness now, because unmarried persons can more readily engage in sexual relationships without social stigma and because the financial security of marriage has been undermined by high rates of divorce. With higher rates of single living, the social stigma of divorce is decreasing (Marks, 1996:917).

Gender, Race, and Class

More women than men marry sometime over the life course. Still, women are more likely to be alone for some or all of their lives from their middle years on (Figure 12.3). 43 million women are now single. This is more than 40 percent of all adult females, up from 30 percent in 1960 (Edwards, 2000:48). Of course, the rise in single women encompasses other important trends, and a growing number are being more open about lesbian relationships. Still, singlehood is not always a matter of choice. Demography and culture combine to create a condition known as the "marriage squeeze." This is an imbalance in the number of women and men available for marriage. Because women tend to marry men who are somewhat older than themselves, there are more women than men who are looking for a partner. The older women become, the greater the imbalance. Among persons aged sixty-five and older, men are a minority and unmarried men are a minority within that minority (although in the specifically never-married population men outnumber women until the age of sixty-five). In the *total* elderly single population, comprising the widowed and divorced together with the never married, unmarried women begin to outnumber men by the age of thirty-five (Fowlkes, 1994:154). The single woman has come into her own. Not long ago, she would live a temporary existence—a rented apartment shared with a girlfriend or two. Adult life—a house, a car, travel, and children—only came with a husband. Today 60 percent of single women own their own homes, more than half of adventure travelers are women, and two in five business travelers are women (Edwards, 2000:48).

As women acquire higher levels of education and income, the female singles category grows ever larger. Demographers project that more than 20 percent of college-educated women currently in their thirties will never marry, representing a dramatic increase from any previous cohort of American women. The irony of this development is that men who are statistically available are the least educated. So we have a puzzle with completely mismatched pieces. As Jessie Bernard put it years ago, in the pool of eligibles, the men are at the "bottom of the barrel" and the women are the "cream of the crop" (quoted in Doudna and McBride, 1981:23).

The proportion of never-married has increased for Whites, Blacks, and Hispanics. Among Whites, the proportion increased from 16 percent to 21 percent between 1970 and 1996. Thirty-nine percent of Black adults in 1996 had never been married, up from 21 percent in 1970. For Hispanics the proportion rose from 19 to 30 percent during this period (Saluter and Lugaila, 1998:2).

Many would say that fewer Black women marry because there are not enough eligible men. However, many Black women remain single by choice. Sociologist Elizabeth Higginbotham, who studied the priorities of educated Black women in the contemporary United States, found important class differences in women's life preferences. Women from established middle-class families were expected both to marry and to complete college, but women from lower-middle-class families were expected to finish college before they married (Higginbotham, 1981).

Although women are more likely to remain single, research suggests that long-term singlehood has often been a more positive state for women than for men, and that women who remain single are superior to single men in terms of education, occupation, and mental health (summarized in Marks, 1996). After divorce, men are at greater risk of emotional disorder. They also remarry more quickly and more frequently than women (Fowlkes, 1994:157). There is evidence that unmarried women remain outside marriage in different ways and for different reasons than men do. Fowlkes summarizes the research findings:

> Permanently single men give every indication of living out socially and emotionally undeveloped lives compared to their married counterparts. . . . Women who remain single identify the advantages of preserving and fully developing their personal and social autonomy by not accommodating to the secondary status of the traditional wife role (Fowlkes, 1994:159).

Barbara Levy Simon's study *Never Married Women* (1987) provides a corrective to the myth that never-married women are lonely and embittered "old maids." Simon conducted interviews with fifty never-married women born between 1884 and 1918. She included women of diverse racial, ethnic, and religious backgrounds in her study. Thirty-eight of her fifty elderly respondents (76 percent) actively chose singlehood.

Although they gave varied reasons for their choice, the theme of freedom (freedom from the demands embedded in the wife's role) emerged repeatedly in the interviews as a major reason to remain single. Intensely involved in the social networks of their jobs and voluntary service, these women were "agents contributing to their own history" (Simon, 1987:38). Recent studies also suggest that mature single women are beginning to report more advantages to single status in terms of personal autonomy and growth than might have been true in the past (Marks, 1996:921).

Experiencing Single Life

Singlehood's new respectability has not dispelled myths and stereotypes about single people. Stereotypes about singles abound in a society in which marriage is idealized. Old beliefs about unmarried people being somehow flawed have given way to newer stereotypes. Two of the more prominent stereotypes are that singles must be terribly lonely and that they are "swingers" (i.e., sexually nonexclusive). A study conducted by Leonard Cargan in the mid-1980s examined these two stereotypes by comparing the responses of single people with those of married people to determine whether singles felt undesirable, lonely, and incomplete. The singles included both never-married and divorced women and men. The stereotype of loneliness was shown to be true, in that singles had no one with whom to share happy or sad moments or with whom to discuss problems. But these findings were qualified by the relatively large numbers of the married who also felt these facets of loneliness. The other stereotype of sexual "swinging" was upheld in the sense that singles have more sexual partners. However, it was the divorced singles, not single people in general, who tended to be sexually nonexclusive. Furthermore, "swingers" appeared in all of the categories examined (Cargan, 1984:546–557).

Do singles still swing in the twenty-first century? Apparently, they do somewhat. As the median age of the U.S. population has increased, the singles scene is maturing. Today upwardly mobile singles are as likely to meet in fitness clubs, libraries, amateur theatrical groups, running clubs, churches, coffee bars, and, of course, online, in chat rooms, and though e-mail (Stapinski, 1999). These settings give singles a way of meeting people who have more in common than a pitcher of beer (*American Demographics*, 1992:22).

Like other nontraditional alternatives, singlehood can be an ambivalent experience: autonomous and euphoric at some times, lonely and unconnected at other times (Gordon, 1994). Even amid the joys of self-discovery, people require companionship. A growing number of adults are opting to live by themselves while maintaining a stable relationship. Other "singles" are, in fact, living with a partner without being married. Today, what it means to be single is no longer clear. In the next section, we examine how the lives of millions of unmarried women and men resemble those of married people.

HETEROSEXUAL COHABITATION

The term "heterosexual cohabitation" refers to the practice of a couple sharing a household in a marriage-like relationship. Once considered "living in sin," this arrangement is becoming an increasingly routine phase leading to marriage as well as a variation on formal marriage. Whereas cohabitation has recently become common in the United States, it is an old custom in many Scandinavian countries (see Box 12.1). The relationship category "unmarried partner of the opposite sex" was added to the 1990 Census questionnaire to help identify this type of living arrangement (Kalish, 1994a:3). The number of unmarried couple households surged from 1.3 million in 1978 to 3.0 million in 1998. Between 1970

BOX 12.1 Families in Global Perspective: Universal Cohabitation before Marriage

Cohabitation before marriage has long been the norm in Sweden. For Swedish couples, it is both a trial before marriage and an alternative to marriage. Thirty-four percent of women born between 1936 and 1940 and eighty-three percent of women born between 1951 and 1955 lived with a partner before marriage. Since the mid-1980s, about half of all children are born outside of marriage, mainly into cohabiting unions.

Swedish policies tend to see cohabitation as equal to marriage. Thus, many of the regulations of marriage apply to cohabitation. These regulations help provide protection to the economically weaker person in the relationship. This is in stark contrast to the United States where, in both marriage and cohabitation, the economically disadvantaged person is often not protected. The norm of cohabiting is supported through Sweden's governmental policies in many ways. For example, the concept of illegitimacy has been removed from Swedish legislation. Child custody rights apply to both married and cohabiting couples. Children inherit from both parents equally, whether born within marriage or not. Parents, as a rule, establish joint custody of their children in the case of separation. Joint custody is actually the default policy in Sweden. Also, the same regulations apply to both married and cohabiting couples in the case of a dissolution. And, cohabiting couples have the option of signing a written cohabitation agreement which is regulated through Swedish law.

Historically, in Sweden, it was the daughters of manual workers who started the trend of cohabitation. They were more likely to view cohabitation as an alternative to marriage (including childbearing) rather than a trial marriage or a new form of union living. Cohabitation was often preferred since law did not protect the legal rights of married women to their own earnings. For example, married women were not granted the legal right to enter into work contracts and to control their own earnings until the marriage act of 1920. Also, until 1920, a husband had ownership rights over his wife's earnings. The possibility that a husband might take her earnings and spend them on alcohol, for example, made working women prefer cohabitation to marriage. These living arrangements were referred to as "Stockholm marriages."

The historical beginnings of working women cohabiting still holds true today. Research found that early experiences influence whether or not women stay in cohabiting relationships or if they eventually marry. Women in cohabiting relationships with manual working mothers are less likely to marry. On the other hand, women in cohabiting relationships from rural communities and women who are religiously active are more likely to marry. Economic and social factors also play a role in whether cohabiting couples decide to marry.

Although many couples still choose to marry, cohabitation—whether it be a precursor to marriage, as an alternative to marriage, or as a way to leave options open—is the norm. Researchers have found that the normal family career starts with cohabitation. Sweden's government has recognized this family pattern by implementing policies that support cohabiting couples, thus providing them with legal, economic, and social benefits and legitimacy.

(continued)

(continued from previous page)

References

Duvander, Ann-Zofie E. (1999). "The Transition from Cohabitation to Marriage: A Longitudinal Study of the Propensity to Marry in Sweden in the Early 1990s." *Journal of Family Issues* 20 (5) (September): 698–717.

Gustaffsson, Siv (1995). "Single Mothers in Sweden: Why Is Poverty Less Severe? In *Poverty, Inequality, and the Future of Social Policy,* Katherine McFate, Roger Lawson, and William Julius Wilson (eds.). New York: Russell Sage Foundation, pp. 292–294.

Source: Angela YH Pok. Department of Sociology, Michigan State University, 2001. This essay was written expressly for the sixth edition of *Diversity in Families.*

and 1998, the share of unmarried couple households rose from 1 percent to 5 percent. Experts estimate that more than half of all couples who married after 1985 began their relationship as cohabitors (Bianchi and Casper, 2000:18). (See also Table 12.1, below.)

The Rise of Cohabitation

Noted demographer Larry Bumpass asks, "How has it happened that what was once morally reprehensible has become the majority experience in just two decades?" (Bumpass, 1990:486). Sociologists point to several trends that explain why cohabitation is now the majority experience among cohorts of marriageable age, including the later age at which young people marry, changing norms about sexual relations outside of marriage, new living arrangements after divorce and before remarriage, and increasing individualism and secularization (Bianchi and Casper, 2000; Bumpass and Lu, 2000b). These developments underlie the growing acceptability of living together. Bumpass explains:

> . . . shacking up was offensive after all, not because couples were sharing cooking and the laundry, but because they were sharing a bed. The revolution in the sexual experience of unmarried persons over the same period has seriously weakened the basis for disapproving of cohabitation. Only one-fifth of young adults now disapprove of cohabitation under any circumstances (Bumpass, 1990:486).

Not only have social norms changed, other conditions have promoted the increase in cohabitation. The trends associated with singlehood and living away from parents in dormitories and apartments open up new possibilities for women and men. Women have attained financial and personal options beyond marriage, while men no longer face the same pressures from employers to be married (Goldscheider and Waite, 1991:61).

Something else has changed to make living together a common experience. People are much less confident about marital stability. Many choose cohabitation because they worry about marriage, given the high divorce rate. Bumpass

"I joined this gym because I wanted a firm body, strong muscles, and a big chest—I never dreamed I'd get them on the first day!"

reports that in a series of questions about reasons for cohabitation, couples reported wanting to make sure that they are compatible before getting married. This reason was indicated far more than any other options offered (Bumpass, 1990:407).

Still other reasons for cohabitation lie in the economic and emotional benefits it offers. It is a means by which two persons can pool their resources to share the costs of rent, food, and utilities. Even among the elderly, economic incentives may encourage cohabitation and inhibit marriage (Chevan, 1996). In addition, this arrangement provides some of the emotional advantages of marriage with few of its economic and legal restrictions (Spain and Bianchi, 1996:32).

Who Are Cohabitors?

Cohabitation is not a new phenomenon. Throughout American history, some couples have lived together without formal marriage. In the past, the practice was concentrated among the poor. But as cohabitation has become common-place, cohabitors are not a distinct population. Researchers can no longer pro-vide profiles of those who live together without being married. Nevertheless we can make some generalizations about the social characteristics of cohabitors (summarized in McLanahan and Casper, 1995; Spain and Bianchi, 1996; and Seltzer, 2001):

- They were mostly young adults. Although the increase in cohabitation occurred among all age groups (including older adults), it was greatest among women and men in their late twenties and early thirties.
- A sizable proportion had divorced. Over two-thirds of cohabiting couples in the mid-1990s included at least one divorced person, an increase from one-half from 1981.
- Increasing proportions of cohabiting couples today include children in their households. Today, two-thirds of children spend some time living with their mother and a cohabiting partner.

The general assumption is that those individuals who cohabit before mar-riage are somehow different types of people—less traditional, more willing to experiment. However, this assumption tells us little about the social circum-stances that go beyond individual choices to facilitate cohabitation. Nor does it provide insight into the properties of the cohabitating partnership itself. Not enough research has been done to substantiate the advantages and disadvan-tages of cohabitation as (1) a temporary premarital experience, (2) a trial mar-riage, or (3) a stable, nonmarital alternative (Baber and Allen, 1992:41; Fowlkes, 1994:157; Seltzer, 2001). Despite its dramatic increase in the past two decades, cohabitation for many remains an ambiguous arrangement, often lacking in pre-dictability and clear understanding between partners as to their hopes, expecta-tions, and role definitions for the relationship (Fowlkes, 1994:158).

Gender, Class, and Race

Cohabitation, like other domestic arrangements, is shaped by gender, class, and race. For example, gender is an important variable in how cohabitation is expe-rienced. Some research shows that men tend to view cohabitation in pragmatic terms, with less emotional involvement and less personal commitment than women, who tend to define the arrangement as a step toward a stable, long-term relationship (Jackson, 1983; Macklin, 1983). Women cohabitors are more likely than men to desire marriage (Blumstein and Schwartz, 1983; Lyness et al., 1972:308). This tendency may be greater among previously unmarried women. Blumstein and Schwartz found cohabiting women who had been married before less eager to marry than women who had never been married, but previous mar-riage had no negative impact on the men. Other findings also suggest different consequences of marriage for women and men. Cohabiting may be a better deal for men than for women if women end up with the responsibilities of marriage without the legal protections. Some research find that women who cohabit are more prone to depression than married women, especially if children are involved. If some women constantly worry that the union could dissolve, the instability is detrimental to their well-being (Peterson, 2000a:2D).

Compared with married couples, cohabitors tend to be more egalitarian and to have less traditional attitudes toward family life. In four out of five cohabiting couples both partners work outside the home, compared with three in five married couples. Nevertheless, there are differences in the household division of labor. The strong tendency is for household duties to be split along traditional gender lines, with women doing more domestic chores (Blumstein and Schwartz, 1983:148; Shelton and John, 1993a; Seltzer, 2001). Despite this gender gap, research finds a smaller gap among cohabitors than among those who are formally married because cohabitating women spend less time on housework than do married women. Men's time spent in housework is not significantly different among cohabitors and those who are formally married (Shelton and John, 1993a:401). Housework is another indication that cohabitation may be more advantageous to men than to women, even though women in this arrangement spend less time on household duties.

Although the rise in cohabitation is characteristic of all social and economic groups, it continues to be more common among those with less education and for whom economic resources are more constrained (Bumpass and Sweet, 1989; Bumpass and Lu, 2000b:32) Perhaps this is because cohabiting unions require less initial commitment to fulfill long-term economic responsibilities. Because "marriage includes expectations about economic roles, couples may think that they should reach specific financial goals such as steady employment or housing of a certain quality before it is appropriate to marry" (Seltzer, 2000:469). Economic factors have produced a long history of consensual unions among African Americans and some Latino groups. These patterns differ in important ways from the majority patterns. Recent research finds that informal unions among Puerto Ricans in New York City are widespread. Almost half of the first unions of young Puerto Ricans aged fifteen to twenty-nine begin informally. Such unions are similar to marriage especially insofar as childbearing behavior is concerned. Young Puerto Ricans' high rates of cohabitation reflect a set of economic conditions, including low rates of labor force participation, low earnings, and other factors that discourage entry into legal marriage. Their unions, however, are much like marriage and can be considered a distinctive family form (Landale and Fennelly, 1992).

Cohabitation has risen in all racial groups. However, the rates of growth have varied in the last three decades. In 1978, single White women were least likely to live with a partner outside of marriage, while single Hispanic women were most likely to cohabit. By 1998, 10 percent of single White women lived with a male partner, compared with 9 percent of single Hispanic and 7 percent of single Black women. In 1998, cohabiting couples were also more than twice as likely to be of different races than married couples: 13 percent compared to 5 percent. About half of the interracial unmarried couples consisted of a White woman and a man who was African American, Latino, or another racial group (Bianchi and Casper, 2000:16).

Is Cohabitation a Prelude to Marriage or a Substitute for Marriage?

Differences in the nature of cohabitation prompt questions about how this widely accepted practice should be viewed in relation to marriage. In the family field, scholars are debating whether cohabitation is a precursor to formal marriage, a trial period before marriage, or a replacement for formal marriage.

Many see cohabitation as simply a new stage in the American courtship process, a now-common premarital step. They argue that cohabitation is an extension of marriage because it allows people to "try out" potential marriage partners. As reasonable as this sounds, some cohabitation patterns raise questions about this perspective. First, not all cohabiting couples anticipate marriage. In fact, many cohabitation arrangements are relatively short-lived—only 1.5 years (Bumpass, 1990:487; Bumpass and Lu, 2000b). Cohabitation before marriage may even increase the risk of divorce (McLanahan and Casper, 1995; Spain and Bianchi, 1996). (See Table 12.1.)

Another perspective holds that cohabitation is not a prelude to formal marriage at all. Instead, it is a family form in its own right for cohabiting couples who do not necessarily reject marriage. They are "less likely to see marriage as the defining characteristic of their family lives" (Seltzer, 2001:470). In many racial-ethnic settings, informal unions are surrounded by standard expectation much like those that apply to married couples. And the fact that minority cohabiting couples are more likely to have children than White cohabiting couples "suggests that cohabitation has become more of a substitute for marriage in minority communities than in White communities" (McLanahan and Casper, 1995:29).

Which of these contrasting views is most correct? Is cohabitation a temporary step on the way to marriage, or is it a distinctive family type? No doubt both

TABLE 12.1

Unmarried Couples by Relationship Type in 1987–1988, and after Five to Seven Years

Type of Relationship in 1987–1988	All Couples Percent	Outcome of relationship after 5 to 7 years		
		Still Live Together[1]	Married[2]	Separated[3]
All unmarried couples	100	21	40	39
Substitute for marriage	10	39	25	35
Precursor to marriage	46	17	52	31
Trial marriage	15	21	28	51
Coresidential dating	29	21	33	46

Note: Couples were interviewed between 1987 and 1988 and again from 1992 to 1994.

[1]Couple was still cohabiting at the time of the second survey.

[2]Got married some time between the two surveys (may or may not be currently married).

[3]No longer cohabiting.

Source: Suzanne M. Bianchi and Lynne M. Casper, 2000. "American Families," *Population Bulletin* 55 (December 2000), Population Reference Bureau. p. 17.

"I said I'm ready to make a commitment."

perspectives are correct. Each captures a distinctive feature of cohabitation with different purposes and meanings. Considering these differences, we must not treat cohabitants as one homogeneous group. Comparisons between cohabitating and noncohabitating couples imply that all cohabitating relationships are alike, which is not true.

Given the increasing numbers of cohabiting couples and the fact that many do not intend to marry their partner eventually, does this mean that the institution of marriage is in jeopardy? Bumpass, after reviewing the evidence, does not think so. However, he notes several implications of cohabitation for marriage (from Bumpass, 1990:48):

1. Cohabitation changes the meaning of "single." Singlehood (and the rapid decline of marriage) no longer means unattached living.

2. Marriage is now a less specific marker of other transitions, such as sex, living arrangements, and parenting.

3. Cohabitation requires a new way of marking those unions that eventually become marriages. For some couples, "marriage" began when they started living together, whereas others avoid an unstable marriage by splitting up before they reach the altar.

4. "Premarital divorces" help keep the divorce rate from going even higher, since many couples are using cohabitation to test their relationship.

5. Not all cohabitations are part of the marriage process. Some are better characterized as relationships of convenience in which marriage is not an issue.

Does cohabitation enhance marital stability and lessen the likelihood of divorce? Although the association between cohabitation and marital outcome is not well understood, the current answer to this question is a qualified no. Research conducted on large samples demonstrates that cohabitation is negatively related to marital stability. Why? Perhaps cohabitors enter marriage in the same way that they enter cohabitation, with the notion that a relationship should be ended if either partner is dissatisfied.

Whether or not cohabitation weakens marriage, it is redefining family life. Among its many affects on family boundaries, none is more profound than its implications for children's lives. Living together now often involves children from previous marriages as well as non marital births occurring in cohabiting unions. As a consequence, about two-fifths of all children spend time in a cohabiting family, and the greater instability of families begun by cohabitation means that children are also more likely to experience marital disruption (Bumpass and Lu, 2000b:29).

⌒AME-SEX PARTNERS AND FAMILIES

Before the gay liberation movement of the 1970s and the AIDS epidemic that first appeared in the 1980s, gay men and lesbians were largely invisible. Before that time most gay men and lesbians sought to avoid the risk of disclosing their **sexual orientation.** Today, lesbian women and gay men are a well-established presence in the public consciousness. Same-sex partnerships are an important part of growing family diversity in the United States and the world.

The social movement for gay civil rights was catalyzed by the 1969 **Stonewall riots,** when police raided a gay bar in New York City. Instead of dispersing, the 200 homosexual patrons who had never collectively resisted the police before, fought back. This gave impetus to collective efforts by gays to publicize police harassment, job discrimination, and other indignities that lesbians and gays routinely face. By 1980, more than 4000 gay rights organizations existed in the United States. This provided the political basis for challenging various forms of same-sex oppression.

By the end of the twenty-first century, thirty years after Stonewall and three decades of gay rights activities, homosexuals had achieved recognition as a distinct social group. This has worked both to their advantage and disadvantage. No longer closeted or hidden from view, those inside the community find support for their sexual preference that has never before existed. However, securing a legitimate public identity has not eliminated prejudice. There is a long tradition of fear and hatred of homosexuality in Western society (termed *homophobia*). Most religious groups are unyielding. The military continues to discriminate. Many employers subtly discriminate. The U.S. Supreme Court remains unsympathetic. Bias toward gays is far more accepted among larger numbers of Americans than is bias against other groups. In surveys, about three-fourths of homosexuals say they have been harassed by people calling them names, and as many as one in four say they have been physically assaulted.

On the other hand, two and a half decades of struggle for gay rights have produced modest gains. Some court decisions have been favorable; some gay rights ordinances have been passed by progressive legislatures and city commissions. Some religious leaders and a few congregations accept gays and lesbians and have worked to change attitudes and move homosexuals closer to the mainstream. The American Psychiatric Association has removed homosexuality from its list of mental illnesses. Still, huge obstacles remain.

The success of gay rights political activists has not achieved the ultimate goal—full acceptance of same-sex relationships. Many, if not most, lesbians and gay men express the desire for an enduring love relationship with a partner of the same gender. Research findings suggest that many are successful in creating such relationships. Survey data suggest that 40 to 60 percent of gay men and 45 to 80 percent of lesbians are currently involved in steady romantic relationships (Patterson, 2001:272). Yet same-sex marriage is vehemently opposed by those who believe that homosexuality is morally offensive and dangerous. In Chapter 8 we examined the political debate over same-sex marriage and the mainstream political resistance for legalizing gay marriage. As for public opinion on gay marriage, although it is more negative than positive, it is divided. "In December 1995, a Roper poll showed that 56 percent of Americans disapproved of gay marriage and only 30 percent approved. The rest were undecided (Schwartz and Rutter, 1998:186).

Despite resistance and discrimination, lesbians and gay men *are* creating and sustaining families. Not only are gay families here to stay, family has become a frontier issue in the struggle for gay rights. It may seem odd to identify a family, rather than an individual, as gay. Nevertheless, this historically new category of family is a vital part of family diversification that is now taking place in the nation and the world (Stacey, 1998:118).

Who Is Gay and What Are Gay Families?

Important questions revolve around the numbers of gay men and lesbian women in the United States. The numbers of homosexuals are unknown and perhaps unknowable, because many never reveal their sexual orientation and live lives that appear to be heterosexually oriented. The common estimates by researchers range from 4 to 10 percent of adults in the total population that are exclusively or substantially homosexual. Pioneering research by Alfred Kinsey and his associates first on men, in 1948, and then on women, in 1953, made it clear that homosexuality was much more common than anyone had suspected. Since Kinsey's studies, the 10 percent figure has been widely used, prompting the phrase, "one in ten," meaning that one in ten persons in the United States is gay or lesbian. In fact, Kinsey argued that it was impossible to answer the question of how many gays and lesbians are in the population. The authors of *Sex in America* (Michael et al., 1994), the book based on the national sex survey (see Chapter 7), explain that the answer to the gay numbers question is subtle and shaded with gray. They give three reasons why we cannot say that a person is gay or not gay: first, people often change their sexual behavior during their lifetime, making it impossible to state that a particular set of behaviors defines a person as gay; second, there is no one set of sexual desires or self-identification that uniquely defines homosexuality; and third, homosexual behavior is not easily measured. Persecution means that many people never reveal their sexual orientation (Michael et al., 1994:172).

Problems of definition also apply to gay families, because individuals and not families have sexual orientations. Typically, in families of origin, family members have different sexual orientations. Katherine Allen and David Demo suggest that we can define lesbian and gay families by the presence of two or more people who share a same-sex orientation (e.g., a couple), or by the presence of at least one lesbian or gay adult rearing a child. This definition represents families that are influenced by issues and dynamics associated with homosexuality (Allen and Demo, 1995:113). Others refer to lesbian and gay cohabiting couples as families even though they are not considered families according to official definition because they are not legally married (Bianchi and Casper, 2000:10). Although the matter of what constitutes a gay family is important, family researchers extend the discussion to include the following (from Savin-Williams and Esterberg, 2000:199):

- families in which parents are heterosexual but the children are lesbian or gay
- children of lesbian and gay parents and how these children have fared, both psychologically and socially (see Chapter 9)
- lesbian and gay parents who are making the decision to parent and the relationships they have with each other
- public policies that have, with relatively few exceptions, neglected the needs of gay and lesbian families (see Chapter 13)

Many same-sex couples misrepresent their relationships in surveys and their households come in different shapes, and compositions, so "gay families" are difficult to count. We do not have systematic or comprehensive data on gay and lesbian households because the U.S. Census Bureau does not identify the sexual orientation of those it surveys. By conservative estimates, families of lesbians and gay men make up at least 5 percent of U.S. families (Stacey, 1996:129). Social scientists are now developing solid demographic studies to describe the gay and lesbian population and inform policy debates (Black et al., 2000).

Gay Couples and Families

The idea that we should go beyond "homosexual lifestyles" to study the *family relations* of lesbians and gays is new even in the family field. "We have yet to reach a point where lesbians and gays are viewed as family members who happen to be gay" (Allen and Demo, 1995:116). Until recently, much of what we knew about gays and lesbians came from classic studies of homosexual partnerships (e.g., Bell and Weinberg, 1978; Harry, 1983; Peplau, 1981; Blumstein and Schwartz, 1983), but a newly published report on the demographics of the lesbian and gay population has constructed the first real portrait of cohabiting couples (From Black et al. 2000; and Bianchi and Casper, 2000:10–11):

1. Lesbian and gay couples are highly urban. About 45 percent of lesbian couples and 60 percent of gay couples were concentrated in twenty cities in 1990. The greatest proportion lived in San Francisco, Washington, D.C., Los Angeles, Atlanta, and New York City.
2. Many couples include children: 22 percent of lesbian couples and 5 percent of gay couples, compared with 59 percent of married couple families.
3. Gays and lesbians who live with partners have higher educational attainment than men and women in heterosexual marriages. In 1990, 13 percent of cohabiting gay men ages twenty-five to thirty-four had a postgraduate education, compared with 17 percent of married men. Sixteen percent of cohabiting lesbians had some postgraduate education compared with 5 percent of married women.
4. Gay men who live with a partner tend to earn less than other men, whereas cohabiting lesbians generally earn more than other women.
5. The rate of home ownership is lower for gay and lesbian couples than for married couple families. Among those who own a home, however, gay and lesbian couples tend to own more expensive homes than married couples.

In their classic study, Blumstein and Schwartz (1983) found that lesbian couples and gay male couples faced many of the same issues confronting heterosexual couples who live together, married or not. They must work out issues related to the division of household labor, power and authority, and emotional obligations. Homosexual couples, however, face additional problems. Because of the general antipathy toward homosexuality in American society, gay men and lesbian women are not encouraged to be open about their sexual preferences and their relationships. Hence, they may feel restricted in showing affection toward their lovers in public. They are seldom extended such commonplace courtesies as having a partner invited to an office party or to a retirement banquet. Even heterosexuals who might like to welcome a gay friend's partner may not know how to go about doing so. Blumstein and Schwartz contend that the "couple" status of homosexuals is always in jeopardy:

> The problem with gay male culture is that much of it is organized around single-hood or maintaining one's sexual marketability. Meeting places like bars and baths promote casual sex rather than couple activities. The problem with the lesbian world is quite different. Women are often in tight-knit friendship groups where

friends and acquaintances spend so much intimate time together that, it seems to us, opportunities arise for respect and companionship to turn into love and a meaningful affair (Blumstein and Schwartz, 1983:322–323).

Current research on lesbian and gay couples points to a number of similarities and differences between homosexual and heterosexual couples, some of which contradict the prevailing stereotypes. For example, lesbians and gay men report as much satisfaction with their relationships as do heterosexual couples. For the most part, they describe themselves as happy. When they do experience problems in their relationships, they often stem from the difficulties that heterosexuals face, that is, different backgrounds, job-related problems, financial pressures, and friction with extended family networks. On the other hand, the lack of formalized social supports for committed lesbian and gay relationships might lead to higher break-up rates than are found in married couples (Kurdek, 1998). In her summary of research, Charlotte Patterson concludes: "In general, the picture of lesbian and gay relationships emerging from this body of work is one of positive adjustment even in the face of stressful conditions (Patterson, 2001:271).

Gender

In Chapter 7 we saw that gender is important in the intimate relationships of lesbians and gays, but in ways that contradict common stereotypes. For example, lesbians are commonly depicted as masculine women, whereas gay men are depicted as effeminate men. In reality, lesbians and gays are not inverts of heterosexuals. Lesbians and heterosexual women are more alike than different, as are gay and heterosexual men. Nevertheless, in the values and behaviors that link love and sex, lesbians and gays have identifiable gender-linked behaviors (Fowlkes, 1994:172). To simplify, "men are like men, and women are like women despite differences in sexual orientation" (Hovedt, 1982:182, cited in Fowlkes, 1994:172).

Studies comparing lesbian, gay, and heterosexual couples find important contrasts in their characteristic patterns of intimacy. Gender shapes domestic values and practices more strongly than sexual identity (Stacey, 1998:139). For example, lesbians have been found to be more sexually exclusive than gay men. Data collected before and after the HIV/AIDS epidemic had attracted public attention revealed that most lesbians experienced monogamous sexual relationships whereas gay men did not (reported in Patterson, 2001:273). The tendency for gay men to be less sexually exclusive than lesbian women parallels the difference in heterosexual males and females. This difference is related to gender role socialization in society, where "males are socialized to engage in sexual behaviors both with and without affection while women are expected to combine the two" (Harry, 1983:226).

In a major departure from the heterosexual pattern, homosexual couples tend to be egalitarian (Allen and Demo, 1995). Studies have found that heterosexual couples, whether in cohabitation or marriage relationships, tend to accept the traditional gender roles for men and women. In contrast, homosexual couples are much more likely to share in the decision making and in household duties. This was recently confirmed by Lawrence Kurdek (1993), who found that married, gay, and lesbian couples followed different strategies for allocating household labor. As reported in other studies (Thompson and Walker, 1991), married couples allocated housework primarily on the basis of gender. In other words, wives did most of the housework. Although partners in gay couples and married couples were equally likely to be specialized in task performance, gay couples tended to distribute the pattern of specialization equally so that, unlike married couples, one partner did not do all the work. Partners in gay couples specialized in task performance on the basis of skill, interest, and work schedule, while Lesbians typically followed an ethic of equality (Kurdek, 1993).

An important implication of the equality found in homosexual relationships is that, contrary to the stereotype, the partners do not take the role of either "husband" or "wife." The prevailing assumption is that one takes the masculine role and is dominant in sexual activities and decision making, while the other does the "feminine" household tasks and is submissive to the first. Research consistently refutes this "butch/femme" notion, noting that only a small minority of couples reflect the stereotype.

Voluntarily Chosen Kinship Networks

In conventional thinking, "family" is a heterosexually based unit, formed through legal marriage. By assuming that homosexuals are incapable of procreation, parenting, and kinship, gay and lesbian relationships are thought to be incompatible with family life. It is true that gay rights movements once sought to escape the constraints of a heterosexist institution. In the 1990s, however, family issues are at the forefront of lesbian and gay struggles for social justice (D'Emilio, 1996). New research is finding networks of support that operate like families. Partners and friends are more reliable sources of social and emotional support than families of origin (Allen and Demo, 1995:420). These networks are an emergent feature of lesbian and gay family life.

Same-sex networks of support are the subject of the book *Families We Choose*, by anthropologist Kath Weston (1991). This book is based on a study conducted in San Francisco in the late 1980s. During a two-year period, Weston conducted interviews and engaged in participant observation with forty lesbians and forty gay men from diverse racial-ethnic backgrounds (Box 12.2). She discovered kinship networks among gays and lesbians who are creating relationships they define as family. Weston calls such kin arrangements "chosen" families. Kinship is based not on procreation ties, but on networks of friends, lovers, co-parents, children conceived through artificial insemination, adopted children, children from previous heterosexual relationships, and blood kin (in other words, "fictive kin").

The families that gays and lesbians were creating in the Bay Area had extremely fluid boundaries, much like kinship organization among sectors of racial-ethnic and White working-class families (see Chapters 3 and 5). One of Weston's informants, a lesbian named Toni Williams, gave the following account of the people she called kin:

> In my family, all of us kids are godparents to each others' kids, okay? So we're very connected that way. But when I go have a kid, I'm not gonna have my sisters as godparents. I'm gonna have people around me that are gay. That are straight. I

BOX 12.2   Researching Families: Fieldwork in Gay Communities

Kath Weston describes the methods she used to select and study lesbians and gay men in San Francisco.

The fieldwork that provides the basis for my analysis was conducted in the San Francisco Bay Area during 1985–1986, with a follow-up visit in 1987. . . .

With its unique history and reputation as a gay city, San Francisco hardly presents a "typical" lesbian and gay population for study. Yet the Bay Area proved to be a valuable field site because it brought together gay men and lesbians from very different colors and classes, identities and backgrounds.

In addition to the long hours of participant-observation so central to anthropological fieldwork, my analysis draws on 80 in-depth interviews conducted while in the field. Interview participants were divided evenly between women and men, with all but two identifying themselves as lesbian or gay. Random sampling is clearly an impossibility for a population that is not only partially hidden or "closeted," but also lacks consensus as to the criteria for membership. In general, I let self-identification be my guide for inclusion. Determined to avoid the race, class, and organizational bias that has characterized so many studies of gay men and lesbians, I made my initial connections through personal contacts developed over the six years I had lived in San Francisco previous to the time the project got underway. The alternative-gaining entree through agencies, college classes, and advertisements-tends to weight a sample for "joiners," professional interviewees, the highly educated, persons with an overtly political analysis, and individuals who see themselves as central (rather than marginal) to the population in question.

By asking each person interviewed for names of potential participants, I utilized techniques of friendship pyramiding and snowball sampling to arrive at a sample varied in race, ethnicity, class, and class background. While the Bay Area is perhaps more generally politicized than other regions of the nation, the majority of interview participants would not have portrayed themselves as political activists. Approximately 36 percent were people of color; of the 64 percent who were white, 11 (or 14 percent of the total) were Jewish. Slightly over 50 percent came from working-class backgrounds, with an overlapping 58 percent employed in working-class occupations at the time of the interview.

Of the 82 people contacted, only two turned down my request for an interview. A few individuals made an effort to find me after hearing of the study, but most were far from self-selecting. The vast majority demanded great persistence and flexibility in scheduling (and rescheduling) on my part to convince them to participate. I believe this persistence is one reason this study includes voices not customarily heard when lesbians and gay men appear in the pages of books and journals: people who had constructed exceedingly private lives and could scarcely get over their disbelief at allowing themselves to be interviewed, people convinced that their experiences were uneventful or unworthy of note, people fearful that a researcher would go away and write an account lacking in respect for their identities or their perceptions.

To offset the tendency of earlier studies to focus on the white and wealthier sectors of lesbian and gay population, I also utilized theoretic sampling. From a grow-

(continued)

(continued from previous page)

ing pool of contacts I deliberately selected people of color, people from working-class backgrounds, and individuals employed in working-class occupations.

In any sample this diverse, with so many different combinations of identities, theoretic sampling cannot hope to be "representative." To treat each individual as a representative of his or her race, for instance, would be a form of tokenism that glosses over the differences of gender, class, age, national origin, language, religion, and ability which crosscut race and ethnicity. At the same time, I am not interested in these categories as demographic variables, or as reified pigeonholes for people, but rather as identities meaningful to participants themselves.

Source: Kath Weston, *Families We Choose*. New York: Columbia University Press, 1991, pp. 7–10.

don't have that many straight friends, but certainly I would integrate them in my life. They would help me. They would babysit my child, or . . . like my kitty, I'm not calling up my family and saying, "Hey Mom, can you watch my cat?" No, I call on my inner family; my community, or whatever to help me with my life.

So there's definitely a family. And you're building it; it keeps getting bigger and bigger. Next thing you know, you have hundreds of people as your family (Weston, 1991:108).

Weston's study is important because it challenges the conventional notion that homosexuals lack family ties. It also reveals some of the ways in which lesbians and gays are broadening the definition of family by including domestic partnerships and friendship networks.

The Domestic Partner Movement

Controversies over gay and lesbian families continue to be debated in U.S. electoral politics and in the nation's courts. No state permits marriage between members of the same sex. (See Chapter 8.) The only industrial nations that permit "registered partnerships" (thus giving official recognition to homosexual marriages) are Denmark, Norway, Sweden, and the Netherlands. Aside from the emotional benefits of marriage, homosexuals are also denied significant legal and economic benefits of marriage: coverage under their spouses' health and pension plans, rights of inheritance and community property, and potential savings from joint tax returns. Gay and lesbian partners face a "catch-22": "They legally cannot wed and yet they face discrimination because they are not married. Until recently, the courts have rules consistently to deny these benefits to same-sex partners in long-term relationships. In 2000, a Vermont law went into effect establishing the institution of civil union for lesbian and gay couples with all the rights afforded to married couples under state law. It is the first law of its kind in the United States. Under it, lesbian and gay partners who enter civil unions will be eligible to receive the same benefits for their spouses, including

Gay couples often do not enjoy all the benefits of marriage such as domestic partnership.

health insurance, as are now offered to married couples by their employers (Human Rights Campaign Foundation, 2000:18).

The family has become the newest battleground for lesbian and gay rights. In the last two decades, two developments made the economic and legal discrimination against gay and lesbian families hit home. The first is AIDS. As partners and friends have died, homosexuals have grown more aware of their lack of family rights. They have not been able to have their partners included in their companies' health plans and have had no claims on their lovers' property. The second development is the growing number of gay and lesbian couples having and adopting children (Horn, 1990:9). These changes have mobilized lesbians and gays to take legal and political action in their quest for family rights.

The **domestic partner movement** has entered the courts, legislatures, and workplaces to qualify for some of the legal benefits accorded married heterosexuals. Activists argue that "family" can no longer be defined by marriage alone but by sharing lives in intimate and committed relationships of mutual caring. Several landmark developments have greatly expanded the definition of what constitutes a family. In 1982, the *Village Voice,* a New York city weekly, became the first U.S. employer to offer health insurance benefits to the domestic partners of its lesbian and gay employees. As more employers added the benefits through the 1990s, others followed. By 2000, over 3500 private companies, colleges and

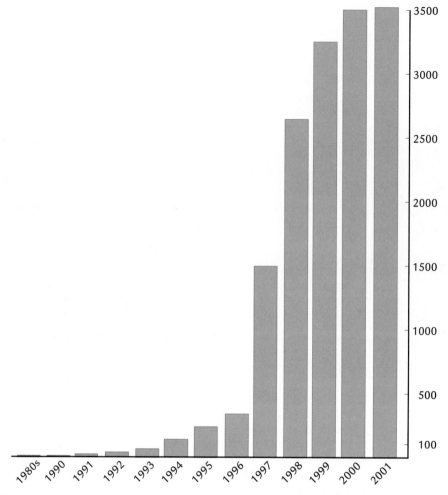

Figure 12.4

Number of employers who offer domestic partner health benefits, by year.

Source: Human Rights Campaign Foundation, *The State of the Workplace for Lesbian, Gay, Bisexual, and Transgendered Americans 2000*. Washington, DC: Human Rights Campaign Foundation, 2000, p. 23.

universities, and state and local governments offered domestic partnerships health insurance to their employees (see Figure 12.4). Employers who offer domestic partnership benefits operate in all fifty states (Human Rights Campaign Foundation, 2000:23–24).

Generally, employers require one declaration of long-term commitment from participants along with a shared mortgage or lease and other evidence, such as a joint bank account or credit card (Hodges, 1996:A6). Cohabiting heterosexuals also benefit from the new legislation. Many are using domestic partner plans as well. Not only has the gay rights movement transformed our understanding of human sexuality; it is also expanding the definition of what constitutes a family.

FAMILIES SEPARATED BY TIME AND SPACE

Global changes in labor force participation are profoundly altering family arrangements and contributing to growing family diversity. As more family members seek employment in market economies, families throughout the world are becoming more dispersed (Bruce et al., 1995). To conclude this chapter, we consider briefly two family forms that are characterized by temporal and spatial separation: transnational families and commuter marriages in the United States. Both forms rearrange interactions between family members and require a redefinition of family.

Transnational Families

In Chapter 4 we discussed some of the family consequences that are emerging from immigration. As migrants separate themselves from families, homes, jobs, and communities, they must adjust to new surroundings. One of the ways they do this is through their family connections. Instead of severing family ties, they retain strong family bonds that sustain them across time, space, and national boundaries. **Transnational families** are those with one or more members in the United States and one or more members "back home" in another country (Chavez, 1992:119).

Many studies highlight the tremendous costs encumbered by transnational arrangements. Anthropologist Leo Chavez has found that split families experience emotional, financial, and physical stress as a result of the migrant's absence:

> Migrants are subject to many life-threatening experiences in crossing the border and then in working in the United States. As a consequence, parents in transnational families wait expectantly for the migrant's return, as do spouses and children. Wives not only fear for their husbands' safety, but often worry that their husbands will meet other women, causing them to forget their families back home. . . . Family members left behind often must assume tasks and roles belonging to the missing spouse. Although this can be quite burdensome, many families left behind do not reunite with migrants in the United States. Others, however, find the pressures too great to bear and choose to join the family members in the United States (Chavez, 1992:119).

A growing U.S. market for Latina domestic and child-care workers is reshaping motherhood as it reshapes families. Hondagneu-Soteo and Avila's (1996) research focuses on transnational mothering among Latina domestic workers, where mothers work in the United States while their children remain in Mexico or Central America. Sometimes these immigrant women did not bring their children with them because they worked as live-in maids or child-care providers, and these types of employment made it impossible for them to live with their children. Other mothers found that they could provide better for their children by a transnational mothering arrangement because U.S. dollars stretched farther in Central America and Mexico than in the United States. This arrangement is difficult for parents and children, but it is sometimes the only choice if one is to take advantage of better wages in the United States. Latinos living in the United States have a long history of family flexibility, yet Hondagneu-Soteo and Avila argue that transnational mothering is radically different from many other family adaptations because it is now women with young children who are recruited for U.S. jobs that pay far less than a "family wage." When men come north and leave their families in Mexico, they are fulfilling familial obligations defined as bread-winning for the family. When women do so, they are embarking not only on an immigration journey, but on a more radical gender transformative odyssey. They are initiating separations of space and time from their communities of origin, homes, children, and sometimes husbands. In doing so, they must cope with stigma, guilt, and criticism from others. Furthermore, caring for other people's children is not always compatible with doing daily care for one's own family (Hondagneu-Soteo and Avila, 1997:7).

Filipina migrants also fill the international need for domestic work. In more than 100 countries today, they do housework and other forms of caretaking for more privileged women. At the same time, they hire low-wage women workers in the Philippines to care for their children they left behind. This represents an international division of reproductive labor that extends to family life among (1) middle-class women in receiving nations, (2) migrant domestic workers, and (3) Third World women who are too poor to migrate. The Filipina domestic work-ers who are "in the middle" of this division of labor suffer the pain of family sep-aration, even as they provide caregiving for other families in post industrial soci-eties (Parrenas, 2000).

Immigrant families are fractured in other ways. For example, many immi-grant mothers of newly born children must send their infants "home" to their countries of origin to be cared for by extended-family members. This is a com-mon practice is New York's Chinatown where immigrants work long hours in garment factories for paltry pay, leaving them no time to care for children (Sen-gupta, 1999).

As we think about how immigrant families adapt themselves to the new social and economic realities they face, it is important to keep the following two points in mind. First, transnational families are closely linked with the global-ization of economies that create increasing demands for immigrant labor. Sec-ond, transnational families require major adaptations in all areas of family life to cope with the problems of immigration and withstand temporal and spatial sep-aration. Gender relations are deeply affected by migration, separation, and the reuniting of family members (see Box 12.3).

Commuter Marriages

Commuter marriage is another arrangement arising out of changing labor force trends. Wives and husbands maintain separate households as a way of solving the dilemmas of dual-career families. Two demanding careers in different loca-tions means that couples commute to one or the other household between peri-ods of separation that are devoted to work. Most commuting couples do not see

Inside the Worlds of Diverse Families: Strategy and Strain in a Multinational Family

Anthropologist Leo Chavez describes family separation as a survival strategy. He uses the story of Felicia and Héctor Gómez to illustrate some of the experiences of families that are stretched across time, space, and national boundaries.

Héctor left Mexico for the United States in 1972, when he was about 26 and Felicia about 21, with two children and another on the way. Héctor and Felicia lived, at that time, in a rancho called Cabellito, in the state of Aguascalientes. Héctor had always worked in agriculture. Both his and Felicia's parents were farmers. Although his father owned a piece of land, it provided the family with little income. Héctor said, "We were very poor. I never had schooling. My father was poor and the work I had to do was to help him." Héctor did not have his own land after he married Felicia. His father's land was given to his brother. "I didn't have land. I was just a field hand," Héctor noted. "Sometimes I worked and sometimes I didn't." Faced with irregular work and the economic demands of a family, Héctor decided to migrate to San Diego County, where his cousin worked.

> I worked very much, very much [in Aguascalientes]. And we tried to save to buy things, a chimney for the house. We didn't have these things. We didn't have anything to buy them with. So, I had a dream to come here because I knew that here one could earn a little more. So, I said to myself, "I'm going to the United States. I'm going to try."

For five years Héctor migrated back and forth between an avocado farm in Escondido and his family in Aguascalientes. Héctor would see his family in Mexico once a year, as he said, "for a month, or a couple of weeks, or 15 days, depending upon when there was little work. Then I'd return to Escondido when there was more work." Felicia and Héctor had two more children during this period of brief encounters.

As Felicia remembers it,

> The first time he came here I was left alone [with two children] and pregnant. Then he came back when my daughter was born. Then he returned [to the United States] while I raised her. During the time I was raising her he came back again and I got pregnant again. He returned when the boy was two months old. Then I raised the boy and he returned and I got pregnant with the other girl.

Héctor's absences meant extra work for Felicia. The rancho she lived in was very rural. Felicia had to perform physically demanding chores daily, such as carrying water from a well or nearby river to the house. She had to take care of all household responsibilities alone, as well as care for their growing family.

> My life was full, of a lot of work, cutting wood, hauling water to bathe my children, and all of the work. Well, I had to do my husband's work and mine, too, because all of the men there would gather the wood and haul water to the house. But because he was absent, I had to do it. And I had to do my work, which was caring for my children, making tortillas, and preparing food for them. So, it was too much suffering for me to have to carry the whole weight, fetching the water, gathering wood, washing. Because I couldn't carry a lot of water at once. I had to bathe them [the children] with what little water I had and with the remaining water I wash the clothes. All day long,

(continued)

(continued from previous page)

this went on. One day I would fetch five or six buckets of water. The next day I would wash, because it wasn't possible to do everything at once.

Héctor's separation from Felicia and their children was a physical strain on Felicia. But his absence also created an emotional gulf between Héctor and his children. Since he saw them for only one short period during the entire year, his children were growing up without his presence. As Felicia noted,

The children didn't know him because he could only stay two weeks in Mexico. So, when he arrived the children cried because they didn't know him. They didn't know their father. For them, their father was only a picture.

Héctor felt saddened by the emotional distance between himself and his children. He lamented the lack of affection his children held for him. They were almost like strangers.

The first years, I was fine. But then the time came, after four years, that I would go to visit my family and my children didn't know me. I would try to hold them and they wouldn't allow it. They would cry. They weren't comfortable with me. I noticed that they didn't have any affection for me, nor I for them.

Despite these problems, Héctor did not consider bringing his family to the United States. His work on an avocado farm earned him only about $1.50 an hour, and he did not have housing suitable for a family. It was his employer who kept insisting that Héctor bring his family. Over the years, the employer, who did not live on the farm, gave Héctor increasing responsibility for its daily operations. Héctor noted that when he would suggest going back to see his family, the employer "didn't like it because I was in charge of the trees. He said, 'I don't like it that you go so often. Look, send for your family.'"

After his pay was raised to $2.50 an hour, Héctor finally decided to bring his family north. "I thought I must make a decision. It was very hard for me to continue living here alone. My family occupied my thoughts; when would I be able to see them on a continual basis?" In 1977, Héctor returned to Aguascalientes and brought his family back with him to Escondido. "I brought them and they were all very happy. My children and I could finally be together."

For the Gómezes, Héctor's life as a migrant meant that he lived more in San Diego than at home in Mexico. They viewed the effect of this separation on Felicia and the children as a major problem facing the family and its future. Their solution was to move the entire family to San Diego, where they would face new problems as undocumented immigrants. But for the Gómezes, these were challenges they could face together, as a family.

Source: Leo R. Chavez, *Shadowed Lives: Undocumented Immigrants in American Society.* Orlando, FL: Harcourt Brace College Publishers, 1992, p. 134.

their decision to commute as a matter of choice. Instead, living apart is a necessary accommodation to their careers. Like many innovations, couples view commuting as a temporary lifestyle (Baber and Allen, 1992:38). The patterns for this type of relationship vary. Some couples are together each weekend; others are together only once a month. Some couples are a day's drive away; others fly across the country.

Marital separation is not entirely new. In the past, there have always been circumstances under which husbands and wives lived in different locations. These have included war, immigration, economic need, and specific occupations such as those of pilots, truck drivers, politicians, entertainers, salespeople, and executives. These lifestyles have not usually required separate households. Furthermore, in these examples, it is typically the husband's work that separates the married couple. New commuter marriages are the result of *women's* professional roles. Most often, wives set up a temporary residence in a different geographic location. This contrasts sharply with the traditional pattern of wives giving up their jobs to live with their husbands.

Married couples who live apart view the careers of husband and wife as being equally important. Their work and family arrangements promote women's equality by making it acceptable for women to be dedicated to their careers, to individual freedom, and to personal growth. According to Naomi Gerstel and Harriet Engel Gross, who have studied this extensively, it takes great effort to live this way. Individuals' needs are pitted against family needs, and most commuters are ambivalent about their way of life (1987a). Yet most commuting couples feel that the strains in separate living are outweighed by the individual rewards they gain in their careers.

Studies of commuting couples have found both benefits and challenges for those involved. (The following is based on Jackson et al., 2000.) Benefits of commuting include: (1) increased sense of autonomy, achievement and satisfaction; (2) greater self-esteem and confidence; (3) ability to pursue careers without immediate and everyday family constraints, and other opportunities associated with compartmentalizing work and family roles (Chang and Wood, 1996; Douvan and Pleck, 1978; Groves and Horm-Winegerd, 1991).

Commuters tend to compartmentalize their lives into two areas: work and marriage. This may restrict interaction with people outside these realms and impose unique strains on the couple's relationship. Unlike the habituated togetherness of most married couples, commuters must work out the patterns of communication, sex, and domestic maintenance during their infrequent visits. This can be a gain for couples as an interacting unit. "They invest themselves heavily in their marital relationship when they are together, and often regard this shared time as a special, important time to concentrate on the relationship. As a result, there is less trivial conflict" (Gerstel, 1977:364). The separation may provide a unique support for dual-career relationships, in that it offers a balance between separation and togetherness by easing the stress of unrelieved companionship (Douvan and Pleck, 1978:138). A study by Bunker et al. (1992) found greater work-life satisfaction among commuting couples than among dual-career single-residence couples.

The other side of this career-enhancing autonomy includes the following challenges: (1) stresses from trying to balance family and career responsibilities, (2) loneliness and lack of companionship, (3) lack of understanding of this family arrangement, and (4) hectic schedules associated with greater separation of work and family responsibilities (Jackson et al., 2000:23).

Gerstel and Gross (1987b) found that career and family characteristics interact to influence couples' commuting experiences. They identified three types of commuting couples who experience commuting differently based on the length of the marriage and the presence of children:

1. *Adjusting couples.* These were young couples in the early stages of both careers and marriages. They spent a good deal of effort "adjusting."
2. *Balancing couples.* These couples were older and more advanced in their careers, contending more with conflict over the increased childcare and domestic responsibilities of who stays home with the children. They struggled to strike a balance between the demands of their jobs and their families.
3. *Established couples.* These couples were freed from their childbearing responsibilities. At least one partner was well established in a career. With children no longer in the home, they had fewest stresses and saw the greatest advantages in commuting.

Commuter marriages are becoming more common for couples of various racial backgrounds, but little research has addressed the experiences of racial-ethnic couples in this arrangement. Anita Jackson and her colleagues Ronald P. Brown and Karen E. Patterson-Stewart studied African American couples in commuter marriages to see how they managed commuting and how their families and careers were affected. These couples experienced many of the same advantages and disadvantages as noted in studies of White couples (see Table 12.2), but the study also suggests that commuting may have distinctive benefits for African Americans:

Commuting is a strategy for engaging in meaningful work when such opportunities are not in close proximity to one's family residence. For African Americans, this opportunity may be of particular significance considering their long history of oppressed employment opportunities and the finding in this study that commuting was viewed as a way to combat obstacles, such as employment limitations, restrictive assumptions about one's skills and abilities, and racial stereotypes and oppression. Throughout history, African Americans have traveled long distances from their families to obtain gainful employment, such as during the large migration of African Americans from the rural south to the northern cities in the early part of the 20th century (Staples and Johnson, 1993). Today, with a greater range of educational and occupational opportunities available to them, coupled with a competitive workforce, African American men and women may be choosing to commute in order to obtain not only employment but employment that matches their skills and abilities and is personally meaningful (Jackson et al., 2000:31).

Gender

Commuting is a solution to the incompatible demands of career and family, but it creates new problems depending on the couples' stage of family and career. Although some commuters as a group view their adaptation as a complex mixture of costs and benefits, women in general tend to evaluate the overall arrangement less negatively. Apparently, the freedom from schedules and household chores and the ability to work without interruption works to the advantage of

TABLE 12.1

Advantages and Disadvantages of the Commuter Lifestyle in the Lives of African American Couples

Advantages	Disadvantages
Meaningful personal expression	Stress of complex lifestyle
Personal fulfillment	Hectic schedules
Enhanced identity	Driving
Autonomy	Financial hardship
Enhanced family dynamics	Sexual advances
Effective interactions	Alienation and isolation
Quality use of time	Loneliness
Career advantages	Guilt
Combat employment limitations, assumptions, racial stereotypes/ oppression	Misperceptions of the lifestyle
	Lack of community

Source: Anita P. Jackson, Ronald P. Brown, and Karen E. Patterson-Stewart, 2000. "African Americans in Dual-career Commuter Marriages: An Investigation of Their Experiences," *The Family Journal: Counseling and Therapy for Couples and Families* 8 (1) (January 2000): 26.

women more than men. Gerstel and Gross (1987b) found that women increased the amount of time they spent on professional work, but because commuting equalizes the division of domestic responsibilities, men did more household labor than they had done in the past. This made men more dissatisfied with the arrangement.

Still, most studies have found varied sources of strain for husbands and wives (Gerstel, 1977; Gross, 1984; Kirschner and Walum, 1978; Jackson et al., 2000). According to Gross, wives miss the emotional protection that they expected from the ideal husband, and they sense that this loss is the cost of their gain in independence. "More so than husbands in our culture, wives are programmed to think of marriage as an intimacy oasis, an emotionally close relationship that will be total" (Gross, 1984:473). Though highly career oriented, these women still give interpersonal relations, as compared to work-related rewards, a primacy in their lives that their husbands do not. Husbands, on the other hand, are less likely to express as much unhappiness about the loss of emotional closeness that living apart can produce. They do feel guilty about not providing the emotional closeness they sense their wives need. But in spite of women's expressed loss of intimacy, wives are more comfortable with the arrangement because it validates their equal rights in work and marriage.

The study of African American couples found that while commuting produced stronger identities for both husbands and wives, gender differences were also present. Commuting strengthened husbands' family provider identities, while wives new identities centered on their confidence in managing home, career, and travel responsibilities (Jackson et al., 2000:32).

CHAPTER REVIEW

1. Family boundaries are becoming more ambiguous. Marriage is no longer the basis of family life. This decline has been ushered in by global changes, especially new social practices regarding sex, childbearing, divorce, and women's labor force participation.

2. Emerging family forms have not replaced nuclear families but coexist as increasingly legitimate social arrangements.

3. The rise in new family arrangements shows the importance of both structure and agency. Social, economic, and demographic changes have created opportunities for individuals to choose from a wide variety of household and family options.

4. A growing share of adults are spending more of their lives in an unmarried status. Approximately 10 percent of adults will never marry. The increased number of singles is rooted in historical circumstances, including the independence from birth families fostered by urbanization and industrialization.

5. There are many ways of being single. Long-term singlehood is generally a more positive state for women than for men. Yet demographic and cultural factors combine to create a "marriage squeeze" that increases the number of single women, including those who are not single by choice.

6. The imbalanced sex ratio among Black men and women creates greater difficulties for Black women desiring marriage than for White and Latina women.

7. A quarter of Americans have cohabited at some point during their lives. Several possible factors explain the increasing acceptance and practice of a formerly unthinkable phenomenon, including postponement of marriage and the tendency of divorced individuals to choose cohabitation over remarriage.

8. Cohabitation exhibits great diversity. For some, it is a prelude to marriage. For others, it is a practical domestic arrangement.

9. Some cohabitation arrangements differ from marriage in the following ways: presumption of the length of the relationship; the symbolic privatism of marriage; and the lack of institutionalization of cohabitation. Cohabitation does not lessen the likelihood of divorce. Among minorities, however, cohabitation often resembles marriage in important respects.

10. Although popular estimates of the gay and lesbian population are about 10 percent of the population, lesbian and gay couples are not easily counted. Despite the new struggles for gay rights, discrimination is pervasive in U.S. society.

11. Gender differentials in same-sex relationships are important. Sexual exclusivity is more likely among lesbians than among gay men. This parallels the behavior of heterosexual males and females. Same-sex couples tend to be more egalitarian than heterosexual couples.

12. Lesbians and gay men have begun to establish families of choice, constructing their own notions of kinship and thereby expanding the definition of family.

13. Gay and lesbian partners are denied the symbolic and financial benefits of legal marriage. Domestic partnerships offering benefits for heterosexual and same-sex partners are now recognized in private companies, colleges and universities, and state and local governments throughout the United States.

14. New patterns of family dispersal stem from changes in work opportunities in the United States and the world. Transnational families and commuter marriages are two emerging family forms that require radical changes in family living as women and men adapt to temporal and spatial separation. Immigration creates transnational families, while commuter marriage is the result of U.S. women's increased entry into professional occupations. Both family forms entail difficult costs and strains that accompany women's and men's new roles.

RELATED WEB SITES

http://www.lovemakesafamily.org/

LOVE MAKES A FAMILY: Lesbian, Gay, Bisexual, and Transgender People and Their Families: The Love Makes a Family photo-text exhibit is distributed by Family Diversity Projects, Inc., which was founded in 1996 by photographer Gigi Kaeser, and writer, Peggy Gillespie. In order to help create safe schools for gay and lesbian youth and children of gays and lesbians, Family Diversity Projects distributes a special version of Love Makes a Family designed especially for elementary school students (K–6) with age-appropriate text. Family Diversity Projects also provides speakers and workshop leaders for conferences and exhibit venues. At the most basic level, Love Makes a Family combats homophobia by breaking silence and making the invisible visible, thereby making the world a safer place for all families.

http://www.familydiv.org/inourfamily/

IN OUR FAMILY is a touring photo-text exhibit created by the award-winning Family Diversity Projects, Inc. With photos by Gigi Kaeser and interviews by Rebekah Boyd, Peggy Gillespie, and Jeane Beard. This exhibit celebrates families of every kind, including: Adoptive families, Foster families, Divorced families and stepfamilies, Single-parent families, Multiracial families, Families dealing with illness and/or death, Lesbian and Gay parented families, Interfaith families, Multi-generational families, Immigrant families, Families facing physical challenges, and Families facing mental challenges. Each family photograph is accompanied by the words of parents and children in these families who speak candidly about life. Together, the images and the text reveal the common thread present in this tapestry of families: love. IN OUR FAMILY is an easy-to-hang display consisting of 20 photos with accompanying laminated text panels that can be easily transported.

http://www.unmarried.org/

Alternatives to Marriage Project: Alternatives to Marriage Project is a national organization for unmarried people, including people who choose not to marry, are prevented from marrying, or are among the majority of people who live together before marriage. This project work for greater understanding and acceptance of unmarried people. The Alternatives to Marriage Project is open to everyone, including singles, couples, married people, people in relationships with more than two people, and people of all genders and sexual orientations.

http://www.singlesrights.com/

American Association for Single People: AASP protects the legal rights of single people whether they live alone or with someone else, whether they are straight, gay, or bisexual, whether they are young or old, with or without a disability, and regardless of their race or ethnicity.

http://www.parentsplace.com/family/singleparent/

Single Mothers By Choice (SMC) was founded in 1981 by Jane Mattes, C.S.W. and psychotherapist. SMC is devoted to providing information and support to single mothers as well as those contemplating or trying to achieve single motherhood.

http://www.ssc.wisc.edu/nsfh/

The National Survey of Families and Households includes interviews with 13,007 respondents from a national sample. The sample includes a main cross-section of 9,637 households plus an oversampling of blacks, Puerto Ricans, Mexican Americans, single-parent families, families with step-children, cohabiting couples and recently married persons.

CHAPTER **13**

Family Policy for the Twenty-First Century

Myths and Realities

Myth: Since abortions became legal, the number and rate of abortions have steadily risen.

Reality: The number of abortions annually has steadied after dropping since 1980. The abortion rate (number per 1000 adult women) has dropped from over 29 in 1980 to less than 23 in 1997.

Myth: Welfare to the poor has risen steadily and it is a significant part of the federal budget.

Reality: Welfare to the poor has declined dramatically since 1980. Before the welfare legislation was passed in 1996, welfare to the poor constituted about 5 percent of the federal budget. Since 1996 the money spent on the impoverished has declined further.

Myth: Poor people are undeserving because they do not help themselves.

Reality: Research shows that most welfare recipients earn extra money from various informal jobs. Also, there are not enough jobs in many locales, such as the inner cities and rural areas.

454

Myth: The majority of welfare recipients are African American.

Reality: Whites outnumber African Americans and Latinos among welfare recients.

Myth: The proportion of children in poverty is lower than the proportion of elderly who are poor.

Reality: The proportion of poor children is almost twice as high as it is for the elderly.

Myth: Because the United States has the world's best medical system, it ranks at or near the top on the basic health indicators for children.

Reality: Compared to other industrialized nations, the United States ranks relatively low in overall infant mortality and ranks last in children covered by medical insurance.

Myth: The money spent on welfare for poor children is a bad investment.

Reality: Research shows that money spent on childhood poverty programs (immunization, prenatal health care, preschool education) saves society many times more money than is spent on welfare.

Myth: Preschool programs for high-risk children are a waste because intelligence is fixed genetically.

Reality: Research shows that preschool programs for at-risk children have long-term positive effects on IQ scores (the earlier the intervention, the better the results).

Two fundamental themes have guided this sociological inquiry of families: Family forms are increasingly diverse, and the forms families take are the products of social, political, and economic forces in the larger society. In this final chapter we ask: What is the role of government regarding families? Should government actions move us back to the "modern family" of a bread-winning husband, his homemaker wife, and their children, or should the government assist families to cope with the social, political, and economic forces that affect them so greatly? These are policy issues that generate considerable heat in today's political climate.

We use Aldous and Dumon's definition of **family policy:** "family policy refers to objectives concerning family well-being and the specific measures taken by governmental bodies to achieve them" (1991:467). This definition requires clarification. First, it can be argued reasonably that all government policies affect families—for example, taxes, education, subsidies, health, warfare, and welfare. Although this is true to a degree, we concentrate on those policies aimed specifically at families. Second, "the United States has no overall, official family policy" (Zimmerman, 1992:4). This is to say that the U.S. government and the state governments have no plan regarding families but rather a potpourri of laws, regulations, and policies that lack coherence. This does not mean, however, that an overall family policy is impossible to attain. Third, the very notion of a government plan regarding families is abhorrent to some because it implies government intrusion into family life. This reminds us that public policies regarding families divide Americans along ideological lines.

This chapter begins with a discussion of the ideological fault lines, to use an earthquake metaphor, that divide Americans and their governmental officials on family issues. This background is important for understanding why the United States as a society takes some actions regarding families and avoids others. The heart of this chapter focuses on four crucial and hotly contested public policy issues: family planning (contraception and abortion), helping the impoverished, meeting the needs of disadvantaged children, and relieving burdens for working parents. The chapter concludes with a personal note—the principles that we believe should guide the formulation of pro-family social policies.

THE IDEOLOGICAL FAULT LINES

People are rarely neutral about family issues. They respond with passion because family issues are at the heart of religious, political, and philosophical ideologies. Progressives and conservatives are quickly divided over welfare, homosexual rights, abortion, sex education in schools, condom distribution, parental leave, and the like. These issues are debated with passion in legislatures as conservatives and progressives confront each other with opposing views and opposing solutions.

The Conservatives

Conservatives, or, as they are sometimes called, **"the moral right,"** believe that the family is the basic building block of society. The family is where members' basic needs are met, where children learn their most important lessons, and where individuals are loved unconditionally. The conservative ideology is pro-family, but not just any family form. The ideal family is a married couple in a life-long monogamous relationship; the husband is the disciplinarian and economic provider while the wife is a homemaker in charge of raising the children (for the intellectual foundations of the conservative position see, for example, Murray, 1984; Wilson, 1993; Whitehead, 1993). As Reverend Jerry Falwell, a spokesperson for the moral conservatives, says, "The family is the God-ordained institution of the marriage of one man and one woman together for a lifetime with their biological or adopted children" (Falwell, 1980:104). From this perspective,

> . . . the family is seen as God-given but also as based upon essential biological differences between men, women and children and their differing needs. Women are seen as biologically needing to be mothers and fulfilling themselves through motherhood. Biological mothering is also seen as the foundation of the social role of women, who are the ones "naturally" committed to caring for children. Children are seen as needing family support during a prolonged childhood and parents are seen as those best able to guide their children's moral and social development (Abbott and Wallace, 1992:10).

The conservatives are alarmed and appalled by what they consider the breakdown of the family (Furstenberg, 1999). The following facts illustrate the changes in families that frighten conservatives.

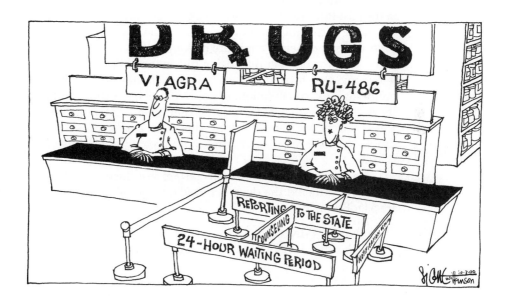

- *Premarital sex:* Relatively few young people wait until they marry to initiate sex.
- *Cohabitation:* More and more couples choose cohabitation as the initial stage of family formation.
- *Abortion:* Each year 1.2 million abortions are performed in the United States.
- *Out-of-wedlock childbearing:* One-third of all births in the United States—more than a million babies a year—are born to unmarried women.

- *Divorce:* One-half of all marriages now end in divorce, and each year more than a million children are affected by their parents' separation or divorce. One in three of us is a member of a stepfamily.
- *Fatherlessness:* Divorce, single parenthood, and desertion translate into an estimated 35 percent of all households with children but without fathers present.
- *Nonparental child care:* More than six in ten mothers with children under the age of one year are in the labor force; almost three-fourths of the mothers with children between one and eighteen years are in the labor force. This requires, of course, that parents entrust their children to other caregivers during working hours.

Abbott and Wallace say that

> . . . the Moral Right is best conceptualized as a backlash movement, reacting to social changes that have taken place since World War Two, especially in the areas of morality, welfare spending and the role of women; . . . [It] combines a nostalgia for the past with a zeal to save the [nation] from what is perceived as [its] current economic and moral sickness (Abbott and Wallace, 1992:19).

According to the conservative credo, the principal causes of family decline in the past three decades or so have been cultural and political. The primary reason is the decline of traditional family values, which has led to the moral decay of society's members. People are making selfish decisions (e.g., women working in the labor force rather than being full-time mothers, or accepting welfare rather than providing for themselves and their family) or behaving immorally (e.g., premarital sex, cohabitation, extramarital sex, abortion, and homosexuality). In short, "The conservative position is that, as a result of hedonistic individualism, we are letting our 'family values' slip away, and what is needed now is nothing short of a moral rearmament on behalf of parental responsibility" (Mason et al., 1998:3)

The members of the moral right are also incensed at government policies that have furthered the decline of the traditional family. Some of these policies are as follows:

- No-fault divorce laws that make divorce easy to obtain
- The 1973 U.S. Supreme Court decision (*Roe v. Wade*) that made abortion legal
- Decisions by local authorities to provide contraceptives and birth control counseling and compulsory sex education in the public schools
- Local decisions that encourage homosexuality (passage of homosexual rights legislation, granting homosexual unions legal status, allowing gay couples or lesbian couples to adopt children)
- Policies of the welfare state that encourage people to rely on the state rather than on their own initiative
- High welfare spending, which causes high levels of taxation, which, in turn, forces married women into the labor market
- Government subsidies for child care, which encourage mothers to work outside the home.

Political Action

The political result of the morality crusade is that there is a virtuous "us" and an immoral "them." This moral framing of social troubles means that the morally "virtuous" are convinced of their "rightness" (Morone, 1996). This feeling of moral superiority and certitude results in resistance to negotiation and compromise, and intolerance toward those who are not only wrong but immoral. The result is a zeal to promote and support traditional values and the traditional family.

Although there is some diversity within this political movement to stop the moral decline and restore the traditional family, at the center it is very organized. Leading the charge is the religious right and its leader, Reverend Pat Robertson, who founded the Christian Coalition in 1989. This organization is well funded and has about 2 million members. The goal of the Christian Coalition is to have evangelicals elected at the local, state, and national levels so that public policies can be changed to conform with a Bible-based agenda. The organization provides a manual and leadership schools to teach members how to organize and win campaigns. They organize cadres of church-based workers as volunteers to disseminate political information to people most likely to be compatible with their religious and political views. They supply millions of voter guides through church networks that promote candidates in tune with traditional family values. The Christian Right includes a number of organized groups that are actively involved in the media and promoting their ideology in Washington, D.C., and in the various state legislatures. Some of these organizations are James Dobson's Focus on the Family, Beverly LaHaye's Concerned Women of America, Phyllis Schlafly's The Eagle Forum, and Gary Bauer's Family Research Council.

The concern of conservatives about families includes how families are described and analyzed in college textbooks. In a critique of twenty current textbooks on family and marriage, sociologist Norval Glenn (1997), sponsored by the conservative Institute for American Values, expressed grave concern that each of these textbooks describes the diversity of family forms that have emerged without ample consideration for the negative consequences emanating from them, especially for children. Moreover, these books, according to Glenn, are antimarriage because they minimize the beneficial consequences of marriage to individuals and society. Implicit in Glenn's critique is that current textbooks, ours included, celebrate new family forms while denigrating the modern family of working father, homemaking mother, and their children.

The Progressives

For progressives the traditional family is not a given. Rather, family forms are socially and historically constructed, not monolithic universals that exist for all times and places. The family that conservative writers uphold as "legitimate" is no less a product of social structure and culture; it emerged as a result of social and economic conditions that are no longer operative for most Americans and that never were operative for many poor Americans and people of color (Baca Zinn and Eitzen, 1998; Dill et al., 1993:14).

Thus, one critical difference between the conservatives and progressives is causation: What is the cause of family changes over the past forty years or so? As we have seen, the conservatives believe that these changes result from a shift in values, accompanied by government policies congruent with the new values. Progressives disagree with that view.

> The [conservatives] have it backward when they argue that the collapse of traditional family values is at the heart of our social decay. The losses in real earnings and in breadwinner jobs, the persistence of low-wage work for women and the corporate greed that has accompanied global economic restructuring have wreaked far more havoc on Ozzie and Harriet Land than have the combined effects of feminism, sexual revolution, gay liberation, the counterculture, narcissism and every other value flip of the past half-century (Stacey, 1994:120–121).

Because families come in so many varieties, progressives argue also that to speak of "the family" obscures more than it reveals. Families today may be two-parent, single-parent, stepfamilies, gay and lesbian families, and foster families, with different forms within each of these categories. Indeed, 93 percent of contemporary families *do not* fit the traditional family model held as the ideal by conservatives—two parents, a breadwinning husband and homemaking wife, with their children. Also, "different families, located at different points in the American social structure, face different problems and pose different policy challenges" (Mason et al., 1998:1). To focus on an idealized family based on a nostalgic view of the past, as the conservatives do, leads policy makers in the wrong direction—that is, away from focusing on the actual problems experienced by most families now. Progressives, therefore, seek ways that society might maximize the love, care, and nurturance within various types of families. Some possibilities are subsidized daycare, universal health insurance, the legalization of gay and lesbian marriages, and the economic support for poor single mothers. As an example of the latter, the poverty of single mothers is not a result of never marrying or divorce but a combination of factors, including secondary job markets, low wages, the loss of their spouse's wage, and no health insurance. In sum,

> [There is] no evidence whatsoever that if your parents divorce *instead* of suffering together you will thereafter be worse off than if they forgo divorce on your behalf, especially were society to offer responsible child support, public day care, and economic opportunities for all citizens, which, of course, ought to be the family values agenda (Z *Magazine*, 1993:4).

The key for progressives is the impact of social forces on families. Examples include the following:

- Young pregnant women get married if the father has a decent job (Wilson, 1987).
- Poverty threatens the well-being and development of children.
- The recent surge of women in the labor force is really a White middle-class phenomenon because women of color and working-class women rarely have had the option of staying home to raise their children (Dill et al., 1993).
- Family trends in the United States over the past three decades have occurred in every other Western nation. "The trends are rooted in the development of the advanced industrial societies" (Skolnick and Rosen-crantz, 1994:65).

Progressives believe that society, through the government, should come to the aid of families, promoting diversity, eliminating institutional racism and sexism, assisting single mothers, allowing a woman's right to choose whether to have a baby, meeting the basic needs of children, and promoting such policies as universal health insurance.

Political Action

The progressives are much less organized than the conservatives. There is one national organization, the National Organization for Women (NOW), which lobbies in Washington and files lawsuits on behalf of women's rights, and local chapters work for the progressive agenda at the state and local levels. There also are organizations focused on special issues. Most prominent are pro-choice organizations such as the National Abortion and Reproductive Rights Action League. There is no progressive media network, although the conservatives claim that the progressive agenda is widely promoted by a liberal bias in newspapers and television.

To summarize, issues surrounding the family divide conservatives and progressives on questions such as: Why are family forms changing—is the reason cultural or structural? What actions should be taken to address problems surrounding family issues—are these best left to private choices or are they public choices? If they are public choices, what is the proper role of government? Keep these questions in mind as we address several important family policy issues, beginning with the most volatile one—issues surrounding family planning.

THE GOVERNMENT AND REPRODUCTIVE RIGHTS

Contraceptives

The state and federal governments have a long history of involvement in reproductive matters. Historically, some states with Catholic majorities outlawed the use of contraceptives. That prohibition was lifted in 1968 when the U.S. Supreme Court, in *Griswold v. Connecticut*, ruled that a state statute making the use of contraceptives by married couples a criminal offense was unconstitutional. This court decision did not, however, end the controversy.

About 60 percent of all pregnancies in the United States are unplanned, occurring because the people involved misuse contraceptives, use unreliable contraceptives, or do not use contraceptives at all. Among the poor, about three-fourths of pregnancies are unplanned. If the poor wish to use contraceptives, the expense is sometimes prohibitive. The cost of a Norplant kit, which offers five years of pregnancy protection, is $365 plus $300 for implanting and removing the device. Depo Provera injections, which provide three months of protection, cost $30 or $120 for a year's worth of injections. A month's supply of oral contraceptives can be purchased for about $13 from a local Planned Parenthood clinic. In sharp contrast, a woman in the Netherlands can purchase *a year's supply* of oral contraceptives for about $8.

One solution is to supply condoms free in high schools, colleges, and health clinics. This is challenged by the moral right because, in their view, it encourages

Choices in Sex Education

sexual promiscuity. Research comparing rates of condom use and sexual activity among public high school students in New York, where condoms are offered, and Chicago, where they are not, found, however, that sex education and condoms do not increase sexual activity (reported in Richardson, 1997). Similarly, a Rand Corporation study conducted in Los Angeles found that a free-condom program in high school increased sexual safety without any corresponding increase in sexual activity (reported in Maugh, 1998). Condom use does decrease rates of pregnancy (and, indirectly, abortion rates), sexually transmitted diseases, and HIV infections. These reductions are crucial, because about 40,000 new HIV infections and 3 million other sexually transmitted diseases occur annually among teenagers (Nelson, 1997). Concerning teen pregnancy, the United States has the highest rate of any developed nation (more than double that of the next highest Western developed nation, New Zealand, and almost ten times higher than in the Netherlands) (Pollitt, 1995). Because of these facts and the recognition that two-thirds of teenagers are sexually active by the time they graduate from high school (56 percent of girls and 73 percent of boys), the American Academy of Pediatrics, which represents more than 40,000 pediatricians, officially recommended in 1995 that high schools distribute condoms. As of 1997, only 431 public schools nationwide made condoms available, which represents 2.2 percent of all public high schools.

The federal government has taken a position opposite that of the American Academy of Pediatrics in an effort to reduce teen pregnancy. The 1996 welfare law included $250 million to states (which would match every $4 in federal money with $3 in state money) for sex education based on abstinence. Under the new federal rules the abstinence programs should teach that sex outside of marriage is likely to have harmful psychological and physical effects. Information about contraception (the pill and condoms) is precluded by the abstinence-only message required by the law.

Abortion

Abortion was a common procedure in the United States until the last third of the nineteenth century (the following historical information is from Reagan, 1997). Prior to criminalization, abortions were permitted until the fetus was felt to move in the uterus (about the fourth month of pregnancy). Beginning about 1867, the American Medical Association began a crusade against abortion (ironically, that same organization was instrumental in the legalization of abortion a century later). This state-by-state effort was successful so that by 1900, all states had antiabortion legislation. Sixty years later the situation began to reverse as some state legislatures passed legislation permitting abortions under certain conditions. Thus, for most of the twentieth century, abortions were illegal, and countless women sought illicit and often unsafe abortions.

In 1973, the U.S. Supreme Court, in *Roe v. Wade,* invalidated all state laws against abortion. Most significant, the Court ruled that the fetus is not a person and therefore is not guaranteed the protection and rights provided persons by the Constitution. This ruling raises one of the most highly charged emotional and political issues in the United States. Pro-choice and antiabortion forces clash over whose rights are to be protected—those of the woman or those of the fetus. Abortions are interpreted by one side as a viable option for the woman to control her life and by the other side as murder.

As a result of *Roe v. Wade,* approximately 1.18 million (1997) legal abortions occur per year, ending about 23 percent of all pregnancies. The U.S. abortion rate has been declining since 1980. The annual U.S. abortion rate is 22.9 per 1000 women age fifteen to forty-four, which is higher than in most developed societies (see Box 13.1).

The antiabortion forces were incensed by the *Roe v. Wade* decision and have directed their efforts since to weakening or changing it. They have engaged in intense lobbying and have worked hard to elect candidates who favor what they call the "prolife" position. Especially important in this crusade has been working for the election of Presidents who will nominate Supreme Court justices opposed to abortion. Antiabortion advocates have also engaged in demonstrations and acts of civil disobedience, including "rescue" squads that harass abortion patients and providers. Occasional zealots have even firebombed abortion clinics and murdered workers at abortion clinics. The hassles and dangers for doctors who perform abortions are so great that many decline to engage in that activity. As a result, the number of abortion providers has dropped by 30 percent since 1982, and some 86 percent of counties in the United States have no abortion services (*New York Times,* 2000).

Following *Roe v. Wade* in 1973, a number of legislative, judicial, and executive actions have made abortions more difficult to obtain. In 1976, Congress

BOX 13.1   Families in Global Perspective: A Global Abortion View

More than one in five pregnancies worldwide end in abortion, and abortion is common even where it is illegal and unsafe, says the most comprehensive report yet on abortion around the world.

Nearly 80,000 women die from abortion complications each year, mostly in poor countries where abortion is illegal, says the report from the Alan Guttmacher Institute in New York.

"It is clear that women the world over go to great lengths to terminate an unplanned pregnancy," says Guttmacher president Jeannie Rosoff.

The nonprofit institute regularly produces studies and policy analysis on abortion, contraception and other reproductive health issues.

The new report is based on studies and government statistics that Guttmacher says have varying reliability: Countries where abortion is legal generally have the most reliable numbers, because abortions are officially reported. In some other countries, the numbers are based on surveys of small numbers of women.

Worldwide, 35 of every 1,000 women have abortions each year, Guttmacher estimates. That rate is similar in the developed and developing world. But regional and country-by-country rates vary widely.

Western Europe has the lowest rate, 11 per 1,000; eastern Europe has the highest, 90 per 1,000. Cuba and Vietnam, where abortion is legal and widely available, have high rates, but so do Chile and Peru, where the procedure is illegal and often performed in underground clinics.

The U.S. rate is 23 per 1,000.

Access to contraception and attitudes about ideal family size seem more important than legality and safety in determining abortion rates, says Susheela Singh, head of research at Guttmacher.

"We are seeing a lot of change in the average family size in a lot of countries. What are you going to use if you don't have good contraception?"

Modern contraception has been slow to make it into communist countries of eastern Europe, where abortion has long been the primary means of limiting family size, Singh says.

The report says 25% of the world's women live in countries where abortion is prohibited or allowed only to save a woman's life; 41% live in countries where women can get abortions for any reason, at least in early pregnancy; and the rest live in countries where abortion is somewhat restricted.

The researchers estimate that 12% of pregnancies in Africa end in abortion, as do 23% in Latin America, 30% in East Asia, 57% in eastern Europe, 21% in the rest of Europe and 23% in the USA, Canada, Australia, New Zealand and Japan.

Olivia Gans, a spokeswoman for the National Right to Life Committee in Washington, D.C., says she believes the numbers in the report are unreliable, even for countries where abortion is legal. And, she calls the report part of a "strong-armed imperialist effort" to legalize abortion in countries "where there is a strong cultural or religious feeling against it."

The best way to help women and children in poor countries is to improve basic health care, she says.

But supporters of abortion rights say legal, safe abortion is a part of basic health care.

(continued)

(continued from previous page)

A comparison of rates: estimated abortion rates in selected countries.

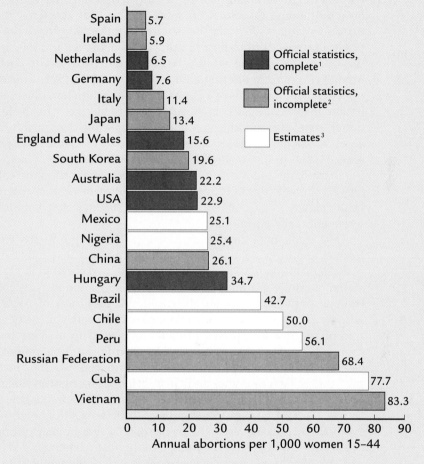

Country	Rate
Spain	5.7
Ireland	5.9
Netherlands	6.5
Germany	7.6
Italy	11.4
Japan	13.4
England and Wales	15.6
South Korea	19.6
Australia	22.2
USA	22.9
Mexico	25.1
Nigeria	25.4
China	26.1
Hungary	34.7
Brazil	42.7
Chile	50.0
Peru	56.1
Russian Federation	68.4
Cuba	77.7
Vietnam	83.3

Legend:
- Official statistics, complete[1]
- Official statistics, incomplete[2]
- Estimates[3]

Annual abortions per 1,000 women 15–44

[1] From countries where at least 80% of abortions are thought to be reported to the government.
[2] From countries where fewer than 80% of abortions are thought to be reported, presumed to be underestimates.

"Worldwide, we don't value women's lives enough to make sure they have the information, the technology and the access to carry out responsible decisions," says Kate Michelman, president of the National Abortion and Reproductive Rights Action League in Washington, D.C. "It boggles my mind."

The report says the worldwide trend is toward liberalization of abortion laws.

Source: Kim Painter, "A Global Abortion View," *USA Today,* January 21, 1999, p. 8D.

passed the Hyde amendment, which cut off federal funds for all abortions except for pregnancies resulting from rape, incest, or that endangered a woman's life. The Supreme Court has supported this by ruling that a woman, although possessing the right to have an abortion, does not have a constitutional right to have the federal government pay for it. Similarly, a majority of the states now have laws prohibiting the use of tax monies to pay for abortions. In 1989, the Court ruled in *Webster v. Reproductive Services* that the states have the right to prohibit public employees from participating in an abortion. In 1990, in *Rust v. Sullivan*, the Court upheld the administration's right to prevent doctors at federally funded clinics from offering advice on abortion. In 1991, a federal appeals court upheld most provisions of a Pennsylvania abortion law, one of the strictest in the nation. In 1994, the Supreme Court ruled that judges can create carefully drawn buffer zones around abortion clinics to prohibit demonstrators from blocking access to patients and staff members, while, at the same time, protecting the free speech rights of demonstrators outside the buffer zones. The Court in 2000, by a 6–3 margin, upheld the right of states to restrict abortion protests through "bubble" laws that keep protesters at least 8 feet from women entering reproductive health clinics. The Court, by a 5–4 vote, in 2000 rejected Nebraska's ban on what opponents call "partial-birth abortion."

The ideology of the president clearly affects reproductive rights policies. The Reagan and Bush administrations took a number of actions that affected family planning. During the Reagan years, some 16 percent of federal funds for the provision of family planning clinics were cut. Both the Reagan and Bush administrations opposed sex counseling and the provision of contraceptives in the schools. During the 1980s, federal monies for research on the development of contraceptives and educational programs designed to increase their correct usage dropped by about half. The Food and Drug Administration under President George Herbert Walker Bush banned the import of RU-486, the French "abortion pill" that is legal in France and Great Britain. The right-to-life groups called this drug the "French death pill" because it terminates pregnancy *after* sexual intercourse. The Reagan and Bush administrations also banned the use of federal funds for fetal-tissue research (the use of fetal cells appears promising for victims of Parkinson's disease and could possibly treat Alzheimer's, diabetes, leukemia, and spinal cord injuries). The younger Bush has allowed limited research.

President Clinton reversed or at least neutralized some of the actions by his predecessors. His appointment of two justices to the U.S. Supreme Court tipped the balance against overturning *Roe v. Wade*. He first permitted the testing of RU-486 (mifepristone) in the United States, and later his administration's Food and Drug Administration approved its use. Moreover, the Clinton administration ruled that federal funds could be used for research involving stem cells derived from human embryos. Also, President Clinton vetoed bills that would have outlawed late-term abortions (the so-called partial-birth abortions).

The pro-choice decisions by the Clinton administration are fragile and in danger of being reversed with the shift to a Republican president, George W. Bush in 2001. President Bush has consistently taken the conservative position on contraceptive and abortion issues. In his first few days in office, he used an executive order to reverse President Clinton's earlier executive order, reinstating the ban on federal aid to international agencies that provide abortion counseling or otherwise help women obtain abortions. Further, Bush has criticized the use of RU-486; he is anti-abortion, and he has condemned the Supreme Court's rejection of Nebraska's ban on partial-birth abortion. President Bush has the power to rescind various rules supporting pro-choice. He can nominate justices to the Supreme Court who want to overturn *Roe v. Wade*. This will be difficult, however, with the shift to a Democrat-controlled Senate in mid-2001.

Prior to President George W. Bush, the battle for abortion rights had been won, tentatively, at the federal level in the laws and in the courts, but it had been lost in many of the states. Although abortion is a legal option, many states have put up roadblocks to this practice. These obstacles imposed by many of the states include imposing waiting periods, mandating counseling, and requiring parental notification and consent before abortions can be performed (*New York Times*, 2000). In 1999, state legislatures enacted more than fifty measures to restrict choice. Some thirty-one states have enacted bans on "partial birth abortions." The public, meanwhile, for the most part, supports abortion.

> Over the past three decades, about 35 to 40 percent of voters have supported abortion without significant restrictions, 10 to 20 percent have opposed it under all circumstances, and the remaining 40 to 55 percent have favored abortion rights with some restrictions. . . (Judis, 2000:12).

Bias against the Poor

According to the Hyde amendment, mothers on public assistance cannot obtain abortions through Medicaid. Pro-abortion advocates argue that the federal and state decisions denying public funding for abortions make the abortion option less feasible for those women least able to afford children. Faced with the high cost of an abortion, poor women are either forced to have the baby and keep it, to have the baby and place it for adoption, or to attempt self-induced abortions. The result is that about four in ten poor teens have abortions, compared to seven in ten higher-income teens (Goodman, 1995). The irony, of course, is that poor women who want abortions but cannot afford them have their babies and then are vilified for having babies to increase their welfare checks. In terms of social policy, public funding of reproductive services would save dollars.

> Every public dollar spent on family planning saves $4 on medical and welfare costs. So does every dollar spent on abortion. Funding Medicaid abortions would save $612 million over two years. Not by encouraging abortion, but by enabling poor women to make their own choices. Just like women who aren't poor (Goodman, 1995:A8).

WELFARE

In 1999 some 11.8 percent of the population (32.3 million people) were below the poverty line of $13,290 for a family of three and $17,029 for a four-person family (U.S. Bureau of the Census, 2000). Since the 1930s the United States has had a fairly comprehensive welfare program to help those in need. This changed in 1996, when the federal government cut federal aid to the poor and eliminated welfare to poor women with children. Let's first examine the welfare system in place until 1996 and then review the changes and consequences resulting from the recent welfare legislation.

The Shrinking Welfare State

From 1935 to 1996 the United States had a minimal welfare program for those in need. The New Deal under President Roosevelt and the Great Society under President Johnson created the minimum wage, federal aid to education, health and nutrition programs, food stamps, energy assistance, subsidized housing, and Aid to Families with Dependent Children (Moen and Forest, 1999:644-647). Beginning with President Nixon and accelerating under President Reagan, this welfare program was gradually dismantled. This dismemberment quickened appreciably in 1996, when the federal government made welfare assistance to families temporary and withdrew $55 billion of federal aid to the poor.

The Personal Responsibility and Work Opportunity Reconciliation Act of 1996

The welfare system prior to 1996 needed an overhaul. Its provisions encouraged dependency because recipients who got off welfare lost Medicaid. It provided disincentives to work because money earned was subtracted from welfare payments. By leaving the distribution of benefits for many programs to the states, there were wide disparities. And the benefits provided were never enough to lift many people out of poverty. The welfare system, however, did help many on the economic margins to receive enough to get by. A study by the Center on Budget and Policy Priorities showed that federal and state antipoverty programs lifted many out of poverty.

> The study found that without such assistance, 57.6 million people would have been poor in 1995. "But when government benefits are counted, including food stamps, housing assistance, school lunch support and benefits provided through the earned-income tax credit, *the number of poor people drops to 30.3 million*" (reported in Herbert,1996:68A, emphasis added).

Although this difference is certainly important, the government could do much better if it chose to do so. For example, France and the United States both would have child poverty rates of about 25 percent if it were not for government assistance. With the generous government assistance provided in France, the child poverty rate is just 6.5 percent. The minimal U.S. welfare program, on the other hand, reduces the child poverty rate to only about 21 percent (Raspberry, 1997).

Conservatives and progressives wanted to reform the welfare system, but rather than reform, in 1996 the Republican-dominated Congress and a middle-of-the-road Democratic President passed a sweeping welfare law that ended the sixty-one-year-old safety net for the poor, completing the "Reagan Revolution" (Watts, 1997:409). The major provisions of this law (as later amended) include the following (much of the description of the new welfare law and its consequences is from the Children's Defense Fund, 1997; Edelman, 1997; Schorr, 1997; Watts, 1997; Pavetti, 2000; and Eitzen, 1996):

1. States, through federal block grants, are given a fixed sum of money and considerable flexibility in how to spend it.
2. The law insisted on work. The states were required to demand that parents work within two years of receiving cash assistance, although the states had the right to shorten the period before welfare recipients must work.
3. The law mandated a five-year lifetime limit on the receipt of assistance, which states can reduce if they wish.
4. The law required that unmarried teen parents must live at home or in another adult-supervised setting and attend school to receive welfare assistance. The states again had the option of ending assistance for teen parents who have children outside marriage.
5. Various federal assistance programs targeted for the poor were cut by $54.5 billion over six years. Included in these budget cuts were $27 billion from the food stamp program, $7 billion from the children's portion of the Supplemental Security Income program, $3 billion over six years for child nutrition, and a six-year total of $2.5 billion for social services. Cuts were also made by tightening the qualifying criteria for being defined as a disabled child. Ironically, the narrowed eligibility requirements result in the loss of coverage for some children who if they were adults would be considered disabled" (Edelman, 1997:48).
6. The welfare law denied a broad range of public benefits to legal immigrants. All legal immigrants were cut off from food stamps, and those who entered the country after the welfare bill was signed were ineligible for federal programs such as Supplemental Security Income and state-run programs such as temporary welfare and Medicaid.
7. The federal money given to the states is now capped at $16.4 billion annually. This is significant because it means that there is no adjustment for inflation and population growth. In effect, by 2002 the states will have considerably less federal money to spend on welfare than they did under the old welfare provisions.

In sum, this new welfare legislation ended the entitlement, which guaranteed that states must give help to all needy families with children. Now assistance for poor families was temporary (Aid to Families with Dependent Children—AFDC—was replaced by Temporary Assistance for Needy Families—TANF), with parents required to work. Assuming the passage of the 1996 Welfare Act, *The Nation* (a progressive publication) editorialized, "There is now a bipartisan agreement that the United States bears no responsibility for its poorest families" (*The Nation*, 1995:371).

The Conservative Assumptions Guiding Current Welfare Policy and the Progressive Response

Assumptions from conservative ideology provide the bedrock of the 1996 welfare law. First, there is the assumption that welfare programs establish perverse incentives that keep the beneficiaries from working and encourage them to have babies outside marriage. That is, welfare is so generous that it makes sense to stay on welfare rather than go to work. Moreover, because the benefits increase with each child, women on welfare make the rational decision to have more children. Progressives argue that this reasoning is fallacious because it ignores five facts: (1) the average monthly AFDC payment, accounting for inflation, had withered by almost 50 percent since 1970, yet the birth rate for unmarried mothers soared during this period; (2) the average monthly AFDC payment plus food stamps provided benefits that were much below the poverty line; (3) states with low welfare benefits had higher illegitimacy rates than states with higher welfare benefits; (4) New Jersey's 1993 law that ended the practice of increasing a welfare check when a recipient had another baby did *not* drive down birth rates among women on welfare (Healy, 1997); and (5) the much more generous welfare states of Canada, Western Europe, and Scandinavia have much lower out-of-wedlock birth rates than found in the United States.

A second assumption of the lawmakers is that when poor people are confronted with a "sink or swim" world, they will develop the motivation and the skill to stay afloat (Murray, 1984). If welfare recipients are forced off welfare, their only recourse will be to work, resulting in productive people rather than parasites. Progressives, however, note that under current societal conditions many of the poor will "sink" even if they want to "swim." There are not enough jobs. Many of the jobs that are available do not lift the poor out of poverty. And many who are being pushed "into the pool" cannot "swim" because of some disability.

Third, welfare dependency is assumed to be the source of poverty, illegitimacy, laziness, crime, unemployment, and other social pathologies. Progressives, however, point to the nations with much more generous welfare systems than in the United States (Canada, Scandinavia, and Western Europe), noting that cities in those countries are much safer and that violent crime is much lower than in the United States, as is the rate of teenage pregnancy.

Fourth, the United States is an individualistic and competitive society. The obvious result of competition and a market economy is inequality, and that is good because it motivates people to compete and weeds out the weak. Following this logic of the conservatives, losers are responsible for their situation. Therefore, it is not the responsibility of society to take care of them. Progressives argue, to the contrary, that the causes of poverty are complex, involving social location (class, race, gender), the changing economy, the lack of good jobs, institutional racism and sexism, the maldistribution of resources for schools, and inadequate pay and benefits for low-end jobs. Thus, a cure for poverty involves much more than greater individual effort and elimination of the welfare system. It requires structural changes in society.

A final assumption underlying the welfare legislation of 1996 is that the able poor must work. Many poor people are labeled as undeserving because it does not appear that they help themselves. That belief, however, is false. It assumes, for example, that welfare mothers are unable or unwilling to work. Research from a number of studies shows that most welfare recipients earn extra money from various activities, such as house cleaning, doing laundry, repairing clothing, childcare, and selling items that they have made. For example, sociologist Kathleen Harris, summarizing her findings from a nationally representative sample of single mothers who received welfare, says that

> I found exclusive dependence on welfare to be rare. More than half of the single mothers whom I studied worked while they were on welfare, and two-thirds left the welfare rolls when they could support themselves with jobs. However, more than half (57 percent) of the women who worked their way off public assistance later returned because their jobs ended or they still could not make ends meet (Harris, 1996:B7).

This outside work to supplement welfare is necessary because welfare payments are insufficient to meet their economic necessities. This gap is made up through various strategies (agency), including income-producing work and help from family, friends, neighbors, boyfriends, and absent fathers.

A question arising from the requirement that all welfare recipients work is whether a single mother is "able" to work (McLarin, 1995). Traditionally, she was not considered so. AFDC was created in 1935 with the goal of keeping women at home with their children. The new legislation has changed that, forcing poor women with children to work, without training, without jobs, and without child care. Through twisted logic, the same politicians who want poor mothers to work want middle-class mothers to give up their jobs because a stay-at-home mother is positive for children.

Another issue regarding work has to do with its availability. During the Great Depression the federal government provided jobs to the poor. These jobs included constructing roads, bridges, and buildings; planting trees to stop wind erosion; and the like. This government jobs program was successful. The jobs provided society with important projects and needy individuals with income and skill development. The situation is different now. The new legislation mandates that poor people work, but *without* providing the jobs.

> This punitive overhaul [of the welfare system] sends [welfare recipients] off on their own to secure work in a world of downsizing, layoffs and capital flight. Where are the welfare recipients going to find stable jobs? How can they pay for health insurance and child care when they earn the minimum wage? What will happen to their children? (*The Nation*, 1995:372.)

Underscoring one of the preceding points is that working for the minimum wage, which most former welfare recipients do, gives a full-time worker an annual income that is more than $2500 *below* the poverty line for a family of three.

The Consequences of the 1996 Welfare Legislation for Families

Although the time has been relatively short since the 1996 welfare legislation, we can examine some preliminary results and anticipate the legislation's longer-term effects. During the four years after the enactment of the welfare legislation, 6.6 million people left welfare for work. Thus, it appears, the 1996 welfare legislation was working by replacing welfare with work. This interpretation is much too optimistic for at least five reasons. First, those who left the welfare rolls initially were likely the easiest to place in jobs (that is, they had some secondary education and job experience). The much more difficult task will be to find jobs for those who have little education, work experience, or job skills or who are functionally disabled. In 2000 there were still 6.9 million on welfare, and these will be the most difficult to place in the labor market.

Second, the welfare legislation was passed at a propitious historical moment—during an economic expansion, when jobs were being created and unemployment was low. During the four years after passage the unemployment rate ranged between 4 and 5 percent, the lowest rates in a quarter-century. Because of a growing economy the welfare rolls declined by 10 percent in the two years *before* the 1996 legislation (Jencks and Swingle, 2000). And, from 1994 to 2001, the welfare rolls were cut in half. But is this significant reduction because of welfare reform that forces single mothers to work, or is it the product of an extraordinary economic boom that allowed millions of low-skilled women to increase their incomes? What will happen when the employment rate goes up to 7 or 8 percent, or worse, when there is an economic recession? In either situation there will be layoffs, which means that the last to be hired (the workers only recently off welfare) will be the first to be fired. If these former employees had used up their time limits for welfare, they will be on their own without a safety net—with nowhere to turn for rent, utilities, food, and health care.

When the economy slows down, as it inevitably will, many of the working poor and former welfare recipients will lose their jobs. What will happen to them when they cannot pay their rents or house payments, or their utility bills, or medical bills? Under the previous welfare system, many families were just a lost job, divorce, or medical disaster away from losing their housing. The fastest growing category of homeless during the late 1980s and early 1990s was families (Timmer et al., 1994). Under the new welfare law, and especially when society experiences an economic downturn, will increasing numbers of families have to move into substandard housing or even into homeless shelters? According to Peter Edelman,

> There will be suffering. Some of the damage will be obvious—more homelessness, for example, with more demand on already strapped shelters and soup kitchens. The ensuing problems will also appear as increases in the incidence of other problems, directly but perhaps not probably owing to the impact of the welfare bill. There will be more malnuitrition and more crime, increased infant mortality, and increased drug and alcohol abuse. There will be increased family violence and abuse against children and women, and a consequent significant spillover of the problem into the already overloaded child-welfare system and battered women's shelters (Edelman, 1997:53).

Third, and related to the second reason, the availability of low-end jobs is distributed unevenly. Some social categories have more difficulty getting low-wage employment than others. Women make up almost 60 percent of the low-wage sector. "And not surprisingly, in the fierce competition for jobs in that sector, individuals who are young, black and non-college educated fare the worst" (Herbert, 1997b:70). When the unemployment rate was 5.2 percent in 1996, unemployment among young African American women (ages fifteen to twenty-five with a high school diploma) was 19.7 percent (Economic Policy Report, cited in Herbert, 1997b).

The job squeeze also occurs geographically. Some states have relatively little difficulty in moving people from welfare to work, whereas others face difficulties in doing so. Some regions (the coal mining region in Appalachia), states such as California, and cities such as New York have to overcome a mismatch—huge numbers on welfare and relatively few jobs. There are many pockets of rural poverty where jobs are few and poverty high. In the eleven delta counties of Mississippi, for example, the poverty rate is 41 percent and unemployment more than double the national rate. Frank Howell of Mississippi State University has estimated that for every 254 families leaving welfare in those counties, only one new job will be created (cited in DeParle, 1997b).

Fourth, 40 percent of those who have been forced off of welfare are *not* working (Rogers-Dillon, 2001). Now they have neither welfare nor work. Peter Edelman, assistant secretary for planning and evaluation at the Department of Health and Human Services in the Clinton administration who resigned his post in protest to the 1996 welfare legislation, said this about the former welfare recipients who do not work:

> The math goes like this. About 2.5 million women have left the welfare rolls. About 60 percent of those—more in some states, less in others—have jobs. That means that about 1.5 million of those women are employed. But it also means that 40 percent, or about a million, don't. With their children, that's 3 million people. They are America's disappeared. We don't know what has happened to them, although it is easy enough to find them one by one on a visit to any transitional shelter for homeless families in any major city (Edelman, 2000:3).

Fifth, the jobs that many former welfare recipients get pay less than subsistence wages and have little if any benefits. A study by the Center on Budget and Policy Priorities found that after the first year of welfare reform, the income of the poorest 10 percent of female-headed families *fell* an average of $580, which represented about one-seventh of their income. This study included in the definition of income, food stamps, housing subsidies, the Earned Income Tax Credit, and similar benefits (reported in Sawyer, 1999). Over 1.25 million, the majority of whom were children, lost Medicaid coverage and became uninsured due to welfare reform. Moreover, the meager take-home pay is reduced further for those who must pay for child care. In short, leaving welfare for a job does not, for many, end poverty.

If, however, mandatory employment is coupled with extra benefits such as child care and housing subsidies, the results for children are positive. Research on children three to twelve years old in California, Florida, Georgia, Michigan, Minnesota, and Wisconsin found that employment of the parents alone did not foster the healthy development of children (reported in Pear, 2001). When employment and other benefits increase family income above their former welfare income, children do better in school than children in similar poor families that simply receive cash assistance under the old welfare rules. The key, then, is family income. If it rises, children do better in school. If it falls, as will happen in an economic downturn, then the school performance of the children affected will decline.

A major concern with the welfare legislation is that by pushing the poor into an already crowded workforce, wages for low-end jobs will be driven down.

This hurts those leaving welfare as well as the working poor. There are 38 million working poor who receive $7.50 or less an hour for work and usually have no health insurance. What will happen to their wages and jobs when the remainder of those people on welfare are added to the workforce, as mandated by the law? Employers are prohibited from firing existing workers to hire welfare recipients whose compensation is subsidized by the state. However, employers can reduce working hours, wages, and benefits for existing workers, a likely occurrence. The plight of the working poor, always marginal, thus becomes worse because of welfare reform. Researchers at the Economic Policy Institute estimate that with the addition of 1 million new low-wage workers, the income of the bottom 30 percent of earners will be reduced on average by 11.9 percent. This drop in wages will be even more severe in those states and locales with large numbers of people on welfare (McCrate, 1997). This has at least three additional negative consequences. First, it weakens those labor unions that organize low-pay workers such as janitors, municipal workers, and food handlers. This weakness reinforces low wages and minimal benefits for the economically marginal. Second, the anger of the working poor most likely will be directed at the former welfare recipients, not the economic system that limits their opportunities and exploits them. Third, and related to the second, the anger of the working poor will likely be overtly racist, as the working poor perceive their economic situation reduced by racial minorities and immigrants, whom they believe are the majority of welfare recipients (a belief that is false—Whites outnumber African Americans and Latinos among welfare recipients).

In the past the newly unemployed and the poor were eligible for food stamps and other benefits. Under the new policy, however, able-bodied adults under age fifty without children can receive food stamps for only three months in any three-year period. Benefits for parents will be cut off after two years. What will be the consequences for the poor, and especially their children, of being cut off from food stamps, child nutrition programs, school lunch programs, and housing subsidy programs? Two consequences are increases in hunger and homelessness. A survey of twenty-five cities by the U.S. Conference of Mayors found that the demanded for hunger assistance in those cities increased by 18 percent in 1998 and another 17 percent in 1999. Similar spikes in requests also occurred in the demand for emergency shelter (reported in Halladay, 2000).

For those who experience poverty because of the welfare legislation there are negative effects on their families. Stephanie Coontz summarizes what previous research predicts:

> Poor couples are twice as likely to divorce as more affluent ones. Jobless individuals are three to four times less likely to marry. And teens who live in areas of high unemployment and inferior school systems are six to seven times more likely to become unwed parents than more fortunate teens. Dozens of research studies show that the most effective deterrent to early childbearing is access to, among other things, good schools and steady jobs (Coontz, 1994:19).

Is the answer to these poverty-related problems a more feeble welfare system or a more robust one? Progressives argue that the only way to help the poor is to spend more money, not less, as the government has done since the Reagan administration. This money would be spent on helping people with child care, increasing the minimum wage, increasing the Earned Income Tax Credit, providing job training and education programs, providing universal health care (at present we provide some health care for the poor through Medicaid but do not help the working poor—clearly, a perverse incentive system), and reducing the tax burden on the poor who are trying to work their way out of poverty.

The new welfare legislation hits several social categories particularly hard. Legal immigrants arriving after August 1996 are denied Supplemental Security Income, and all legal immigrants, regardless of time of entry, are denied food stamps (930,000 on the day the ban went into effect). Another group disadvantaged by the new welfare law was the 135,000 disabled children who were denied welfare assistance under the more rigorous definitions employed in the new law. In terms of numbers, the new welfare legislation primarily affects women and their children, the prime recipients of AFDC. This law contains no provisions requiring the states to provide educational or job-training programs. Without education,

> . . . women's wages will not grow, and without growth in their wages, welfare mothers will never be able to afford child care or health care. . . . Eliminating welfare without improving the pay and benefits of the jobs they can get—or improving their ability to get better jobs—can have only one result: an increase in poverty among women and children (Harris, 1996:B7).

Finally, there is a major concern with the abdication of federal responsibility for welfare. As a result of turning over welfare to the states, we have fifty different welfare programs. This devolution has the effect of making benefits very uneven, as some states will be relatively generous and others will be much less so. States' rights have not always worked in the past. "States failed in the past to take the lead in trying to end racial discrimination or to alleviate unemployment and poverty. That's why the country needs the New Deal, civil rights legislation, and social welfare programs" (Hettleman, 1997:24; see also Schlesinger, quoted in Shanker, 1995:E7).

What Is Missing in the New Welfare Legislation?

Foremost, the legislation ignored the conclusions of social science research (Astone, 1997). This research documents, for example, that 70 percent of ADFC recipients left welfare within two years. We also know that nearly three-fourths of those who left end up back on welfare because of inadequate pay, the lack of medical benefits, or their lack of job skills. Social science research also informs us of the detrimental effects of poverty on marriage relationships, the increased probability of spouse and child abuse, and the dismal future for many children of the poor.

Second, while focusing on the replacement of work for welfare, there is no provision for jobs, and if one finds work, there is no assistance for transportation (two-thirds of all new jobs are in the suburbs, while three-quarters of welfare recipients live in central cities or rural areas); and there is only a modest child-care subsidy.

Third, the welfare legislation targeted single mothers, forcing them off welfare. Missing was any effort to protect their children from the pernicious effects of poverty (Lerner et al., 1999). The U.S. Department of Health and Human Services, using optimistic assumptions that two-thirds of long-term welfare recipients would find jobs after two years and that the states would maintain their current levels of financial support, predicted that the new welfare would move 2.6 million people, including 1.1 million children, into poverty. Moreover, more than 8 million families with children would lose an average of $1300 per family (cited in Edelman, 1997:46). Thus, more children than ever will be further impoverished, which will have serious debilitating consequences for them. As Marian Wright Edelman has stated, "The elimination of the national guarantee to protect children is a moral outrage . . . a massive betrayal that places the lives of many of our youngest and most vulnerable citizens in grave danger" (Edelman, 1996:1).

The fourth missing ingredient in the new welfare legislation is an understanding of the structural sources of poverty and meeting the challenges of a rapidly changing economy.

Fifth, the welfare legislation did not address the real issue—ending poverty. "Many of us had assumed that welfare reform was fueled by a desire to eliminate poverty. This is not the case. Under the new law, welfare is seen as an issue in and of itself, divorced from issues of poverty. *Ending welfare had nothing to do with addressing poverty*" (Watts, 1997:412).

And, sixth, the program is not adequately funded. Minnesota's welfare reform program is generously funded so that former recipients retain some of the benefits after they go to work, receive tax credits, health insurance, and childcare assistance (Wolf, 2000a). This program costs from $1900 to $3800 more per family each year than the state's former welfare program. In return, research shows that for those in the program, income was higher, poverty reduced, and families strengthened. Tommy Thompson, the former governor of Wisconsin and Secretary of Health and Human Services under President George W. Bush, said in his confirmation hearings that for "welfare reform to be successful, you have to make an investment up front. It can't be done on the cheap. You can't expect welfare mothers to go to work unless they have child care. They've got to have health insurance, transportation and training. All cost money. The savings to taxpayers, and they are substantial, come later as caseloads decline" (quoted in Pear, 2001:3).

MEETING THE NEEDS OF DISADVANTAGED CHILDREN

Poor children are at great risk in the United States and are the most neglected in the developed world.

Children in the United States are 1.6 times more likely to be poor than those in Canada, two times more likely than those in Britain, and three times more likely than those in France or Germany, even though the United States is the wealthiest of these nations and has lower unemployment levels (Children's Defense Fund, 1997:17).

In 1999 there were 12.1 million children under age eighteen (16.9 percent) below the poverty line (U.S. Bureau of the Census, 2000). Children under age six living in a household headed by a single woman had a poverty rate of 50.3 percent compared to the rate (9.0 percent) for children in married-couple families. While only 8 percent of White children under age eighteen were poor, 23 percent of Latino children, were, as were 33 percent of African American children. These differences in child poverty by race are more severe if we consider deep poverty (i.e., those families with incomes below one-half the poverty threshold), with Latino (8 percent) and African American (15 percent) children much more likely to be very poor than White children (3 percent).

Poor Children at Risk

Each of the problems mentioned in this section hits poor children the hardest. They are more likely than privileged children to suffer from low birth weight, more likely to be exposed to toxic chemicals, and the least likely to receive good nutrition and decent medical care, including immunization against contagious diseases. They are also more likely to miss out on preschool education.

> Childhood poverty impairs physical growth, cognitive ability (e.g., reading ability), and socioemotional functioning (e.g., behavioral problems, depression). . . . The incidence, duration, and chronicity of childhood poverty also have large negative effects on children's IQ, educational achievement, and later adult productivity (Lichter, 1997:122).

Infant Mortality

Family poverty is strongly correlated with premature delivery; postnatal, infant, and childhood mortality; malnutrition; and ill-health (Leach, 1994:188). The United States ranks low among the industrialized nations in infant mortality (an overall rate in 1998 of 7.2 deaths per 1000 live births). Infant mortality is an important measure of the well-being of infants, children, and pregnant women because it is closely related with such factors as maternal health, quality of access to medical care, social class, and public health practices (the following data are from Federal Interagency Forum on Child and Family Statistics, 2000). As a result of the confluence of these factors, *African American babies are more than two times more likely to die as White infants* (a rate of 13.7 for African Americans, compared with 6.0 for Whites).* Infant mortality results, for the most part, because children are born too soon or too small. Those who survive low birth weight are more likely to grow up deaf, blind, or mentally retarded than normal-birth-weight babies. Again, the rate of African American low birth weight (13.2 percent in 1998) is *more than twice that of Whites* (6.6 percent). Among Latinos, women of Mexican origin have the lowest percentage of low-birth-weight infants (6.0 percent) and Puerto Ricans the highest (9.7 percent). Among Asian Americans, low birth weight was lowest for births to women of Chinese origin (5.3 percent) and highest for women of Filipino origin (8.2 percent).

*The maternal death rate (deaths per 100,000 live births) is 7.7 for women generally. For African American women the maternal death rate is four times the rate for Whites (Spake, 1999).

Much of infant mortality is preventable. One-third of pregnant women (about 1.3 million women a year, with 30 percent of Latino women and 27 percent of African American women) receive inadequate prenatal care, mostly because they lack economic resources, including medical insurance. In 1998 some 43 million people in the United States did not have health insurance, including 11 million children. By race/ethnicity, 30 percent of Latino children were not covered by health insurance, 20 percent of African American children were not covered, compared to 11 percent of White children who were uninsured (Federal Interagency Forum on Child and Family Statistics, 2000).

Infectious Diseases

The most recent data (1998) show that 79 percent of children ages nineteen to thirty-five months were appropriately immunized. Those children not immunized were disproportionately the poor and racial minorities. This situation has improved markedly since 1993, when Congress passed the Vaccines for Children program, which subsidized vaccinations for uninsured, Medicaid-eligible, and Native American children.

Exposure to Toxic Chemicals

Poor children often live in environmentally unsafe situations. Affordable housing for the poor and the near-poor is often found where the air, water, and land are polluted. Especially dangerous for young children is exposure to lead, which is related to behavioral problems, reduced intelligence, and problems with speech. Substances such as PCBs (polychlorinated biphenyls) and mercury, the by-products of chemical and industrial production, not only cause cancer and birth defects, but there is evidence tying these compounds to lack of coordination, diminished intelligence, and poor memory in children (Kaplan and Morris, 2000). Children can also be exposed to pesticides and herbicides in the air or from the food they ingest.

Hunger and Malnutrition

The good health and development of children depend on a diet sufficient in nutrients and calories. In 1999, 3.8 percent of children lived in diet-insufficient households. Nine out of ten of these children were in households below the federal poverty level. Quality of food, as measured by the government's Healthy Eating Index, appears to be a problem for most U.S. children, a problem that worsens as they move toward adolescence. That is, most children do not eat enough fruit and vegetables and eat too much saturated fat and sugar. Children in families below the poverty level are less likely than higher-income families to have a diet rated as good (Federal Interagency Forum on Child and Family Statistics, 2000).

Educational Deficits

One result of these problems—exposure to toxic chemicals, lack of adequate health care, inadequate diet—is that when poor children start school, they are already behind. "At age 5, poor children are often less alert, less curious, and less effective at interacting with their peers than are more privileged youngsters"

(Hewlett, 1991:56). Moreover, poor children are more likely than privileged children to attend schools that are poorly staffed, overcrowded, and ill equipped, because schools are financed primarily through the property wealth of the districts. The consequence for them and for society is that they will likely be underachievers.

The Societal Response to Disadvantaged Children

What do we do about the 12.1 million impoverished children and the many millions more whose families are just above the government's poverty line? There is strong evidence that poor children—hungry, ill housed, and unhealthy—will not do as well as their more privileged peers in school and will be more likely to fall into self-destructive and nonproductive activities as they grow up. Clearly, the conditions of poverty will likely keep them from reaching their potential. These facts do not jibe with the great value Americans place on "equal opportunity."

If we choose, we can reduce or even eliminate poverty for children and their parents. Other societies have chosen to do this (e.g., the social democracies of Europe) with success. The United States has actually taken the opposite position by eliminating AFDC payments, by cutting back on nutrition programs, by making only token efforts at job training, and by keeping the minimum wage too low.

Reducing Poverty for the Elderly while Increasing Poverty for the Young

As a nation, the United States has taken deliberate actions to reduce poverty among older Americans while simultaneously allowing childhood poverty to increase. In 1970, the proportion of elderly in poverty was double the national average, yet by 1999 the poverty rate among the elderly was below the national average (9.7 percent compared to the national rate of 11.8 percent). The poverty rate for children under age eighteen in 1970 was over one-third lower than that for the elderly. By 1999, this situation had changed, with 16.9 percent of children under age eighteen living in poverty (U.S. Bureau of the Census, 2000) (see Figure 13.1).

During the last twenty years, federal benefits to the elderly have risen from one-sixth of the federal budget to 30 percent (to about $300 billion annually). This increase occurred because federal policy makers created programs such as Medicare and Medicaid and because Social Security benefits were indexed to offset inflation. Conversely, however, these same decision makers did not provide adequately for needy families with children. The government actually reduced or eliminated the programs targeted to benefit children (e.g., the children's share of Medicaid, Aid to Families with Dependent Children, Head Start, food stamps, child nutrition, and federal aid to education).

Childhood poverty is especially acute for racial minorities. The bias against children in federal programs is heightened for minority children. Former Senator Daniel Patrick Moynihan pointed out that there are two ways in which the federal government provides benefits to children in single-parent families. The first is Aid to Families with Dependent Children. The majority of the children receiving this type of aid are African American or Latino. Since 1970, the gov-

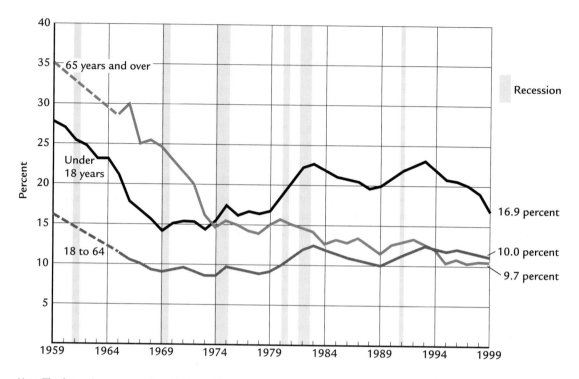

Figure 13.1

Poverty rates by age: 1959 to 1999

Note: The data points represent the midpoints of the respective years. The latest recession began in July 1990 and ended in March 1991. Data for people 18 to 64 and 65 and older are not available from 1960 to 1965.

Source: U.S Bureau of the Census, "Poverty in the United States: 1999," *Current Population Reports,* P60-210 (September 2000), p. ix.

ernment has decreased the real benefits by 13 percent, and in 1996 it placed a two-year limit on benefits. The other form of assistance is Survivors Insurance (SI), which is part of Social Security. The majority of children receiving SI benefits are White, and these benefits have increased by 53 percent since 1970 (adjusted for inflation). Moynihan, writing eight years before the 1996 welfare legislation, said:

> To those who say we don't care about children in our country, may I note that the average provision for children under SI has been rising five times as fast as average family income since 1970. We do care about some children. Majority children. It is minority children—not only but mostly—who are left behind (Moynihan, 1988:5).

Another telling illustration is that while Congress in 1996 eliminated AFDC and severely cut food stamps and school nutrition programs for the poor, it did not cut cash and food programs for poor senior citizens.

The decisions to help the elderly disproportionately reflect the electoral power that the elderly have compared to the young. The elderly are organized, with several national organizations dedicated to political action that will benefit their interests. The American Association of Retired Persons, for example, is the nation's largest special-interest organization, with close to 40 million members. With the elderly making up 16 percent of the voting public (and much more in states such as Florida and Arizona, which have high concentrations of elderly people), politicians pay attention to their special needs.

Children, on the other hand, have no electoral power and few advocates (an exception is the Children's Defense Fund). Their parents, especially those who are poor, are not organized. So, in a time of fiscal austerity, the needs of children—prenatal care for poor women, nutritional and health care, daycare, and better schools—are underfunded. The irony here is that the political right wing, which claims to be pro-family, limits its political agenda to antiabortion legislation and court cases and ignores or resists governmental assistance to needy children and their struggling parents.

The argument here is not that the elderly and the young should compete for scarce resources and that one or the other should win. Rather, both age groups are dependents and are in need. The test of a civilization is the condition of its dependents. So far the United States has opted to care moderately well for one and not at all well for the other.

Inadequate Government Programs for Impoverished Youth

Although the evidence is clear that investing in children saves money in the long run (Children's Defense Fund, 1997; *Denver Post*, 2000), government programs continue either to neglect the needs of poor children or to provide only modestly for them. Examples include the following:

- Government support for prenatal care among high-risk groups has declined significantly since 1980.
- The U.S. health care system is based on the principle that the users of services pay fees either directly or through insurance. Those who cannot afford these fees may seek public assistance. The services provided to those seeking assistance are defined differently by each state, as are the rules of eligibility. The result is that only about half of all poor children qualify for such help.
- The Centers for Disease Control have recommended that all children under the age of six be screened for lead in the blood, yet only one child in ten receives such testing.
- The Special Supplemental Food Program for Women, Infants, and Children (WIC) provides mothers with vouchers to buy infant formula and wholesome foods (at a cost of about $30 a month), yet government funds support only about 60 percent of women and infants who qualify for the program. Congress reduced the funds for WIC for fiscal 1997.
- Only about 40 percent of the children eligible for Head Start actually participate because the program is underfunded.

The Special Case of Preschool Programs to Enhance Cognitive Ability

Children from impoverished backgrounds tend to do less well than their more privileged counterparts in school (grades, scoring on intelligence tests, deportment). This, of course, disadvantages them in school and in opportunities when they complete school. The reasons for this deficit are complex. Some of the possibilities are as follows. (1) Their home environments are less likely to involve reading and other cognitive stimulation that is useful in school. (2) Their experiences outside the neighborhood are more limited (e.g., trips to museums, zoos, national parks). (3) They are less likely to have computers and other recent technologies at home. (4) The language spoken at home may not be English or, if English, it may not be grammatically correct. (5) The tests are biased for middle-class experiences. (6) Children of the affluent are more likely to attend early childhood development programs, which prepares them for school, than are children of the poor. (7) Poor children usually attend inferior schools. (8) Some would even argue that the poor are genetically disadvantaged. This last point is the old social Darwinism argument that the poor are poor because they do not have what it takes to succeed. In other words, in a competitive society they are where they should be.

This brings us to the serious question: Is intelligence immutable, or is it possible to boost cognitive development? Head Start is one federally funded program that has documented positive effects for economically disadvantaged children. Lisbeth Schorr has summarized what is known about this excellent program:

> The basic Head Start model has proved to be sound. When three- to five-year-old children are systematically helped to think, reason, and speak clearly; when they are provided hot meals, social services, health evaluations, and health care; when families become partners in their children's learning experiences, are helped toward self-sufficiency, and gain greater confidence in themselves as parents and as contributing members of the community, the results are measurable and dramatic (Schorr, 1988:192; see Schorr, 1997).

In effect, a number of studies have shown that Head Start programs raise IQ scores among poor children by as much as 10 points. These results, however, fade out entirely by the sixth grade. Yet this rise and fall of IQ scores makes the case for the role of environmental factors in cognitive development. As Maschinot has argued,

> [The critics of Head Start] ignore the obvious fact that once they leave Head Start, poor students typically attend substandard schools from the first grade onward. The fact that IQ scores drop again after this experience should lead one logically to conclude that intelligence as defined by IQ tests is highly responsive to environmental manipulations, not the reverse (Maschinot, 1995:33).

Research outside of Head Start provides further justification for the Head Start model. The Abecedarian Project, conducted at the University of North Carolina, reinforces the belief that the early education of poor children pays off in cognitive advancement. This project has been rigorously researched (see Box 13.2) to assess the effects of assisting poor children in their preschool years and during their school years. By the time the children reached age twenty-one, research shows that they benefitted by delayed parenthood, higher IQs, higher reading and math scores, and more years of formal education (Ramey et al., 1999).

A second study, by the Robert Wood Johnson Foundation, of low-birth-weight infants followed their development for three years. The researchers found that the ones who had a stimulating daycare environment had, on aver-

Researching Families: Nature Versus Nurture: Can IQ Be Raised?

There is a longstanding debate on the role of the environment on intelligence (see Herrnstein and Murray, 1994; and Maschinot, 1995). Do impoverished children have different IQs than privileged children because of heredity, or is it environment? Let's examine one test to see whether environment makes a difference on IQ scores.

The Abecedarian Project used an experimental design to assess the effects of environment (the following information is from Campbell and Ramey, 1994). Ramey and his associates began with educationally high-risk children from 120 families. The IQs of the biological mothers averaged 85; 98 percent of the children were African American; the average maternal age was 19.9 years when the target child was born; maternal education averaged 10.6 years; the median earned family income was none; and three-fourths of the families were single-parent. From four months onward, half of these children (the experimental group) were randomly placed in a preschool where the staff focused on language development, preliteracy skills, and social development. The other half (the control group) stayed at home. When the children in the two groups reached kindergarten age, they were randomly divided again. Half of the experimental group received no further special treatment. The other half of the experimental group and half of the control group received help in school for the next eight years. This help was a Home School Resource Teacher assigned to work with the parents of each child on individualized sets of educational activities to target basic skills. To summarize the procedures, there are four randomly selected groups: one received an enriched program for twelve years; another received this program for the first four years of life; another did not receive it for four years but did for the next eight; and one did not receive any enrichment at all. The results are as follows: (1) by age three the children in the experimental group averaged 17 points higher than the control group on IQ tests (101 versus 84); (2) these differences, although less pronounced, persisted more than a decade later (the difference was now about 10 IQ points). Campbell and Ramey concluded that

> . . . for impoverished children, the earlier in the life span education occurs, the greater its benefit is likely to be. . . . The most important policy implication of these findings is that early educational intervention for impoverished children can have long-lasting benefits, in terms of improved cognitive performance. This underscores the critical importance of good early environments and suggests that the focus of debate should now be shifted from whether government should play a role in encouraging good early environments to how these environments can be assured (Campbell and Ramey, 1994:694–695).

age, a 13-point higher IQ score than the babies who did not receive those experiences (reported in Richmond, 1994).

As a final example, there is a study of high-risk African American children in Ypsilanti, Michigan. The children were divided randomly into two groups. One group received a high-quality active learning program as three- and four-year-olds. The other group got no preschool education. The groups were compared when they were age twenty-seven, with these results:

> By age 27, those who had received the preschool education had half as many arrests as the comparison group. Four times as many were earning $2,000 or more a

month. Three times as many owned their own homes. One-third more had gradu-ated from high school on schedule. One-fourth fewer of them needed welfare as adults. And they had one-third fewer children born out of wedlock. Analysis of the data collected about these young people over the years shows that every dollar spent on their preschool education has netted $7.16 saving later on for taxpayers (Beck, 1995:7B).

The good news is that we know that early education helps poor youth pre-pare for school—and the earlier this education occurs, the better the results. The problem is that the majority of children from poor families do not have preschool programs to prepare them for school. Head Start, the major government pro-gram, is underfunded, reaching only two in five eligible children, and only about 30 percent of programs operate year-round.

The neglect of children, especially poor children, in their earliest years is a crisis, resulting in millions who grow up to live stunted lives. Lisbeth Schorr pro-vides a fundamental reason for our neglect:

> Our national failure to act on what we know about the early years is the product, at least in part, of our commitment to rugged individualism. The notion that every family should be able to care for its own, without outside help, has made the U.S. the only industrialized country in the world without universal preschools, paid parental leave, and income support for families with young children (Schorr, 1997:235).

Paid parental leave and income support for working families with young chil-dren are two of the topics considered in the following section.

WORKING PARENTS

1998 marked the first time since the U.S. Census Bureau began tracking the num-bers that families with both parents in the labor force became the majority (51 percent of married couples, up from 33 percent in 1976) (reported in Lewin, 2000). Among the many problems facing working parents, two are critical: (1) obtaining job-protected leaves for family emergencies, including birth; and (2) finding and funding satisfactory care for children while parents are at work. In both instances, the policies of the federal and state governments lag behind the child support policies of other Western nations (Jaffe, 1999).

Parental Leave

Some businesses provide generous parental leave policies for their employees so that parents can have children, remain at home for some time after the birth of a child, or meet the emergency health needs of their families without losing their jobs, benefits, or sometimes even wages. Other employers have less generous programs or no programs at all for their employees (see Chapter 6). Likewise, some states require maternity leaves, whereas others do not.

Given the random nature of possible benefits in this area, some have advo-cated that the government mandate that businesses provide uniform benefits to their workers. In 1993, after seven years of legislative efforts and two presidential vetoes by conservative presidents, a federal policy concerning parental leaves was enacted. This policy required firms with more than fifty employees to provide their employees with unpaid maternity leaves of up to twelve weeks, guaranteed jobs (the same or an equivalent job after the leave), and the retention of job benefits during the leave.

Although this legislation is a progressive step, it is a relatively small step with two large problems. First, this policy does not cover 40 percent of the workers in the United States (those who work for businesses with fewer than fifty employees). Second, unpaid leave is a severe financial hardship for many mothers. Almost all other industrial countries provide new mothers and sometimes fathers with paid maternity leave (a range of four months to a year at 80 to 90 percent of normal pay). The two biggest economic competitors of the United States—Japan and Germany—each guarantee at least three months of paid leave, with additional unpaid leave if desired. Moreover, most of the other industrial countries offer parental leave to care for sick children (from ten weeks to three years, usually with low or no pay).

In 1997 President Clinton granted federal employees up to 24 hours of unpaid leave each year for family matters and emergencies. At the same time he urged Congress to extend the same benefit to all workers by expanding the Family and Medical Leave Act. Republicans have resisted this expansion, offering instead a bill that would allow employers to offer workers paid by the hour a chance to take comparable time off instead of the overtime pay they might otherwise be due. These contrasting positions represent the confrontation between the political interests of labor and those of business. Labor-friendly Democrats do not trust management, fearing that they will save money by cutting out the overtime they now must pay. The Republicans and their business backers, on the other hand, do not trust ordinary workers, fearing that they will invent excuses to cheat employers out of the hired labor on which they depend (Means, 1997). The resulting impasse leaves workers without the necessary flexibility to meet their family demands.

Child Care

Probably the biggest problem facing most of these working parents is finding accessible and acceptable child care. The word "accessible" refers to cost, proximity, and compatibility with work schedules; "acceptable" refers to various dimensions of adequacy, such as sanitation, safety, stimulation, and caring supervision. Each of these variables is important, but the most immediate concerns are availability and cost: child care is very expensive. It is the largest single work-related expense for working mothers (costing in most urban areas more to send a four-year-old to child care than it does to pay public college tuition for a nineteen-year-old (Folbre, 2000). This means, of course, that the more affluent are able to take advantage of higher-quality facilities that emphasize child development and learning opportunities. Those less well off are more prone to use less costly child-care facilities that are likely to be overcrowded, unlicensed, and even unhealthy.

Despite the cost of child care, governments can provide such programs if they choose (the following examples are from Folbre, 2000). For example, in France, at an annual cost of $5500 per child, there is a universal nursery for children ages three to five. The cost is fully subsidized by the government, and nearly 100 percent of children attend. Within the United States, Georgia has a very progressive and universal prekindergarten program for four-year-olds, funded fully by money from the state lottery. This programs serves 80 percent of the state's four-year-olds and has a robust public approval rating of 85 percent.

The United States has no comprehensive child-care system. This lack of a system differentiates us from the other industrialized nations. Currently the federal government is involved modestly in providing for child care through two programs. First, it permits the deduction of child-care payments on income tax returns. This amounts to about a $4 billion tax credit, which is considerable. The problem, however, is that by being tied to taxes, it has negligible effects on the poor because they do not earn enough to take advantage of it.

Second, the welfare legislation of 1996 included approximately $4 billion in new child-care funds over six years. "But the new law forces so many parents into the work force that this increase falls far short of what is needed to meet the new demand for child care generated by the law, much less to ensure that vulnerable children receive good care" (Children's Defense Fund, 1997:38).

The government's less-than-adequate child-care programs are fundamentally flawed in at least two respects. Foremost, they are underfunded. The amounts the federal government promised simply do not meet child care needs. The other problem is that they rely on the states to implement the programs and to match the federal grants if they are to receive the monies. The states, through their governors, legislatures, and social service bureaucracies, vary greatly in their enthusiasm for child care, their licensing and monitoring of child-care programs, the standards they set to ensure quality in child care, and their ability to fund child-care programs. If history is a guide, then it is likely that many states will not commit the greater resources needed to receive the federal funds.

The decision makers at the state level vary in their views about child care. Some take the politically conservative position that the government should not interfere with parents' decisions regarding their children. Other conservatives object to the government's subsidization of child care because that encourages mothers to be in the workforce rather than at home with their children (a principle they are willing to overlook when it comes to poor single mothers). Progressives stand in strong opposition to the traditional laissez-faire government attitude regarding daycare. Daycare centers, they argue, must be provided as the right of parents and children and as the obligation of society.

The need for daycare is obvious and is becoming greater as the proportion of mothers who have preschool children and who are employed in the labor force continues to grow. The need for subsidized child care for poor parents, who typically are single mothers, is especially acute.

The need for child care is not limited to preschool children. Working parents are also faced with taking care of their school-aged children after school, but this usually conflicts with their work schedules. A common response is to let the children fend for themselves or be supervised by an older sibling until a parent gets home from work. The problem is exacerbated by schools that dismiss children at 2:30 or 3:00 p.m., hours before the end of the normal workday. The result is that about 7 million **latchkey children** go home alone after school. Research shows that latchkey children are more likely than adult-supervised children to experiment with illicit drugs, to be sexually active, and to vandalize property and commit other crimes. Consider these facts (from Herbert, 1997a): (1) the peak hour for juvenile crime is the first hour after school; and (2) the hours immediately after school are the peak hours for the conception of teenage pregnancies. A report to the Attorney General said this:

> When we send millions of young people out on the streets after school with no responsible supervision or constructive activities, we reap a massive dose of juvenile crime. If, instead, we were to provide students with quality after-school programs, safe havens from negative influences, and constructive recreational, academic enrichment and community service activities, we would dramatically reduce crime while helping students develop the values and skills they need to become good neighbors and responsible adults (cited in Herbert, 1997a:15).

Work-Related Policies and Gender Inequality

Businesses and governments in the United States have been slow to respond to the needs of women in the labor force. This reluctance on the part of those in power (almost always men) to provide support for parents (usually mothers) who need special help to combine the roles of worker and parent has two sources. One is a cultural attitude, the common belief that women really belong

at home and should not be encouraged by government or their employers to have children *and* to work outside the home. Another source is structural: women are relatively powerless, and it is to the advantage of the powerful to keep women in marginal and low-paying jobs. The irony, of course, is that Americans place the highest value on both work and family, yet they do little to help make the two compatible for women.

Women are also disadvantaged in the workplace when they use the work-related rules put in place by governments or businesses. Women are the ones taking leave for childbirth and staying with the newborn for the first weeks or months. Women also are the ones who typically request a leave to take care of sick family members. When these women take their leaves they may have their job back (as now required by law for large firms), but they may also face two obstacles. One might be their co-workers, who may resent having to carry the load for them while they were absent. The second hindrance may come from management, which chooses men over women for promotions because men are more "reliable" and they appear to have a greater commitment to their careers than women appear to have.

PRINCIPLES TO GUIDE FAMILY POLICY: AN IMMODEST PROPOSAL

We have noted a number of structural problems affecting contemporary families. Although these problems are formidable, we can do something about them. If we, as a society, have the will, we have the resources to come to aid of our children, provide universal health care, universal preschool training, daycare and after-school care, job training, and other costly programs (Reich, 2001). Early in 2001 the federal government estimated a budget surplus of $5.6 trillion over ten years. What will we do with this huge windfall? This question quickly divides conservatives and progressives. The conservative response is to use the surplus to reduce taxes. The progressive answer, in contrast, is to put significant amounts toward sustaining and nourishing families through schools, social, and health services.

If we have the resources and the will, what steps should we take as a society to sustain and nourish families? The first step must be to determine the facts. This requires that we challenge the myths that often guide public opinion and our policy makers. Providing the facts and demythologizing families have been major goals of this book.

The second step is to establish, as a society, principles that will guide family policies. This, we realize, is politically impossible at the moment, for at least two reasons. First, government decisions are determined largely by campaign contributions, gifts, lobbying, and media blitzes. Until the public demands effective campaign finance reform and lobbying reform, decisions will be made that benefit the most affluent among us and, conversely, work to the disadvantage of those who have no effective political voice (the poor, children, women, minorities). Second, the majorities in the federal and state legislatures (and the politician of either major political party who serves as president) tend to be political conservatives, which means that they opt for reducing the helpful functions of government while expanding the repressive ones (Ehrenreich, 1997).

Assuming that we can overcome the bias of money in politics and the political power of the moral right, dubious assumptions at best, let us propose some principles that we believe ought to guide family policies (we realize, of course, that this is a controversial exercise, but we ask you to ponder these proposals and improve on them).

1.   We call for policies and behaviors that enhance our moral obligation to others, to our neighbors (broadly defined) and their children, to those unlike us as well as those similar to us, and to future generations. This principle runs counter to our heritage, since the Constitution of the United States is based on individualism. The reigning philosophy of that time celebrated individualism, and the focus was on removing constraints on individual freedom. To this day, political quarrels about family policy can be traced to a conflict between concern for the individual and concern for the well-being of the family group (Anderson, 1991:237).

The celebration of individualism, we argue, leads to exacerbated inequality, the tolerance of inferior housing, schools, and services for "others," and public policies that are punitive to the disadvantaged. Moreover, exaggerated individualism is the antithesis of cooperation and solidarity—the requirements of community.

There is a flaw in the individualistic credo. We cannot go it alone entirely—our fate depends on others. Thus, it is in our individual interest to have a collective interest. As Alan Wolfe, discussing the Scandinavian countries, has put it:

> The strength of the welfare state—indeed, the accomplishment that makes the welfare state the great success story of modern liberal democracy—is the recognition that the living conditions of people who are strangers to us are nonetheless our business (Wolfe, 1989:133).

The key question for U.S. society is: How much do we limit individual freedom for the collective good? Or, put another way: How willing are we to sacrifice (in taxes) so that the fate of others will be improved?

2.   Acceptance of the first principle leads to the second, a call for government programs that provide for people who cannot provide for themselves. Economic inequality is undermining the quality of family life, especially those living near or below the poverty line. Frank Furstenberg, Jr., says:

> The incivilities of poverty are evident in inner-city communities, blighted suburban areas and rural enclaves. They assume the form of inadequate housing, schools, social and recreational services, as well as the absence of commercial enterprises. The misallocation of resources in American society through a market system that provides unlimited rewards to the privileged at the same time as it excludes others from the benefits of prosperity is a potential problem for families struggling to maintain a decent life (Furstenberg, 1999:37).

Thus, society must bring all members of society up to a minimum standard of dignity. At a minimum, this includes universal health insurance, jobs, a minimum wage that places one above the poverty line, and adequate pensions.

3.   Acceptance of the preceding principles leads to a third, a special commitment to children (all children) and to implementing this commitment with viable, universal programs. In Jay Belsky's words:

> The time has come for this nation to regard child care as an infrastructure issue and make the same kind of investment in it that we talk about making in our bridges and roads and that we initially made in these vital transportation systems. We need to recognize that, in the same way that the massive capital investment in transportation and communication systems resulted in huge capital gains that we continue even to this day to realize, investment in child care can bring with it comparable long-term benefits. To gain insight into the costs, specifically foregone opportunity costs of not endeavoring to improve child care and increase options for families, imagine for a moment an America with the automobile but without paved roads (Belsky, 1990:11).

Such a commitment to children involves providing prenatal and postnatal medical care, childhood immunization, protection from exposure to toxic chemicals, adequate nutrition, the elimination of child poverty, universal access to preschool programs, safe neighborhoods, and equally financed schools.

Most significant, children should be wanted by their parents. Unwanted pregnancies should be kept at a minimum through universal sex education in the schools and the easy availability of contraceptives. Abortion is legal. It should be readily available to those who choose this option and subsidized for those who cannot afford it.

4.   A similar commitment to the one made for children must be made for women as well. Young single mothers need parenting skills, education, jobs, and subsidized daycare. Divorced women need fair treatment by the courts, adequate child support from their former husbands, education, job skills, and jobs. All women in the labor force must have equity with men (equal pay for equal work, chance for promotion, and benefits), maternity leave with pay, reliable child care, and flexible work schedules without prejudice from management.

5.   Although some family policies should be made and administered at the local level, others must be largely financed and organized by the federal government. This principle is based on the assumption that some issues are national in scope and require uniform standards (e.g., nutrition guidelines, immunization timetables, preschool goals, the certification of daycare providers, and eligibility for health care). Other policies, such as reducing poverty, require the massive infusion of money and compensatory programs, coupled with centralized planning. This principle runs counter to the current mood of Congress, which wants to return most programs to the states. The problem with this strategy, as we have mentioned, is that policies will be uneven in funding and goals, making them less effective and less fair.

6.   We call for "progressive family policies that reflect the realities of all kinds of families—including families of color, lesbian and gay families, single-parent and blended families, two-parent families, families in which a member has a disability, and families of all social classes" (Fried and Reinelt, 1993:66). This principle recognizes the family diversity present in contemporary society.

The reality is that rather than return to the 'modern family" of the 1950s, families are becoming more diverse. These diverse forms should be recognized and nurtured by society rather than vilified and denigrated, as is now often the case.

These may seem like radical proposals, but they are not. Most of these suggestions in one form or another are found in each of the Western democracies *except* the United States. Can we learn from them? Should we learn from them? Can we afford them? Can we afford *not* to adopt these proposals?

*C*HAPTER REVIEW

1. Family policy refers to objectives concerning family well-being and the specific measures taken by governmental bodies to achieve them.

2. Conservatives and progressives differ in their concept of families: For the former, families are the building blocks of society; for the latter, families are socially and historically constructed. For conservatives, the traditional family, with working father, homemaker mother, and their children, is the way families are supposed to be. For progressives, families change as the society changes.

3. Abortion was legalized by the U.S. Supreme Court in 1973. In 1997 approximately 1.18 million legal abortions were performed, terminating slightly less than one-fourth of all pregnancies. The annual number of abortions and the abortion rate have been declining since 1980.

4. Reproductive rights policies are unfair to the poor, making it more likely that they will have unwanted babies. This bias takes two forms: (a) the relatively high cost of contraceptives; and (b) federal law and many state laws, which make it illegal for public money to be spent for abortions.

5. Although much less generous than found in other industrialized nations, the United States had a fairly comprehensive welfare program to help those in need from 1935 to 1996. This changed with the welfare legislation passed in 1996, which ended Aid to Families with Dependent Children, required welfare recipients to work within two years, placed a five-year lifetime limit on receiving welfare, required unmarried teen parents to live in an adult-supervised setting, gave the states great latitude in administering and funding welfare, cut $54.5 billion in funding over six years, and limited the benefits of legal immigrants.

6. Four years after passage of the welfare bill, it appeared to be a success, with 6.6 million people leaving welfare for work. This interpretation is overly optimistic because (a) those who left welfare early were the easiest to place because they were more skilled and more educated; (b) people left welfare for work *before* 1996 because the economy was robust and jobs were plentiful; (c) low-end jobs are not distributed evenly—some social categories, such as the young, women, and racial minorities, fare the worst, and some regions, states, and cities have a severe mismatch, with too few jobs and too many on welfare; (d) 40 percent of those who have been forced off welfare are *not* working; and (e) Those who work likely work at less than a subsistence wage with little if any benefits.

7. More than 12 million children (1999), some 16.9 percent of those under age eighteen and 24 percent of those under age six, are living below the poverty line. Racial minorities are disproportionately poor, with 33 percent of African American children and 23 percent of Latino children poor, compared to 8 percent of White children. The difference in child poverty by race is even more severe when deep poverty is considered (i.e., those families with incomes below one-half the poverty threshold).

8. Compared with other industrialized nations, the United States ranks relatively low in infant mortality (with African

American babies more than two times more likely to die in their first year as White infants) and last in the number covered by health insurance.

9. Poverty among the elderly has been reduced by government programs (Social Security indexed for inflation), while poverty for children has increased because government actions have reduced programs to help children.

10. The unwillingness of society to help poor children is costly in the long run (cost of medical costs, welfare, crime). Preschool programs for at-risk children are important for improving IQ scores and school performance.

11. Parental leave (for birth or sickness) is now federal policy for firms with more than fifty employees. Although this policy is progressive, it lags behind those of other industrial nations because the leave is *unpaid* and does not cover the 40 percent of U.S. workers who work for small businesses.

12. Unlike the other Western democracies, the United States has no comprehensive child-care system. Daycare provisions for working parents is a special problem that is not met by government and many businesses.

13. Women are disadvantaged in the workplace when they use the work-related rules such as family leave. Particularly, management may treat such women differently from men because managers assume that these women are less committed to their careers.

14. We propose six principles to guide pro-family policies: (a) policies and behaviors that enhance our moral obligation to others; (b) the government provision of benefits to people who cannot provide for themselves; (c) a special commitment to all children to ensure health, safety, preparation for school, and equal funding for schools; (d) a commitment to equality for women; (e) addressing many problems with federal money, standards, and administration; and (f) a recognition, acceptance, and nurturing of the diverse forms of families present in contemporary society.

RELATED WEB SITES

http://www.icomm.ca/workfare/links.htm

International Welfare/Workfare links page: This home page contains 50 kb of links that document welfare reform and workfare internationally. New links are added regularly.

http://www.mathematica-mpr.com/

Mathematica Policy Research, Inc.: Mathematica Policy Research, Inc., is a leader in policy research and analysis. It was founded in 1968 to conduct the first major social policy research experiment in the United States. Since then, they have conducted some of the most important evaluations of policies and programs in health care, welfare, education, nutrition, employment, and early childhood development.

http://www.epn.org/ideacentral/welfare/

Idea Central: Welfare and Families carries new articles, reports, and other information about the national debate over welfare reform and family issues, much of the material from leading policy research and advocacy organizations.

http://www.communitychange.org

Center for Community Change (CCC): CCC helps poor people to improve their communities and change policies and institutions that affect their lives by developing their own strong organizations.

http://www.clasp.org

Center for Law and Social Policy (CLASP): "CLASP is a national non-profit organization with expertise in both law and policy affecting the poor. Through education, policy research and advocacy, CLASP seeks to improve the economic security of low-income families with children and secure access for low-income persons to our civil justice system."

http://www.libertynet.org/~kwru

Poor People's Summit: The Poor People's Summit, held in Philadelphia from October 9–11th, 1999, brought together poor and homeless leaders from across the country. The Summit was sponsored the North-South Dialogue and hosted by the Kensington Welfare Rights Union and the Temple University School of Social Work. Over 300 people came to Philadelphia, representing poor people's organizations from around the country and over 60 schools of social work and other allied organizations. The Poor People's Summit is a part of the Economic Human Rights Campaign, where poor people are documenting and organizing against the human rights violations occurring because of welfare reform, downsizing and poverty.

http://www.welfareinfo.org

Welfare Information Network: "The Welfare Information Network (WIN)—WIN provides information on policy choices, promising practices, program and financial data, funding sources, federal and state legislation and plans, program and management tools, and technical assistance. WIN's web site provides one stop access to over 9,000 links on more than 400 web sites."

http://www.span-online.org/

"The Social Policy Action Network develops effective social policy by transforming the findings of research and the insights of front-line practitioners into concrete action agendas for policymakers. SPAN then crafts strategies to build public will for these policy ideas, providing clear messages for the public and compelling stories for the newsmedia. Our work focuses on some of the most critical issues of the nation's social policy agenda, including welfare reform, fatherhood, teen pregnancy and parenting, child welfare, and early childhood education and care. SPAN is an intermediary—a small and strategic organization whose work complements and promotes the efforts of larger organizations."

http://www.ccsd.ca/

The Canadian Council on Social Development (CCSD) is one of Canada's most authoritative voices promoting better social and economic security for all Canadians. A national, self-supporting, non-profit organization, the CCSD's main product is information and its main activity is research, focussing on concerns such as in-come security, employment, poverty, child welfare, pensions and government social policies.

http://www.urban.org

The Urban Institute is a nonpartisan economic and social policy research organization that investigates social and economic problems. It is relevant to families and welfare, immigration, violence, crime, and health care.

http://www.naral.org/

National Abortion Rights Action League (NARAL): The goal at NARAL is to help find sane, workable answers that will ultimately reduce the need for abortions. Ignoring the problems regarding contraception, reproductive health care and sex education while ripping away a woman's right to choose whether or not to continue a pregnancy will only result in more unintended pregnancies and more abortions. This shortsighted approach is neither American nor life affirming. Until we achieve our goal, it is critical that those who value the freedom and independence we enjoy in this country work hard now to protect a woman's right to choose.

http://gseweb.harvard.edu/%7Ehfrp/about/history.html

Harvard Family Research Project: The Harvard Family Research Project was founded in 1983 at the Harvard Graduate School of Education. The Harvard Family Research Project (HFRP) works to increase the effectiveness of public and private organizations and of communities as they promote child development, student achievement, healthy family functioning, and community building. Its role is to build capacity and to support high performance through solid research and evaluation. The audiences for HFRP's work include policymakers, practitioners, philanthropists, and concerned individuals.

http://www.aclu.org/issues/gay/dpmodel.html

Model Domestic Partnerships: Developed by the ACLU, this web page details model laws and policies that you can use to get your government or company to adopt a domestic partnerships plan. For a detailed account on how to lobby, pressure, and win passage of domestic partnership plans, see related links on this page.

http://www.equalrights.org

Equal Rights Advocates: "Equal Rights Advocates (ERA) is celebrating its 25th Anniversary this year. Based in San Francisco, ERA works to achieve women's economic security through litigation, public education, legislative advocacy, public policy analysis and advice & counseling. ERA works in coalition with other organizations to achieve public policy goals that reflect the concerns and needs of diverse communities."

http://www.crlp.org/

The Center for Reproductive Law and Policy (CRLP) is a non-profit legal and policy advocacy organization dedicated to promoting women's reproductive rights. CRLP's domestic and international programs engage in litigation, policy analysis, legal research, and public education seeking to achieve women's equality in society and ensure that all women have access to appropriate and freely chosen reproductive health services.

http://epinet.org/

The Economic Policy Institute: This website provides information and data on various policy alternatives.

http://arc.org/

The Applied Research Center: This website focuses on the consequences of welfare reform.

http://fightcrime.org/

Fight Crime.Org discusses the benefits to society if all children were to get pre-school training.

http://www.frc.org

Family Research Council: The Family Research Council is the "nation's leading pro-family public policy organization."

Glossary

abortion Expulsion of a fetus or embryo from the uterus, either spontaneously or via a medical procedure.

abuse Behavior aimed primarily at hurting another person, either verbally or physically.

acculturation Process whereby ethnic groups adopt the values, attitudes, and behaviors of the dominant group.

achieved status Position in a social organization attained through personal effort.

ageism Discrimination against the elderly.

agency The ability of human beings to create viable lives even when they are constrained by social forces.

aggregate data analysis A research technique that analyzes quantitative data at different times (e.g., births, deaths, work histories) in order to understand trends.

AIDS Acquired immune deficiency syndrome, an incurable disease that attacks the immune system.

alienation An individual's feeling of separation from the surrounding society.

alimony Income paid to support a divorced spouse.

amniocentesis Medical test performed during pregnancy to determine the presence of birth defects and the sex of the child.

androgyny State of having both male and female characteristics.

anomie Social condition characterized by the absence of norms or conflicting norms.

ascribed status Social position based on such factors as age, race, and family, over which the individual has no control.

assimilation Process by which individuals or groups voluntarily or involuntarily adopt the culture of another group, losing their original identity.

assortive mating The process in mate selection of people marrying others like themselves.

baby boom A fifteen-year period in American history following World War II, when an extraordinary number of babies were born.

backstage behavior Erving Goffman's term denoting that people act differently in private because they have fewer constraints.

bilateral model of parent–child relations The assumption that there is an equal degree of agency to the parent and child.

binational family Family of mixed legal status, such as an undocumented immigrant and a U.S. citizen or legal resident.

birth control Any method used to avoid pregnancy.

birth dearth Period following the baby-boom years, characterized by low birth rates.

birth order Sibling position based on age.

blaming the victim The belief that some individuals are poor, criminals, school dropouts, or otherwise deviant because they have a flaw within them.

bureaucracy System of administration that is characterized by specialized roles, explicit rules, and a hierarchy of authority.

bureaucratization Trend toward greater use of the bureaucratic mode of organization within society.

capital flight Investment choices that involve the movement of corporate monies from one investment to another.

capitalism Economic system based on private ownership of property, guided by the seeking of maximum profits.

capitalist patriarchy Condition of capitalism in which male supremacy keeps women in subordinate roles at work and in the home.

child abuse "The distinctive acts of violence and nonviolence and acts of omission and comission that place children at risk" (Gelles, 1976:136).

class privilege Advantages, prerogatives, and options available to those in an affluent economic situation.

cohabitation Practice of living together as a couple without being married.

cohabitation (heterosexual) Practice of sharing a household by an unmarried male and female in an emotional and physical relationship.

cohabitation (homosexual) Practice of sharing a household by two persons of the same sex in an emotional and physical relationship.

cohort Group of persons who are born at approximately the same time and who subsequently go through life stages together.

colonialism (internal) Use of power by the dominant group in society to oppress a racial minority.

commuter marriage A marriage in which spouses live apart because their jobs require that they live in different locations.

comparable worth Basis of legislative and court actions to equalize pay for traditional "male" and "female" jobs that require equal skills and training.

compulsory heterosexuality The beliefs and practices that define and enforce heterosexual (other sex attraction) behavior as the only natural and permissible form of sexual expression.

conflict perspective View of society that posits conflict as a normal feature of social life, influencing the distribution of power and the direction and magnitude of social change.

conspicuous consumption Purchase and obvious display of material goods to impress others with one's wealth and assumed status.

consumption work A form of invisible work for women as they select goods and make purchases for the family.

coping The active process by individuals to manipulate their role expectations and behaviors to deal with stressful situations.

corporal punishment Use of physical harm or pain but not injury for the purpose of correction or control.

courtship Process of selection and attachment between potential mates that leads to the formation of strong emotional and sexual ties and possibly marriage.

Cult of True Womanhood Ideology by which women are judged by their piety, purity, submissiveness, and domesticity.

cultural approach View that assumes that families in society are the products of the culture in which they are embedded. Families, for example, differ by social class because of the distinctive values found in each class.

cultural tyranny Socialization process that forces narrow behavioral and attitudinal traits on persons.

culture Knowledge that the members of a social organization share.

culture of poverty View that the poor are qualitatively different in values and lifestyles from the rest of society and that these cultural differences explain continued poverty.

deep poverty One-half the poverty threshold and below.

deferred gratification Willingness to sacrifice in the present for expected future rewards.

deflation Part of the economic cycle when the amount of money in circulation is down, resulting in low prices and unemployment.

deindustrialization Widespread systematic diversion of capital (finance, plant, and equipment) from productive investment in the nation's basic industries into unproductive speculation, mergers, acquisitions, and foreign investment.

demography The study of population.

deskilling A consequence of job specialization and technological advances, in which jobs require narrower and more repetitive tasks, resulting in lower pay, less prestige, and less autonomy.

deviance Behavior that violates the expectations of society.

differential fertility Variation in childbearing rates by social class or some other social characteristic.

discretionary income Uncommitted income that persons or families can spend as they please.

discrimination Process of acting toward a person or group with partiality, typically because the individual or group belongs to a minority.

disinvestment Corporate decision to remove capital from an operation (e.g., shutting down a manufacturing plant).

divorce Legal termination of a marriage.

doctrine of two spheres The belief that married women should spend their life within the home, while married men should devote their time outside the home to earning a living for the family.

domestic partner movement The effort to allow homosexuals to register as married. Official recognition of gay partners provides them with the legal and economic benefits of marriage.

double standard Different standards of appropriate sexual behaviors for women and men, with men given more freedom.

dual-earner marriage Marriage in which the husband and wife are both employed outside the home.

dual-welfare system Two systems of welfare, one providing assistance to the needy and the other providing subsidies to the well-to-do.

dyad Two-member group.

economy The social institution that ensures the maintenance of society by producing and distributing the necessary goods and services.

egalitarian Relationship in which the partners share equally in practical responsibilities and decision making.

emotion work Arlie Hochschild's term for the work that women do to keep right feelings in relationships.

empty nest syndrome State of psychological depression or search for new roles that occurs among many full-time housewives whose children have grown up and left home.

ethnic group Social group with a common culture distinct from the culture of the majority because of race, religion, or national origin.

ethnic stratification System of inequality in which race, religion, or national origin is the major criterion for rank and rewards.

ethnicity The condition of being culturally distinct on the basis of race, religion, or national origin.

extended family Several generations of kin that constitute a single family unit, in both living arrangements and obligations.

false consciousness In Marxian theory, the idea that the oppressed may hold beliefs damaging to their interests.

false universalization Incorrect generalization that people experience the family in uniform ways.

familism The attachment to one's nuclear family and to the extended family.

family Particular societal construct whereby persons are related by ancestry, marriage, or adoption.

Family and Medical Leave Act of 1993 Federal law providing workers in establishments with more than fifty workers the right to unpaid job-protected leave to meet family health needs.

family-based economy Mode of production common in the colonial period wherein the household was the basic economic unit.

family-consumer economy Extension of the family-wage economy wherein families specialize in consumption supported by a male wage earner.

family cycle Changes that take place in the family unit as it moves from stage to stage as its members age.

family Darwinism The belief that families survive or sink by their own resources and fitness, not for structural reasons.

family imagery An idealized picture of the family attained by distorting reality.

family policy Objectives concerning family well-being and the specific measures taken by governmental bodies to achieve them.

family reconstitution A research tool that uses every available fragment of information to reconstruct family and household patterns.

family strategies Conscious and unconscious solutions to the constraints imposed on families by economic and social structures.

"family values" The conservative term supporting the two-parent family, with the husband as the breadwinner and the wife as mother and homemaker. The implication is that all other family arrangements are the source of social problems.

family wage Income that men derive from work outside the home that is sufficient to allow women to stay home, raise children, and maintain a family.

family-wage economy Family members making a living by earning wages working outside the home, producing goods and services for employers.

fecundity Ability to have children.

feminization of poverty Rapid rise in the numbers of female-headed households living in poverty.

fertility Frequency of actual births in a population.

fictive kin People treated like family even though they are not related by blood or marriage.

frontstage behavior The formal playing of roles.

flextime Employer–employee arrangement that permits the employee to choose his or her work schedule within specific limits.

functionalism The dominant sociological paradigm of the 1950s and 1960s. It posited that the nuclear family was the basis of social organization and cohesion in society, and essential for the socialization of children and for the division of labor that enabled women and men to perform their social roles in an orderly manner.

Gay Male whose sexual preference is for someone of the same sex.

gender Cultural and social definition of feminine and masculine. It differs from sex, which is the biological fact of femaleness or maleness.

gender strategies Couples in relationships develop myths—versions of reality that emphasize sharing in order to preserve harmony and camouflage conflict.

gendered Behavior patterned according to sex.

gendered institution Gender is present in the processes, practices, images, ideologies, and distributions of power in the various sectors of social life.

gendered institutions approach Emphasizes the features of social organization that produce gender inequality.

gendered labor Work apportioned according to sex. Traditionally this has meant that women do the household chores of cooking, cleaning, and child care, while men do yardwork and home repairs.

genetic engineering Scientific effort to manipulate DNA molecules in plants and animals.

godly family The ideal colonial community based on patriarchy. The family was ruled by the father, who had authority over his wife, children, and servants, much as God the Father ruled over His children.

golden age of the family Mythical, idealized image of how the family once was.

graying of America Demographic trend toward an ever-increasing proportion of the population being old.

Head Start A federally funded program to educate disadvantaged preschool children.

"her" marriage Marriage as experienced by the woman.

hidden economy Practice by which people work at legitimate occupations but evade taxes.

hidden labor Unpaid household labor performed by wives, which serves to reproduce the paid labor force.

hierarchy Arrangement of people or objects in order of importance.

"his" marriage Marriage as experienced by the man.

homogamy When marriage partners are alike in various characteristics, such as race, ethnicity, religion, educational attainment, social class, and age.

homophobia Fear and hatred of homosexuals.

household Residential unit in which members share resources. These units vary in membership and composition. A household is not always a family (parents and children), and a family is not always a household (because it may be separated geographically).

household augmentation The strategy among the poor to double up in households to share expenses.

househusband A husband who stays home to care for the house and family while his wife works for pay outside the home.

human agency Individuals, acting alone or with others, shape, resist, challenge, and sometimes change their social environments.

hypergamy Marriage in which the female marries upward into a higher social stratum.

hypogamy Marriage in which the female marries downward into a lower social stratum.

ideology Shared beliefs about the physical, social, or metaphysical world.

illegal economy Goods and services produced and distributed outside the law.

illegitimacy Birth of a child to an unmarried woman.

immigrant analogy Assumption that racial minorities are just like European immigrants in that they will eventually become assimilated.

incest Sexual behaviors between persons so closely related that marriage between them is prohibited by law.

industrialization Process by which societies become increasingly organized around the production of goods and technology by machines.

inflation Situation in which too much money purchases too few goods, resulting in rising prices.

institution Social arrangement that channels behavior in an important area of societal life.

institutional racism Established and customary ways that exclude people of color from full and equal participation in the institutions of the dominant society. This occurs independent of prejudice or discrimination on the part of individuals.

institutional sexism Practice by which the social arrangements and accepted ways of doing things in society disadvantage females.

institutional violence Situation that occurs when the normal workings of the society do harm to a social category.

interaction work The effort by women to sustain communication with their mates.

intergenerational downward mobility Individuals who, when compared to the socioeconomic status of their parents, do not measure up.

internalization In socialization, the process by which society's demands become part of the individual, acting to control his or her behavior.

intimacy Emotionally charged relationship in which the participants are closely connected.

intragenerational downward mobility Individuals who, in the course of their adult lives, decline in socioeconomic status.

irregular economy Goods and services produced in unrecorded establishments to evade taxes.

kin Network of persons who are related by birth, adoption, or marriage.

kin work The work that women do to sustain family (visits, letters, telephone calls, presents, and cards).

latchkey children Children under age thirteen who have no adult supervision after school.

latent function Unintended consequence of a social arrangement or social action.

learned helplessness Theory that when individuals perceive that the negative things happening to them are not their fault, they tend to give up trying to change the situation.

lesbian Female whose sexual preference is for someone of the same sex.

life chances Opportunities throughout one's life cycle to live and experience the good things in society.

lifestyle Relational patterns around which individuals organize their living arrangements.

machismo (macho) Stereotypic description of Latino men, referring to male dominance, posturing, physical daring, and an exploitative attitude toward women.

macro level Large-scale structures and processes of society, including the institutions and the system of stratification.

majority group Social category in society holding superordinate power and successfully imposing their will on less powerful (minority) groups.

male chauvinism Exaggerated beliefs about the superiority of the male and the resulting discrimination against females.

male privilege Advantages and prerogatives that systematically benefit men and are denied to women.

manifest function Intended consequence of a social arrangement or social action.

marital contract Legal document drawn up prior to a marriage, specifying rights and duties of the partners and especially the disposition of property in case of death or divorce.

marital power Manner in which decision making is distributed between a husband and wife.

marriage Socially approved sexual union between two persons (monogamy) or more than two (polygamy).

marriage squeeze Excess of women at the most marriageable age.

mating gradient Tendency for males to marry down and for females to marry up in age, education, and social class.

matriarchal family A family form in which the woman holds the power.

matrix of domination The systems of inequality (race, class, and gender) in which each of us exists.

micro level Social organization and process of small-scale social groups.

minority Social category composed of persons who differ from the majority, are relatively powerless, and are the objects of unfair and unequal treatment.

miscegenation laws Laws forbidding people of different races from marrying. Abolished by the U.S. Supreme Court in 1967.

modern family The nuclear family that emerged in response to the requirements of an urban, industrial society consisting of an intact nuclear household unit with a male breadwinner, his full-time homemaker wife, and their dependent children.

"mommy track" The employment of women in work positions that are less difficult but less prestigious, less lucrative, and limited in advancement potential. These positions do make it easier for women to care for their families.

monogamy Form of marriage in which an individual cannot be married to more than one person at a time.

monolithic family form Mythical belief that assumes a single, uniform family experience.

monopolistic capitalism Form of capitalism prevalent in the contemporary United States, in which a few large corporations control the key industries, destroying competition and the market mechanisms that would ordinarily keep prices low and help consumers.

Moral Right A conservative political movement reacting to social changes that have taken place since World War II, especially in the areas of morality, welfare spending, and the role of women.

mores Important societal norms, the violation of which results in severe punishment.

mortality rate Frequency of actual deaths in a population.

Moynihan report The controversial report by Daniel Patrick Moynihan in 1965 that argued that the source of problems in the African American community was African Amerian families.

mystification Deliberate misdefinition of a situation.

myth Idealized version about the way things are or were. These are beliefs that are held uncritically and without examination or scrutiny.

"myth of peaceful progress" Erroneous belief based on two assumptions: (1) that the diverse groups in society have learned to compromise and live in harmony; and (2) that any group can gain its share of power, prosperity, and respectability merely by playing the game according to the rules.

"network families" Support network of friends that some single people establish for themselves. These provide a familial alternative to those people without traditional families.

new federalism Current federal policy of withdrawing monies for social programs for the needy, leaving states and local governments with the responsibility to provide for them.

new poor Those who are downwardly mobile because their skills are no longer needed. They are much more trapped in poverty than were the "old poor" of previous generations.

no-fault divorce Laws providing for divorce by mutual consent of the partners.

nonfamily household Persons who live alone or with unrelated individuals.

norm Part of culture that refers to rules that specify appropriate and inappropriate behavior; in other words, the shared expectations for behavior.

nuclear family Kinship unit composed of husband, wife, and children.

nuptiality The proportion of married persons.

official violence Those governmental actions that do harm.

old poor The poor of previous generations, who had more hope of upward mobility than the poor of today; the old poor had the advantages of an expanding economy and a need for unskilled labor.

order model Conception of society as a social system characterized by cohesion, consensus, cooperation, reciprocity, stability, and persistence.

paradigm The basic assumptions that scholars have of the social worlds they study.

parental leave Policies of businesses that allow their employees to have children, take care of children, and meet emergency home needs without losing their jobs.

participatory socialization Mode of socialization in which parents encourage their children to explore, experiment, and question.

patriarchal family Family structure in which the father is dominant.

patriarchal terrorism Violence initiated by men as a way of gaining and maintaining total control over their female partners.

patriarchy Social relations in which men are dominant over women.

patriarchy (private) Male dominance in the interpersonal relations between women and men.

patriarchy (public) Male dominance in the institutions of the larger society.

pedophilia Sexual interest in children.

peer group Friends, usually of the same age and socioeconomic status.

pink-collar jobs Low-status, low-paying jobs reserved primarily for women.

postmodern family The multiplicity of family and household arrangements that has emerged as a result of a number of social factors, such as women in the labor force, divorce, remarriage, and cohabitation arrangements.

poverty Standard of living below the minimum needed for the maintenance of adequate diet, health, and shelter.

power Ability of one person or group to get another person or group to act on its wishes whether the other person or group agrees to or not.

prestige Respect of an individual or social category as a result of social status.

primary group Small group characterized by intimate, face-to-face interaction.

principle of least interest Argument that the partner with the least interest in the relationship is the one who is more apt to exploit the other.

privilege The distribution of goods and services, situations, and experiences that are highly valued and beneficial.

pronatalism The strong positive value a society places on having children.

psychosocial interference The transfer of moods from one social setting (e.g., work) to another (e.g., family).

qualitative methods Research techniques based on subjective analysis.

quantitative methods Research based on the analysis of numerical data.

quinceanera rites This Mexican American ritual presents young women on their fifteenth birthday to the ethnic community as now eligible for marriage.

race Socially defined category on the basis of a presumed common genetic heritage resulting in distinguishing physical characteristics.

racial-ethnic groups Groups labeled as "races" by the wider society and bound together by their common social and economic conditions resulting in distinctive cultural and ethnic characteristics.

racial formation The sociohistorical process by which races are continually being shaped and transformed.

racial stratification System of inequality in which race is the major criterion for rank and rewards.

racism Domination and discrimination of one racial group by the majority.

reconstituted family (blended family) Family form created by a remarriage that involves one or more children from the previous marriage of either spouse.

religion Social institution that encompasses beliefs and practices regarding the sacred.

remarriage Marriage by anyone who has been previously married.

repressive socialization Mode of socialization in which parents demand rigid conformity in their children, enforced by physical punishment.

revisionist perspective New scholarship that challenges the traditional interpretations.

role Behavioral expectations and requirements attached to a position in a social organization.

role performance (role behavior) Actual behavior of persons occupying particular positions in a social organization.

second shift The term referring to women's responsibilities for housework, child care, and home management that women must do in addition to their labor in the workforce.

secondary group Large, impersonal, and formally organized group.

segmented labor market The capitalist economy divided into two distinct sectors: one in which production and working conditions are relatively stable and secure, the other composed of marginal firms in which working conditions are poor and wages and job security are low.

segregation Separation of one group from another.

self-esteem One's opinion of oneself.

self-fulfilling prophecy Event that occurs because it was predicted. The prophecy is confirmed because people alter their behavior to conform to the prediction.

sequencing Adjusting the timing of events over the life course by eliminating or postponing activities in one sphere, either work or family, until a later stage.

sex-gender system System of stratification that operates by ranking and rewarding women's and men's roles unequally (see *patriarchy*).

sex ratio Number of males per hundred females in a population.

sex roles approach Treats gender differences as learned.

sexism Individual actions and institutional arrangements that discriminate against women.

sexual orientation The sex of those to whom one is attracted.

sexual stratification Hierarchical arrangement based on gender.

shared monopoly Control by four or fewer firms of 50 percent or more of a particular market.

sibling A brother or sister.

significant others Those individuals who are most important to a person, such as parents and close friends

social class Number of persons who occupy the same relative economic rank in the stratification system.

social constructionist approach to families The assumption that families are shaped by specific historical, social, and material conditions.

social control Regulation of human behavior in any social group.

social Darwinism The belief that the principle of the survival of the fittest applies to human societies, especially the system of stratification.

social differentiation Process of categorizing persons by some personal attribute.

social inequality Ranking of persons by wealth, family background, race, ethnicity, or sex.

social interaction Process by which individuals act toward or respond to each other.

social location One's position in society based on family background, race, socioeconomic status, religion, sexuality, or other relevant social characteristics.

social mobility Movement by an individual from one social class or status group to another.

social movement Collective attempt to promote or resist change.

social organization Order of a social group as evidenced by the positions, roles, norms, and other constraints that control behavior and ensure predictability.

social production The varied ways in which people make a living.

social reproduction The maintenance of life on a daily basis, including food, clothing, shelter, and emotional activity.

social stratification Ranking of people in a hierarchy that differentiates them as superior or inferior.

social structure Patterned and recurrent relationships among people and parts of a social organization.

social system Differentiated group whose parts are interrelated in an orderly arrangement, bound by geographic space or membership.

socialization Process of learning the culture.

socialization agents Those individuals, groups, and institutions responsible for transmitting the culture of a society to newcomers.

society Largest social organization to which individuals owe their allegiance. The entity is located geographically, has a common culture, and is relatively self-sufficient.

socioeconomic status (SES) The measure of social status that takes into account several prestige factors, such as income, education, and occupation.

sociology Scholarly discipline concerned with the systematic study of social organizations.

spillover Carrying over the concerns, responsibilities, and demands of one part of life to another (e.g., the conditions of work that affect family life).

split-shift parenting When working parents share child care, one parent takes care of the children while the other works.

status Socially defined position in a social organization.

status group Collection of social equals.

stepchild Child of one's husband or wife by a former marriage.

stepparent Person who occupies the parent role for the children by a former marriage of his or her spouse.

stereotype Exaggerated generalization about some social category.

stigma Label of social disgrace.

Stonewall riots In 1969, after the police raided a gay bar in New York City, the homosexual patrons fought back. This event marks the beginning of the modern gay movement.

structural diversity approach Assumption that families are shaped by the structure of society (e.g., the availability of work, remuneration for work, opportunities by race and gender).

structural determinism View that structural

conditions control the destiny of individuals and groups.

structural interference Time constraints imposed by the demands of work and family roles.

structured social inequality Patterns of superiority and inferiority, the distribution of rewards, and the belief systems that reinforce the inequalities of society.

subculture Relatively cohesive cultural system that varies in form and substance from the dominant culture.

sunrise industries Sectors of economic potential, increased output, and rising employment.

sunset industries Economic sectors experiencing declining output and employment.

symbol An entity such as a word, a gesture, or physical object that represents something else.

transnational families Families in which the members are located across national boundaries. For example, an undocumented worker leaves his or her family in Mexico to work in the United States.

transience Rapid turnover in things, places, and people.

underclass Assumption that the poor have a set of distinctively negative values, psychological attributes, and maladaptive behaviors (see *culture of poverty*).

underemployment Being employed at a job below one's level of training and expertise.

underground economy The hidden, irregular, and illegal economies.

undocumented immigrant Immigrant who has entered the United States illegally.

urbanization The movement of people from rural to urban areas.

value stretch People in the lower classes sharing middle-class values but stretching them as they adjust to conditions of deprivation.

values Shared criteria used in evaluating objects, ideas, acts, feelings, or events as to their relative desirability, merit, or correctness.

venereal diseases Diseases transmitted by sexual contact.

voluntary childlessness The decision by some couples not to have children.

welfare Economic aid provided to those in need by the federal, state, and local governments.

widowhood Loss of a spouse by death.

work–family interference The ways in which the connections between jobs and family may be a source of tension for workers and family members.

work–family role system Traditional uneven division of labor in which men's work role takes priority over the family role, and women, even those who work outside the home, are to give priority to the family role.

Bibliography

Abbott, Pamela, and Claire Wallace (1992). *The Family and the New Right*. London: Pluto Press.

Acker, Joan (1973). "Women and Stratification: A Case of Intellectual Sexism." *American Journal of Sociology 78* (January): 936–945.

Acker, Joan (1980). "Women and Stratification: A Review of Recent Literature." *Contemporary Sociology 9* (January): 25–39.

Acker, Joan (1988). "Women and Work in the Social Sciences." In *Women Working*, Ann Helton Stromberg and Shirley Harkess (eds.). Mountain View, CA: Mayfield, pp. 10–24.

Acker, Joan (1992). "Gendered Institutions: From Sex Roles to Gendered Institutions." *Contemporary Sociology 21* (September): 565–568.

Acock, Alan C., and David H. Demo (1994). *Family Diversity and Well-Being*. Thousand Oaks, CA: Sage.

Adam, Barry D. (1993). "Review of Margaret Cruikshank's The Gay and Lesbian Liberation Movement." *Contemporary Sociology 22* (November): 813–814.

Adams, Bert W. (1980). *The Family*. Chicago: Rand McNally.

Aerts, Elaine (1993). "Bringing the Institution Back In." In *Family, Self, and Society: Toward a New Agenda for Family Research*, Philip A Cowan, Dorothy Field, Donald A. Hansen, Arlene Skolnick, and Guy E. Swanson (eds.). Hillsdale, NJ: Lawrence Earlbaum Associates, pp. 3–41.

Ahlburg, Dennis A., and Carol J. De Vita (1992). "New Realities of the American Family." *Population Bulletin 47* (August): entire issue.

Ahrons, Constance (1994). *The Good Divorce: Keeping Your Family Together When Your Marriage Comes Apart*. New York: HarperCollins.

Albelda, Randy (1992). "Whose Values, Which Families?" *Dollars & Sense* No. 182. (December): 6–9.

Aldous, Joan (1991). "In the Families' Ways." *Contemporary Sociology 20* (September): 660–662.

Aldous, Joan, and Wilfried Dumon (1991). "Family Policy in the 1980s: Controversy and Consensus." In *Contemporary Families: Looking Forward, Looking Back*, Alan Booth (ed.). Minneapolis: National Council on Family Relations, pp. 466–481.

Allen, Katherine (1997). "Lesbian and Gay Families." In *Contemporary Parenting: Challenges and Issues*, Terry Arendell (ed.). Thousand Oaks, CA: Sage, pp. 196–218.

Allen, Katherine, and David H. Demo (1995). "The Families of Lesbians and Gay Men: A New Frontier in Family Research." *Journal of Marriage and the Family 57* (February): 111–127.

Allen, Mike, and Nancy Burrell (1996). "Comparing the Impact of Homosexual and Heterosexual Parents on Children." *Journal of Homosexuality 32* (2): 19–35.

Allen, Walter P. (1978). "The Search for Applicable Theories of Black Family Life." *Journal of Marriage and the Family 40*(1): 117–129.

Alvirez, David, and Frank D. Bean (1976). "The Mexican–American Family." In *Ethnic Families in America*, Charles H. Mindel and Robert W. Habenstein (eds.). New York: Elsevier, pp. 271–292.

Amato, Paul R. (2001). "The Consequences of Divorce for Adults and Children." In *Understanding Families into the New Millennium: A Decade in Review*, Robert M. Milardo (ed.). Minneapolis: National Council on Family Relations, pp. 1269–1287.

Amato, Paul R., and Alan Booth (1996). "A Prospective Study of Divorce and Parent–Child Relationships." *Journal of Marriage and the Family 58* (May): 356–365.

Amato, Paul R., and Alan Booth (1997). *A Generation at Risk: Growing Up in an Era of Family Upheaval*. Cambridge, MA: Harvard University Press.

Amato, Paul R., and Bruce Keith (1991). "Parental Divorce and Well–Being of Children: A Meta-Analysis." *Psychological Bulletin 110*: 26–46.

Ambert, Anne-Marie (1992). *The Effect of Children on Parents*. New York: Haworth Press.

American Bar Association (1997). "Multidisciplinary Responses to Domestic Violence." Chicago: ABA Commission on Domestic Violence.

American Demographics (1992). "The Singles Scene." Desk Reference Series (July): 18–23.

AmeriStat (2000a). "Fertility: Having Children Later or Not at All." <http://AmeriStat.org/fertility/HavingChildrenLaterNot.html>

AmeriStat (2000b). "Fertility: Births to Unmarried Women—End of the Increase?" <http://AmeriStat.org/fertility/ births-UnmarriedWomenEndIncrease.html>

AmeriStat (2000c). "Fertility: Declining Fertility Among Teenagers." <http://AmeriStat.org/fertility/Declining-FertilityAmongTeenagers.html>

AmeriStat (2000d). "Children: Two–Parent Families on the Decline." <http://AmeriStat.org/children/TwoParentFamiliesDecline.html>

AmeriStat (2000e). "Marriage and Family: Nuclear Meltdown." <http://AmeriStat.org/marfam/trad-fam. htm>

Ammons, Paul, Josie Nelson, and John Wodarski (1982). "Surviving Corporate Moves: Sources of Stress and Adaptation among Corporate Executive Families." *Family Relations* 32 (April): 207–212.

Amott, Teresa, and Julie Matthaei (1991). *Race, Gender, and Work: A Multicultural Economic History of Women in the United States.* Boston: South End Press.

Andersen, Margaret L. (1988). "Moving Our Minds: Studying Women of Color and Reconstructing Sociology." *Teaching Sociology* 16 (April): 123–132.

Andersen, Margaret L. (1991). "Feminism and the American Family Ideal." *Journal of Contemporary Family Studies* 22 (Summer): 235–246.

Andersen, Margaret L. (1997). *Thinking about Women: Sociological Perspectives on Sex and Gender,* 4th ed. Boston: Allyn and Bacon.

Andersen, Margaret L., and Patricia Hill Collins (eds.) (1995). *Race, Class, and Gender: An Anthology,* 2nd ed. Belmont, CA: Wadsworth.

Andersen, Margaret L. and Patricia Hill Collins. (2001) "Introduction." in *Race, Class, and Gender: An Anthology.* Margaret L. Andersen and Patricia Hill Collins (eds.) Belmont, CA: Wadsworth/Thompson Learning.

Anderson, Elaine A. (1991). "The Future of Family Policy: A Postscript." In *The Reconstruction of Family Policy,* Elaine A. Anderson and Richard C. Hule (eds.). New York: Greenwood Press, pp. 237–240.

Anderson, Elijah (1990). *Streetwise.* Chicago: University of Chicago Press.

Angel, Ronald, and Marta Tienda (1982). "Determinants of Extended Household Structure: Cultural Pattern or Economic Need?" *American Journal of Sociology* 87 (6): 1360–1383.

Angier, Natalie (1991). "The Biology of What It Means to Be Gay." *New York Times,* September 1, pp. E1, E4.

Annin, Peter (1996). "Slumbering Around." *Newsweek,* November 4, p. 57.

Aponte, Robert (1991). "Urban Hispanic Poverty: Disaggregation and Exploration." *Social Problems* 38 (November): 516–528.

Apter, Terri (1993). *Working Women Don't Have Wives: Professional Success in the 1990s.* New York: St. Martin's Press.

Arendell, Terry (1997). "A Social Constructionist Approach to Parenting." In *Contemporary Parenting: Challenges and Issues,* Terry Arendell (ed.). Thousand Oaks, CA: Sage, pp. 1–44.

Aries, Phillippe (1965). *Centuries of Childhood: A Social History of Family Life.* New York: Knopf and Random House.

Armas, Genaro C. (2000). "Asians, Hispanics Increase in U.S." Rocky Mountain News, August 30, p. 34A.

Arrighi, Barbara, and David J. Maume (2000). *Journal of Family Issues* 21 (May): 464–487.

Aschenbrenner, Joyce, and Carolyn Hamecdah Carr (1980). "Conjugal Relations in the Context of the Black Extended Family." *Alternative Lifestyles* 3 (4): 463–484.

Associated Press (1995). "Sweden Has First Gay Rites" (January 3).

Associated Press (1997). "Cities: Too Few Jobs to Handle Welfare Load" (November 22).

Associated Press (2000). "EU's Parliament Backs Gay Unions" (March 18).

Astone, Nan Marie (1993). "Thinking about Teenage Childbearing." Report from the Institute for Philosophy and Public Policy, University of Maryland (Summer): 8–13.

Astone, Nan Marie (1997). "Review of the Personal Responsibility and Work Opportunity Reconciliation Act of 1996." *Contemporary Sociology* 26 (July): 413–415.

Baber, Kristine M., and Katherine R. Allen (1992). *Women and Families: Feminist Reconstructions.* New York: Guilford Press.

Baca Zinn, Maxine (1975). "Political Familism: Toward Sex Role Equality in Chicano Families." *Aztlan* 6 (1): 13–26.

Baca Zinn, Maxine (1980). "Employment and Education of Mexican American Women: The Interplay of Modernity and Ethnicity in Eight Families." *Harvard Educational Review* 50 (1): 47–62.

Baca Zinn, Maxine (1989). "Family, Race, and Poverty in the Eighties." *Signs: Journal of Women in Culture and Society* 14 (4): 856–874.

Baca Zinn, Maxine (1990). "Family, Feminism, and Race in America." *Gender & Society* 14 (March): 62–86.

Baca Zinn, Maxine (1994). "Feminist Rethinking from Racial Ethnic Families." In *Women of Color in U.S. Society,* Maxine Baca Zinn and Bonnie Thornton Dill (eds.). Philadelphia: Temple University Press, pp. 303–314.

Baca Zinn, Maxine (2000). "Feminism and Family Studies for a New Century." *The Annals of the American Academy of Political and Social Science* 571 (September): 42–56.

Baca Zinn, Maxine, and Bonnie Thornton Dill (1994). "Difference and Domination." In *Women of Color in U.S. Society,* Maxine Baca Zinn and Bonnie Thornton Dill (eds.). Philadelphia: Temple University Press, pp. 3–12.

Baca Zinn, Maxine, and Bonnie Thornton Dill (1996). "Theorizing Difference from Multicultural Feminism." *Feminist Studies* 22 (Summer): 1–11.

Baca Zinn, Maxine, and D. Stanley Eitzen (1993). "The Demographic Transformation and the Sociological Enterprise." *The American Sociologist* 24 (Summer): 5–12.

Baca Zinn, Maxine and D. Stanley Eitzen (1996). *Diversity in Families,* 4th ed. New York: HarperCollins.

Baca Zinn, Maxine, and D. Stanley Eitzen (1998). "Missing Paradigm Shift in Family Sociology." *Footnotes* (American Sociological Association Newsletter) (January).

Baca Zinn, Maxine, Pierrette Hondagneu-Sotelo, and Michael A. Messner (eds.) (1997). *Through the Prism of Difference: Readings on Sex and Gender.* Boston: Allyn & Bacon.

Baca Zinn, Maxine, and Barbara Wells (2000). "Diversity within Latino Families: New Lessons for Family Studies." In *Handbook of Family Diversity*, David H. Demo, Katherine R. Allen, and Mark A. Fine (eds.). New York: Oxford University Press, pp. 252–273.

Bachman, Ronet (1994). *Violence against Women.* Washington, DC: U.S. Department of Justice (NCJ-145325).

Bachman, Ronet, and L. E. Saltzman (1996). "Violence against Women." Rockville, MD: U.S. Department of Justice (NCJ No. 154348).

Balswick, Jack, and Charles Peek (1971). "The Inexpressive Male: A Tragedy of American Society." *Family Coordinator* 20: 363–368.

Barnett, Ola W., Cindy L. Miller-Perrin, and Robin D. Perrin (1997). *Family Violence across the Lifespan.* Thousand Oaks, CA: Sage.

Barrera, Mario (1979). *Race and Class in the Southwest.* Notre Dame: University of Notre Dame Press.

Barten, Patty (1999). "Your Next Job." *Newsweek,* February 1, pp. 43–45.

Bartfield, Judi (2000). "Child Support and the Postdivorce Economic Well-Being of Mothers, Fathers, and Children." *Demography* 37 (May): 203–213.

Bartholet. E. (1993). *Family Bonds: Adoption and the Practice of Parenting.* New York: Houghton Mifflin.

Barton, Jane Hughes (1994). *Remarriage after 50: What Women, Men and Adult Children Need to Know.* New York: Roger Thomas Press.

Basow, Susan (1992). *Gender Stereotypes and Roles,* 3rd ed. Pacific Grove, CA: Brooks/Cole.

Bateson, Mary Catherine (2000). *Full Circles, Overlapping Lives: Culture and Generation in Transition.* New York: Random House.

Beck, Joan (1995). "Preschool Can Help Close the Poverty Gap." *Denver Post,* January 19, p. 7B.

Beckett, Joyce O. (1976). "Working Wives: A Racial Comparison." *Social Work* 21 (November): 463–471.

Begley, Sharon (2001). "Brave New Monkey." *Newsweek,* January 22, pp. 50–52.

Belkin, Lisa (2000). "Your Kids Are Their Problem." <http://nytimes.com/library/magazine/home/20000723mag-kids.html>

Bell, Alan P., and Martin S. Weinberg (1978). *Homosexualities: A Study of Human Diversity.* New York: Simon & Schuster.

Belluck, Pam (1997). "Hispanics' Lawsuit Cracks Housing Bias." *Denver Post,* August 8, p. 2A.

Belsky, Jay (1990). "Infant Day Care, Child Development, and Family Polity." *Society* (July/August): 10–12.

Belsky, Jay (1991). "Parental and Nonparental Child Care and Children's Socioemotional Development." In *Contemporary Families: Looking Forward, Looking Back,* Alan Booth (ed.). Minneapolis: National Council on Family Relations, pp. 122–140.

Belsky, Jay, and John Kelly (1994). *The Transition to Parenthood: How a First Child Changes a Marriage; Why Some Couples Grow Closer and Others Apart.* New York: Delacorte Press.

Benett, Jeanne, and Selwyn Jones (1993). "Labor Force Occupation." *Current Population Reports,* Series P23-185 (May): 24–25.

Bengtson, Vern L., Carolyn Rosenthal, and Linda Burton (1990). "Families and Aging: Diversity and Heterogeneity." In *Handbook of Aging and Social Sciences,* 3rd ed., Robert H. Binstock and Linda K. George (eds.). San Diego, CA: Academic Press, pp. 263–287.

Benin, Mary Holland, and Linda B. Robinson (1997). "Marital Happiness across the Family Life Cycle: A Longitudinal Analysis," a paper presented at the American Sociological Association (August).

Bequaert, Lucia H. (1976). *Single Women: Alone and Together.* Boston: Beacon Press.

Berardo, Felix M. (1991). "Family Research in the 1980s: Recent Trends and Future Directions." In *Contemporary Families: Looking Forward, Looking Back,* Alan Booth (ed.). Minneapolis: National Council on Family Relations, pp. 1–11.

Berardo, Felix M. (1998). "Family Privacy: Issues and Concepts," *Journal of Family Issues* 19 (January): 4–19.

Berger, Peter L., and Hansfried Kellner (1975). "Marriage and the Construction of Reality." In *Life as Theatre,* Dennis Brissett and Charles Edgley (eds.). New York: Aldine De Gruyter, pp. 219–233.

Berk, Sarah Fenstermaker (1988). "Women's Unpaid Labor: Home and Community." In *Women Working,* Ann Helton Stromberg and Shirley Harkess (eds.). Mountain View, CA: Mayfield, pp. 287–302.

Bernard, Jessie (1971). "The Paradox of the Happy Marriage." In *Woman in Sexist Society,* Vivian Gornick and Barbara K. Moran (eds.). New York: Basic Books, pp. 145–162.

Bernard, Jessie (1972). *The Future of Marriage.* New York: Bantam.

Bernard, Jessie (1984). "The Good Provider Role: Its Rise

and Fall." In *Work and Family*, Patricia Voydanoff (ed.). Palo Alto, CA: Mayfield, pp. 43–60.

Bernard, Joan Kelly (1994). "Living with Your Parents Can Cool Romance." *Coloradoan*, November 28, p. B1.

Berry, John (1999). "The Family Crunch Gets Tighter." *Washington Post National Weekly Edition*, May 31, p. 34.

Bianchi, Suzanne M. (1995). "Changing Economic Roles of Women and Men." In *State of the Union: America in the 1990s*, Vol. 1, Reynolds Farley (ed.). New York: Russell Sage, pp. 107–154.

Bianchi, Suzanne M., and Lynn M. Casper (2000). "American Families." *Population Bulletin* 55 (December): entire issue.

Bianchi, Suzanne M., and Daphne Spain (1996). "Women, Work, and Family in America." *Population Bulletin* 51 (December): entire issue.

Bianchi, Suzanne M., L. Subaiya, and J. R. Kahn (1999). "The Gender Gap in the Economic Well-Being of Nonresident Fathers and Custodial Mothers." *Demography* 36:195–203.

Biggs, Simon, Chris Phillipson, and Paul Kingston (1995). *Elderly Abuse in Perspective*. Philadelphia: Open University Press.

Billingsley, Andrew (1992). *Climbing Jacob's Ladder*. New York: Simon & Schuster.

Biondo, Brenda (2000). "Think Your Day Care Is Expensive?" *USA Weekend*, February 4, p. 10.

Birdwhistell, Ray L. (1980). "The Idealized Model of the American Family." In *Marriage and Family in a Changing Society*, James M. Henslin (ed.). New York: Free Press, pp. 562–567.

Black, Dan, Gary Gates, Seth Sanders, and Lowell Taylor (2000). "Demographics of the Gay and Lesbian Population in the United States: Evidence from Available Systemic Sources." *Demography* 37 (May):139–154.

Blake, Judith (1989). *Family Size and Achievement*. Berkeley: University of California Press.

Blassingame, John (1977). *Slave Testimony: Two Centuries of Letters, Speeches, Interviews and Autobiographies*. Baton Rouge: Louisiana State University Press.

Blauner, Robert (1972). *Racial Oppression in America*. New York: Harper & Row.

Block, Sandra (1999). "Living Together? Commit to Contract." *USA Today*, October 15, p. 3B.

Blumberg, Paul M., and P. W. Paul (1975). "Continuities and Discontinuities in Upper-Class Marriages." *Journal of Marriage and the Family* 37 (December): 63–78.

Blumstein, Philip, and Pepper Schwartz (1983). *American Couples: Money, Work, Sex*. New York: William Morrow.

Bogenschneider, Karen (2001). "Has Family Policy Come of Age? A Decade Review of the State of U.S. Family Policy in the 1990s." In *Understanding Families into the New Millennium*, Robert M. Milardo (ed.).

Minneapolis: National Council on Family Relations, pp. 355–378.

Bohannan, Paul, and Rosemary Erickson (1978). "Stepping In." *Psychology Today* 11 (January): 53–54, 59.

Booth, Alan, and Paul R. Amato (1994). "Parental Gender Role Nontraditionalism and Offspring Outcomes." *Journal of Marriage and the Family* 56 (November): 865–875.

Booth, Alan, and John Edwards (1985). "Age at Marriage and Marital Instability." *Journal of Marriage and the Family* 47: 67–75.

Boss, Pauline, and Barrie Thorne (1989). "Family Sociology and Family Therapy: A Feminist Linkage." In *Women in Families*, Monica McGoldrick, Carol M. Anderson, and Froma Walsh (eds.). New York: W. W. Norton, pp. 78–96.

Boudreau, Frances A. (1993). "Elder Abuse." In *Family Violence: Prevention and Treatment*, Robert L. Hampton, Thomas P. Gullotta, Gerald R. Adams, Earl H. Potter, and Roger P. Weissberg (eds.). Newbury Park, CA: Sage, pp. 142–158.

Boulding, Elise (1983). "Familia Faber: The Family as Maker of the Future." *Journal of Marriage and the Family* 45 (May): 257–266.

Breines, Wini, and Linda Gordon (1983). "The New Scholarship on Family Violence." *Signs* 8 (Spring): 490–531.

Bridenthal, Renate (1981). "The Family Tree: Contemporary Patterns in the United States." In *Household and Kin*, Amy Swerdlow, Renate Bridenthal, Joan Kelly, and Phyllis Vine (eds.). Old Westbury, NY: The Feminist Press, pp. 47–105.

Briggs, Bill (1997). "Curtail TV Habits, Group Urges." *Denver Post*, April 15, p. E1.

Briggs, Bill (2000). "Pampered Parents?" *Denver Post*, July 9, pp. F1,F3.

Bronfenbrenner, Urie, Peter McClelland, Elaine Wethington, Phyllis Moen, and Stephen J. Ceci (1996). *The State of Americans*. New York: The Free Press.

Brown, Susan L., and Alan Booth (1996). "Cohabitation versus Marriage: A Comparison of Relationship Quality." *Journal of Marriage and the Family* 58 (August): 668–678.

Brown–Smith, Naima (1998). "Family Secrets," *Journal of Family Issues* 14 (January): 20–42.

Bruce, Judith, Cynthia B. Lloyd, and Ann Leonard (1995). *Introduction to Families in Focus: New Perspectives on Mothers, Fathers, and Children*. New York: The Population Council.

Brumberg, Joan Jacobs (1997). *The Body Project: An Intimate History of American Girls*. New York: Random House.

Bryson, Ken, and Lynne M. Casper (1999). "Coresident Grandparents and Grandchildren." *Current Population Reports: Special Studies*, P-23-198 (May).

Bumpass, Larry L. (1990). "What's Happening to the Family? Interactions between Demographic and Institutional Change." *Demography* 27 (November): 483–498.

Bumpass, Larry, and Hsien-Hen Lu (2000a). "Cohabitation: How the Families of U.S. Children are Changing." *Focus* 21 (Spring): 5–8.

Bumpass, Larry, and Hsien-Hen Lu (2000b). "Trends in Cohabitation and Implications for Children's Family Contexts in the United States." *Population Studies* 54: 29–41.

Bumpass, Larry L., Ronald R. Rindfuss, and Richard B. Janosik (1978). "Age and Marital Status at First Birth and the Pace of Subsequent Fertility." *Demography* 15 (February): 75–86.

Bumpass, Larry L., and James A. Sweet (1989). "National Estimates on Cohabitation." *Demography* 26: 615–625.

Bumpass, Larry L., James A. Sweet, and Andrew Cherlin (1991). "The Role of Cohabitation in Declining Marriage Rates." *Journal of Marriage and the Family* 53 (4): 913–927.

Bumpass, Larry L., James A. Sweet, and Teresa Castro Martin (1990). "Changing Patterns of Remarriage." *Journal of Marriage and the Family* 52 (August): 747–756.

Bunker, B. B., J. M. Zubek, V. J. Vanderslice, and R. W. Rice (1992). "Quality of Life in Dual-Career Families: Commuting versus Single-Residence Couples." *Journal of Marriage and the Family* 54: 339–406.

Burchinal, Margaret R. (1999). "Child Care Experiences and Developmental Outcomes." *The Annals* 563 (May): 73–97.

Buriel, Raymond, and Terri De Ment (1997). "Immigration and Sociocultural Change in Mexican, Chinese, and Vietnamese American Families." In *Immigration and the Family*, Alan Booth, Ann C. Crouter, and Nancy Landale (eds.). Mahwah, NJ: Lawrence Erlbaum Associates, pp. 165–200.

Burkett, Elinor (2000). *The Baby Boon*. New York: The Free Press.

Burr, Chandler (1993). "Homosexuality and Biology." *The Atlantic Monthly* 271 (March): 47–65.

Business Week (2000a). "The New World of Work." (January 10): 36.

Business Week (2000b). "The 21st Century Corporation." (August 28): 278.

Butler, Sandra (1978). *Conspiracy of Silence: The Trauma of Incest*. San Francisco: New Glide.

Calhoun, Arthur W. (1945). *A Social History of the American Family*, 3 vols. New York: Barnes and Noble.

Camarillo, Albert (1979). *Chicanos in a Changing Society: From Mexican Pueblos to American Barrios in Santa Barbara and Southern California, 1848–1930*. Cambridge, MA: Harvard University Press.

Campbell, Frances A., and Craig T. Ramey (1994). "Effects of Early Intervention on Intellectual and Academic Achievement: A Follow-up Study of Children from Low-Income Families." *Child Development* 65 (April): 684–698.

Campbell, J. C., L. Rose, J. Kub, and D. Nedd. (1998). "Voices of Strength and Resistence: A Contextual and Longitudinal Analysis of Women's Responses to Battering." *Journal of Interpersonal Violence* 13: 743–762.

Cancian, Francesca M. (1987). *Love in America: Gender and Self Development*. New York: Cambridge University Press.

Caplow, Theodore, Louis Hicks, and Ben J. Wattenberg (2001). *The First Measured Century*. Washington, DC: The AEI Press.

Cargan, Leonard (1984). "Singles: An Examination of Two Stereotypes." In *Family in Transition*, 4th ed., Arlene S. Skolnick and Jerome H. Skolnick (eds.). Boston: Little, Brown, pp. 546–556.

Carlson, Christopher (1990). *Perspectives on the Family: History, Class, and Feminism*. Belmont, CA: Wadsworth.

Carman, Diane (2000). "No Answer to Divorce Question." *Denver Post*, July 1, p. B1.

Carr, Lois Green, and Lorena S. Walsh (1979). "The Planter's Wife: The Experience of White Women in Seventeenth–Century Maryland." In *A Heritage of Her Own*, Nancy F. Cott and Elizabeth H. Pleck (eds.). New York: Simon & Schuster, pp. 25–58.

Catanzarite, Liza, and Vilma Ortiz (1996). "Family Matters, Work Matters? Poverty among Women of Color and White Women." In *For Crying out Loud: Women's Poverty in the U.S.*, Diane Dujon and Ann Withorn (eds.). Boston: South End Press, pp. 122–139.

Caulfield, Minna Davis (1974). "Imperialism, the Family, and Cultures of Resistance." *Socialist Revolution* 20: 67–85.

Cazenave, Noel A. (1980). "Alternative Intimacy, Marriage and Family Lifestyles among Low Income Black Americans." *Alternative Lifestyles*, 3 (4): 425–444.

Chafetz, Janet Saltzman (1997). "'I Need a Traditional Wife!': Employment Family Conflicts." In *Workplace/Women's Place*, Dana Dunn (ed.). Los Angeles: Roxbury, pp. 116–123.

Chang, C. Y., and A. M. Wood (1996). "Dual-Career Commuter Marriages: Balancing Commitments to Self, Spouse, Family and Work." Paper presented at the National Conference of the American Counseling Association, Pittsburgh, PA.

Chasin, Barbara H. (1997). *Inequality and Violence in the United States*. Atlantic Highlands, NJ: Humanities Press.

Chavez, Leo R. (1992). *Shadowed Lives: Undocumented Immigrants in American Society*. Orlando, FL: Harcourt Brace.

Cheal, David (1991). *Family and the State of Theory.* Toronto: University of Toronto Press.

Cherlin, Andrew J. (1978). "Remarriage as an Incomplete Institution." *American Journal of Sociology* 84 (November): 634–651.

Cherlin, Andrew J. (1981). *Marriage, Divorce, Remarriage.* Cambridge, MA: Harvard University Press.

Cherlin, Andrew J. (1992). *Marriage, Divorce, Remarriage,* revised and enlarged edition. Cambridge, MA: Harvard University Press.

Cherlin, Andrew J. (1999a). "Going to Extremes: Family Structure, Children's Well-Being and Social Science." *Demography* 36 (November): 421–428.

Cherlin, Andrew J. (1999b). *Public and Private Families.* Boston: McGraw-Hill.

Cherlin, Andrew J. (2000). "Generation Ex." *The Nation,* December 11, pp. 62–68.

Cherlin, Andrew J., and Frank F. Furstenberg, Jr. (1994). "Stepfamilies in the United States: A Reconsideration." *Annual Review of Sociology* 20: 359–381.

Chevan, Albert (1996). "As Cheaply as One: Cohabitation in the Older Population." *Journal of Marriage and the Family* 58 (August): 656–667.

Chideya, Farai (1999). "A Nation of Minorities: America in 2050." *Civil Rights Digest* 4 (Fall):35–41.

Children for the Future (2000). <http://childrenforthefuture.org/fertility>.

Children's Defense Fund (1997). *The State of American's Children Yearbook: 1997.* Washington, DC: Children's Defense Fund.

Christensen, Kathleen (1988). *Women and Home-Based Work.* New York: Henry Holt.

Clifford, Mark, and Manjeet Kripalani (2000). "Different Countries, Adjoining Cubicles." *Business Week,* August 28, pp. 182–184.

Cody, Cheryl Ann (1983). "Naming, Kinship and Estate Dispersal: Notes on Slave Family Life on a South Carolina Plantation, 1786 to 1833." In *The American Family in Social Historical Perspective,* 3rd ed., Michael Gordon (ed.). New York: St. Martin's Press, pp. 440–458.

Cohen, Theodore F. (1993). "What Do Fathers Provide? Reconsidering the Economic and Nurturant Dimensions of Men as Parents." In *Men, Work, and Family,* Jane Hood (ed.). Newbury Park, CA: Sage, pp. 1–22.

Coker, Donna (1999). "Enhancing Autonomy for Battered Women: Lessons from Navajo Peacemaking." *UCLA Law Review* 47 (1): 39–41.

Cole, David (1994). "Five Myths about Immigration." *The Nation,* October 17, pp. 410–412.

Coleman, Margaret (1998). "Homemaker vs. Worker in the United States." *Challenge* 41 (November/ December): 75–87.

Coleman, Marilyn, and Lawrence H. Ganong (1991). "Remarriage and Stepfamily Research in the 1980s: Increased Interest in an Old Family Form." In *Contemporary Families: Looking Forward, Looking Back,* Alan Booth (ed.). Minneapolis: National Council on Family Relations, pp. 192–207.

Coleman, Marilyn, Lawrence H. Ganong, and Mark Fine (2001). "Reinvestigating Remarriage: Another Decade of Progress." In *Understanding Families into the New Millennium: A Decade in Review,* Robert M. Milardo (ed.). Minneapolis: National Council on Family Relations, pp. 507–526.

Collier, Jane, Michelle Z. Rosaldo, and Sylvia Yanagisako (1982). "Is There a Family? New Anthropological Views." In *Rethinking the Family: Some Feminist Questions,* Barrie Thorne and Marilyn Yalom (eds.). New York: Longman, pp. 25–39.

Collins, Chuck, Betsy Leondar-Wright, and Holly Sklar (1999). *Shifting Fortunes: The Perils of the Growing Wealth Gap.* Boston: United for a Fair Economy.

Collins, Patricia Hill (1990). *Black Feminist Thought.* Cambridge, MA: Unwin Hyman.

Collins, Patricia Hill (1997). "Comment on Heckman's 'Truth and Method: Feminist Standpoint Theory Revisited': Where's the Power?" *Signs: Journal of Women in Culture and Society* 22 (2): 375–381.

Collins, Patricia Hill (2000). *Black Feminist Thought: Knowledge, Consciousness, and the Politics of Empowerment,* 2nd ed. New York: Routledge.

Collins, Randall (1988a). *Sociology of Marriage & the Family,* 2nd ed. Chicago: Nelson-Hall.

Collins, Randall (1988b). "Women and Men in the Class Structure." *Journal of Family Issues* 9 (1) (March): 27–50.

Collins, Randall, and Scott Coltrane (1995). *Sociology of Marriage and the Family* 4th ed. Chicago: Nelson-Hall.

Coltrane, Scott (1996). *Family Man: Fatherhood, Housework, and Gender Equity.* New York: Oxford University Press.

Coltrane, Scott (1998). *Gender and Families.* Thousand Oaks, CA: Pine Forge Press.

Coltrane, Scott, and Elsa O. Valdez (1993). "Reluctant Compliance: Work–Family Role Allocation in Dual Earner Chicano Families." In *Men, Work, and Family,* Jane Hood (ed.). Newbury Park, CA: Sage, pp. 151–175.

Connell, Robert W. (1992). "A Very Straight Gay: Masculinity, Homosexual Experience, and the Dynamics of Gender." *American Sociological Review* 57: 735–751.

Connell, R. W., D. J. Ashenden, S. Kessler, and G. W. Dowsett (1982). *Making the Difference.* Boston: Allen & Unwin.

Cook, Christopher D. (2000). "Temps Demand a New Deal." *The Nation,* March 27, pp. 13–20.

Coontz, Stephanie (1992). *The Way We Never Were: American Families and the Nostalgia Trap.* New York: HarperCollins.

Coontz, Stephanie (1994). "The Welfare Discussion We Really Need." *The Christian Science Monitor,* December 29, p. 19.

Coontz, Stephanie (1997). *The Way We Really Are: Coming to Terms with America's Changing Families*. New York: Basic Books.

Coontz, Stephanie (1999a). "The American Family." *Life,* November, pp. 79–94.

Coontz, Stephanie (1999b). "Introduction." In *American Families: A Multicultural Reader,* Stephanie Coontz, with Maya Polson, and Gabrielle Raley (eds.). New York: Routledge, pp. ix–xxix.

Coontz, Stephanie (2000). "Historical Perspectives on Family Diversity." In *Handbook of Family Diversity,* David H. Demo, Katherine R. Allen, and Mark A. Fine (eds.). New York: Oxford University Press, pp. 15–31.

Coontz, Stephanie (2001). "Historical Perspectives on Family Studies." In *Understanding Families into the New Millennium: A Decade in Review,* Robert Milardo (ed.). Minneapolis: The National Council on Family Relations, pp. 80–94.

Cooper, Sheila McIssac (1999). "Historical Analysis of the Family." In *Handbook of Marriage and the Family,* 2nd ed, Marvin B. Sussman, Suzanne K. Steinmetz, and Gary W. Peterson (eds.). New York: Plenum Press, pp. 13–38.

Corliss, Richard (2000). "Clint Does It the Old Way." *Time,* August 14, p. 70.

Cott, Nancy F. (1979). "Eighteenth-Century Family and Social Life Revealed in Massachusetts Divorce Records." In *A Heritage of Her Own: Families, Work, and Feminism in America,* Nancy F. Cott and Elizabeth H. Pleck (eds.). New York: Simon & Schuster, pp. 107–135.

Coy, Peter (2000). "The Creative Economy." *Business Week,* August 28, pp. 76–82.

Crenshaw, Albert B. (1999). "Give Credit When Due." *Washington Post National Weekly Edition,* May 10, p. 20.

Crenshaw, Albert B. (2000). "The Higher Cost of Higher Education." *Washington Post National Weekly Edition,* July 3, p. 35.

Crispell, Diane (1992). "The Brave New World of Men." *American Demographics* 14 (January): 38–43.

Crispell, Diane (1995). "Why Working Teens Get into Trouble." *American Demographics* 17 (February): 19–20.

Crispell, Diane (1996). "The Sibling Syndrome." *American Demographics* 18 (August): 24–30.

Crosby, John F. (1985). *Reply to Myth: Perspectives on Intimacy*. New York: Wiley.

Cuber, John F., and Peggy Haroff (1965). *Sex and the Significant Americans*. Baltimore: Penguin.

Cuber, John F., Martha Tyler John, and Kenneth S. Thompson (1975). "Should Traditional Sex Modes and Values Be Changed?" In *Controversial Issues in the Social Studies,* Raymond H. Muessig (ed.). Washington, DC: National Council for the Social Studies, pp. 87–121.

Currie, Elliott (1998). *Crime and Punishment in America.* New York: Metropolitan Books.

Curry, Timothy Jon (1991). "Fraternal Bonding in the Locker Room: A Profeminist Analysis of Talk about Competition and Women." *Sociology of Sport Journal* 8: 119–135.

Daniels, Arlene Kaplan (1987). *Invisible Careers: Women, Civic Leaders*. Chicago: University of Chicago Press.

Darling, Carol A., David J. Kallen, and Joyce VanDusen (1989). "Sex in Transition, 1900–1980." In *Family in Transition,* 6th ed., Arlene S. Skolnick and Jerome H. Skolnick (eds.). Glenview, IL: Scott, Foresman, pp. 236–244.

Davis, Robert (1994). "Abuse Knows No Social Boundaries." *USA Today,* June 20, p. 3A.

Dawson, John M., and Patrick A. Langen (1994). "Murder in Families." Bureau of Justice Statistics Special Report (July).

Day, Jennifer Cheeseman (1996). "Projections of the Number of Households and Families in the United States: 1995 to 2010." *Current Population Reports,* Series P-25-1129. Washington, DC: U.S. Government Printing Office.

Degler, Carl (1980). *At Odds: Women and the Family in America from the Revolution to the Present*. New York: Oxford University Press.

DeJarnett, Sandra, and Bertram H. Raven (1981). "The Balance, Bases and Modes of Interpersonal Power in Black Couples: The Role of Sex and Socioeconomic Circumstances." *The Journal of Black Psychology* 7 (2): 51–66.

Delgado, Richard, and David Yun (1997). "The Lessons of Loving vs. Virginia." *Rocky Mountain News,* June 27, p. 57A.

D'Emilio, John (1996). "Commentary: What Is a Family?" *Sociologists' Lesbian and Gay Caucus Newsletter* (Summer): 3–4.

D'Emilio, John, and Estelle B. Freedman (1988). *Intimate Matters: A History of Sexuality in America*. New York: Harper & Row.

Demo, David (2000). "Children's Experience of Family Diversity." *Phi Kappa Phi Journal* 80 (Summer): 16–20.

Demo, David H., and Alan C. Acock (1991)."The Impact of Divorce on Children." In *Contemporary Families: Looking Forward, Looking Back,* Alan Booth (ed.). Minneapolis: National Council on Family Relations, pp. 162–191.

Demo, David H., and Martha J. Cox (2001). "Families with Young Children: A Review of Research in the 1990s." In *Understanding Families in the New Millennium,* Robert M. Milardo (ed.). Minneapolis: National Council on Family Relations, pp. 95–114.

Demos, John (1970). *A Little Commonwealth*. New York: Oxford University Press.

Demos, John (1972). "Demography and Psychology in the Historical Study of Family-Life: A Personal Report." In *Household and Family in Past Time*, Peter Laslett and Richard Wall (eds.). Cambridge, UK: Cambridge University Press, pp. 561–570.

Demos, John (1977). "The American Family of Past Time." In *Family in Transition*, 2nd ed., Arlene S. Skolnick and Jerome H. Skolnick (eds.). Boston: Little, Brown, pp. 59–77.

Demos, John (1979). "Images of the American Family, Then and Now." In *Changing Images of the Family*, Virginia Tufte and Barbara Meyerhoff (eds.). New Haven, CT: Yale University Press, pp. 43–60.

Demos, John (1981). "Family Membership in Plymouth Colony." In *Family Life in America, 1620–2000*, Mel Albin and Dominick Cavallo (eds.). St. James, NY: Revisionary Press, pp. 3–13.

Demos, John (1986). *Past, Present, and Personal*. New York: Oxford University Press.

Demos, John, and Virginia Demos (1973). "Adolescence in Historical Perspective." In *The American Family in Social Historical Perspective*, Michael Gordon (ed.). New York: St. Martin's Press, pp. 209–222.

Denver Post (2000). "Invest in Children." (May 30): 10B.

DeParle, Jason (1997a). "A Sharp Decrease in Welfare Cases Is Gathering Speed." *New York Times*, February 2, pp. 1A, 12A.

DeParle, Jason (1997b). "Welfare Law Weights Heavily on Delta, Where the Jobs Are Few." *New York Times*, October 16, p. 1A.

Deutsch, Francine M. (1999). *Halving It All: How Equally Shared Parenting Works*. Cambridge, MA: Harvard University Press.

DeVault, Marjorie L. (1991). *Feeding the Family. The Social Organization of Caring as Gendered Work*. Chicago: University of Chicago Press.

De Vita, Carol J. (1996) "The United States at Mid-Decade." *Population Bulletin* 50 (March):entire issue.

di Leonardo, Micaela (1987). "The Female World of Cards and Holidays: Women, Families, and the Work of Kinship." *Signs: Journal of Women in Culture and Society* 12: 440–453.

Dill, Bonnie Thornton (1983). "On the Hem of Life: Race, Class, and the Prospects for Sisterhood." In *Class, Race, and Sex: The Dynamics of Control*, Amy Swerdlow and Hanna Leisinger (eds.). Boston: G. K. Hall, pp. 173–188.

Dill, Bonnie Thornton (1988). "Our Mothers' Grief: Racial Ethnic Women and the Maintenance of Families." *Journal of Family History* 13 (4): 415–431.

Dill, Bonnie Thornton (1994). "Fictive Kin, Paper Sons, and Compadrazgo: Women of Color and the Struggle for Survival." In *Women of Color in U.S. Society*, Maxine Baca Zinn and Bonnie Thornton Dill (eds.). Philadelphia: Temple University Press, pp. 149–169.

Dill, Bonnie, Thorton (1998). "Economic Disparity Is Key for Minorities." *The Chronicle of Higher Education* (October 2): B7–B8.

Dill, Bonnie Thornton, Maxine Baca Zinn, and Sandra Patton (1993). "Feminism, Race, and the Politics of Family Values." *Report from the Institute for Philosophy and Public Policy*, University of Maryland 13 (Summer): 13–18.

Dill, Bonnie Thornton, Maxine Baca Zinn, and Sandra Patton (1998). "Race, Family Values, and Welfare Reform," *Sage Race Relations* 23 (Fall): 4–31.

Dobash, Russell P., and R. Emerson Dobash (1979). *Violence against Wives*. New York: Free Press.

Dobash, Russell P., and R. Emerson Dobash (1981). "Community Response to Violence Against Wives: Charivari, Abstract Justice and Patriarchy." *Social Problems* 28 (June): 563–581.

Dodds, Paisley (1997). "Church Cites Bible in Decision to End Day Care." *Rocky Mountain News*, April 5, p. 36A.

Domhoff, G. William (1970). *The Higher Circles: The Governing Class in America*. New York: Random House.

Dorrington, C. (1995). "Central American Refugees in Los Angeles: Adjustment of Children and Families." In *Understanding Latino Families: Scholarship, Policy, and Practice*, R. Zambrana (ed.). Thousand Oaks, CA: Sage, pp. 107–129.

Doudna, Christine, and Fern McBride (1981). "Where Are the Men for the Women at the Top?" In *Single Life*, Peter J. Stein (ed.). New York: St. Martin's Press, pp. 21–33.

Douvan, Elizabeth, and Joseph Pleck (1978). "Separation as Support." In *Working Couples*, Robert and Rhona Rapoport (eds.). New York: Harper Colophon, pp. 138–146.

Downey, Douglas B. (1995). "When Bigger Is Not Better: Family Size, Parental Resources, and Children's Educational Performance." *American Sociological Review* 60 (October):746–761.

Drucker, Peter F. (1993). *The Post-Capitalist Society*. New York: HarperCollins.

Drucker, Peter F. (1999). "Beyond the Information Revolution." *The Atlantic Monthly* 284 (October):47–57.

Dubeck, Paula J. (1998). "The Need and Challenge to Better Integrate Work and Family in the Twenty-First Century." In *Challenges for Work and Family in the Twenty-First Century*, Dana Vannoy, and Paula J. Dubeck (eds.). Hawthorne, NY: Aldine de Gruyter, pp. 3–8.

Dunn, William (1991). "'I Do' is Repeat Refrain for Half of Newlyweds." *USA Today*, February 15, p. A1.

Duvander, Ann-Zofie E. (1999). "The Transition from Cohabitation to Marriage: A Longitudinal Study of the Propensity to Marry in Sweden in the Early 1990s." *Journal of Family Issues* 20 (September): 698–717.

Dworkin, Andrea. (1981). *Pornography: Men Possessing Women*. New York: Perigree Books.

Dyer, Everett D. (1979). *The American Family: Variety and Change.* New York: McGraw-Hill.

Early, Frances H. (1983). "The French-Canadian Family Economy and Standard of Living in Lowell, Massachusetts, 1870." In *The American Family in Social Historical Perspective,* 3rd ed., Michael Gordon (ed.). New York: St. Martin's Press, pp. 482–503.

Economist, The (1993). "The Other America." (July 10): 17–18.

Edelman, Marian Wright (1996). "Need for State Advocacy Intensifies." *Children's Defense Fund Reports* 17 (September): 1.

Edelman, Peter (1997). "The Worst Thing Bill Clinton Has Done." *The Atlantic Monthly* 279 (March): 43–58.

Edelman, Peter (2000). "America's 'Disappeared.'" *Salon.* http://salon.com/news/feature/2000/01/14/poverty/index.html>.

Edin, Kathryn (2000). "Few Good Men." *The American Prospect* (January 3): 26–31.

Edin, Kathryn, and Laura Lein (1997). *Making Ends Meet.* New York: Russell Sage Foundation.

Edwards, Tamala (2000). "Flying Solo." *Time,* August 28, pp. 47–53.

Ehrenreich, Barbara (1997). "When Government Gets Mean: Confessions of a Recovering Statist." *The Nation,* November 17, pp. 11–16.

Ehrenreich, Barbara (2000). "Maid to Order." *Harper's Magazine* 300 (April): 59–70.

Ehrenreich, Barbara, and Diedra English (1978). *For Her Own Good: 150 Years of the Experts' Advice to Women.* Garden City, NY: Doubleday/Anchor.

Eichler, Margrit (1981). "The Inadequacy of the Monolithic Model of the Family." *Canadian Journal of Sociology* 6 (Summer): 367–388.

Eitzen, D. Stanley (1974). *Social Structure and Social Problems.* Boston: Allyn & Bacon.

Eitzen, D. Stanley (1996). "Dismantling the Welfare State." *Vital Speeches of the Day* 62 (June 15): 532–536.

Eitzen, D. Stanley, and Maxine Baca Zinn (1989). "The Forces Reshaping America." In *The Reshaping of America: Social Consequences of the Changing Economy,* D. S. Eitzen and Maxine Baca Zinn (eds.). Englewood Cliffs, NJ: Prentice Hall, pp. 1–13.

Eitzen, D. Stanley, and Maxine Baca Zinn (2001). *In Conflict and Order: Understanding Society,* 9th ed. Boston: Allyn & Bacon.

Elder, Glen H., Jr. (1969). "Appearance and Education in Marriage Mobility." *American Sociological Review* 34 (August): 519–532.

Elliott, Michael (1994/1995). "Forward to the Past." *Newsweek,* December 26/January 2, pp. 130–133.

Elliott, Pam (1996). "Shattering Illusions: Same-Sex Violence." In *Violence in Gay and Lesbian Domestic Partnerships,* Claire M. Renzetti and Charles Harvey Miley (eds.). New York: Harrington Park, pp. 1–8.

El Nasser, Haya (2000). "When Growth Gets Limited, So Does Housing." *USA Today,* May 18, p. 14A.

Eng, P. (1990). "Woman Battering in Asian Immigrant Communities in the U.S." Paper presented at the Fourth International Interdisciplinary Congress on Women, New York.

Eng, P. (1995). "Domestic Violence in Asian/Pacific Islander Communities." In *Health Issues for Women of Color,* D. L. Adams (ed.). Thousand Oaks, CA: Sage, pp. 78–88.

Engels, Friedrich (1942). *The Origin of the Family, Private Property, and the State.* New York: International Publishers (original work published in 1884).

England, Paula, and Nancy Folbre (1999). "Who Should Pay for the Kids?" *The Annals* 563 (May): 194–207.

Epstein, Steven (1994). "A Queer Encounter: Sociology and the Study of Sexuality." *Sociological Theory* 12 (July): 188–202.

Erbe, Bonnie (2000). "Child-Free and Not Complaining." *Rocky Mountain News,* July 25, p. 37A.

Escobar, Gabriel (1999). "Transforming a Nation in Just One Generation." *Washington Post National Weekly Edition,* January 18, p. 29.

Eshleman, J. Ross (2000). *The Family,* 9th ed. Boston: Allyn & Bacon.

Espin, Olivia (1984). "Influences on Sexuality in Hispanic/Latina Women." In *Pleasure and Danger: Exploring Female Sexuality,* Carole S. Vance (ed.). Boston: Routledge and Kegan Paul, pp. 149–164.

Eve, Raymond A., and Donald G. Renslow (1980). "An Exploratory Study of Private Sexual Behaviors among College Students: Some Implications for a Theory of Class Differences in Sexual Behavior." *Social Behavior and Personality* 8 (1): 97–105.

Falwell, Jerry (1980). *Listen America.* New York: Doubleday.

Faragher, Johnny, and Christine Stansell (1979). "Women and Their Families on the Overland Trail to California and Oregon, 1842–1868." In *A Heritage of Her Own,* Nancy F. Cott and Elizabeth H. Pleck (eds.). New York: Simon & Schuster, pp. 246–267.

Farber, Bernard (1973). "Family and Community Structure: Salem in 1800." In *The American Family in Social Historical Perspective,* Michael Gordon (ed.). New York: St. Martin's Press, pp. 100–110.

Farley, Reynolds (1996). *The New American Reality.* New York: Russell Sage Foundation.

Fasinger, Polly A. (1993). "Meanings of Housework for Single Fathers and Mothers: Insights into Gender Inequality." In *Men, Work, and Family,* Jane Hood (ed.). Newbury Park, CA: Sage, pp. 195–216.

Faust, Kimberly A., and Jerome N. McKibben (1999). In *Handbook of Marriage and the Family,* 2nd ed., Marvin Sussman, Suzanne K. Steinmetz, and Gary W. Peterson (eds.). New York: Plenum Press, pp. 475–499.

Feagin, Joe R. (1986). *Social Problems: A Critical Power-Conflict Perspective,* 2nd ed. Englewood Cliffs, NJ: Prentice Hall.

Federal Interagency Forum on child and Family Statistics (2000). *America's Children: Key National Indicators of Well-Being, 2000.* Washington, DC: U.S. Government Printing Office.

Fernandez-Kelly, M. Patricia (1990). "Delicate Transactions, Gender, Home, and Employment among Hispanic Women." In *Uncertain Terms,* Gaye Ginsberg and Anna Lowenhaupt Tsing (eds.). Boston: Beacon Press.

Fernandez-Kelly, M. Patricia., and A. M. Garcia (1990). "Power Surrendered, Power Restored: The Politics of Home and Work among Hispanic Women in Southern California and Southern Florida." In *Women and Politics in America,* Louise Tilly and Patricia Gurin (eds.). New York: Russell Sage Foundation.

Ferree, Myra Marx (1987). "Family and Job for Working-Class Women: Gender and Class Systems Seen from Below." In *Families and Work,* Naomi Gerstel and Harriet Engel Gross (eds.). Philadelphia: Temple University Press, pp. 289–301.

Ferree, Myra Marx (1991). "Feminism and Family Research." In *Contemporary Families: Looking Forward, Looking Back,* Alan Booth (ed.). Minneapolis: National Council on Family Relations, pp. 103–121.

Figart, Deborah M., and Ellen Mutari (1998). "Degendering Work Time in Comparative Perspective: Alternative Policy Frameworks." *Review of Social Economy* 56: 460–480.

Fine, Michelle (1981). "Injustice by Any Other Name." *Victimology* 6 (Nos. 1B4): 48–58.

Finkelhor, David (1993). "Epidemiological Factors in the Clinical Identification of Child Sexual Abuse." *Child Abuse and Neglect* 17: 67–70.

Fishman, Katharine Davis (1992). "Problem Adoptions." *Atlantic Monthly* 270 (September): 37–69.

Fishman, Pamela M. (1978). "Interaction: The Work Women Do." *Social Problems* 25 (April): 397–406.

Fitzpatrick, Mary Anne (1988). *Between Husbands and Wives: Communication in Marriage.* Beverly Hills, CA: Sage.

Fletcher, Michael A. (1998). "All Fighting for a Piece of the Dream." *Washington Post National Weekly Edition,* May 18, pp. 8–9.

Folbre, Nancy (2000). "Universal Childcare: It's Time." *The Nation,* July 3, pp. 21–23.

Forbes (2000). "Forbes 400 Richest People in America, 1999: The Families." http://www.forbes.com/toolbox/rich400/asf/families.asp?.year+1999>.

Forward, Susan, and Craig Buck (1978). *Betrayal of Innocence: Incest and Its Devastation.* Los Angeles: J. P. Tarcher.

Fowlkes, Martha R. (1987). "The Myth of Merit and Male Professional Careers." In *Families and Work,* Naomi Gerstel and Harriet Engel Gross (eds.). Philadelphia: Temple University Press, pp. 347–360.

Fowlkes, Martha R. (1994). "Single Worlds and Homosexual Lifestyles: Patterns of Sexuality and Intimacy." In *Sexuality across the Life Course,* Alice S. Rossi (ed.),. Chicago: The University of Chicago Press, pp. 151–184.

Frank, Ellen, and Carol Anderson (1989). "The Sexual Stages of Marriage." In *Marriage and Family in a Changing Society,* James M. Henslin (ed.). New York: The Free Press, pp. 190–195.

Frankenberg, Ruth (1993). *The Social Construction of Whiteness: White Women, Race Matters.* Minneapolis: University of Minnesota Press.

Frazier, E. Franklin (1939). *The Negro Family in the United States.* Chicago: University of Chicago Press.

Frerking, Beth (1994). "How Could a Mom Kill Her Own Children?" *Rocky Mountain News,* November 5, p. 56A.

Frey, William H. (1999). "'New Sun Belt' Metros and Suburbs Are Magnets for Retirees." *Population Today* 27 (October): 1–3.

Fried, Mindy, and Claire Reinelt (1993). "A Family Policy for All Kinds of Families." *Social Policy* 23 (Summer): 64–71.

Frisco, Michelle, Chandra Muller, and Daniel Powers (2000). "Adolescent Sexual Initiation and Academic Attainment." Unpublished paper presented at the American Sociological Association Meetings, Washington, DC.

Fuchs, Rachel (1984). *Abandoned Children.* Albany: State University of New York Press.

Fuller–Thomson, Meredith Minkler, and Diane Driver (1997). "A Profile of Grandparents Raising Grandchildren in the United States." *The Gerontologist* 37 (3): 406–411.

Funk, Allie, and Margaret McLean Hughes (1996). "Shift Work and Child Care." In *Women and Work: A Handbook,* Paula J. Dubek and Katherine Borman (eds.). New York: Longman, pp. 406–407.

Furstenberg, Frank F., Jr. (1987). "Race Differences in Teenage Sexuality, Pregnancy, and Adolescent Childbearing." *The Milbank Quarterly* 65, Supplement 2: 381–403.

Furstenberg, Frank F., Jr. (1990). "Divorce and the American Family," *Annual Review of Sociology* 16: 379–403.

Furstenberg, Frank F., Jr. (1996). "The Future of Marriage." *American Demographics* 18: 34–40.

Furstenberg, Frank F., Jr. (1999). "Is the Modern Family a Threat to Children's Health?" *Society* 36 (July/August): 31–37.

Furstenberg, Frank F., Jr. (2001). "A Sociology of Adolescence and Youth in the 1990s." In *Understanding Families into the New Millennium,* Robert M. Milardo (ed.). Minneapolis: National Council on Family Relations, pp. 115–129.

Furstenberg, Frank F., Jr., and Andrew J. Cherlin (1991). *Divided Families: What Happens to Children When Parents Part.* Cambridge, MA: Harvard University Press.

Furstenberg, Frank F., Jr., and Julien O. Teitler (1994). "Reconsidering the Effects of Marital Disruption." *Journal of Family Issues* 15 (June): 173–190.

Gagnon, John (1983). "On the Sources of Sexual Change." In *Promoting Sexual Responsibility and Preventing Sexual Problems,* George W. Albee, Sol Gordon, and Harold Leitenberg (eds.). Hanover, NH: University Press of New England, pp. 157–170.

Galinsky, Ellen (1986). "Family Life and Corporate Policies." In *Support of Families,* Michael Yogman and T. Berry Brazelton (eds.). Cambridge, MA: Harvard University Press.

Galinsky, Ellen, and James T. Bond (1996). "Work and Family: The Experiences of Mothers and Fathers in the U.S. Workforce." In *The American Woman, 1996–97,* Cynthia Costello and Barbara Kivimae Krimgold (eds.). New York: W. W. Norton, pp. 79–103.

Galvin, Kathleen M., and Bernard J. Brommel (1999). *Family Communication: Cohesion and Change,* 5th ed. New York: Longman.

Gans, Herbert J. (1962). *The Urban Villagers.* New York: The Free Press.

Gans, Herbert J. (1990). "Second Generation Decline." *Ethnic Racial Studies* 15: 173–192.

Garcia, Mario T. (1980). "La Familia: The Mexican Immigrant Family, 1900–1930. In *Work, Family, Sex Roles, Language,* Mario Barrera, Alberto Camarillo, and Francis Hernandez (eds.). Berkeley: Tonativa-Quinto Sol International, pp. 117–140.

Garekik, Glenn (1991). "Teach Your Parents Well." *USA Weekend,* August 9, pp. 4–5.

Garey, Anita 1995). "Constructing Motherhood on the Night Shift: 'Working Mothers' as Stay-at-Home Moms." *Qualitative Sociology* 18 (4): 415–437.

Garey, Anita (1999). *Weaving Work and Motherhood.* Philadelphia: Temple University Press.

Garey, Anita, and Karen Hanson (1998). "Introduction: Analyzing Families with a Feminist Sociological Imagination." In *Families in the U.S.: Kinship and Domestic Politics.* Philadelphia: Temple University Press, pp. xii–xv.

Gaylord, Maxine (1979). "Relocation and the Corporate Family: Unexplored Issues." *Social Work* 24 (May): 186–191.

Gecas, Viktor, and Monica A. Seff (1991). "Families and Adolescents:" In *Contemporary Families: Looking Forward , Looking Back,* Alan Booth (ed.). Minneapolis: National Council on Family Relations, pp. 208–225.

Geiser, Robert L. (1979). *Hidden Victims: The Sexual Abuse of Children.* Boston: Beacon.

Gelles, Richard J. (1976). "Demythologizing Child Abuse." *The Family Coordinator* 25 (April).

Gelles, Richard J. (1977). "No Place to Go: The Social Dynamics of Marital Violence." In *Battered Women,* Maria Roy (ed.). New York: Van Nostrand, pp. 46–62.

Gelles, Richard J. (1990). "Domestic Violence and Child Abuse." In *Violence: Patterns, Causes, and Public Policy,* Neil Alan Weiner, Margaret A. Zahn, and Rita J. Sagi (eds.). San Diego: Harcourt, Brace, Jovanovich.

Gelles, Richard J. (1993). "Family Violence." In *Family Violence: Prevention and Treatment,* Robert J. Hampton, Thomas P. Gullotta, Gerald R. Adams, Earl H. Potter, and Roger P. Weissberg (eds.). Newbury Park, CA: Sage.

Gelles, Richard J. (1995). *Contemporary Families: A Sociological View.* Thousand Oak, CA: Sage.

Gelles, Richard J., and Jon R. Conte (1991). "Domestic Violence and Sexual Abuse of Children." In *Contemporary Families: Looking Forward, Looking Back,* Alan Booth (ed.). Minneapolis: National Council on Family Relations, pp. 327–340.

Gelles, Richard J., Regina Lackner, and Glenn D. Wolfner (1994). "Men Who Batter: The Risk Markers." *Violence Update* 4 (August): 1–2, 4, 10.

Gelles, Richard J., and Murray A. Straus (1979). "Determinants of Violence in the Family." In *Contemporary Theories About the Family,* Vol. 1, Wesley R. Burr, Reuben Hill, F. Ivan Nye, and Ira L. Reiss (eds.). New York: The Free Press, pp. 549–581.

Gelles, Richard J., and Murray A. Straus (1988). *Intimate Violence.* New York: Simon & Schuster.

Gelman, David (1990). "A Much Riskier Passage." *Newsweek Special Issue,* Summer/Fall, pp. 10–17.

Gelman, David (1992). "Born or Bred?" *Newsweek,* February 24, pp. 46–53.

Genovese, Eugene D. (1981). "Husbands and Fathers, Wives and Mothers during Slavery." In *Family Life in America, 1620–2000,* Mel Albin and Dominick Cavello (eds.). New York: Revisionary Press, pp. 237–251.

Geronimus, Arline T. (1992). "The Socioeconomic Consequences of Teen Childbearing Reconsidered." *Quarterly Journal of Economics* 107 (4): 1187–1214.

Gerson, Kathleen (1993). *No Man's Land.* New York: Basic Books.

Gerson, Kathleen (2000). "Resolving Family Dilemmas and Conflicts: Beyond Utopia." *Contemporary Sociology* 29 (January): 181–187.

Gerstel, Naomi R. (1977). "The Feasibility of Commuter Marriage." In *The Family: Functions, Conflicts, and Symbols,* Peter J. Stein, Judith Richman, and Natalie Hannon (eds.). Reading, MA: Addison-Wesley, pp. 357–365.

Gerstel, Naomi, and Harriet Engel Gross (eds.) (1987a), "Commuter Marriage: A Microcosm of Career and

Family Conflict." In *Families and Work,* Naomi Gerstel and Harriet Engel Gross (eds.). Philadelphia: Temple University Press, pp. 222–233.

Gerstel, Naomi, and Harriet Engel Gross (eds.) (1987b). *Families and Work.* Philadelphia: Temple University Press.

Giarrusso, Roseann, Merrel Silverstein, and Du Feng (2000). "Psychological Costs and Benefits of Raising Grandchildren." In *To Grandmother's House We Go and Stay,* Carole B. Cox (ed.). New York: Springer, pp. 71–90.

Giddens, Anthony (1992). *The Transformation of Intimacy: Sexuality, Love, and Eroticism in Modern Societies.* Stanford, CA: Stanford University Press.

Gilbert, Dennis, and Joseph A. Kahl (1982). *The American Class Structure, A New Synthesis.* Homewood, IL: Dorsey Press.

Gilbert, Susan (2000). 'Kids' Earlier Sex Vexes Parents." *Denver Post,* November 5, pp. 42A–43A.

Gillespie, Dair (1972). "Who Has the Power? The Marital Struggle." In *Family Marriage and the Struggle of the Sexes,* Hans Peter Dreitzel (ed.). New York: Macmillan, pp. 121–150.

Gillis, John R. (1996). *A World of Their Own Making.* Cambridge, MA: Harvard University Press.

Gitlin, Todd (1994). "Imagebusters: The Hollow Crusade against TV Violence." *The American Prospect,* No. 16 (Winter): 42–49.

Gladin, Howard (1977). "Private Lives and Public Order: A Critical View of the History of Intimate Relations in the United States." In *Close Relationships,* George Levinger and Harold L. Rauch (eds.). Amherst: University of Massachusetts Press, pp. 33–72.

Glenn, Evelyn Nakano (1983). "Split Household, Small Producer and Dual Wage Earner: An Analysis of Chinese-American Family Strategies." *Journal of Marriage and the Family* 45 (1) (February): 35–46.

Glenn, Evelyn Nakano (1985). "Racial-Ethnic Women's Labor: The Intersection of Race, Gender, and Class Oppression." *Review of Radical Political Economy* 17: 86–109.

Glenn, Evelyn Nakano (1987). "Racial-Ethnic Women's Labor: The Intersection of Race, Gender and Class Oppression." In *Hidden Aspects of Women's Work,* Christine Bose, Roslyn Feldberg, and Natalie Sokoloff with the Women and Work Research Group (eds.). New York: Praeger, pp. 46–73.

Glenn, Evelyn Nakano (1992). "From Servitude to Service Work: Historical Continuities in the Racial Division of Paid Reproductive Labor," *Signs: Journal of Women in Culture and Society* 18 (1) (Autumn): 1–43.

Glenn, Evelyn Nakano (1994). "Social Construction of Mothering." In *Mothering, Ideology, Experience, and Agency,* Evelyn Nakano Glenn, Grace Chang, and Linda Rennie Forey (eds.). New York: Routledge, pp. 1–29.

Glenn, Norval D. (1989), "Duration of Marriage, Family Composition, Marital Happiness." *National Journal of Sociology* 3: 3–34.

Glenn, Norval D. (1996). "Values, Attitudes, and the State of American Marriage." In *Promises to Keep: Decline and Renewal of Marriage in America,* David Popenoe, J. B. Elshtain, and David Blankenhorn (eds.). Lanham, MD: Rowman and Littlefield, pp. 15–34.

Glenn, Norval D. (1997). "A Critique of Twenty Family and Marriage Textbooks." *Family Relations* 46 (July): 197–208.

Glick, Jennifer E. (1999). "Economic Support From and To Extended Kin: A Comparison of Mexican Americans and Mexican Immigrants." *International Migration Review* 33 (Fall): 745–765.

Glick, Jennifer E., Frank D. Bean, and Jennifer V. W. Van Hook (1997). "Immigration and Changing Patterns of Extended Family Household Structures in the United States: 1970–1990." *Journal of Marriage and the Family* 59 (February): 177–191.

Gober, Patricia (1993). "Americans on the Move." *Population Bulletin* 48 (November): entire issue.

Goffman, Erving (1959). *The Presentation of Self in Everyday Life.* Garden City, NY: Doubleday.

Goldscheider, Frances K., and Calvin Goldscheider (1994). "Leaving and Returning Home in 20th Century America." *Population Bulletin* 48 (March).

Goldscheider, Frances K., and Linda J. Waite (1991). *New Families, No Families? The Transformation of the American Home.* Berkeley: University of California Press.

Goldstein, Joshua R. (1999). "The Leveling of Divorce in the United States." *Demography* 36 (August): 409–414.

Gonzalas, Kathleen M. (1928). *The Mexican Family in San Antonio, Texas.* The University of Texas. (Reprinted by R. and E. Research Associates, San Francisco, 1971.)

Goode, William J. (1959). "The Theoretical Importance of Love." *American Sociological Review* 24 (February): 38–47.

Goode, William J. (1963). *World Revolution and Family Patterns.* New York: The Free Press.

Goode, William J. (1971). "Force and Violence in the Family." *Journal of Marriage and the Family* 33 (November): 624–636.

Goode, William J. (1983). "World Revolution in Family Patterns." In *Family in Transition,* 4th ed., Arlene Skolnick and Jerome Skolnick (eds.). Boston: Little, Brown, pp. 43–52.

Goodman, Ellen (1995). "Now We're Against Paying for Welfare and Abortions." *Coloradoan,* January 20, p. A8.

Gordon, Michael, ed. (1983). *The American Family in Social-Historical Perspective.* New York: St. Martin's Press.

Gordon, Tula (1994). *Single Women: On the Margins?* New York: New York University Press.

Gorman, Christine (1991a). "Are Gay Men Born That Way?" *Time,* September 9, pp. 60–61.

Grabill, Wilson H., Clyde V. Kiser, and Pascal K. Whelpton (1973). "A Long View." In *The American Family in Social-Historical Perspective,* Michael Gordon (ed.). New York: St. Martin's Press, pp. 374–396.

Graff, E. J. (1999). "Same-Sex Spouses in Canada." *The Nation,* July 12, pp. 23–24.

Granrose, Cherlyn Skromme (1996). "Planning to Combine Work and Childbearing." In *Women and Work: A Handbook,* Paula J. Dubek and Katherine Borman (eds.). New York: Longman, pp. 401–403.

Greenberg, Susan H., and Karen Springen (2000). "Back to Day Care." *Newsweek,* October 16, pp. 61–62.

Greenberger, Ellen, and Laurence Steinberg (1986). *When Teenagers Work: The Psychological and Social Costs of Adolescent Employment.* New York: Basic Books.

Greenwald, John (1999). "Elder Care: Making the Right Choice." *Time,* August 30, pp. 52–56.

Greven, Phillip J. (1970). *Four Generations: Population, Land, and Family in Colonial Andover, Mass.* Ithaca, NY: Cornell University Press.

Griffith, James, and Sandra Villavicienco (1985). "Relationships among Acculturation, Sociodemographic Characteristics, and Social Supports in Mexican American Adults." *Hispanic Journal of Behavioral Science* 7: 75–92.

Griswold del Castillo, Richard (1984). *La Familia.* Notre Dame, IN: University of Notre Dame Press.

Gross, Harriet Engel (1984). "Dual-Career Couples Who Live Apart." In *Framing the Family,* Bert N. Adams and John L. Campbell (eds.). Prospect Heights, IL: Waveland Press, pp. 468–482.

Groves, M. M., and D. M. Horn-Wingerd (1991). "Commuter Marriages: Personal, Family, and Career Issues." *Sociology and Social Research* 75 (4): 212–217.

Grundy, Lea, and Netsy Firestein (1997). *Work, Family, and the Labor Movement.* Cambridge, MA: Radcliffe Public Policy Institute.

Guo, Guang, and Kathleen Mullan Harris (2000). "The Mechanisms Mediating the Effects of Poverty on Children's Intellectual Development." *Demography* 37 (November): 431–447.

Gutman, Herbert (1976). *The Black Family in Slavery and Freedom, 1750–1925.* New York: Pantheon.

Haas, Linda (1999). "Families and Work." In *Handbook of Marriaige and the Family,* 2nd ed., Marvin B. Sussman, Suzanne K. Steinmetz, and Gary Peterson (eds.). New York: Plenum, pp. 571–612.

Halladay, Jessie (2000). "Demand Up for Services for the Poor." *USA Today,* December 14, p. 21A.

Halle, David (1984). *America's Working Man.* Chicago: University of Chicago Press.

Hamburg, David A. (1993). "The American Family Transformed." *Society* 31 (January/February): 60–69.

Handlin, Oscar (1951). *The Uprooted.* Boston: Little, Brown.

Hareven, Tamara K. (1975). "Family Time and Industrial Time." *Journal of Urban History* 1 (May): 365–389.

Hareven, Tamara K. (1976a). "Modernization and Family History: Perspectives on Social Change." *Signs: Journal of Women in Culture and Society* 2: 190–206.

Hareven, Tamara K. (1976b). "Women and Men: Changing Roles." In *Women and Men: Changing Roles, Relationships, and Perceptions,* Libby A. Cater, Anne Firor Scott, and Wendy Martyna (eds.). Queenstown, MD: Aspen Institute for Humanistic Studies, pp. 93–118.

Hareven, Tamara K. (1977). *Family and Kin in Urban Communities, 1700–1930.* New York: New Viewpoints.

Hareven, Tamara K. (1987). "Historical Analysis of the Family." In *Handbook of Marriage and the Family,* Marvin B. Sussman and Suzanne K. Steinmetz (eds.). New York: Plenum, pp. 37–57.

Hareven, Tamara K., and Maris A. Vinovskis (eds.) (1978). *Introduction to Family and Population in Nineteenth-Century America.* Princeton, NJ: Princeton University Press.

Harrington, Michael (1984). *The New American Poverty.* New York: Holt, Rinehart & Winston.

Harris, Kathleen Mullan (1996). "The Reforms Will Hurt, Not Help, Poor Women and Children." *The Chronicle of Higher Education* (October 4): 37.

Harry, Joseph (1983). "Gay Male and Lesbian Relationships." In *Contemporary Families and Alternative Lifestyles,* Eleanor D. Macklin and Roger H. Rubin (eds.). Beverly Hills, CA: Sage, pp. 216–234.

Hartley, Shirley Foster (1973). "Our Growing Problem: Population." *Social Problems* 21 (Fall).

Hartmann, Heidi I. (1981). "The Family as the Locus of Gender, Class, and Political Struggle: The Example of Housework." *Signs: Journal of Women in Culture and Society* 6 (3): 366–394.

Hatfield, Elaine (1983). "What Do Women and Men Want from Love and Sex?" In *Changing Boundaries, Gender Roles and Sexual Behavior,* Elizabeth Rice Allgeier and Naomi B. McCormick (eds.). Palo Alto, CA: Mayfield, pp. 106–134.

Hayes, Cherly D., John L. Palmer, and Martha J. Zaslow (eds.) (1990). *Who Cares For America's Children? Child Care Policy for the 1990s.* Washington, DC: National Academy Press.

Hayghe, Howard (1990). "Family Members in the Workforce." *Monthly Labor Review* 113 (March): 14–19.

Healy, Melissa (1997). "Welfare 'Family Caps' Fail Test." *Denver Post,* September 12, p. 23A.

Heaton, Tim B. (1986). "How Does Religion Influence Fertility? The Case of Mormons." *Journal of the Scientific Study of Religion* 25: 248–258.

Heaton, Tim B. (1990). "Marital Stability Throughout the Child-Rearing Years." *Demography* 27 (February): 55–63.

Heaton, Tim B., Karen Davis Boyd, Kennion D. Jolley, and Brent C. Miller (1996). "Influences of Children's Number, Age, Relatedness, Gender, and Problems on Parental and Marital Relationships." *Family Perspectives* 30 (2): 131–159.

Heinz, James, and Nancy Folbre (2000). *The Ultimate Field Guide to the U.S. Economy.* New York: The New Press.

Helburn, Suzanne W. (1999). "The Silent Crisis in U.S. Child Care." *The Annals* 563 (May): 8–19.

Heller, Celia (1966). *Mexican American Youth: Forgotten Youth at the Crossroads.* New York: Random House.

Henretta, James A. (1973). *The Evolution of American Society, 1780–1815.* Lexington, MA: D. C. Heath.

Herbert, Bob (1997a). "3:00, Nowhere to Go." *New York Times,* October 26, p. 15.

Herbert, Bob (1997b). "Not All Enjoy Highs of Low Jobless Rate." *New York Times,* November 21, p. 70A.

Herbert, Bob (2000a). "This Is Class Warfare?" *New York Times,* http://nytimes.com/library/opinion/ herbert/ 082100.herb.html>.

Herbert, Bob (2000b). "Working Harder, Longer." *New York Times,* <htty://090400herb.html>.

Herbert, Wray (1999). "Not Tonight Dear." *U.S. News & World Report,* February 22, pp. 57–59.

Herman, Judith, and Lisa Hirschman (1981). *Father–Daughter Incest.* Cambridge, MA: Harvard University Press.

Hernandez, Donald J. (1993). "Jobs, Poverty, and Family Breakup." *USA Today* (magazine) 122 (November): 28–29.

Herrnstein, Richard J., and Charles Murray (1994). *The Bell Curve: Intelligence and Class Structure in American Life.* New York: The Free Press.

Herz, Diane E., and Barbara H. Wootton (1996). "Women in the Workforce: An Overview." In *The American Woman, 1996–97,* Cynthia Costello and Barbara Kivimae Krimgold (eds.). New York: W. W. Norton, pp. 44–78.

Hetherington, E. Mavis, and Margaret Stanley-Hagan (2000). "Diversity among Stepfamilies." In *Handbook of Family Diversity,* David H. Demo, Katherine R. Allen, and Mark A. Fine (eds.). New York: Oxford University Press, pp. 173–196.

Hettleman, Kalman R. (1997). "States' Rights, School Wrongs." *The Nation,* March 10, pp. 23–24.

Hewlett, Sylvia Ann (1991). *When the Bough Breaks: The Cost of Neglecting Our Children.* New York: Basic Books.

Hewlett, Sylvia Ann and Cornel West (1998). *The War against Parents: What We Can Do for America's Beleaguered Moms and Dads.* Boston: Houghton Mifflin.

Heyl, Barbara (1996). "Homosexuality: A Social Phenomena." In *The Meaning of Difference,* Karen E. Rosenblum and Toni-Michelle C. Travis (eds.). New York: McGraw–Hill, pp. 120–129.

Higginbotham, Elizabeth (1981). "Is Marriage a Priority?" In *Single Life: Unmarried Adults in Social Context,* Peter J. Stein (ed.). New York: St. Martin's Press, pp. 259–267.

Hill, Robert B. (1977). *Informal Adoption among Black Families.* Washington, DC: National Urban League Research Department.

Hill, Robert B. (1993). *Research on the African American Family.* Westport, CT: Auburn House.

Hine, Thomas (1999). "The Rise and Decline of the American Teenager." *American Heritage* (September): 69–82.

Hochschild, Arlie Russell, (1975) "Inside the Clockwork of Male Careers," In *Women and the Power to Change,* Florence Howe, (ed.) New York: McGraw Hill, pp. 47–80.

Hochschild, Arlie Russell (1983a). "Attending to, Codifying and Managing Feelings: Sex Differences in Love." In *Feminist Frontiers,* Laurel Richardson and Verta Taylor (eds.). Reading MA: Addison-Wesley, pp. 250–262.

Hochschild, Arlie Russell (1983b). *The Managed Heart.* Berkeley: University of California Press.

Hochschild, Arlie Russell, with Anne Machung (1989). *The Second Shift.* New York: Viking Penguin, 1989.

Hochschild, Arlie Russell (1997). *The Time Bind.* New York: Metropolitan Books.

Hochschild, Arlie Russell (2000). "The Nanny Chain." *The American Prospect* (January 3): 32–36.

Hodges, Jill (1996). "Partner Benefits May Not Apply to Heterosexuals." *Minneapolis Star Tribune,* June 7, p. 1.

Hoffman, Lois W. (1987). "The Effects of Children on Maternal and Parental Employment." In *Families and Work,* Naomi Gerstel and Harriet Engel Gross (eds.). Philadelphia: Temple University Press, pp. 362–368.

Holstein, James A., and Jay Gubrium (1999). "What Is Family? Further Thoughts on a Social Constructionist Approach." *Marriage and Family Review* 28 (3/4): 3–20.

Hondagneu-Sotelo, Pierrette (1992). "Overcoming Patriarchal Constraints: The Reconstruction of Gender Relations among Mexican Immigrant Women and Men." *Gender & Society* 6 (September): 393–415.

Hondagneu-Sotelo, Pierrette (1994). *Gendered Transitions: Mexican Experiences of Immigration.* Berkeley: University of California Press.

Hondagneu-Sotelo, Pierrette (1995). *Women and Children First: New Directions in Anti-Immigrant Politics. Socialist Review* 25 (1): 169–190.

Hondagneu-Sotelo, Pierrette, and Ernestine Avila (1996). "Transnational Motherhood: The Means of Spatial and Temporal Separations." (Unpublished manuscript.)

Hondagneu-Sotelo, Pierrette, and Ernestine Avila (1997). "I'm Here, But I'm There: The Meanings of Latina Transnational Motherhood." *Gender & Society,* 11 (October): 548–571.

Hondagneu-Sotelo, Pierrette, and Michael A. Messner (1994). "Gender Display and Men's Power: The 'New Man' and the Mexican Immigrant Man." In *Theorizing Masculinities,* Harry Brod and Michael Kaufman (eds.). Newbury Park, CA: Sage, pp. 200–218.

Hood, Jane C. (ed.). (1994). *Men, Work, and Family.* Newbury Park, CA: Sage.

Hoppe, Sue Kier, and Peter L. Heller (1975). "Alienation, Familism, and the Utilization of Health Services by Mexican-Americans." *Journal of Health and Social Behavior* 16: 304–314.

Hopper, D. Ian (2000). "Report: Nearly 25% of Women Have Been Assaulted by Partner." Associated Press, July 14.

Horn, Patricia (1990). "To Love and Cherish." *Dollars & Sense,* No. 157 (June): 9–22.

Horovitz, Bruce. (1999). "Selling Beautiful Babies." *USA Today,* October 25, pp. 1A–2A.

House Select Committee on Children, Youth, and Families (1984). *Federal Programs Affecting Children.* Washington, DC: U.S. Government Printing Office.

Houseknecht, Sharon K., and Jaya Sastry (1996). "Family 'Decline' and Child Well-Being." *Journal of Marriage and the Family* 58 (August): 726–739.

Hovedt, M. E. (1982). "Life Adaptations." In *Homosexuality: Social, Psychological, and Biological Issues.* W. Paul, J. Weinrich, J.C. Gonsiorek, and M.E. Hovedt (eds.). Beverly Hills, CA: Sage, pp. 288–289.

Howe, Louise Kapp (1972). *The Future of the Family.* New York: Simon & Schuster.

Huber, Joan (1993). "Gender Role Change in Families: A Macro-Sociological View." In *Family Relations: Challenges for the Future,* Timothy H. Brubaker (ed). Newbury Park, CA: Sage, pp. 41–58.

Hughes, Diane, Ellen Galinsky, and Anne Morris (1992). "The Effect of Job Characteristics on Marital Quality: Specifying Linking Mechanisms." *Journal of Marriage and the Family* 54 (February): 31–42.

Huisman, Kimberly A. (1996). "Wife Battering in Asian American Communities." *Violence against Women* 2 (September): 260–283.

Hull, Jon D. (1995). "The State of the Union." *Time,* January 30, pp. 53–75.

Human Rights Campaign Foundation (2000). *The State of the Workplace for Lesbian, Gay, Bisexual, and Transgendered Americans.* Washington, DC: Human Rights Campaign Foundation.

Hunter, A. G., and M. E. Ensminger (1992). "Diversity and Fluidity in Children's Living Arrangements." *Journal of Marriage and the Family* 54: 418–426.

Hurst, Charles E. (2001). *Social Inequality: Forms, Causes, and Consequences.* Boston: Allyn & Bacon.

Hurtado, A. (1995). "Variations, Combinations, and Evolutions: Latino Families in the United States." In *Understanding Latino Families,* R. E. Zambrana (ed.). Thousand Oaks, CA: Sage, pp. 40–61.

Hutchinson, I. W., J. D. Hirschel, and C. E. Pesackis (1994). "Family Violence and Police Utilization." *Violence and Victims* 9: 299–313.

Hutter, Mark (1981). *The Changing Family.* New York: Wiley.

Hutter, Mark (1991). "Immigrant Families in the City." In *The Family Experience,* Mark Hutter (ed.). New York: Macmillan, pp. 170–177.

Hutter, Mark (1998). *The Changing Family,* 3rd ed. Boston: Allyn & Bacon.

Iglitzen, Lynne B. (1972). *Violent Conflict in American History.* San Francisco: Chandler.

Imber-Black, Evan (2000). "The Power of Secrets." In *Annual Editions: Marriage and the Family 2000/2001,* Kathleen R. Gilbert (ed.). Guilford, CT: Dushkin/McGraw-Hill, pp. 216–219.

Ingrassia, Michelle (1993). "Living on Dracula Time." *Newsweek,* July 12, pp. 68–69.

Ingrassia, Michelle (1994). "Virgin Cool." *Newsweek,* October 17, pp. 59–64.

Ingrassia, Michelle, and Melinda Berk (1994). "Patterns of Abuse." *Newsweek,* July 4, pp. 26–33.

Ishii-Kuntz, Masako (2000). "Diversity within Asian American Families." In *Handbook of Family Diversity,* David H. Demo, Katherine R. Allen, and Mark A. Fine (eds.). New York: Oxford University Press, pp. 274–292.

Island, David, and Patrick Letellier (1991). *Men Who Beat the Men Who Love Them: Battered Gay Men and Domestic Violence.* New York: Harrington Park Press.

Jackson, Anita P., Ronald P. Brown, and Karen E. Patterson-Stewart (2000). "African Americans in Dual-Career Commuter Marriages.": *The Family Journal: Counseling and Therapy for Couples and Families* 8 (January): 23–36.

Jackson, Maggie (1998). "Work–Family Study Finds Many Firms without Policies." *Denver Post,* July 15, p. 3.

Jackson, Patrick G. (1983). "On Living Together Unmarried: Awareness Contexts and Social Interaction." *Journal of Family Issues* 4 (March): 35–39.

Jacobsen, Linda, and Brad Edmondson (1993). "Father Figures." *American Demographics* 15 (August): 22–27, 62.

Jaffe, Kenneth (1999). "Small Children, Sizable Needs." *Forum for Applied Research and Public Policy* 14 (Winter): 84–87.

Jagger, Alison M., and Paula S. Rothenberg (1984). *Feminist Frameworks*. New York: McGraw-Hill.

James, Kerrie, and Laurie MacKinnon (1990). "The 'Incestuous Family' Revisited: A Critical Analysis of Family Therapy Myths." *Journal of Marital and Family Therapy* 16 (January): 71–88.

Jarrett, Robin (1994). "Living Poor: Family Life among Single Parent African American Women." *Social Problems* 41 (February): 30–49.

Jeffries, Vincent, and H. Edward Ransford (1980). *Social Stratification, A Multiple Hierarchy Approach*. Boston: Allyn & Bacon.

Jencks, Christopher, and Joseph Swingle (2000). "Without a Net: Whom the New Welfare Law Helps and Hurts." *The American Prospect* (January 3): 37–41.

Johnson, Dirk (1996). "No-Fault Divorce Is Under Attack." *New York Times*, "Themes of the Times" (Fall): 8.

Johnson, Kevin (1999). "Can 'Child Support' Live Up to Its Name?" *USA Today*, October 20, p. 12A.

Johnson, Michael P. (1995). "Patriarchal Terrorism and Common Couple Violence: Two Forms of Violence against Women." *Journal of Marriage and the Family* 57 (May): 283–294.

Johnson, Michael P., and Kathleen J. Ferraro (2001). "Research on Domestic Violence in the 1990s: Making Distinctions." In *Understanding Families into the New Millennium: A Decade in Review*, Robert M. Milardo (ed.). Minneapolis: National Council on Family Relations, pp. 167–182.

Jones, Ann (1994). *Next Time, She'll Be Dead: Battering and How to Stop It*. Boston: Beacon.

Jones, Barry (1982). *Sleepers Awake! Technology and the Future of Work*. Melbourne: Oxford University Press.

Jones, Barry (1990). *Sleepers Awake! Technology and the Future of Work*, new ed. Melbourne: Oxford University Press.

Jones, Rachel L. (1996) "Hispanic Children Biggest Minority." *Denver Post*, July 2, pp. A1, A11.

Jorgensen, Helene, and Hans Riemer (2000). "Permatemps." *The American Prospect*, August 14, pp. 38–40.

Judis, John B. (2000). "The New Politics of Abortion." *The American Prospect*, July 31, pp. 12–13.

Judson, David (1997). "Buried in Bankruptcies." *Coloradoan*, April 20, pp. E1, E4.

Juster, Susan, and Maris A. Vinovskis (1987). "Changing Perspectives on the American Family in the Past." *Annual Review of Sociology* 13: 193–216.

Kagan, Jerome (1977). "The Child in the Family." *Daedalus* 106 (Spring): 33–56.

Kahl, Joseph A. (1957). *The American Class Structure*. New York: Holt, Rinehart.

Kain, Edward L. (1990). *The Myth of Family Decline: Understanding Families in a World of Rapid Social Change*. Lexington, MA: Lexington Books.

Kalish, Susan (1994a). "Fewer and Fewer 'Traditional' U.S. Households," *Population Today* 22 (November): 3.

Kammeyer, Kenneth C. W. (1981). "The Decline of Divorce in America." Paper presented at the meetings of the Midwest Sociological Society (April).

Kammeyer, Kenneth C. W. (1987). *Marriage and Family*. Boston: Allyn & Bacon.

Kammeyer, Kenneth C. W., George Ritzer, and Norman R. Yetman (1990). Sociology: Experiencing Changing Societies, 3rd ed. Boston: Allyn & Bacon.

Kamo, Yoshinori, and Min Zhou (1994). "Living Arrangements of Elderly Chinese and Japanese in the United States." *Journal of Marriage and the Family* 56 (August): 544–558.

Kandiyoti, Deniz (1988). "Bargaining with Patriarchy." *Gender & Society* 2: 274–290.

Kanter, Rosabeth Moss (1984). "Jobs and Families: Impact of Working Roles on Family Life." In *Work and Family*, Patricia Voydanoff (ed.). Palo Alto, CA: Mayfield, pp. 111–118.

Kaplan, Sheila, and Jim Morris (2000). "Kids at Risk." *U.S. News & World Report*, June 19, pp. 47–53.

Kass, Leon R. (2000). "The End of Courtship." *In the Public Interest* 141 (Fall). http://www. thepublicinterest.com/main.html>.

Katz, Jonathan Ned (1990). "The Invention of Heterosexuality." *Socialist Review* 20 (January/March): 7–34.

Keefe, Susan (1984). "Real and Ideal Extended Familism among Mexican American and Anglo Americans: On the Meaning of 'Close' Family Ties." *Human Organization* 43: 65–70.

Kennedy, David M. (1996). "Can We Still Afford to Be a Nation of Immigrants?" *Atlantic Monthly*, November, pp. 51–80.

Kenniston, Kenneth (1977). *All Our Children: The American Family under Pressure*. New York: Harcourt Brace Jovanovich.

Kertzer, David I. (1991). "Household History and Sociological Theory." *Annual Review of Sociology* 17: 155–179.

Kibria, Nazli (1990). "Power, Patriarchy, and Gender Conflict in the Vietnamese Immigrant Community." *Gender & Society* 4 (March): 9–24.

Kibria, Nazli (1993). *Family Tightrope: The Changing Lives of Vietnamese Americans*. Princeton, NJ: Princeton University Press.

Kibria, Nazli (1994). "Migration and Vietnamese American Women: Remaking Ethnicity." In *Women of Color in U.S. Society*, Maxine Baca Zinn and Bonnie Thornton Dill (eds.). Philadelphia: Temple University Press, pp. 247–261.

Kibria, Nazli (1997). "The Concept of 'Bicultural Families' and Its Implications for Research on Immigrant and Ethnic Families." In *Immigration and the Family*, Alan Booth, Ann C. Crouter and Nancy Landale (eds.). Mahwah, NJ: Lawrence Erlbaum Associates, pp. 205–210.

Kilborn, Peter T. (1994). "More Women Take Low-Wage Jobs Just So Their Families Can Get By." *New York Times*, March 13, p. 11.

Kimmel, Michael, and Michael A. Messner (1995). *Men's Lives*, 3rd ed. Boston: Allyn & Bacon.

Kinsey, Alfred S., Wardell B., Pomeroy and Clyde E. Martin, and the staff of the Institute for Sex Research. (1948). *Sexual Behavior in the Human Male*. Philadelphia: Saunders.

Kinsey, Alfred S., Wardell B., Pomeroy and Clyde E. Martin, and the staff of the Institute for Sex Research. (1953). *Sexual Behavior in the Human Female*. Philadelphia: Saunders.

Kirn, Walter (2000). "Should You Stay Together for the Kids?" *Time*, September 25, pp. 75–88.

Kirschner, Bette Frankle, and Laurel Richardson Walum (1978). "Two-Location Families." *Alternative Lifestyles* 1 (November): 513–525.

Komorovsky, Mirra (1962). *Blue Collar Marriage*. New York: Vintage.

Koop, C. Everett (1989). "Violence against Women: A Global Problem." Paper presented at the Pan American Health Organization. Geneva, Switzerland (May).

Kornblum, William (1991). "Who Is the Underclass?" *Dissent* 38 (Spring): 202–211.

Krain, Mark, Drew Cannon, and Jeffrey Bagford (1977). "Rating-Dating or Simple Prestige Homogamy: Data on Dating in the Greek System on a Midwestern Campus." *Journal of Marriage and the Family* 39 (November): 663–674.

Kuczynski, Leon, Lori Harach, and Silvia C. Bernardine (1999). "Psychology's Child Meets Sociology's Child: Agency, Influence and Power in Parent–Child Relationships." In *Contemporary Perspectives on Family Research*, Vol. 1. Stamford, CT: JAI Press, pp. 21–52.

Kurdek, Lawrence. 1993. "The Allocation of Household Labor in Gay, Lesbian, and Heterosexual Married Couples." *Journal of Social Issues* 49 (3): 127–139.

Kurdek, Lawrence A. (1998) "Relationship Outcomes and Their Predictors: Longitudinal Evidence from Heterosexual Married, Gay Cohabiting, and Lesbian Couples." *Journal of Marriage and the Family* 60 (August): 553–568.

Ladner, Joyce A. (1971). *Tomorrow's Tomorrow: The Black Woman*. Garden City, NY: Doubleday.

Lamb, Michael E. (1987). *The Fathers Role: Cross-Cultural Perspectives*. Hillsdale, NJ: Lawrence Erlbaum Associates.

Lamphere, Louise, Patricia Zavella, and Felipe Gonzales with Peter B. Evans (1993). *Sunbelt Working Mothers*. Ithaca, NY: Cornell University Press.

Landale, Nancy S., and Katherine Fennelly (1992). "Informal Unions among Mainland Puerto Ricans:

Cohabitation or an Alternative to Legal Marriage?" *Journal of Marriage and the Family* 54 (May): 269–280.

Landale, Nancy. S., and R. S. Oropesa (1995). "Immigrant Children and the Children of Immigrants: Inter- and Intra-Ethnic Group Differences in the United States." Population Research Group Paper 95-2. East Lansing, MI: Institute for Public Policy and Social Research, Michigan State University.

Landers, Ann (1996). "Culture Dictates Marriage between a Man/a Woman." *Denver Post*, July 21, p. 12D.

Laner, Mary Riege, and Nicole A. Ventrone (1998). "Egalitarian Daters/Traditionalist Dates." *Journal of Family Issues* 19(4): 468–477.

Lang, John (1998). "Suits Take a Swing at Paddling," *Rocky Mountain News*, May 2, pp. 2A, 58A.

Langman, Lauren (1987). "Social Stratification." In *Handbook of Marriage and the Family*, Marvin B. Sussman and Suzanne L. Steinmetz (eds.). New York: Plenum, pp. 211–249.

Lantz, Herman, Margaret Britton, Raymond L. Schmitt, and Eloise Snyder (1968). "Preindustrial Patterns in the Colonial Family in America: A Content Analysis of Colonial Magazines." *American Sociological Review* 33: 413–426.

Lardner, George, Jr. (2000). "How Prices Go through the Roof." *Washington Post National Weekly Edition*, June 19, p. 20.

Larkin, Jack (1988). *The Reshaping of Everyday Life*, New York: Harper & Row.

LaRossa, Ralph (1997). *The Modernization of Fatherhood: A Social and Political History*. Chicago: University of Chicago Press.

Larson, Reed, and Maryse Richards (1994). *Divergent Realities: The Emotional Lives of Mothers, Fathers, and Adolescents*. New York: Basic Books.

Lasch, Christopher (1975). "The Family and History." *New York Review of Books* 8 (November 13): 33–38.

Lasch, Christopher (1977). *Haven in a Heartless World: The Family Besieged*. New York: Basic Books.

Laslett, Peter (1971). *The World We Have Lost*, 2nd ed. New York: Scribners.

Latham, Lisa Moricoli (2000). "Southern Governors Declare War on Divorce." http://salon.com/mwt/feature/2000/01/24/divorce/index.html>.

Laumann, Edward O., John H. Gagnon, Robert T. Michael, and Stuart Michaels (1994). *The Social Organization of Sexuality*. Chicago: University of Chicago Press.

Lawson, Annette, and Deborah L. Rhode (1993). "Introduction." In *The Politics of Pregnancy*, Annette Lawson and Deborah L. Rhode (eds.). New Haven, CT: Yale University Press, pp. 1–19.

Leach, Penelope (1994). *Children First: What Our Society Must Do—And Is Not Doing—for Our Children Today*. New York: Knopf.

Lee, Louise (2000). "The Shine is off the Golden State." *Business Week,* September 11, p. 44.

Lee, Sharon M. (1998). "Asian Americans: Diverse and Growing." *Population Bulletin* 53 (June):entire issue.

Lee, Thea M. (1989). "Rational Expectations: A New Look at the Economics of Teen Pregnancy." *Dollars & Sense* No. 144 (March): 10–11.

Leibowitz, Lila (1978). *Females, Males, Families: A Biosocial Approach.* North Scituate, MA: Duxbury.

Leland, John (2000). "Silence Ending about Abuse in Gay Relationships." http://nytimes.com/2000/11/06/national/06ABUS.html>.

Lemann, Nicholas (1986). "The Origins of the Underclass." *The Atlantic Monthly,* Part I (June): 31–55; Part II (July): 54–68.

Lempert, Lora Bey, and Marjorie L. De Vault (2000). "Special Issue on Emergent and Reconfigured Forms of Family Life." *Gender & Society* 14 (February): 6–10.

Leonhardt, David (2000). "Lingering Job Worries amid a Sea of Plenty." http://nytimes.com/library/tech/yr/mo/biztech/articles/29worry.html>.

Lerner, Gerda (1979). "The Lady and the Mill Girl: Changes in the Status of Women in the Age of Jackson 1800–1840." In *A Heritage of Her Own,* Nancy F. Cott and Elizabeth Pleck (eds.). New York: Simon & Schuster, pp. 182–196.

Lerner, Michael (1982). "Recapturing the Family Issue." *The Nation,* February, pp. 141–143.

Lerner, Richard M., Elizabeth E. Sparks, and Laurie D. McCubbin (1999). *Family Diversity and Family Policy.* Boston: Kluwer Academic.

Levine, Art (1990). "The Second Time Around: Realities of Remarriage." *U.S. News & World Report,* January 29, pp. 50–51.

Levine, Heidi, and Nancy J. Evans (1996). "The Development of Gay, Lesbian, and Bisexual Identities." In *The Meaning of Difference,* Karen E. Rosenblum and Toni-Michelle Travis (eds.). New York: McGraw-Hill, pp. 130–136.

Lewin, Tamar (1994). "Case Might Fit Pattern of Abuse, Experts Say." *New York Times,* June 19, p. 21.

Lewin, Tamar (2000). "Majority of Married Couples with Children Now Both Work." *Denver Rocky Mountain News,* October 24, p. 2A.

Lewis, Oscar (1959). *Five Families: Mexican Case Studies in the Culture of Poverty.* New York: Basic Books.

Lewis, Oscar (1966). *La Vida.* New York: Random House.

Lichter, Daniel T. (1997). "Poverty and Inequality among Children." *Annual Review of Sociology* 23: 121–145.

Lichter, Daniel T., and Nancy S. Landale (1995). "Parental Work, Family Structure, and Poverty among Latino Children," *Journal of Marriage and The Family.* 57 (May): 346–353.

Lindholm, Kathryn, and Richard Willey (1983). *Child Abuse and Ethnicity: Patterns of Similarities and Differences.* Los Angeles: Spanish Speaking Mental Health Research Center, occasional paper No. 18.

Longworth, R. C. (1999). "Middle Class Reaping Least Benefit from 90s Boom." *The Times-Picayne* (New Orleans), September 6, p. A3.

LoPiccolo, Joseph (1983). "The Prevention of Sexual Problems in Men." In *Promoting Sexual Responsibility and Preventing Sexual Problems,* George W. Albee, Sol Gordon, and Harold Leitchberg (eds.). Hanover, NH: University Press of New England, pp. 39–65.

Lorber, Judith (1994). *Paradoxes of Gender.* New Haven, CT: Yale University Press.

Love, Alice Ann (2000). "Survey Shows 46% of Couples Work Different Shifts." *Albuquerque Journal,* March 10, p. A1.

Lucal, Betsy (1996). "Oppression and Privilege: Toward a Relational Conceptualization of Race." *Teaching Sociology* 24 (July): 245–255.

Lugaila, Terry A. (1998). "Marital Status and Living Arrangements." *Current Population Reports,* Series P-23-194. Washington, DC: U.S. Government Printing Office (September).

Luker, Kristin (1996). *Dubious Conceptions: The Politics of Teenage Pregnancy.* Cambridge, MA: Harvard University Press.

Lyness, J. F., M. E. Lipetz, and K. E. Davis (1972). "Living Together: An Alternative to Marriage." *Journal of Marriage and the Family* 34: 305–311.

Mackay, Judith. (2000) *The Penguin Atlas of Human Sexual Behavior.* New York: Penguin Putnam.

MacKinnon, Catherine A. (1989). *Toward a Feminist Theory of the State.* Cambridge, MA: Harvard University Press.

Macklin, Eleanor D. (1983). "Nonmarital Heterosexual Cohabitation." In *Family and Transition,* 4th ed., Arlene S. Skolnick and Jerome H. Skolnick (eds.). Boston: Little, Brown, pp. 264–265.

Madsen, William (1964). *The Mexican-Americans of South Texas.* New York: Holt, Rinehart and Winston.

Males, Mike (1996). *The Scapegoat Generation: America's War on Adolescents.* Monroe, ME: Common Courage Press.

Mann, Susan A., Michael D. Grimes, Alice Abel Kemp, and Pamela J. Jenkins (1997). "Paradigm Shifts in Family Sociology?: Evidence from Three Decades of Family Textbooks." *Journal of Family Issues* 18 (May): 315–349.

Manning, Anita (1997). "Teen Girls No Longer Enjoy an Age of Innocence." *USA Today,* October 6, p. 4D.

Mantsios, Gregory (1996). "Rewards and Opportunities: The Politics and Economics of Class in the U.S." In *The Meaning of Difference,* Karen E. Rosenblum and Toni-Michelle Travis (eds.). New York: McGraw-Hill, pp. 97–103.

March, Karen, and Charlene Miall (2000). "Adoption as a Family Form." *Family Relations* 49 (October): 359–362.

Marks, Carole (1991). "The Urban Underclass." *Annual Review of Sociology* 17: 445–466.

Marks, Nadine F. (1996). "Flying Solo at Midlife: Gender, Marital Status, and Psychological Well-Being." *Journal of Marriage and the Family* 58 (November): 917–932.

Marsiglio, William, Paul Amato, Ronald D. Day, and Michael E. Lamb (2001). "Scholarship on Fatherhood in the 1990s and Beyond." In *Understanding Families into the New Millennium: A Decade in Review,* Robert M. Milardo (ed.). Minneapolis: National Council on Family Relations, pp. 392–410.

Martin, Philip, and Elizabeth Midgley (1994). "Immigration to the United States: Journey to an Uncertain Destination." *Population Bulletin* 49 (September).

Martin, Philip, and Elizabeth Midgley (1999). "Immigration to the United States." *Population Bulletin* 54 (June):entire issue.

Martin, Teresa Castro, and Larry L. Bumpass (1989). "Recent Trends in Marital Disruption." *Demography* 26: 37–51.

Maschinot, Beth (1995). "Behind the Curve." *In These Times,* February 6, pp. 31–34.

Mason, Mary Ann, and Jane Mauldon (1996). "The New Stepfamily Requires a New Public Policy." *Journal of Social Issues* 52 (Fall): 11–27.

Mason, Mary Ann, Arlene Skolnick, and Stephen D. Sugarman (1998). "Introduction." In *All Our Families: New Policies for a New Century,* Mary Ann Mason, Arlene Skolnick, and Stephen D. Sugarman (eds.). New York: Oxford University Press, pp. 1–12.

Matthaei, Julie A. (1982). *An Economic History of Women in America.* New York: Schoken.

Matthews, Tony (1999). http://3.ns.sympatico.ca/tands.matthews/christdivorce.html>.

Maugh, Thomas H. II (1998). 'Free Condoms: Safety Up, Sex Not." *Denver Post,* April 14, p. 2A.

May, Martha (1990). "The Historical Problem of the Family Wage: The Ford Motor Company and the Five Dollar Day." In *Unequal Sisters: A Multi-cultural Reader in U.S. Women's History*, Ellen Carol DuBois and Vicki L. Ruiz (eds.). New York: Routledge, pp. 275–291.

McAdoo, Harriette Pipes (1978). "Factors Related to Stability in Upwardly Mobile Black Families." *Journal of Marriage and the Family* 40 (4): 761–776.

Maccaffrey, Shannon (2000). "Rent Rates Outpace Minimum Wage." *Rocky Mountain News,* September 22, p. 7AA.

McCollum, Audrey T. (1990). *The Trauma of Moving.* Newbury Park, CA: Sage.

McCrate, Elaine (1997). "Hitting Bottom: Welfare 'Reform' and Labor Markets." *Dollars and Sense,* No. 213 (September/October): 34–35.

McEnroe, Jennifer (1991). "Split-Shift Parenting." *American Demographics* 13 (February): 50–52.

McFalls, Joseph A., Jr. (1998). "Population: A Lively Introduction." *Population Bulletin* 53 (September):entire issue.

McGinn, Daniel, and John McCormick (1999). "Your Next Job." *Newsweek,* February 1, pp. 43–45.

McIntosh, Peggy (1992). "White Privilege and Male Privilege: A Personal Account of Coming to See Correspondences through Work in Women's Studies." In *Race, Class, and Gender,* Margaret L. Andersen and Patricia Hill Collins (eds.). Belmont, CA: Wadsworth, pp. 70–81.

McKay, Judith (2000). *The Penguin Atlas of Human Sexual Behavior.* New York: Penguin Reference.

McKinley, Donald Gilbert (1964). *Social Class and Family Life.* Glencoe, IL: Free Press of Glencoe.

McLanahan, Sara, and Karen Booth (1991). "Mother-Only Families." In *Contemporary Families: Looking Forward, Looking Back,* Alan Booth (ed.), Minneapolis: National Council on Family Relations, pp. 405–428.

McLanahan, Sara, and Larry Bumpass (1988). "Intergenerational Consequences of Family Disruption." *American Journal of Sociology* 94: 130–152.

McLanahan, Sara, and Lynne Casper (1995). "Growing Diversity and Inequality in the American Family." In *State of the Union: America in the 1990s,* Vol. 2, Reynolds Farley (ed.). New York: Russell Sage Foundation, pp. 1–46.

McLanahan, Sara, and G. D. Sandefur (1994). *Growing up with a Single Parent: What Hurts, What Helps.* Cambridge, MA: Harvard University Press.

McLarin, Kimberly J. (1995). "For the Poor, Defining Who Deserves What." *New York Times,* September 17, p. 4E.

McLean, Elys A. (1995). "U.S. Children in Poverty." *USA Today,* January 31, p. 5A.

McLoyd, Vonnie C., Ana Mari Cauce, David Takeuchi, and Leon Wilson. (2001) "Marital Processes and Parental Socialization in Families of Color: A Decade Review of Research." in *Understanding Families into the New Millennium: A Decade in Review,* Robert M. Milardo, (ed.). Minneapolis, MN: National Council on Family Relations, pp. 466–487.

Means, Marianne (1997). "Frazzled Families Could Use a Break." *Rocky Mountain News,* May 19, p. 39A.

Meier, Diane E., and R. Sean Morrison (1999). "Old Age and Care near the End of Life." *Generations* 23 (Spring): 6–11.

Menaghan, Elizabeth G. (1989). "Escaping from the Family Realm: Reasons to Resist Claims for its Uniqueness." *Journal of Marriage and the Family* 51 (August): 805–816.

Menaghan, Elizabeth G. (1996). "Maternal Occupational Conditions and Children's Family Environments." In *Women and Work: A Handbook,* Paula J. Dubek and Kaktherine Borman (eds.). New York: Longman, pp. 409–412.

Menaghan, Elizabeth G., and Toby L. Parcel (1991). "Parental Employment and Family Life." In *Contemporary Families: Looking Forward, Looking Back, Alan Booth* (ed.). Minneapolis: National Council on Family Relations, pp. 361–380.

Messner, Michael A. (1996). "Studying up on Sex." *Sociology of Sport Journal* 13: 221–237.

Meyer, Jan (1990). "Guess Who's Coming to Dinner This Time? A Study of Gay Intimate Relationships and the Support for Those Relationships." In *Homosexuality and Family Relations*, Fredrick Bozett and Marvin B. Sussman (eds.). New York: Harrington Press, pp. 59–81.

Michael, Robert T., John H. Gagnon, Edward O. Laumann, and Gina Kolata (1994). *Sex in America*. Boston: Little, Brown.

Michigan State Medical Society (1993). *Reaching Out: Intervening in Partner Abuse*. East Lansing, MI: Michigan State Medical Society.

Milkie, Melissa A., and Pia Peltola (1999). "Playing All the Roles: Gender and the Work–Family Balancing Act." *Journal of Marriage and the Family* 61 (May): 476–490.

Miller, JoAnn Langley, and Dean D. Knudsen (1999). "Family Abuse and Violence." In *Handbook of Marriage and the Family*, 2nd ed., Marvin Sussman, Suzanne K. Steinmetz, and Gary W. Peterson (eds.). New York: Plenum Press, pp. 705–741.

Miller, Louisa (1993). "Marriage, Divorce, and Remarriage." *Current Population Reports*, Series P-23-185: 22–23.

Miller, Melodie I., Phillis Moen, and Donna Dempster-McClain (1991). "Motherhood, Multiple Roles, and Maternal Well-Being: Women of the 1950s." *Gender & Society* 5 (December): 565–582.

Miller, S. M. (1972). "Confusions of a Middle-Class Husband." In *The Future of the Family*, Louise Kapp Howe (ed.). New York: Touchstone, pp. 95–108.

Miller, S. M., and F. R. Riessman (1964). "The Working Class Subculture: A New View." In *Blue Collar Worlds: Studies of the American Worker*, A. B. Shostack and W. Bomberg (eds.). Englewood Cliffs, NJ: Prentice Hall, pp. 24–36.

Millman, Marcia (1991). *Warm Hearts and Cold Cash: The Intimate Dynamics of Families and Money*. New York: The Free Press.

Mills, C. Wright (1940). "Methodological Consequences of the Sociology of Knowledge." *American Journal of Sociology* 46 (November): 316–330. Reprinted (1963) in *Power, Politics and People: The Collected Essays of C. Wright Mills*, Irving L. Horowitz (ed.). New York: Ballantine, pp. 453–468.

Mindel, Charles H. (1980). "Extended Familism among Urban Mexican-Americans, Anglos and Blacks." *Hispanic Journal of Behavioral Sciences* 2: 21–34.

Mintz, Steven, and Susan Kellogg (1988). *Domestic Revolutions: A Social History of American Family Life*. New York: The Free Press.

Mishel, Lawrence, Jared Bernstein, and John Schmitt (2000). *The State of Working America 2000–2001*, Executive Summary, Economic Policy Institute (September 3). <epinet.org/books/swa2000/swa2000intro.html>.

Mitchell, Juliett. (1966) "Women, The Longest Revolution." *New Left Review* No. 44.

Moberg, David (1995). "Reviving the Public Sector." *In These Times*, October 16, pp. 22–24.

Modell, John (1978). "Patterns of Consumption, Acculturation, and Family Income Strategies in Late Nineteenth-Century America." In *Family and Population in Nineteenth Century America*, Tamara K. Hareven and Maris A. Vinovskis (eds.). Princeton, NJ: Princeton University Press, pp. 206–240.

Modell, John, and Tamara K. Hareven (1977). "Urbanization and the Malleable Household: An Examination of Boarding and Lodging in American Families." In *Family and Kin in Urban Communities, 1700–1930*. New York: New Viewpoints, pp. 167–186.

Moen, Phyllis (1999). *The Cornell Couples and Careers Study*. Cornell Employment and Family Careers Institute. Ithaca, NY: Cornell University Press.

Moen, Phyllis, and Kay B. Forest (1999). "Strengthening Families: Policy Issues for the Twenty-First Century." In *Handbook of Marriage and the Family*, 2nd ed. Marvin Sussman, Suzanne K. Steinmetz, and Gary W. Peterson (eds.). New York: Plenum, pp. 633–663.

Moen, Phyllis, and Elaine Wethington (1992). "The Concept of Family Adaptive Strategies," *Annual Review of Sociology* 18: 233–251.

Moen, Phyllis, and Yan Yu (2000). "Effective Work/Life Strategies: Working Couples, Work Conditions, Gender, and Life Quality." *Social Problems* 47 (August): 291–326.

Mogelonsky, Marcia (1996). "The Rocky Road to Adulthood." *American Demographics* 18 (May): 26–35, 56.

Montague, Bill (1997). "Rising Consumer Credit Lurks as Economy Killer." *USA Today*, May 15, p. 1B.

Moore, Joan W., and Raquel Pinderhughes (eds.) (1993). *In the Barrios: Latinos and the Underclass Debate*. New York: Russell Sage Foundation.

Morin, Richard (1998). "Wanted: Some Time for Their Families." *Washington Post National Weekly Edition*, March 2, p. 35.

Morone, James A. (1996). "The Corrosive Politics of Virtue." *The American Prospect*, No. 26 (May/June): 30–39.

Mortimer, Jeylan T., and Michael D. Finch (1996). "Work, Family, and Adolescent Development." In *Adolescents, Work, and Family*, Jeylan T. Mortimer and Michael D. Finch (eds.). Newbury Park, CA: Sage, pp. 1–24.

Moynihan, Daniel P. (1965). *The Negro Family: The Case*

for National Action. Washington, DC: Office of Policy Planning and Research, U.S. Department of Labor.

Moynihan, Daniel. (1988). "Our Poorest Citizens—Children." *Focus* 11 (Spring): 5–6.

Mullings, Lieth (1986b). "Uneven Development: Class, Race, and Gender in the U.S. before 1900." In *Women's Work,* Eleanor Leacock, Helen I. Safa, and contributors. South Hadley, MA: Bergin and Garvey, pp. 41–57.

Mullings, Lieth (1997). *On Our Own Terms: Race, Class, and Gender in the Lives of African American Women.* New York: Routledge.

Murray, Charles (1984). *Losing Ground.* New York: Basic Books.

Myers, Scott M., and Alan Booth (1996). "Men's Retirement and Marital Quality." *Journal of Marriage and the Family* 17 (May): 336–357.

Nakonezny, Paul A., Robert D. Shull, and Joseph Lee Rodgers (1995). "The Effect of No-Fault Divorce Law on the Divorce Rate across the 50 States and Its Relation to Income, Education, and Religiosity." *Journal of Marriage and the Family* 57 (November): 477–488.

Naples, Nancy A. (1992). "Activist Mothering: Cross Generational Continuity in the Community Work of Women from Low-Income Urban Neighborhoods." *Gender & Society* 6 (September): 441–463.

The Nation (1995). "Welfare Cheat." (October 9): 371–372.

National Center on Elder Abuse (1998). *National Elder Abuse Incidence Study: Final Report.* Washington, DC: American Public Health Services Association.

Neergaard, Lauran (2000). "Alzheimer's Alarm Sounded." *Denver Post,* July 10, p. 2A.

Nelson, Jill (1997). "Condom Opponents Must Face Reality." *USA Today,* October 3, p. 13A.

Neugarten, Bernice L. (1980). "Grow Old along With Me! The Best Is Yet to Be." In *Growing Old in America,* Beth Hess (ed.). New Brunswick, NJ: Transaction Books, pp. 180–197.

Newman, Cathy (2000). "Race Divides the Fortunes of Older Americans." *Denver Post,* August 10, p. 3A.

Newman, Katherine S. (1988). *Falling from Grace: The Experience of Downward Mobility in the American Middle Class.* New York: The Free Press.

Newman, Katherine S. (1993). *Declining Fortunes: The Withering of the American Dream.* New York: Basic Books.

Newman, Katherine S. (1994). "Troubled Times: The Cultural Dimensions of Economic Decline." In *Understanding American Economic Decline,* Michael A. Bernstein and David E. Adler (eds.). New York: Cambridge University Press, pp. 330–357.

Newsweek (1998). "The Face of the Nation." (November 2): 63.

Newton, Jan M. (1973). "The Political Economy of Women's Oppression." In *Women on the Move: A Feminist Perspective,* Jean Ramage Lepaluoto (ed.). Eugene: University of Oregon Press, pp. 117–128.

New York Times (1994). "Health Data Show AIDS Spreading at Lower Rate." (February 3): A9.

New York Times (2000). "The Enduring Battle over Choice." http://nytimes/2000/10/11/opinion/11wed1.html>.

Nicholson, Linda (1997). "The Myth of the Traditional Family." In *Feminism and Families,* Hilde Lindemann Nelson (ed.). New York: Routledge, pp. 27–42.

Nock, Steven L., James D. Wright, and Laura Saanchez (1999). "America's Divorce Problem." *Society* 36 (May/June): 43–52.

Norment, Lynn (1999). "Black Women White Men, White Women Black Men: What's Behind the Escalating Trend? *Ebony,* November, pp. 217–222.

Norris, Pippa (1984). "Women in Poverty: Britain and America." *Social Policy* 14 (Spring): 41–43.

Norton, Arthur J., and Louisa F. Miller (1992). "Marriage, Divorce, and Remarriage in the 1990s." *Current Population Reports,* Series P23-180.

Norwegian Parliament (1991). "The Marriage Act," Act No. 47 of 4 July 1991 Relating to Marriage.

Occupational Outlook Quarterly (1999–2000) 43, no. 4(Winter): 33–34. Washington, DC: U.S. Department of Labor, Bureau of Labor Statistics.

O'Connell, Martin (1993). "Where's Papa? Fathers' Role in Child Care." *Population Trends and Public Policy* (September). Washington, DC: Population Reference Bureau.

O'Connell, Martin and David E. Bloom (1987). *Juggling Jobs and Babies: America's Child Care Challenge,* Washington, DC: Population Reference Bureau.

O'Hare, William P. (1992). "America's Minorities: The Demographics of Diversity." *Population Bulletin* 47 (December): entire issue.

O'Hare, William P. (1993). "Diversity Trend: More Minorities Looking Less Alike." *Population Today* 21 (April): 1–2.

O'Hare, William P. (1996). "A New Look at Poverty." *Population Bulletin* 51 (September): entire issue.

Okin, Susan Moller (1989). *Justice, Gender, and the Family.* New York: Basic Books.

Oliver, Melvin L., and Thomas M. Shapiro (1995). *Black Wealth/White Wealth: A New Perspective on Racial Equality.* New York: Routledge.

Omi, Michael, and Howard Winant (1994). *Racial Formation in the United States,* 2nd ed. London: Routledge.

Ortiz, Judith Coffer (2000). "The Myth of the Latin Woman: I Just Met a Girl Named Maria." In *Race, Class, and Gender: An Anthology,* 4th ed. Margaret L. Andersen and Patricia Hill Collins (eds.). Belmont, CA: Wadsworth, pp. 342–346.

Osmond, Marie Withers (1996). "Work-Family Linkages in Early Industrialization: The Public-Private Split." In *Women and Work: A Handbook,* Paula J. Dubek and Kathryn Borman (eds). New York: Longman, pp. 385–391.

Osmond, Marie Withers, and Barrie Thorne (1993). "Feminist Theories: The Social Construction of Gender in Families and Society." In *Sourcebook of Family Theories and Methods: A Contextual Approach,* P. G. Boss, W. J. Doherty, R. LaRossa, W. R. Schumm and S. K. Steinmetz (eds.). New York: Plenum, pp. 591–623.

Ostrander, Susan A. (1984). *Women of the Upper Class.* Philadelphia: Temple University Press.

Parade (1999). "Day-Care Costs, from Top to Bottom." (March 28): 10.

Parrenas, Rhacel Salazar (2000). "Migrant Filipina Domestic Workers and the International Division of Labor." *Gender & Society* 14 (August): 560–581.

Parsons, Talcott (1955). "The American Family: Its Relations to Personality and the Social Structure." In *Family Socialization and Interaction Process,* Talcott Parsons and Robert F. Bales (eds.). New York: The Free Press, pp. 31–21.

Patterson, Charlotte J. (1992). "Children of Lesbian and Gay Parents." *Child Development* 63 (October): 1025–1042.

Patterson, Charlotte J. (2001). "Family Relationships of Lesbian and Gay Men." In *Understanding Families into the New Millennium: A Decade in Review,* Robert M. Milardo (ed.). Minneapolis: National Council on Family Relations, pp. 271–288.

Patterson, Charlotte J., and Richard E. Redding (1996). "Lesbian and Gay Families with Children." *Journal of Social Issues* 52 (Fall): 29–50.

Pavetti, LaDonna (2000). "Welfare Policy in Transition: Redefining the Social Contract for Poor Citizen Families with Children." *Focus* 21 (Fall): 44–50.

Pear, Robert (1993). "Poverty Is Cited as Divorce Factor." *New York Times,* January 15, p. A6.

Pear, Robert (2001). "Gains Reported for Children of Welfare-to-Work Families." http://nytimes. com/2001/01/23/national/23WELF.html>.

Pence, Elaine, and Michael Paymar (1993). *Education Groups for Men Who Batter: The Duluth Model.* New York: Springer.

Peplau, Letitia Anne (1981). "What Homosexuals Want." *Psychology Today* 15 (March): 28–38.

Perry-Jenkins, Maureen, and Karen Polk (1994). "Class, Couples, and Conflict: Effects of the Division of Labor on Assessments of Marriage in Dual-Earner Families." *Journal of Marriage and the Family* 56 (February): 165–180.

Peters, Marie F., and Harriette P. McAdoo (1983). "The Present and Future of Alternative Lifestyles in Ethnic American Cultures." In *Contemporary Families and Alternative Lifestyles,* Eleanor D. Macklin and Roger Roben (eds.). Beverly Hills, CA: Sage, pp. 288–307.

Peters, Tom (2000). "What Will We Do for Work?" *Time,* May 22, pp. 68–71.

Peterson, Karen S. (1993a). "Couples Who Cohabitated More Likely to Divorce." *USA Today,* October 7, p. D1.

Peterson, Karen S. (1993b). "Guys Wed for Better, Wives, for Worse." *USA Today,* October 11, pp. D1–2.

Peterson, Karen S. (1996a). "Typical Family Is a Modern-Day Oxymoron." *USA Today,* November 27, p. 4D.

Peterson, Karen S. (1997). "Interracial Dating." *USA Today* (November 3): 1A–2A, 10A.

Peterson, Karen S. (2000). "Changing the Shape of the American Family." *USA Today,* April 18, pp. 1D–2D.

Peterson, Karen S. (2000). "Sex For Many Teens, Oral Doesn't Count." *USA Today,* November 16, pp. 1D–2D.

Peterson, Richard R. (1996). "A Re-evaluation of the Economic Consequences of Divorce." *American Sociological Review* 61 (June): 528–536.

Peyser, Marc (1999). "Home of the Gray." *Newsweek,* March 1, pp. 50–53.

Pillemer, Karl A. (1993). "Abuse Is Caused by the Deviance and Dependence of Abusive Caregivers." In *Current Controversies on Family Violence,* Richard J. Gelles and Donileen R. Loseke (eds.). Newbury Park, CA: Sage, pp. 237–249.

Piorkowski, Geraldine K. (2000). "Back Off." In *Annual Editions: Marriage and Family: 2000–2001.* Guilford, CT: Dushkin/ McGraw-Hill, pp. 37–40.

Piotrkowski, Chaya (1978). *Work and the Family System.* New York: The Free Press.

Piven, Frances Fox (1996). "An Interview Conducted by Barbara Ehrenreich." *The Progressive* 60 (November): 34–36.

Planned Parenthood Foundation of America, Inc. 2000 Fact Sheet (2000). "Helping Young People to Delay Sexual Intercourse." http://www. plannedparenthood.org/library/teen-pregnancy/helpyoung.html>.

Pleck, Elizabeth H. (1973). "The Two-Parent Household: Black Family Structure in Late Nineteenth-Century Boston." In *The American Family in Social-Historical Perspective,* Michael Gordon (ed.). New York: St. Martin's, pp. 152–178.

Pleck, Joseph H. (1977). "The Work-Family Role System." *Social Problems* 24 (April): 417–427.

Pleck, Joseph H. (1993). "Are Family Supportive Employer Policies Relevant to Men?" In Men, Work, and Family, Jane Hood (ed.). Newbury Park, CA: Sage, pp. 217–237.

Polakow, Valerie (1993). Lives on the Edge: Single Mothers and Their Children in the Other America. Chicago: University of Chicago Press.

Pollard, Kelvin M., and William P. O'Hare. (1999) "America's Racial and Ethnic Minorities." *Population Bulletin* 54 (September):entire issue.

Pollitt, Katha (1995). "Subject to Debate." *The Nation,* February 27, p. 265.

Pollitt, Katha (1996). "Adoption Fantasy." *The Nation,* July 8, p. 9.

Popenoe, David (1993). "American Family Decline, 1960–1990: A Review and Appraisal." *Journal of Marriage and the Family* 55: 527–541.

Popenoe, David (1997). "Family Trouble." *The American Prospect,* no. 34 (September/October): 18–19.

Population Reference Bureau (1999). "America's Diversity: On the Edge of Two Centuries." *Reports on America* 1 (May): entire issue.

Population Today (1997a). "Population Update." Vol. 25 (September): 6.

Population Today (1997b). "24-Hour Economy Changing How We Work and Live." Volume 25 (December): 1–2.

Population Today (1999). "Intergroup Married Couples: 1998." Vol. 27 (February): 6.

Population Today (1999). "The '90s Family—Nuclear Meltdown?" Vol. 27 (September): 5.

Population Today (2000a). "U.S. Population Update." Vol. 28 (February/March): 7.

Population Today (2000b). "Hispanics' Contribution to U.S. Fertility." Vol. 28 (May/June): 7.

Portes, Alejandro, and Robert L. Beck (1985). *Latin Journey.* Berkeley: University of California Press.

Portes, Alejandro, and Rubén G. Rumbaut (1990). *Immigrant America: A Portrait.* Berkeley: University of California Press.

Portes, Alejandro, and Min Zhou (1993). "The New Second Generation: Segmented Assimilation and Its Variants." *Annals of the American Academy of Political and Social Science* 530: 74–96.

Presser, Harriet B. (1993). "The Housework Gender Gap." *Population Today* 21 (July/August): 5.

Price, Sharon J., and Patrick C. McKenry (1988). *Divorce.* Beverly Hills, CA: Sage.

Purdum, Todd S. (2000). "Shift in the Mix Alters the Face of California." http://nytimes.com/library/national/070400ca-latin.html>.

Qian, Zhenchao (1997). "Breaking the Racial Barriers: Variations in Interracial Marriage between 1980 and 1990." *Demography* 34 (May): 263–276.

Queen, Stuart A., and Robert W. Habenstein (1974). *The Family in Various Cultures,* 4th ed. Philadelphia: Lippincott.

Rainwater, Lee (1966). "Some Aspects of Lower Class Sexual Behavior." *Journal of Social Issues* 12 (April): 96–108.

Ramey, C. T., F. A. Campbell, M. Burchinal, M. L. Skinner, D. M. Gardner, and S. L. Ramey (1999). "Persistent Effects of Early Intervention on High-Risk Children and Their Mothers." *Applied Developmental Science* 4: 2–14.

Ramirez, Oscar (1980). "Extended Family Support and Mental Health Status among Mexicans in Detroit." *La Red,* a monthly newsletter of the National Chicano Research Network, No. 28 (March 1980): 2.

Ramirez, Oscar, and Carlos H. Arce (1981). "The Contemporary Chicano Family: An Empirically Based Review." In *Explorations in Chicano Psychology.* Augustine Baron, Jr. (ed.). New York: Praeger, pp. 3–28.

Rank, Mark R. (2000). "Poverty and Economic Hardship in Families." In *Handbook on Family Diversity,* David H. Demo, Katherine R. Allen, and Mark A. Find (eds.). New York: Oxford University Press, pp. 293–315.

Rapp, Rayna (1982). "Family and Class in Contemporary America: Notes toward an Understanding of Ideology." In *Rethinking the Family: Some Feminist Questions,* Barrie Thorne and Marilyn Yalom (eds.). New York: Longman, pp. 168–187.

Raspberry, William (1997). "Poor—and Different from You and Me." *Washington Post National Weekly Edition,* November 24, p. 26.

Rawlings, Steve (1993). "Households and Families." *Current Population Reports,* Series P-23-185: 16–17.

Rawlings, Steve (1995). "Households and Families." *Population Profile of The United States: 1995. Current Population Reports,* Series P1-23-189: 28.

Reagan, Leslie J. (1997). *When Abortion Was a Crime: Women, Medicine, and Law in the United States, 1867–1973.* Berkeley: University of California Press.

Rebchook, John (2000). "Cost of Housing Rising Faster than Incomes." *Rocky Mountain News,* August 29, pp. 1B, 6B.

Reich, Robert B. (2000a). "It's the Year 2000 Economy, Stupid." *The American Prospect,* January 3, p. 64.

Reich, Robert B. (2000b). "Is Scrooge a Democrat Now?" *The American Prospect,* June 19–July 3, p. 96.

Reich, Robert B. (2001). "The New Economy as a Decent Society." *The American Prospect,* February 12, pp. 20–23.

Reisberg, Leo (1999). "Average Tuition and Fees at College Rose Less Than 5% This Year." *Chronicle of Higher Education,* October 15, p. A52.

Rennison, Callie Marie, and Sarah Welchans (2000). "Intimate Partner Violence," *Bureau of Justice Statistics* (NCJ 178247).

Renzetti, Claire M. (1992). *Violent Betrayal: Partner Abuse in Lesbian Relationships.* Newbury Park, CA: Sage.

Renzetti, Claire M. (1997). "Violence and Abuse Among Same-Sex Couples." In *Violence between Intimate Partners,* Albert P. Cardarelli (ed.). Boston: Allyn & Bacon, pp. 70–89.

Riche, Martha Farnsworth (1991). "The Future of the Family." *American Demographics* 13 (March): 44–47.

Riche, Martha Farnsworth (2000). "America's Diversity and Growth: Signposts for the 21st Century." *Population Bulletin* 55 (June): entire issue.

Richardson, Lynda (1997). "Study Supports Schools That Offer Condoms." *Denver Post,* September 30, pp. 3A, 42A.

Richmond, Julius B. (1994). "Give Children an Earlier Head Start." *USA Today,* April 12, p. 13A.

Rindfuss, Ronald R., S. Philip Morgan, and Kate Offutt (1996). "Education and the Changing Age Pattern of American Fertility: 1963–1989." *Demography* 33 (August): 277–290.

Risman, Barbara J. (1998). *Gender Vertigo: American Families in Transition.* New Haven, CT: Yale University Press.

Risman, Barbara J., and Myra Marx Ferree (1995). "Making Gender Visible." *American Sociological Review* 60: 775–782.

Risman, Barbara J., and Pepper Schwartz (1988). "Sociological Research on Male and Female Homosexuality." *Annual Review of Sociology* 14: 125–147.

Robinson, Paul (1994). "The Way We Do the Things We Do." *New York Times Book Review,* October 30, pp. 3, 22.

Rochelle, Ann (1997). *No More Kin: Exploring Race, Class, and Gender in Family Networks.* Thousand Oaks, CA: Pine Forge.

Rodman, Hyman (1964). "Middle-Class Misconceptions about Lower Class Families." In *Blue Collar World: Studies of the American Worker,* Arthur B. Shostak and William Gomberg (eds.). Englewood Cliffs, NJ: Prentice Hall, pp. 59–69.

Rogers-Dillon, Robin H. (2001). "What Do We Really Know about Welfare Reform?" *Society* 38 (January/February): 7–15.

Rollins, Judith (1985). *Between Women: Domestics and Their Employers.* Philadephia: Temple University Press.

Romero, Mary (1992). *Maid in The U.S.A.* New York: Routledge.

Rosenblum, Karen E., and Toni-Michelle C. Travis (eds.) (1996). "Introduction." In *The Meaning of Difference,* Karen E. Rosenblum and Toni-Michelle C. Travis (eds.). New York: McGraw-Hill, pp. 1–34.

Rossi, Alice S. (1994). "Eros and Caritas: A Biopsychosocial Approach to Human Sexuality and Reproduction." In *Sexuality across the Life Course,* Alice S. Rossi (ed.). Chicago: University of Chicago Press, pp. 3–38.

Rouse, L. P. (1997). "Domestic Violence: Hitting Us Where We Live." In *Analyzing Social Problems: Essays and Exercises,* D. Dunn and D. V. Walker (eds.). Upper Saddle River, NJ: Prentice-Hall, pp. 17–22.

Rubel, Arthur J. (1966). *Across the Tracks: Mexican Americans in a Texas City.* Austin: University of Texas Press.

Rubin, Gayle (1984). "Thinking Sex: Notes for a Radical Theory of Politics and Sexuality." In *Pleasure and Danger,* Carol Vance (ed.). Boston: Routledge and Kegan Paul, pp. 267–320.

Rubin, Lillian B. (1976). *Worlds of Pain: Life in the Working-Class Family.* New York: Basic Books.

Rubin, Lillian B. (1983). *Intimate Strangers: Men and Women Together.* New York: Harper & Row.

Rubin, Lillian B. (1990). *Erotic Wars: What Ever Happened to the Sexual Revolution?* New York: HarperCollins.

Rubin, Lillian B. (1994). *Families on the Fault Line: America's Working Class Speaks about the Family, the Economy, Race, and Ethnicity.* New York: HarperCollins.

Rumbaut, Ruben G. (1997). "Ties That Bind: Immigration and Immigrant Families in the United States." In *Immigration and the Family,* Alan Booth, Ann C. Crouter, and Nancy Landale (eds.). Mahway, NJ: Lawrence Erlbaum Associates, pp. 3–46.

Rutter, Virginia (1994). "Lessons from Step-Families." *Psychology Today* 27 (May/June): 30–33, 60, 62, 64, 66, 68–69.

Ryan, Mary P. (1983). *Womanhood in America: From Colonial Times to the Present,* 3d ed. New York: Franklin Watts.

Saluter, Arlene F., and Terry A. Lugaila (1998). "Marital Status and Living Arrangements." *Current Population Reports,* Series P-20-1496. Washington, DC: U.S. Government Printing Office.

Samora, Julian and Richard Lamana (1967). "Mexican Americans in a Midwest Metropolis: A Study of East Chicago." UCLA Study Project Advance Report.

Sanchez, George J. (1990). "Go after the Women: Americanization and the Mexican Immigrant Woman, 1915–1929." In *Unequal Sisters: A Multicultural Reader in U.S. Women's History,* Ellen Carol DuBois and Vicki L. Ruiz (eds.). New York: Routledge, pp. 250–263.

Sattel, Jack W. (1976). "The Inexpressive Male: Tragedy or Sexual Politics?" *Social Problems* 23 (April): 469–477.

Savin-Williams, Ritch C., and Kristin G. Esterberg (2000). "Lesbian, Gay, and Bisexual Families." In *Handbook of Family Diversity,* David H. Demo, Katherine R. Allen, and Mark A. Fine (eds.). New York: Oxford University Press, pp. 197–215.

Sawyer, Kathy (1999). "The Poorest Get Poorer." *Washington Post National Weekly Edition,* August 30, p. 34.

Scarr, Sandra (1997). "New Research on Day Care Should Spur Scholars to Reconsider Old Ideas." *Chronicle of Higher Education,* August 8, p. A48.

Scheper-Hughes, Nancy (1992). *Death without Weeping: Mother Love and Child Death in Northwest Brazil.* Berkeley: University of California Press.

Schneider, Elizabeth M. (2000). *Battered Women and Feminist Lawmaking.* New Haven, CT: Yale University Press.

Schor, Juliet B. (1998). *The Overspent American: Upscaling, Downshifting, and the New Consumer*. New York: Basic Books.

Schorr, Lisbeth B. (1997). *Common Purpose: Strengthening Families and Neighborhoods to Rebuild America*. New York: Doubleday Anchor Books.

Schumpeter, Joseph (1950). *Capitalism, Socialism, and Democracy*, 3rd ed. New York: Harper.

Schvaneveldt, Jay D., Robert S. Pickett, and Margaret H. Young (1993). "Historical Methods in Family Research." In *Sourcebook of Family Theories and Methods: A Contextual Approach*, P. G. Boss, W. J. Doherty, R. LaRossa, W. R. Schum, and S. K. Steinmetz (eds.). New York: Plenum, pp. 591–623.

Schwartz, John (1997). "The Sobering Impact of Marriage." *Washington Post National Weekly Edition*, February 10, p. 35.

Schwartz, Pepper (1994). "Modernizing Marriage." *Psychology Today* 27 (September/October): 54–59, 86.

Schwartz, Pepper (2000). "Creating Sexual Pleasure and Sexual Justice in the Twenty-First Century." *Contemporary Sociology* 29 (January): 213–219.

Schwartz, Pepper, and Virginia Rutter (1998). *The Gender of Sexuality*. Thousand Oaks, CA: Pine Forge.

Scott, Donald M., and Bernard Wishy (1982). *America's Families: A Documentary History*. New York: Harper & Row.

Scott, John Finley (1965). "The American College Sorority: Its Role in Class and Ethnic Endogamy." *American Sociological Review* 30 (August): 514–527.

Seccombe, Karen (2001). "Families in Poverty in the 1990s: Trends, Causes, Consequences, and Lessons Learned." In *Understanding Families into the New Millennium: A Decade in Review*, Robert M. Milardo (ed.). Minneapolis: National Council on Family Relations, pp. 313–332.

Seltzer, Judith A. (1994). "Consequences of Marital Dissolution for Children." *Annual Review of Sociology* 20: 235–266.

Seltzer, Judith A. (2001). "Families Formed outside of Marriage." In *Understanding Families into the New Millennium: A Decade in Review*, Robert M. Milardo (ed.). Minneapolis, MN: National Council on Family Relations, pp. 466–487.

Sengupta, Somini (1999). "Women Keep Garment Jobs by Sending Babies to China." *New York Times*, September 14, pp. 1A, 21A.

Sennett, Richard, and Jonathan Cobb (1972). *The Hidden Injuries of Class*. New York: Vintage.

Seward, Rudy Ray (1978). *The American Family: A Demographic History*. Beverly Hills, CA: Sage.

Shanker, Albert (1995). "In Defense of Government." *New York Times*, November 5, p. E7.

Shapiro, Andrew (1992). *We're Number One: Where America Stands—and Falls—in the New World Order*. New York: Random House Vintage.

Shapiro, Laura (1977). "Violence: The Most Obscene Fantasy." *Mother Jones* 2 (December): 11.

Shehan, Constance L. (1999). "No Longer a Place for Innocence: The Re-Submergence of Childhood in Post-industrial Societies." *Contemporary Perspectives on Family Research*, Vol. 1. Stamford, CT: JAI Press.

Shehan, Constance L., and Kenneth C. W. Kammeyer (1997). *Marriages and Families: Reflections of a Gendered Society*. Boston: Allyn & Bacon.

Shelton, Beth Anne (1992). *Women, Men, and Time: Gender Difference in Paid Work, Housework, and Leisure*. New York: Glenn-wood.

Shelton, Beth Anne, and Daphene John (1993a). 'Does Marital Status Make a Difference?" *Journal of Family Issues* 14 (3): 401–420.

Shelton, Beth Anne, and Daphene John (1993b). "Ethnicity, Race, and Difference: A Comparison of White, Black and Hispanic Men's Household Labor Time." In *Men, Work, and Family*, Jane Hood (ed.). Newbury Park, CA: Sage, pp. 1–22.

Sherman, Lawrence W., and Richard A. Berk (1984). "The Specific Deterrent Effects of Arrest for Domestic Violence." *American Sociological Review* 49: 261–272.

Shorter, Edward (1975). *The Making of the Modern Family*. New York: Basic Books.

Sidel, Ruth (1996). *Keeping Women and Children Last*. New York: Penguin.

Simpson, Bob (1998). *Changing Families: An Ethnographic Approach to Divorce and Separation*. Oxford, UK: Berg.

Simpson, Kevin (2000). "A Closet Is a Closet." *Denver Post*, August 20, pp. 1A, 10A–11A.

Simon, Barbara L. (1987). *Never Married Women*. Philadelphia: Temple University Press.

Sklar, Holly (1999). "For CEOs, a Minimum Wage in the Millions." *Z Magazine* 12 (July/August): 63–66.

Skolnick, Arlene (1983). *The Intimate Environment*, 3rd ed. Boston: Little, Brown.

Skolnick, Arlene S. (1987). The Intimate Environment: Exploring Marriage and the Family, 4th ed. Boston: Little, Brown.

Skolnick, Arlene S. (1993). "Changes of Heart: Family Dynamics in Historical Perspective." In *Family, Self, and Society: Toward a New Agenda for Family Research*, Philip A. Cowan, Dorothy Field, Donald A. Hansen, Arlene Skolnick, and Guy Swanson (eds.). Hillsdale, NJ: Lawrence Erlbaum Associates, pp. 43–68.

Skolnick, Arlene S. (1997a). "Family Feud: Arlene Skolnick Responds," *The American Prospect*, no. 33 (July–August): 16.

Skolnick, Arlene S. (1997b). "Family Trouble: Arlene Skolnick Responds," *The American Prospect*, no. 34 (September–October): 19–21.

Skolnick, Arlene S. (1997c). "Family Values: The Sequel," *The American Prospect*, no. 32 (May–June): 86–94.

Skolnick, Arlene S., and Stacey Rosencrantz (1994). "The New Crusade for the Old Family." *The American Prospect*, No. 18 (Summer): 59–65.

Skolnick, Arlene S., and Jerome H. Skolnick (eds.). (1983). *Family in Transition*, 4th ed. Boston: Little, Brown.

Smith, Daniel Blake (1983a). "Autonomy and Affection: Parents and Children in Chesapeake Families." In *The American Family in Social-Historical Perspective*, 3rd ed., Michael Gordon (ed.). New York: St. Martin's, pp. 209–228.

Smith, Daniel Scott (1983b). "Parental Power and Marriage Patterns: An Analysis of Historical Trends in Hingham, Massachusetts." In *The American Family in Social-Historical Perspective*, 3rd ed., Michael Gordon (ed.). New York: St. Martin's, pp. 255–268.

Smith, Dorothy (1993). "The Standard North American Family." *Journal of Family Issues* 14 (March): 50–65.

Smith, Marcia (1997). "When Violence Strikes Home." *The Nation*, June 30, pp. 23–24.

Smock, Pamela J. (1990). "Remarriage Patterns of Black and White Women: Reassessing the Role of Educational Attainment." *Demography* 27 (August): 467–473.

Smock, Pamela J. (1993). "The Economic Costs of Marital Disruption for Young Women Over the Past Two Decades." *Demography* 30 (August): 353–371.

Smolowe, Jill (1995). "Adoption in Black and White." *Time*, August 14, pp. 50–51.

Snipp, C. Matthew (1989). *American Indians: The First of the Land*. New York: Russell Sage Foundation.

Society (2001). "Racial Divide in Domestic Violence." Vol. 38 (January/February): 2.

Sorenson, S. B., and C. A. Telles (1991). "Self-reports of Spousal Violence in a Mexican American and a non-Hispanic White Population." *Violence and Victims* 6: 3–16.

Sorrentino, Constance (1990). "The Changing Family in International Perspective." *Monthly Labor Review* 113 (March): 41–58.

Spain, Daphne, and Suzanne M. Bianchi (1996a). "Most U.S. Unwed Mothers Are Not Teenagers." *Population Today* 24 (November): 3.

Spain, Daphne, and Suzanne M. Bianchi (1996b). *Balancing Act*. New York: Russell Sage Foundation.

Spake, Amanda (1999). "The Perils of Motherhood." *U.S. News & World Report*, June 28, p. 60.

Spitze, Glenna (1991). "Women's Employment and Family Relations." In *Contemporary Families: Looking Forward, Looking Back*, Alan Booth (ed.). Minneapolis: National Council on Family Relations, pp. 381–404.

Sprey, Jetse (2001). "Theorizing in Family Studies: Discovering Process." In *Understanding Families into the New Millennium: A Decade in Review*, Robert M. Milardo (ed.). Minneapolis, MN: National Council on Family Relations, pp. 1–14.

Stacey, Judith (1990). *Brave New Families: Stories of Domestic Upheaval in Late Twentieth-Century America*. New York: Basic Books.

Stacey, Judith (1991). "Backward toward the Postmodern Family: Reflections on Gender, Kinship, and Class in the Silicon Valley." In *America at Century's End*, Alan Wolfe (ed.). Berkeley, CA: University of California Press, pp. 17–34.

Stacey, Judith (1994). "The New Family Values Crusaders." *The Nation*, July 25/August 1, pp. 119–122.

Stacey, Judith (1996). *In The Name of the Family: Rethinking Family Values in the Postmodern Age*. Boston: Beacon.

Stacey, Judith (1998). "Gay and Lesbian Families: Queer Like Us." In *All Our Families: New Policies for a New Century*, Mary Ann Mason, Arlene Skolnick, and Stephen D. Sugarman (eds.). New York: Oxford University Press, pp. 117–143.

Stacey, Carol, and Timothy J. Biblarz (2001). "(How) Does the Sexual Orientation of Parents Matter?" *American Sociological Review* 66 (April): 159–183.

Stack, Carol (1974). *All Our Kin: Strategies for Survival in a Black Community*. New York: Harper & Row.

Stack, Carol, and Linda M. Burton (1994). "Kinscripts: Reflections on Family, Generation, and Culture." In *Mothering: Ideology, Experience, and Agency*. Evelyn Nakano Glenn, Grace Chang, and Linda Rennie Forcey (eds.). New York: Routledge, pp. 33–44.

Stains, G. L., and J. L. Pleck (1983). *The Impact of Work Schedule on Family Life*. Ann Arbor: University of Michigan.

Stapinski, Helene (1999). "Y Not Love?" *American Demographics* (February): 62–68.

Staples, Robert (1978). "The Myth of Black Sexual Superiority: A Re-examination." *The Black Scholar* 9 (April): 16–23.

Staples, Robert (1982). *Black Masculinity: The Black Male Role in American Society*. San Francisco: The Black Scholar Press.

Staples, Robert, and Leonore B. Johnson (1993). *Black Families at the Crossroads: Challenges and Prospects*. San Francisco: Jossey-Bass.

Stein, Peter J. (1981). *Single Life: Unmarried Adults in Social Context*. New York: St. Martin's.

Stein, Peter, J., Judith Richman, and Natalie Hannon (1977). *The Family: Functions, Conflicts and Symbols*. Reading, MA: Addison-Wesley.

Steinberg, Stephen (1981). *The Ethnic Myth*. Boston: Beacon Press.

Steinmetz, Suzanne K. (1978). "Battered Parents." *Society* 15 (July/August).

Steinmetz, Suzanne K., and Murray A. Straus (1974). *Violence in the Family*. New York: Harper & Row.

Stephen, Elizabeth Hervey (1999). "Assisted Reproduction Technologies: Is the Price Too High?" *Population Today* 27 (May): 1–3.

Stiehm, Judith (1976). "Invidious Intimacy." *Social Policy* (March/April): 12–16.

Stith, Sandra M., Karen H. Rosen, Kimberly A. Middleton, Amy L. Busch, Kirsten Lundeberg, and Russell P. Carleton (2000). "The Intergenerational Transmission of Spouse Abuse: A Meta-Analysis." *Journal of Marriage and the Family* 62 (August): 640–654.

Stolberg, Sheryl Gay (1999). "U.S. Birth Rate Hits Record Low." *Denver Post,* April 2, p. 3A.

Straus, Murray A. (1977). "A Sociological Perspective on the Prevention and Treatment of Wifebeating." In *Battered Women,* Maria Roy (ed.). New York: Van Nostrand.

Straus, Murray A. (1977–1978). "Wife Beating: How Common and Why?" *Victimology* 2 (3–4), pp. 443–458.

Straus, Murray A., and Denise A. Donnelly (1994). *Beating the Devil out of Them: Corporal Punishment in American Families.* New York: Lexington Books.

Straus, Murray A., and Richard J. Gelles (1986). "Societal Change and Change in Family Violence from 1975 to 1985 as Revealed by Two National Surveys." *Journal of Marriage and the Family* 48 (August): 465–479.

Straus, Murray A., Richard Gelles, and Suzanne K. Steinmetz (1980). *Behind Closed Doors: Violence in the American Family.* New York: Anchor/Doubleday.

Straus, Murray A., and Christine Smith (1989). "Violence in Hispanic Families in the United States: Incidence Rates and Structural Interpretations." In *Physical Violence in American Families: Risk Factors and Adaptations to Violence in 8,145 Families,* Murray A. Straus and Richard J. Gelles (eds.). New York: Transaction Books.

Straus, Murray A., and Christine Smith (1990). "Family Patterns and Child Abuse." In *Physical Violence in American Families.* New Brunswick, NJ: Transaction Books, pp. 245–261.

Straus, Murray A., and Carrie L. Yodanis (1996). "Corporal Punishment in Adolescence and Physical Assaults on Spouses in Later Life: What Accounts for the Link?" *Journal of Marriage and the Family* 58 (November): 825–841.

Sullivan, Mercer L. (1993). "Puerto Ricans in Sunset Park, Brooklyn: Poverty amidst Ethnic and Economic Diversity." In *In the Barrios: Latinos and the Underclass Debate,* Joan W. Moore and Raquel Pinderhughes (eds.). New York: Russell Sage Foundation, pp. 1–26.

Suro, Roberto (1999). "Mixed Doubles." *American Demographics* 21 (November): 57–62.

Surra, Catherine A. (1991). "Research and Theory on Mate Selection and Premarital Relationships in the 1980s." In *Contemporary Families: Looking Forward, Looking Back,* Alan Booth (ed.), Minneapolis, MN: National Council on Family Relations, pp. 54–75.

Swingle, Chris (2000). "Only But Not Lonely Child." *Coloradoan,* February 10, pp. C1, C7.

Swoboda, Frank, and Amy Joyce (2000). "No Such Thing as an Average Weekday." *Washington Post National Weekly Edition,* March 20, p. 20.

Szinovacz, Maximiliane E. (1987). "Family Power." In *Handbook of Marriage and the Family.* New York: Plenum, pp. 651–693.

Taft, Donald (1936). *Human Migration.* New York: Ronald Press.

Talbot, Margaret (2000). "The Price of Divorce." http://nytimes.com/books/00/10/01/reviews/001001.01talbot.html>.

Tannen, Deborah (1990). *You Just Don't Understand: Women and Men in Conversation.* New York: Ballantine Books.

Taylor, Peggy (1992). "The Way We Never Were: A New Age Journal Interview with Stephanie Coontz." *New Age Journal,* September/October, pp. 64–69.

Taylor, Robert Joseph, Linda M. Chutters, M. Belinda Tucker, and Edith Lewis (1991). "Developments in Research on Black Families." In *Contemporary Families, Looking Forward, Looking Back,* Alan Booth (ed.). Minneapolis, MN: National Council on Family Relations. pp. 275–296.

Taylor, Ronald L. (2000). "Diversity Within African American Families." In *The Handbook of Family Diversity,* David H. Demo, Katherine R. Allen, and Mark A. Fine (eds.) New York: Oxford University Press, pp. 232–251.

Tentler, Leslie Woodcock (1979). *Wage-Earning Women.* Oxford, UK: Oxford University Press.

Terwilliger, Cate (2000). "Halting the Drop into Debt." *Denver Post,* July 23, pp. 1F, 10F.

Thompson, Linda, and Alexis J. Walker (1991). "Gender in Families." In *Contemporary Families: Looking Forward, Looking Back.* Alan Booth (ed.). Minneapolis, MN: National Council on Family Relations, pp. 76–102.

Thorne, Barrie (1982). "Feminist Thinking on the Family: An Overview." In *Rethinking the Family: Some Feminist Questions.* Barrie Thorne and Marilyn Yalom (eds.). New York: Longman, pp. 1–24.

Thorne, Barrie (1992). "Feminism and the Family: Two Decades of Thought." In *Rethinking the Family: Some Feminist Questions,* 2nd ed., Barrie Thorne and Marilyn Yalom (eds.). Boston: Northeastern University Press, pp. 3–30.

Tilly, Louise, and Joan W. Scott (1978). *Women, Work, and Family.* New York: Holt.

Timmer, Doug A., D. Stanley Eitzen, and Kathryn D. Talley (1994). *Paths to Homelessness: Extreme Poverty and the Urban Housing Crisis.* Boulder, CO: Westview.

Tjaden, P., and N. Thoennes (1999). *Extent, Nature, and Consequences of Intimate Partner Violence.* Washington,

DC: National Institute of Justice/Center for Disease Control and Prevention.

Torres, S. (1987). "Hispanic-American Battered Women: Why Consider Cultural Differences?" *Response* 10: 20–21.

Treas, Judith. 1995. "Older Americans in the 1990s and Beyond." *Population Bulletin* 50 (May): entire issue.

Tufte, Virginia, and Barbara Meyerhoff (eds.). (1979). *Changing Images of the Family*. New Haven, CT: Yale University Press.

Tumin, Melvin (1973). *Patterns of Society*. Boston: Little, Brown.

Turbett, Patrick, and Richard O'Toole (1980). "Physicians' Recognition of Child Abuse." Paper presented at the annual meeting of the American Sociological Association (New York).

Turkle, Sherry (1995). *Life on the Screen*. New York: Simon and Schuster.

Tyson, Laura D'Andrea (1999). "Why Medicare Must Do More at the Drugstore." *Business Week,* March 22, p. 26.

Tzeng, J. M., and R. D. Mare (1995). "Labor Market and Socioeconomic Effects on Martial Stability." *Social Science Research* 24: 329–351.

Uchitelle, Louis, and N. R. Kleinfield (1996). "The Price of Jobs Lost." In *New York Times, The Downsizing of America*. New York: Times Books, pp. 3–36.

Udry, J. Richard, and Benjamin C. Campbell (1994): "Getting Started on Sexual Behavior." In *Sexuality across the Life Course*, Alice S. Rossi (ed.). Chicago: University of Chicago Press, pp. 209–232.

Uhlenberg, Peter (1972). "Marital Instability among Mexican-Americans: Following the Pattern of Blacks?" *Social Problems* 20 (Summer): 49–56.

United Nations (1999). *Demographic Yearbook 1997*. New York: United Nations, Department of Economic and Social Affairs.

USA Today (1994). "When Will Society Take Spouse Abuse Seriously?" (June 20): 14A.

USA Today (1996). "Smoke and Mirrors Can't Cure Fast-Failing Medicare." (June 6): 12A.

USA Today (1999). "A Small But Useful Start on Providing Long-Term Care." (January 5): 16A.

USA Today (2000). "Aging-Parent Trap: Caregivers Feel Stress." (September 25): 9D.

U.S. Bureau of the Census (1996). "Population Projection of the United States by Age, Sex, Race, and Hispanic Origin: 1995 to 2050." *Current Population Reports,* Serios P-25-113.

U.S. Bureau of the Census (1999a). "Marital Status and Living Arrangements: March 1998." *Current Population Reports,* Series P20-514.

U.S. Bureau of the Census (1999b). "Poverty in the United States: 1998." *Current Population Reports,* Series P60-207.

U.S. Bureau of the Census (1999c). *Statistical Abstract of the United States, 1999,* 119th ed. Washington, DC: U.S. Government Printing Office.

U.S. Bureau of the Census (2000). "The Asian and Pacific Islander Population in the United States, 1999." *Current Population Reports,* Series P-20-529.

U.S. Department of Health and Human Services (1999). *Health, United States 1999.* DHHS publication 99-1232. Washington, DC: U.S. Government Printing Office.

U.S. Department of Labor (2000a). *20 Facts on Women Workers.* Washington, DC: Division of Labor Statistics.

U.S. Department of Labor (2000b). "Women's Jobs: 1964–1999." http://www.dol.gov/dol/wb/public/jobs6497.htm>.

U.S. Department of Labor (2000c). "Annual Average Tables." *Employment and Earnings.* Washington, DC: Office of Employment and Unemployment Statistics.

U.S. Department of Labor, Women's Bureau (1993). *Twenty Facts on Women Workers.* Washington, DC: Division of Labor Statistics.

U.S. Department of Labor, Women's Bureau (1994). *Working Women Count, Executive Summary.* Washington DC: Division of Labor Statistics.

Usdansky, Margaret L. (1993). "Teen-Age Birth Rates Go Back up." *USA Today,* May 14, p. 1.

Uttal, Lynet (1999). "Using Kin for Child Care: Embedment in the Socioeconomic Networks of Extended Families." *Journal of Marriage and the Family* 61 (November): 845–857.

Valdmanis, Thor (2000). "Big Merger Wave Appears to be Winding Down to a Trickle." *USA Today,* January 2, p. 2B.

Valenzuela, Angela, and Sanford Dornbush (1994). "Familism and Social Capital in the Academic Achievement of Mexican Origin and Anglo Adolescents. *Social Science Quarterly* 75: 18–36.

Vance, Carole S. (1984). *Pleasure and Danger*. Boston: Routledge and Kegan Paul.

Vander Zanden, Ronald (1966). *American Minority Relations*. New York: Ronald Press.

Vandeven, Andrea M., and Eli H. Newberger (1994). "Child Abuse." *Annual Review of Public Health* 15: 367–379.

Vanneman, Reeve, and Lynn Weber Cannon (1987). *The American Perception of Class*. Philadelphia: Temple University Press.

Vecoli, Rudolph J. (1964). "Contadini in Chicago: A Critique of the Uprooted." *Journal of American History* 51: 405–417.

Veevers, J. E. (1980). *Childless by Choice*. Toronto: Butterworths.

Vega, William A. (1990). "Hispanic Families in the 1980s:

A Decade of Research." *Journal of Marriage and the Family* 52: 1015–1024.

Vega, William A. (1995). "The Study of Latino Families: A Point of Departure." In *Understanding Latino Families,* Ruth E. Zambrana (ed.). Thousand Oaks, CA: Sage, pp. 1–17.

Velez-Ibanez, Carlos (1993). "U.S. Mexicans in the Borderlands: Being Poor without the Underclass." In *The Barrios: Latinos and the Underclass Debate,* Joan Moore and Raquel Pinderhughes (eds.). New York: Russell Sage Foundation, pp. 195–220.

Velez-Ibanez, Carlos G. (1996). *Border Visions.* Tucson: University of Arizona Press.

Ventura, Stephanie, Sally Curtin, and T. J. Mathews (2000). "Variation in Teenage Birth Rates, 1990–1999: National and State Trends." *National Vital Statistics Reports* 48 (6). Hyattsville, MD: Center for Disease Control and Prevention.

Verdin, Tom (2000). "Minorities in the Majority." Associated Press (August 31).

Vobejda, Barbara, and Judith Havemann (1997). "On the Rolls but Working off the Books." *The Washington Post National Weekly Edition,* November 10, p. 29.

Voydanoff, Patricia (1984). "Introduction." In *Work and Family,* Patricia Voydanoff (ed.). Palo Alto, CA: Mayfield, pp. 2–7.

Voydanoff, Patricia (1987). *Work and Family Life.* Beverly Hills, CA: Sage.

Waite, Linda (1995). "Does Marriage Matter?" *Demography* 32 (November): 483–507.

Waite, Linda (1999). "The Importance of Marriage Is Being Overlooked." *USA Today: The Magazine of the American Scene,* January, pp. 46–48.

Waite, Linda (2000). "Trends in Men's and Women's Well–Being in Marriage." In *The Ties That Bind: Perspectives on Marriage and Cohabitation,* Linda Waite (ed.). New York: Aldine de Gruyter, pp. 368–392.

Waite, Linda, and Maggie Gallagher (2000). *The Case for Marriage: Why Married People Are Happier, Healthier, and Better Off Financially.* New York: Doubleday.

Waite, Linda, and Frances K. Goldscheider (1992). "Work in the Home: The Productive Context of Family Relationships." In *The Changing American Family,* Scott J. South and Stewart E. Tolnay (eds.). Boulder, CO: Westview, pp. 267–299.

Waite, Linda, G. Haggstrom, and D. E. Kanouse (1986). "The Effects of Parenthood on Career Orientation and Job Characteristics of Young Adults." *Social Forces* 65 (1): 28–43.

Waldron, Charlene M. (1996). "Lesbians of Color and the Domestic Violence Movement." In *Violence in Gay and Lesbian Domestic Partnerships,* Claire M. Renzetti and Charles Harvey Miley (eds.). New York: Harrington Park, pp. 43–51.

Walker, Lenore E. (1979). *The Battered Woman.* New York: Harper & Row.

Waller, Willard (1937). "The Rating and Dating Complex." *American Sociological Review* 2 (October): 727–734.

Wallerstein, Judith, Julia Lewis, and Sandra Blakeslee (2000). *The Unexpected Legacy of Divorce.* New York: Hyperion.

Ward, Russell, and Glenna Spitze (1996). "Will the Children Ever Leave?" *Journal of Family Issues* 17 (July): 514–539.

Waters, Mary C., and Karl Eschbach (1995). "Immigration and Ethnic and Racial Inequality in the United States." *Annual of Review of Sociology* 21: 419–446.

Watts, Jerry (1997). "The End of Work and the End of Welfare." *Contemporary Sociology* 26 (July): 409–412.

Weber, Lynn (1998). "A Conceptual Framework for Understanding Race, Class, Gender, and Sexuality." *Psychology of Women Quarterly* 22: 13–32.

Weber, Lynn (2001). *Understanding Race, Class, Gender, and Sexuality: A Conceptual Framework.* New York: McGraw-Hill.

Wegar, Katarina (2000). "Adoption, Family Ideology, and Social Stigma." *Family Relations* 49 (October): 363–370.

Weinbaum, Batya, and Amy Bridges (1979). "The Other Side of the Paycheck: Monopoly Capital and the Structure of Consumption." In *Capitalist Patriarchy and the Case for Socialist Feminism,* Zillah R. Eisenstein (ed.). New York: Monthly Review Press, pp. 190–205.

Weise, D., and D. Daro (1995). *Current Trends in Child Abuse Reporting and Fatalities.* Chicago: National Committee to Prevent Child Abuse.

Weissbourd, Richard (1994). "Divided Families, Whole Children." *The American Prospect,* No. 18 (Summer): 66–72.

Weitzman, Lenore (1985). *The Divorce Revolution: The Unexpected Social and Economic Consequences for Women and Children in America.* New York: The Free Press.

Wells, Barbara, and Maxine Baca Zinn (2000). "Spatial Inequality and Marriage Matters." Unpublished paper.

Wells, Miriam J. (1976). "Emigrants from the Migrant Stream: Environment and Incentive in Relocation." *Aztlan: International Journal of Chicano Studies Research* 7: 267–290.

Wells, Robert V. (1991). "Demographic Change and Family Life in American History: Some Reflections." In *The Family Experience,* Mark Hutter (ed.). New York: Macmillan.

Wellstone, Paul (1998). "The People's Trust Fund." *The Nation,* July 27/August 3, pp. 4–5.

Welter, Barbara (1973). "The Cult of True Womanhood: 1820–1860." In *The American Family in Social-Histori-*

cal Perspective, Michael Gordon (ed.). New York: St. Martin's, pp. 224–250.

West, Candace (2000). "Social Accessibility and Involvement." *Contemporary Sociology* 29 (July): 584–590.

West, Cornel (1996). "Black Sexuality: The Taboo Subject." In *The Meaning of Difference,* Karen E. Rosenblum and Toni Michelle C. Travis, (eds.). New York: McGraw-Hill, pp. 225–230.

Westheimer, Ruth K. (1989). "Are You Having Fun Together?" *Redbook* 172 (January): 116–118.

Weston, Kath (1991). *Families We Choose.* New York: Columbia University Press.

White, Lynn K. (1990). "Determinants of Divorce: A Review of Research in the Eighties." *Journal of Marriage and the Family* 52 (November): 904–912.

Whitebook, Marcy (1999). "Child Care Workers: High Demand, Low Wages." *The Annals* 563 (May): 146–161.

Whitehead, Barbara Dafoe (1993). "Dan Quayle Was Right." *Atlantic Monthly* 271 (April): 47–84.

Whitmire, Richard (1994). "Odds Often Steep for Stepchildren." *Coloradoan,* September 3, p. A7.

Whyte, Martin King (1990). *Dating, Mating, and Marriage.* New York: Aldine De Gruyter.

Whyte, Martin King (1992). "Choosing Mates—The American Way." *Society* 29 (March/April): 71–77.

Wiehe, Vernon R. (1998). *Understanding Family Violence.* Thousand Oaks, CA: Sage.

Williams, Annette Leslie (1999). "Interracial Marriage for Black Women, Too." *USA Today,* October 8, p. 19A.

Williams, Gertrude (1980). "Toward the Eradication of Child Abuse and Neglect at Home." In *Traumatic Abuse and the Neglect of Children at Home,* Gertrude Williams and John Money (eds.). Baltimore, MD: Johns Hopkins University Press, pp. 588–605.

Williams, Norma (1990). *The Mexican American Family: Tradition and Change.* Dix Hills, NY: General Hall.

Wilson, Everitt K. (1966). *Sociology: Rules, Roles, and Relationships.* Homewood, IL: Dorsey.

Wilson, James Q. (1993). "The Family-Values Debate." *Commentary* 95 (April): 24–31.

Wilson, William Julius (1987). *The Truly Disadvantaged: The Inner City, the Underclass, and Public Policy.* Chicago: University of Chicago Press.

Wilson, William Julius (1996). *When Work Disappears: The World of the New Urban Poor.* New York: Knopf.

Wolf, Richard (2000). "Surprise Benefits in Welfare Reform." *USA Today,* June 1, p. 3A.

Wolf, Rosalie S. (2000). "The Nature and Scope of Elder Abuse." *Generations* 24 (Summer): 6–12.

Wolfe, Alan (1994). "The Gender Question." *The New Republic* (June 6): 27–34.

Wolfe, Diane L. (1990). "Daughters, Decisions, and Domination: An Empirical and Conceptual Critique of Household Strategies." *Development and Change* 21: 43–74.

Wolfe, Diane L. (1992). *Factory Daughters.* Berkeley: University of California Press.

Wolfinger, Nicholas H. (1999). "Trends in the Intergenerational Transmission of Divorce." *Demography* 36 (August): 415–420.

Woodward, Kenneth (1990). "Young Beyond Their Years." *Newsweek,* (Special Edition, Winter/Spring): 54–60.

Wright, Erik Olin, David Hachen, Cynthia Costello, and Joey Sprague (1982). "The American Class Structure." *American Sociological Review* 47 (December): 709–726.

Yans-McLaughlin, Virginia (1973). "Patterns of Work and Family Organization." In *The Family in History,* T. K. Rabb and R. I. Rotborg (eds.). New York: Harper & Row.

Ybarra, Lea (1977). "Conjugal Role Relationships in the Chicano Family." Ph.D. dissertation, University of California at Berkeley.

Young, Iris Marion (1994). "Making Single Motherhood Normal." *Dissent* 41 (Winter): 88–93.

Z Magazine (1993). "Family Values" Vol. 6 (May): 4.

Zaretsky, Eli (1976). *Capitalism, the Family, and Personal Life.* New York: Harper & Row.

Zavella, Patricia (1987). *Women's Work and Chicano Families.* Ithaca, NY: Cornell University Press.

Zhou, Min (1997). "Growing up American: The Challenge Confronting Immigrant Children and Children of Immigrants." *Annual Review of Sociology* 23: 63–95.

Zick, C. D., and K. R. Smith (1991). "Marital Transitions, Poverty, and Gender Differences in Mortality." *Journal of Marriage and the Family* 53: 327–336.

Zimmerman, Shirley L. (1992). *Family Policies and Family Well-Being: The Role of Political Culture.* Newbury Park, CA: Sage.

Zoglin, Richard (1996). "Chips Ahoy." *Time,* February 19, pp. 58–61.

Zuckerman, Gregory (2000a). "Bullish U. S. on Credit Binge." *Denver Post,* July 9, pp. 1G, 8G.

Zuckerman, Mortimer B. (2000b). "Whistling While We Work." *U.S. News & World Report,* January 24, p. 72.

Photo Credits

Page 4: Stock Boston (top), FPG International (bottom); Page 5: Stock Boston (top and bottom); Page 13: FPG International; Page 14: CBS/Shooting Star (top left and top right), Fox/Shooting Star (bottom); Page 31: The Seaver Collection, Los Angeles County Museum of Natural History; Page 33: Solomon D. Butcher Collection, Nebraska State Historical Society; Page 34: Solomon D. Butcher Collection, Nebraska State Historical Society; Page 44: Abby Aldrich Rockefeller Folk Art Collection, Colonial Williamsburg Foundation; Page 48: National Gallery of Art, Washington, DC; Page 53: Baker Library, Harvard Graduate School of Business Administration, Boston, MA; Pages 56, 61, 67, and 78: Val Berryman Collection; Page 79: Huntington Library, San Marino, CA; Page 81: Library of Congress, Russel Lee; Page 85: Abby Aldrich Rockefeller Folk Art Collection, Colonial Williamsburg Foundation; Page 93: FPG International; Page 95: Drawing by David Horsey, Reprinted with permission of Tribune Media Services, All rights reserved; Page 117: Steve Gold, 1995; Page 119, Lisa Falk; Page 129: FPG International; Page 140: Drawing by Leo Cullum, Copyright © 1993 The New Yorker Magazine, Inc.; Page 151: Stock Boston; Page 155: Guiliano Colliva, The Image Bank; Page 158: Jacqueline Lalley, Family Resource Coalition; Page 171: Val Berryman Collection; Page 183: Stock Boston; Page 189: Drawing by Pat Hardin; Page 193: FPG International; Page 194: Drawing by David Horsey, Seattle Post Intelligencer; Page 204: Drawing by Reilly, Copyright © 1965 The New Yorker Magazine, Inc.; Page 208: Drawing by Pat Hardin; Page 229: Drawing by Pat Hardin; Page 230: Stock Boston; Page 236: Drawing by Koren, Copyright © The New Yorker Magazine, Inc.; Page 249: Stock Boston; Page 253: Drawing by Pat Hardin; Page 259: Stock Boston; Page 260: Steven Simpson, FPG International; Page 270: Stock Boston; Page 273: Drawing by Smaller, Copyright © 2000, New Yorker Magazine; Page 284: Drawing by Crawford, Copyright © 2000 The New Yorker Magazine, Inc.; Page 306: Drawing by Pat Hardin; Page 309: Stephen Simpson, FPG International; Page 317: Drawing by Pat Hardin; Page 320: Dick Luria, FPG International; Page 324: Stock Boston; Page 342: Drawing by Kevin Siers, © 2000 The Charlotte Observer, reprinted with permission; Pages 354 and 370: United Way of America; Page 392: Maslin, Copyright © 1996 The New Yorker Magazine, Inc. ; Page 396: Drawing by Weyant, Copyright © 2001 The New Yorker Magazine Inc.; Page 398: Drawing by Mort Gerberg, Copyright © 1993 The New Yorker Magazine, Inc.; Page 404: Drawing by Pat Hardin; 429: Stephanie Rausser, FPG International; Page 424: Drawing by Leo Cullum, Copyright © 2001 The New Yorker Magazine Inc.; Page 430: Drawing by Pat Hardin; Page 434: Copyright © 2000 New Yorker Magazine Inc.; Page 443: Stock Boston; Page 457: (top), Drawing by Dana Summers, Orlando Sentinel, (bottom), Drawing by Signe Wilkinson, Philadelphia Daily News; Page 462: Drawing by Danziger; Page 487, Drawing by Kirk.

Text Credits

Box 1.1: Frank F. Furstenberg, Jr., "Is the Modern Family a Threat to Children's Health?" SOCIETY (July/August 1999). Reprinted with permission.

"Inside the Worlds of Diverse Families" by Barbara Wells, 2001. Department of Sociology, Maryville College. Written expressly for the sixth Edition of Diversity in Families.

THE PSYCHOSOCIAL INTERIOR OF THE FAMILY, 4E by Gerald Handel and Gail Whitechurch. Copyright © 1994 by Walter de Gruyter, Inc. Used by permission from Aldine de Gruyter.

"Historical Methods in Family Research," SOURCEBOOK OF FAMILY THEORIES AND METHODS: A CONTEXTUAL APPROACH by Schvaneveldt et al. Copyright © 1993 by Plenum Press. Reprinted by permission.

DOMESTIC REVOLUTIONS: A Social History of American Family Life by Steven Mintz and Susan Kellogg. Copyright © 1988 by The Free Press. Used by permission from the Free Press, an imprint of Simon & Schuster.

"Eighteenth Century Family and Social Life Revealed in Massachusetts Divorce Records" by Nancy F. Cott, JOURNAL OF SOCIAL HISTORY 10, Fall 1976. Used by permission of Carnegie Mellon University.

LIVES ON THE EDGE by Valerie Polakow. Copyright © 1993 by Chicago: The University of Chicago Press. Reprinted by permission of The University of Chicago Press.

"Persistent Myths About The Afro-American Family" by Herbert B. Gutman in THE AMERICAN FAMILY IN SOCIAL-HISTORICAL PERSPECTIVE, edited by Michael Gordon. New York: St. Martin's Press, 1983. Reprinted by permission.

"Changes in Capitalism Render One-Earner Families Extinct," by Lester C. Thurow, USA TODAY, January 27, 1997. Copyright © 1997 by Lester C. Thurow. Used by permission of author.

FALLING FROM GRACE: The Experience of Downward Mobility in the American Middle Class by Katherine S. Newman. Copyright © 1988 by Katherine S. Newman. Used by permission of the Free Press, an imprint of Simon & Schuster.

Figure 4.1: Copyright 1999, USA TODAY. Reprinted with permission.

Figure 4.3: Copyright 2000, USA TODAY. Reprinted with permission.

Box 5.2, "Inside the Worlds of Diverse Families": by Kathryn Edin and Laura Lein, MAKING ENDS MEET, © 1997 Russell Sage Foundation, New York, New York.

Figure 5.2: Reprinted with permission of the Population Reference Bureau.

"Progress for Women's Rights Worldwide? Beijing Plus Five": Panel essay written expressly for the sixth edition of DIVERSITY IN FAMILIES, 2001.

Figure 6.3: Reprinted with permission of the Population Reference Bureau.

THE TIME BIND: WHEN WORK BECOMES HOME AND HOME BECOMES WORK by Arlie Russel Hochschild. Copyright © 1997 by Arlie Russell Hochschild. Reprinted by arrangement with Henry Holt and Company.

Figure 6.4: Alice Love, March 10, 2000. Reprinted by permission of the Associated Press.

"Constructing Motherhood on the Night Shift: Working Mothers as Stay-at-Home Moms," by Anita Ilta Garey in QUALITATIVE SOCIOLOGY, Vol. 18, No. 4. Used by permission of Plenum Publishing Corporation.

Name Index

Subject Index